Andalucia

Palm trees exploded darkly overhead, and orange trees bore fruit and blossom together, giving out mixed odours of spring and Christmas. On the broad pavement below the palms, scarlet-skirted little girls skipped in haloes of honeyed dust.

Laurie Lee
A Rose for Winter (Hogarth Press)

Travel Publications

38 Clarendon Road – WATFORD Herts WD1 1SX - U.K.
Tel. (01923) 415 000
www.michelin-travel.com
TheGreenGuide-uk@uk.michelin.com

Manufacture française des pneumatiques Michelin

Société en commandite par actions au capital de 2 000 000 000 de francs
Place des Carmes-Déchaux – 63 Clermont-Ferrand (France)
R.C.S. Clermont-Fd B 855 200 507

© Michelin et Cie, Propriétaires-Éditeurs 2000
Dépôt légal novembre 2000 – ISBN 2-06-158301-6 – ISSN 0763-1383

Compogravure : LE SANGLIER, Charleville-Mézières
Impression : KAPP Lahure Jombart, Évreux
Brochage : DIGUET DENY, Breteuil-sur-Iton

Cover design: Carré Noir, Paris 17ᵉ arr.

THE GREEN GUIDE:
The Spirit of Discovery

*The exhilaration of new horizons,
the fun of seeing the world, the
excitement of discovery: this is what
we seek to share with you. To help
you make the most of your travel
experience, we offer first-hand
knowledge and turn a discerning
eye on places to visit.*

*This wealth of information gives you
the expertise to plan your own
enriching adventure. With THE
GREEN GUIDE showing you the
way, you can explore new
destinations with confidence or
rediscover old ones.*

*Leisure time spent with THE GREEN
GUIDE is also a time for refreshing
your spirit and enjoying yourself.*

*So turn the page and open a window
on the world. Join THE GREEN
GUIDE in the spirit of discovery.*

Contents

Giralda, Sevilla

Fishing boats, Málaga

Sights 64

Practical Information 332

Door knocker. Écija

Geranium-adorned doorway. Frigiliana

Maps and plans

COMPANION PUBLICATIONS

Map of Andalucia no 446

– a 1:400 000 scale map of Andalucia with an index of place names

Travelling around Andalucia

Spain/Portugal Road Atlas

– a useful 1:400 000 scale, spiral-bound atlas with a full index of place names and numerous town plans

Spain/Portugal Map no 990

– a 1:1 000 000 scale map of the Iberian Peninsula

www.michelin-travel.com

– Michelin offers motorists a complete route planning service (fastest, shortest etc) on its comprehensive web site

LIST OF MAPS AND PLANS

Main maps

Town/City maps

Plans of monuments and archeological sites

Maps with descriptions of driving tours

Using this guide

● The summary maps at the front of this guide have been designed to assist you in planning your trip. The **Map of principal sights** identifies major attractions, classified according to Michelin's star system, while the **Map of driving tours** proposes a number of driving itineraries.

● This guide is divided into three sections: **Introduction, Sights,** and **Practical Information.**

● The **Introduction** gives interesting background information on Andalucian history, the arts and traditional culture.

● Andalucia's principal natural and cultural attractions are presented in alphabetical order in the **Sights** section. The clock symbol ⊙, placed after sight names, indicates that opening hours and prices for that sight are included in the **Admission times and charges** section at the back of the guide.

● In the **Travellers' addresses** section, listed under a number of cities within this guide, you will find selected hotel, restaurant and bar recommendations, as well as a wealth of information on shopping and leisure activities.

● General information of a more practical nature, such as transport, accommodation, beaches, sports, entertainment, local holidays etc, is contained within the **Practical Information** section.

● The index at the back of this guide contains a comprehensive list of specific place names, historical figures and practical information.

● We greatly appreciate comments and suggestions from our readers. Contact us at:

Michelin Travel Publications, 38 Clarendon Road,
Watford, Herts, WD1 1SX, England.
☎ 01923 415 000
Fax 01923 415 250
TheGreenGuide-uk@uk.michelin.com
www.michelin-travel.com

B. Touillon/STOCK PHOTOS

Key

★★★ **Worth a journey**

★★ **Worth a detour**

★ **Interesting**

Tourism

⊙	Admission Times and Charges listed at the end of the guide	►►	Visit if time permits
⊙━ ⟹	Sightseeing route with departure point indicated	AZ B	Map co-ordinates locating sights
⛪ ♦ ⛪ ♦	Ecclesiastical building	🛈	Tourist information
🔯 🕌	Synagogue – Mosque	⋗ ⋰	Historic house, castle – Ruins
🏛	Building (with main entrance)	∪ ☼	Dam – Factory or power station
■	Statue, small building	☆ ∩	Fort – Cave
⊥	Wayside cross	⛏	Prehistoric site
◎	Fountain	▼ ₩	Viewing table – View
━●━■━	Fortified walls – Tower – Gate	▲	Miscellaneous sight

Recreation

🏇	Racecourse	🏃	Waymarked footpath
⛸	Skating rink	◈	Outdoor leisure park/centre
≋ ▥	Outdoor, indoor swimming pool	🎢	Theme/Amusement park
⚓	Marina, moorings	🐃	Wildlife/Safari park, zoo
⛺	Mountain refuge hut	🌳	Gardens, park, arboretum
▫━▫━▫	Overhead cable-car	🦜	Aviary, bird sanctuary
🚂	Tourist or steam railway		

Additional symbols

══ ══	Motorway (unclassified)	✉ ☎	Post office – Telephone centre
❶ ❶	Junction: complete, limited	⊠	Covered market
▭▭ ▭▭	Pedestrian street	⋅✕⋅	Barracks
ı═════ı	Unsuitable for traffic, street subject to restrictions	△	Swing bridge
⊞⊞⊞ ----	Steps – Footpath	∪ ✕	Quarry – Mine
🚆 🚍	Railway – Coach station	Ⓑ Ⓕ	Ferry (river and lake crossings)
□┼┼┼┼□	Funicular – Rack-railway	⟱	Ferry services: Passengers and cars
━⊢⊦ ◉	Tram – Metro, Underground	⟹	Foot passengers only
Bert (R.)...	Main shopping street	③	Access route number common to MICHELIN maps and town plans

Abbreviations and special symbols

D	Provincial council (Diputación)	**U**	University (Universidad)
G	Central government representation (Delegación del Gobierno)	🛡	Civil Guard (Guardia Civil)
H	Town hall (Ayuntamiento)	🏠	Accommodation
J	Law courts/Courthouse (Palacio de Justicia)	℗	Parador (hotel run by the State)
M	Museum (Museo)	🐂	Bullring
POL.	Police station (Policía)	🌿	Olive grove
T	Theatre (Teatro)	🍊	Orange Grove

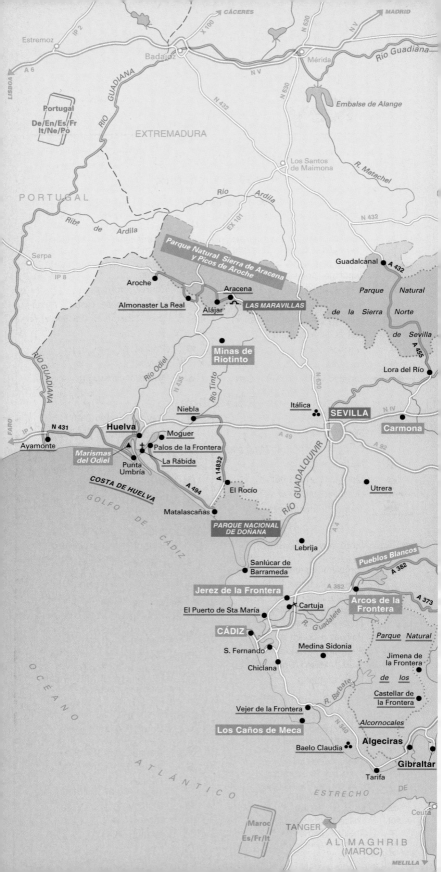

Driving tours

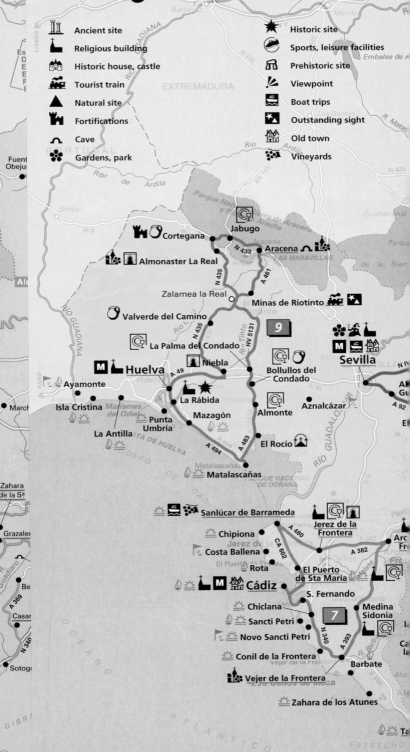

Symbol	Description
	Ancient site
	Religious building
	Historic house, castle
	Tourist train
	Natural site
	Fortifications
	Cave
	Gardens, park
	Historic site
	Sports, leisure facilities
	Prehistoric site
	Viewpoint
	Boat trips
	Outstanding sight
	Old town
	Vineyards

CÁCERES

EXTREMADURA

PORTUGAL

Badajoz

Mérida

Embalse de A

Parque Natur

Fuente Obejul

Almo

Cortegana
Almonaster La Real
Jabugo
Aracena
Zalamea la Real
Valverde del Camino
Minas de Riotinto
La Palma del Condado
Niebla
Bollullos del Condado
Sevilla
Huelva
La Rábida
Mazagón
Almonte
Aznalcázar
Ayamonte
Isla Cristina
Punta Umbría
La Antilla
El Rocío
Matalascañas

9

7

Sanlúcar de Barrameda
Jerez de la Frontera
Chipiona
Costa Ballena
Rota
El Puerto de Sta María
Cádiz
S. Fernando
Medina Sidonia
Chiclana
Sancti Petri
Novo Sancti Petri
Conil de la Frontera
Barbate
Vejer de la Frontera
Zahara de los Atunes

Zahara de la Sª
Grazale
Arc Fr

OCÉANO ATLÁNTICO

GIBR

ESTRECHO

TANGER

Sotog

Casar

PARQUE NACIONAL DE DOÑANA

GOLFO DE CÁDIZ

Legend

Picturesque village	
M	Museum, art gallery
	Regional specialities
	Theme park
	Cave dwelling
	Crafts
	Place of pilgrimage
	Hispano-Moorish architecture

MADRID
N 430
Guadiana
Embalse de Orellana
Embalse de Serena
R. Guadiana
R. Gua
Río Valdeazogues
Río Zújar
Río Jabalón
N 430
Puertollano
Ciu

CASTILLA - LA MAN

Parque Natural Sierra de Andújar

Montoro
Adamuz
Marmolejo
Medina Azahara
Las Ermitas
A 421
N IV
El Carpio
Almodóvar del Río
A 431
Moratalla
CP 234
Villaseca
Córdoba
M
Jaén
Palma del Río
Baena
Jabalcuz
Carmona
Écija
Zuheros
Luque
La Guardia de Jaén
N IV
Río
Virgen de la Sierra
Los Murciélagos
á de la daira
A 351
Cabra
Carcabuey
Priego de Córdoba
Alcalá la Real
Marchena
Lucena
A 92
Virgen de Araceli
Rute
A 333
rahal
Paradas
A 92
Osuna
A 92
Estepa
Iznájar
R. Genil
Santa Fé
Loja
A 92
Loja
Archidona
Alhama de Granada
Antequera
N 331
de la tera
Ronda
Tolox
Málaga
Rincón de la Victoria
N 340
Frigiliana
Nerja
Gaucín
A 376
Tolox
Torremolinos
Torre del Mar
Torrox-costa
Almuñécar
S. Pedro de Alcántara
Marbella
Benalmádena Costa
ena de ontera
A 369
Puerto Banús
ellar de ontera
Estepona
Fuengirola
La Duquesa
N 340
Sotogrande
COSTA
San Roque
Algeciras
M
Gibraltar
Ceuta
MELILLA
MEDITERRANE

1	Renaissance buildings in the land of olive groves
2	Cave dwellers and their landscapes
3	Deserts and beaches of Almería
4	Towns and villages of the Parque Natural de las Sierras Subbéticas

5
6
10
8
4

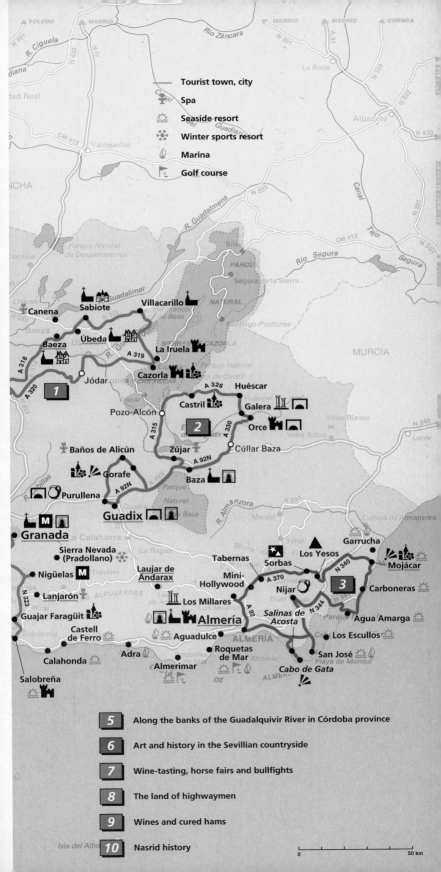

Tourist town, city

Spa

Seaside resort

Winter sports resort

Marina

Golf course

TOLEDO
MADRID
Río Záncara
MADRID
MADRID
CUENCA

R. Ciguela
N 301
A 31
La Roda
N 320

ad Real
Albacete
N 430

VALENCIA

diana

Valdepeñas
CM 412
NCHA

Río Guadalmena
CM 412
Tajo
N 301

N 322

Parque Natural
de Despeñaperros
PARQUE
Río Segura
Segura

Carolina

Sila
Segura de la Sierra

R. Guadalimar
Villacarillo
NATURAL

Canena
Sabiote

Baeza
Úbeda
La Iruela
Santiago-Pontones

Baeza
A 319
MURCIA

A 316
Jódar
Cazorla
1
A 326
Huéscar

A 320
Pozo-Alcón
Castril
Galera
Vélez Blanco
N 340

A 315
2
Orce
Lorca
Vélez Rubio

Baños de Alicún
Zújar
A 330
Cúllar Baza

Gorafe
A 92N
Baza

Purullena
A 92N
Cuevas de Almanzora

Guadix

Granada
La Calahorra
R. Almanzora
Garrucha

Sierra Nevada
(Pradollano)
Tabernas
Los Yesos
Mojácar

Nigüelas
Sorbas
N 340

Lanjarón
Mini-
Hollywood
Nijar
Carboneras

Guajar Faragüit
Laujar de
Andarax
N 344

Castell
de Ferro
Los Millares
Salinas de
Acosta
Agua Amarga

N 323
Almería
Los Escullos

Calahonda
Aguadulce
ALMERÍA

Adra
Roquetas
de Mar
San José

Salobreña
Almerimar
Cabo de Gata

Isla del Albo

---

5   Along the banks of the Guadalquivir River in Córdoba province

6   Art and history in the Sevillian countryside

7   Wine-tasting, horse fairs and bullfights

8   The land of highwaymen

9   Wines and cured hams

10   Nasrid history

0   50 km

Casares

Introduction

Andalucia

Spain's most southerly autonomous community *(comunidad autónoma)* covers a total area of 87 300km²/33 706sq mi and is similar in size to Portugal and Switzerland. This figure represents 17.3% of the country's total area. Over 7 million people (18% of the Spanish population) live in this historic region, which acts as a bridge between Europe and Africa and between the East and West.
The lands of Andalucia, which for centuries were a source of fascination for successive waves of colonisers, extend north-south from the Sierra Morena – a range of mountains separating the region from the communities of Extremadura and Castilla La Mancha – to the Mediterranean coast; and west-east from the Guadiana river – a natural border with Portugal – to the community of Murcia.

GEOLOGY

In geological terms, Andalucia is a young region which has replaced the large sea situated between the continental masses of Eurasia and Goswana. The Cordilleras Béticas, which rose up as a result of Alpine movements during the Tertiary Era, and the Guadalquivir River, with its slow sedimentation, cut off the sea, leaving just a 14km/8mi-wide stretch of water, the Straits of Gibraltar, which, with the exception of the Suez Canal, is the only navigable gateway to the Mediterranean.

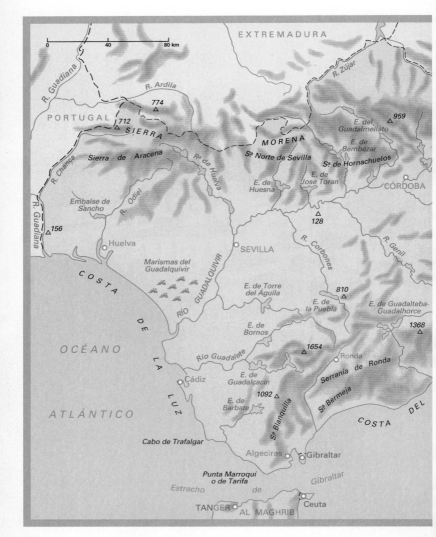

LANDSCAPE

Contrary to popular belief, Andalucia is a land of sharp contrasts, both in terms of its climate and landscape. The fertile Guadalquivir Valley, which has always been considered to be the region's most representative area, is set between two high mountain ranges, the Sierra Morena to the north and the Cordilleras Béticas to the south, while Andalucia's coastal areas, lapped by the waters of the Atlantic and the Mediterranean, have their own varied landscapes.

Sierra Morena

The modern-day name of this mountain range remains something of an enigma. There are those who believe that the name evolves from the Sierra Mariana (from Mario, a praetor in Roman Hispania), while others are of the opinion that the name alludes to the dark colour of its landscape, with its predominance of slate.

Yet despite its rugged, mountainous appearance, it is not a true *sierra* or *cordillera*, but the southern extension of the Castilian Meseta, which descends sharply into the Guadalquivir depression. Starting its life to the north of Jaén, where it reaches its maximum altitude (Sierra Madrona – 1 323m/4 339ft) it extends west to form the Sierra de Hornachuelos in the province of Córdoba, the Sierra Norte in the province of Sevilla and the Sierra de Aracena in the province of Huelva.

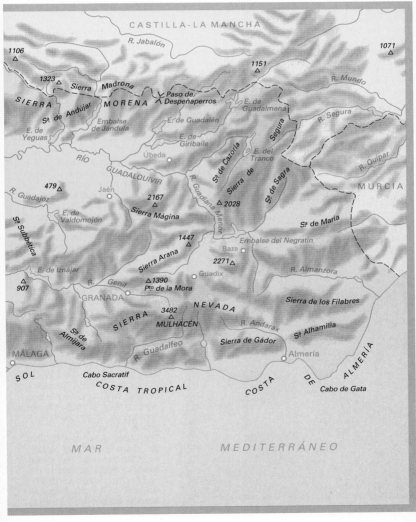

Through the ages, the approach to Andalucia from the Meseta has been via the **Despeñaperros pass**, a defile cut by the river of the same name in an area of astonishing geological formations covered with cork, holm and gall oaks. As a result of work carried out in recent years, the road traversing the pass is much less arduous than in times past, and is almost as spectacular as the route created by the French architect, Le Maur, in 1779.

In addition to its significant importance in terms of game, with areas which are abundant in deer and wild boar, the Sierra Morena is also home to a wealth of protected fauna such as wolves, Iberian lynx, imperial eagles, and black and tawny vultures.

The mountain range contains three natural parks. Two of these are found in the province of Jaén, **Despeñaperros** and the **Sierras de Andújar**, the third in the north of Huelva province. The latter, the **Sierra de Aracena y Picos de Aroche**, is one of the largest in the whole of Andalucia (184 000ha/454 664 acres), set in a mountainous area with varied vegetation, covering 28 small communities with a total population of 41 000 inhabitants. Each of these wealthy communities earns its livelihood from cork oak (from which cork is obtained), the rearing of black pigs (the best hams in Spain are produced in Jabugo, Cortegana and Cumbres Mayores) and, in recent years, from rural tourism (mainly from the province of Sevilla), which is increasing in importance throughout the region.

The Parque Natural de las Sierras de Andújar occupies the heart of the Sierra Morena and is an excellent example of a Mediterranean ecosystem with its varied, abundant vegetation and large swathes of forest and Mediterranean scrub.

Guadalquivir Depression

The Guadalquivir River running through Córdoba province

The spine of Andalucia, as it is known, runs between the Sierra Morena to the north and the Cordilleras Béticas to the south. This former area of Tartessian settlement forms a triangle of flat landscapes whose highest point is found to the east, in the province of Jaén, descending to the lowest part of the depression along the Gulf of Cádiz, where the Atlantic exerts its considerable influence.

The whole valley, which covers 65% of Andalucia, is a densely populated, predominantly agricultural area owing to its deep, fertile black soil, which is well served by the water brought from the tributaries of the Guadalquivir. As a result, the valley is home to plantations of fruits and vegetables, large areas devoted to the growing of cereal crops, olive groves and vineyards.

The Guadalquivir depression is also home to two of Spain's most historic cities, namely **Córdoba** and **Sevilla**, as well as one of Europe's most impressive national parks, the **Parque Nacional de Doñana**, with its abundance of flora and fauna.

Ch. Sappa/HOA QUI

Guadalquivir River

The Romans called it Betis, while to the Moors it was known as the Great River (Guad-al-Quivir in Arabic); irrespective of its name, however, it has always been the soul of Andalucia, and is the only river (670km/419mi) which flows exclusively through the region. Due to the thrust of the powerful Cordilleras Béticas to the south, its path has gradually shifted northwards, to such an extent that it now flows at the very foot of the Sierra Morena.

The Guadalquivir rises in the **Sierra de Cazorla** (Jaén), at an altitude of 1 600m/5 248ft. After a brief journey through the mountains, it then enters the Baetica Depression, gently flowing from an altitude of 100m/328ft in the province of Córdoba to just 10m/32ft in Sevilla. With the additional waters of its tributary, the Genil, the river is navigable from the city of Sevilla to the Atlantic, where it forms a huge marshland area (Doñana), which the Romans named Lacus Ligustinus.

Although the Guadalquivir's tributaries flowing down from the Sierra Morena (the Viar, Bembézar and Guadiato) all follow a short course and are particularly erosive, those starting life in the Cordilleras Béticas, the Guadiana Menor and Genil in particular, carry a far greater volume of water.

The rivers of Andalucia

In addition to the Guadalquivir basin, the region's hydrographic network consists of a variety of rivers, the volume of which can vary enormously from one season to the next. The reservoirs built during the second half of the 20C have enabled their flow to be regulated, thus increasing areas under cultivation.

Andalucia's major Atlantic rivers, such as the Guadiana, Tinto, Odiel and Guadalete, are all of significant length, carry relatively large volumes of water, and form estuaries and sand bars where they flow into the ocean.

The rivers descending to the Mediterranean coast (Guadiaro, Guadalhorce, Guadalfeo, Adra, Almería and Almanzora) begin their life in the Cordilleras Béticas, are shorter in length, and, in general, form deltas at their point of entry into the sea. During periods of low water in the provinces of Granada and Almería, the wide, deep gullies known as **ramblas**, which are in fact the beds of rivers, remain empty of water, to such an extent that during longer periods of drought, local people often use these *ramblas* for planting crops and even for building. Needless to say, during periods of heavy rain, the torrents of water cascading down these erstwhile dry beds destroy everything in their path, resulting in huge losses of material possessions and even loss of life.

Mention should also be made of Andalucia's large wetland areas, including the Ría del Tinto-Odiel, the Bay of Cádiz, Adra and the Doñana National Park, as well as the region's salt marshes and lagoons, underground aquifers, and inland areas dotted with lakes, such as **Fuente de Piedra** (Málaga).

Cordilleras Béticas

This chain is the highest to be found in Andalucia and acts as a natural barrier between the Guadalquivir and the coast. It occupies almost all of eastern Andalucia and is formed by two ranges of Alpine-type ranges: the Cordillera Subbética to the north and the Cordillera Penibética to the south. An inner corridor, known as the **Depresión Penibética**, runs between the two.

This depression widens out to the east, forming the **Depresión de Granada**, irrigated by the Genil, continuing along the **Guadix** and Baza basins, before skirting either side of the **Sierra de Filabres**, forming the Almanzora Valley and the Almería depressions.

The **Sistema Subbético**, which connects with the Sierra Morena to the east, is less well defined, however. The highest sections of this chain are the Sierras de Cazorla, **Segura** and **Las Villas** (600m/1 968ft – 2 100m/6 888ft), which together have been designated a natural park. This particular area, dotted with oak, arbutus (strawberry tree) and rowan trees, is a haven for birds of prey, mountain goats and various types of game. The **Cordillera Penibética**, which is higher than the Cazorla, Segura and Las Villas ranges, extends parallel to the coast from the **Serranía de Ronda** to the west, in the province of Málaga, as far as Murcia. The highest summits in Andalucia are found in the **Sierra Nevada**, near Granada, with a cluster of 14 peaks over 3 000m/9 840ft, including **Monte Veleta** (3 392m/11 125ft) and **Mulhacén** (3 481m/11 418ft), the highest peak on the Iberian Peninsula. On its southern flank is the historic **Alpujarras** region, renowned for its wilderness and difficult access. To the east, behind the **Sierra de Los Filabres** and the **Sierra de Gádor** in the province of Almería, lies a large volcanic region, the **Cabo de Gata-Níjar**, with its spectacular landscapes which provide a dramatic contrast with the deep blue sea.

The Coast

Andalucia's 900km/562mi of coastline is one of Europe's most visited tourist areas. Its beaches, where many centuries ago merchants from the East and invaders from North Africa first set foot on European soil, are now the domain of visitors with more peaceful intentions from Spain and abroad who wish to spend an enjoyable holiday in the sun or retire here away from the colder climates of Northern Europe.

Costa de Almería

The coastline extending from the Portuguese border to the Straits of Gibraltar is known as the **Costa de la Luz** (Coast of Light), and enjoys the slightly cooler influence of the Atlantic. Until recently, these vast beaches of fine sand were deserted apart from a handful of small resorts such as La Antilla and Matalascañas in Huelva, which were popular with Spanish families, particularly from Sevilla. Over the past few years, a number of new large tourist complexes have begun to attract more foreign visitors, such as Zahara de los Atunes, Caños de Meca and Tarifa, a town popular with surfers from around the world.

The beaches of the Mediterranean are neither as long nor as open as their Atlantic counterparts; they are, however, far better known, undoubtedly because visitors can be guaranteed fine weather almost all year round. The beaches around Marbella, the capital of the famous **Costa del Sol** (Sun Coast), are not as attractive as those in Rincón de la Victoria, also in the province of Málaga; however the luxurious infrastructure and sporting facilities of this glamorous resort more than make up for this. The **Costa Tropical**, to the south of Granada, is a rocky coast with crystal-clear water perfect for snorkelling and scuba diving, while the **Costa de Almería** further east, with its quieter beaches, some with protected status, such as those at Los Genoveses and Cabo de Gata, is the ideal coastline for visitors with environmental issues at heart.

CLIMATE, VEGETATION AND FAUNA

Climate

In general terms, the climate of Andalucia is Mediterranean in nature with dry summers and relatively mild winters, during which the region receives the majority of its somewhat scarce and irregular precipitation. The region's average annual temperature is 16.8°C/63°F.

Because of the size of Andalucia and the presence of high mountain ranges skirting an extensive stretch of coastline along two huge bodies of water, closer analysis of the Andalucian climate shows significant differences between areas. As an example, although the Guadalquivir Valley has a climate that could be described as typically Mediterranean, neighbouring mountain areas are much colder and receive far greater precipitation. Along the coast, a marked contrast can also be seen between the beaches of the Mediterranean, with its calm, warm waters, and those of the more open Atlantic coast, characterised by colder waters and frequent strong winds, particularly around Tarifa on the Straits of Gibraltar, a paradise for windsurfers, where the average wind strength is 30.6kph/19mph.

Closer study of specific areas clearly shows the region's climatic differences; this can be seen along a line stretching from Andújar through Córdoba to Sevilla, where temperatures in summer often exceed 40°C/104°F and where spring, considered to be the best time of the year, starts at the end of February. The most westerly parts of the Sierra Morena, such as the Sierra de Cádiz and the Sierra de Málaga, in the Cordilleras Béticas, are the wettest areas of Andalucia due to the influence of Atlantic winds, while the Sierra de Grazalema registers precipitation levels above 4 000l per year, the highest in Spain. The region's coldest temperatures have been recorded in the Sierra Nevada, where snow remains on the highest peaks all year round and where the ski slopes stay open until May. In complete contrast, the startling Campo de Níjar area in the province of Almería is arid, volcanic and desert-like, with temperatures to match.

Vegetation

Andalucia is also home to a huge variety of plants and flowers. Perhaps the most representative landscapes of the region are the mountain ranges skirting the Mediterranean, with their small shrubs and bushes such as rockrose, lentisk (mastic tree) and juniper, aromatic plants (thyme, lavender and rosemary), and trees belonging to the Quercus family, including evergreen, gall and cork oak. Carobs, chestnuts, and wild olives, the latter occasionally attaining an impressive size, can often be seen in areas covered by forests of oak.

Pine trees are more prevalent at higher altitudes, as well as in coastal regions. Several species, including the umbrella and maritime pines, used to prevent sand dune erosion along the Atlantic coast, are found in these areas, as are the resistant holm oak and larch. Many of these trees, along with the ubiquitous eucalyptus, are the result of reafforestation schemes undertaken at a time when little thought was given to vegetation native to these areas. The **Spanish fir**, a tree considered to be a relic from the Tertiary era, is also common to the region, although it is generally only found in the woods around Grazalema (Cádiz), and in the Sierra de las Nieves and Sierra Bermeja mountains, both of which are in the province of Málaga.

Forests of ash, willow and poplar all grow alongside rivers, streams and lakes, while wetland areas are the natural habitat for various species of reeds, salt cedars and coarse grasses – ideal nesting grounds for aquatic birds.

Andalucia's myriad protected habitats are also home to a breathtaking variety of vegetation (the oak forests of Sierra Quintana, near Andújar, and the cork oak groves in the province of Cádiz), much of which is endemic to the region and has already disappeared from the rest of Europe.

Olive tree

Umbrella pine

M. Janvier/MICHELIN

Fauna

The region has an equally rich and varied fauna, which includes a number of protected species, some of which are either extinct or dying out in the rest of the world, such as the monk seal, found on the Chafarinas islands (Almería), and the malvasia duck, whose habitat is found in the lakes of the Sierra Subbética in the province of Córdoba. In addition to species of game such as wild boar, stag, deer, mountain goat and the mouflon (particularly abundant in the Sierra de Cazorla and Sierra de Segura), large populations of **lynx** and **ichneumon**, both of which are carefully protected, are also found in the region.

Andalucia's birdlife warrants special mention, given the presence of 184 different species of birds which nest in the region, in addition to the fifty or so others which spend their winters here. The area's numerous aquatic birds include the **pink flamingo**, which flourishes only in Fuente de Piedra (Málaga) and the French Camargue, and the eastern glossy ibis, a bird found only in Andalucia. Birds of prey, such as the magnificent **imperial eagle**, the Egyptian vulture and the black vulture tend to nest in the more inaccessible parts of the region.

PROTECTED AREAS

Although man has spent several millennia exploiting the mineral and agricultural wealth of Andalucia and raising cattle on its land, and despite the environmental damage caused during the course of the 20C, 1 500 000ha/3 700 000 acres of land, or 17% of the region's total area, are currently designated as protected areas – a percentage that is one of the highest in Europe.

Each of these distinct 82 areas is a natural paradise in which man shares the land with protected fauna and flora in perfect harmony. As is the case elsewhere, serious ecological disasters still occur; however, the majority of Andalucia's population are conscious of the fact that their survival and evolution depends upon maintaining the environmental balance of their land.

See list of protected areas on p 346.

Andalucia today

POLITICAL AND ADMINISTRATIVE ORGANISATION

Once democracy was restored to Spain after the death of General Franco in 1975, Andalucia was the fourth *comunidad* to be recognised within the Spanish state, which is now made up of 17 autonomous communities.
The Statute of Autonomy, approved in 1981, was a response to the wishes of the Andalucian people as expressed in the referendum on 28 February 1980.

Political organisation – The **Junta de Andalucía** is the autonomous executive body that coordinates and manages the administration of the region. Its president works in collaboration with the Consejo de Gobierno (Cabinet), currently made up of 13 ministers each responsible for a separate department.
Legislative functions are performed by the **Andalucian Parliament** (Parlamento de Andalucía), the seat of which is in Sevilla. Its 109 members are elected by universal suffrage every four years.
The region's highest court is the **Tribunal Superior de Justicia** in Granada.
Centralised administration is the responsibility of the government's delegate for Andalucia (Delegado del Gobierno), whose office is based in Sevilla, beneath whom affairs are managed by a network of provincial subdelegates *(subdelegados)*.

Administrative organisation – The Autonomous Community of Andalucia comprises eight

> ### Blas Infante (1885-1936)
>
> During the Second Republic, this politician made his name as the leader of the Andalucian Movement. He participated in the drafting of the preliminary bill for the Statute of Andalucia (1933) and presided over the assembly formed to ensure the recognition of the Confederate Andalucian State. The author of *El ideal andaluz* (1915) among other works, he was shot shortly after the outbreak of the Spanish Civil War.

provinces: Almería, Cádiz, Córdoba, Huelva, Jaén, Granada, Málaga and Sevilla. The administrative boundaries of these *provincias* have stayed the same since they were established as part of the reforms of Javier de Burgos in the middle of the 19C; each is governed by its own provincial parliament *(diputación)*. The basic territorial unit is the *municipio*, governed by a town hall *(ayuntamiento)*. Some municipalities with economic or social problems have merged to form larger communities or *mancomunidades*, enabling them to obtain better services at reduced cost.

The three symbols of Andalucia: the flag, the coat of arms and the anthem

Although definitively approved by a law passed by the Andalucian Parliament as part of the new democratic process, the three symbols of Andalucia are not a new creation. In fact, the Statute of Andalucia (1982) clearly stated that the anthem, coat of arms and green and white flag would be those defined by the Assembly of Ronda in 1918 and by the Juntas Liberalistas de Andalucía in 1933. The Andalucian people have fully embraced these "insignia of Andalucia", as referred to by Blas Infante, the creator of this trilogy.
The region's flag consists of three horizontal bands: green, white and green.
The coat of arms, inspired by the escutcheon of the city of Cádiz, shows Hercules between two columns subduing two lions. Above him is the Latin inscription *Dominator Hercules Fundator* and at his feet the motto *Andaluc'a, por s', para Espa–a y para la Humanidad* (Andalucia by itself, for Spain and for Humanity).
The anthem, the third symbol of Andalucian nationality, embraces the traditional claims of its people, reaffirming their love of peace and their desire for a future in which they regain the privileged position they occupied in the past.

ECONOMY

To express his admiration for the immense natural riches of Andalucia, the Greek geographer Strabo compared the region with the Elysian Fields. How is it possible, therefore, that in centuries to come, peasants were plunged into starvation and then forced to emigrate?

Agricultural decadence began with the expulsion of the Moors. Land was abandoned while new settlers, fewer in number than those who had already left, showed greater enthusiasm for warfare and the colonisation of America than for agricultural work. In years to come, large landowners *(caciques)* and the ruling classes did little to improve the situation. However, there are those who believe that the "traditional" underdevelopment of Andalucia is in reality a relatively new phenomenon which began in the second half of the 19C. In fact, at the beginning of the 19C the distribution of wealth was reasonably uniform across the whole country. The development of the Hispanic capitalist society had an extremely detrimental effect on the lands of southern Spain, to the extent that in 1935 the per capita income in Andalucia was just 717 pesetas, against 1 307 pesetas in the rest of the country. The problems intensified in the post-war period, when the most impoverished were forced to emigrate to other Spanish regions (mainly Catalonia and the Basque Country) and to various European countries (particularly Germany, France and Switzerland). During the 1960s, over 900 000 Andalucians left their native region.

This situation slowly began to improve during the 1970s, although the endemic problems besetting the region remained: the unequal distribution of land into large estates *(latifundios)*, low levels of industrial investment and poor professional training for workers. During the second half of the 1980s, the region enjoyed another economic revival, particularly in the provinces along the Mediterranean coast.

1992 was to be a key year in Andalucia's economic development. The World Expo in Sevilla, which received 40 million visitors, brought with it tremendous economic benefits to the region's capital and coastal towns and cities, and had a positive effect on other provinces, with the construction of the motorway linking Sevilla, Córdoba, Granada and Málaga and the creation of the AVE high-speed rail link between Madrid and Sevilla via Córdoba.

Following the euphoria of 1992, a new industrial crisis hit the region, exacerbated by problems linked to drought, forest fires and unemployment.

In recent years, growth in Andalucia has been similar to the national average, while the region's official unemployment rate, although the highest in Spain, has been significantly reduced to 13%.

Agriculture – This sector is the mainstay of the region's economy. Cereal production is concentrated in the province of Sevilla (the country's leading province for cereals), Cádiz, Almería and Granada; fruits (particularly citrus fruits) and vegetables are mainly produced in the fertile lowlands of Granada; olives in Jaén and Granada; vines in Jerez, Montilla and Málaga; and cotton in Córdoba and Sevilla. Over the past few years, the provinces of Huelva and Almería have become covered with a sea of plastic, used to protect early crops and a range of other produce.

Animal breeding – The majority of farms are concentrated on the pasturelands of the Sierra Morena, the Sierra de Cádiz and the Cordillera Subbética. In the main, these fenced-in lands have been stripped of their low bushes and scrub and, in places, of their natural vegetation of holm and cork oak. These areas constitute an agro-forestry system which is unique in Europe, where in addition to animal breeding, firewood, cork and honey are also produced.

Traditional breeding, which is extensive in nature, takes advantage of natural pasture to raise select and, in many cases, exclusively Andalucian, breeds, such as the Cartujana horse, merino sheep, Iberian pig and the fighting bull.

Industry – Andalucia is a region with limited industry, where the majority of plants and factories are located in and around the major cities. The province of Cádiz is known for its chemical and petrochemical plants, particularly around Algeciras, while the processing of agricultural products is a vital part of the region's economy as a result of the huge production of excellent-quality olive oil and wine. The wines from the provinces of Cádiz (sherry and brandy around Jerez, in particular), Córdoba and Málaga are famous the world over, while the province of Jaén produces more olive oil than any other Spanish province.

Mining – Although lead is still mined in Jaén, Almería and Córdoba, pyrites and manganese in Huelva and iron in Granada, Sevilla and Almería, the mines of Andalucia are now a mere shadow of their former selves. Gone are the days when, at the end of the 19C, the English company which acquired the mines at Riotinto (Huelva) employed over 10 000 workers or when, at the time of the Phoenicians, the kingdom of Tartessus enjoyed great prosperity due to the mineral and metal deposits found in its soil.

Fishing – Andalucia is Spain's second largest fishing region, after Galicia, with a total annual catch of 68 000 tonnes of fish (tuna and sardines, in particular), 12 600 tonnes of molluscs (clams, cockles), and 3 200 tonnes of crustaceans (shrimps, prawns).

Tourism – The majority of the 15 million people who visit the region every year stay mainly along the Costa del Sol. In terms of visitors, Andalucia is Spain's third most important destination for foreign tourists and the number one choice for the Spanish.

Historical table and notes

The Phoenicians

Towards the end of the second millennium BC, at the same time as the first Indo-European tribes were crossing the Pyrenees, navigators from the far east of the Mediterranean were landing on the southern coast of Spain. The discovery of riches in the south of the peninsula (silver, gold, copper and tin) led the **Phoenicians** to found their colonies here first.

1100 BC	Foundation of Gadir (Cádiz), the largest Phoenician colony in the Western Mediterranean. Minerals extracted from the Riotinto and Aznalcóllar mines were exported from here.
8C-7C BC	The apogee of the kingdom of Tartessus, which trades with Phoenician and Greek colonies established in the southern part of the peninsula.

The Kingdom of Tartessus (?8C-6C BC)

This kingdom, which later came to be identified with the biblical Tarsis, and whose legendary status is equal to that of Atlantica, reached its pinnacle in the 9C and 8C BC and died out in the 6C BC, either a victim of the Carthaginian invasion or simply as a result of the major crisis which affected the Mediterranean after the conquest of the city of Tyre by Nebuchadnezzar (573 BC). The wealth of this kingdom dazzled the Greeks and Phoenicians and has amazed modern archeologists, who have discovered numerous remains of this civilisation in Huelva, Sevilla and Córdoba.

Greek and Latin writers date the mythical foundation of Tartessus to around the year 1200 BC. Others believed that the Tartessian monarchy had two different dynasties. The first was founded by Geryon – a creature with three heads and three bodies – who was defeated by Hercules, and the second by Gargoris and his son Habis, the inventor of agriculture.

Modern researchers believe the Tartessian civilisation evolved from the Megalithic culture of southern Spain. The civilisation developed to such a degree that it had its own written laws, a well-organised society comprising seven social groups and an excellent knowledge of the techniques for transforming metal. The dynasty's only historical king was Arganthonios, who ruled during the 7C BC and was praised by writers such as Herodotus, Anacreon and Pliny. Despite the many archeological findings, the exact location of the civilisation's capital is still uncertain, although it is thought to have been situated close to Sanlúcar de Barrameda (Cádiz).

The Carthaginians

6C-4C BC	Various **Iberian tribes** continue to inhabit the peninsula. Andalucia remains the most homogenous region. The **Carthaginians** gradually settle in southern Spain, replacing the Phoenicians. Cádiz develops into a major port and a prosperous city, while the Mediterranean coast of Andalucia experiences increasing growth.
264-241	**First Punic War**. Rome defeats Carthage and significantly reduces its freedom of movement and its income in the Mediterranean.
237	The Carthaginian general **Hamilcar Barca** lands in Cádiz, makes a pact with the Iberians and establishes an operational base against the Romans in southern Spain. He is followed by **Hasdrubal**, who commandeers richer lands in the region and founds his capital at Nova Carthago (Cartagena, Murcia). The Carthaginians improve agricultural techniques in the Guadalquivir Valley, which they transform into an important grain-producing area. Carthaginian fishing boats ply the Andalucian coast and set up a flourishing salting industry.
218-201	**Second Punic War**. Rome is victorious once more and the Carthaginians are forced to relinquish their Spanish territory.

Roman domination

197	The Romans conquer Cádiz, the last Carthaginian stronghold in Spain.
83-45	Hispania is the stage for the civil war between Sertorius and Sulla and for the Pompeyan wars, which are brought to an end by Caesar's victory in Munda (Montilla) in 45 BC.
40	Caius Octavius **Augustus** is declared Roman Emperor. This heralds the integration of Hispania into Roman politics.

Romanisation – With the rise of Julius Caesar to power, Rome begins to establish a determined policy of colonisation, which involves the founding and regeneration of cities. Augustus divides the peninsula into three large provinces: Tarraconensis, Lusitania and **Baetica** (Andalucia). As a result of its greater degree of Romanisation, the latter comes to depend on the Senate even though the other provinces remain under the control of the Emperor. Perhaps in order to compensate for the bloodshed suffered in previous years, as well as to house veterans of the civil wars, many cities in Baetica receive special treatment, including Corduba (the capital), Gadir, Hispalis (Sevilla), and Itálica. The region quickly adopts Roman habits and customs: Roman soldiers are granted land, become farmers and marry Iberian women. In order to facilitate the movement of troops and trade to the cities (metals, wine, oil and salted products) a number of roads are built; one of these is the Vía Augusta, which runs parallel to the Mediterranean coast and crosses Baetica from east to west. Andalucia enjoys a period of peace spanning several centuries.

14-37 AD	During the rule of Tiberius a number of Hispanic patricians obtain Roman citizenship and move to Rome. Inhabitants of Baetica who later became famous were among them, such as the philosopher **Seneca**, born in Córdoba in 4 BC, and his nephew **Lucan** (b 39). Both men committed suicide in the imperial city in 65, on the orders of Nero.
74	**Vespasian** grants the right of citizenship to Hispanics in recognition of the part played by the peninsula during the crisis which followed Nero's assassination.
98-117	Rule of Marcus Ulpius **Trajan**, born in Itálica in 53, the first Emperor to be neither Roman nor Italian.
117-138	Rule of **Hadrian**, also originally from Itálica. Baetica and the rest of Hispania reach their zenith.
3C	The arrival of Christianity, probably from North Africa. Rome moves its commercial axis to the East and the slow decline of Hispania begins.
300-314	Council of the Hispanic bishops in Elvira (Granada).
395	Death of **Theodosius**, the last great Roman Emperor, probably born in Itálica.

The pantry of Europe

During their occupation of Hispania the Romans exploited the mines of the Sierra Morena and Riotinto (Huelva), the marble quarries at Macael (Almería), and encouraged the development of agriculture in Baetica. Wines from Cádiz were exported to various parts of the Empire (especially to Italy and the south of France), olive oil was sold in the markets of Rome, Gaul, Germania and Britain, and there was an increase in the raising of livestock in the north of Huelva and on the mud flats of the Guadalquivir. In addition, the fish salting industry in Hispalis and Córdoba experienced the greatest development as a result of the many marine species found along the Andalucian coast. Despite its wealth, Baetica, along with the rest of the peninsula, tended to export the majority of its local products and resources.

Visigothic domination

411-425	The Vandals and Alans occupy Andalucia for a short period until the Visigoths, allied with Rome, and led by Athaulf, succeed in expelling them to North Africa.
441	The Swabian king Rekhila conquers Sevilla.
484-507	The Visigothic occupation of Andalucia is consolidated during the reign of **Alaric II**.
522	The Byzantine Emperor **Justinian** establishes a Byzantine province in the southeast of the peninsula, which is later reconquered by the Visigoths.
568-586	During the reign of Leovigild, Andalucia supports the revolt of **Hermenigild** against his father.
589	Third Council of Toledo and the conversion of the Goths to Catholicism.
615	**Sisebut** implements the first official attempt at eradicating Judaism from the Iberian Peninsula.
8C	During this period, under the influence of **St Leander** (d 600) and **St Isidore** (d 636), who dedicates his *Etymologies* to King Sisebut, Baetica is the only sizeable cultural region in Latin Christendom. Syrian and Greek merchants trade with the south of the peninsula. Jews begin to settle in Córdoba, Sevilla and Málaga. Roman Law is abandoned and the patricians are replaced by bishops and judges.
710	Death of King **Witiza**. Faced with the claims to the throne of **Roderick**, Duke of Baetica, Witiza's followers turn to abroad for assistance.

Muslim Andalucia or al-Andalus (8C-15C)

At the beginning of the 8C the Umayyad Caliphate from Damascus conquers the Berber lands of North Africa. This Caliphate had outgrown the lands of the Arabian Peninsula and the concept of holy war enabled it to express its aggression. The dominant tribes adhere to the Islamic faith and join together with the powerful Muslim forces.

711 An army of 7 000 men under the command of the Berber **Tarik-ibn-Zeyad**, the governor of Tangiers, crosses the Straits and defeats King Roderick near the Guadalete River, or the La Janda lagoons. They march north to conquer Toledo, the capital of the Visigothic kingdom, marking the beginning of Muslim domination in Spain.

712 18 000 soldiers land in Andalucia led by the governor Musa, Tariq's superior.

Damascus increases in size as a result of the Arab conquests. The Caliphs respect the local governments set up in the conquered territories. In 719 the Caliph troops attempt to conquer the south of France but are repulsed in Poitiers by Charles Martel. The Arabs settle in the Guadalquivir Valley and leave the Berbers the less productive lands of Castilla, León and Galicia.

740-750 Confrontations between the various ethnic groups of Islamic faith occupying the peninsula.
In Arabia the Abbasid dynasty assassinates the Umayyads and seizes power from them.

The Emirate of Córdoba (756-929) – The al-Andalus kingdom is created, eventually embracing almost the entire Iberian Peninsula. Although theoretically subject to the authority of the new Abbasid capital of Baghdad, the Andalucian Emirs are practically independent.

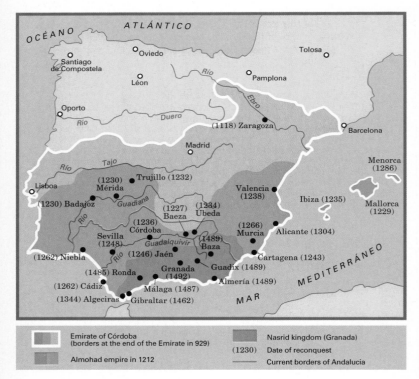

Emirate of Córdoba (borders at the end of the Emirate in 929)	Nasrid kingdom (Granada)
Almohad empire in 1212	(1230) Date of reconquest
	Current borders of Andalucia

755 Abd ar-Rahman, the only remaining member of the Umayyad family, lands in southern Spain and in a short space of time succeeds in uniting all Muslims. A year later he settles in Córdoba and proclaims himself emir. **Abd ar-Rahman I** lays the foundation of the al-Andalus kingdom.

784 Construction of the Mezquita in Córdoba begins.

788-929 On the death of Abd ar-Rahman I, the seemingly resolved tensions explode and internal conflict breaks out between ethnic groups (Arabs, Berbers, Jews, Christians converted to Islam *(muladíes)* and Mozarabs). The Emirate is weakened and the Christian kingdoms of the north strike a number of major blows against the al-Andalus army.

The Caliphate of Córdoba (929-1031) – The new Caliphate, which had finally broken all ties with Baghdad, becomes the most powerful kingdom in the West and its court the most cultured and refined. Spain regains its commercial impetus in the Mediterranean, which had practically been paralysed during the period of Visigothic domination. Muslims and Christians mount raids on each other's territory throughout the peninsula and a network of castles and watchtowers is built to keep an eye on the enemy.

929	Beginning of the rule of **Abd ar-Rahman III** (912-61) who declares himself Caliph and Commander of the Believers, brings peace to his kingdom and strengthens the military border areas of Toledo, Badajoz and Zaragoza.
936	Construction of the city of Medina Azahara begins.
978	General **Almanzor** seizes power and establishes himself as Prime Minister. The Caliph becomes a symbolic figurehead.
1002	The death of Almanzor in Calatañazor. The first outbreaks of civil war destabilise the Caliphate.
1031	End of the Umayyad dynasty. Rebellion of the Cordoban nobility and the destruction of Medina Azahara. The provinces and cities become independent and a number of autonomous kingdoms are created.

First Taifa kingdoms and Almoravid supremacy (1009-1110) – The *taifa* (group or faction in Arabic) kingdoms which appeared at the beginning of the 11C are organised according to ethnic criteria, with the Berbers controlling the coast from the Guadalquivir River to Granada, the Slavs dominating the southeast (Almería and the eastern provinces) and the Arabs holding power in Córdoba and Sevilla.

At first the *taifa* kingdoms make alliances with their neighbours, although some of them also enter into pacts with the Christians where necessary, even to the extent of paying taxes in order to remain on their own land.

The Christian monarchs exploit their enemies' weaknesses and succeed in conquering a number of large towns.

1042	Construction of the Alcázar begins in Sevilla.
1064	Work begins on the Alcazaba in Málaga.
1085	**Alfonso VI** of Castilla and León conquers Toledo. Lengthy Christian campaigns are waged against Sevilla and Badajoz. **Al-Mutamid**, king of Sevilla, feels threatened and calls upon the Almoravids of North Africa for assistance. Yusuf Ibn Tashunin responds to the plea for help, crosses the Straits of Gibraltar and in a short time manages to assume control of all the *taifa* kingdoms.
1118	The expeditions of **Alfonso I** *(El Batallador)* in Andalucia expose the weakness of the Almoravids at a time when the Almohad movement is beginning to gain ground in Morocco.

Second Taifa kingdoms (1144-70) and Almohad supremacy – For a short period of time the *taifa* kingdoms reappear, taking advantage of the decline of the Almoravids. They were soon to disappear once more, this time as a result of the Almohad invasion led by Abd al-Mumin (the *Miramamolin* of Christian chronicles).

1147	Almohad troops occupy Marrakech, Tarifa and Algeciras. Overcoming Christian resistance and that of the Moorish kings in the eastern provinces, the Almohads manage to take control of southern Spain.
1163	Sevilla becomes the capital of Al-Andalus.
1184	Work starts on the Great Mosque *(Mezquita Mayor)* in Sevilla, whose minaret is later known as the Giralda.
1195	The Battle of Alarcos (Ciudad Real), in which Al-Mansur is victorious over the Castilian king **Alfonso VIII**, is the last great triumph of the Almohad army. This moment marks the beginning of the decline of the Muslim invaders.
1212	**Battle of Las Navas de Tolosa**. The armies of Castilla, Aragón and Navarra finally defeat the Almohads.

The Nasrid kingdom (1232-1492) – During the last phase of declining Almohad power, Mohammed I, of the Banu Nasr or Nasríes (Nasrid) dynasty, succeeds in uniting the territories of Granada, Málaga and Almería to create a kingdom that was to last for two and a half centuries, protected by the sea and the mountains. In order to secure power, he initially accepts his position as a vassal of the Castilian kings and fights alongside them during the conquest of Sevilla. However, he subsequently takes advantage of the expulsion of the Moors by the Christians to build up a highly populated and productive kingdom.

The reigns of the 23 Nasrid kings were often beset with interminable internal strife, with the fall of the Nasrid kingdom brought about by the violent disputes between the Cegri and Abencerraje families.

1237	Work starts on the Alcazaba, the oldest part of the Alhambra palace.
1313	Construction of the Generalife begins.
1248	The **Conquest of Sevilla** by the Christian troops establishes a frontier which remains unchanged until the 15C.
1410	Don Fernando, the Castilian Infante, takes Antequera.
1462	**Enrique IV** conquers Gibraltar and Archidona. The Nasrids appeal for assistance from various Muslim countries, but no help is forthcoming.
1464-82	Reign of **Muley Hacén** (Abu l-Hasan in Arabic), who provokes the animosity of his people by introducing high taxes.
1482-92	Boabdil, son of Muley Hacén, deposes his father and accedes to the throne. He decides to attack Lucena but is taken prisoner by the Catholic Kings, who release him in exchange for his continuing opposition to his father. Muley Hacén dies and is succeeded by his brother, El Zagal. The Nasrids suffer a series of defeats.
1492	**Boabdil** surrenders and retires to the Alpujarras seigniory made available to him by his victors. Shortly after he moves to the Maghreb and settles in Fez.

The Reconquest (12C-15C)

The break up of the Caliphate and the proclamation of the Kingdom of Taifas weakens Moorish power. Muslim troops from the various kingdoms concentrate their efforts on fighting over territory rather than holding back the Christian advance.

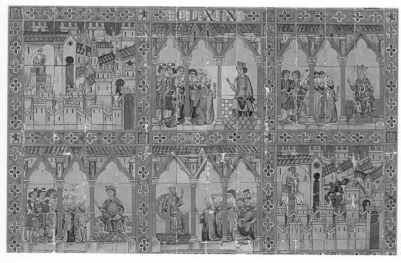

R. Mattès

1158-1214	Reign of **Alfonso VIII**. Beginning of the Christian campaigns in Andalucia. Castilla seizes the Sierra Morena. The Almohads are defeated at Las Navas de Tolosa.
1217-52	**Fernando III the Saint**, King of Castilla, takes a decisive step towards the reconquest of Andalucia by first seizing eastern Andalucia, culminating in his entry into Córdoba in 1236, and then western Andalucia (including Sevilla in 1248).
1252-84	Fernando III's son, **Alfonso X the Wise**, conquers the kingdom of Niebla (Huelva), consolidates the Castilian dominions in Lower Andalucia, suppresses revolts in Cádiz and Jerez and expels large numbers of Muslims.
1284-1469	The Reconquest advances slowly and is halted from the middle of the 14C to the beginning of the 15C. The 15C sees Christian victories during the reigns of Juan II and Enrique IV.
1469	The marriage of **Isabel of Castilla** and **Fernando of Aragón**, to whom the Valencian pope Alexander VI grants the title of the Catholic Monarchs in 1496. Beginning of the unification of the Christian kingdoms.
1481	The Inquisition holds the first *auto-da-fé* in Sevilla.
1482-92	The **Catholic Monarchs** begin their major offensive against the Nasrid kingdom of Granada. Muslim cities fall to the Christians one after the other: Ronda (1485), Málaga (1487), Baza (1489), Almería and Guadix (1489).
2 January 1492	**Boabdil** hands over the keys of the city of Granada to the Catholic Monarchs. As part of the surrender agreement, the Christian monarchs promise to respect the religion, laws and customs of those who wish to remain in the country.

Consequences of the Reconquest

In the 13C the repopulation of Andalucia took place in two stages: the first during the reign of Fernando III and the second during that of Alfonso X; those Moors who resisted were forced to emigrate. It is thought that between 1240 and 1270 more than 300 000 Muslims fled their homes in order to settle, almost exclusively, in Granada. Immediately after the revolt of 1262 and the resulting expulsion of Muslims, the workforce was substantially reduced and the region saw an increase in the development of huge estates *(latifundios)*. The reconquest of the kingdom of Granada had very similar consequences. However, on this occasion the majority of inhabitants remained in their towns and villages as a result of the agreement signed by the Catholic Monarchs promising to respect their religion, laws and customs. The breaking of this promise by the Christians provoked two rebellions in the Alpujarras mountains, which were violently put down. In 1570 the Moors were forced to disperse throughout Castilla. The final expulsion was ordered in 1609.

The Golden Age of Andalucia

Trade with **America** brought wealth to Sevilla and the surrounding region, including Córdoba and Málaga. The city was transformed into a major Spanish city and a paradise for powerful merchants, adventurers and those on the margins of society. The situation in the rest of Andalucia was different. The arrival of new products from the Indies (cochineal, indigo) had an effect on the region's traditional textile industry, while Granada's silk industry, which produced satin, velvet and damask, suffered immeasurably from the austere clothing policy imposed on the Spanish Empire by the Habsburgs. However, Córdoba began to specialise in the production of harnesses and cordovans made from American leather, while the mercury from the mines of Almadén, used in the production of silver amalgams, became indispensable for exploiting the silver mines of Mexico and Peru. On the other hand, the continuous increases in taxes and the relentless demand for agricultural produce helped to concentrate land in the hands of the most powerful.

1492	**Christopher Columbus** sets sail from the port of Palos de la Frontera (Huelva). On 12 October he arrives at Guanahani Island (Bahamas). **Expulsion of the Jews** who have not converted to Christianity. More than 150 000 people are forced to leave Sefarad (Spain). The majority of them settle in Mediterranean countries, where they form Sephardic communities in which the inhabitants continue to speak the Spanish of that period.
1499-1501	**First Alpujarras rebellion**. The intransigence of Cardinal Cisneros provokes an uprising by Muslims from the Albaicín in Granada. This soon spreads to the Alpujarras region, the Sierra de los Filabres and the Serranía de Ronda.
1502	Publication of a decree which forces the Muslim rebels to convert to Christianity or leave the country. The majority opt for baptism. From this moment on, Moors who convert are known as **Moriscos**.
1503	The Casa de Contratación, which monopolises the colonial market, is founded in Sevilla.
1516	**Carlos I**, later to become Emperor under the name Carlos V, inherits the Spanish throne on the death of his grandfather Fernando the Catholic.

1520-22	The Spanish, incensed by Carlos V's largely Flemish court advisers and the increasing number of taxes, rise up in arms. The emperor quells **Comuneros** revolts in Andalucia.
1530	Construction of Carlos V's palace begins in the Alhambra.
1556	Carlos V abdicates in favour of his son **Felipe II**.

The Spanish Inquisition

The Court of the Inquisition was set up in 1468 in order to punish converted Jews who continued to practice their religion in secret; ultimately, its use was gradually extended to include the suppression of all kinds of moral or heretic deviations. Its extensive and complex organisation was made up of a council of the Supreme Inquisition and local, fiscal and domestic inquisitors. All methods were considered suitable for extracting a confession from the accused; however, once condemned, the offender was handed over to the secular branch of the organisation to carry out the sentence. During the four centuries of the Inquisition (it was abolished by the Cádiz courts in 1813) it was a highly effective tool of suppression used by both the Church and the State, especially in the period up to the 18C.

1568-71	**Second Alpujarras rebellion**. Afraid that the Moors would ally themselves with the Turks and Berbers, Felipe II outlaws the use of Arabic and the observance of the Islamic religion. Revolts erupt throughout the region. The Moors from Granada disperse throughout Spain.
1599	The painter **Diego Velázquez** is born in Sevilla, where he will work until 1622.

The Crises of the 17C-18C

The first half of the 17C witnessed the beginning of Andalucia's decline. One of the causes was the drop in population, decimated by four major plagues (in 1649 the population of Sevilla was reduced by half) and by the final expulsion of the *moriscos*, whose work was of fundamental importance to agriculture. In the next few years the situation in the Andalucian countryside continued to decline, with most of the land falling into the hands of large landowners. More than 80% of agricultural workers were day labourers and only 7% of land belonged to those who worked it. Gradually the wealthy created a powerful rural oligarchy closely connected to the municipal administration which completely controlled the life of the people. Industry in Sevilla, closely bound to maritime trade, collapsed after the silting up of the Guadalquivir at Sanlúcar, preventing large ships from navigating upstream.

1610	**Decree of expulsion** of the *morisco* population.
1621	**Felipe IV** ascends to the throne.
1641	Riots in the region's main towns and cities are the result of the people's discontent with the economic crisis.
1680	Cádiz becomes an Atlantic trading port, taking over the role previously held by Sevilla.
1700	**Carlos II**, the last monarch of the House of Austria, dies in Madrid.
1702	Beginning of the **War of the Spanish Succession** between Felipe V and Carlos of Habsburg. In the course of the struggle, the British, who supported the Archduke Carlos, take **Gibraltar**. The Treaty of Utrecht (1713) ratifies English control of the Rock.
1767	**Carlos III** begins the repopulation of the Sierra Morena *(see p 19)*.
1788	The colonial monopoly of Cádiz is abolished.

The social conflicts of the 19C

At the beginning of the century there was little industrial development in Andalucia. The mining of natural resources began towards the middle of the century, although in 1868 the mining industry was taken over by foreign monopolies. At the same time, the shipbuilding industry experienced significant growth in Cádiz, agricultural produce began to be sold commercially and large sections of the railway network were built. Continued trade with the colonies, which was to last until 1898, also enabled exchanges with a number of European countries. As a result of these contacts, groups of middle-class liberals began to develop in major towns and cities.

1808	The French army enters Spain. Beginning of the **War of Independence** (Peninsular War). On 19 July General Dupont is defeated at **Bailén**.
1812	During the French invasion the **Cortes de Cádiz** (Cádiz Parliament) is convened and the liberal **Constitution of Cádiz** is drawn up.
1814	End of the War of Independence.
1820	**Rafael del Riego** leads a liberal revolt in Andalucia and forces King Fernando VII to reinstate the 1812 constitution.

1835-37	The minister Mendizábal orders the disentailment *(desamortización)* of the property of the Church and town councils.
1840	Andalucian peasants, the victims of liberalism and disentailment, organise themselves in order to improve their living conditions.
1863	Pérez del Álamo, a veterinary surgeon, starts a major Republican uprising which spreads to Málaga, Granada, Jaén and Almería.
1873	Proclamation of the **First Republic**. Tentative efforts at land redistribution. General Pavía suppresses a number of attempts to create the cantons of Sevilla, Cádiz, Granada and Jerez.
1875	**Restoration** of the monarchy (Alfonso XII). Andalucian anarchism develops into terrorism, resulting in an increase in terrorist attacks.

20C

1900-31	Strikes and social struggles continue unabated, led by the trade unions, particularly the CNT and FAI.
1931	Proclamation of the **Second Republic** and minor attempts at agrarian reform which do not satisfy Andalucian farm workers, who are beset by hunger and unemployment.
January 1933	The **Casas Viejas** incident in Cádiz. The revolutionary general strike which started in Cádiz comes to a tragic end when the Civil Guard and riot police set fire to the house in which the anarchist leaders had taken refuge. This brings about the Socialists' defeat in the elections of the same year.
1936-39	In the early days of the **Civil War**, most of Andalucia is held by the military garrisons of the region's cities (Cádiz, Granada, Córdoba and Sevilla), while the east of the region remains loyal to the Republic.
1960	This decade sees an increase in **emigration** to the more industrialised regions of Spain (Basque Country and Catalonia) and to a number of European countries (West Germany, France and Switzerland).
1975	Death of Francisco Franco. **Juan Carlos I** is declared king.
1977	The Spanish Socialist Workers Party (PSOE) wins the elections in Andalucia.
1978	The government of Adolfo Suárez approves the pre-autonomous status of the region and the Junta de Andalucía is established.
1980	Andalucian autonomy is approved by referendum.
1982	The **Autonomous Statute of Andalucia** comes into force. First elections for the Andalucian Parliament. **Rafael Escuredo** becomes the first President of the Junta de Andalucía.
1984	Presidency of Juan Rodríguez de la Borbolla.
1990	Presidency of Manuel Chaves.
1992	World Expo at Sevilla. Inauguration of the Madrid-Sevilla high-speed train (AVE).
August 1999	World Athletics Championships are held in Sevilla.

World Athletics Championships

Art and architecture

Prehistory and Antiquity

Very few regions in Europe possess quite as many vestiges of their prehistoric past as Andalucia. Some of these have been discovered as recently as the 1950s, and it is likely that many more will be discovered in the future. Most of these finds are in areas where access is difficult, such as the hills and mountains in the provinces of Córdoba, Granada, Cádiz, Málaga and Almería.

Of prime importance from the **Paleolithic era** (30000-9000 BC) are the **Pileta caves** at Benaoján (Málaga), with their miles of galleries decorated with paintings of animals and somewhat later symbolic drawings, and the caves at Nerja (Málaga); both of these have been afforded special protection. Meanwhile, at the Ambrosio cave in Vélez Blanco (Almería), the decorative engraved frieze on one of the cave's walls is an unusual example of an open-air sanctuary. The **Neolithic era** saw the development of more schematic anthropomorphous and zoomorphic figures alongside drawings of the sun, idols and various symbols. The caves at Tajo de las Figuras (Cádiz), La Graja (Jaén) and Los Letreros (Vélez Blanco, Almería) all date from this period.

Menga dolmen

B. Kaufmann/MICHELIN

The third millennium BC saw the influx of civilisations from the Mediterranean, heralding the beginning of the **Megalithic culture**, which reached its zenith in the second millennium; the most striking example of this period can be found at **Los Millares** (Gádor, Almería). This large complex of walls and collective sepulchres shows that the people who built it not only knew how to work metals, but also had significant knowledge of ceramics, basket-making and weaving. The Megalithic monuments dating from the second millennium BC are worthy of special note, in particular the collective Menga, Viera and Romeral dolmens at **Antequera**, those at Castilleja de Guzmán and the 4C-3C BC Dolmen del Soto at Trigueros. All of these Megalithic constructions are considered to be the finest to be found anywhere in Spain, both in terms of their size and the high level of culture they reflect.

Oriental influences

Phoenicians – Oriental art came to Andalucia via the Phoenicians who, having founded Gades (Cádiz), established outposts on either side of the Straits of Gibraltar in preparation for further advances along the Mediterranean coast. The oldest Phoenician remains discovered are those from the settlement at Morro de Mezquitilla (Málaga), dating from the 9C BC. A number of other vestiges of the Phoenician culture have also been unearthed in the provinces of Cádiz, Málaga (the tombs at Trayamar) and Almería (Sexi necropolis).

Greeks – Cádiz and Huelva contain the richest examples of Greek ceramics in Andalucia, despite the fact that neither province was home to Greek settlements of any importance. It is highly probable that many of these discoveries were in fact gifts that the Phoenicians bestowed upon the native inhabitants to earn their friendship.

Tartessians – The kingdom of Tartessus (9C-4C BC), which maintained close relations with the Phoenicians, produced a variety of objects made from bronze and ceramic (jugs, water pitchers, amphorae), as well as delicate pieces of goldware (diadems, belts, pendants) decorated with distinctive motifs. Although their function is still unclear, archeologists believe that their use is linked to the worship of various divinities.

Iberians – The earliest examples of Iberian **sculpture** date from the 5C BC and show clear influences from Greek and Phoenician art, with rigid figures represented face on. These artefacts are generally funerary in nature and were used to protect the dead, whose remains were cremated and deposited in urns or sarcophagi, which were then placed in large stone mausoleums, as can be seen at La Toya (Jaén), Baza (Granada) and Villaricos (Almería). The apogee of local sculptural art was from the 5C-4C BC, during which works with clear Hellenic influences were created, such as the magnificent **Dama de Baza**. Iberian **ceramics** also incorporated the salient features introduced by foreign civilisations in Andalucia, in particular the red glaze used by the Phoenicians and vases produced by the Greeks. Their varied designs developed from primitive bands and circumferences to complex drawings of leaves and flowers interspersed with geometric motifs.

Oriental art in museums – The most important archeological finds can now be seen in the museums found in every provincial capital in Andalucia. The Museo Arqueológico in **Granada** contains the most impressive finds from the Phoenician necropolis at Almuñecar, as well as Egyptian alabaster and Greek and Phoenician vases, while the archeological section in the Museo Provincial in **Cádiz** displays several magnificent Egyptian sarcophagi, an impressive small statue of the god Melkart, and various anthropomorphous sarcophagi of Phoenician origin. The kingdom of Tartessus is magnificently represented in the provincial museum in **Huelva**, although the Museo Arqueológico in **Sevilla** has by far the most complete collection of this mythical civilisation, with a number of quite extraordinary exhibits from the Carambolo, Ebora and Mairena treasures. Iberian art also has pride of place in the Museo Provincial in **Jaén**, whose exhibits include pre-5C BC carvings from Porcuna, including warriors, men and women in ceremonial costume, high priests etc.

Roman art (1C BC-4C AD)

In accordance with their custom, the Romans who came to Hispania in the 2C BC immediately introduced the official art from their imperial capital into their new lands through artists accompanying the occupying forces. Although, with the passing of time, many of these works were completed or created entirely on the Iberian peninsula, it is not possible to talk of truly Hispano-Roman art, but of Roman art created in Hispania.

Baetica, the most advanced region on the Iberian peninsula during the period of Roman domination, began to experience significant growth with the development of new settlements, particularly along the Guadalquivir River (Betis under the Romans), planned according to the grid system employed in Rome. Córdoba, the capital of the province, could not match the splendour of **Itálica**, which attained maximum development under the emperors Trajan and Hadrian, both of whom were of Andalucian extraction. In addition, the cities of **Hispalis** (Sevilla), **Carmona** and **Acinipo** (Ronda la Vieja) also contained opulent patrician mansions and large public buildings built using marble from Macael (Almería).

In Roman **sculpture**, representations of emperors (Trajan, Hadrian and Vespasian) and their families were common, as were sculpted figures of goddesses (Venus in Itálica, for example).

Ephebus of Antequera

The decoration of patrician mansions also imitated that of Rome. Multicoloured **mosaics** took up the themes developed in line with the function of the room in which they were laid; small bronze figures reproduced the work created by slaves brought from Africa (standard-holders, candelabra); while the tiny statues of household gods (lares) governed daily activities.

Mention should also be made of the importance of **agricultural villas** – a Roman creation whose layout and design were to inspire popular Andalucian architecture.

Hispano-Roman ceramics

The export of agricultural products to the Italian peninsula encouraged the development of the ceramic industry in Baetica. Production activities specialised in the manufacture of amphorae, which today are known as Dressel 20. To date, over 70 ovens used for this purpose have been discovered in the lower Guadalquivir Valley.

Other workshops, always located outside of towns and cities to reduce the risk of fire, were used to produce a type of widely used domestic ceramic known as **sigillata hispanica**. Typical pieces were bright red in colour and decorated with plant or animal motifs.

Hispano-Visigothic art (6C-8C)

The Visigoths who invaded Spain in the 5C were nomadic tribes who did not possess their own form of architecture. Consequently, paleo-Christian traditions, which had already integrated Byzantine and Oriental influence, remained alive throughout Roman Baetica until the end of the 6C.

The third Council of State in Toledo (589), which proclaimed the unity of the kingdom, marked a starting point for new architectural forms which consolidated to acquire undisputed uniformity.

In religious buildings, the classical basilican plan, albeit slightly modified, as in Alcalá de los Gazules, developed into a cruciform shape. Aisles were separated by columns or pillars supporting **horseshoe arches**. The vaults were generally semicircular in form, while the aisles often had a **wooden armature**. The decoration on the walls, imposts and capitals showed a marked **Oriental influence** with a predominance of **geometric motifs** as opposed to vegetal and very few human figures. The exterior of Visigothic temples were devoid of buttresses of any kind.

Given that almost every Visigothic temple was modified at a later date, the plan of these primitive edifices can now be recognised in just a few buildings, such as in San Pedro de Alcántara (Málaga), El Germo (Córdoba) and Gerena (Sevilla).

The most recognisable feature of Visigothic art is its **gold and silverwork**, which reached its peak of perfection in the 7C. Craftsmen produced two types of work: liturgical items (processional crosses and votive objects such as their famous crowns) and articles of a personal nature (clasps, bracelets, necklaces and pendants). Some of the pieces now exhibited in the region's museums, such as those from **Torredonjimeno** (Jaén), belong to treasure buried by the Visigoths prior to the Moorish conquest.

Hispano-Moorish art (8C-15C)

The Moorish invasion, which may initially have appeared as a terrible tragedy, was in reality the beginning of a magnificent era in which the region's inhabitants manifested

their true creativity and vitality once they came into contact with the aesthetic ideas of Islam.

However, throughout the eight centuries of Moorish occupation in Spain, Andalucian art always retained a series of basic artistic characteristics which clearly distinguished it from all other artistic trends of the period.

Arches – During the early days of Moorish rule, the **horseshoe arch**, with its Visigothic and Oriental influence and alternating red (brick) and white (plaster with lime) voussoirs, was the main feature used in Moorish buildings. The arches had a dual purpose: as an element of support and as a decorative feature, for example to act as a border for a blind arch. The development of intercrossing arches gave rise to the pointed horseshoe-shaped arch, which was extensively used from the 12C onwards.

As time passed, the **foliated arch**, which was already in evidence in the Mezquita in Córdoba, evolved into the highly complex **multifoil arch**.

The **alfiz**, the rectangular moulding surrounding the arch, was another of the recurrent themes of Moorish art, and was to have a major influence on Mudéjar art in subsequent centuries.

Vaults, armatures and artesonado work – Hispano-Moorish vaults took their influence from Oriental Islamic art. Unlike those used in Christian art (arris and fan vaults), their ribs do not cross in the centre of the vault. Perhaps one of the best examples of this can be seen in the enclosure of the mihrab in Córdoba's Mezquita.

Yet, despite the uniqueness of Andalucian vaults, it is undoubtedly the widely used wooden armature which can be considered as the architectural feature which best displays the Moor's technical and aesthetic expertise. Wooden coverings evolved from simple

Ataurique motif

paired and knuckle armatures to the most sophisticated of *artesonado* work decorated with stars to form attractive *lacería* ornamentation.

Decoration: materials and motifs – Hidden behind the austerity of their external walls, the interiors of Andalucian palaces were often of extraordinary splendour, although the rendering used within them often completely masked the poor quality of the construction materials.

The refined aesthetic sense of the Hispano-Moors managed to successfully combine techniques as disparate as **azulejos** and **alicatados** (decorative sections of tiling), panels of stone or sculpted plasterwork, mosaics with Oriental influence, wood worked to form latticework, and exquisite *artesonado*, to create surprisingly sumptuous effects.

The decorative motifs used can be classified into three main groups:

Geometric designs, mainly used in the decoration of glazed ceramic friezes and in the ornamentation of wood (doors, latticework and *artesonados*), in which the lines are broken up by polygons and stars.

Plant motifs, which were known as **atauriques**, used to decorate sculpted stone or plaster wall panels. With the passing of time, these motifs (palm leaves, grapevines) were styled to create extremely complex designs. One of the most common techniques used was the stylisation of the tree of life – vegetal decoration arranged around a vertical axis. **Mocárabes**, decorative motifs resembling stalactites, were used to decorate arches and cupolas.

Epigraphs fulfilled the same informative function as images used by other architectural styles, with **Kufic script**, characterised by its large, angled lettering, and **Nesjí script**, with its more free-flowing characters, the most widely used.

Applied arts – Andalucian decorative art produced a variety of elaborate objects which can be separated into two distinct groups, namely household and luxury items, the latter created to satisfy the demand of a more refined ruling class who afforded greater importance to interior decoration and who took great pleasure in bestowing unique and sumptuous gifts on foreign visitors.

In terms of **ceramics**, the following stand out: the earthenware known as **green and manganese**, the so-called **cuerda seca** ceramics *(azulejos)* used as wall decoration, and the gilded work known as **reflejo metálico** (lustre work). The latter, production of which began in Córdoba in the 9C, attained its full glory during the Nasrid period in the production centres in and around Málaga.

In addition to Córdoba, where Abd ar-Rahman II founded the Casa del Tiraz or Royal Silk Factory, Almería specialised in the production of exquisite **fabrics**; during the 14C and 15C, the workshops of Granada also produced impressive silk fabrics entwined with gold thread. In general, intense colours predominated in these fabrics, which were decorated with inscriptions and architectural motifs.

Nasrid **gold and silversmiths** showed a special predilection for ceremonial swords, the hilts and guards of which were decorated with extraordinary combinations of marble, filigree and polychrome enamel.

To complete the full picture of Hispano-Moorish artistry, mention should also be made of the highly delicate **marble carvings**, which were popular decorative features used by the Caliphate, **taraceas** (marble-inlaid wood and wood of varying colours) used to decorate Nasrid furniture, and leatherwork (**cordovans** made from goatskin and embossed **guadamecíes** made from sheepskin).

Many of these items remained popular over the centuries due to their continued use by the Christians, who praised their quality and value. As an example to illustrate this, the sculpted marble boxes and chests used by Muslim women to keep their jewels and perfume were subsequently used to preserve the relics of saints.

Cordoban period (8C-10C)

The Mezquita in Córdoba and the Medina Azahara palace, the two great monuments from this period, contain all the features associated with early Hispano-Moorish art, which developed during the three centuries in which Córdoba was the capital of al-Andalus.

In accordance with their custom of assimilating the culture of those they conquered, the Moors used techniques and features from both Visigothic and Roman art, which they skilfully combined with the oriental traditions of the Arabian Peninsula.

The major imports from Caliphal art were the **foliated arch** and the **alfiz**, the rectangular surround of a horseshoe arch. In terms of decoration, the early geometric motifs containing squares and diamonds gradually evolved into designs encompassing floral motifs (vine leaves, bunches of grapes, acanthus leaves, palm trees and rosettes) inspired by the Umayyads; these motifs were later replaced by heart-shaped floral drawings which took their inspiration from the Abbasids.

B. Kauffmann/MICHELIN

Caliphal capital

The Caliphate's economic prosperity was reflected in the materials used (ashlar stone and worked marble) and the opulence of the metallic lustre **Byzantine mosaics** created by foreign craftsmen.

Other Caliphal buildings

During the Caliphal period, other constructions included the minarets of San Juan and Santa Clara (Córdoba), El Salvador (Sevilla) and San José (Granada), in addition to the fortifications in Tarifa and the Pinos Bridge (Granada).

Taifa period (11C)

Despite the political dispersion which was a feature of the *taifa* (faction) kingdoms, Andalucian art of the period showed great unity, given that Andalucia had become isolated from the rest of Islam and, as such, removed from Oriental influence. The artists from the erstwhile Caliphate of Córdoba emigrated to the courts of various *taifas* where they continued the Cordoban tradition.

Economic decadence resulted in the abandoning of noble materials such as ashlar stone on walls, and columns and pillars made from marble in favour of **brick**, **plaster** and **mortar**. To compensate for this, **decorative motifs** attained unexpected heights (epigraphic, geometric and plant designs) and varied combinations of **arches** (**foliated**, **mixtilinear**, semicircular, pointed, intercrossing etc) started to be used to form arabesque features. During this period, religious architecture was less important than both civil (numerous **public baths** such as the so-called Bañuelo de Granada) and military architecture (the *alcazabas* in Málaga, Granada and Almería).

Almoravid period (12C)

Following the arrival of the Almoravids on the Iberian Peninsula, Andalucian art spread throughout the Maghreb. Marrakech and Sevilla developed into the capitals of a new kingdom on either side of the Straits of Gibraltar, gradually introducing new trends resulting from mutual influence between the peoples of the two continents.

Arches began to develop ever more complicated styles, as did **cupolas**, some of which contained openwork and others which were decorated with *mocárabe* motifs. This era heralded the appearance of geometric decoration in the form of networks of **sebka** or diamond-shaped designs; combinations of epigraphic and *lacería* motifs also increased in complexity.

Almost all the buildings dating from this period have either disappeared or have been swallowed up beneath additions introduced by the Almohads, although experts believe that they are able to recognise features of the Almoravid style in the mihrab in one of the *mezquitas* in Almería (the present-day Iglesia de San Juan).

Almohad period (13C)

The basic religious principles of the Almohads, which were based on purity and austerity, were reflected in the **simplicity** and **monumental nature** of their buildings, the majority of which were defensive in character, such as the Alcázar and the Torre del Oro in Sevilla. This type of fortified construction, with its delimiting gateways and defensive towers *(albarranas)* separated from the fortified buildings, would later be adopted by the Christians as a model for their own castles.

The new arrivals used the same construction materials as their predecessors, namely brick, mortar, plaster and wood, but opted for **more sober decoration**, with large empty spaces and **geometric adornments** replacing plant motifs. The traditional horseshoe arch was practically abandoned, except in exceptional circumstances, and replaced by **pointed horseshoe** and foiled arches.

Without doubt, the most representative monument from this period is the Giralda in Sevilla which, in its day, was the minaret for the main *mezquita* in the capital of the Almohad kingdom.

Nasrid period (13C-15C)

In the eyes of many specialists, this era represents the greatest period in Andalucian art. For many years, these same experts highlighted the poverty of the materials used in Nasrid art, and their contrast with their abundance of decoration. Nowadays it is known that the function of the building determined the choice of materials used in its construction.

Patio de los Leones, Alhambra

Consequently, in baths, as well as fortresses such as the Alcazaba in Granada, ashlar stone, bricks and mortar (consisting of its characteristic red colour) were used, while palaces such as the Alhambra used **marble** on the floors and for its columns, **glazed ceramics** *(azule-jos)* in areas exposed to friction, elaborate **plaster and stucco** decoration, **wooden vaults** and **artesonados** and **mocárabe vaults**.

Capitals were generally of two types: the first had a cylindrical base decorated with plain leaves which supported a parallelepiped adorned with additional foliage; the second type were *mocárabe* in style and derived from Oriental art. Although less spectacular nowadays due to the weathering effects of time, colour was the other main feature of Nasrid buildings, the in-

---

Nasrid epigraphic inscriptions

Buildings in the kingdom of Granada contained three types of inscriptions: those of an informative nature relating to the origin of the building; religious inscriptions, taken from the Koran; and literary and poetic inscriptions.

---

teriors of which, in their prime, must have looked like an Impressionist painting. In addition to the friezes of *azulejos*, the plaster and wood used to cover walls were painted in red, blue, green and gold tones, at a time when different coloured marble was also used for capitals and columns. Given that the present-day appearance of the Alhambra continues to impress and amaze millions of visitors, we can only imagine how impressive it must have looked during its period of ultimate splendour.

The use of water in Andalucian architecture

Throughout the kingdom of al-Andalus, that scarce commodity – water – played a fundamental role in architecture. Water had a triple function: practical, religious and aesthetic. Practical, because of its necessity for life (the irrigation of fields and the supply of bath water); religious, because the Koran states that a series of ablutions must be carried out prior to prayer; and aesthetic, because water stored in pools and basins reflected the elegant decoration of the walls and ceilings, while water running through channels, fountains and gutters produced a relaxing murmuring and provided welcome cool. Water also enabled gardens to be created that were so well integrated into the surrounding architecture that it is difficult to know where nature ends and where the works created by man begin.

Medieval Andalucian art

Mudéjar art (13C-16C) – Following the conquest of Córdoba and Sevilla in the first half of the 13C, Christian models were imposed on those buildings under the yoke of the kingdom of Castilla, although their construction was entrusted to skilled Muslim craftsmen. This resulted in the development of the typically Spanish Mudéjar art, the fusion of Islamic and Western artistic concepts.

Mudéjar architecture evolved over the centuries, adapting to the dominant features of each area, in such a way that the Mudéjar style in Andalucia is different from that of other Spanish regions. Despite these differences, in general it can be said that it remains loyal to Muslim traditions in terms of the materials used (plaster, brick and wood), its construction techniques (walls, horseshoe arches and wood ceilings) and decoration (fine *artesonado* work, the use of alfiz, and complicated plasterwork).

In the main, the churches of Sevilla (San Marcos, San Pablo and Santa Marina) are built using brick, with *artesonados* and traditional features of Almohad decoration.

Major examples of civil architecture, in which roofs with two or four slopes predominate, include the Alcázar in Sevilla, which Pedro I rebuilt in 1366, the Torre de Don Fadrique (Sevilla), the Torre de El Carpio (Córdoba), the Castillo de San Romualdo (San Fernando, Cádiz) and the Casa de Pilatos (Sevilla).

Gothic art (13C-15C) – Early Andalucian Gothic art, which was inspired by the Cistercian model (large rose windows on the façades and a central nave with two side aisles of lower height with ogival vaults), produced works of great interest such as the so-called *fernandina* churches of Córdoba (Santa Marina, San Miguel and San Lorenzo). The construction of Sevilla Cathedral started in 1401. This edifice is the largest Gothic building in Andalucia and was one of the last Spanish Gothic churches to be built. The Flemish artists

Rose window, San Lorenzo church (Córdoba)

who worked on this ambitious project introduced a series of innovations, such as a rectangular floor plan, a flat apsidal end with a small apse, slender fasciated pillars, complex star-shaped vaults and abundant decoration.

During the reign of Isabel the Catholic, the **Isabelline style** developed, halfway between Gothic and Renaissance, exuberantly combining Flamboyant and Mudéjar features. The Capilla Real in Granada, a work by Enrique Egas, is the best example of the Isabelline style portrayed in Andalucia.

Foreign artists who came to Sevilla in the 15C brought Flemish influence, with its deep realism, to Andalucian sculpture. **Lorenzo Mercadante**, who was born in Brittany, is one of the best exponents of this Andalucian Gothic style. He worked mainly on the cathedral in Sevilla and introduced the baked clay technique, which was later used by numerous local artists. Spanish artists of the period worthy of mention include **Pedro Millán**, creator of the statue of the Virgin of the Pillar *(Virgen del Pilar)* in the same cathedral.

The Renaissance (16C)

Architecture – The arrival of the Renaissance in Spain coincided with a new period of splendour in Andalucia, with Sevilla, which had a monopoly on trade with the New World, and Córdoba and Granada all developing into cultural and artistic centres of great renown. Initially, the magnificence of late-Gothic architecture and Mudéjar tradition prevented the total adoption of Renaissance ideas; in fact, the first three decades of the 16C saw the development of the **Plateresque style**, so called because its lavish decoration was reminiscent of silverwork *(plata*: silver). The semicircular arch, bossed features, balustrades, classical capitals and the presence of medallions and escutcheons on the façades of buildings are the most characteristic features of this style, which is magnificently represented by the Town Hall *(Ayuntamiento)* in Sevilla, a work by Diego de Riaño.

As the century evolved, greater importance was attributed to proportions than ornamentation, resulting in the total abandonment of Gothic ideas. Barrel, oval and oven vaulting became predominant features, along with the almost exclusive use of the semicircular arch; decorative motifs also increased in size at a time when the trend was for the concentration of decoration in specific areas to allow for the development of vast open areas.

Three names stand out in Renaissance architecture in the region. **Diego de Siloé** (1495-1563) completed the work on Granada Cathedral, having modified the Gothic plans set out by Enrique de Egas. The edifice, one of the most significant from this period, served as a model for the cathedrals in both Málaga and Guadix. The architect and painter **Pedro Machuca** (d 1550) always remained faithful to his Italian training.

O. Torres/MARCO POLO

Patio of Carlos V's palace, Alhambra

Carlos V's palace in the Alhambra, his most impressive work, is a work of total innovation which was completely misunderstood at the time. **Andrés de Vandelvira** (d 1575), who worked closely with Diego de Siloé, left his audacious mark on Jaén Cathedral and other buildings in the same province, particularly in Úbeda (Iglesia del Salvador) and Baeza.

The most important figures of the Renaissance in Sevilla were **Martín Gaínza**, the architect for the chapel royal in the city's cathedral, and **Hernán Ruiz**, who was responsible for the facing and pinnacle of the Giralda.

The last third of the 16C in Spain also saw the strong influence of the **Herreran style** created by **Juan de Herrera**, as seen at El Escorial. Sevilla is also home to a work by Felipe II's favourite architect: the Archivo de Indias which, with its sober, rectilinear façade, encompasses all the characteristic features of Counter Reformation art.

Sculpture – Realism and expression are the dominant sculptural themes from the Renaissance period, which was already providing a foretaste of Baroque imagery. Given that most projects were commissioned by the Church, religious figures predominate. It should also be remembered that the Counter Reformation was initiated in the last third of the century, on behalf of which Felipe II was determined to mount a strong defence. The vast majority of works were carved in polychrome wood; marble, alabaster and stone were only used for rare secular figures, funereal and monumental art. As was the case during the Gothic period, the Renaissance in Andalucia saw an abundance of altars decorated with large-dimensioned retables.

Of the numerous Italian artists who worked in the region, the following stand out: **Domenico Fancelli** (1469-1518), the sculptor of the tombs of the Catholic Monarchs in the Chapel Royal in Granada Cathedral; **Jacobo Florentino** (1476-1526), who created the Burial of Christ (Entierro de Cristo) exhibited in the Museo de Bellas Artes in the city; and **Pietro Torrigiano**, whose penitent St Jerome (Museo de Bellas Artes, Sevilla) was to exert great influence on Sevilla's Baroque sculptors. The Burgundian **Felipe Vigarny** (d 1543) mainly worked in Castilla in collaboration with Berruguete; however, he created one of his best works in Granada, namely the altarpiece for the city's Chapel Royal.

Although he died young, the most important Spanish sculptor of the period was **Bartolomé Ordóñez** (d 1520), who was trained in Italy and died in Carrara while he was working on the tombs of Juana la Loca (Joan the Mad) and Felipe el Hermoso (Philip the Handsome) for the Capilla Real in Granada.

Painting – As with the sculpture of the period, religious rather than secular themes dominated Renaissance painting. It could be said that in the whole of Andalucia, the only city to stand apart was Sevilla, where several families with large fortunes decorated their mansions with secular, mythological and allegorical canvases (Casa de Pilatos). During the early decades of the century the Flemish influence, with its characteristic taste for concrete images, remained ever present. However, Tuscan mannerism and Raphael's classicism gradually paved the way for the arrival of Venetian painting.

The best exponent of the early Sevillian Renaissance was **Alejo Fernández** (?1475-1546), an artist of German extraction who adopted the Spanish surname of his wife. In line with the themes popular with Flemish painters, he was first attracted by the effects of perspective and by the arrangement of space. During this period, when his studio was in Córdoba, he painted his famous *Flagellation* (Museo del Prado, Madrid) and *Christ Tied to the Column* (Museo de Bellas Artes, Córdoba). When he moved to Sevilla, his interest evolved to the human form, with works such as the *Virgin of the Rose* (Iglesia de Santa Ana) and the *Virgin of the Navigators*, his most famous painting of the period, on display in the Alcázar in Sevilla.

The Sevillian artist **Luis de Vargas** (1506-68), who trained in Italy with a disciple of Raphael, took his inspiration from the mannerism of Vasari and the delicate touch of Correggio. His most renowned work is the *Generación temporal de Cristo* in the city's cathedral, which was given the nickname of *La Gamba* due to the beauty of Adam's leg (*gamba* in Italian).

In the eyes of many, **Luis de Morales** (?1520-?86), an artist from Extremadura with close ties with Andalucia, is the most interesting painter of his era, whose highly personal works manifest both Flemish and Italian influence. The gentleness of his feminine characters and the expressiveness of his ailing Christs (*Ecce Homo* in the Academia de San Fernando, Madrid) made him the most admired artist of the time and subject to imitation by his peers.

During the 16C, Sevilla became popular with many Flemish artists who were attracted by

---

Italian ceramics in Andalucia

Glazed and painted ceramics from Italy, which co-existed with those created according to Mudéjar traditions, were brought to Andalucia at the beginning of the 16C by the Pisan, Francisco Niculoso, who was responsible for two interesting works in Sevilla: the portal of the church of the Convento de Santa Paula and the altarpiece in the oratory of the Alcázar. This type of decoration was inspired by the work of the Della Robbia family.

---

the wealth and riches of the city and by the possibility of commissions in America. These included Peter Kempeneer, known as **Pedro de Campaña** (1503-63), who painted the impressively large *Descent from the Cross* in the city's cathedral, and Hernando Sturbio (d 1577), the creator of the *Retable of the Evangelists* in the same edifice.

Baroque (17C-18C)

Spanish Baroque shone forth in every aspect of art. During the first half of the 17C, the influence of the Herreran style remained: churches with a very simple rectangular plan, ornamental plaster motifs and occasionally façades decorated with panels of *azulejos* (Hospital de la Caridad, Sevilla). This austerity gradually softened, as buildings started to be covered with more ornate decoration, even though the structures themselves remained simple in design and many cupolas were deceptive in that they were often composed of a wooden arcature with a plaster facing instead of being made of stone. It was during the course of this century that the architect, sculptor and painter **Alonso Cano** created Granada Cathedral.

Around 1700, a period coinciding with the rise to power of the Bourbons, Andalucian Baroque entered into its most sumptuous phase, during which the overflowing imagination of artists knew no bounds. Concave and convex structures gave undulating movement to façades, while decorative motifs such as volutes, floral bands and Solomonic columns adorned every surface.

Beneath the common denominator of exuberance, architects felt free to interpret Baroque according to their own personal preferences. Moorish influence and a fantasy of colour were the prime influences behind the ostentatious Sagrario in the Carthusian monastery (Cartuja) in Granada, designed by **Francisco Hurtado** (1669-1725). Meanwhile, **Vicente Acero**, the architect of the Real Fábrica de Tabacos (Royal Tobacco Factory), was inspired by Siloé's Renaissance cathedral in Granada, when he embarked upon Spain's last great cathedral, in Cádiz, built between 1722 and 1729.

The Sevillian **Leonardo de Figueroa** (1650-1730), the creator of a number of important civic buildings such as the Palacio de San Telmo (today the seat of the Andalucian parliament) and the Hospital de Venerables, was also responsible for several fine churches, including the Iglesia del Salvador and the Iglesia de San Luis de los Franceses; the latter, with its central plan and Solomonic columns, demonstrates his great ability to combine brick, ceramics and coloured plaster.

Sculpture – Although marble and bronze statues inspired by allegorical and mythological themes were popular in both Italy and France, in Andalucia as in the rest of Spain sculpture was used as a tool of the Counter Reformation, with realism as its dominant theme.

At the beginning of the 20C, the region became a fundamental focal point for religious sculpture – times were difficult and people were looking towards religion as a solution to their problems. Communities of monks and nuns developed, multiplying the need for sculpted images and groups of statues, both to be venerated at the altar and held aloft in street processions such as those during Holy Week. These increasingly realistic and expressive works continued to be carved from polychrome wood, although the colours became increasingly natural. In many cases fabric covered the whole body, so that only the face and hands were carved; it was also known for glass eyes and tears to be added as a final touch of authenticity.

In Sevilla, the finest representative of the zenith of Andalucian sculpture was **Juan Martínez Montañés** (1568-1648), the master of a large generation of artists. More influenced by Renaissance ideas than his contemporaries, the faces he carved always depicted great serenity. As well as numerous Mannerist-inspired *retablos* (Santos Juanes in the Iglesia de San Leandro), he also created some exquisitely beautiful statues of the Virgin Mary in a dream-like pose as seen in Sevilla Cathedral, and countless images of Christ and saints (his best work is his Christ of Clemency in Sevilla Cathedral), including tiny marble figurines. Among the disciples of Montañés, mention should be made of the Cordoban **Juan de Mesa** (1583-1627), who was more dramatic in style than his master and who created the venerated *Jesœs del Gran Poder* (Jesus of Great Power).

The Granada School was headed by the multi-faceted **Alonso Cano** (1601-67), an architect and artist as well as a sculptor, who trained alongside Martínez Montañés. His simple, delicate figures would later be reinterpreted by his numerous pupils, such as Pedro de Mena, the sculptor of the choir stalls in Málaga Cathedral, and José de Mora, whose psychological imbalance – he was to die insane – remain entrenched in several of his works. During the course of the 17C, and particularly at the beginning of the 18C, Italian influence began to manifest itself, inspired by the style employed by Bernini. Agitation, movement and a sense of the dramatic in the scenes portrayed are the dominant features of this style subsequently copied by Andalucian artists. Alongside José de Arce (d 1666), who introduced this new trend, **Pedro Roldán** (1624-70), who mainly worked in Sevilla (the *Entombment* in the Hospital de la Caridad), and Pedro Duque Cornejo, the creator of many works for Carthusian monasteries in and around Sevilla, stand out.

The long list of Baroque sculptors from the Granada School should also include Torcuato Ruiz del Peral, who carved highly expressive heads of saints and the choir stalls in Guadix Cathedral.

> ## La Roldana's cribs
>
> The tradition of cribs *(nacimientos)*, which would appear to have been started by St Francis of Assisi, has always been very popular in Spain. During the Baroque period, many sculptors created, and inspired through their work, a huge variety of popular figures made from polychrome fired clay, which became part of the country's cultural heritage. La Roldana, the daughter of Pedro Roldán, was one of the finest exponents of this art form in the Andalucian School.

Painting – The 17C is without doubt the Golden Age of Andalucian painting, which started out loyal to the dominant Flemish tradition of the 16C before developing its own expression through opulence and light. From the middle of the century onwards, Sevilla and Madrid became the undisputed capitals of Spanish painting. The renown of Sevillian artists in the early decades of the 17C, such as Francisco Pacheco, the father-in-law of Velázquez, has remained obscured by the brilliance of three undisputed masters: Velázquez, Zurbarán and Murillo.

Diego Velázquez spent the majority of his professional life in Madrid as a portrait painter to the Court. However, neither fame nor the influence of Italian artists whom he admired greatly, in particular Titian, could bring him to forget his training in Sevilla. It was during this period in the city (1617-23) that he painted works with predominantly religious themes and or in the *costumbrismo* genre (*Adoration of the Kings*, Museo del Prado, Madrid). **Francisco de Zurbarán** (1598-1664), from Extremadura, interpreted themes of monastic life, but also painted more popular themes, representing reality in the simplest of ways possible. His academy was one of the largest in Sevilla, exporting more works to the Americas than any other in the city. **Bartolomé Murillo** (1617-82), whose works of a religious nature *(Virgin Mary, Infant Jesus)* have been reproduced time and time again, was the most famous Spanish artist of the period.

P. Feria Fernández/MUSEO DE BELLAS ARTES DE SEVILLA

St Hugh and Carthusian Monks at Table, Zurbarán (Museo de Bellas Artes, Sevilla)

The delicate touch and warmth of his paintings cannot hide the qualities of an extraordinary painter who was a great master of both technique and colour. In complete contrast, **Juan Valdés Leal** (1662-1695) concentrated on expression and the macabre, as seen in *Las Postrimerías* (Dying Moments) in Sevilla's Hospital de la Caridad.

In Granada, the aforementioned **Alonso Cano** (1661-67), a great friend of Velázquez, was the most classical of all Baroque painters. His most famous work is a series of canvases representing the Life of the Virgin (Granada Cathedral), showing the major influence of the Venetian masters, whose work he became familiar with when he worked under the protection of the Count-Duke of Olivares.

19C-20C

After several centuries of artistic splendour, Andalucian creativity appeared to run out of steam as it entered the 19C. The severe economic crisis in the region was reflected in a dearth of commissions and the absence of prestigious projects. Despite this, a few Andalucian artists still managed to make their mark in Spain.

Painting – In Romantic painting, several Sevillian artists stand out. These include Antonio Martínez Esquivel, José Gutiérrez de la Vega and Valeriano Domínguez Bécquer; the latter, the brother of the poet Gustavo Adolfo Bécquer, was inspired by *costumbrismo*, with its joyful scenes so alien to his personal experiences of sadness. **Manuel Rodríguez de Guzmán** is worthy of special interest as a result of the huge excitement generated by his excellent sketches of Andalucian life. His warm portrayals of life in southern Spain, which were greatly admired by foreigners, helped to perpetuate the romantic image of Andalucia.

In the last quarter of the century, the realist **Julio Romero de Torres** (1880-1930) was born in Córdoba. This artist specialised in painting Andalucian women of great beauty and restrained sensuality *(Oranges and Lemons)*. Although his work was criticised in certain quarters, such was his popularity that shortly after his death a museum was created in the house in which he was born.

Very different from Romero de Torres, both in terms of his style and his life outside Spain, was the Málaga-born **Picasso** (1881-1973) who is undoubtedly the most famous figure of contemporary Spanish pictorial art. Although he lived in his native Andalucia for just eight years, he maintained close ties with his own region and kept alive his passion for bullfighting from afar.

Two artists who made their names in the early part of the 20C were Daniel Vázquez Díaz (1882-1969), who took his inspiration from Cubism to create works such as the frescoes in the Monasterio de la Rábida (Huelva), and Rafael Zabaleta (1907-60), an artist known for his stylised, rustic expressionism.

Other artists born towards the middle of the 20C include Luis Gordillo (1934) and Guillermo Pérez Villalta (1948), who both became involved in the trend back towards figurative representation, Alfonso Fraile, Vicente Vela, Alfonso Albacete, Carmen Laffon, Chema Cobo and the Granada-born José Guerrero.

Sculpture – **Mateo Inurria** (1869-1924), the creator of the statue of El Gran Capitán in Córdoba, and **Jacinto Higueras** were the leading Andalucian sculptors from the first half of the 20C. **Miguel Berrocal** (1933), who in his early works manifested his keen interest in abstract forms, later moved onto more figurative subjects.

Architecture – The widespread changes within the field of architecture were slow to take root in Andalucia. Modernismo merely produced a few strange examples of the genre within bourgeois society (the interiors of houses and small shops), particularly in the province of Cádiz. At the same time, and inspired by the Costurero de la Reina lodge (Sevilla, 1893), the historicist and revivalist movement was born, which came to the fore at the 1929 Ibero-American Exhibition, with its ornate pavilions. Other official buildings, such as the Palacio Provincial in Jaén and a number of cinemas and theatres, including the Teatro Falla in Cádiz and the Aliatar in Granada are further examples of this movement.

The architecture of recent decades, which has openly embraced these new trends, is a clear reflection of the positive development of the Andalucian economy. Since the sixties, during which the School of Architecture was created in Sevilla, a number of public buildings, tourist complexes and housing developments have been built, designed by the best architects from Andalucia and elsewhere in Spain (Saénz de Oiza, Moneo, de La-Hoz, García de Paredes, Cano Lasso etc).

The urban projects completed for the 1992 World Expo in Sevilla are further proof of the architectural renaissance which has taken place in the region.

Puente de la Barqueta (Sevilla)

ARCHITECTURAL TERMS

Alcazaba: fortified military settlement.

Alcázar: Moorish royal palace.

Alfiz: rectangular surround to a horseshoe-shaped arch in Muslim architecture.

Alicatado: technique of Persian origin consisting of cutting sheets of ceramic tiles *(azulejos)* in such a way as to form geometric patterns.

Altarpiece: also retable. Decorative screen above and behind the altar.

Apse: far end of a church housing the high altar; can be semi-circular, polygonal or horseshoe.

Arabesque: a Romantic term used to express the ornamental effect of Islamic art.

Archivolt: each of the concentric ornamental mouldings on the outer edge of a splayed arch.

Artesonado: marquetry ceiling in which raised fillets outline honeycomb-like cells in the shape of stars.

Ataurique: stylised plant ornamentation inspired by the acanthus leaf, a feature of Moorish art.

Azulejo: glazed, patterned, ceramic tiles.

Cabecera: east or apsidal end of a Christian church, containing the chancel.

Caliphal: architectural style developed in Córdoba under the Caliphate (8C-11C) of which the finest example is the Mezquita.

Camarín: small chapel on the first floor behind the altarpiece or retable. It is lavishly decorated and very often contains a lavishly costumed statue of the Virgin Mary.

Capilla Mayor: area of the high altar containing the **retablo mayor** or monumental altarpiece which often rises to the roof.

Churrigueresque: in the style of the Churrigueras, an 18C family of architects. Richly ornate Baroque decoration.

Coro: chancel in Spanish canonical churches often built in the middle of the nave. It contains the **stalls** *(sillería)* used by members of religious orders. When placed in a tribune or gallery it is known as the **coro alto**.

Crucero: transept. The part of a church at right angles to the nave which gives the church the shape of a cross. It consists of the transept crossing and arms.

Cuerda seca: glazed ceramic technique.

Estípite: pilaster in the shape of a truncated inverted pyramid.

Grotesque: typical Renaissance decoration combining vegetation, imaginary figures and animals.

Kiblah: sacred wall of a mosque from which the *mihrab* is hollowed, facing towards Mecca.

Kufic: Arabic script originating from the city of Kufa, characterised by large angled letters.

Lacerías: geometric decoration formed by intersecting straight lines making star-shaped and polygonal figures. Characteristic of Moorish architecture.

Lantern: an architectural feature in the highest part of a cupola admitting light to the area below.

Madraza: a Moorish university or religious academy.

Mihrab: richly decorated prayer-niche in the sacred wall *(kiblah)* in a mosque.

Minaret: tower of the mosque *(mezquita)*, from which the muezzin calls the faithful to prayer.

Mocárabes: decorative motifs of Muslim architecture formed by assembled prisms ending in concave surfaces. They resemble stalactites or pendants and adorn vaults and cornices.

Modillion: a bracket or console used to support a cornice, the springing of an arch etc.

Mozarabic: the work of Christians living under Arab rule after the Moorish invasion of 711. On being persecuted in the 9C, they sought refuge in Christian areas bringing with them Moorish artistic traditions.

Mudéjar: the work of Muslims living in Christian territory following the Reconquest (13C-14C).

Plateresque: term derived from *platero* (silversmith), and used to describe the early style of the Renaissance characterised by finely carved decoration.

Predella: the lower part of an altarpiece.

Presbytery: the space in front of the main altar, separated from the nave by steps or a partition.

Sagrario: chapel containing the Holy Sacrament. May sometimes be a separate church.

Sebka: type of brick decoration developed under the Almohads consisting of an apparently endless series of small arches forming a network of diamond shapes.

Stucco: type of moulding mix consisting mainly of plaster, used for coating surfaces. It plays a fundamental role in wall decoration in Hispano-Muslim architecture.

Trasaltar: back wall of the *capilla mayor* in front of which sculptures or tombs are often found.

Trascoro: the wall, often carved and decorated, which encloses the *coro*.

Triforium: arcade above the side aisles which opens onto the central nave of a church.

Tympanum: inner surface of a pediment. This often ornamented space is bounded by the archivolt and the lintel of the doors of churches.

Yesería: plasterwork used in sculptured decoration.

Al-Andalus

THE MOORS

The inhabitants of al-Andalus, as the region was known during the period of Moorish occupation, were of different origins and therefore had different physical characteristics. As the years passed the distinction between natives and foreigners lessened as the newcomers imposed their structures on the conquered territories. The natives were Hispano-Roman Visigoths, both Christian and Jewish, of Latin culture and organised according to a feudal system. The foreigners were Arabs and Berbers, of Muslim faith and Arab culture.

The process of islamisation and arabisation imposed by those in authority gave rise to a relatively uniform Moorish society which was both Arabic and Muslim. Initially this society comprised two main social groups: the upper *(jassa)* and lower *(amma)* classes, with major differences between the two which were even reflected in legal matters; a member of the nobility was not punished in the same way as a member of the lower class. A middle class, which continued to increase in size, came into existence around the 11C. The poor *(miskin)* survived through taking on occasional work as labourers on farms and during harvests. The clients or *maulas* were free servants who were bound to a master, from whom they could take their name. The largest number of slaves belonged to the siqlabi group *(esclavos)*, who were purchased on the international market or taken prisoner in times of war; these usually worked for the most important nobles. Negro slaves *(abid)*, who worked mainly in the army, originated from the African slave market.

ORIGINS

Arabs – They arrived in the peninsula in two main waves – the first in the 8C and the second during the Almohad period in the 12C – and always occupied the most powerful positions. Their aim from the beginning was to islamise the native population. In the later period, in order to be recognised as an Arab it was enough to bear a suitable name, which could be acquired relatively easily for those with the right contacts.

Berbers – The first main contingent of this North-African ethnic group crossed the Straits of Gibraltar in the 8C, led by the generals Tarik and Musa. In the second half of the 10C and beginning of the 11C, many of the same faith followed and eventually found themselves in control of some of the *taifa* kingdoms, including Granada. Although many of them obtained positions of responsibility, the vast majority worked as agricultural labourers, cattle breeders and craftsmen.

Mozarabs – The Christians used this term to describe the arabised Christians who stayed on their land and remained true to their religion after the arrival of the Muslims. The Arabs referred to them as *nazarenos (naara)*.

Muladíes – These were Christians who converted to Islam and, in a number of cases, managed to obtain prominent positions. During the 11C they altered their family tree in order to create an ostensible Arab line that would allow them to retain their privileged position in society.

Jews – Badly treated by the Visigoths, they greeted the arrival of the Muslims with delight. They integrated into Islamic culture perfectly and experienced no major problems until the Almohad invasion.

DAILY LIFE

Towns

The Moors made profound changes to Hispano-Visigothic society which, having experienced a long period of decline, was extremely rural in character. This eminently urban Islamic civilisation founded a number of towns, some of which were quite sizeable; Córdoba, for example, became the largest and one of the most important cities in Europe at the time, both in terms of population and cultural activity. It should be noted that Andalucian cities of the period were equipped with sewerage systems, public lighting and various communal services. In fact, they were blessed with far more amenities than their contemporary Christian counterparts.

The Moorish **medina** (al-Madinat), the old walled centre of the city, followed an organised pattern within the chaos of its narrow streets and alleyways which developed as a result of a lack of building regulations. The districts *(harat)* were inhabited by craftsmen of the same guild or by families of the same religion (Jews and Mozarabs). The interior of the medina housed markets now known in Spanish as *zocos* (from the Arabic *suq*), public baths *(hamam)*, mosques and restaurants, and even included a university or *madraza* in larger towns and cities.

More modern districts or **arrabales** *(al-Rabad)* were situated around the medina and were soon walled. The **cemetery** *(maqbara)* was located outside the city walls, not far from the roads leading into the city, as was the **sa'ría**, a large esplanade that was occasionally used as a military training area *(musalla)*, and sometimes as a meeting place for the faithful *(musara)* to celebrate the end of Ramadan; this often replaced the main mosque in smaller settlements. During the Christian period these esplanades were subsequently used to thresh the grain and were known as *eras* (threshing floors).

The civil and military authorities, as well as the army and their families, lived in the **alcazaba** *(al-Qasaba)*, an independent walled fortress equipped with its own services which was never a part of the main city.

LIVING QUARTERS

In general only one Moorish family lived in each house. The wealthy could afford to have many wives, but for the rest of the population monogamous marriage was the norm. The surface area of those Moorish houses which have been excavated by archeologists varies from 50 to 300m2/538 to 3 229sq ft.

The most obvious feature of Moorish houses is the desire for privacy. Each individual built his house to meet his own needs, but nearly all houses were away from the road in order to avoid noise. Only the Jews built houses grouped together around a yard, with a joint entrance situated at the end of a cul-de-sac. Protected by a very plain façade, with few openings covered with shutters, Moorish houses were organised around a patio which was reached across a hallway. All houses had a privy, a kitchen and one or more rooms, as well as a barn. Water was stored in a cistern or drawn from a well in the patio. Fireplaces were not common as the houses were heated with braziers and the women cooked over fires contained in earthenware pots.

Household furnishings were simple: ceramic and earthenware utensils, chests, carpets, and tapestries and cushions, which could be made from cotton, wool or silk depending on the financial standing of the family.

R. Corbel/MICHELIN

THE MARKET OR ZOCO

Although it also existed in rural areas, the *zoco* was mainly an urban feature. Cities had specialised markets which sold and even manufactured products which came from the countryside. Articles of high quality and value were sold in special markets known as **alcaicerías**. These were also centres of export to much larger areas, such as the Mediterranean, Islamic countries, the Maghreb and other African markets.

The market overseer, known as the *almotacn*, controlled commercial activity, which was regulated down to the smallest detail, in order to avoid illegal practices and abuse.

Alhóndigas were used to store products and to house merchants. The Spanish word *fonda*, meaning inn, has evolved from the Arabic word for this particular building *(funduq)*. The Corral del Carbón in Granada is an old reconstructed *alhóndiga*.

BATHS

Every district in the towns and cities of al-Andalus would have had its own *hamam* or public bath (it is said that Córdoba had over 600) to meet the demands of a population with a great penchant for water and a desire to fulfil the Islamic obligations of spiritual and bodily cleanliness. As well as centres of hygiene with specialised staff, baths also acted as a place in which to meet and relax – in the mornings for men, and the afternoons for women and children.

The exteriors of the baths were topped with vaults with small skylights to enable the diffusion of a thin, but pleasant, light. The interior, covered with *azulejos*, was divided into four main areas whose temperature progressively increased. In the first, visitors would undress once they had obtained towels and the obligatory wooden shoes. They would then enter a second section, a cold room, housing the latrines, where the bathing process would begin, before continuing to the remaining two rooms, one hot, the other warm. The purpose of the hot room was to open up the pores, while the warm room would have been used for massages. Men would take advantage of their visit to the baths to have their hair cut and beard trimmed, while women would apply a range of beauty products, such as depilatory creams, jasmine-scented perfume, henna to colour the hair and kohl to darken the area around the eyes.

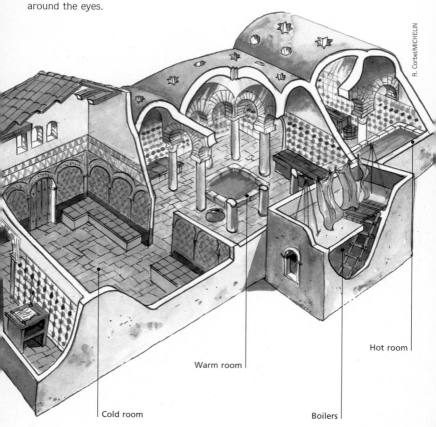

R. Corbel/MICHELIN

Hot room

Warm room

Cold room

Boilers

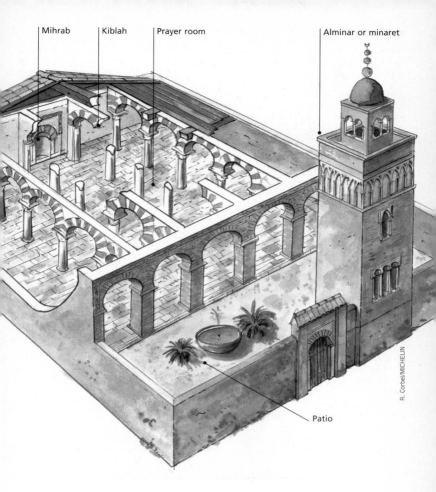

Mihrab | Kiblah | Prayer room | Alminar or minaret

Patio

R. Corbel/MICHELIN

THE MOSQUE

The mosque *(mezquita)* is not a temple inhabited by God, but a house of prayer in which Muslims over the age of 16 were called to midday prayer on Fridays. Towns would have small, local mosques, as well as larger ones, known as *aljamas*, as in Córdoba. In line with other parts of the Islamic world, mezquitas in al-Andalus were also used as large civic centres, similar to the Roman forum and the public squares of the Middle Ages. Here, documents of interest to the community could be read and flags would be blessed prior to the departure of a new military expedition. Initially, the mezquita would have also have been used as a teaching centre and the office of the town's treasury.

The layout of the mezquita was inspired by the house in Medina where the prophet Muhammad lived and imparted his teaching. As a result, in keeping with the design of a traditional house, it consisted of two clearly defined areas: the **covered area** or prayer room *(haram)*, with its floor covered in matting, and the **patio** *(shan)*, with a fountain or pool *(sabil)* for ritual ablutions. Other basic features included:

The **kiblah**, or main wall of the room, facing Mecca. Strangely, mezquitas in al-Andalus faced southwards rather than southeast, which would have been the direction towards Mecca from Andalucia. Some experts believe that this was due to Syrian influence, while others consider that the route to Mecca would first have involved a journey south.

The **mihrab**, an empty niche in the centre of the *kiblah* to remind the faithful of the place where Mohammed prayed.

The **maqsura**, an area surrounded by latticework screens located in front of the mihrab. It would appear that this area was reserved for the Caliph.

The **mimbar**, a type of wooden pulpit used by the imam to conduct Friday prayers *(jutba)*.

The **alminar** or minaret, the most symbolic feature of Islamic architecture, is a tower attached to one of the walls of the patio, the upper part of which is used by the muezzin to call the faithful to prayer. A typical Andalucian alminar would be crowned with three gilded spheres *(yamur)* of decreasing sizes and a fleur-de-lis.

49

The countryside

The outskirts of large cities were dotted with farms known as **almunias**. The beauty of these luxurious mansions with their own gardens, orchards, pools and fountains was said to rival that of some of the most sumptuous royal palaces. A fine example of this was the *almunia* of al-Rusafa, to the northeast of Córdoba.

Although sovereigns and leading figures in Islamic life owned extensive land farmed by labourers, independent farmers and cattle breeders were also commonplace in al-Andalus. They lived within small communities known as **alquerías** which were generally protected by a castle. These hamlets included houses, outbuildings, farmland and barns. Larger ones were often surrounded by fortifications and had their own common amenities similar to those found in urban areas.

AGRICULTURE

The introduction of sophisticated hydraulic techniques had a significant effect on the Mediterranean ecosystem of Andalucia. Although some of these techniques originated from the Roman period, such as the river water-wheel, it is impossible to deny that the Moors were superbly skilled in extracting water from below ground and pumping it through a system of channels to extensive areas of farmland. In fact, modern-day Spanish contains a number of agricultural terms which directly descend from Arabic. In addition to terrace farming, the Moors also introduced animal-powered wheels and an irrigation system of Oriental origin consisting of boring various holes in the ground until a source was discovered; once found, the wells were used to control the pressure of the water which was then channelled to those areas requiring irrigation.

R. Corbel/MICHELIN

Islamic law controlled the provision of water, which was considered a common asset. The *zabacequia* would settle any disputes and would establish the irrigation timetable which was scrupulously respected. If a farmer failed to make use of his slot, it would be channelled to other land; nobody, however, had the right to pass on their water as a gift, sell it or exchange it.

In addition to the region's traditional crops (olives, cereals and vines), the Moors also grew other products imported from the East such as rice, pomegranates, cotton and saffron, as well as what were considered to be luxury items (spices, mulberry trees to feed silkworms etc). The fertile irrigated land *(huertas)* overflowed with high-quality products, many of which had been introduced by the Moors, such as the aubergine, artichoke, chicory and asparagus. Meanwhile, the magnificent gardens traditionally associated with Moorish culture were a feast of colour with stock, roses, honeysuckle and jasmine.

ANIMAL BREEDING

The Moors were great breeders of animals which were used for riding, for pulling agricultural equipment, and the table. As an illustration of their importance, the **Andalucian horse**, whose origins can be traced back to the Moors, is now famous the world over. The leather industry was one of the most flourishing sectors of the region's economy. Documentary evidence has also shown that flocks of sheep were of enormous size during the period of Arab domination. It is also strange to note that although Muslims were prohibited from eating pork, old texts refer to the breeding of pigs and of payment to farmers for them. The main breeding areas were the marshlands of the lower Guadalquivir and the area to the east of Córdoba.

DEFENSIVE ARCHITECTURE

The Moors built a number of military installations both as a form of defence and as a base from which to attack their Christian and fellow Muslim rivals. Many of these constructions were reused after the Reconquest and some are still standing today.

Besides the *alcazaba*, the most typical defensive buildings were the castles built along the border with Christian-held territory. As a general rule, they were built with an east-west orientation and comprised two clearly defined sections: the *alcázar* or fortress, organised around a central patio, and a large esplanade in which the barracks for troops would have been located. On the outer limits of the central castle, and separate from it, there would have been a series of smaller fortresses in constant communication with a number of **watchtowers**.

The **walls** were strengthened by the construction of towers, used as a garrison and a strategic point from which to harass the enemy, and pyramid-shaped merlons. Communication around the walls was via an inner circular path.

The 11C saw the construction of the first **barbicans**, defensive walls positioned in front of the main walls, and the first moats. Later on, during the period of Almohad domination, **turrets**, such as the Torre del Oro in Sevilla, began to be seen. These defensive constructions were independent of the main fortified area, but connected to it via a wall with a narrow path *(coracha)*.

In the early days of Moorish rule, the gateways along the walls were strengthened using metal plates and leather. In the 11C, however, these gateways began to be built in the towers themselves, while later refinements saw the introduction of **machicolations** and platforms consisting of small raised structures erected on the external façade of the defensive wall.

Obviously, construction techniques evolved over the centuries. During the Caliphate of Córdoba, for example, ashlar stone was predominantly used, to be subsequently replaced by the more resistant clay mortar, a mixture of sand, lime and gravel made into moulds and then covered with brightly coloured plaster to physically dazzle the enemy.

R. Corbel/MICHELIN

A LAND OF SCHOLARS, POETS AND PHILOSOPHERS

For eight centuries al-Andalus was an important centre of artistic and scientific culture. While sovereigns elsewhere on the Iberian Peninsula were living in sombre castles, in which they were surrounded by men interested in nothing but warfare, Moorish emirs, caliphs and monarchs were inhabiting luxurious palaces and encouraging cultural development, where scientists, philosophers, poets and artists acted as the best possible ambassadors for the power and refinement of their Moorish rulers. Nor should it be forgotten that those at the vanguard of Andalucian culture were not isolated figures, for they carried out their work alongside a team of assistants within the Court itself. This research would either have taken place in large libraries, such as the one created by Al-Hakam II, with over 300 000 volumes, or in the *madrazas* (universities) created for this very purpose.

From the 9C onwards, Arabic was the most widely used language across the entire peninsula; and although Christians and Jews preserved their own languages, they used Arabic in daily life and in their artistic and scientific work. Another feature of Moorish culture was the constant interchange with other areas, from the eastern boundaries of Islamic influence – on journeys to and from Mecca – to North Africa, particularly during the Almoravid and Almohad periods.

Much of the credit for the preservation of Muslim knowledge, which was highly valued by the Western world throughout the Renaissance and even beyond, is due to the efforts of Alfonso X. With the cooperation of Mozarabs and Jews alike, this Christian monarch had Arabic manuscripts copied and corrected following his conquests and those of his father, Fernando III.

THE SCIENCES

Moorish scientists took an interest in every conceivable aspect of science. **Alchemists** studied the behaviour of metallic substances and slowly discovered their basic processes; agronomists wrote agricultural papers including detailed information on the rearing of carrier pigeons, which at the time were the fastest and most efficient form of communication; **naturalists** created zoos housing unusual species; while **mathematicians**, such as Avempace, who was also a great astronomer, were noted for their work on trigonometry.

The field of **medicine** reached new heights through the work of specialists who published their scientific findings in encyclopaedia. Through these publications, it is known that they were able to perform somewhat complex surgery and were aware of illnesses such as haemophilia. As well as the most famous physician of them all, **Averroës**, who was also a great philosopher, mention should also be made of the five generations of the **Avenzoar** family. Medical science was strictly linked with **botany** – another field in which spectacular advances were also made. An example of this can be seen in the work of Ibn al-Baytar, from Málaga, the author of a compendium in which he lists 1 400 plant- and mineral-based medicines which were of great importance during the Renaissance.

R. Corbel/MICHELIN

The extensive knowledge of Moorish scientists resulted in the development of **inventions** revolutionary in their time. These ranged from the construction of astrolabes and quadrants – fundamental to navigation – to refrigeration systems, lighting effects created via bowls of mercury, anaphoric clocks (moved by water) – very useful for fixing the hours of prayer – and even mechanical toys. The Moors also adopted Chinese paper manufacturing techniques, resulting in the production of paper in Córdoba from the 10C onwards, and were responsible for introducing the so-called **Arabic numerals**. It should also be noted that the Spanish words *guarismo* (a number or figure) and *algoritmo* (algorithm) derive from the name of the mathematician al-Khuwarizmi.

LITERATURE

In Arabic literature, poetry was of greater importance than prose. Arab writers improvised; in other words they composed their poetry out loud, and on many occasions forced their slaves to learn poems by heart in order to sell them at a higher price.

Early divans (collections of poems) solely consisted of **qasidas** – classical, monorhymed love poems made up of three parts: the evocation of the beloved woman, the description of a journey and a eulogy of the poem's subject. At the end of the 9C, a poet from Cabra invented the **moaxaja**, with one part written in classical Arabic, the other in romantic ballads *(jarchas)*. The romantic couplets which appeared as **jarchas** in Arabic *moaxajas* are the oldest expression of European lyrical poetry. The zejel, seemingly invented by **Avempace**, was the other type of poetic composition frequently used in al-Andalus; these were written in the vernacular language and were generally narrative in character.

Al-Mutamid, the king of Sevilla during the *taifa* period, was considered one of the finest of Moorish writers, although the poet cited most by critics was the Cordoban Ibn Zaydun, the lover of Wallada, an Umayyad princess, who herself was also a brilliant poet. In terms of literary prose, during the Caliphal period the most significant written work was the *El collar œnico* (The Single Necklace), by Abd al-Rabbini, who also wrote numerous epistles. However, the best-known writer of the period was the jurist and theologian **Ibn Hazm**, to whom we owe *The Dove's Necklace* on poetic diction and psychological truth, which has been translated into a number of languages. In it, he narrates various amorous adventures set in the court of Córdoba, but always with exemplary, moral zeal. The 14C saw the rise to literary prominence of **Ibn Zamrak**, whose verses are engraved in the walls of the Alhambra.

It is highly probable that Greek philosophy, particularly that inspired by Aristotle, would not have been bequeathed to us without **Averroës** (Ibn Rusd), the intellectual heir to Avicena. This great Cordoban (1126-98), who was a magistrate in Sevilla and Córdoba and who even became physician to the court, based his work on the texts of Greek thinkers to develop his own philosophy from the pre-ordained ideas of Islamic religion. This physician, musician, astronomer, mathematician and poet was without doubt the most complete character in Moorish culture.

Religions

Islam – The Umayyad rulers who invaded Spain in the 8C were noted for their tolerance towards other religions; however, this did not prevent them from attempting to islamise the country's native inhabitants from the very outset, offering them incentives such as exemption from the payment of religious taxes. It would appear that in the 10C, 50% of the region's inhabitants were Muslims, a percentage that increased to 90% two centuries later. The al-Andalus kingdom of three religions only really existed during the first four hundred years of Moorish rule, after which Muslims were in the minority.

Christianity – Those who opted to retain their own religion were placed into the category of *tributarios (dimm')*. They had their own hierarchies but were subject to Muslim authority and had to pay a special tax *(yizya)*.
The crisis enveloping Christianity in al-Andalus began with the arrival of the Almoravids. This period saw the initiation of compulsory conversions, emigration to Christian territories, and even deportations to various parts of the Maghreb.

Judaism – In line with Christians, Jews could continue to practise their religion after the arrival of the Moors provided they paid a tribute; as can be seen in the Jewish quarters of Andalucia today, they generally lived in enclaves in the heart of towns and cities. Following the decree implemented by the first Almohad king forcing Jews to convert to Islam or face expulsion, many settled in other Jewish communities across the Maghreb and in Egypt. Those who converted and remained in al-Andalus were forced to wear distinctive clothing or signs such as a yellow cap and a special belt.

Popular architecture

The popular architecture of Andalucia is as varied as its landscape. In spite of this, it can be said that many towns and villages have a number of features in common, such as narrow streets, whitewashed façades, niches with statues of saints or the Virgin Mary, windows with wrought-iron grilles, as well as balconies, sun porches and drying galleries. Once through the main door, access to the house is often via a hallway through to the patio; these two parts of the entrance area create an air circulation system which helps to temper the extreme heat of high summer. The kitchen and lounge are normally found on the ground floor; the bedrooms on the first floor; and the attic or *soberao*, used as a storeroom and an area for drying hams and sausages at the very top. Those with both the means and space may have two types of sleeping quarters: bedrooms on the ground floor for the summer and others on the upper floors for the winter months. Roofing varies from one province to the next, with flat roofs (used as terraces), as seen in Almería in particular, equally as common as those with sloping sides.

Plants and flowers

A lack of plants and flowers is not a criticism that can be levelled against Andalucian houses. Around the region, patios, balconies and terraces are bedecked in greenery, while streets and squares carry the scent of citrus blossom in spring and the enchanting aroma of jasmine in summer.

The patios of mansion houses are resplendent with plants of every type, from leafy ferns to hyacinths, gladioli, tuberose and violets. In smaller abodes, the simplicity of the accommodation is often hidden behind whitewashed walls covered with myriad species of plants such as single, double, scented and ivy geraniums, carnations and jasmine.

The selection of the most suitable plants for different times of the year and their ground and wall arrangement is an art form which has been completely mastered by Andalucian women. Dark corners are ideal for aspidistras, while sun traps are perfect places for geraniums; carnations and other plants which are not particularly attractive when not in flower are left to grow on terraces and then brought onto patios when in bloom. As a general rule, plants are not purchased; instead, seeds and cuttings are passed on by friends and neighbours and then nurtured in pots of every description, from jam jars to magnificent ceramic flowerpots.

In the countryside of Córdoba and Sevilla, areas where large estates or *latifundios* are the norm, *cortijos* (homesteads), *haciendas* and *lagares* (wine and olive estates) can be seen dotted around the landscape; as a result, these farms and ranches are now wrongly perceived as the archetypal "casa andaluza". These large rural units usually consist of a large patio surrounded by stables, storehouses and the accommodation provided for staff and some farm workers, and a smaller patio with the owner's homestead built around it.

Whitewashing a house in Frigiliana

Up until the 19C, towns and cities were comprised of individual houses. However emigration from the countryside and smaller towns resulted in the revision of this policy and the construction of new types of housing. It was from this time that the so-called "neighbourhood corrals" *(corrales de vecindad)* evolved, occasionally created in abandoned convents and monasteries. Today, following substantial renovation, some of these corrals have been converted into expensive seigniorial residences popular with artists and high-earning professionals. At the lower end of the economic scale, blocks of flats began to be built at the beginning of the 20C.

However, Andalucia also contains a number of unique types of housing such as the caves in Granada, Almería and in particular Guadix; the ranches of the Doñana National Park, built from a wooden frame covered with rushes; the houses of the Alpujarras (Granada and Almería), the direct inheritors of Moorish architecture; the small houses tucked away down alleyways and under the arches of villages in the Axarquía region (Málaga); and the incomparable beauty of the *pueblos blancos* (white villages) of Cádiz and Málaga.

Andalucia
a source of inspiration

Andalucia has produced countless figures of renown in the world of culture. From the Roman philosopher **Seneca** to winners of the Nobel Prize for Literature, such as **Juan Ramón Jiménez** and **Vicente Aleixandre**, and writers of the stature of **Luis de Góngora**, the list of Andalucia's celebrities is endless. Some of these remained on their home soil or maintained close ties with it; others earned their living far from their region of birth. However, there have also been those from elsewhere who have had a deep attraction for the soul of this complex region so full of contrasts. We can but state just a few of these worthy men and women who have found their source of inspiration in this magnificent land.

Literature

Tirso de Molina (1579-1684), the probable author of *Don Juan*, set the conquests of the legendary Don Juan Tenorio on the banks of the Guadalquivir. Alongside Don Quixote and Faust, this great lover was to become one of the great figures of world literature thanks to the playwright José Zorrilla. The latter, a prolific Romantic author, was a contemporary of a group of foreign writers who found the exoticism and mystery they were searching for in Andalucia. Writers from Britain, such as **Richard Ford** and **George Borrow**; France, including **Théophile Gautier**, Victor Hugo and Latour; North America **(Washington Irving)**; and Italy (Edmundo d'Amicis) were the first foreign tourists to travel to the south of Spain. Between them they created the myth of Andalucia – with its outlaws, bullfighters, heartless gypsies and a carefree people – which had little in common with the reality of the region but which met with great success. Meanwhile, elsewhere in Spain the Sevillian poet **Gustavo Adolfo Bécquer** was penning his famous *Rimas* (Rhymes) which some writers considered to be the perfect union of German *lied* and Andalucian *siguiriyas* and fandango.

The poetry of Andalucia reached its headiest heights in the early decades of the 20C, through the writing of several members of the Generation of '27. **Antonio Machado** (1875-1939), author of *Cantares* y *Coplas elegidas*, and forever nostalgic for his childhood in Sevilla, and his brother **Manuel Machado**, who wrote *Cante Jondo*, were both able to reflect the true sense of the region. For his part, **Federico García Lorca** (1898-1936), a man of strong personality, lifted Andalucian lyricism to its peak with the *Gypsy Ballads*, *Blood Wedding* and *The House of Bernarda Alba*. The poems of the painter and poet **Rafael Alberti** (1902-99), the heir to Góngora, Bécquer, Juan Ramón Jiménez and Antonio Machado, were highly personal, gracious and popular in style, as well as typically Andalucian *(Marinero en tierra)*. The second half of the 20C saw the rise to notoriety of Andalucian writers such as **Félix Grande**, **José Caballero Bonald**, **Antonio Muñoz Molina** and, above all, **Antonio Gala**, the great Cordoban writer who perhaps painted a better picture than anyone of the realities of modern Andalucia and the grandeur of its past.

Music

Three great Spanish classical composers on the margins of popular music yet directly inspired by it reflected the soul of Andalucia in their compositions. Strangely, just one of them was a native of the south; the other two were both Catalan.

Manuel de Falla (1876-1946), born in Cádiz, is surely the most illustrious Spanish composer of the 20C. With his studious approach to musical ethnography, yet without making concessions to picturesque folklore, the passion of gypsy song and the brilliance of flamenco are both present in his two most famous works, *El amor brujo* (Love, the Magician) and *The Three-Cornered Hat*.

The Gerona-born **Isaac Albéniz** (1860-1909), one of the major representatives of the Spanish nationalist movement, dedicated some of his best works to Andalucia, such as *Caprichos andaluces* and a major part of his *Iberia*. Another widely known Catalan, **Enrique Granados** (1867-1916), dedicated one of his three Spanish *Danzas* to Andalucia. Nor should we forget some of the great operas set in the region, including Bizet's *Carmen* and Mozart's *Don Giovanni*.

Cinema

Since its very early days, Hispanic cinema has often found inspiration in Andalucian themes, which are considered as being some of the most representative in Spain. This trend, which Berlanga caricatured in his unforgettable *Bienvenido Mr Marshall*, was to gradually disappear until Carlos Saura put Andalucian folklore back on the map with works such as *Bodas de sangre*, *Flamenco* y *Sevillanas*.

In recent times, following his success with *Solas*, critics have singled out **Benito Zambrano** as the standard bearer of new Andalucian cinema.

Popular traditions

The people of Andalucia are renowned for their tradition of *fiestas*, which they celebrate in a unique way, usually involving the entire village, town or city. Through the course of the year over 3000 festivals are held around the region, the majority of which are of a religious nature (processions and *romer'as*), although special mention needs to be made of the famous fairs *(ferias)*, carnivals and Moorish and Christian *fiestas*.

The Feria

The Andalucian *feria* is a celebration encompassing all the colour, music, dance and exuberance of the region. Its origins can be found in the traditional spring and autumn cattle fairs which were first held, as in the rest of Spain, during the Middle Ages. As these fairs developed over the centuries, they lost their early significance and evolved into general celebrations where everyone would dress up in their finery, bring out their finest horses and carriages, and above all, enjoy themselves to the full. Although every *feria* has its own specific characteristics, they also have many features in common.

April Fair

B. Morandi/DIAF

Strangely, Sevilla's April Fair, the best known of all Andalucia's festivals and one which was to serve as a model for other important modern *ferias* such as those held in Córdoba, Málaga and Jerez, is relatively recent, as it is was only created in 1847.

The area used to host the *feria* is generally enclosed with access via a large entrance gateway decorated with myriad coloured lights. Inside, the fairground is separated into distinct zones: the so-called **calle del Infierno** (literally, the Street of Hell); the **Recreo** (entertainment area); **Los Cacharritos**, home to a number of typical fairground attractions (Ferris wheel, roller coaster, shooting ranges, tombolas etc); the shopping area, or Rastro, (only generally found in small towns and villages); and the *feria*'s **Real** area, with its succession of flimsy, ephemeral entertainment booths known as **casetas**, decorated with lamps, pictures and furniture designed for the simple pleasures of eating, drinking and dancing day and night. Some of these booths are private, where entrance is strictly for members or for those with tickets, while others are open to everyone.

Although it may not appear obvious to first-time visitors, there is a strict programme for the *feria*, as is the case with every traditional celebration in Andalucia. From noon until around four in the afternoon, everyone gathers in the *Real* dressed in typical costume. As music starts up in the *casetas*, encouraging the more energetic early birds to dance a *sevillana* or two, others parade through the streets on magnificent horses with elaborately decorated harnesses and saddles or in elegant open carriages. The period after the siesta or the traditional bullfight is the time for children to make the most of the festivities before darkness falls and more visitors return to the *feria*, in normal dress, for more eating, drinking and dancing until the early hours of the morning. Such is the typical routine during *feria* week – a time for little sleep and significant reserves of energy.

Semana Santa

Gold-embroidered capes glistening in the candlelight, sumptuous statues lit up by the moon carried reverently along streets lined by orange trees, the resonant beating of drums, sacred flamenco *saetas* sung from a balcony as the Virgin and Child passes beneath it... such is the image of Semana Santa (Holy Week), the most important *fiesta* in the Andalucian calendar.

The large cities of Málaga, Sevilla and Granada, as well as villages and towns across the whole of Andalucia, all commemorate the Passion and the Death of Christ in their own way, carrying in procession works of art created by famous sculptors such as Alonso Cano, Martínez Montañés and Pedro de Mena. These images are transported on a variety of floats known as **pasos** in Sevilla and **tronos** in Málaga, all of which are decorated with richly sculpted wood, engraved silver and a multitude of flowers. Underneath, hidden by velvet flaps, the bearers or **costaleros** advance slowly with their load, weighing around three tonnes, with each carrier supporting a weight of approximately 80kg/140lb. To prepare for this arduous task, teams train for three months between Christmas and Semana Santa, during which the younger members cover the route to be taken with a structure similar in weight and size to the one they will be carrying on their shoulders on the day of the procession.

A Holy Week procession

In Andalucia there are close to a thousand **Passion brotherhoods** or **fraternities** responsible for the building and maintaining of these floats. Individual donations and raffles provide the financial means necessary to ensure that these *pasos* are impeccable and increasingly sumptuous in appearance. The statues of the Virgins themselves also have an extensive wardrobe which the *santera* (statue keeper) will choose from according to the occasion.

As the processions wind their way through the streets, onlookers place themselves at strategic points to admire the illuminated floats as they emerge from a dark alley and the skill of the carriers beneath. With this endless toing and froing the streets and bars of neighbouring terraces are quickly swamped with people in a friendly, yet exuberant atmosphere which is such a part of religious feeling in Andalucia.

"Al cielo con Ella"! (To heaven with Her!), the cry goes up as the float is lifted and the procession starts its slow, tortuous journey.

Romerías

Devotion to the Virgin is without doubt the most characteristic feature of Andalucian religious fervour, to the extent that it is said that "Andalucia is the land of the Blessed Mary". The region is home to countless sanctuaries with names advocating every possible veneration of the Virgin: de la Cabeza (the head), de la Bella (the beautiful) de la Regla (the rule), del Sol (the sun), de la Luna (the moon), de la Peña (pain) and de la Sierra (the mountain), to name but a few.

Every *romer'a* (religious pilgrimage) has its own idiosyncratic features, some of which are particularly strange, but in general it consists of a pilgrimage to a church, often on decorated carts and horseback, a religious ceremony with a procession, followed by dinner outdoors with dancing and singing until dawn, and occasionally continuing into the following day.

The most famous of all Andalucia's *romer'as* is to **El Rocío** (Huelva), an event attracting close to one million pilgrims and visitors from around Spain as well as from several European countries *(see p 273)*.

Cruces de Mayo

The Festival of the Crosses (cruces), held on 3 May every year, celebrates the Discovery of the Holy Cross. According to tradition, in the 4C the mother of the Emperor Constantine discovered the cross (Lignum crucis) on which Christ had died and divided it into small fragments which she then distributed throughout the Christian world.

The Cruces de Mayo are celebrated throughout Andalucia, although veneration varies from province to province. In some areas, the crosses are fixed and venerated all year round, such as in La Palma del Condado in the province of Huelva, while in others crosses are erected specifically for the celebration, as in Conil de la Frontera (Cádiz). In every case, the crosses are adorned with branches of rosemary and flowers, religious ceremonies are held, followed by singing and dancing well into the night. In Córdoba, the Cruces de Mayo are erected around the city and are particularly renowned for their imagination and stunning beauty.

Carnival

In most of Andalucia's provincial capitals, the *fiestas* during Carnival have a long tradition initiated by Sevilla during its Golden Age and further developed by Cádiz, more than any other city in the region. Carnival is a time of excess for the imagination and an opportunity for extravagant celebration. It is the culmination of months of hard practice and costume design in readiness for the event. The main participants are known as **comparsas** – groups of people dressed in similar costume who make their way through the streets singing ironic and humorous songs based on political and current affairs.

The Carnival celebrations held in towns and villages closer to the Meseta and the borders with Castilla tend to more restrained in nature, with more importance attributed to the so-called "burial of the sardine", in reference to the fish eaten during Lent.

In the eyes of many, the most spectacular Carnival takes place in **Cádiz**, as Sevilla prefers to devote its energies to Holy Week and its April Fair.

Traditional costume

Each of Andalucia's provinces has its own regional costume, which varies significantly from one area to the next. In Málaga, for example, part of the **verdiales** costume consists of a garish hat totally covered with flowers and a variety of coloured bands; this contrasts with the **piconera** costume in Cádiz, with its satin skirt, white blouse, black apron and hairnets of arbutus flowers; and the costume of the Alpujarras mountains (Granada), with its multicoloured striped skirt, long-sleeved blouse and flowery shawl. However, what is considered to be the Andalucian costume par excellence is the one traditionally worn in Córdoba and Sevilla which saw various modifications during the second half of the 20C. In fact, the so-called Andalucian costume is perhaps the only one in the world with its own fashion, which varies from year to year in terms of its colour, number and length of pleated ruffles, the shape of the sleeves etc.

Variations apart, the **traje de faralaes** or flamenco costume worn by women is characterised by bright colours and a tight-fitting design which highlights the figure; the wide neck and ruffles which finish off the inner part of the dress add to the attractive look. The costume is sometimes accompanied by a shawl, earrings and bracelets of similar colour to the dress, as well as real or artificial flowers in the hair. When on horseback, the *campero* costume is worn, consisting of an equestrian skirt, a blouse with a lace apron, and a black jacket.

The men's costume, generally black, grey or dark brown in colour, consists of a short jacket, white shirt without a tie, tight-fitting trousers and leather boots. The traditional headgear is either the wide-brimmed *sombrero cordobs* or the lower-crowned *sombrero sevillano*.

Bullfighting

The world of bullfighting, which excites the passions of its enthusiastic followers and staunch opponents alike, is another aspect of culture indelibly associated with Andalucian life. Irrespective of the views of visitors to the region, it is a part of life which is impossible to ignore.

The region's *fiestas* are dependent upon the **ganaderías** (ranches) such as Miura, Pablo Romero and Concha Sierra which breed the famous fighting bulls *(toro de lidia)* for the bullring. Andalucia's ranches are also famous for the magnificent **horses** used on the region's farms and homesteads and seen in the streets during popular and religious festivals. The famous **toreros** (bullfighters) have inspired poets and songwriters in their composition of works which are now considered to be classics, such as García Lorca's *Lament on the death of a bullfighter*, *paso dobles* and songs which have become part of the culture of the region and the entire country.

Bullfighters are still seen by many as idols, risking their lives in what supporters view as the ultimate battle between man and beast. The modern-day face of bullfighting is changing. It is now a multi-billion peseta industry generating huge income and employing many thousands of people. A further example of this change was the recent elevation of the first female bullfighter to the professional ranks.

Bullfighting has also given rise to magnificent architecture as is best admired in the *plaza de toros* in Ronda; sumptuous, brightly coloured "suits of light" *(trajes de luces)* with beautiful gold and silk embroidery; and the traditional **bullfighting posters** which on occasion are veritable works of art.

R. Mattès

Other types of fight – **Capeas** are popular festivals during which young amateurs match their skills against bulls in village squares and smaller provincial bullrings. At **novilladas**, young three-year-old bulls or *novillos* are fought by apprentice bullfighters known as *novilleros*. A **rejoneador** is a mounted bullfighter who takes part in the traditional three-act corrida.

Flamenco

Flamenco is the most genuine expression of Andalucian art, created towards the middle of the 19C from a combination of pre-existing musical forms with Jewish, Byzantine, Moorish and even Hindu influence. Experts fail to agree on the scale of this influence, but what does seem clear is that it developed in Lower Andalucia (Jerez, Utrera, Lebrija, Cadiz etc) via a number of families who passed on the art from generation to generation. Although it has been admitted that flamenco is not gypsy in origin, the *gitanos* have incorporated their own personality and their considerable interpretative capacity into flamenco.

B. Gardel/HEMISPHERES

For a long time considered to be an art form associated with those of "ill repute" – a view expressed at the turn of the century by writers such as Miguel de Unamuno – initiatives led by leading cultural figures such as Federico García Lorca and Manuel de Falla elevated flamenco to the status of the cultural expression of the Andalucian people.

Since that time, flamenco has seen the rise to fame of singers such as Antonio Mairena, Fosforito, la Niña de la Puebla and, in more recent times, **Camarón de la Isla**, renowned guitarists such as **Paco de Lucía** and dancers of the quality of Cristina Hoyos.

The new generations have demonstrated that flamenco remains a living art and that it is capable of evolving and assimilating new rhythms. Purists do not agree, but groups such as Ketama and Navajita Plateá, guitarists such as Raimundo Amador and dancers of international renown such as Joaquín Cortés and Antonio Canales are ready to show that flamenco is able to explore new avenues.

Although to many observers and listeners the individual aspects of flamenco may be somewhat difficult to comprehend and interpret, it is impossible not to be moved by the passion of this truly Andalucian art form.

Handicrafts

Andalucia's handicrafts cover a wide range of products. Although many of these vary considerably from area to area, particularly with regard to pottery and ceramics, many of the region's traditions are common to most provinces. Over the past few years, strenuous efforts have been made to rediscover old techniques and decorative motifs that have been in danger of disappearing; sadly, however, some aspects of ornamental art, such as decorative work on silk – such a common feature during Moorish times – have now been lost forever.

Iron and metalwork – In many areas, iron is still worked in accordance with traditional methods, using the forge and anvil, to produce grilles, fences and staircases. The towns of Arcos de la Frontera (Cádiz) and Torredonjimeno (Jáen) are both reputed for this type of metalwork; meanwhile, some smaller towns in the province of Málaga, such as Arroyo de la Miel, Cártama and Estepona all specialise in the production of artistic locksmith work. Also worthy of mention are the imaginative tin and glass lamps from Úbeda, the unusual cowbells made in Cortegana (Huelva), and the attractive carriages from Bollulos del Condado with their combination of iron and woodwork.

Leather goods – Because of the huge importance of horses to the region's economy, a large equestrian equipment industry has developed in Andalucia which produces saddles, riding breeches, leather pouches and other items used for horse riding and hunting. The leading leather centres are found in Jerez de la Frontera, Alcalá de los Gazules and Villamartín (Cádiz); Almodóvar del Río (Córdoba) and various towns and villages in Huelva, particularly Almonte and Zalamea la Real.

Ubrique and Prado del Rey (Cádiz) have developed into the capitals for leather fashion accessories with a number of workshops producing a range of bags, belts and gloves for leading companies around the world.

Shoes are also important to the local economy, as seen in Valverde del Camino (boots) and Montoro (handmade shoes).

This list is not complete, however, without mentioning the magnificent cordovans (embossed leather) with their traditional and modern decoration produced, as the name would suggest, in the workshops of Córdoba.

Woodwork – The manufacture of furniture has become a feature of Andalucian industry, establishing itself alongside sculptural art with a tradition dating back several centuries and whose work is inspired by the creations of sculptors such as Martínez Montañés and Pedro Roldán.

In the 19C, following the arrival of a number of English wine and sherry producers, the coopers of Sanlúcar de Barrameda and San Fernando near the city of Cádiz, who had hitherto concentrated on barrelmaking, found it easy to develop their work to English tastes and create a range of high-quality mahogany furniture. Further to the east, the town of Ronda has made its name for the production of a more rustic style of furniture. Granada is famous for its inlaid (marquetry with inlaid bone, mother-of-pearl, amber or marble) and gilded work. Over the course of time, some villages within the province have also developed an excellent reputation for furniture produced in the Mudéjar (Capileira) and Renaissance styles (Baza).

The so-called "Sevilla chairs", with their bright colours and flower motifs, are manufactured in several towns and villages in the province of Huelva, including Valverde, Galorza and Zalamea.

Pottery and ceramics – Andalucia's pottery and ceramics industries produce an almost unlimited choice, ranging from items of everyday use (pitchers, jars and bowls) to those used for decorative purposes only, such as the high-quality Pickman-La Cartuja de Sevilla porcelain, with its delightful grey, pink and green decorative motifs.

Andalucian handicrafts

The kilns used in the Almerian villages of Albox, Níjar and Sorbas are almost identical to those used in former times; the province of Granada still retains many of its 19C wood-fuelled kilns; while the potters' wheels in Guadix remain as active as ever.

The numerous workshops in the Triana district of Sevilla still produce their traditional blue, yellow, orange and purple pottery and ceramics, while the village of Sanlúcar la Mayor to the west of the city is now specialising in the reproduction of lustre ceramics with Hispano-Moorish designs.

Jaén, meanwhile, is renowned for the blue and white ceramics of Andújar. Not to be outdone, the province of Córdoba has made its name with Caliphal ceramics decorated with geometric, plant and animal motifs.

Other artisanal industries found in Andalucia include marble from Macael; *jarapas* (handwoven rugs and blankets) from Níjar (Almería); blankets from Grazalema (Cádiz); handmade carpets produced in Málaga, Marbella and Estepona; basketwork from Lanjarón; jewellery from Córdoba; fans, shawls and ornamental combs from Sevilla; regional costume from Antequera (Málaga); and the guitars manufactured in Granada, Córdoba and Jaén (Marmolejo).

Food and wine

Eight centuries of Moorish presence have had a profound effect on Andalucian culture, including the region's cuisine. New agricultural techniques, based on maximising the use of water, made it possible to grow crops on hitherto uncultivated land, thus enabling the year-round production of fruits and vegetables. The Moors brought with them a whole range of new crops (rice, aubergines, artichokes, and asparagus) as well as spices which at the time were unknown in the western world (pepper, cinnamon and cumin). They also introduced an order for the presentation of dishes which, until then, had been brought to the table at the same time.

Yet, despite the deep-rooted influence of Arab cuisine on southern Spain, it has failed to displace the traditional Mediterranean cooking of the region, centred around wine and olive oil, which remains to this day. Nowadays, the wines of Andalucia have a well-deserved worldwide reputation, while the region's olive oil industry, including two quality *Denominaciones de Origen* labels – Baena (Córdoba) and Sierra de Segura (Jaén) – is currently enjoying great popularity *(see p 234)*.

The region's cuisine can be divided into two distinct areas: the **coast**, with its emphasis on fish and seafood; and **inland**, where the cooking is dominated by meat dishes, vegetables, hearty soups and stews.

Gazpacho

This chilled, refreshing and healthy soup is by far Andalucia's most famous dish. Its basic ingredients are tomatoes, cucumber, peppers, oil, vinegar, garlic and salt, the quantities of which vary from family to family; many people will also add croutons, onions and even sliced hard-boiled egg. Despite their different flavours, *salmorejo* (bread mashed with tomatoes, garlic, oil, vinegar and salt) and *ajo blanco* (similar to *salmorejo* but made with almonds instead of tomatoes and served with grapes or melon) are considered to be variations on the gazpacho theme, perhaps because both are also served chilled.

Mimo/STOCK PHOTOS

Although fried fish *(pescaíto frito)* is a popular dish in bars along the coast, Andalucian cuisine is mainly based around its stews *(guisos)*, which may also be known as *cocido andaluz*, *olla* or *puchero*. These can be found in every province, with ingredients varying according to local products. Dishes with either pork or chicken, vegetables and chickpeas and/or various type of beans *(judías)* are also popular across Andalucia. The local meat stew known as *pringá* is a popular *tapa* in the bars of Sevilla.

In the more mountainous parts of inland Andalucia, game stews are an important part of the local cuisine, providing the necessary calories and warmth on a cold winter's night. This contrasts with the lighter fish dishes, prepared in every manner possible along the Mediterranean and Atlantic coasts: baked *(cocido)*; grilled *(a la plancha)*, particularly the shrimp and prawns from Sanlúcar de Barrameda; in stews *(guisados)*, such as the seafood stews *(guisos marineros)* from Cádiz; fried *(frito)*, including anchovies, squid and cuttlefish; and barbecued *(asado)*, an ideal way of grilling sardines caught off the Málaga coast.

Another important aspect of Andalucian gastronomy is the wide choice of cured hams and sausages *(embutidos)*. Local

---

Breakfast

In most bars and cafeterias you can try a typical Andalucian breakfast *(desayuno)* consisting of toasted bread with olive oil and *manteca colorá*, a reddy-coloured dripping. If this traditional delicacy fails to whet your appetite, why not try deep-fried *churros*, long strips of doughnut, traditionally served with thick, sweet hot chocolate.

products include *morcón*, a type of blood pudding; the cured legs of hams *(cañas)* from Jabugo (Huelva), one of Spain's main areas for the rearing of acorn-fed pigs for the famous *jamón ibérico*; *morcilla* (black pudding) from Ronda (Málaga) and the renowned sausages and hams from Trévelez, in the province of Granada.

Andalucia's cheeses are generally made from goats' or sheep's milk, although cows' milk is used on rare occasions. Although these predominantly strong-flavoured cheeses are little known outside of the region, they are an ideal accompaniment to a glass of chilled *fino*, *manzanilla* or *oloroso* sherry, but are never eaten after the main course. The main areas of cheese production are the mountains of Almería and Granada, the Serranía de Ronda (Málaga) and in the Sierra de Grazalema (Cádiz).

Moorish and Jewish influence is very evident in the tremendous variety of cakes and pastries produced in the region. Some of the best known, flavoured with cinnamon, almonds and anise, include the *polvorones* and *mantecados* from Estepa (Málaga), which are eaten throughout Spain at Christmas; the delicious *tocinos de cielo* (literally "bacon from heaven"), a custard pudding from Jerez de la Frontera; and flaky round cakes known as *roscos* in a variety of guises such as millefeuilles *(milhojas)* and honeyed fritters *(pestiños)*.

Tapas

The tradition of eating tapas is synonymous with Spain, Andalucia and, more particularly, Sevilla, from where it originated. Although tapas originally consisted of no more than just a thin slice of cured ham, a single prawn or a small piece of Spanish omelette to accompany a glass of wine, as time has passed, tapas have increased in size to such an extent that a selection of tapas or the larger *raciones* are often eaten instead of a full meal.

Nowadays, many of these cakes are produced by nuns according to traditional recipes dating back many centuries. Perhaps this is why many of them have evocative names such as *huesos de santo* (saint's bones), *cabello de ángel* (angel's hair), *suspiro de monja* (nun's sigh) and the aforementioned *tocino de cielo*.

Wine and Sherry

Andalucia has 86 000ha/212 500 acres of vineyards producing wines which have a superb reputation around the world. Almost all of this land is found within designated quality control areas *(denominaciones de origen)*.

The region's wines are mainly produced using two varieties of white grape: Palomino, predominantly grown in and around Jerez de la Frontera, and Sanlúcar de Barrameda; and Pedro Ximénez, which is the main constituent of the sweet wines *(vinos dulces)* produced in Jerez, Málaga and Montilla-Moriles, south of Córdoba.

The region currently has four *denominaciones de origen (D.O.)*: Jerez, Montilla-Moriles, Condado de Huelva and Málaga. Each of these areas concentrates on the production of full-bodied wines, although recent diversification has seen their range expand towards young, light and fruity table wines.

D.O. Jerez (Cádiz) – The sherries of the Jerez area, which include the famous *finos* and *manzanillas* are Andalucia's best known and most prestigious wines. Sherry, as the name suggests (the word sherry is the anglicised form of the town), can only be produced in the designated area around Jerez, while *manzanillas* are the exclusive preserve of Sanlúcar de Barrameda. The Jerez appellation also produces sweet and dry *olorosos*, sweet wines *(vinos dulces)* such as Moscatel and Pedro Ximénez, and amontillados, which undergo a longer oxidisation process in the barrel *(see p 216, 223)*.

D.O. Montilla-Moriles (Córdoba) – These excellent wines produced in the area south of Córdoba have a high alcohol content. Although they are classified according to the same criteria as those wines produced in Jerez, Montilla-Moriles wines are very different to those produced further west *(see p 252)*.

A *bodega* in Jerez

D.O. Málaga – Up until a century ago, sweet Málaga wines could be enjoyed on the finest tables in Europe. Despite their slight decline in fortune due to changing tastes, they are still the perfect accompaniment for dessert or afternoon tea *(see p 229)*.

D.O. Condado (Huelva) – The pale and fruity Condado wines are produced from the Zalema grape. There are two types of Condado: Condado Pálido, reminiscent of the sherries of Jerez and *manzanilla*; and Condado Viejo, similar to an *oloroso*, which can attain an alcohol content of 23 per cent.

In addition to these leading regions, Andalucia also has other, smaller areas of vine-yards producing wines rarely seen elsewhere in Spain or abroad. These include Aljarafe and Los Palacios (Sevilla); Villaviciosa de Córdoba (Córdoba); Bailén, Lopera and Torreperogil (Jaén); Costa-Albondón (Granada) and Laujar (Almería).

Serving suggestions – The sherries of Andalucia are produced according to a special *solera* blending process which guarantees uniform quality over a period of years.

These wines are traditionally served in *catavinos*, narrow, tall glasses which enable the superb qualities of the wine to be enjoyed to the full.

Each variety of sherry should be drunk at a different temperature:

– *finos* are generally chilled to between 8°C and 10°C. Once opened, a bottle should be drunk as quickly as possible;

– *amontillados* should be ideally served between 12°C and 14°C;

– *olorosos* are at their best at a temperature of 18°C.

Brandies and liqueurs

Brandies and liqueurs are also an important feature of the Andalucian economy. Anise, brandy and rum produced in Andalucia are sold throughout Spain and are increasingly being exported abroad.

The early **aniseed-based** liqueurs originated from Ojén (Málaga), next to Spain's very first blast furnace, at a time when it was thought that aniseed had a beneficial effect on respiratory tracts affected by the mining and iron and steel industries. Today, the main areas for anise are in Montilla (Córdoba), which produces liqueurs with a smooth aroma and high alcohol content; Cazalla and Constantina (Sevilla), famous for their strong *cazalla*; and Zalamea la Real and Alosno (Huelva), with its dry and potent *aguardiente*.

Most of the **brandy** served in bars around Spain comes from Jerez de la Frontera, Sanlúcar de Barrameda and Puerto de Santa María, all of which belong to a regulatory body for brandy quality, the *Consejo Regulador del Brandy*. However, it is also distilled in Rute and Montilla (Córdoba), Málaga and in La Palma del Condado (Huelva).

It should also be remembered that the distilling and production techniques for **rum**, which is now considered to be a typically Caribbean drink, and its main ingredient – sugar cane – were exported to Cuba from Spain. Centuries later, when Fidel Castro came to power on the island, some Cuban producers transferred their production plants to Andalucia, particularly to Málaga and Granada, the only parts of Europe where sugar cane is grown.

Patio de los Leones, Alhambra (Granada)

Sights

AGUILAR DE LA FRONTERA★

Córdoba – Population 13 397
Michelin map 446 T 16

The whitewashed houses of Aguilar de la Frontera extend up a small hill, creating an attractive contrast with the greenery of the vineyards surrounding the town.
After the Reconquest in the 13C, the Moorish town of Bulay was renamed Aguilar; the suffix *de la Frontera* was added soon after, due to the town's proximity to the borders of the kingdom of Granada. Its history is indelibly linked with the Fernández de Córdoba family, who have been the lords of Aguilar since 1370.

Leave your car in llano de las Coronadas, next to paseo de Vicente Aranda, a verdant garden in the heart of the town. The historical centre *(casco antiguo)* contains a number of fine seigniorial houses and Baroque churches, particularly in **calle Arrabal**, with several mansions dating from the 17C and 19C (nos 5, 11 and 13).

Head towards placilla Vieja, then climb the cuesta de Jesús hill.

Aguilar's famous pastries

During your visit, why not try the delicious *risaos* made with almonds, sugar, egg yolk and lemon, or the equally tasty coffee or strawberry meringues *(merengas)*.

★**Parroquia de Nuestra Señora del Soterraño** ⊘ – The town's main church is dedicated to its patron saint. The present building was built in the 16C on the orders of Catalina Fernández de Córdoba.

Exterior – The exterior has two stone doorways. The Baroque portal to the left originates from an earlier church and is typical of the 17C. A number of similar doorways can be seen around the town. The finely sculpted doorway to the right is Plateresque.

Interior – The interior is surprising in the rich decoration of its chapels. The three aisles, separated by ogival arches, rest on cruciform pillars. As is usual in this area, the church has a straight triple apse. The main nave has a Mudéjar ceiling which has preserved part of its *artesonado* work, while the high altar is crowned by a Gothic pointed vault. A large Baroque altarpiece with seven sculptures, dominated by an image of the town's patron saint, can be admired in the presbytery.
An 18C lectern and some attractive walnut **choir stalls** dating from the same century can be seen towards the rear of the central aisle. The back of every seat is adorned with an octagonal medallion depicting figures in relief, including saints, apostles and images of the Virgin Mary. In spite of the somewhat primitive technique used, they all manage to convey great expression and emotion.
The **Capilla del Sagrario**★ and the **Capilla de la Inmaculada** *(to the left and right of the Capilla Mayor)* contain some particularly impressive 17C stuccowork. A **high-relief of the Last Supper** in the Capilla del Sagrario is particularly worthy of note.
The **Capilla de Jesús Nazareno**★, an impressive mid-18C Baroque chapel in the Epistle nave, contains the venerated statue of Jesus of Nazareth. The chapel is topped by an echinus-adorned cupola completely covered with stuccowork. The lavishly decorated *camarín* (prayer-niche) can be seen to the rear of the chapel.
The ruins of a castle, the Castillo de Poley, are visible on a small hill behind the church.
From Llano de las Coronadas, follow calle Santa Brígida.

Iglesia del Hospital de Santa Brígida – This church dates from the 16C, although it underwent significant restoration in the 17C and 18C. The unusual façade, with its central tower flanked by simple Baroque doorways, is of particular interest. The 18C tower is neo-Classical in style, in contrast to the largely Baroque characteristics of other church towers in the area.
Return to Llano de las Coronadas and take calle Moralejo.

Convento de las Carmelitas (Monasterio de San José y San Roque) – This Carmelite monastery was founded in 1668 and its construction continued until 1761. The interior of the church *(only open during religious services)* is surprisingly rich in decoration and is considered to be the town's Baroque masterpiece. This sumptuous style can be seen throughout the church with its retables, oil paintings, stucco foliage, volutes and angels, creating a scene that has retained great unity of style.
A number of fine seigniorial mansions can be seen in calle Moralejo and calle Carrera.
From calle Moralejo, either take calle Granada or calle Mercaderes.

★**Plaza de San José** – This large, neo-Classical square, completed in 1810, is accessed via four vaulted arches. It is dominated by the town hall *(ayuntamiento)*, and is one of very few examples of an octagonal square in Spain. Its main charm lies in its simplicity and harmony.
Leave plaza de San José via calle Don Teodoro.

★**Torre del Reloj** – This 18C Baroque tower rises majestically above the plaza de los Desamparados, but was never part of a church. It was in fact built for civil use, although it remained a model for Andalucian bell-towers of the period. Additional features include a cupola with *azulejo* decoration and a turret.

Calle del Carmen – This street is reached via calle Desamparados. The houses here enjoy superb views of the surrounding vineyards. In **placita del Carmen**, a small square fronted by the church of the same name, stands a small Christ of the Lanterns, similar in style to the one found in Córdoba.

Return to calle Moralejo and head along calle Vicente Núñez.

Note, at no 2, the somewhat unusual **Casa Señorial del Caballo de Santiago**, a seigniorial mansion which takes its name from a depiction of St James *(Santiago)* on horseback *(a caballo)* on the central balcony.

B. Kaufmann/MICHELIN

Torre del Reloj

EXCURSIONS

Laguna de Zónar – *Follow the A 309 towards Puente Genil.* The **Centro de Visitantes de Zonas Húmedas El Lagar** at Km 75.8 is a visitor centre providing information on the geographical characteristics and flora and fauna of this wetland ecosystem formed by three lakes, while the nearby **Centro de Visitantes Zoñar** ⊙ at Km 76.6 has an interactive exhibition on the lagoon. A viewpoint enables visitors to get a closer look at the lagoon, which is home to the **malvasía duck**, a protected species which until a few decades ago was threatened with extinction.

Puente Genil – *18km/11mi along the A 309.* This small country town takes its name from the Genil River which runs through it, and its 16C bridge, built by Hernán Ruiz. A pleasant walkway runs alongside the river. This region is renowned for its quinces, a fruit used to produce a variety of local specialities.

The centre of the town is home to several old mansion houses, particularly those in calle Don Gonzalo, and the **Museo Arqueológico y Etnográfico** ⊙, a small archeological and ethnographical museum displaying finds discovered during excavations of the surrounding area. A number of interesting churches are also dotted around the historical centre, including the 17C **Nuestra Señora de la Concepción**, with its tower-flanked portal and polychrome stucco main altarpiece; the **Iglesia de la Purificación**, with its attractive 19C bell-tower and spire, and an Immaculate Conception by Pedro Duque Cornejo; the **Iglesia del Convento de San Francisco**, with its fine sculptures (Nuestra Señora de los Ángeles by La Roldana); and the **Iglesia de Jesús Nazareno**, decorated with paintings by local 19C artists, and housing a venerated image of Jesus of Nazareth, Puente Genil's patron saint.

Holy Week

As you wander through the streets of Puente Genil, you will perhaps notice the strange signs outside some of its houses such as Imperio Romano, Cien Luces, Los Levitas etc. These are the headquarters of the 65 associations or brotherhoods that participate in the Holy Week festivities. The processions displaying characters from the Old and New Testaments are a feature of Aguilar's Semana Santa.

ALCALÁ LA REAL★

Jaén – Population 21 493
Michelin map 446 T 18

Alcalá la Real is situated to the south of Jaén province in a mountainous area of undulating hills and extensive olive groves. The town's origins date back to prehistoric times; however, due to its strategic position on the border between Christian- and Muslim-held lands, it became synonymous with fierce battles between the two adversaries. During the period of Moorish domination, which lasted over 600 years, *Qalat*, (a fortified settlement in Arabic) as it was then known, reached the pinnacle of its splendour, until its reconquest by Alfonso XI in 1341.

Nowadays, this attractive town is an active agricultural and commercial centre with numerous shops, most of which are concentrated along calle San Fernando. Typical local dishes include *pollo a la secretaria*, a chicken dish with peppers, peas and an onion and saffron sauce.

Fortaleza de la Mota, Alcalá la Real

Alcalá la Real's native sons include the poet Juan Ruiz, known as the **Arcipreste de Hita**, and the medieval sculptors **Juan Martínez Montañés** and **Pablo de Rojas**.

★★ **Fortaleza de la Mota** – The fortress stands on the hill of the same name, offering magnificent **views★** of the town and surrounding area. It is difficult to distinguish the crags and rocks from the castle walls, which have preserved their seven entrance gates. The Puerta de la Imagen, very similar in appearance to the Puerta de la Justicia in the Alhambra (Granada), is particularly worthy of note.

The fortress is divided into two sections dating from different periods: the Moorish *alcazaba* and the abbey churches. The first is a castle with three towers: the Torre de Mocha, Torre de la Campana and Torre del Homenaje. Inside the castle, built on the remains of the former mosque, stands the **Iglesia de Santo Domingo★**, a Gothic-Mudéjar church built by Alfonso XI. It has preserved the tower of the former minaret – one of the most characteristic features of Alcalá – as well as a fine 15C retable.

The **Iglesia de Santa María la Mayor**, badly damaged during the War of Independence, can be seen on a esplanade of the fortress. It has, nevertheless, retained an attractive Renaissance **façade**, Plateresque in style, on which Diego de Siloé is known to have worked. This monumental complex also houses the interesting **Museo Arqueológico** ⊘, inside the Torre del Homenaje, with its collection of archeological exhibits from Alcalá and the surrounding locality.

Paseo de los Álamos

This delightful avenue is the ideal place to relax at the end of a long day and enjoy a chilled glass of the local wine on the outdoor terraces of its numerous tapas bars.

Iglesia de Nuestra Señora de las Angustias – This impressive, octagonal church built by Ventura Rodríguez in the 13C contains an exceptional set of medieval painted wooden **tablets★** and the font where the artists Martínez Montañés and de Rojas were baptised.

WHERE TO STAY

MODERATE

Río de Oro – *Abad Moya, 2* – ☎ *953 58 03 37* – *10 rooms* – *4 000pts*. This family-run hotel has a good location in the town centre. Well-appointed rooms, some of which have a balcony overlooking a square and park. Good value for money.

Torrepalma – *Conde de Torrepalma, 2* – ☎ *953 58 18 00* – *fax 953 58 17 12* – *38 rooms* – *7 000pts*. A modern hotel with spacious, comfortable rooms. The only slight inconvenience is its location along one of Alcalá's busiest and noisiest shopping streets.

EATING OUT

El Curro – *Ramón y Cajal, 6* – ☎ *953 58 30 50*. The first thing you see on entering El Curro is the bar, frequented by locals. Although there is a dining room, (albeit somewhat dreary in appearance), regulars eat in a more attractive room with a low ceiling and fireplace. Specialities include grilled meats and ham.

Town Hall – The *ayuntamiento*, situated on the pleasant **plaza del Arcipreste de Hita**, occupies a charming 18C Baroque building flanked by two towers. Opposite stands an artistic **sundial★** by Fernando Tapia.

Palacio Abacial – The abbot's palace, in front of the attractive Los Álamos fountain at one end of the paseo of the same name *(see below)*, is housed in a sober neo-Classical building, the façade of which has a Renaissance-inspired balcony and an elegant doorway with reliefs and coats of arms of noble families.

EXCURSIONS

Castillo de Locubín – *12km/8mi north on the J 2340*. The road winds its way to the Puerto del Castillo pass, the setting for this small, whitewashed settlement, with its superb **views★** of the San Juan River and Víboras Reservoir *(embalse)*. It is worth visiting the remains of the old **Moorish castle** which, along with the fortresses at Alcaudete and Alcalá la Real, was part of the defensive system on the border with the kingdom occupied by the Moors.

Alcaudete – *26km/16mi northeast on the N 432*. Alcaudete is nestled in the folds of a small promontory, hidden amid olive groves. It was conquered by the Infante Don Fernando de Antequera in 1408, from which time it became one of the most important points along the border with the kingdom of Granada. It is renowned for its pastries: *hojaldrinas*, cider *empanadillas* and *roscos de vino*, doughnut-like cakes made by the nuns from the Convento de Santa Clara.

Castle ruins – The Moorish *alcazaba* was built on the site of a former Roman fortress and has preserved several vestiges of its walls and keep.

Iglesia de Santa María – The solemn silhouette of this Gothic church with its Plateresque side portal stands at the foot of the castle. Inside the church, note the fine coffered *artesonado* ceiling, the Renaissance grilles in front of the high altar and the doors of the sacristy.

Iglesia de San Pedro – This 16C Mudéjar-style church contains an interesting altarpiece.

Plaza Mayor – The main square is situated at the heart of a labyrinth of narrow streets with a number of shops and bars. The 18C town hall comes into view after passing through an archway known as the Arco de la Villa.

ALGECIRAS

Cádiz – Population 101 972

Michelin map 446 X 13

Algeciras has always been one of Spain's most important ports. The Moors called it *al-Yazirat al-jadra*, meaning "green island", and from the early days of Muslim occupation the town acted as one of the main landing points for Moorish troops. Today, it is Spain's leading passenger port. Its period of greatest splendour coincided with the period of Arab domination (711-1344), during which time it was one of the two administrative districts of the Cádiz region. In the 18C, following the capture of Gibraltar by the British, it regained its strategic importance, resulting in the growth of its population and its development as Spain's counterpoint to British domination in the Straits. In 1906 it played host to the **Algeciras Conference**, at which the major European powers confirmed the division of Morocco into separate zones of influence.

Algeciras may not be one of the most attractive Andalucian cities, yet visitors will be pleasantly surprised to find a friendly town which is full of life, its lack of large monuments more than compensated by the vibrant atmosphere of its streets.

Museo Municipal ⊘ – The municipal museum is installed in a large house within the boundaries of the attractive Parque de las Acacias park. It displays a number of items from the Roman period including amphorae and corks, which bear witness to the significant trade in the waters of the Bay of Algeciras. Also of interest are the exhibits relating to the **Siege of Algeciras** (1342-44), during which the troops of Alfonso XI employed ingenious war techniques and used the first firearms known as *truenos* (thunderclaps).

Market – This iron and concrete structure in the plaza Palma was designed by the Spanish engineer **Eduardo Torroja** in the 1950s. The roof is supported at just four points, a most unusual feature for the period, and one which undoubtedly required great technical innovation at the time.

Plaza Alta – This square in the heart of Algeciras is the city's most famous landmark. Note the attractive 1930s Mudéjar-style *azulejo* and brick fountain surrounded by palm trees. Two churches border the square: the 18C **Iglesia de Nuestra Señora de la Palma**, a mixture of Baroque and neo-Classical styles, and the **Iglesia de Nuestra Señora de la Aurora**, a smaller Baroque edifice.

Merenid baths (Baños Meriníes) – In 1999 the town hall transferred the remains of the 13C Moorish baths, originally part of the residence of the Merenid dynasty in Algeciras, to the **Parque María Cristina**. A Moorish-style wheel and well have also been rebuilt to illustrate how the baths operated.

EXCURSIONS

The road to Tarifa – This short 21km/13mi section separating Algeciras and Tarifa is the most southerly road in Europe and offers some stunning **views★★★** of the North African coast. Cars can stop at the **Mirador del Estrecho**, a viewpoint 13km/8mi along the road, although the views are better nearer to Algeciras. To the right of the road, note the quixotic landscape of modern **wind turbines**.

La Línea de la Concepción – *17km/10.5mi west of Algeciras.* La Línea's origins only date back to the 18C, making it one of the youngest towns in Spain. Following the British invasion of Gibraltar, a defensive line needed to be established which was subsequently named Línea de Gibraltar. Gradually, a small settlement developed alongside these defences, acquiring town status in 1870. From then on it was known as La Línea de la Concepción, in honour of the Virgin Mary, at that time the patron saint of the army.

The town has little to offer tourists. The heavily urbanised centre is laid out around calle Real and the Iglesia de la Inmaculada Concepción, built in 1879.

Almadraba – *Los Caireles, 2* – ☎ *956 17 55 66* – fax *956 17 15 63* – *84 rooms* – *11 450pts.* Facing the Rock of Gibraltar. Modern, spacious rooms with balconies overlooking the Rock. Out of season a suite costs the same as the hotel's standard rooms.

★Gibraltar

20km/12.5mi east. A British crown colony. Passport required for entry. First and foremost, Gibraltar is famous for its magnificent rock which, although rising a mere 423m/1 388ft above the sea, is visible from all around the bay. It acquires even greater dimension and beauty at close quarters, as its individual features come into clearer view.

View of the Rock of Gibraltar

The history of Gibraltar is intimately linked to its strategic position. It was here that **Tarik-ibn-Zeyad** landed in AD 711 at the head of the Moorish troops who were to conquer almost all of the Iberian Peninsula. In Antiquity, Gibraltar was known as Calpe, one of the Pillars of Hercules; however, the modern name derives from the Arabic *Djebel Tarik*, meaning "Tariq's Mountain". During the 14C, Gibraltar was the scene of numerous battles between Moors and Christians and in 1462 it was permanently conquered by the Duke of Medina Sidonia. Its importance waned until the early 18C when it was invaded by the British during the **War of the Spanish Succession**, after which Felipe V and Carlos III attempted unsuccessfully to regain control of it.

Visitors are advised to check the entry situation before arrival as long queues (one hour or more) occasionally develop for motorists entering and leaving Gibraltar. On these occasions, it is worth leaving your car on the Spanish side and walking across the border.

Gibraltar Museum ⊘ – The museum is close to the Tourist Office in the centre of the town and is an ideal place to start your visit. It is housed in a simple colonial building above some interesting 14C **Moorish baths★** and contains extensive exhibits on the history of the Rock, ranging from the famous **Gibraltar skull** of a Neanderthal woman discovered in 1848, to Gibraltar's role in the Second World War. The enormous **model★** of the Rock, created in 1865, is also worthy of note.

> ### Gibraltarians
> The inhabitants of Gibraltar descend from a melting pot of races, religions and cultures, making the Rock a highly cosmopolitan place to live and visit. Most of these native Gibraltarians speak both Spanish and English.

Main Street – Gibraltar's main thoroughfare is lined by literally hundreds of shops, banks and bars, popular with the thousands of daily visitors. Although the local currency is the Gibraltar pound, the majority of shops and bars will also accept pesetas. Main Street is home to **St Mary's Catholic Cathedral**, built above the former main mosque, and the **Convento**, the residence of Gibraltar's governor since 1728, where the Changing of the Guard can be seen several times daily.

To the far south of the Rock stands the **Europa Point lighthouse**, from where visitors can enjoy **superb views of Africa**. The Shrine of Our Lady of Europe, the patron saint of Gibraltar, and Ibrahim-al-Ibrahim's mosque can both be seen nearby.

WHERE TO STAY

Cannon – *9 Cannon Lane – ☏ 350 51711 – fax 350 51789 – 18 rooms – £34.50.* Close to Main Street. Basic but adequate rooms (no TV or phone). English breakfast is served on a small patio.

EATING OUT

Water Front – *Queensway Quay.* A large restaurant with a terrace overlooking the sea. House specialities include grilled meats and kebabs.

Bunters – *1 College Lane – ☏ 350 70482 – closed in August.* This typically British restaurant off Main Street is both popular and friendly.

Upper Rock ⊙ – The Upper Rock, designated a **Nature Reserve**, is home to some of Gibraltar's most interesting sights, including the famous Barbary apes, brought here by British troops from North Africa at the end of the 18C.

Moorish castle – The castle occupies a strategic position overlooking the bay. The building visible today was built in the 14C, although the early origins of the fortress date back to a castle constructed in the 8C. Its most impressive feature is its keep.

The ascent to this part of the Upper Rock is possible by taking the **cable-car** ⊙ or one of the numerous taxis available for hire in Main Street.

The Great Siege Tunnels – Visitors interested in military history should not miss the Great Siege Tunnels, some 60km/37mi of underground galleries built by the British to defend the Rock during the Great Siege of 1779-83.

St Michael's Cave – Legend says that the cave is endless and that a tunnel runs from it, linking Gibraltar with the African coast. In fact, this limestone cave has a height of 62m/203ft at its highest point and features some spectacular formations of stalactites and stalagmites. The main cavern has been transformed into an auditorium for concerts and theatre performances.

ALHAMA DE GRANADA★

Granada – Population 5 894

Michelin map 446 U-V 18

Alhama de Granada is one of Andalucia's most attractive small towns, with its whitewashed houses and narrow streets. Its location, literally hanging above a gorge, has inspired poets and travellers alike through the centuries. The Moors named it Al-Hamma, meaning "hot spring", due to the thermal waters found here. Its renown was such that during the period of the Reconquest, Christians paid enormous sums of money to take the waters here.

★MOORISH QUARTER

Alhama has preserved an interesting Moorish quarter which can be easily explored on foot. A viewpoint behind the **Iglesia del Carmen** provides a pleasant introduction to the town with its impressive **view**★ over the famous gorge of the Alhama River. Walk around the church to the delightful Baroque Capilla de Jesús Nazareno, passing an old Arab fortress which was extensively restored in the 19C. Head up calle Baja de la Iglesia until you reach the imposing tower of the **Iglesia de la Encarnación**, which rises above the neighbouring whitewashed houses.

★**Iglesia de la Encarnación** ⊙ – The church, whose name symbolises the incarnation of the Christian faith over Islam, is built above a former mosque, several stones of which can still be distinguished on the south façade. The Baroque portal conceals an early Gothic façade decorated with plant motifs and fantastic animals. The single-nave interior is somewhat sober in style and topped by a complex pointed vault. The sacristy contains a small museum in which a set of valuable 16C priests' garments *(ternos)* are the prize exhibits.

Upon leaving the church, admire the **Casa de la Inquisición** *(right)*, an Isabelline Gothic-style building used as a House of the Inquisition. It was demolished and subsequently rebuilt in the 1950s. The enchanting plaza de los Presos can be seen

WHERE TO STAY

MODERATE

El Ventorro – *3km/2mi from Alhama de Granada towards Jatar on the GR 141* – ☎ *958 35 04 38 – 19 rooms – 6 000pts*. This hotel on the banks of the Alhama River has small, sober rooms which have nonetheless been tastefully decorated. The restaurant serves simple but tasty cuisine.

MID-RANGE

Hotel Balneario – *Carretera del Balneario. Less than 1km/0.6mi from Alhama on the Granada road* – ☎ *958 35 00 11 – fax 958 35 02 97 – 110 rooms – 9 500pts – open May to Oct*. The origins of these springs date back to Roman times, although they acquired great renown during the Caliphal period. The present building was built in the 19C. The most spectacular feature is the *aljibe*, a delightful **Moorish cistern**★ into which the spring's thermal waters gush at a temperature of 47°C/116°F. It is contained within a room built over a Roman basement with an octagonal vault supported by 11C Caliphal arches. The owners have a second hotel, the **Baño Nuevo**, nearby, with rooms priced at 5 000pts. The clientele here tends to be elderly.

Moorish cistern, Hotel Balneario

on the other side of the tower with, to the right, the former 17C **prison**, and opposite, the well-preserved façade of the 16C **granary**. Calle Vendederas leads to what was once the kingdom of Granada's first military field hospital, built in 1485, and now housing the town's **Tourist Office**.

Walk around the outside of the Tourist Office and follow calle Caño Wamba.

Here, an unusual 16C fountain can be seen, along with the ruins of the **Iglesia de las Angustias** a little further along the street.

Head down calle de la Mina as far as the so-called Moorish dungeons (mazmorras árabes).

These cavities, excavated out of the rock, were used in the past as both a prison and as silos for grain.

A valuable prize

Alhama was captured from the Moors by Christian troops under the Castilian leader **Ponce de León** in 1482, signalling the start of the **War of Granada**, which ended with the capture of the Nasrid capital ten years later. Due to its magnificent, almost impregnable position, the fertile fields surrounding it and, above all, its springs of thermal water, the qualities of which have been known since Roman times, Alhama was considered one of the jewels in the Nasrid crown. As such, its capture by the Christians was a mighty blow.

ALMERÍA

Population 168 025
Michelin map 446 V 22

The white town of Almería spreads out between the sea and an arid hill upon which stands its impressive fortress *(alcazaba)*. The capital of a historically isolated province with the sea as its only means of communication, Almería has undergone significant changes with the creation of a modern transport infrastructure and the development of advanced agrarian techniques which have placed it at the forefront of Spanish agriculture. The city's superb climate has encouraged tourism, the other main sector of the local economy.

HISTORICAL NOTES

The province of Almería was home to large prehistoric settlements such as Los Millares and El Argar. The area was later colonised by the Phoenicians, Carthaginians and Romans.

The Moorish city – Almería was founded in the 9C by Abd ar-Rahman II. A century later, Abd ar-Rahman III built the *alcazaba* and the walls, transforming the city into one of the most important ports in al-Andalus. After the fall of the Caliphate in the 11C, it became the capital of a *taifa* kingdom governed by Jairán, who developed the city's textile industry, with the introduction of over 10 000 looms. Because its power threatened the Kingdom of Aragón's domination of the Mediterranean, the Aragonese mounted a number of attacks against the city. In one of these, Alfonso VII succeeded in temporarily seizing the city. Following its reconquest by the Moors, Almería became part of the Nasrid kingdom of Granada until its definitive submission to the Catholic Monarchs in 1489.

A period of decline – Almería's decline started in the 16C with Berber attacks on the city, coupled with natural disasters such as the earthquakes of 1512, 1522 and 1550 which decimated the population. The 1522 earthquake destroyed the entire city. The definitive expulsion of the *moriscos* (Moors who had converted to Christianity) worsened an already difficult situation.

The city's resurgence – This dark period in Almería's history continued until the 19C, when the city underwent an economic revival with the discovery of abundant mineral resources in the region. As the city grew, the old walls were demolished and new districts sprang up. The First World War dealt a severe blow to the mining sector and, consequently, the city itself, with the withdrawal of mining companies, the majority of

---

Fiestas

Although Almería is not as well known as other Andalucian cities, it has its own solemn **Semana Santa** celebrations, with its numerous processions and the singing of traditional and moving *saetas* as the floats are carried aloft through its streets.
On 3 May, the city hosts its annual **Cruces de Mayo** festival, during which crosses *(cruces)* adorned with flowers can be seen.
On the **night of St John** (the evening of 23 June) traditional bonfires are lit on the city's beaches, accompanied by lively singing and dancing.
Almería's **Feria** is held at the end of August in honour of its patron, Our Lady of the Sea.

---

which were foreign owned. Having survived this crisis, Almería is now looking optimistically to the future, supported by a flourishing tourism industry and a modern agricultural sector.

SIGHTS

★**Alcazaba** ⊘ – Abd ar-Rahman III ordered the construction of this fortress on a hill overlooking Almería and its bay in the 10C. It was subsequently enlarged by Almotacín, who built a splendid Moorish palace, and by the Catholic Kings, who erected a Christian palace after they had regained control of the town. The fortress was badly damaged in the 1522 earthquake.
Access to the *alcazaba* is via an arch and a ramp leading to three walled enclosures.

Almería

WHERE TO STAY

The centrally situated placita de Flores is the best area to look for accommodation as it has three hotels of different standards (**Torreluz**, **Torreluz II** and **AM Torreluz**), a restaurant and a tapas bar.

MODERATE

Nixar – *Antonio Vico, 14* – ☎ *950 23 72 55* – *40 rooms* – *5 500pts*. Despite this small hotel's lack of character, the rooms are well appointed and reasonably priced. Those overlooking the street have a balcony and are a little brighter than those to the rear. No lift.

MID-RANGE

Torreluz II – *Placita de Flores, 3* – ☎/fax *950 23 43 99* – *64 rooms* – *10 674pts*. A modern hotel with spacious rooms. The nearby Hotel Torreluz is owned by the same proprietors but is of a lower standard, with double rooms costing 8 266pts.

Costasol – *Paseo de Almería, 58* – ☎/fax *950 23 40 11* – *55 rooms* – *10 425pts*. The Costasol is located in Almería's busiest shopping street. Attractive, spacious rooms, some with balcony. Private car park.

AM Torreluz – *Placita de Flores, 5* – ☎/fax *950 23 49 99* – *105 rooms* – *17 000pts*. A luxury hotel in the heart of the city. Facilities include a private garage, piano-bar, restaurant, swimming pool and fitness room.

EATING OUT

Balzac – *Gerona, 29* – ☎ *950 26 61 60* – *closed Sun.* An unusual restaurant, both in terms of its medieval decor (wrought-iron grilles, armour and swords) and its delicious Mediterranean cooking prepared by a native of Marseille.

La Gruta – *At Km 436 along the N 340* – ☎ *950 23 93 35* – *only open in the evening.* Over 700m²/7 500sq ft of caves and a wine cellar containing 4 000 bottles give an idea of the scale of this restaurant. Grilled meats are the house speciality, prepared as they have been for centuries at the entrance to the cave.

TAPAS

Las Botas – *Fructuoso Pérez, 3* – ☎ *950 26 22 72*. A tapas bar adorned with a bull's head, barrels instead of tables and photos of bullfights on the walls. Good tapas popular with locals. The **Valentín** restaurant in calle Tenor Iribarne belongs to the same owners.

The **first enclosure** *(recinto)*, now occupied by pleasant gardens, is also home to the cistern *(aljibe)*. A wall, the Muro de la Vela, crowned by a belfry, separates the first enclosure from the second. The bell would have been sounded to warn the population of impending attack by pirates. The walls connecting the fortress with San Cristóbal hill can be seen to the north.

The **second enclosure** housed the royal residence. Several features have been preserved, including the Caliphal cistern room (now used to house exhibitions), a Mudéjar hermitage, a reconstruction of a Muslim house, a pool and the baths used by the troops. The large esplanade was the parade ground for the Palacio de Almotacín. The private baths of the Caliph's wife can be seen in one corner.

The **third enclosure**, located in the most westerly part of the complex, is occupied by the castle built by order of the Catholic Monarchs. The large parade ground is dominated by an imposing keep with a Gothic doorway.

The impressive **view**★ from the battlements takes in the city and port, with its backdrop of arid hills and a shimmering azure sea. The working-class district of **La Chanca**, with its simple, brightly painted troglodyte houses can also be seen.

★**Cathedral** ⊙ – The city's unique cathedral, more akin to a fortress than a place of worship, was built in the 16C on top of the former mosque. Frequent attacks by Barbary pirates explain its external appearance with its merloned towers and solid walls supported by large buttresses. To the side, where the main doorway is situated, a large 17C tower is crowned by a small belfry.

The impressive **main doorway**★, Renaissance in style, contrasts with the austerity of the façade, its rich decoration unable to disguise its classical lines. The escutcheon of the founding bishop can be seen on the door pediment, and that of Carlos I, with its characteristic two-headed eagle, on the upper floor. St Peter and St Paul are depicted on the medallions. The door at the front of the church, similar in style, is of a simpler design.

Before entering the cathedral, admire the unusual relief of the **Portocarrero sun**★ – an animated sunburst, the symbol of the city – at the east end.

ALMERÍA

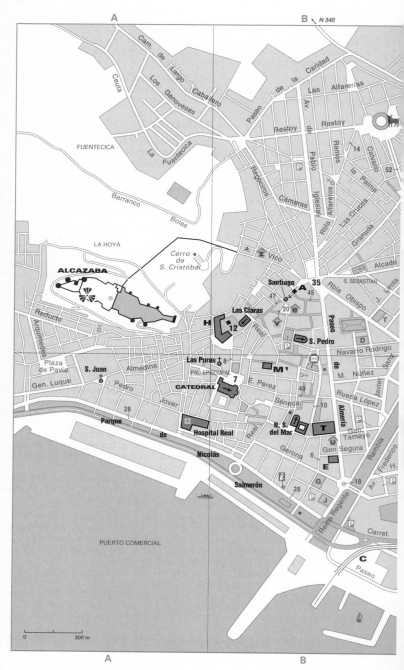

ALMERÍA

Detail, choir stalls

Interior – The three Gothic aisles, of similar height, are topped with star vaults supported by fasciated pillars. The chancel, which has preserved its Gothic vault, was remodelled in the 18C, as were the tabernacle, retable and ambulatory arches.

The Renaissance **choir stalls** are particularly worthy of note with their exceptional medallions of profiled faces in the upper stalls and full-bodied reliefs displaying great movement; the neo-Classical back wall, in marble of various colours, was designed by Ventura Rodríguez. The transept contains a Flamboyant Gothic door which formerly led to the cloisters.

The **ambulatory** has three chapels: the axial chapel is Gothic in appearance and houses the venerated statue of Cristo de la Escucha, while those to the side are Renaissance in style. St Indalecio, the patron saint of Almería, can be seen in the right-hand chapel, and various canvases by Alonso Cano in the chapel to the left.

The late-19C Palacio Episcopal (Bishop's Palace) and the Iglesia de las Puras, part of an old convent founded in the 16C, front the **plaza de la Catedral**.

Santo Cristo de la Escucha

Legend describes how the statue of Christ continued to repeat the word *escucha* (listen) when imprisoned to prevent the city from falling into Muslim hands. Once the city had been reconquered by the Christians, whenever this word was heard from a wall, his image appeared, hence the unusual name.

Iglesia de las Puras – The church and tower are both 17C. Note the escutcheon on the doorway flanked by the heads of two lions and large urns decorated with the sun and the moon. The interior contains a Baroque altarpiece with an Immaculate Conception by Alonso Cano.

Plaza Vieja or Plaza de la Constitución – This pleasant, arcaded square is dominated by the **town hall**. Its present layout dates from the 19C, although a square lined by administrative buildings and bazaars already existed here during the Moorish period. The commemorative column at its centre remembers those liberals who lost their lives in a revolt against Fernando VII in 1824.

Iglesia de las Claras – This small, 17C church, hidden behind a simple, yet elegant doorway, is noteworthy for its cupola above the transept decorated with stuccowork and escutcheons.

Iglesia de San Pedro – Although founded by the Catholic Monarchs, the present-day church was built in the 18C in neo-Classical style. In the interior, the length of its wide central nave is accentuated by the balcony running beneath the lunette-adorned barrel vault.

Iglesia de Santiago – The 16C church of St James, one of the smallest in the city, is situated in the small calle de las Tiendas with its many shops. Its impressive **Renaissance portal★** shows clear similarities in both layout and technique with the doorways of the cathedrals and is dominated by a magnificent depiction of St James Slayer of the Moors *(Santiago Matamoros)*. The symbols of the saint – scallop shells and crosses of St James – decorate the space between the columns. At the foot of the church note the solid tower pierced by arches in its lower section.

In the nearby calle Tenor Iribarne, the 11C **Moorish cisterns** which would have supplied water to the city are well worth a visit if open.

Puerta de Purchena – This square, a busy crossroads, is at the very heart of Almerian life. Many of its seigniorial buildings date from the late 19C.

Paseo de Almería – The city's main avenue is fronted by a mixture of 20C buildings and modern tower blocks and includes a range of shops, banks, cafeterias and bars. The **Círculo Mercantil**, which has preserved its 1920s ceilings, stuccowork and *azulejo* panelling, is one of its most attractive buildings; behind it stands the **Teatro Cervantes**, one of the city's landmarks, opened in 1921. The nearby **Basílica de Nuestra Señora del Mar** houses the venerated statue of Almería's patron saint; its attractive 18C cloister is now home to the city's **Arts and Crafts School**.

Return to paseo de Almería.

At no 64 stands the former casino, a 19C building with a central patio and seigniorial rooms, now the headquarters of the **Delegación del Gobierno de la Junta**, the provincial government. At the end of the street, next to the plaza Emilio Pérez, is the somewhat surprising and unusual Casa Montoya, built in an architectural style more associated with the province of Santander in northern Spain.

Parque de Nicolás Salmerón – This pleasant strip of greenery with its fountains and pools runs parallel to the port in an area formerly occupied by warehouses.

Hospital Real – Although the hospital was founded in the 16C, the façade and doorway of this large 18C building are distinctly neo-Classical in style.

Iglesia de San Juan – The church's exterior, with its sober portal of ringed columns, a pediment and coat of arms, is more reminiscent of a civil building than a place of worship. The interior contains a number of surprises for visitors with its 12C *mihrab* and *quibla* wall – vestiges of the former 10C mosque built on the same site.

ADDITIONAL SIGHTS

Museo de Almería – While awaiting the construction of new premises, part of the museum's collection is on display in the Biblioteca Villaespesa and the Archivo Histórico.

Biblioteca Villaespesa ⊘ – The Villaespesa Library has on exhibit a number of finds from archeological excavations around the province, notably those of the prehistoric settlements of El Argar and Los Millares.

Archivo Histórico ⊘ – The Historical Archives building, housed in the 19C former palace of the Viscounts of Almansa, contains an interesting collection of artefacts from the various civilisations that colonised Almería, including Greek and Roman ceramics, mosaics, sarcophagi etc.

Railway Station – The railway station is an attractive brick building dating from the end of the 19C with ceramic and wrought-iron decoration.

Cable Inglés – The English Cable, as it is known, is an extension to the railway line, built in the early 20C to carry goods from the rail terminus to the docks. It consists of a stone bridge and an iron mechanism which was used for loading.

EXCURSION

★**Los Millares** ⊘ – *12km/7.5mi along the A 32, and then 7km/4.5mi along the A 348 (a reception hut is located at Km 42)*. This Copper Age settlement is the most important to have been discovered in Europe, both in terms of its surface area and the remains found here. It was founded around 2700 BC and was abandoned some 900 years later. It is believed that between 1 000 and 1 500 people lived at Los Millares, denoting a society that was already developing an advanced urban model. Its inhabitants included arable and livestock farmers, as well as those who worked copper and produced ceramics with their own individual characteristics which would have been used for ritual ceremonies. The tableland upon which it sits, dominating the Andarax Valley, would have been a prestigious site, with a wetter Mediterranean climate and a less arid landscape than today, along with fertile fields, an abundance of game and the copper mines in the nearby Sierra de Gádor.

Remains of a complex defensive system with a number of walls and small forts have also been unearthed here. The external wall is the longest known construction dating from this period with semicircular towers at irregular intervals. The settlement's dwellings consisted of circular huts, with diameters varying from 4m/13ft to 7m/23ft. The finds uncovered in the **necropolis** – almost 100 collective tombs – are of particular interest. In one of these, it is possible to admire the structure of a perfectly preserved tomb with its atrium, a corridor with various sections separated by perforated slate tiles and a circular chamber covered with a false cupola. The entire construction would have then been covered on the outside by a mound of earth.

Castillo de ALMODÓVAR DEL RÍO★★
Córdoba
Michelin map 446 S 14

The name Almodóvar originates from the Arabic *al-Mudawwar* meaning "the round one", a clear reference to the hill upon which the castle has been built. In the 8C, under Moorish rule, a large fortress stood here. Almódovar was subsequently governed by various *taifa* kingdoms before its reconquest by Fernando III in 1240.

Follow the road skirting the town until you approach the castle. It is possible to drive up to the fortress along a dirt track.

The present-day **castle** ⊘ was erected in the 14C in Gothic style and is considered one of the most important in Andalucia because of its beauty and excellent state of repair. It was restored at the beginning of the 20C when a neo-Gothic mansion was added to its interior. The town nestles at its feet on the south side along the banks of the Guadalquivir River.

Castillo de ALMODÓVAR DEL RÍO

B. Kaufmann/MICHELIN

From the castle the **views**★ of the river and the Cordoban countryside are quite magnificent. The edifice consists of two walled enclosures – one in the form of a barbican – with eight towers of varying proportions. The largest of the eight, known as the *torre del homenaje* (keep), is in fact a turret. A stroll inside the castle, with its battlements, towers and parade ground, will transport visitors back in time.

The legend of Princess Zaida

According to legend, every 28 March a woman dressed in white appears, wailing from one of the towers. It is said that this is the ghost of Princess Zaida, who was taken prisoner by the Almoravids and who died from grief in the castle's dungeon upon hearing of the death of her husband in battle.

EXCURSION

Embalse de la Breña – *5km/3mi. Head back towards the town and take a turning signposted to the left.* The road winds its way across hills carpeted in olive trees to the Breña Reservoir (embalse), whose waters are used by the private Córdoba Sailing Club. On the return journey, after passing a bend in the road, enjoy the magnificent silhouette of the Castillo de Almodóvar.

ALMUÑÉCAR

Granada – Population 20 997
Michelin map 446 V 18

The Romans named this former Phoenician settlement *Sexi Firmun Julium*, although its present name derives from the Arabic *Hins-al-Monacar*, or "fortress city", a reference to its strategic position on top of a hill. Nowadays, its perfect location in the fertile valley of the Verde River, where it is protected from cold weather systems by the mountain range skirting the coast and tempered by the warm winds from North Africa, makes it an ideal year-round holiday destination. This hot climate is also the reason for the proliferation of fruits, vegetables and flowers – the other important feature of the local economy – grown under plastic all along this part of the Mediterranean.

SIGHTS

Palacete de la Najarra: Tourist Office ⊘ – This small, neo-Moorish palace, built in the second third of the 19C, is now home to the Tourist Office and is an ideal starting point for a visit of Almuñécar. Note the exotic garden inside the palace.

★**Castillo de San Miguel** ⊘ – This castle of Roman origin bears witness to the succession of occupiers who took up residence here: the Umayyads, Almoravids, Almohads, Nasrids and Christians. It suffered considerable damage in the war against the French in 1808, resulting in the abandonment of the castle until recent times. Under the Nasrids, it served as a palace for the monarchs of the kingdom of

WHERE TO STAY

MODERATE

Casablanca – *Plaza San Cristóbal, 4 –* ☎ *9586355 75 – fax 958635589 – 15 rooms – 9 000pts.* This small hotel with a terrace overlooking an attractive square is just 30m/100ft from the sea. The **Hotel Playa de San Cristóbal** (☎ *958633612*) next door has rooms costing 6 500pts, albeit inferior in quality. A small ornithological park can also be visited on the square.

EATING OUT

Antonio – *Bajos del Paseo, 12 –* ☎ *958630020.* A restaurant with a solid reputation specialising in fish and seafood for the past 30 years. In the words of its owner: "We never use frozen products, only the freshest ingredients". The lobster, swordfish and Jabugo cured ham are particularly recommended.

Los Geranios – *Plaza de la Rosa, 4 –* ☎ *958630724 – closed Sun and from 15 Nov to 15 Dec.* This eatery looks out onto a small pedestrianised square and is popular with foreign visitors. Specialities include *pollo al limón* (chicken with lemon), *brochetas de bacalao* (cod kebabs) and *paella*.

Granada. Inside, the dungeon and a single house have survived from this period; the fortified entrance towers were built during the reign of Carlos V. The small museum displays some interesting **models** of the Almuñécar area.

Cueva de los Siete Palacios: Museo Arqueológico ⊘ – The town's archeological museum is housed in a basement of Roman origin. Exhibits include various artefacts unearthed in the Phoenician necropolises of Laurita and Puente Noy, the most outstanding of which is the Egyptian **funerary urn★** of Apophis I in grey marble, containing the oldest written document found in Spain.

Parque "El Majuelo" – These small botanical gardens contain a wonderful array of sub-tropical plants, including 400 species of palm tree. The ruins of an old **Phoenician salting factory** are visible inside the gardens. This particular industry attained such enormous prestige during the period of Greek occupation that figures such as Strabo and Galen refer to **garum** *(see p 321)*, a special condiment, which was produced here.

La Herradura – *8km/5mi west of Almuñécar.* This spectacular bay is situated between **La Punta de la Mona** and **Cerro Gordo**, two watchtowers protecting the **Playa de La Herradura**. Here, as is the case all along the coast in Granada province, the rugged mountains descend to the sea, creating a setting

---

Scuba diving

La Herradura has developed into an important centre for scuba diving. A number of dive companies operate here, offering courses for all levels.

Buceo La Herradura: *Puerto deportivo de Marina del Este –* ☎ *958827083.*

Granada Sub: *Paseo Andrés Segovia, 6 –* ☎ *958640281.*

---

of extraordinary beauty. La Punta de la Mona is home to a pleasure port, the **Puerto Deportivo Marina del Este**. The road continues to offer stunning **views** as it heads towards Cerro Gordo.

EXCURSIONS

Costa Tropical – The Costa Tropical is the name used to describe the 100km/62mi stretch of coastline between La Herradura and La Rábita, characterised by steep descents where mountains swoop down to the sea forming delightful coves, albeit difficult to reach. From **Motril**, the road runs parallel to the Mediterranean, passing through Torrenueva, **Carchuna**, **Calahonda** and Castell de Ferro. The beaches here are longer and wider than those around Almuñécar. In addition, several medieval watchtowers, such as the Torre de Carchuna, Torrenueva and La Rábita, are visible from the road. From the town of La Rábita, it is worth making the short detour *(5km/3mi)* to **Albuñol**, a *pueblo blanco* nestled in the Sierra de la Contraviesa.

★Salobreña – *15km/9mi east of Almuñécar.* Salobreña is situated by the sea on top of a hill crowned by an imposing **castle**. It is surrounded by fields of sugar cane and orchards and is probably the most attractive of the towns along the stretch of coast within the boundaries of Granada province. Its swathe of whitewashed houses dominate the hillside, its narrow streets awash with colourful bougainvillaea. The town's main attractions are its castle, the **Iglesia de la Virgen del Rosario** church and its splendid beaches, such as the **Playa de El Peñón**.

WHERE TO STAY

Salobreña – *At Km 323 on the Málaga–Almería road, 3km/2mi from Salobreña towards Málaga* – ☎ *958 61 02 61* – *fax 958 61 01 01* – *192 rooms* – *10 500pts.* This large tourist complex, with its gardens and swimming pool, comprises several modern buildings with rooms overlooking the sea, known here as the Costa Rocosa (Rocky Coast). The views of the Mediterranean are superb, with nothing more than the background noise of waves breaking on the shore.

EATING OUT

El Peñón – *Playa de El Peñón* – ☎ *958 61 05 38* – *open 10am to midnight.* A small, romantic restaurant at the end of the Playa de Salobreña from where you can enjoy the spectacular sunsets. Specialities include *paella* and fresh fish.

Castle ⊙ – *The best view of the castle is from the Almuñécar road.* Although records show that a castle existed here as early as the 10C, its greatest period of splendour coincided with the reign of the Nasrids, who transformed it into a luxurious residence which also served as a royal prison.

Access to the interior is via a corner doorway, which leads to the first defensive enclosure. The *alcazaba* (fortress), with its two underground caverns and keep, is at the very heart of the castle.

A castle of legends

Washington Irving wrote that the princesses Zaida, Zoraida and Zorahaida, the daughters of the king of Granada, Mohammed IX, were confined to this sumptuous palace for many years by their father who, following the advice of his astrologers, decided to protect them from everyday temptation, not least that of meeting an undesirable suitor. The three princesses lived here surrounded by luxury, their every need attended to, until their father took them to his palace at the Alhambra. Destiny dictated that they encountered such a temptation on the journey to Granada, when the party fell upon three Christian prisoners who immediately fell in love with the three young princesses.

Motril – *21km/13mi east of Almuñécar.* Today, this sizeable community of 50 000 inhabitants is the largest town along the Costa Tropical, although this was not always the case. Up until the 18C, when sugar cane was introduced here, resulting in its nickname of "Little Cuba", Motril was nothing more than a small village known only as the residence of the mother of Boabdil, the last king of Granada. Sadly, it has little to offer tourists, who tend to flock to the hotels along the **Playa de Poniente**, 4km/2.5mi to the southeast.

Las ALPUJARRAS★

Granada - Almería

Michelin map 446 V-19-20-21

The Alpujarras became the final stronghold of the Nasrids following the Christian conquest of Granada and the focal point of a rebellion by the *moriscos* in 1568. A backwater for three centuries, this magnificent mountain range was subsequently rediscovered by 19C Romantic travellers, and today has developed into one of Andalucia's most popular tourist destinations. Despite this influx of visitors, it has still managed to preserve many of its charms, customs and traditions. Straddled across the provinces of Granada and Almería, and demarcated to the south by the **Sierra de la Contraviesa** and **Sierra de Gádor**, and to the north by the **Parque Nacional de Sierra Nevada**, the Alpujarras are characterised by small whitewashed villages, rugged mountains and fertile valleys.

History – The arrival of the first inhabitants in these valleys coincided with the Moorish conquest in the year 711. These early settlers were Berber tribes who were used to the difficult, mountainous terrain of North Africa and began to grow olives and vines and breed silkworms here. The period of greatest prosperity in the Alpujarras was under the Nasrids between the 13C and 15C. The area was divided into administrative districts known as *tahas (see Pitres)*, its population increased and industries such as textiles experienced significant growth. After the conquest of Granada, the Catholic Monarchs ceded this area to the court of Boabdil. However, the increase in religious intolerance against the Muslim population resulted in the first revolt in the Alpujarras. In 1569, a new uprising was led by Fernando de Válor, who later became known as **Abén Humeya**. The war and the subsequent expulsion of the *moriscos* was to have a detrimental effect on the Alpujarras, which then entered a period of decline.

PRACTICAL INFORMATION

Oficina de Información del Legado Andalusí – Lanjarón – *Avenida de Madrid* ☎ *958 77 02 82.* This Tourist Office is able to provide a wealth of information on the area's Moorish history.

Centro de Interpretación del Parque Nacional de Sierra Nevada (NEVADENSIS) – Pampaneira – *Plaza de la Libertad* – ☎ *958 76 33 01.* The Sierra Nevada Information Centre organises activities such as hikes through the Alpujarras, ascents of the Sierra Nevada, descents of mountain ravines and horse trekking.

Centro de Información del Puerto de la Ragua – *On the Puerta de la Ragua road* – ☎ *950 52 40 20.* Activities including cross-country skiing and dog-sleigh excursions can be arranged from this information centre.

Rustic Blue – Bubión – ☎ *958 76 33 81.* A private company dedicated to rural tourism in the province of Granada, including the booking of accommodation and the organising of outdoor activities.

WHERE TO STAY

BUBIÓN

Villa Turística de Bubión – *Barrio Alto* – ☎ *958 76 31 11* – *fax 958 76 31 36* – *43 rooms* – *12 000pts.* Simple, traditional-style apartments with kitchen, lounge, bathroom and bedroom. The restaurant is one of the best in the area with specialities such as kid, trout and locally-made sausages.

BUSQUÍSTAR

Alcazaba de Busquístar – *On the GR 421, 4km/2.5mi from Trevélez towards Juviles* – ☎ *958 85 86 87* – *fax 958 85 86 93* – *44 rooms* – *10 000pts.* A hotel which has used typical local materials in its construction, including stone slabs, baked clay floors and whitewashed walls. The rooms are spacious and have terraces with superb views over the *sierra.*

CÁDIAR

Alquería de Morayma – *On the A 348, 2km/1.2mi from Cádiar towards Torvizcón* – ☎/*fax 958 34 32 21* – *15 rooms* – *7 500pts.* A small country hotel with views of the mountains and the village of Cádiar. Facilities include a bar, restaurant, and a *bodega* decorated with earthenware casks. Good value for money.

LANJARÓN

España – *Avenida de la Alpujarra, 42* – ☎/*fax 958 77 01 87* – *40 rooms* – *5 800pts.* In the centre of Lanjarón. This early-20C hotel has been frequented in the past by illustrious guests such as García Lorca and Manolete. All the rooms have extremely high ceilings.

Cured hams, Trevélez

Hidalgo-Lopesino/MARCO POLO

LAROLES

Refugio de Nevada – *Carretera de Mairena* – ☎ *958 76 03 20* – *fax 958 76 03 04* – *12 rooms* – *6 800pts.* This hotel is situated in the highest part of Laroles. Fairly basic rooms with television and private bathrooms. Sadly, the rooms do not have balconies, as the views from here are magnificent, particularly in winter when the peaks are covered in snow.

TREVÉLEZ

La Fragua – *Barrio Medio, San Antonio, 4* – ☎ *958 85 85 73* – *fax 958 85 86 14* – *several rooms* – *5 500pts.* On a steep, narrow street winding its way between whitewashed houses. Although fairly basic, all the rooms have a telephone and en-suite bathroom. Some also have a terrace with delightful views of the village and surrounding mountains.

SHOPPING

Rugs – The typical local rugs *(jarapas)* of the area, originally made using brightly-coloured sections which were then joined together, are now woven whole according to different patterns. These rugs are generally inexpensive and can be found throughout the Alpujarras. Two workshops in Pampaneira are particularly recommended for the quality of their products: **Hilacar** *(calle Viso –* ☎ *956 76 32 26)* and **La Rueca** *(calle José Antonio, 4 –* ☎ *958 76 30 27).*

Hams – The best place to buy cured hams is in Trevélez, where there are a number of drying sheds. Prices vary between 1 000 and 1 500pts/kg depending upon the length of time the hams have been cured.

★★① THE GRANADA ALPUJARRAS

From Lanjarón to Bayárcal

100km/62mi (127km/79mi including the excursion to Puerto de la Ragua) – allow two days.

Lanjarón – Lanjarón acts as a natural entrance to the area from Granada and is one of the most accessible towns in the Alpujarras. Famous for its medicinal mineral water, it has developed into a popular tourist base, attracting thousands of visitors every year. In addition to its famed waters, the town's other main attraction is its 16C **castle**, guarding the entrance to the valley from its superb elevated position.

The A 348 road offers magnificent views of the arid and imposing Sierra de Lújar.

9km/5.5mi from Lanjarón, before reaching the town of Órgiva, take the GR 421, which crosses the northern stretch of the Alpujarras. Caution is required when driving along this narrow mountain road.

Before reaching Pampaneira, the road passes through three small villages, **Cañar**, with its impressive views, Carataunas and Soportújar, none of which are on the main tourist track.

★★**Pampaneira** – *Leave your car in the car park at the entrance to the town, then continue on foot.* Pampaneira is the first of the three villages in the **Poqueira Valley★★**. Although recently discovered by tourists, it has still managed to preserve its traditional architecture. The main street, with its myriad shops selling local products, leads to the **plaza de la Libertad**, dominated by the 17C Baroque Iglesia de la Santa Cruz. The best way of discovering the charms of these villages is to wander through their narrow streets. In Pampaneira, a number of traditional looms producing the famous Alpujarras rugs *(jarapas)* can still be visited. The village also has a **Visitor Centre** ⊙ *(Centro de Visitantes)*, which is able to organise a number of varied local excursions.

Continue along the GR 421. After 2km/1.2mi, take the turn-off to Bubión (3km/1.8mi) and Capileira (4km/2.4mi).

Bubión – Situated at an altitude of 1 296m/4 250ft, the village of Bubión became famous during the revolt of 1569 when its tower was an important centre for *morisco* resistance. As is the case elsewhere in this valley, its houses, with their rugged whitewashed walls and flat rooftops, are reminiscent of the architecture of North Africa.

Capileira – At 1 436m/ 4 710ft, Capileira is the highest of the three villages in the Poqueira Valley. It has preserved its 16C parish church with an attractive Baroque retable. One of its houses is now home to the **Museo Alpujarreño de Artes y Costumbres Populares** ⊙, a museum recreating 19C Alpujarran life through its popular arts and customs.

B. Kaufmann/MICHELIN

A narrow street in Pampaneira

Return to the junction with the GR 421.

Mecina Fondales – From here several excursions are possible along the valley formed by the Trevélez River. A minor road leads to the village of Ferreirola, a name which refers to the abundance of iron found throughout this region.

The road continues through an area of outstanding beauty before gradually entering the delightful Trevélez Valley.

Pitres – The village is the largest of the seven settlements which make up the *taha* – an old Moorish territorial district comprising Pitres, **Capilerilla**, Mecina, Mecinilla, Fondales, Ferreirola and Atalbéitar.

Pórtugos – Pórtugos is famous for its **Fuente Agria**, a spring of iron-rich water behind the hermitage of Nuestra Señora de las Angustias, on the exit to the village. Tradition says that the water from one of the five pipes has a different taste to that of the others. The best way of testing this theory is to try the water yourself! Opposite, some steps lead to **El Chorreón**, a reddish-coloured waterfall which bears witness to the ferrous qualities of the soil in this area.

Alpujarran houses

The local architecture is perhaps the best example of the region's Moorish past. Those visitors who have set foot in North Africa will be surprised by the strong similarities, with the predominance of south-facing houses searching for the warmth of the sun and often following the relief of this mountainous landscape. The houses are usually built on different levels, forming regularly spaced terraces and steep narrow streets acting as a conduit for rainwater. Traditionally they comprise two floors, the walls of which are completely covered with lime. Their most typical feature is the flat roof, known as a *terrao*, made using large beams of chestnut and battens *(alfarjías)*, on top of which a layer of bluish-grey clay *(launa)* is added. Upon contact with water, this layer of clay solidifies to provide a waterproof covering. In the past, these flat roof terraces were used as meeting areas, although nowadays they are predominantly used for storage or for drying clothes, curing food etc.

Busquístar – This quiet, Mozarabic-style village is the first *pueblo* in the spectacular **Trevélez river valley★**. From here the road ascends the left-hand side of the valley to the village which has given its name to the entire valley. However, its dazzlingly white houses are of less interest than its neighbours in the Poqueira Valley.

★**Trevélez** – Trevélez is formed by three districts, each at a different altitude, and is the highest municipality in Spain (1 600m/5 248ft in the *barrio alto*). Its whitewashed houses and narrow alleyways are spread out across the landscape like a thick blanket of snow. Behind the village the impressive silhouette of **Mulhacén**, the highest peak on the Iberian Peninsula (3 482m/11 424ft), stands guard.

Beyond Trevélez, the GR 421 once more descends the eastern side of the valley. After 6km/4mi, bear right on the GR 413. Once past the abandoned mines of Conjuro, the road links up with the village of Torvizcón and the A 348 running across the southern section of the Alpujarras. If you wish to continue heading east, follow the GR 421 until you reach Juviles.

Juviles – At this point the scenery undergoes a radical change, the verdant nature of the previous two valleys giving way to a wilder landscape. The 16C **Iglesia de Santa María de Gracia** is one of the prettiest churches to be found anywhere in the Granada Alpujarras.

Upon leaving Bérchules, bear left onto the A 348.

Mecina Bombarón – The landscape here is notably drier, with the appearance of a more Mediterranean-type vegetation, particularly in the **Contraviesa** area to the south, which is famous for its wines. The village, formerly known as Mecina Buenvarón, is dissected by small ravines which act as natural barriers between the different sections of the village. Upon leaving the village, note the Roman bridge over the Mecina River, alongside a more modern construction.

Yegen – This village owes its renown to **Gerald Brenan** – the author of *South from Granada*, a marvellous portrayal of the traditions and customs of the Alpujarras – who spent seven years here between 1923 and 1934. A plaque marks the house in which he lived during this period.

Trevélez cured ham

Ever since **Queen Isabel II** extolled the virtues of its **cured ham** *(jamón)* in the 19C, the name of Trevélez has been synonymous with this gastronomic treat. The secret of its drying sheds *(secaderos)* lies in their special climatic conditions (dry and cold) and the exclusive use of sea salt. White-coloured pigs are bred to produce these large hams (up to 10kg/22lb in weight), which are slightly rounded in shape.

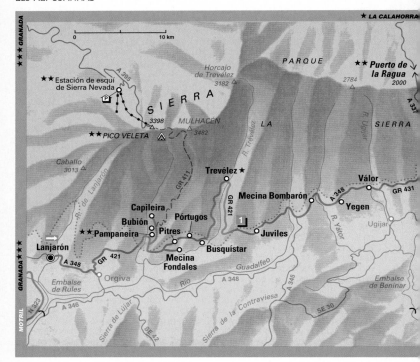

WHERE TO STAY

Laujar de Andarax

Almirez – *1.6km/1mi from the village towards Alcolea on the Laujar–Órgiva road – ☎/fax 950 51 35 14 – 20 rooms – 5 000pts.* A small hotel with a restaurant. Nothing out of the ordinary, but reasonably priced and well-appointed.

Villa Turística de Laujar – *Camino del Caleche – ☎ 950 51 30 27 – fax 950 51 35 54 – 47 rooms – 9 600pts.* A hotel complex on the outskirts of the village with apartments sleeping between one and six guests. The lack of charm here is compensated by the comfortable rooms.

Válor – Válor is the largest settlement in this part of the Granada Alpujarras. Along with many other churches in this area, the 16C **Iglesia de San José** has been built in Mudéjar style. A late-18C fountain in the square is worthy of particular note. The leader of the *morisco* rebellion in 1568, Don Fernando de Córdoba, known as **Abén Humeya**, was born and lived in Válor.

Shortly after leaving Válor, bear left onto the GR 431.

Laroles – Laroles stands at the foot of the Ragua Pass. Note the unusual tower of its parish church. The hamlets of Picena and Cherín are visible to the south.

2km/1.2mi beyond Laroles, an extremely narrow road provides a direct link with Bayárcal, the first village in the Almería Alpujarras. The A 337 heading north leads to the Ragua Pass; this road is the only thoroughfare connecting the northern and southern sections of the Sierra Nevada (closed in winter).

★★**Puerto de la Ragua** – As far as the summit (1 993m/6 537ft) the road ascends a gentle slope, along which the landscape gradually acquires a mountainous appearance. Once over the pass, the road narrows and steepens as it descends towards the Guadix Plateau, offering magnificent views of the **Castillo de la Calahorra** ★★ *(see p 204).*

Turn around and head back towards Bayárcal along the eastern slopes of the valley.

★2 THE ALMERÍA ALPUJARRAS

From Bayárcal to Alhama de Almería – *73km/45mi – allow 3hr*

Bayárcal – Bayárcal is the highest village in Almería at an altitude of 1 275m/4 182ft. The oak grove within its boundaries is one of the largest in the province. It is well worth exploring the village on foot to enjoy the superb views. The 16C Mudéjar-style **Iglesia de San Francisco Javier** contains several interesting canvases: San Francisco Javier, the town's patron saint, an Immaculate Conception by Alonso Cano and an *Ecce Homo*.

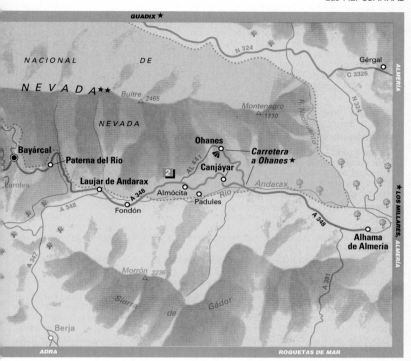

Paterna del Río – *7km/4.5mi west.* The village is surrounded by forests of chestnut, oak and poplar. The **Iglesia de San Juan Bautista** has preserved an interesting Mudéjar *artesonado* ceiling.

Laujar de Andarax – Laujar, the capital of the Almería Alpujarras, is situated by the source of the Andarax River, with the Sierra Nevada to the north and the Sierra de Gádor to the south. Several 16C-17C seigniorial houses and a number of fountains adorn the streets of the town, which was the birthplace of the writer **Francisco Villaespesa** (1877-1936). He is remembered by two plaques: one at the Mirador de la Vega, next to the plaza de la Alpujarra; the other on the house in which he was born.

> **Abén Humeya**
>
> The leader of the 1568 *moriscos* revolt in the Alpujarras *(see p 32)*, **Abén Humeya** was assassinated in Laujar by his followers on 20 October 1569. Once the revolt had finally been quashed in 1571, the *moriscos* were expelled from the kingdom of Granada.

Iglesia Parroquial de la Encarnación – This 16C brick parish church has a bell-tower at its east end. The high altar in the single-nave interior is adorned with an attractive Baroque altarpiece, including a statue of the Immaculate Conception attributed to Alonso Cano.

Town Hall – The façade of the 18C *ayuntamiento*, also constructed of brick, is both sober and harmonious in style. To the left stands the **Pilar de los Cuatro Caños**, a public fountain made of stone dating from the 17C.

Source of the Andarax River – *1.5km/1mi from Laujar. Follow the signposts to the "Nacimiento", to the left of the square.* The river's source is situated in an attractive location with an abundance of pine trees, picnic tables and barbecue stands.

Follow the A 348.

Laujar to Canjáyar road – This *carretera* runs through the fertile Andarax Valley between terraces of orange trees, prickly pears and several vineyards which grow the highly prized Almería grape.

The 20km/12mi stretch of road between Laujar de Andarax and Canjáyar passes through **Fondón** and **Almócita**, two typical Almerian villages with whitewashed houses and attractive parish churches.

The road offers a delightful view of **Padules**, with its 16C church dominating this hillside village.

> A **rosé wine** is produced in Laujar by a number of private estates and one organic producer, the Cortijo del Cura, located on the outskirts of the town.

> ### A strange devotion
>
> In many places such as Laujar, Fondón, Ohanes and Canjáyar, small her-
> mitages known as *ánimas* (souls) are visible as you come into or leave the
> village. These small chapels are adorned with an altar containing a picture
> representing the Virgen del Carmen extracting souls from flames with the
> help of angels. The entrance doorway often has a peephole to enable visitors
> to peer inside.

Canjáyar – This whitewashed village sits on a hillside at the foot of the Ermita de San
Blas, its streets still retaining a certain *morisco* air. Note the parish church of Santa Cruz.
Continue along the A 348. After 3km/2mi take the turn-off to Ohanes.

★**Ohanes road** – The road up to the village of Ohanes (958m/3 142ft) circles the mountain, winding along a sinuous route offering increasingly spectacular **views**★ as it climbs
upwards. Not a single trace of habitation is visible here, adding even greater charm to
this virgin landscape. The panorama is vast, even encompassing the Sierra de Gata in
the far distance. The village comes into view after a bend in the road.

Ohanes – Ohanes enjoys a magnificent **site**★ dominating the Andarax Valley from on
high, its houses forming a blanket of white against the verdant mountain backdrop;
the village's stone parish church adds a final flourish to this superb scene. The
narrow, winding streets, seemingly suspended in a vacuum, stand out against the
intense blue of the Almerian sky.
The entire mountain slope at the foot of the village side is planted with terrace upon
terrace of vineyards.
Return to the A 348 along the same road or via Beires.

Alhama de Almería – *19km/11mi from Canjáyar towards Almería.* The contrast in
landscape surrounding Alhama is particularly interesting, with the desert-like
Tabernas and the lush Andarax Valley on one side, and the Sierra de Gádor on the
other. The village has its own natural baths with therapeutic waters at a temperature of around 46°C/115°F, several seigniorial houses and an old café, the Tertulia,
dating from the early 20C. Alhama was also the birthplace in 1838 of **Nicolás
Salmerón**, the president of the First Republic, who resigned from his post in order
not to have to sign a death warrant. Before leaving Alhama de Almería, it is well
worth tasting the local ring-shaped pastries *(rosquillas)*.

Ohanes

ANDÚJAR★

Jaén – Population 35 803
Michelin map 446 R 17

Andújar is considered to be Spain's leading olive-growing centre. First occupied by the Iberians, who named it Isturgis, it was later colonised by the Romans and the Moors, who built its monumental walls in the 9C. It was finally reconquered by Fernando III in 1225. This unassuming yet pleasant town attracted a number of illustrious visitors in its past, such as Francisco de Quevedo, who made plans here for a journey by Felipe IV; Cosimo de' Medici, whose entourage passed through Andújar on his return to Italy from Córdoba; and later, in the 18C and 19C, Joseph Townsend – the celebrated British traveller – and Prosper Merimée, among others.

Nowadays, Andújar is an important agricultural and industrial town with a historical centre characterised by narrow, winding streets and old buildings. The surrounding area is equally attractive, including the **Parque Natural Sierra de Andújar**, a spectacular protected area of woods and streams, which is home to the popular Santuario de la Virgen de la Cabeza. Mention should also be made of the renowned Andújar ceramics (ashtrays, bowls, plates etc) and the region's delicious cuisine, with appetising dishes such as *ajo blanco* (a sauce made from garlic and breadcrumbs), *flamenquines* (fried veal and ham rolls), and the locally-produced asparagus.

Iglesia de Santa María – Construction of the church, situated on the attractive square of the same name, was started at the end of the 15C but was not completed until two centuries later, hence its interesting, albeit eclectic, architectural styles. The interior, a mixture of pointed, circular and groined vaults, contains several notable works, including an *Assumption of the Virgin* by Pacheco (left-side apse chapel), an Immaculate Conception by Guiseppe Cesari, a manuscript signed by St John of the Cross, and, above all, **Christ in the Garden of Olives**★★ by El Greco, in a chapel to the left, enclosed by a fine 16C **grille**★ by Maestro Bartolomé. This huge canvas, the source of great discussion and interpretation, depicts Christ dressed in an elegant red tunic and illuminated by a light which descends from the sky, isolating the other characters in the painting: an angel dressed in white and the apostles St Peter, St James and St John, who appear to be dozing at his feet.

Town Hall ⊙ – The town hall is housed in a building dating from the mid 17C. The old Corral de Comedias, a theatre formerly used for staging theatrical performances, can be seen inside.

Iglesia de San Miguel – The impressive silhouette of this church dominates the plaza de España, also known as the plaza del Mercado. The interior, decorated with unusual 17C and 18C murals, has an exceptional choir and a fine partition screen, both of which are adorned with delicately carved reliefs.

Palacio de Los Niños de Don Gome ⊙ – This elegant, 16C palace is topped with a sober tower with Indian-influenced decoration. Inside, the most notable features include the pretty porticoed patio and the stables, which have preserved their original stalls.

Iglesia de San Bartolomé – The main attraction of this late-15C church is the façade, its three stone **Gothic portals**★ bearing elegant and exquisitely carved ornamental features.

Torre del Reloj – Along with a small section in the calle Silera and the Fuente Sorda and Tavira towers, this former keep is one of the few remaining vestiges of the Moorish defensive walls.

Oak groves

Although the landscapes of Jaén are dominated by the ubiquitous olive tree, the province is also home to a number of holm oak forests, most notably in the Sierra de Andújar. These noble trees adopt a different appearance depending on the light; this ability has undoubtedly spawned a famous local legend which says that the oak trees dance at night, but are then petrified by the first rays of sunshine early in the morning.

EXCURSIONS

Villanueva de la Reina – *14km/9mi southeast along the JV 2310*. This small, tranquil town on the banks of the Guadalquivir offers contrasting views of the mountains of the Sierra Morena to the north and the flatter landscapes to the south. The old quarter has preserved the 18C **Iglesia de Nuestra Señora de la Natividad**.

★**Centro de Visitantes del Parque Natural Sierra de Andújar** ⊙ – *Leave Andújar to the north along the J 5010*. The road climbs through an impressive landscape of holm oaks, cork oaks, wild olives and arbutus, providing magnificent **views**★★ of the surrounding area.

This protected park in the low foothills of the Sierra Morena above the Guadalquivir Valley is spread over an area covering 60 800ha/150 240 acres. Its varied landscape alternates from open pasture, grazed by fighting bulls, to dark ravines, where the dense vegetation is the ideal habitat for deer, lynx and wild boar. The plentiful Jándula and Yeguas rivers are particularly popular with fishing enthusiasts, while the extensive network of marked paths criss-crossing the park's forests and thickets, carpeted in wild jasmine and mastic trees, are a haven for hikers.

Santuario de la Virgen de la Cabeza ⊙ – *32km/20mi north of Andújar*. The sanctuary is situated at the heart of the park, close to the magnificent **Coto Nacional de Lugar Nuevo**. According to tradition, the Virgin Mary appeared to a shepherd on a rocky head *(cabeza)*. To commemorate this miraculous apparition, a chapel was built here, subsequently replaced in the 16C by a monastery which was destroyed during the Spanish Civil War. Nowadays, the site is one of Andalucia's main places of Marian pilgrimage, and the destination for a huge crowd participating in a popular *romería* on the last Sunday in April.

Where to stay in the Sierra de Andújar

La Mirada – *Santuario Virgen de la Cabeza. Approximately 30km/18mi from Andújar –* ☎ *953 50 21 11 – 15 rooms – 6 000pts.* In the heart of the Parque Natural de Andújar. Clean, modern and well-appointed rooms which can cost up to 100 000pts on the days of the famous *romería* to the Virgen de la Cabeza. A good, reasonably priced hotel the rest of the year.

Bailén – *23km/14mi northeast on the N IV*. The town is famous as the scene of a **battle** that took place here in 1808 during the Peninsular War between the French army, commandered by Dupont, and Spanish troops under the control of General Castaños. The defeat for the French marked the beginning of the end of French presence on Spanish soil.

Bailén has a typically Andalucian feel, with its whitewashed houses and pleasant squares. The town's principal monument is the **Iglesia de la Encarnación**, a 16C church with a combination of Gothic and Renaissance influence, which contains the tomb of General Castaños.

ANTEQUERA★

Málaga – Population 40 239
Michelin map 446 U 16

Known to the Romans as *Anticaria* (the old city), the ancient town of Antequera extends across the foot of the Sierra del Torcal opposite the imposing Peña de los Enamorados Rock, in the heart of Málaga province. Conquered by Fernando of Aragón in 1410, the town enjoyed its period of greatest splendour between the 16C and 18C, as witnessed by the wealth of civil and religious buildings dating from this time. Its cobblestone streets and whitewashed houses, with their flower-decked balconies and wrought-iron grilles, combine harmoniously with its monumental churches, attractive avenues and more modern buildings, preserving the town's individuality. Today, Antequera is an important industrial and agricultural centre, mainly as a result of the fertile soil of the valley in which it lies. The town's **Holy Week** celebrations, renowned for their emotion

WHERE TO STAY

MODERATE

Nuevo Infante – *Infante Don Fernando, 5 – ☎ 952 70 02 93 – fax 952 70 00 86 – 18 rooms – 5 000pts.* A small hotel located in one of the town's main shopping streets. The bedrooms open onto an inner patio, while the reception is on the second floor.

MID-RANGE

Parador de Antequera – *García del Olmo – ☎ 952 84 09 01 – fax 952 84 13 12 – 55 rooms – 13 500pts.* This modern *parador* with its spacious rooms has been built overlooking the valley on the outskirts of Antequera.

EATING OUT

Lozano – *Avenida Principal, 2 – ☎/fax 952 84 27 12.* Although the location in an industrial area is less than attractive, Lozano is one of the best restaurants in Antequera. Specialities include both meat and fish dishes, served in a large, noisy dining-room. Rooms are also available *(6 500pts).*

El Escribano – *Plaza de los Escribanos, 11 – ☎ 670 85 56 64 – open 11am to midnight.* El Escribano is located in the upper part of Antequera, from where its restaurant and terrace-bar overlook the Colegiata de Santa María.

La Espuela – *Plaza de Toros – ☎ 952 70 34 24 – open noon to midnight.* This restaurant, actually located in the bullring, offers a wide range of regional and Spanish dishes.

and beauty, reach their peak on the night of Good Friday, when a moving "farewell" *(despedida)* is celebrated in plaza de San Sebastián between the brotherhoods of Santa Cruz de Jerusalén (Holy Cross of Jerusalem) and Dulce Nombre de Jesús (Divine Name of Jesus), both of which were founded in the 16C. The town also has a rich culinary tradition, including dishes such as *porra antequerana* (a dish similar to *gazpacho* and *salmorejo*), pigs' trotters with chickpeas *(manos de cerdo con garbanzos)* and the almond-flavoured, meringue-like *bienmesabe*, a Moorish-influenced dessert.

Alcazaba ⊘ – The fortress is accessed via an avenue lined by leafy hedges offering expansive **views**★ of the Sierra del Torcal, the Antequera plain, with the Peña de los Enamorados in the background, and of the town itself, with its attractive painted roofs and graceful church towers. This was the first fortress in the kingdom of Granada conquered by the Christians (1410), although it once again fell into Moorish hands soon after. The 15C walls, built with reused Roman materials, enclose a pleasant garden, ideal for a stroll to enjoy the silence which is characteristic of this part of the town. Of the towers which still survive, the most interesting are the Torre de la Estrella, the Torre Blanca and, above all, the Torre del Homenaje, popularly known as the Torre del Papabellotas, crowned by a small chapel housing the Antequera bell.

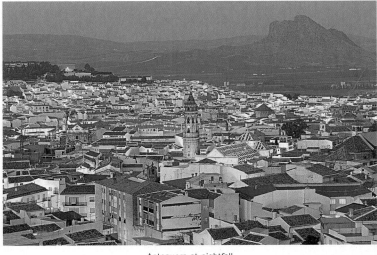

Antequera at nightfall

Peña de los Enamorados

This impressive rock rises up halfway along the road linking Antequera and Archidona. It has given rise to a romantic legend which tells of Tagzona, the daughter of the Moorish leader of the area, who had fallen hopelessly in love with Tello, a young Christian imprisoned near Antequera. They made the decision to elope but were discovered by the guards of Tagzona's father, who chased them to the very top of a rock on the outskirts of the town. Without any hope of escape, and with the arrows of Moorish marksmen bearing down on them, the two lovers launched themselves hand-in-hand into the void below, sealing their love for each other for eternity.

★**Colegiata de Santa María** ⊘ – This 16C collegiate church, situated in the square of the same name, stands at the foot of the castle gardens. It is a fine example of the early Renaissance, a style which also encompasses several late-Gothic features. Access to it is through the 16C **Arco de los Gigantes** (Giants' Arch), which has preserved vestiges of Roman tablets and sculptures found in and around Antequera. The church is a monumental edifice with three naves covered with Mudéjar vaults and separated by semicircular arches resting on Ionic columns. The splendid **façade**, inspired by Roman triumphal arches and adorned with slender pinnacles, is worthy of note, as is the rectangular chancel, with its Gothic-Mudéjar vault. During the Golden Age, it was the seat of the Cátedra de Gramática y Latinidad (Academy of Grammar and Latin), made up of a number of leading poets from Antequera.

Iglesia del Carmen ⊘ – The church is all that remains of a former Carmelite convent. Built in the 16C and 17C, it comprises a wide-proportioned single nave covered by an attractive, Mudéjar-style *artesonado* ceiling. The interior is profusely decorated with paintings and polychrome stuccowork; note the fine retable at the high altar. This superb work, sculpted in the 18C by Antonio Primo, is carved from wood without polychrome adornment; the small chapel at its centre is decorated with more canvases.

Museo Municipal ⊘ – The municipal museum is housed in the **Palacio de Nájera**, a 17C building with an interesting look-out tower. It contains a noteworthy collection of archeological artefacts, the most outstanding item of which is undoubtedly the **Ephebus of Antequera★**. This bronze Roman sculpture from the 1C represents a naked boy whose hands appear to carry an object that has now disappeared. Note the lightness of the work, as well as the child's sublime expression.

Convento de San José ⊘ – The façade is a fine example of Antequera Baroque. It is a highly original ensemble, consisting of a portal with a semicircular arch resting on *estípites* and character-based decoration which, similar to corbels, support a cornice with beautifully sculpted plant motifs and grotesque masks. The interior houses an interesting collection of old paintings.

Convento de la Encarnación – This 16C convent, with its single nave and lofty chancel, shows similarities with a number of Mudéjar churches in Granada. The portal on calle Encarnación is formed by a semicircular arch, the pendentives of which depict the figures of the Angel and the Virgin Mary, forming an Annunciation. The church has also preserved several interesting 18C sculptures.

Iglesia de San Sebastián ⊘ – The main portal of this 16C church is an interesting example of the Plateresque style. Its graceful 18C steeple, with its four sections, is one of Antequera's most emblematic features. Of note inside are a number of works of art, including a 15C sculpture of the Virgin of Hope and various canvases by the Mannerist artist Antonio Mohedano.

"May the sun come out in Antequera..."

At the beginning of the 15C, Antequera still found itself under Moorish domination, at a time when Christian troops continued their advance south to conquer further territory in al-Andalus. Unsure of what the best military stategy should be, the Infante, Don Fernando of Aragón, was confronted one night by an apparition of a beautiful young girl surrounded by lions who said to him: "Tomorrow, may the sun come out in Antequera and may whatever God ordains happen". The following day, 16 September 1410, Christian troops took the town of Antequera, which they dedicated to St Euphemia, the virgin and martyr from Chalcedon who so inspired Don Fernando. Henceforth he became known as *el de Antequera*. Since this time, the Spanish phrase *Salga el sol por Antequera* (May the sun come out in Antequera) has become a popular saying which serves as an inspiration for people to face up to whatever challenges present themselves in life.

Iglesia de San Agustín ⊘ – Built by Diego de Vergara, who also designed Málaga Cathedral, this 16C church has a single nave with pointed Gothic vaulting and a fine 17C-18C tower. The Mannerist-style portal comprises a semicircular arch with a balcony, in which vaulted niches with religious images can be seen. The high altar is adorned with several interesting canvases by Mohedano, narrating the story of St Augustine.

Palacio Municipal – This former Franciscan monastery is fronted by an unusual neo-Baroque façade built as recently as 1953. Its main attraction is the cloister, with two elegant galleries, the lower of which is supported by semicircular arches and arris vaulting, while the upper level is graced with large windows with broken pediments. The Baroque staircase between the two floors has a stucco-adorned vault and polychrome marble decoration.

Convento de Nuestra Señora de los Remedios ⊘ – This 17C church, dedicated to the patron saint of Antequera, has a Latin cross ground plan with two side chapels and sumptuous ornamentation based on Franciscan themes and plant motifs. The high altar is dominated by a fine gilded retable with a niche *(camarín)* decorated with delicate stuccowork and housing a 16C Virgin of the Remedies.

Real Convento de San Zoilo – The rich polychrome stucco decoration highlighting plant and geometric motifs inside this 16C late-Gothic convent is of particular interest. Other outstanding features include the Mudéjar *artesonado* ceiling, an altarpiece comprising 16C Renaissance panels and the so-called Green Christ *(Cristo Verde)*, a Renaissance statue attributed to Pablo de Rojas.

Convento de Belén – The interior of this 18C convent consists of three richly decorated naves. The main nave, with its barrel vault interspersed with lunettes, is flanked by two side aisles, separated by semicircular arches, with a number of small chapels. On either side of the transept, topped by a semicircular cupola, stand two chapels; the one on the Epistle side contains a stucco-adorned niche *(camarín)* housing a statue of Christ by José Mora. The nuns here are renowned for their delicious pastries which can be purchased by visitors.

★**Menga and Viera dolmens** ⊘ – *To the left of the Antequera exit on the A 354, towards Granada.* These enormous burial chambers were built at the foot of the Cerro de la Cruz, taking advantage of the slope provided by a small hillock. The construction techniques used were particularly advanced, involving the use of a line of pillars supporting enormous stone slabs. The **Menga dolmen** (2500 BC) comprises a type of artificial cave with a spacious oval chamber preceded by a gallery almost 25m/82ft long, 7m/23ft wide and 2.70m/9ft high, with 10 vertical monoliths and five horizontal ones. This chamber, covered by an enormous stone slab, contains seven monoliths on each side and a large stone at its head. Note the third vertical monolith on the left side of the gallery with its representations of human figures and solar symbols. The **Viera dolmen** (2200 BC) comprises a long gallery, at the end of which the burial chamber, cube-like in shape and consisting of four vertical monoliths and a large stone slab covering, can be seen.

EXCURSIONS

★**El Romeral dolmen** ⊘ – *4km/2.5mi northeast. Leave Antequera on the A 354. Bear left on the N 331 at a signposted crossroads.* The architecture of the El Romeral cave is more complex than that at Menga or Viera. This dolmen, dating from 1800 BC, consists of projecting ashlar stone walls, two circular chambers and a gallery surmounted by limestone slabs. The first chamber is covered by a false ceiling and enclosed by a large monolithic slab; behind it, a carved door provides access to the second room, containing an altar-like structure for offerings.

★★**Parque Natural de El Torcal** – *14km/9mi southeast. Take the C 3310 towards Villanueva de la Concepción, then bear right onto a signposted road leading to the* **Centro de Recepción "El Torcal"** ⊘. The park, spread over an area in excess of 12ha/30 acres, has some of Spain's most unusual scenery, where erosion by wind and rain have combined to create chasms, obelisks and other strange formations. The park's flora, which includes Spanish squill and Venus's navelwort, is particularly impressive, especially in spring, when the colour and scent of wild flowers and plants is a botanist's delight.

The Reception Centre is the ideal starting-point for any visit, with details on the two signposted walks through the park. The shortest of the two *(1hr there and back)* follows the La Losa footpath to the Maceta corrie *(torca)* and passes the Ventanillas viewpoint *(mirador)* at one of its highest points, from where the **views**★★ are quite exceptional. The longest of the two walks *(3hr there and back)* traverses the Chamorro chasm *(sima)*, the Pizarro Rock *(peñón)* and the Los Topaderos trail *(vereda)*.

Archidona – *19km/11mi northeast. Leave Antequera on the A 354. After the Peña de los Enamorados, follow the A 92 and bear right at a signposted intersection.* The small town of Archidona extends across a slope of the Sierra de Gracia, at the foot of the Pico de Conjuro peak, amid a landscape of undulating olive groves. The old quarter has preserved a number of vestiges from its period of Moorish rule.

★**Plaza Ochavada** – This octagonal square is one of the symbols of the town. Built in the 18C by the architects Francisco Astorga and Antonio González, it combines features inspired by French urban planning with aspects typical of Andalucian architecture. The façades of the buildings fronting the square are a mixture of red brick arches and pilasters and whitewashed masonry, embellished by traditional, flower-decked Andalucian balconies. In the past, this unusually shaped square was used for bullfights.

Ermita de la Virgen de Gracia ⊘ – The chapel is situated in the upper town within the walls of the old Moorish castle, of which only a few walls, the keep, vestiges of a cistern and the restored Puerta del Sol (Sun Gateway) remain. This small 18C chapel has three naves, a hemispherical dome and an elliptical cap with stucco decoration; it has managed to preserve several ornamental features from the mosque which previously stood on the same site. From the chapel there are some delightful views of Archidona and the surrounding countryside.

Iglesia de Santa Ana ⊘ – This predominantly Gothic construction also includes several Baroque features, such as the fine 18C façade. The large, triangular-based tower is capped by a pyramidal pinnacle with glazed green and white roof tiles. The interior contains a number of interesting works of art.

Convento de las Mínimas – The predominant feature of this former 18C convent is the Baroque doorway, flanked by a polygonal red brick tower with glazed ceramic decoration.

Iglesia de las Escuelas Pías ⊘ – This church houses a venerated statue of Jesus of Nazareth.

★**Laguna de la Fuente de Piedra** – *22km/13mi northwest. Leave Antequera on the A 354, then take the A 92 towards Sevilla. Turn right at the Km 132 exit and continue along the MA 701 towards Fuente de Piedra. Once in the town, follow the signposts.* This extensive lagoon is the habitat for a variety of flora (saltwort, suaeda vera, rushes etc) and fauna, including one of the largest colonies of flamingos in Europe, storks, gulls, cranes and egrets. The wonderful spectacle of these birds in flight or massed together on the water is quite remarkable, particularly in the late afternoon.

★VALLE DEL GUADALHORCE

From Antequera to the Cueva de Doña Trinidad Grund

70km/44mi southwest. Allow half a day.

The beautiful Guadalhorce Valley meanders through the Serranía de Ronda and the Montes de Málaga to the Guadalteba-Guadalhorce Reservoir *(embalse)*. It traverses a diverse landscape, with olive groves and fields of crops separating the plain from the mountains, and with hills dotted with whitewashed houses, vegetable gardens and rocky walls, offering superb **views** of the local area.

Leave Antequera on the avenida de la Legión. Turn right at the signposted crossroads, following the A 343 towards Álora. The road winds its way through delightful landscapes, passing through the Abdalajís Valley, before heading south to Álora.

★**Álora** – The town is perched on a hillside on the banks of the Guadalhorce River, at the foot of Monte Hacho. Its typically Andalucian centre, with its maze of narrow streets lined by low, whitewashed houses, is overlooked by the castle, with its fine views of the surrounding area.

★★**Desfiladero de los Gaitanes** – *Leave Álora on the MA 444 towards El Chorro.* The **corniche road**★ crosses some superb mountain scenery before it reaches the incredible Garganta del Chorro defile, the main attraction in the Parque de Ardales. Visitors are advised to leave their car at the El Chorro campsite and to continue on foot along a tarmac track *(30min there and back)* which climbs to a metal bridge offering magnificent **views**★★★ of this incredible natural phenomenon. Here, perched over the defile, the sensation is of being suspended in mid-air above the bed of the river, as its water flows through an incredibly high formation of rock. At the end of the bridge, a flimsy catwalk, the Camino del Rey, made from wood and rope, skirts the rockface to join up with another bridge, in an even worse state of repair.

A word of warning

Given the dangerous nature of the defile and to ensure the safety of visitors, we recommend that you go no further than the metal bridge suspended high above the El Chorro defile.

Bobastro ruins – *Return to the MA 444 and continue towards Ardales. At a signposted junction, bear left onto a narrower track.* This scenic **road**★★ passes through tranquil mountain landscapes before it reaches the Tajo de la Encantada Reservoir *(embalse)*.

Leave your car on the road and continue on foot along a marked path; allow 15min each way. It was at Bobastro that General Omar Ben Hafsun, the descendant of a noble Visigothic family, united Mozarabs and other Islamic groups to defend country life in opposition to the Umayyads. From these inaccessible hilltops, known as the Mesas de Villaverde, this intrepid soldier headed the rebellion against the Emirate of Córdoba, before subsequently embracing the Christian faith. All that remains of Bobastro today are the ruins of the alcázar walls, several caves and, more importantly, an unfinished 10C church with a triple-nave basilical ground plan, transept and three apses. This temple, which has been excavated from sandstone rock, highlights the architectural synthesis which existed between Hispano-Roman, Visgothic and Islamic art.

★**Embalse del Guadelteba-Guadalhorce** – *Return to the MA 444 and continue as far as the campsites and* **Parque de Ardales Information Points** ⊙ *(Puntos de Información) situated in front of the Conde de Guadalhorce reservoir.* This reservoir *(embalse)* is situated in the heart of the Parque de Ardales, a beautiful area of dark woods, light-coloured stone rocks and plentiful camping areas. Along with the neighbouring Gaitejo, Tajo de la Encantada and Conde de Gualhorce reservoirs, this area is perfect for those visitors searching for the peace and quiet of the countryside. A number of footpaths skirt the reservoir's crystal-clear waters, while others criss-cross delightful landscapes where not a soul can be seen. The impressive silence here, particularly in winter, the pure air and perfect climate are the main attractions of an area that can be visited practically all year round. The views from the hills overlooking the reservoir are also impressive.

★**Cueva de Doña Trinidad Grund** ⊙ – *From the Embalse del Conde de Guadalhorce take the MA 444 to Ardales. In order to visit the cave, ask for the keys at the town hall.* The cave, located just 3km/2mi from the village towards Carratraca, runs for a distance of 1 600m/5 248ft underground. It contains archeological discoveries that prove that it was occupied from the Paleolithic period to the Bronze Age. Its main attractions are its wall paintings (54 representations of animals and 130 symbols), which constitute exceptional examples of art from the Quaternary Era. Of particular interest is the depiction of a large female deer, in which the animal's legs and heart are painted a bright red.

ARACENA★

Huelva – Population 6 500
Michelin map 446 S 10

The small town of Aracena, nestled at the heart of the *sierra* of the same name, rises in tiers up a hillside, overlooked by the remains of a Templar castle. The attractive centre is an array of low whitewashed houses which provide a contrast with the more sombre paving of its steets, and larger mansions, their sober doorways adorned with elaborate wrought-iron work providing ideal shelter from the hot summer sun. The **Museo al Aire Libre de Escultura Contemporánea**, an open-air exhibition of modern art displayed in the town's streets and squares, adds a touch of modernity to this picturesque *pueblo*.

The many bars *(mesones)* dotted around Aracena offer ample opportunity to try the local cuisine, particularly the renowned cured ham, **jamón serrano**.

★★★**Gruta de las Maravillas** ⊙ – The entrance to the Cave of Marvels, a spectacular geological formation over 100m/328ft deep, which was the setting for the film *Tarzan and the Mines of King Solomon*, is located in the town centre. The tour of this series of underground caverns, to the accompaniment of pleasant background music, passes through high chambers and narrow passageways of green, blue and pink-toned stalagmites and stalactites, caused by the colouring effects of metal oxides. The system of underground lakes, in which the breathtakingly beautiful limestone ceilings inside the caves are mirrored to superb effect, add an extra dimension to the visit. The main aspects of interest include the "organ chamber" (salón de los órganos); the "cathedral chamber" (sala de la catedral), in which one of its formations can be likened to the figure of the Virgin Mary with a child in her arms; the "emerald lake" (lago de las esmeraldas); the "Sultana's bathroom" (baño de la sultana); the "diamond chamber" (salón de los brillantes), the ceiling of which is covered with myriad twinkling formations; the "nude gallery" (sala de los desnudos); and the outstanding **"God's Crystalware Chamber"**★★ (Salón de la Cristalería de Dios), where the reflections of light produce some quite visual effects. The complex is also home to the **Museo Geológico Minero** ⊙, a geological and mining museum containing an interesting collecction of minerals, rocks and fossils.

Hidalgo-Lopesino/MARCO POLO

Gruta de las Maravillas

Castle ⊙ – The silhouette of this imposing fortress dominates the town of Aracena and its surrounding countryside from the highest point of a nearby promontory. Majestic groves of chestnut trees can be seen extending into the distance, while at closer quarters extensive pine groves act as a protective barrier around the castle, which was built above the remains of a 9C Almohad fortress. The main architectural features include the Gothic church and a **Mudéjar-style tower** – the former minaret – on the north side of which *sebka* panelling similar to that found on the Giralda in Sevilla can be seen.

Iglesia de Nuestra Señora del Mayor Dolor – The Church of Our Lady of Great Suffering was built between the 13C and 14C on an extraordinary site affording superb **views**★★. It contains a sculpture of the Virgin Mary, the town's patron saint, as well as a recumbent statue byPedro Vázquez.

Plaza Alta – This tranquil square, the hub of local life, has several notable buildings, including the Iglesia de Nuestra Señora de la Asunción and the Cabildo Viejo.

Iglesia de Nuestra Señora de la Asunción – The church is a solemn 16C-17C Renaissance-style building with a well-preserved façade with fine decorative detail and refined large windows.

Cabildo Viejo – The town's former municipal storehouse and town hall dates from the 15C. It now houses the **Centro de Información del Parque Natural Sierra de Aracena y Picos de Aroche** ⊙, providing information on the history and evolution of the park and the local area.

WHERE TO STAY

MODERATE

Los Castaños – *Avenida de Huelva, 5* – ☎ *959 12 63 00* – *fax 959 12 62 87* – *55 rooms – 7 000pts.* This attractive, centrally located hotel has modern, tasteful rooms, some of which face onto a large inner patio.

MID-RANGE

Finca Valbono – *Carretera de Carboneras (1km/0.6mi from the town)* – ☎ *959 12 77 11* – *fax 959 12 76 79 – 44 rooms – 8 750pts.* This hotel complex in the heart of the countryside has a choice of standard rooms, bungalows and private houses for rent, which sleep up to eight people. Facilities here include a swimming pool, horse-riding, a basketball court and a terrace, from where groups of the famous *pata negra* pigs *(see p 99)* can be seen. Bicycles are also available for hire.

EATING OUT

La Despensa de José Vicente – *Avenida de Andalucía, 53* – ☎ *959 12 84 55* – *closed Fri and from 1 to 15 June.* One of the best restaurants in the province. According to its owner, only the very best fresh produce is served here. The menu in the small, but tastefully decorated restaurant (and bar) includes locally picked cep mushrooms and a range of cured ham and pork dishes.

TAPAS

Casino de Arias Montano – *Plaza del Marqués de Aracena.* This delightful building dating from 1910, with its columned façade and high ceilings, stands in the main square. A popular meeting-place for Aracena's older generation.

Parque Natural Sierra de ARACENA Y PICOS DE AROCHE★★

Huelva

Michelin map 446 S 9-10

This superb natural park with its mountain landscapes and picturesque villages is a pleasure for the senses. It is a land of contrast, with vast areas of forest occasionally punctuated by slender peaks offering delightful **views** of the *sierra*, where the sound of fast-flowing water blends in with the wind whistling through the treetops.

Information Centres ⊙

– The **Castillo de Aroche** provides detailed information on the black vulture, a species in danger of extinction. This area is home to one of Spain's most important breeding grounds.

– The **Castillo de Cortegana** shows the evolution of defensive architecture in villages and settlements around the park.

– The town hall at **Almonaster** has a whole host of information on activities and excursions available to visitors within the *parque natural*.

– The **Cabildo Viejo** in Aracena has an exhibition of explanatory panels outlining the historical evolution of the area and its immediate surroundings.

From Aroche to Aracena

64km/40mi – allow 1 day.

Aroche – Aroche is one of the oldest towns in the area, as testified by the so-called **Piedras del Diablo** (Devil's Stones), a series of dolmens in a delightful setting 3km/2mi to the southeast along the H 9002, near the chapel *(ermita)* of San Mamés. The town has a pleasing air, with its maze of narrow, twisting alleyways, attractive seigniorial mansions, old buildings and small workshops, specialising in riding saddles, which appear to climb all the way up to the **castle★**, inside of which stands the bullring. The castle, a sober 12C construction used as a refuge by King Sancho IV the Brave, houses an information point for the park. A visit to the 13C **Iglesia de Nuestra Señora de la Asunción** and the **Convento de los Jerónimos**, a Hieronymite monastery, are also recommended.

14km/9mi southeast on the N 433.

Cortegana – This pleasant town, nestled in delightful natural surroundings, is one of the area's main centres for industry and arts and crafts. Its major activities, which include meat production, the manufacture of cork, hand-made weighing instruments and pottery, have transformed Cortegana into an active commercial centre attracting numerous visitors. The town also has several buildings of interest, such as the **Iglesia del Salvador**, an elegant 16C Gothic-Mudéjar church, the Gothic-Renaissance **Iglesia de San Sebastián** and, in particular, its medieval **castle**. This monumental fortress, built in the late 13C, affords impressive **views** of the town and local area. It also contains a park information point.

7km/4.5mi southeast on the A 470.

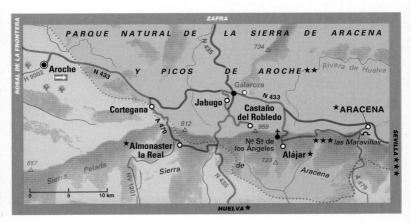

WHERE TO STAY

EL REPILADO

Posada de Cortegana – *On the N 433 – ☎ 959 50 33 01 – 8 000pts*. A number of ham-producing companies are based in El Repilado. The Posada, a complex of several bungalows, enjoys a shady rural setting along a 1km/0.6mi dirt track along which flocks of sheep and herds of *pata negra* pigs can often be seen grazing.

GALAROZA

Galaroza Sierra – *At Km 69.5 on the N 433 Sevilla-Lisbon road – ☎ 959 12 32 15 – fax 959 12 32 36 – 26 rooms – 6 000pts*. A quiet, modern hotel with 20 rooms, six bungalows and a restaurant just a short distance from Jabugo.

★**Almonaster La Real** – Almonaster is a pleasant surprise hidden amid a dense mountainous landscape of chestnut, eucalyptus, cork and holm oak. The white-washed architecture of this exceptional **site** comprises a labyrinth of quiet streets, colonial-style mansions and vestiges of former homesteads where time appears to have stood still. The local gastronomy, mainly based on pork products, and folklore – visitors should not miss the *Cruces de Mayo* festival in May – add to the considerable charms of Almonaster. A **park information point** has been created for tourists in the **town hall**

Interior of the mosque

Hidalgo-Lopesino/MARCO POLO

★**Mosque** ⊘ – The 10C *mezquita*, standing within a walled enclosure, is one of the few examples of Caliphal architecture to have been preserved in this area. The building's reddish walls, supported by the rock beneath, provide visitors with unparalleled views of the mountain sky-line from their privileged vantage-point. The town's unusual bullring *(plaza de toros)* is visible to one side; the castle-fortress, also within the walls, offers **views** of the town below.

Iglesia de San Martín – This sober church is a mix of Gothic and Mudéjar styles.

12km/8mi northeast. Take the A 470 and then follow the N 435.

Castaño del Robledo – The village's secluded set-ting has made it a popular destination for hikers, who come here to walk the net-work of paths criss-cross-ing groves of chestnut trees, to scale the local peaks and to admire the sight of birds of prey gliding through the air.

6km/4mi north along the N 435.

Jabugo – Although this small, tranquil village is hidden away in an isolated moun-tain setting, its name is famous around the world. This renown is due to its prized **cured hams** *(jamones)* and **sausages** *(embutidos)*, which are on sale in the numerous factories here.

13km/8mi southeast. Follow the N 433 towards Fuenteheridos and then bear right.

★**Alájar** – This picturesque whitewashed village of low houses, nestled at the foot of the church with its pointed belfry, enjoys an impressive natural setting popular with walkers. The area around Alájar provides visitors with a complete compendium of the park's attractions, with its dark cork and holm oak forests, steep rugged rocks and stunning views.

Peña Arias Montano – This impressive rock *(peña)* several kilometres to the north of Alájar provides yet more superb **views**★★ of this extraordinary landscape. It owes its name to the learned and erudite Benito Arias Montano, a master to Felipe II, librarian at the monastery of El Escorial, diplomat and royal supervisor for the publica-

> ### Pata negra cured ham
>
> *Pata negra from Jabugo is considered the king of cured hams. This exquisite delicacy has a sublime aroma and taste...and a price to match!*

tion of the *Polyglot Bible*. Following a difficult academic life, this scholar decided to retire here in order to lead a more contemplative existence. The **Ermita de Nuestra Señora de los Ángeles**, a chapel which attracts many visitors, particularly at the weekend, can be seen on a rocky outcrop.

12km/8mi east on the A 470.

★**Aracena** – *See ARACENA.*

ARCOS DE LA FRONTERA★★
Cádiz – Population 27 897
Michelin map 446 V 12

Arcos enjoys one of the most remarkable **settings**★★ in the whole of Andalucia. Perched on top of a steep cliff, its houses appear as though they are about to plunge any moment into the impressive valley formed by the Guadelete River below. This strategic position was not lost on those who have settled here over the millennia. Its present-day name has evolved from the Roman colony of Arx-Arcis, meaning "fortress on high ground", although legend has it that the name derived from Arcobrigán, the arch of Brigo, the grandson of Noah. Arcos was an important Moorish

> ### Views of the town
>
> The most attractive **view**★★ of Arcos is on the A 382 road from Jerez de la Frontera. The A 372 from Grazalema also provides pleasant **views**★ of the town.

town and the capital of a *taifa* kingdom in the 11C. Following an initial incursion by Fernando III, it was finally conquered by Alfonso X in 1264.

WHERE TO STAY

MID-RANGE

El Convento – *Maldonado, 2 – ☎ 956 70 23 33 – fax 956 70 41 28 – 11 rooms – 10 000pts.* As the name suggests, this hotel is housed in a former 17C convent, located in a narrow street in the centre of Arcos. The rooms are quiet; most have views of the valley. The upper section of the hotel has a pleasant terrace.

Marqués de Torresoto – *Marqués de Torresoto, 4 – ☎ 956 70 07 17 – fax 956 70 42 05 – 15 rooms – 10 425pts.* This former 17C palace has a central location in the historical centre. Its architectural features include a small Baroque chapel and an attractive **arcaded patio**. Antique furniture decorates the rooms.

EATING OUT

El Convento – *Marqués de Torresoto, 7 – ☎ 956 70 32 22.* Opposite the Hotel Marqués de Torresoto, in the same building as its namesake hotel, but with a separate entrance. Traditional decor and a columned patio. Specialities include asparagus soup, pheasant *al paraíso* and partridge in an almond sauce.

TAPAS

Alcaraván – *Calle Nueva, 1.* In the walls of the castle and easily identifiable by the numerous flowerpots on its façade. Grilled meats, stuffed peppers and lamb stew are just some of the dishes on the menu, which diners can enjoy to the traditional strains of background flamenco music. Alcaraván is the name of a poetry prize which has been awarded in Arcos de la Frontera for the past 50 years.

99

Harness-making

Guarnicionería – *Paseo de Boliches, 14.* The harness-maker José Moreno has spent his life working with leather, inheriting a long family tradition which has all but disappeared nowadays. In his small workshop, visitors will find a huge selection of horse-riding equipment manufactured according to traditional techniques.

TOUR *2hr*

As in other towns with a similar layout, the best way to enjoy your visit is to wander through the narrow streets. The easiest option is to leave your car in the lower town (paseo de Boliches) and to continue on foot.

Ascend the cuesta de Belén, a hill which connects the bustling commercial heart of Arcos – with its typically 19C architecture – with the upper town. The latter, the nucleus of the medieval city, is characterised by steep-sloped narrow alleyways and whitewashed houses. Pass through the Puerta de Jerez, one of the three entrance gateways providing access to the walled Moorish city. Beyond the **callejón de Juan del Valle**, note the 15C Gothic-Mudéjar **façade★** of the **Palacio del Conde del Águila** to the right, fronted by a magnificent doorway with an *alfiz* surround decorated with finely worked tracery and adorned with two human figures; this is crowned by an attractive mullioned window.

Continue to the right along calle Nueva, which runs parallel to the castle wall.

Plaza del Cabildo – The square, the centre of old Arcos, is dominated by the imposing tower of the **Iglesia de Santa María**. The *plaza* is also lined by the town hall, the *parador*, occupying the former magistrate's house (Casa del Corregidor), and the castle, now a privately owned building. The terrace on the west side offers a magnificent **view★** of the plains below and the Iglesia de San Pedro.

★Iglesia de Santa María de la Asunción ⊘ – This church was built around 1530 above an earlier 14C temple, itself erected on the site of the former Moorish mosque. Its **west façade★**, the work of Don Alonso de Baena, is an extraordinary example of Plateresque art. The interior, accessed via the neo-Classical south façade, has a basilical ground plan with three aisles separated by robust columns supporting star vaults with tiercerons. In the high altar, a 17C **retable**, a work by Jerónimo Hernández and Juan Bautista Vázquez representing the Ascension of the Virgin, stands out. Hidden behind the high altar is the polygonal apse from the earlier Mudéjar church. The **frescoes★** *(The Coronation of the Virgin)* which decorated the earlier high altar were transferred to the wall of the Evangelist nave *(to the left of the altar)* in the 1960s.

Continue along the west façade into the evocative callejón de las Monjas. The flying buttresses now visible were added in the 17C to counteract the movement of the church. Pass the **Renaissance façade★** of the Convento de la Encarnación, continuing along calle del Marqués de Torresoto. Note the 17C Classical-style patio of the **palace-residence of the Marquess of Torresoto** at no 4. The small square at the end of the street, the plazuela Boticas, is fronted by the **Convento de las Mercedarias Descalzas**, where it is possible to buy pastries still produced by the nuns, and the unfinished 18C Jesuit house, now the home of the town's market.

Calle Boticas and calle Nuñez de Prado lead to the other main section of the town.

Façade of the Palacio del Mayorazgo

Hidalgo-Lopesino/MARCO POLO

Close to the Iglesia de San Pedro stand the **Capilla de la Misericordia**, a chapel with a blind pointed arch, and the **Palacio del Mayorazgo**, a palace which now houses the town's conservatory of music and whose wide façade is adorned with an ornate Renaissance loggia.

Iglesia de San Pedro ⊘ – The church dates from the early 15C and for many years rivalled Santa María in importance. The façade is crowned by an impressive neo-Classical bell-tower. The interior ground plan consists of a single nave with a pointed vault with tiercerons.

A ceramics shop is hidden behind the Plateresque façade of no 7 calle San Pedro.

Continue along calle Cadenas.

The street has two interest-

> **Holy Week**
>
> On **Good Friday**, a traditional procession winds its way through the streets of Arcos as part of the **Semana Santa** celebrations. Included in this religious ritual are the *armaos* – local men dressed in typical Roman costume who parade proudly through the town wearing helmets and armour and carrying standards and lances.

ing examples of a noble palace. The first, to the left, in calle Juan de Cuenca, is the palace-residence of the same name; a little further on, in the plaza del Cananeo, stands the former palace of the Marquess and Marchioness of Torresoto.

Continue along calle Bóvedas. On the corner with calle Boticas, note the Casa de los Gamaza.

To return to plaza del Cabildo, you are best advised to continue along calle Boticas until the plazuela de Boticas, and then follow the charming calle de los Escribanos, with its delightful wrought-iron balconies.

ADDITIONAL SIGHT

★**Convento de la Caridad** – The convent stands in the plaza de la Caridad, outside of the walls of the medieval section in the *barrio bajo* (lower town). It was built in the middle of the 18C and exudes a strong colonial influence. The entrance to the church is preceded by an attractive atrium.

La AXARQUÍA★

Málaga
Michelin map 446 V 17–18

The area of La Axarquía is situated at the easternmost point of Málaga province, where its land descends from the southern slopes of the Sierra de Almijara to the Mediterranean. From the end of the Reconquest up to the 18C, this coastline was regularly attacked by Barbary pirates, forcing its inhabitants to settle in the nearby mountains and to build watch-towers – many of which are still visible today – at regular intervals along the coast. Nowadays, the tranquil whitewashed towns and villages inland contrast with the lively, modern coastal resorts, popular with visitors attracted by the region's delightful climate. Agriculture is also an important industry in La Axarquía, with its proliferation of vineyards for the production of wine and raisins, olive groves and fruit orchards. Sub-tropical crops such as sugar cane, avocado, and custard apple, are also a feature here, as are the miles of plastic greenhouses, which are a more familiar sight in Almería province to the east.

FROM MÁLAGA TO NERJA

99km/62mi including detours

Málaga – *See MÁLAGA.*
12.5km/8mi from Málaga along the N 340 – E 15.

Rincón de la Victoria – The town is a popular seaside resort with a large number of tourist apartments and hotels, as well as a sandy beach over 3km/2mi long.

★**Cueva del Tesoro or Cueva del Higuerón** ⊘ – *Follow the signposted road after the first exit to Rincón de la*

Rincón de la Victoria

B. Kaufmann/MICHELIN

101

Rincón de la Victoria

WHERE TO STAY

Molino de Santillán – *At Km 8 on the MA 106 towards Macharaviaya – 952 11 57 80 – fax 952 11 57 82 – 9 rooms – 13 900pts.* This former mill is located in a bucolic setting at the end of a country lane. Guests are advised to arrive in daylight as this farm is not particularly easy to find.

Torrox-Costa

WHERE TO STAY

Cortijo Amaya – ✆ *fax 952 53 02 45 – 14 rooms – 8 000pts.* An old farm-house with views of the Mediterranean and the surrounding countryside. Simple, comfortable rooms, plus a swimming pool and tennis courts.

EATING OUT

The Paseo Marítimo has a mass of shops, bars and restaurants, including **Antonio**, which specialises in fish and seafood.

Victoria. Tradition says that valuable treasure *(tesoro)* was hidden in this cave during Moorish times, although nothing has ever been found here. The cave is of marine origin and has been created by water erosion over the millennia. Some of the beautiful, rounded shapes within its chambers are quite spectacular, and could quite easily have inspired Antoni Gaudí's Casa Milà in Barcelona.

Return to the N 340 – E 15 and continue west for 18km/11mi.

Torre del Mar – This large seaside resort is the closest to the town of Vélez-Málaga. The extensive beach here is bordered by an attractive promenade.

4km/2.5m inland.

Vélez-Málaga – The capital of La Axarquía appears to be dominated by the keep of its former fortress which was destroyed by Napoleon's troops. The **Barrio de la Villa**, a district of Moorish origin extending across the hillside at the foot of the tower, offers superb views over the surrounding plains. The quarter is a maze of steep, narrow streets with whitewashed houses and a 16C Mudéjar-style church, the Iglesia de Santa María, with its fine bell-tower. Access to this *barrio* is from plaza de la Constitución, fronted by the Iglesia de San Juan Bautista, also crowned by an attractive belfry, and containing a number of paintings and remnants of the old walls.

In the town centre, the 17C Palacio de los Marqueses de Beniel, with its sober, elegant façade, is now home to the town hall.

Return to the N 340 – E 15. After 3.5km/2mi bear left and continue for a further 3.5km/2mi.

Algarrobo – The whitewashed houses of Algarrobo rise up on a cliff 190m/623ft above the sea. The layout of the town is typically Moorish with narrow, winding streets leading up to the Ermita de San Sebastián, a chapel with well-tended gardens and views of the sea.

Return once more to the N 340 – E 15. Shortly before a crossroads, bear left towards the signposted Necrópolis de Trayamar.

Necrópolis de Trayamar – The remains of this large necropolis include Punic and Phoenician tombs, some of which date from the 8C and 7C BC.

Return to the N 340 and continue for 9km/5.5mi. Two watch-towers are visible from this stretch of road.

Torrox – The resort of **Torrox Costa** was once the site of a Roman settlement. On the beach, close to the lighthouse *(follow signs to the 'faro')*, excavations have revealed several large basins from this period which were used in the production of *garum (see p 321)*; some of these were subsequently used as burial tombs. The beaches here are particularly pleasant.

The town extends across a hillside *(4km/2.5mi inland)*, from where there are impressive views of the Mediterranean and the nearby terraces of olive groves.

The road to Cómpeta – *14.5km/9mi.* This winding road climbs up along the spurs of the Sierra de la Almijara, dotted with whitewashed villages and farms. A bend in the road affords a delightful view of Cómpeta, its white houses extending across a hillside, dominated by the brick tower of its parish church.

Return to the N 340 – E 15 and continue for 8km/5mi.

★ **Nerja** – *See NERJA.*

Frigiliana

★★**Cueva de Nerja** – See NERJA.
6.5km/4mi inland from Nerja.

★**Frigiliana** – This charming *pueblo blanco* extends across the south-facing slopes of the Sierra de la Almijara. Its upper section, the **Morisco-Mudéjar quarter★★**, is a superb example of popular architecture, with its meticulously maintained whitewashed houses providing a stunning contrast with the bright blue sky. The colourful arrangements of flowers add an extra dash of colour to this enchanting scene. Pedestrianised cobbled and paved streets wind their way up the hillside, past white houses with attractive doorways, picturesque nooks and crannies and viewpoints offering glimpses of the surrounding plains. Panels of *azulejos* adorning several walls provide a reminder of the battles that took place here between Moors and Christians.

AYAMONTE★

Huelva – Population 17 000
Michelin map 446 U 7

The main attraction of this small town is its geographical location at the mouth of the Guadiana, crossed by a modern iron road bridge linking it with Portugal on the opposite bank. Ayamonte is a town of contrasts with an openness which has developed as a result of its status as a port. The noise of its fishing fleet unloading its catch and the hubbub of its fish auctions blend in with the lively conversation of locals enjoying a *paseo* along the paseo de la Ribera, with its numerous outdoor cafés, in front of the port. Beyond the port area, the narrow, paved streets of the old centre extend upwards, flanked by small whitewashed houses with elegant, wrought-iron balconies and porches which provide welcome relief from the summer heat. Ayamonte is also dotted with several charming squares adorned with attractive street lamps, elegant fountains and niches housing religious figures. The colourful colonial-style houses built by Spanish emigrants returning home from the Americas at the end of the 19C are another of the town's typical landmarks.

Ayamonte's gastronomy is also well worth trying, with some excellent fish and seafood, *pestiños* (a type of honey fritter) and the local *coca ayamontina*, a flat biscuit-like cake.

Iglesia de las Angustias – Nestled between small old houses, this 16C church with a colonial air has a spacious triple-nave interior, crowned by a tower which dominates the Ayamonte skyline.

EATING OUT

Casa Barberi – *Plaza de la Constitución* – ☎ *959 47 02 89 – closed Tues.* The Casa Barberi on the main square has been run by the same family since 1917. It is one of the town's best restaurants, specialising in fish and *paella*. The square is also home to a number of other restaurants.

Travellers' addre

Carnival in Ayamonte

The inhabitants of Ayamonte and the surrounding area come to life at carnival time, when the town is the setting for processions, masked balls and dances, many of which continue until the early hours of the morning.

Convento de San Francisco – The main features of this 16C Renaissance monastery are the elegant belfry and the magnificent interior with its fine Mudéjar polychrome wood ceiling, columns decorated with old inscriptions and the large-proportioned retable at the high altar.

Iglesia del Salvador – The 13C building visible today was erected on the site of the old mosque. The portal and tower, with decorative stucco adornments, are of particular interest.

Muelle de Portugal – This modern dock *(muelle)* is the departure point for boats trips across the river to Portugal and to nearby Sanlúcar de Guadiana.

EXCURSIONS

Isla Cristina – *14km/9mi southeast. Take the N 431 towards Lepe. Before reaching El Empalme, bear right on the H 412.* Isla Cristina has an old quarter of low-level houses with *azulejo* decoration, a marina, a series of marshes which have been designated a site of natural beauty and attractive beaches such as Punta del Caimán, Playa Central, Playa del Hoyo, Casita Azul and La Redondela.

Isla Canela – *7km/4.5mi southeast on the H 410.* One of the most popular resorts along the Huelva coast. Various apartment complexes and golf clubs have recently been built along its wide sandy beach.

Punta del Moral – *9km/5.5mi southeast on the H 410.* This small resort is the perfect location for fishing enthusiasts and fish and seafood lovers who can enjoy local specialities at Punta del Moral's numerous beach bars and restaurants.

WHERE TO STAY

Sol y Mar – *Playa Central, Isla Cristina – ☎ 959 33 20 50 – 16 rooms – 10 000pts.* Although the hotel is somewhat lacking in charm and creature comforts, the rooms have terraces overlooking the sea. Two nearby hotels (**Paraíso Playa** and **Los Geranios**) are of a higher standard but are further from the beach.

EATING OUT

Acosta – *Plaza de las Flores, 13, Isla Cristina – ☎ 959 33 14 20.* A family-run restaurant serving mainly fish and seafood in a pretty square. What it lacks in decor it makes up for in the quality of its food.

Casa Rufino – *Avenida de la Playa, Isla Cristina – ☎ 959 33 08 10 – closed in Nov; open lunchtimes only Dec to June; open lunchtimes and evenings July and Aug.* This fish and seafood eatery just a stone's throw from the sea offers a special menu consisting of eight fish dishes (each menu is for four people). Mainly frequented by tourists.

BAENA

Córdoba – Population 20 057

Michelin map 446 T 17

The houses of Baena extend in a white swathe across the hillside, unfurling down to the plain amid a pleasantly undulating landscape of olive groves famous for the production of the local virgin olive oil. The town is separated into two distinct parts: the *barrio alto*, the oldest section, dominated by the tower of Santa María la Mayor parish church; and the *llano*, Baena's modern, commercial heart.

The **drum** *(tambor)*, the emblem of the town, plays a major part in Baena's celebrated and lively Holy Week festivities.

Illustrious sons – Juan Alfonso de Baena, the 16C troubadour who wrote the *Cancionero de Baena*, the de los Ríos family, the writer and politician José Amador, and Demetrio, the architect who initiated the restoration of León Cathedral in northern Spain.

The unmistakable odour of olive oil

As you approach Baena, there is no escaping the smell of this precious golden liquid! Numerous medical studies have demonstrated the beneficial effects that olive oil – one of the main constituents of the Mediterranean diet – has on health. Andalucian *aceite de olivo* is worthy of its widespread acclaim, which dates back to Roman times. The oil produced in Baena is considered one of the best in the region, as testified by the *Denominación de Origen* label guaranteeing its quality. It is produced using a variety of olive known as *picuda*, resulting in a superb, flavoursome olive oil which is ideal both for the table and for frying and as an ingredient for typical Andalucian stews.

BARRIO ALTO

In the Middle Ages, this upper section of narrow, cobbled streets was the town's Moorish quarter. The remains of walls and turrets which were part of the defensive system protecting the Arab city can still be seen here.

Iglesia de Santa María la Mayor – The church stands on the site of the former mosque. Although it dates from the 16C, it has subsequently undergone significant restoration. The portal, known as the Portada del Ángel, is Plateresque in style; its simple, yet elegant decorative features include a network of square decoration around the doorway, three escutcheons and two twisted columns. The slightly leaning bell-tower is the former minaret, and now comprises two Baroque sections crowned by a green and blue *azulejo* spire.

Iglesia del Convento Madre de Dios ⊘ – This convent, which is home to an enclosed order of nuns and is not open to the public, was founded in the early 16C by Don Diego Fernández de Córdoba, the fifth Lord of Baena. Although initially built in Gothic style, Renaissance influence is clearly visible. The single-nave interior has an interesting **east end**★, partly the work of Hernán Ruiz II, although the plan was designed by Diego de Siloé. The chancel is enclosed by a handsome Plateresque grille, while the polygonal apse has several paintings from the Bassano studio in the high altar. The half-dome above it is of note with its sculpted decoration of apostles and angels between echini.

The exterior is fronted by an attractive late-Gothic portal; note the cornices, with their vestiges of wall paintings.

LLANO DISTRICT

Casa del Monte – This imposing three-storey building with its wide façade dates from 1774. It occupies one side of plaza de la Constitución or Coso, which is dominated by the town hall.

Iglesia de Guadalupe ⊘ – *Close to plaza de España.* The main feature of this 16C church is the square chancel with its fine **Mudéjar artesonado**★ ceiling and an 18C Baroque altarpiece. Note also the **Capilla de la Virgen de Guadalupe**, a chapel on the Evangelist side of the church, adorned with a Baroque altar and covered with Mudéjar-style *artesonado* work. The late-15C fresco of the Virgin Mary was transferred here in 1617.

Antiguo Convento de San Francisco – *Now a rest home. On the outskirts of the town heading towards Córdoba. Bear left immediately after the petrol station.* The 18C **Baroque church** ⊘, with its Latin cross ground plan, is crowned with barrel vaults adorned with lunettes. An unusual feature of the building is the oval cupola above the transept which is arranged transversely. The walls are covered with frescoes, although the paintings on the ceiling are restricted to the transept arms. A Baroque altarpiece has pride of place in the east end.

A venerated 18C **Nazarene Christ** stands on the left-hand side of the church which, according to an engraving on a stone tablet, is said to have been fired at 11 times during the Spanish Civil War without suffering any damage.

Zuheros above a sea of olive groves

EXCURSIONS

★**Zuheros** – *17km/10.5mi along the CV 327*. This picturesque village enjoys a superb **setting**★★. Its charm is enhanced by its carefully maintained whitewashed houses lining narrow, cobbled and flower-decked streets.

Plaza de la Paz – This impressive natural viewpoint at a height of 622m/2 040ft provides stunning **views**★★ of hills carpeted in olive groves, with Baena in the distance. A stone dating from pre-Roman times is visible to the left.

Museo Arqueológico ⊘ – The archeological museum displays a number of exhibits from prehistory to the Roman period, discovered at the Cueva de los Murciélagos.

Castle ⊘ – The Romans also founded a fortress on this site. The remains now visible correspond to two different periods: the accessible square tower and battlements are Moorish in origin, while those opposite are from a 16C Renaissance palace. The walls and another isolated tower which was originally part of the walled defensive system can also be seen from the castle.

Cueva de los Murciélagos ⊘ – *4km/2.5mi from Zuheros along a signposted road heading out of the village.* The road leading up to the cave offers more delightful **views**★★. The cave is a superb natural rock formation with several chambers of impressive stalactites and stalagmites. It contains important archeological remains from the Neolithic period, including drawings, engravings, an

interesting burial chamber and myriad work tools, ornaments and pieces of ceramic. The discoveries unearthed here date from between 4300 BC and 3980 BC.

Luque – *5km/3mi from Zuheros along the CO 240*. The village is crowned by a fortress of Moorish origin which has since been restored and modified.
Leave your car in the main square.

The **Parroquia de la Asunción**, a 16C Renaissance-style parish church attributed to Hernán Ruiz II and Hernán Ruiz III has an elegant tower and belfry adorned with columns and a conical roof covered with spherical decorative elements. The chancel houses an 18C Baroque retable dominated by an Assumption.

The remains of the **castle** are visible on a rocky crag behind the town hall. A staircase leading to the base of its walls offers an attractive panorama of Luque and its surrounding area.

BAEZA★★

Jaén – Population 17 691
Michelin map 446 S 19

The town of Baeza stands in a pleasant setting at the centre of Jaén province, a few kilometres to the north of the Guadalquivir River. The gently rolling hills on which it is built – known as La Loma – are surrounded by fields of cereals and olive trees. It was this delightful scenery which was immortalised by the poet Antonio Machado, who wrote: "Oh land of Baeza, I shall dream of you when I cannot see you". This monumental, yet peaceful, town with its rich historical past is nowadays an important economic and commercial centre. The best time to visit Baeza is during **Holy Week** or **Corpus Christi**, when solemn processions are held in the town. The local gastronomy, with its understandable bias towards olive oil, is well worth trying: look out for the *bacalao al estilo de Baeza* (a cod-based dish), *cocido mareado* (a bean stew with garlic, onions and tomatoes), and the typical *ochíos*, made from a dough of bread and oil and sprinkled with paprika.

Historical notes – The origins of Baeza date back to the Bronze Age, although it was under the Romans that it developed into a large settlement known as *Biatia*. During the period of Visigothic domination in the 7C the town was an episcopal see, and later became the capital of a *taifa* kingdom whose area of control stretched from the Guadalquivir to the Sierra Morena mountains; during this period it developed into an important commercial and political centre. Following its reconquest by Fernando III the Saint in 1227, Baeza played a major role in the christianisation of al-Andalus, leading to its nickname of the "royal nest of hawks". Between the 16C and 17C, the town enjoyed its period of greatest splendour, resulting in the construction of handsome Renaissance buildings which now form its historical centre, and the establishment of the prestigious university – an active hub of cultural activity – which was disbanded in the 19C. During the course of these two centuries, numerous intellectuals, architects and poets took up residence in Baeza, including Andrés de Vandelvira and, in particular, St John of the Cross, who completed his celebrated **Spiritual Canticle** here. Between 1912 and 1919, the writer and poet Antonio Machado taught French at the new university, following the death of his wife, Leonor, in Soria.

★★★ ARCHITECTURAL CENTRE *half a day. Route marked on town plan.*

★**Plaza del Pópulo** – Standing in the centre of this small, irregular square is the **Fuente de los Leones** (Fountain of the Lions), one of Baeza's most popular sights. It was built using remains from the ruins of nearby Cástulo and has a statue at its centre which is said to represent Imilce, the wife of Hannibal. The square is fronted by the former abattoir *(carnicería)* and the Casa del Pópulo, the old court building. The **Arco de Villalar**, an arch erected to commemorate Carlos V's victory over the *comuneros* in 1521, stands to one side. Alongside it can be seen another major monument, the **Puerta de Jaén**, which projects onto the Casa del Pópulo via an attractive quarter-circle balcony; this gateway was built to mark the emperor's visit here on his way to Sevilla for his marriage to Isabel of Portugal. It was here that the first Christian mass took place after the reconquest of Baeza.

Former abattoir (Antigua carnicería) – This 16C Renaissance building has an elegant, seigniorial appearance. The façade on the upper level, the seat of the former Tribunal de Justicia, bears a large escutcheon of Carlos V.

WHERE TO STAY

MODERATE

El Patio – *Conde de Romanones, 13 –* ☎ *953 74 02 00 – 14 rooms – 4 000pts.* A somewhat dark and antiquated *hostal*, but with a redeeming patio – as the name suggests – and clean rooms. Suitable for those on a limited budget.

MID-RANGE

Hospedería Fuentenueva – *Paseo Arca del Agua –* ☎ *953 74 31 00 – fax 953 74 32 00 – 12 rooms – 9 100pts.* The former women's prison has been converted into a small hotel with modern rooms located slightly away from the centre on the Úbeda road.

Santa Ana – *Vieja, 9 –* ☎ *953 74 07 65 – fax 953 74 16 57 – 15 rooms – 10 000pts.* An attractive 16C mansion in the heart of the historical quarter. The Santa Ana has several patios, a dining room and rooms furnished in traditional style.

EATING OUT

Vandelvira – *San Francisco, 14 –* ☎ *953 74 81 72 – closed Mon.* An elegant restaurant occupying part of the 16C Monasterio de San Francisco. The entrance is via the impressive cloister. The dining room on the first floor has a 2 100pts fixed menu as well as a selection of à la carte dishes.

BAEZA

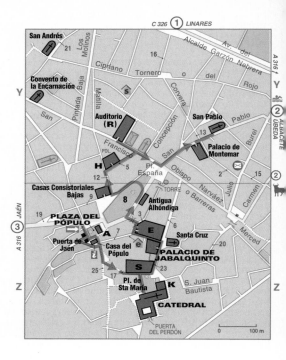

Casa del Pópulo – The former seat of the Caballeros Hijosdalgos de Baeza (Brotherhood of Noble Knights of Baeza) and the Audiencia Civil (Civil Tribunal) were located on the first floor of this building, which now houses the **Tourist Office**. The edifice has harmonious proportions and is decorated with refined detail. The façade, with its adornment of medallions and large windows, is fronted by six doors, each used by a separate clerk of the court in its day.

Plaza de Santa María – The square is dominated by a large **fountain** decorated with

Detail on the pulpit of Baeza Cathedral

caryatids and atlantes by Ginés Martínez. To one side stands the 17C **Seminario de San Felipe Neri**, whose sober façade still bears the inscriptions of students written, according to custom, in bull's blood to celebrate the successful completion of their studies, and, to the left, the **Casas Consistoriales Altas** or Casa Cabrera, emblasoned with the coats of arms of Juana the Mad and Philip the Fair between two attractive mullioned windows.

★**Cathedral** ⊘ – Fernando III ordered the cathedral's construction above the former mosque. In the mid-afternoon, its silhouette casts a dark, mysterious shadow over the narrow cobbled streets behind it.

Exterior – The main façade, Renaissance in style, contrasts with the west side, which has preserved older features such as the 13C Gothic-Mudéjar Puerta de la Luna (Moon Doorway), and the large 14C Gothic rose window. The south wall is broken by the 15C Puerta del Perdón (Pardon Doorway).

★★**Interior** – The exceptional interior, in which the severity of Castilian architecture combines harmoniously with lighter, more graceful Andalucian features, was rebuilt in the 16C according to plans by Andrés de

Vandelvira, who crowned the three aisles with oven vaults. Some of the chapels are outstanding: the Capilla Dorada (Gold Chapel) beside the fonts has a delicate Italianate relief; the Capilla de Santiago (St James's Chapel) on the left side has a fine antique setting; while the Capilla de San José is flanked by caryatids. The fine **Capilla del Sagrario** (Sacrarium Chapel) at the end of the north aisle is particularly interesting with its Baroque silver **monstrance** which is carried in procession on the feast of Corpus Christi. Note also the Plateresque door to the sacristy, with its delicate reliefs, the polychrome beaten metal **pulpit** (1580) in the transept, the Baroque retable at the high altar, and the monumental iron **grille** by Maestro Bartolomé which closes the first bay in the nave. Four Mudéjar chapels adorned with decorative plant motifs *(atauriques)* and Arabic inscriptions have been preserved in the cloisters.

★**Palacio de Jabalquinto** ⊘ – The former residence of Juan Alfonso de Benavides, known as the Capitán de Lorca, is a perfect example of Flamboyant Gothic architecture. Its exceptional **façade★★**, attributed to Juan Guas and Enrique Egas, is a marvel of design which is best seen in the late afternoon when the shadows accentuate its delightful tones. It illustrates the predilection of the nobility at the time for profuse ornamental features, such as projecting pinnacles, stone fleurons, elaborate escutcheons etc. The interior contains a spacious Renaissance patio with marble Corinthian columns and a monumental Baroque staircase.

Façade, Palacio de Jabalquinto

Iglesia de Santa Cruz ⊘ – This small Romanesque church has a Gothic chapel and wall paintings adorning the apse.

Former university (Antigua universidad) ⊘ – To reach the site of the former university, pass through the Arco del Barbudo which, along with the Puerta de Jaén, is the only vestige of the former walls. Founded in the 16C by Rodrigo López and Juan de Ávila, the university was disbanded in 1875 and became a secondary school. Hidden behind the façade, adorned with a medallion of the Holy Trinity, is a handsome Renaissance-style inner **patio**, where Antonio Machado wrote some of his more melancholic poetry.

Plaza del Mercado Viejo or Plaza de la Constitución – The square, the hub of town life, is surrounded by the old corn exchange (*alhóndiga* or *pósito*) and the Casas Consistoriales Bajas, a former civic building. A number of traditional bars and cafés stand side-by-side beneath its arcades.

Former Corn Exchange (Antigua Alhóndiga) – This three-storey building was used as a centre for selling and purchasing grain during the 16C.

Casas Consistoriales Bajas – The members of the town council would sit on the elegant balcony on the façade of this 18C Baroque building to watch bullfights and other celebrations in the square below.

★**Town Hall** – The town hall is housed in a building which formerly existed as the town's law courts and prison. It is Plateresque in style with two floors separated by a wide cornice. The armorial bearings of Felipe II and the magistrate Juan de Borja can be seen between the four balconies on the façade.

Ruins of the Convento de San Francisco – Although this Renaissance convent has suffered extensive damage caused by natural disasters and pillage, in its day it was considered one of Vandelvira's major works. The monumental nature of the transept and apse, its unequal fasciated columns and the majestic carved stone altarpieces remain to give an idea of the beautiful 16C church that once stood here. It is now used as an **auditorium**.

Palacio de Montemar (or Palacio de los Condes de Garcíez) – The main architectural features of this 16C nobleman's palace are its large Gothic windows and a Plateresque inner patio with double arcading.

109

> **The patios of Baeza**
>
> Baeza is a monument in itself, offering surprise after surprise to visitors in the form of elegant palaces, monumental churches, enchanting nooks and crannies and exquisite architectural detail. However, the town's patios – havens of peace and quiet hidden behind the attractive wrought-iron grilles of some of the town's most delightful buildings – are an essential part of any visit here. Every season highlights a different aspect of them: a blaze of colour in spring; an oasis of cool in the heat of summer; the brightness in which they are bathed in the clear light of autumn; and their dazzling architecture, best seen in winter.

Iglesia de San Pablo – The Renaissance façade of this church conceals an interior consisting of three wide aisles supporting Gothic pillars. It has several painted panels and a statue of *Christ of the Expiration*.

ADDITIONAL SIGHTS

Iglesia de San Andrés – Following the Reconquest, Fernando III created in the church the Company of the Two Hundred Crossbowmen of St James, a military institution comprised of noblemen from Baeza who showed allegiance only to the king and who were not permitted to live more than six leagues from the town. The exterior of the building is adorned with a Plateresque doorway; inside, note the **sacristy** ⊙, with its interesting collection of nine **Gothic wood tablets★**, the colours of which bear witness to the technical expertise acquired by Andalucian artists of the time.

Convento de la Encarnación – This convent, built in the transitional Renaissance-Baroque style, is still occupied by discalced Carmelite nuns. It is famous as the place where St John of the Cross completed his *Spiritual Canticle*.

BAZA

Granada – Population 20 113
Michelin map 446 T 21

Baza's origins date back to the 4C BC when native Iberians established the settlement of Basti 2km/1.2mi outside the town. It was here that excavations unearthed the famous **Lady of Baza** (Dama de Baza), a seated sculpture of an Iberian goddess. Following their invasion of the Iberian peninsula, the Moors founded the city of Madinat Bastha on the present-day site; sadly, just a few Arab baths have been preserved from this period of occupation (713-1489). With the expulsion of the *moriscos* at the end of the 16C, the city entered a period of decline. Nowadays, Baza is suffering the consequences of a decline in industry in the area.

Plaza Mayor

SIGHTS

★Colegiata de Santa María de la Encarnación – This sober, fortress-like collegiate church, built on the site of the former main mosque, is sheltered behind an unusual wall of buttresses. The church has a perfect hall-church ground plan with three aisles of equal height and no transept.

The **Plaza Mayor** is fronted by the former town hall, a Renaissance building that now houses the **Museo Municipal** ⊙, which has on display a reproduction of the Dama de Baza, the original of which can be admired in the Museo Arqueológico in Madrid.

B. Kaufmann/MICHELIN

Leave the Plaza Mayor through the Arco de la Magdalena arch on the side of the 18C bell-tower, then follow calle Zapatería to the left to what was once the 'morisco' quarter of Baza.

The narrow alleyways of this *morisco* district are lined by several buildings of interest: the Mudéjar **Iglesia de San Juan Bautista**; the **Convento de la Merced**, housing the *Virgin of Piety*; and a house with an attractive 17C balcony typical of the period.

Return to the Arco de la Magdalena and head down calle Zapatería.

To the left, note the former abattoirs *(antiguas carnicerías)*, dating from 1568.

Continue as far as plaza de Santo Domingo.

The square is dominated by the **Convento de Santo Domingo**, nowadays in a state of poor repair. The better-preserved 17C cloister is concealed on the inside of an early-20C building which once served as a theatre.

Follow calle Dolores.

The façade of the 17C-18C **Iglesia de los Dolores** has an unusual Baroque portal framed between two sturdy Solomonic columns.

Continue along calle Dolores, then bear left onto calle del Agua as far as calle Caniles.

Cascamorras

The origin of this strange *fiesta* dates back to the 15C when, according to legend, an inhabitant of Guadix who was working in an old mozarabic chapel near Baza discovered a fine statue of the Virgin Mary. However, the problem soon arose as to which town would keep the statue. The dispute was settled by the courts, who decided that the Virgin Mary would remain in Baza, but with the proviso that a fiesta in her honour would take place once a year in Guadix. Unfortunately, when the time came for the residents of Guadix – headed by their leader, a figure known as Cascamorras – to assert their rights and reclaim the Virgin Mary, they were chased out of Baza by locals brandishing sticks. Upon their return to Guadix, they were to receive further physical punishment from townspeople angry at their failure. Nowadays, on **6 September** every year, a resident of Guadix dressed in multi-coloured attire plays the part of Cascamorras, and attempts to reach the **Iglesia de la Merced** to steal the image. During the course of his journey, he is jostled and provoked by the inhabitants of both towns in the enactment of this tradition.

★**Moorish baths (Baños árabes)** ⊘ – *In calle Caniles in the Santiago quarter.* These simple baths are situated in the old Jewish quarter, next to the Iglesia de Santiago. They date from the Caliphal period (10C) and are some of the oldest to be found anywhere in Europe. The main room is divided by horseshoe arches supported by slender marble columns. The early vaults, through which light entered via star-shaped openings, have not been preserved. The complex is completed by two rectangular rooms which were probably used as a changing room and a calidarium.

EXCURSION

Parque Natural de Sierra de Baza – *15km/9.5mi towards Guadix along the A 92. Follow the signposts to the park. From the A 92 junction, continue for a further 5km/3mi to the* **Visitor Centre** ⊘ *in Narváez.*
Despite its limited infrastructure, this recently created park is still able to offer a range of interesting walks for hikers. The Sierra de Baza is surprisingly mountainous, with several peaks above 2 000m/6 560ft. The most common trees found here are oak and pine, including the occasional area of wild pine, while typical fauna includes various species of birds of prey.

BELALCÁZAR

Córdoba – Population 3 879
Michelin map 446 Q 14

This small town on the northern fringes of Córdoba province changed its name in the 15C from Gaete to Belalcázar, which derives from Bello Alcázar – a reference to its impressive fortress *(alcázar)*. The town has connections with the Sotomayor family, the rulers of the county of Belalcázar, which was the birthplace of the illustrious *conquistador* **Sebastián de Belalcázar**, who founded the city of Quito, in Ecuador, and also conquered Nicaragua.

Leave your car in plaza de la Constitución.

Iglesia Parroquial de Santiago ⊘ – The parish church of St James stands at one end of the square. Built in the 16C and 17C, its façade dates from its latter period of construction. An incomplete bell-tower rises above the centre of the church. This granite building is striking in its austerity, a sensation enhanced by the sturdy

> ### "La Chiquinina" romería
>
> The *romería* of Nuestra Señora de Gracia de la Alcantarilla, the patron saint of Belalcázar, nicknamed *La Chiquinina*, is held on the last weekend in April. On the Saturday morning, participants head to a chapel 20km/12mi from the town, returning with the image of the saint before sunrise on the Sunday. Were they to fail in this endeavour, the statue of the Virgin Mary would become the property of the town of Monterrubio de la Serena, in the province of Badajoz.

buttresses supporting the sides of the church, giving it a fortress-like appearance. The **interior** has been designed as a church to be used for preaching, with its single nave and side chapels nestling between the buttresses. The east end is of recent construction, following the destruction of the original apsidal end during the Spanish Civil War. The roof visible today was added after the collapse of the previous, higher construction; sadly, this addition breaks the architectural proportions and balance by constraining the windows of the church. Despite this, the interior has retained some of its attraction with its carefully hewn and decorated stone used on arches at the entrance to several chapels.

Town Hall – This 19C granite building dominates Belalcázar's attractive main square. A pediment with a clock adorning the tympanum is a feature of its central section.

Follow calle Sebastián de Belalcázar to the right of the church to reach the **Fuente del Pilar** *(1570), a fountain and water tank formerly used as a drinking trough. From here there is a superb view of the castle.*

★**Castle** – The dominant feature of Belalcázar's skyline is situated on a hillock to the north of the town. The castle was built during the second half of the 15C on what is thought to have been the site of a Roman fortress. It has a quadrangular layout with towers in the corners and in the centre of its walls. A line of modillions run along the uppermost part of the walls and towers.

The imposing keep is worthy of special note with its impressive proportions which dominate the scene. The upper section of the tower has several cylindrical look-out posts decorated with enormous escutcheons with chequered decoration representing the coat of arms of the Sotomayor family, the lords of the castle. These semi-cylindrical features rest on small Flamboyant Gothic ledges.

Belalcázar also has several seigniorial mansions such as the Casa Grande and the Casa de la Administración de los Osuna. A bridge on its outskirts was part of the old Roman road.

Convento de Santa Clara ⊙ – *0.8km/0.5mi towards Hinojosa del Duque, along a road signposted to the left.* Founded in 1476, this monastery was originally created for a community of monks but was subsequently converted into a nunnery in 1483, forcing the monks to found the nearby **Convento de San Francisco**, which is now in ruins. The building is late-Gothic in style and is one of the main convents in the province of Córdoba.

The east end of this single-nave church dominated by a *Christ of the Column* is covered by a star vault with frescoes on the bays between the ribs. The exterior has a segmented arch doorway. The three damaged sculptures above it representing Christ, Mary Magdalene and St Clare, are framed by a trefoiled arch.

> ### Local pastries
>
> Pastry-lovers should not miss out on a visit to the convent of the Poor Clares, where the nuns have developed something of a reputation for their sweet delicacies. Specialities include *flores de almendra* (literally, almond flowers) and *repelaos* (made with eggs and almonds and generally made to order). *Open from 9.30am to 1.30pm and 4.30pm to 6.30pm.*

A **school-workshop** now occupies several of the convent's outbuildings, enabling visitors to admire the work of apprentice masons, carpenters etc *(entrance to the left of the church)*. On the ground floor, the columned room adorned with longitudinal arches is of particular interest; on the upper floor, the rooms originally used as the nuns' dormitories with their original *artesonado* ceiling, and the infirmary with its unusual, deep ceiling in the shaped of an inverted ship's hull, are also worthy of note.

EXCURSION

Hinojosa del Duque – *8.5km/5mi south.* This small town in the Cordoban *sierra* is famous for its parish church *(parroquia)* of San Juan Bautista, the most important monument in the north of the province.

Follow directions to the Catedral de la Sierra.

★**Parroquia de San Juan Bautista** ⊙ – The church, which is more commonly known as the *Catedral de la Sierra*, was built in the 15C and 16C by the Cordoban architects

Hernán Ruiz I, Hernán Ruiz II and Juan de Ochoa.

The impressive **northeast façade★**, the main entrance, comprises a fine Renaissance portal adorned with Corinthian columns. The **sacristy**, to the right of the doorway, is crowned by magnificent **cresting** and three windows which combine to create an attractive ensemble decorated with armorial bearings, scallop shells, caissons etc. To the left of the portal, note the unusual **window** which, as a consequence of the columns and caissons, provides the scene with marked depth. Note also the **bell-tower** (1590), a popular nesting place for a family of storks.

On the **interior**, the stone used in the construction of the arches, pillars and ribbed vaulting contrasts with the whitewashed walls, thereby enhancing the building's architectural features. The central nave is crowned by a fine Mudéjar *artesonado* ceiling, the side aisles with pointed vaulting, and the chancel with a fresco-adorned star vault.

In the main square, to the right of the church's façade, the **Iglesia de la Virgen del Castillo**, a church which has been converted into an exhibition hall, can be seen framed by several houses.

Convento de las Madres Concepcionistas – This convent, which houses an enclosed order of nuns, was built in the 16C. The sober **south façade**, consisting of a series of sturdy buttresses between arches, is crowned by a graceful belfry popular with storks.

BUJALANCE

Córdoba – Population 8 204
Michelin map 446 S 16

This pleasant town in the Cordoban countryside is set in a landscape dominated by the ubiquitous olive. It has preserved much of its popular Andalucian architecture, characterised by a number of noble mansions, most of which were built in the 17C. The Moorish imprint is also visible here in the remains of the fortress *(alcazaba)* and in the name of the town itself: Bujalance derives from *Bury al-Hansh*, which translates as "the serpent's tower".

Follow signs to the town centre (centro ciudad) and park next to the Plaza Mayor.

Plaza Mayor – This sloping, triangular square, with its attractive orange trees, is overlooked by the tower of the Iglesia de la Asunción. The 17C **town hall**, with its heraldic decoration, encloses the upper part of the square, alongside a vaulted arch which leads to the Iglesia de la Asunción.

Iglesia de la Asunción – Entrance through the sacristy *(the first house on the left upon leaving the square through the arch)*. The Church of the Assumption dates from the 16C, although an earlier temple occupied this site. The ground plan is in keeping with the majority of Cordoban churches of the period: three aisles, no transept and a rectilinear apse with three rectangular chapels. The side aisles have retained their original wooden ceiling, unlike the nave which is topped by an 18C vault. The apsidal end has Gothic vaulting, with a star vault in the chancel with tierceron features to the sides.

Works of art in the church include the 16C carved and painted Renaissance altar-piece in the presbytery and the Baroque retable in the chapel on the right side of the apsidal end.

The outstanding feature of the exterior is the fine 18C Baroque **tower** which at 55m/180ft in height is the tallest in the province.

Alcazaba – *Entrance to the left of the main façade of the church*. Despite the fact that it is now in ruins, the towers and curtain wall which were part of the external defences of the former Moorish fortress are still visible. Built during the reign of Abd ar-Rahman III, it was modified after the Reconquest. The castle's seven towers form the basis for the town's coat of arms.

Iglesia de San Francisco – *From the Plaza Mayor, head down calle E Sotomayor to calle Ancha de Palomino*. The church is of new construction, with the exception of the portal and the fine Baroque tower. The earlier building, which was considered a jewel of Cordoban Baroque, was destroyed during the Spanish Civil War.

Ermita de Jesús – *On the outskirts of the town. Follow calle San Antonio to the left of the façade of the Iglesia de San Francisco*. The chapel is situated in the Parque de Jesús, on top of a promontory affording a pleasant view of the olive groves that extend to the horizon. The style corresponds to the 18C, although its origins are earlier. The Baroque portal is adorned with *estípites* and an abundance of minute decoration.

Parque Natural de CABO DE GATA–NÍJAR★★

Almería

Michelin map 446 V 23

The **Cabo de Gata–Níjar** park is a protected area of isolated landscapes and wild beaches to the south of the volcanic Sierra del Cabo de Gata, which runs southwest–northeast parallel to the coast. This extraordinary coastline consists of steep cliffs alternating with beautiful coves and beaches, where the arid landscape is broken only by the sight of prickly pears, agave and a few other species which are able to survive in an area with the lowest rainfall in Spain.

Scuba-diving

The tranquil, crystal-clear waters, pleasant temperatures and breathtaking underwater scenery of the Parque Natural de Cabo de Gata have resulted in the development of one of Europe's most important marine reserves and a paradise for scuba-divers. As a result of the area's natural characteristics (good visibility, a wealth of biological specimens, labyrinthine caves and basalt columns), underwater enthusiasts can choose from several locations: Cala San Pedro, Playazo de Rodalquivar, Cala del Embarcadero (in Los Escullos) etc.

Practical information – Underwater fishing is prohibited within the park. Authorisation is not required for scuba-diving; however, for those wishing to scuba-dive independently, permission should be sought from the Consejería de Medio Ambiente de la Junta de Andalucía. Divers are advised to contact the area's scuba-diving centres for further information.

NÍJAR

Outside the park, to the north.

This pretty town of Moorish origin sits on the fold of a hill on the southern slopes of the Sierra de Alhamilla. From the town, the views of the agricultural plain of **Campo de Níjar** below are particularly impressive. As a result of irrigation, this traditionally arid landscape has been transformed into a fertile area. With its typical whitewashed houses, narrow cobbled alleyways and charming street corners, Níjar is a fine example of popular Andalucian architecture.

B. Kaufmann/MICHELIN

Traditional rugs

Handicrafts – The town has managed to preserve its important tradition of arts and crafts. Its blue and green **pottery**, produced from clay and marl with a kaolin coating, is particular popular. However, perhaps its most typical handicraft is the manufacture of *jarapas*, colourful cotton and wool rugs and blankets.

Iglesia Parroquial ⊘ – The parish church, built in the 15C, is situated alongside the square. Felipe II's coat of arms – the twin-headed eagle – adorns the belltower. The interior, crowned by a wooden ceiling, also contains some fine *artesonado* work.

Watchtower (Torre-vigía) – Walk from the church square to the market square *(plaza del Mercado)*, with its 19C ceramic fountain and four, hundred-year-old elm trees, and then ascend a steep and stony path which rises between the houses *(the last few yards are somewhat difficult)*. The watchtower stands on top of the hill, dominating the town, and offers a commanding **view** encompassing the Níjar plain, with Cabo de Gata and the Mediterranean in the distance.

★★TOUR OF THE PARK

90km/56mi – allow one day.

From Níjar, take the E 15 towards Almería and exit at Km 467. Before reaching Retamar, follow a road heading southwest.

The landscape here is both flat and desert-like, with the sea to the right and the gentle undulations of the mountains in the distance.

Upon reaching a junction, bear right.

The seaside village of **San Miguel de Cabo de Gata** comes into view.

Salinas – The Cabo de Gata saltpans *(salinas)* extend for 4.5km/3mi parallel to the coast to the southeast of Salinas, occupying some 300ha/740 acres. This protected area is of great ecological interest, particularly for limicolous species, and attracts thousands of migratory birds. To make the most of a visit here, binoculars are highly recommended.

Cabo de Gata – The road winds its way up to the lighthouse *(faro)*, providing an opportunity to admire the crystal-clear water and unusual volcanic rock formations with names such as **The Finger** *(El Dedo)* and **Mermaids' Reef** *(Arrecife de las Sirenas)* rising up out of the sea. A viewpoint (Mirador de las Sirenas) and an information point adjoin the lighthouse.

Mermaids' Reef

Return to the junction and take the road to the right.

Centro de Visitantes Amoladeras ⊘ – The nearby visitor centre has an exhibition providing detailed information on the park and a bookshop.

The inland road passes a number of fields under plastic – a typical feature of the Almerian landscape. To the right is the **CEMA** (Michelin Tyre Experimentation Centre), where the company's new tyres are put to the test.

13km/8mi further on, take the turn-off to Los Escullos.

Los Escullos – *5km/3mi.* This small fishing port is situated alongside a delightful long beach with an 18C watchtower known as Calahiguera and a coastal battery from the same period at one end.

Las Salinas

WHERE TO STAY

Las Salinas de Cabo de Gata – *Las Salinas* – ☎ *950 37 01 03* – *fax 950 37 12 39* – *20 rooms* – *14 000pts.* The hotel is lost in a lunar landscape of rocks, sea and salt close to the ruins of a church and a saltpan.

San José

WHERE TO STAY

Puerto Genovés – *Arrastre* – ☎/*fax 950 38 03 20* – *18 rooms* – *5 000pts (8 000pts in Aug).* This small, family-run *pensión* just 200m from the sea has spotless modern rooms, albeit without a phone. Bar with billiards table.

San José – *Correo* – ☎ *950 38 01 16* – *fax 950 38 00 02* – *8 rooms* – *18 400pts (half board)* – *closed from mid-Oct to Mar.* A charming small hotel with rooms overlooking the sea. Half board is compulsory.

EATING OUT

There are a number of fish and seafood restaurants in the port of San José, including the **Mesón El Tempranillo**, offering an excellent *paella* for two.

The road to Rodalquilar passes the **Isleta del Moro** cove and the **Mirador de las Amatistas**, a viewpoint providing pleasant views of the coast, particularly Los Escullos and Isleta del Moro.

Rodalquilar – This mining settlement was abandoned in the 1960s. The old mining installations are still visible in the upper part of the village.

The dirt track leading to the **Playa del Playazo** skirts past several typical constructions: a chain pump, the 16C Rodalquilar or Las Alumbreras tower, and the 18C coastal battery of San Román.

Return to the Los Escullos junction and follow signs to San José. At nearby Pozo de los Frailes, an information point has been created for visitors.

Blood Wedding (Bodas de Sangre)

It was in 1928, at the Cortijo del Fraile, near Rodalquilar, that the tragic event occurred that was to inspire **Federico García Lorca** to write his famous play, *Blood Wedding*. The play recounts the tale of a young woman who fled with her cousin on the day of her wedding. Sadly, this course of action was to end in the assassination of her lover.

San José – The white-washed houses of this small seaside resort, set around an attractive beach, ascend upwards into the hills. Note the half-domed cupolas on some of the buildings – a typical feature of Almerian architecture designed to cool the temperature inside. The port is also home to a small marina.

Beaches – Two superb beaches, the Playa de los Genoveses and the Playa de Monsul, are located away from the centre on the edge of San José. Both are well-signposted at the entrance to the resort. The **Playa de los Genoveses★** lines a wide bay 2km/1.2mi from the centre to the left of a passable dirt track; the **Playa de Monsul★**, 2.5km/1.5mi from San José, is a stretch of fine sand nestled between two mountain spurs which descend to the sea. The large rock at its centre adds additional charm to the setting. A sand dune to the left and the Ensenada de la Media Luna (Half-Moon Cove) complete the scene.

CABRA

Córdoba – Population 20 057
Michelin map 446 T 16

The town, surrounded by a landscape of rolling hills carpeted with olive groves, appears as a swathe of white across the *sierra* of the same name. Its castle and parish church (Parroquia de la Asunción y Ángeles) stand on top of a rise above the town.

The Virgin of the Sierra – During the course of the year, several religious pilgrimages *(romerías)* are made to the Santuario de la Virgen de la Sierra, to venerate Cabra's patron saint. However, the town's most important fiesta is the Feria of Nuestra Señora de la Sierra *(3-8 September)* when the image of the Virgin Mary is brought down to the town.

PLAZA ALTA

From the plaza Vieja, a street winds its way past cypress and palm trees to an esplanade fronted by the Parroquia de la Asunción y Ángeles and the remains of the castle. On the way up, a close look at the stone benches and walls will reveal several fossils contained within them.

Parroquia de la Asunción y Ángeles – Cabra's main church was built above the former mosque; this probably explains the five aisles. The building visible today is the result of a series of modifications started in the apsidal end in the 17C and completed in the aisles in the 19C. On the exterior, the colourful brick tower and the marble Baroque side portal, adorned with *estípites* and Solomonic columns, stand out. The marble-like altarpieces, the stalls, and the cover of the baptismal font, a work by Benlliure, are the outstanding features of the interior.

The opposite side of the esplanade is enclosed by a section of wall topped with merlons.

Torre del Homenaje – The keep, along with the walls, belonged to the castle of the Counts of Cabra, a former Moorish fortress that was rebuilt after the Reconquest. Nowadays, the restored tower forms part of a school, the Colegio de las Madres Escolapias. For a closer look, walk into the patio of the school *(knock first at the gate)*. The inside contains an octagonal room with neo-Mudéjar decoration which was renovated in 1887.

Bizcotelas

For those with a sweet tooth, the boxes of iced cakes *(bizcotelas)* on sale at the Convento de las Madres Agustinas in plaza de San Agustín are a local speciality.

Barrio de la Villa – This quarter *(barrio)* spreads out behind the church, within the town walls. Calle Villa extends as far as a lookout garden encircled by the battlements.

ADDITIONAL SIGHTS

"El Cerro" Moorish quarter – *On the Cuesta de San Juan hill*. The narrow, cobbled streets of this *barrio* with their whitewashed houses and arches, including the **Puerta del Sol** (Sun Gate), wind their way up this hill, providing a reminder of Cabra's Moorish past.

Iglesia de Santo Domingo – The church belongs to a convent founded in the 15C. Despite later modification, the façade has retained two interesting Baroque marble portals, added in the 18C. The simple structure of the main doorway is adorned with balustered Solomonic columns.

Instituto Aguilar y Eslava – An image of the Immaculate Conception is the predominant feature of the elegant 17C red marble doorway adorned with heraldic decoration. The glass ceiling above the patio bears the escutcheon of the Counts of Cabra.

The 18C **Iglesia de la Virgen de la Soledad** opposite is fronted by a stone façade crowned by a belfry. The church interior has stucco decoration in both the cupola and the Virgin Mary chapel *(camarín)*.

> ### A native son
>
> The writer **Juan Velera** (1824-1905) was born into a noble family at no 13, calle Solís. This cultured, refined figure frequented Madrid high society and wrote a number of well-known novels, including *Pepita Jiménez* and *Juanita la Larga*.

Seigniorial mansions – A number of fine noble houses have been preserved in the centre of Cabra, particularly in calle Priego and calle José Solís.

Museo Arqueológico ⊙ – *Calle Martín Belda*. The archeological museum displays exhibits unearthed during excavations of the local area. This well-presented exhibition has been adapted for the visually impaired.

Parque Alcántara-Romero – Also known as the Paseo, this leafy rectangular park was laid out in the middle of the 19C and is an ideal place for a late-afternoon stroll or to escape the intense summer heat.

EXCURSIONS

★**Ermita de la Virgen de la Sierra** ⊙ – *Take the C 336 towards Priego de Córdoba. After 5km/3mi, bear left at a signposted junction.* The winding road climbs upwards for 7km/4.5mi through an arid and rocky landscape, where the major hazard comes from sheep wandering into the road. The sanctuary stands in a delightful **setting★**, at the highest point of the Sierra de Cabra (1 223m/4 011ft), affording expansive **views★★** of the Sierras Subbéticas and the Cordoban countryside. The mirador, to the left of the chapel, next to the communications antenna, has an orientation table. The chapel was rebuilt in the 16C, although its origins date back to the Middle Ages. The main feature is the rich 17C altarpiece and the *camarín* housing a sumptuously dressed image of the town's patron saint, the Virgin of the Sierra. The cloister was added in the 18C.

Parque Natural de las Sierras Subbéticas – The park extends across the municipalities of Cabra, Carcabuey, Doña Mencía, Zuheros, Luque, Priego de Córdoba, Iznájar and Rute.

Centro de Acogida Santa Rita – *At Km 57 along the A 340*. This reception centre, which is located at the Mojón Pass, provides visitors with information on paths, camping grounds and other aspects relating to the park.

The impressive mid-mountain scenery, with its precipitous drops and steep slopes, can be divided into three areas: the Cabra Massif *(macizo)*, the Carcabuey corridor *(pasillo)* and the Sierra de Rute and Sierra de la Horconera.

The Macizo de Cabra is a limestone massif which includes several naturally sculpted rocks – Lapiaz de Las Lanchas, Los Hoyones and La Nava (at the foot of the Ermita de la Virgen de la Sierra) – and the **Cueva de los Murciélagos** *(see p 106)*. In the Carcabuey corridor, home to most of the villages in the park, and in the Sierra de Rute and Sierra de la Horconera, olive groves predominate, but only up to a certain altitude. These two mountain ranges contain the park's most spectacular scenery, culminating in the Pico de La Tiñosa (1 570m/5 150ft).

CÁDIZ ★★

Cádiz – Population 143 129
Michelin map 446 W 11

Cádiz, a bastion ringed by the sea, is attached to the mainland by a narrow isthmus of sand. Its outstanding site and vast sheltered bay have attracted settlers for the past 3 000 years. The inhabitants of Cádiz, the *gaditanos*, are justifiably proud of this historical city which, although perhaps lacking major monuments, is one of Andalucia's most delightful and undiscovered treasures.

Historical notes – Legend suggests that Cádiz was the first city on the European continent. The city was colonised in 1100 BC by Phoenicians from Tyre who, for economic reasons and following unsuccessful incursions along the Granada and Málaga coasts, landed on a small islet surrounded by water on three sides, and founded the city of Gadir (meaning "fortress"). This first settlement extended from the castle of Santa Catalina to the island of Sancti Petri. For five centuries, Gadir was an important commercial centre, initially as a dependency of Tyre and later Carthage, until 206 BC when it came under Roman rule, during which time the renamed Gades developed into an important port for the exchange of goods between Baetica and Rome. After this period, little is known of the city's history and it would appear that the city was of no significant importance either under the Visigoths or the Moors. It was conquered in 1240 by Fernando III the Saint and permanently occupied in 1262 by his son, Alfonso X the Wise, who transformed the city into a port of relative economic and strategic importance. This resurgence involved the development of the Pópulo district which was surrounded by walls, from which time three of the four original gateways still remain (**Arco de los Blancos**, **Arco del Pópulo** and **Arco de la Rosa**). In the late 15C, following the discovery of America, Cádiz experimented with a process of urban expansion which initially resulted in the creation of the present-day district of Santa María. This boom period, fuelled by profitable overseas trade, was halted when the Earl of Essex sacked Cádiz in 1596, destroying much of the city in the process. During the 17C, Cádiz underwent considerable growth, as testified by the numerous examples of Baroque architecture still visible today. However, it was following the transfer of the Casa de Contratación (Exchange) from Sevilla to Cádiz in 1717 that the city enjoyed its finest period, when it became the port of entry for all trade crossing the Atlantic.

The city of the 1800s

The delightful city we see before us today would have been a disappointment for 18C travellers, as Cádiz was far from being the romantic city with an illustrious history that they had perhaps imagined. Nothing was visible of Gerion's mythical fortress, nor were there any vestiges of the period of Moorish occupation; all that was left was the occasional medieval remnant, and certainly nothing that could compare Cádiz with Europe's more glorious cities. Nowadays, however, the charm of Cádiz lies in its ordered 19C layout, its lofty, brightly coloured buildings, its long, straight streets and its myriad squares with their exotic vegetation and colonial air.

1 Around Santa María and the Pópulo district

This walk passes through two of the city's most typical gypsy quarters, where the traditions of flamenco, guitar and dance are part of everyday life. The Pópulo district occupies the early medieval section of the city, while Santa María developed in the 15C beyond the Arco de los Blancos. However, in spite of their unquestionable beauty, they remain the poorest and most run-down districts of Cádiz. Fortunately, a number of redevelopment and restoration projects have been undertaken in recent years on the houses – many of which date from the 17C – and streets in both areas.

Plaza de San Juan de Dios – This 16C square, formerly known as the plaza de la Corredera, is, along with plaza de San Antonio, the oldest in the city. Its strategic position, facing the port, resulted in its development as the hub of Cádiz life; for a long time the square was also the site of the city's market. On one side stands the neo-Classical façade of the **town hall** dating from 1799, a work by Torcuato Benjumeda; next to it, the Baroque tower of the **Iglesia de San Juan de Dios** can also be seen. The square is also home to the city's **Tourist Office** *(no 11)*, housed in an attractive neo-Classical building.
Take calle Sopranis, to the left of the Iglesia de San Juan de Dios.

Calle Sopranis – The street contains some of the best examples of Baroque civil architecture in Cádiz. The façades of nos 9-10 (known as the Houses of the Lilacs because of the decoration on the doorway) and the patio of nos 17-19, with its interesting staircase, are particularly worthy of note. At the end of the street, to the left, at the intersection with Calle Plocia, note the former **tobacco factory**. This iron and brick building, a superb example of 19C industrial architecture, is now home to the city's conference centre *(Palacio de Congresos)*. Opposite stands the **Convento de Santo Domingo**.

WHERE TO STAY

MODERATE

Fantoni – *Flamenco, 5 –* ☎ *956 28 27 04 – 17 rooms – 5 500pts.* Why spend a fortune when you can stay in this simple but pleasant *hostal*? The rooms with en-suite bathrooms are recommended as they overlook a pedestrianised alleyway. Several similar *pensiones* are dotted around this area.

MID-RANGE

Bahía – *Plocia, 5 –* ☎ *956 25 91 10 – fax 956 25 90 61 – 21 rooms – 8 100pts.* A small hotel with an excellent location in the historical centre. Clean, modern rooms. Good value for money.

Francia y París – *Plaza de San Francisco, 2 –* ☎ *956 21 23 18 – fax 956 22 24 31 – 57 rooms – 10 000pts.* An early-20C hotel with pleasant rooms fronting a pedestrianised square in the centre of the city. Facilities include an American bar.

Parador H. Atlántico – *Avenida Duque de Nájera, 9 –* ☎ *956 22 69 05 – fax 956 21 45 82 – 15 000pts.* This modern *parador* has an excellent location at one end of the Parque Genovés.

EATING OUT

El Faro de Cádiz – *San Félix, 15 –* ☎ *956 21 10 68.* A high-quality restaurant and tapas bar. Modern, wooden decor and refined cuisine. The owner's children manage two other restaurants, both known as El Faro: the first is on the San Fernando road; the second is in El Puerto de Santa María.

Terraza – *Plaza de la Catedral, 3 –* ☎ *956 28 26 05.* The Terraza specialises in fish and seafood at its central location on the pedestrianised cathedral square. An unpretentious restaurant with somewhat sober decor.

La Marea – *Paseo Marítimo, 1 –* ☎ *956 28 03 47.* Right on the beach, just a stone's throw from the Hotel Meliá. Unsurprisingly, given the location, fish and seafood (sold by the weight) top the menu.

TAPAS

Taberna Manteca – *Corralón de los Carros, 66 –* ☎ *956 21 36 03.* The faded posters on the walls are a reminder that the owner of this traditional-style bar is a former bullfighter. The Manteca is renowned for its good selection of chorizos, hams and sausages.

El Cañón – *Rosario, 49 –* ☎ *956 28 50 05.* A small, traditional bar dating back to the 19C with a counter selling cured hams and local wines. **La Manzanilla**, on the opposite pavement, is the ideal place to try the wines of the area.

Joselito – *San Francisco, 38 –* ☎ *956 25 45 57.* Despite somewhat lacking in charm, the Joselito is one of the city's best-known addresses, specialising in prawns and other types of seafood. The bar also has a small terrace on paseo de Canalejas.

Aurelio – *Zorrilla, 1 –* ☎ *956 22 10 31.* A popular tapas bar mainly serving fish and seafood. Because of its small size, it soon fills up.

CAFÉS, BARS & NIGHT-LIFE

During the winter, social life is concentrated around the **centre**, especially the streets and squares in the commercial section of Cádiz. During the summer months, the action transfers to the **Playa de la Victoria** and its **Paseo Marítimo**. In this beach area, many of the bars popular with a younger clientele are found in **calle General Muñoz Arenillas**. The **Punta de San Vicente** at the other end of the city is another popular meeting-place for young people.

Café Parisien – *Plaza de San Francisco, 1. Open daily, 9am to 11pm.* This old café on a quiet square is popular with people of all ages, who converge on the highly sought-after outside tables. The café also serves a selection of meals.

El Café de Levante – *Rosario. Open daily, 4pm to 3am.* A quiet café with tasteful modern decor on one of the old quarter's most typical streets. Its relaxed atmosphere attracts an eclectic crowd who come here to enjoy a quiet chat with friends. A variety of concerts are regularly held here on Thursday evenings.

La Mirilla – *Plaza Asdrúbal, 8-9. Open daily, 4pm to around midnight*. A good location overlooking the ocean for a quiet beer or a coffee from the extensive bar list.

O´Connells – *Calle Sagasta, close to the plaza de San Francisco. Open daily, 1pm to 3.30am*. This welcoming Irish pub is popular with local *gaditanos* and foreigners alike. A huge range of beers and whiskies, with meals available until the early hours.

Yogui – *General Muñoz Arenillas, 9. Open daily, 10pm to 4am*. This area, particularly favoured by young people in summer, is the setting for this attractively decorated bar which tends to attract a slightly older crowd. The beer list here offers a choice of 80 different brands. Karaoke on Thursdays and Sundays. At other times, the playlist concentrates on Spanish music from the 1980s and popular classics.

SHOPPING

The best shopping area in Cádiz is concentrated along a few streets in the old part of the city, where the long, narrow streets and squares, particularly **San Francisco**, **Columela**, **Compañía** and **Pelota**, in addition to **calle Ancha** and **plaza de San Antonio**, are crammed full of both traditional stores and more modern boutiques. Typical shops selling traditional cakes and pastries are a feature of this part of the town, such as **Horno Compañía** *(calle Compañía, 7)*, where local specialities such as *pan de Cádiz* can be purchased.

Markets – Arts and crafts markets are regular events in the city. To experience this facet of Cádiz, head to the Sunday market near the **Arco de Pópulo**, or the market which is popularly known as **El Piojito** (The Little Flea), which adds atmosphere to avenida de la Bahía on Monday mornings and where you can buy virtually anything.

O. Torres/MARCO POLO

Cádiz carnival

ENTERTAINMENT

Information – The town hall *(ayuntamiento)* publishes **Cádiz entre columnas**, a monthly guide with details of all cultural activities in the city. This free guide is available from cultural centres, tourist offices etc.
The city's cultural life is as active in winter as it is in summer. The **Gran Teatro Falla** *(plaza Falla)* organises a programme of theatre and concerts throughout the year (except in summer), while the city's five **cultural centres** (El Palillero, El Bidón, La Viña, La Lechera), host a wide range of exhibitions, workshops, etc, as well as flamenco concerts at the fifth venue, the **Baluarte de la Candelaria** *(alameda de Apodaca)*.

TRANSPORT

Airport – The airport at Jerez de la Frontera is just 30min away on the A 4. ☎ 956 15 00 00.

Trains – The railway station is located in plaza de Sevilla, near the centre and close to the port. Services operate to most major cities in Spain, including Sevilla, Madrid and Barcelona, with local trains to other towns in the province running every 30min or so. ☎ 956 25 43 01.

Inter-city buses – These depart from three bus depots:

– **Transportes Generales Comes** *(plaza de la Hispanidad, 1)* offer services throughout Cádiz province and to Sevilla. ☎ 956 21 17 63.

– **Transportes Los Amarillos** *(avenida de Ramón de Carranza, 31)* has frequent departures to destinations in the provinces of Sevilla and Málaga. ☎ 956 28 58 52.

– **Sevibus** *(plaza Elios, 1)* serves Sevilla and Madrid. ☎ 956 25 74 15.

Local buses – The main bus stops in the centre of Cádiz are in plaza de España and close to the port. A single-journey ticket costs 115pts, while a ten-trip ticket is on sale for 830pts. ☎ 956 28 38 04.

Taxis – ☎ 956 21 21 21; 956 21 21 22; 956 21 21 23.

Horse-drawn carriages – In summer, visitors can hire carriages in plaza de San Juan de Dios for a one-hour trip through the tourist section of the city. The cost of the excursions is approximately 4 000pts.

Follow calle Botica as far as calle Concepción Arenal.

★**Cárcel Real** – The royal jail was the first neo-Classical building to be constructed in the city and is one of the best examples of this style in the whole of Andalucia. It was built in 1792 by the local architect Torcuato Benjumeda. The centre of the single-section façade consists of an avant-corps, similar to a triumphal arch, with four large Tuscan-style engaged columns and two lions flanking the escutcheon of the Spanish monarchy. The interior, restored in 1990 for use as law courts, is set around one large central patio and two side ones.

Take calle Santa María to the church of the same name.

Iglesia de Santa María – This 17C church was part of the old Convento de Santa María and has given its name to the quarter in which it stands. Its façade can be seen at the end of the street of the same name. This Mannerist edifice is a work by Alonso de Vandelvira, the son of the famous Renaissance architect Andrés de Vandelvira *(see p 214)*, although the influence of Juan de Herrera can be detected. It is crowned by a belfry topped with an *azulejo*-adorned spire. On the inside of the church, note the dynamism of the Baroque altarpiece, as well as the **Delft ceramics** (Netherlands) covering the base of the Capilla del Nazareno.

The marble **Casa Lasquetty** in calle Santa María *(no 11)* is an example of early-18C civil Baroque architecture.

Cross calle Félix Soto to the 18C **Arco de los Blancos**, an arch formerly known as the Puerta de Tierra which leads into the working-class Pópulo district.

Pass through the arch and continue along calle Mesón Nuevo to plazuela de San Martín.

Casa del Almirante – This fine example of a Baroque palace was built by Admiral *(almirante)* Don Diego de Barrios at the end of the 17C. In keeping with many similar buildings of the period, the most important feature is the double-section Genoa marble **doorway**★★, with its combination of Tuscan and Solomonic columns on the lower and upper storeys respectively.

Turn left along calle Obispo José María Rancés to the small plaza de Fray Félix.

This, the religious heart of the city, is now occupied by the Iglesia de Santa Cruz on the site of the Moorish mosque.

Note the Baroque Casa de Estopiñán on plaza de Fray Félix *(no 1)*.

★**Iglesia de Santa Cruz** ⊘ – Known to *gaditanos* as the *catedral vieja*, this late-16C church was the city's second cathedral, built on the site of the first. The sober exterior is broken only by the glazed ceramics covering its umbrella cupolas. The finely proportioned interior consists of three aisles separated by robust Tuscan-style columns.

★**Casa de la Contaduría: Museo Catedralicio** ⊘ – This complex of four buildings has been superbly restored to house the cathedral museum, with a particularly fine 16C **Mudéjar patio**★. The museum has a variety of liturgical objects, vestments and documents on display, including a letter bearing the signature of St Teresa of Jesus.

121

Façade, Cádiz Cathedral

Among other objects of interest are the 16C **Custodia del Cogollo**★, a gold-plated silver monstrance attributed to Enrique Arfe, and the so-called 17C **Custodia del Millón**, the name of which derives from the number of precious stones it contains.

Teatro Romano ⊘ – The Roman theatre, located immediately behind the Iglesia de Santa Cruz, has managed to preserve much of its seating area and several underground galleries.

From plaza de Fray Félix head down the charming callejón de los Piratas to the plaza de la Catedral.

★★ **Cathedral** ⊘ – Cádiz Cathedral is quite unique. Its construction started in 1722, in a pure Baroque style, but due to a succession of problems was only completed in 1883. The brightness and movement of its lines are particularly evident in its façade, which consists of a series of both concave and convex features flanked by two towers crowned by pavilions which have the appearance of astronomical observatories. The large half-orange cupola above the transept, which appears to float high above the city when sea mist envelops Cádiz in winter, was completed in 1844. The interior, with its Latin cross ground plan and ambulatory, is surprisingly light and spacious.

> **Plaza San Juan de Dios**
>
> This square is popular with locals and visitors alike. Enjoy a break from sightseeing at two of the city's most popular cafés: the traditional-style **Novelty Café**, and **La Caleta**, with its boat-shaped counter.

The popular calle de la Pelota leads to plaza de San Juan de Dios.

② From Plaza San Juan de Dios to the Cathedral

Follow calle Nueva, then turn left onto calle Cristóbal Colón.

Casa de las Cadenas – This mansion was built in the late 17C in accordance with the Baroque style of the period. The marble **doorway**★ was made in Genoa. The building is very similar to the Casa del Almirante, but is distinguished from the latter by the pair of Solomonic columns framing the main entrance.

Continue along calle Cristóbal Colón, turn right onto calle Cobos then left along calle Nicaragua to plaza de la Candelaria.

Plaza de la Candelaria – The major features of interest around the square are the late-19C iron- and glass-fronted building at no 6, and the small Isabelline-style palace at no 15. Note to one side of the square the birthplace of the Spanish politician Emilio Castelar, whose bust adorns its centre.

From the square, continue along calle Santo Cristo as far as calle Nueva. Continue on foot to plaza de San Agustín.

Plaza de San Agustín – The Baroque church and an attractive neo-Classical **patio**, now part of a school, are all that remain of the Convento de San Agustín.

Take calle Rosario.

★**Oratorio de la Santa Cueva** ⊙ – This small neo-Classical jewel is a feast of decoration. The upper part, elliptical in design, consists of a cupola illuminated by lunettes and supported by Ionic columns. In 1795 Goya painted three **canvases★★**, which have been recently restored, to decorate this chapel.

Plaza de San Francisco – The **Iglesia de San Francisco** ⊙, with its simple façade on which the 18C tower is separated from the central section, stands to one side of this small square. Although originally created in the 16C, the interior was restored in the 18C in Baroque style with the addition of stucco and rocaille work. Beneath the pendentive-supported false ceiling, note the lamp-bearing angels, attributed to Pedro Roldán. On the corner of calle Sagasta and callejón del Tinte stands an **elegant building** with attractive windows. This Baroque edifice was subsequently modified in the 19C in Isabelline style. Continuing along callejón del Tinte, note the fine example of neo-Classical architecture at no 2, and the impressive, thousand-year-old dragon tree opposite.

★★**Plaza de Mina** – The 19C saw the creation of several squares on land expropriated from religious orders. One of these was the plaza de Mina, which was created in 1838 on the vegetable garden of the nearby Convento de San Francisco. Today, it is one of the city's most charming squares with its colonial feel, verdant appearance and fine examples of Isabelline-style architecture, particularly the houses at nos 11 and 16.

★**Museo de Cádiz** ⊙ – The city's museum is housed in a small neo-Classical palace with a sober façade built midway through the 19C. The clearly presented archeological displays are worthy of special note, in particular the section dedicated to the Phoenicians, including two **anthropoidal sarcophagi★★** in white marble dating from the 5C BC, which imitate Egyptian models and were almost certainly carved by Greek craftsmen; it should be noted that the realism of the face and hands was believed to be the best way of ensuring the immortality of the dead. In the fine arts section, the outstanding collection of nine **panels★** painted by Zurbarán between 1638 and 1639 for the sacrarium in the Cartuja monastery in Jerez is undoubtedly the star exhibit; note the artist's skill in his mastery of light and shade.

Plaza de San Antonio – This spacious square is one of the oldest in Cádiz. Despite its lack of ornamentation, it was a popular place of residence for the local bourgeoisie in the 1600s; even in the 19C it was still considered to be the city's main square. Over the centuries it has been used for events as diverse as bullfights and outdoor shows. The Baroque façade of the **Iglesia de San Antonio** can be seen on one side, while the rest of the square is fronted by elegant 19C buildings and, at no 15, the Casino de Cádiz, with its impressive neo-Mudéjar patio.

Continue along calle San José to plaza San Felipe Neri. Note the attractive example of Art Nouveau architecture at no 34 calle San José.

Oratorio de San Felipe Neri ⊙ – This Baroque oratory is one of the few examples in Andalucia of a church with an elliptical ground plan. It was built between 1688 and 1719, although the cupola was badly damaged in the Lisbon earthquake of 1755 and was restored in 1764. The interior has two levels: the main features of the lower level are the eight richly decorated chapels and a high altar with an altarpiece dominated by an unusual **Immaculate Conception** in which the Virgin Mary is dark-skinned – sadly the artist was killed in an accident while creating this work. The Tuscan-ordered upper level, in the form of a bullfighting tribune, supports a lightweight cane-framed cupola. The church has gone down in history as a place of liberalism, as it was here that the Cortes gathered in 1812 to proclaim a liberal constitution following the invasion of San Fernando by French troops.

Follow calle Santa Inés to calle Sagasta.

Iglesia de San Lorenzo – This sober Baroque-style church has a polygonal tower decorated with typical blue and white *azulejos*.

Return to calle del Hospital de Mujeres.

Cádiz in 1777

In 1777 Carlos III entrusted the military engineer Alfonso Ximénez and the ubiquitous Sabatini to produce a 1:250 scale **model★** of the city of Cádiz. This apparent royal whim was to result in a magnificent 25m²/82sq ft maquette made from mahogany, ebony and marble. Such was the precision of this superb work that even the smallest detail is represented on it. The majority of buildings standing today can be made out on the model, which also provides an insight into the development of several open spaces within the city, such as the plaza de Mina and the plaza de la Catedral. The model is one of the exhibits at the **Museo Iconográfico e Histórico de las Cortes y Sitio de Cádiz** ⊙ – *Calle Santa Inés, 9.*

CÁDIZ

★**Hospital de Mujeres** ⊘ – The Hospital for Women is one of the major Baroque buildings in Cádiz. In order to overcome the problem of space, the architect designed a narrow façade, but with significant expansion of the building behind it. It is laid out around two patios linked via an extraordinary Imperial-style **stairway**★★

Watchtowers

In cities such as Cádiz with its narrow streets and high buildings, the longing for height to provide additional natural light, space and views was a preoccupation for the majority of the population. During the 17C and 18C, the merchants of Cádiz built over 160 towers to watch over the arrival of their ships and, above all, to act as a symbol of their prosperity and prestige. Although their design varies, the tops of the towers were generally similar in appearance.

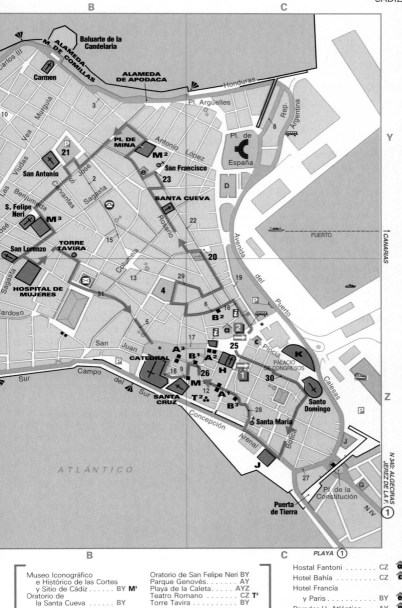

with a cane-framed vault above it. The 18C *Vía Crucis* created from Triana *azulejos* in the patio is particularly attractive. The church *(ask at the porter's lodge for access)* contains a painting of **St Francis** by El Greco.

★**Torre Tavira** ⊙ – The tower's position in the highest part of the city resulted in its designation as an official watchtower in 1778, from where the entry and departure of ships would have been controlled by a complex system of flags. The very first **camera obscura** in Spain, an ingenious device capturing real-time images of the city's movements, was installed in the tower in 1995.

Head down to plaza del Mercado. The plaza de las Flores is located behind the brick Correos (main post office).

Plaza de las Flores – The Square of the Flowers is also known locally as the plaza Topete. The numerous flower and plant stalls, cafés and shops contribute to the delightful atmosphere in one of the city's liveliest squares. A number of shopping streets, such as Calle Columela and Calle Compañía, branch off from here.

Mackerel

Summer is the season for this tasty blue fish, which is sold on the streets of the Barrio de la Viña. A good place to try mackerel is the simple bar on the **plaza del Tío de la Tiza**.

ADDITIONAL SIGHTS

Barrio de la Viña – This working-class district *(barrio)*, created in the early 18C away from the port area and shops in a part of the city exposed to the elements, is one of the most typical quarters of Cádiz. Today, it is renowned as the setting for the **Cádiz carnival★★**, without doubt the most colourful and lively in Spain, which takes place every February.

Iglesia de la Palma – Built at the beginning of the 18C, this circular Baroque-style church soon developed into the main church in this quarter. A number of tapas bars nearby serve excellent fish.

Playa de la Caleta – In former times this beach was the city's natural harbour; today it is the only beach in the old part of the city. At one end, on a small island connected to the city by a small causeway, is the **Castillo de San Sebastián**, a castle built in the 18C and still used for military purposes. Legend has it that this was the site of the temple of Kronos. In 1925, the recently refurbished **Balneario de la Palma**, a spa building, was built in the middle of the beach.

Castillo de Santa Catalina ⊘ – This castle is situated at the opposite end of Caleta beach. Built by Cristóbal de Rojas in 1598 following the sacking of Cádiz by the Earl of Essex, this military fortification has an unusual star shape. It is currently under restoration.

★**Parque Genovés** – The park was formerly known as the paseo del Perejil. Nowadays, it is the city's main area of greenery and a delightful setting for a quiet stroll. The former barracks of Carlos III opposite have been converted into the main building for the University of Cádiz.

Belfry, Iglesia del Carmen

Baluarte de la Candelaria – Built in the 17C, this bulwark *(baluarte)* formed part of the defensive wall which enclosed and protected Cádiz on three sides and was initially constructed as a platform for cannons. In the 19C, it underwent significant restoration, particularly its inner façade, resulting in its present-day neo-Classical appearance.

Iglesia del Carmen – This is the most Latin American of the city's churches and provides clear evidence of the reciprocal influences which existed between Spain and its colonies. Built in the mid 18C, the main interest is centred on its **Baroque façade★**. The sober marble doorway is brought to life by the two exuberant belfries decorated with volutes and *estípites*.

EXCURSIONS

San Fernando – *9km/5.5mi southeast along the N IV*. For centuries, San Fernando and Cádiz have always enjoyed close ties. San Fernando began to develop importance as a military and commercial outpost in the 18C, at the same time as Cádiz was enjoying its period of greatest splendour. In 1766 Carlos III transferred the headquarters of the Navy here, since which time the city has been indelibly linked with the Spanish armed forces. Between 1810 and 1811, Spanish members of parliament convened here to promulgate the first Spanish constitution; in recognition of its resistance to the French during the Peninsular War, Fernando VII conferred the title of **San Fernando** upon the city.

San Fernando is centred around the calle Real, the home of the town hall, the **Iglesia del Carmen** and the **Museo Histórico Municipal** ⊘. The neo-Classical **Iglesia Mayor**, dedicated to St Peter and St Paul, and the Teatro de las Cortes, where members of the Spanish parliament sat in 1811, can be seen in the nearby plaza de la Iglesia.

The city's most important civil building is the **Observatorio Astronómico de la Marina**, a naval observatory built in neo-Classical style in 1753 by Jorge Juan. This observatory was the predecessor of the observatory in Madrid.

A Roman bridge, the **Puente de Suazo**, is visible upon leaving San Fernando. Until recently, the bridge was the only link between San Fernando and the rest of Spain.

Chiclana de la Frontera – *25km/15.5mi southeast along the N IV*. Despite being surrounded by saltpans and agricultural land, Chiclana is home to one of Andalucia's best beaches, the delightful **Playa de la Barrosa★★**, an 8km/5mi stretch of fine sand just 7km/4.5mi from Chiclana. The beach has a number of hotels and some excellent leisure facilities, particularly in **Sancti Petri** and **Novo Sancti Petri**. Chiclana's attractive main square *(plaza mayor)* is dominated by the imposing neo-Classical **Iglesia de San Juan Bautista**, a work by Torcuato Cayón.

CARMONA★★
Sevilla – Population 25 326
Michelin map 446 T 13

Carmona, one of Andalucia's oldest towns, stands proudly on a hill overlooking an expansive and fertile plain irrigated by the Corbones River. It was initially founded by the Carthaginians, and later developed into an important municipality which played an active political role during the period of Roman occupation. This role continued under the Moors, and later, following its reconquest, under the Christians. Vestiges of Carmona's past are clearly visible in its old quarter *(casco antiguo)*, an area of monumental buildings, including elegant palaces, seigniorial houses and solemn places of worship.

The town's **Carnival** is renowned throughout the province, as is its famous **Holy Week**, an opportunity to admire the sumptuous processions that wind their way through the tranquil narrow streets of the old quarter.

WHERE TO STAY

MODERATE

Pensión Comercio – *Torre del Oro, 30 – ☎ 954 14 00 18 – 13 rooms – 5 000pts*. The same family has run this small *pensión* dating from the 16C for the past four generations. An attractive patio, and basic but clean rooms.

MID-RANGE

Parador de Turismo de Carmona – *In the Alcázar – ☎ 954 14 10 10 – fax 954 14 17 12 – 63 rooms – 18 500pts*. This magnificent *parador*, with its superb views of the fertile Corbones plain, is housed in the former residence of the Catholic Monarchs. Even if you don't get the chance to stay here, try and eat in the restaurant, one of the most attractively decorated of the entire Spanish *parador* network. Specialities include Carmona spinach *(espinaca)* and partridge *(perdiz)*.

LUXURY

Casa de Carmona – *Plaza de Lasso, 1 – ☎ 954 19 10 00 – fax 954 19 01 89 – 29 rooms – 23 000pts*. A charming 16C palace located in the old part of Carmona. Large aristocratic lounges, a patio, fountain and Moorish garden. The building formerly belonged to Lasso de la Vega, the governor of Chile.

EATING OUT

La Almazara – *Santa Ana, 33 – ☎ 954 19 00 76*. This bar is housed in an old oil mill. Stylish decor, with its vaults and a wooden ceiling. Local spinach, partridge and suckling pig *(cochinillo)* all feature prominently on the menu.

Puerta de Sevilla

★OLD QUARTER *allow half a day*

Leave your car in the lower part of town, near the Puerta de Sevilla.

Walls – The double Moorish-arched **Puerta de Sevilla★** is one of the few remains from the old lower fortress *(alcázar de abajo)*, which served as an entrance to the old quarter. Vestiges of the impressive walls built by the Carthaginians and strengthened by the Romans can also be seen dotted around this district. One of the most impressive features of the old town is the **Puerta de Córdoba★**, where two superb octagonal towers of Roman origin and a gateway added in the 17C can be admired.

★**Iglesia de San Pedro** ⊘ – The Church of St Peter stands along the paseo del Estatuto. This 15C building, which was heavily restored during the Baroque period, has a fine **bell-tower★**, similar to the Giralda in Sevilla, from which it has taken the name of "Giraldilla". The most interesting features inside the church are the **Capilla del Sagrario**, the sacrarium chapel with its rich decorative detail, and an extraordinary 16C green ceramic **baptismal font**.

Convento de la Concepción ⊘ – The convent contains a charming **cloisters** and a Mudéjar-style church.

Walk through the Puerta de Sevilla.

Iglesia de San Bartolomé – This church of Gothic origin, rebuilt in the 17C and 18C, has a basilical ground plan and a graceful neo-Classical tower. The interior contains an interesting chapel covered with Renaissance *azulejos* to the left of the high altar.

★**Iglesia de San Felipe** – A fine example of 14C Mudéjar architecture with its handsome tower, interior *artesonado* work bearing the coat of arms of the Hurtado de Mendoza family, and a chancel adorned with colourful 16C *azulejos*.

Plaza Mayor or Plaza de San Fernando – This attractive square is fronted by elegant Mudéjar and Renaissance mansions.

Town Hall ⊘ – The interesting Baroque *ayuntamiento* in the heart of the old quarter has preserved a peaceful inner patio and an attractive Roman **mosaic**.

Iglesia del Salvador ⊘ – The handsome plaza de Cristo Rey is fronted by this large Baroque building with a Latin cross ground plan constructed between the 17C and 19C on top of the remains of an earlier church. Note the impressive Churrigueresque **altarpiece** and the interesting collection of paintings, retables and religious gold and silverware from the 17C and 18C.

★**Iglesia de Santa María la Mayor** ⊘ – This large 15C Gothic church was built on the site of the former mosque in the lively calle San Ildefonso. Despite its restoration in Renaissance and Baroque style, the Patio de los Naranjos (Orange Tree Patio), which was part of the original Moorish building, and some beautiful horseshoe arches have been preserved. The 6C **Visigothic calendar**, on the shaft of one of the columns, is particularly interesting.

The triple-nave interior is dominated by a monumental **Plateresque altarpiece★** depicting exquisitely sculpted scenes of the Passion. The side chapels also contain magnificent retables – such as the Christ of the Martyrs – visible behind 16C **Plateresque grilles** designed according to a precise iconographic plan. The sacristy houses a valuable collection of gold and silverwork, including a Renaissance-style processional monstrance, a work by Alfaro.

> ### Carmona's pastries
>
> No visit to Carmona is complete without buying some of the delicious pastries produced by the town's numerous convents. Local specialities here include the sponge-like *bizcochos marroquíes*, the honeyed doughnuts known as *roscos almibarados*, a range of tarts *(tortas)* and *bollos de aceite*, literally "olive oil buns".

★**Convento de las Descalzas** – This magnificent example of 18C Sevillian Baroque has a Latin cross ground plan, a tower with a double campanile and *azulejo* decoration.

Convento de Santa Clara ⓥ – The Convent of St Clare was founded in the middle of the 15C. It is embellished by two pleasant cloisters and an attractive Mudéjar church with several canvases by Valdés Leal, as well as a fine collection of female portraits in the style of Zurbarán.

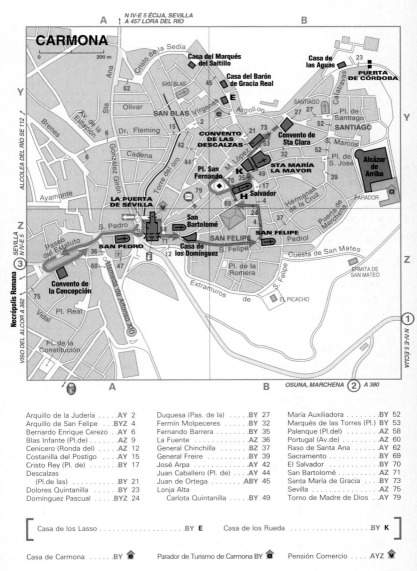

Seigniorial mansions – A number of 17C and 18C noble residences are dotted around the town's squares. Of these, the most attractive are the Casa de los **Rueda**, Casa de los **Domínguez**, Casa del **Barón de Gracia Real**, Casa del **Marqués del Saltillo**, Casa de los **Lasso** and the Casa de las **Aguas**. These elegant mansions add a refined air to Carmona and provide an interesting contrast with the older buildings in the heart of the old quarter.

ADDITIONAL SIGHTS

Upper fortress – This old Roman fortress *(alcázar de arriba)* offers superb **views**★ of the countryside around Carmona. It was extended by the Almoravids, and later converted into the palace of Pedro I. Only a few sections of wall, the odd tower and the parade ground, where a **parador** now stands, have been preserved from the original building and enclosure.

★**Roman necropolis** ⊘ – *At the end of calle Jorge Bonsor. Access is indicated on the road to Sevilla*. This impressive archeological site, one of the most important in Andalucia, dates from the 1C AD. Over 300 tombs, mausoleums and cremation kilns have been discovered here, most of which are contained within vaulted funerary chambers with niches for the urns. The most interesting are the **Tumba del Elefante** (so-called on account of the statue of an elephant) with three dining rooms and a kitchen; the **Tumba de Servilia**, which is the size of a patrician villa; the columbarium and a large circular mausoleum. Other discoveries found within the confines of the necropolis include an amphitheatre and a small museum displaying an interesting collection of items unearthed here.

EXCURSIONS

Viso del Alcor – *12km/8mi southwest along the A 392*. This town of Celtic origin is located at the highest point in the Sierra de los Alcores. Viso's major architectural feature is the **Iglesia de Santa María del Alcor**, a fine example of late-Mudéjar with three aisles with pointed vaulting and a sober Renaissance cupola in the presbytery. It houses a statue of Santa María del Alcor and an interesting collection of 17C paintings from the Venetian School. The 15C **Iglesia de la Merced** is also noteworthy for its unusual collection of 17C and 18C pictorial and sculpted altarpieces.

Mairena del Alcor – *16km/10mi southwest along the A 392*. Mairena del Alcor is a peaceful small town of whitewashed houses nestled on a small plain and protected by the remains of a Moorish fortress, of which only the the odd tower and an access gateway remain. The town's main attraction is the excessively restored, Mudéjar-style **Iglesia de la Asunción**. The interior of the church contains a handsome 17C-18C **main altarpiece** and several Baroque canvases hanging in the sacristy.

Alcolea del Río – *17km/10.5mi north. Take the SE 112 towards Guadajoz then bear onto the SE 129*. Situated on the banks of the Guadalquivir, between the Sierra Morena and the flat landscapes of the Sevillian countryside, Alcolea has two windmills, the Molino de la Aceña and the Molino de la Peña de la Sal, which bear witness to the town's past reliance on the river as a source of income. Alcolea has two churches of note: the Iglesia del Cristo, an 18C Baroque building; and the **Iglesia de San Juan Bautista**, a fine example of 15C Mudéjar architecture housing the image of the Virgen del Consuelo (Virgin of Solace), the town's patron saint, where the famous flamenco singer La Niña de los Peines was baptised.

La CAROLINA

Jaén – Population 14 674

Michelin map 446 R 19

La Carolina is situated 10km/6mi to the south of the **Parque Natural de Despeñaperros**★ *(see p 171)*. It owes it name to the plan aimed at repopulating the Sierra Morena introduced by Carlos III in 1767, who made the town the capital of a group of settlements dispersed across the mountains. Its wide, perpendicular streets bear witness to the taste for order and regularity in the urban planning of the time. The mystical theologian and poet **St John of the Cross** lived in La Carolina for a period of time in the 16C, an event commemorated by the statue of him in plaza del General Moscardó.

Iglesia de la Inmaculada Concepción ⊘ – The church is built above the vestiges of the former Convento de La Peñuela, where St John of the Cross spent time while in La Carolina. Its simple portal leads to an amply proportioned interior containing a fine 15C image of the Virgen de los Dolores (Virgin of Pain) and a *Martyrdom of St Dominic*, a work from the Ribera School.

Palacio del Intendente Olavide – This palace belonged to Don Pablo de Olavide, who was responsible for the colonisation of the area. The monumental neo-Classical façade is adorned with a large royal coat of arms.

Jail – The old jail *(cárcel)* is a neo-Classical building in which General Rafael del Riego *(see Introduction)* was imprisoned before being sent to Madrid to be executed (1823).

CAZORLA★

Jaén – Population 8 527

Michelin map 446 S 20

Colonised by the Romans, who named it Carcesa, and later overrun by the Moors, Cazorla occupies an outstanding **site★** nestled below the Peña de los Halcones in the heart of the **Parque Natural Sierras de Cazorla, Segura y Las Villas★★★** *(see p 132)*. Its well-kept streets with their whitewashed houses and balconies replete with flowers are the perfect place for a quiet stroll, perhaps stopping en route to browse in one of the many craft shops or to enjoy a refreshing drink in one of the attractive squares dotted around the town. On summer evenings, Cazorla comes to life when visitors head for the town's tapas bars and outdoor terraces.

On the night of **14 May**, the date of the *romería* of San Isicio, the façades of Cazorla's houses are adorned with the typical *caracoladas*, snail shells filled with oil which are stuck onto walls with clay and lit up to form attractive geometric displays of light.

Castillo de la Yedra ⊘ – *Access by car via the street running parallel to the Cerezuelo River.* This old fortress of Roman origin stands at the highest point of Cazorla. It was subsequently modified by the Moors and then by the Christians in the 14C. The delightful **views** from the keep take in the town and the surrounding area. A chapel inside the castle contains a life-size Romanesque-Byzantine image of Christ, surrounded by 12 paintings representing the apostles.

Plaza de Santa María – This pleasant square at the heart of the old quarter has at its centre the monumental **Fuente de las Cadenas**, a Renaissance-style fountain. The ruins of the Iglesia de Santa María, a large church designed by Vandelvira and now used as an auditorium, stand to one side.

Town Hall – The town's *ayuntamiento* is housed in the former Convento de la Merced (Convent of Mercy). It is an impressive masonry and brick edifice with a large arcade on the ground floor and a graceful tower.

Iglesia de San Francisco – As the name suggests, the church was part of an old 17C Franciscan monastery. It contains a statue of the locally venerated Santísimo Cristo del Consuelo (Holy Christ of Solace).

WHERE TO STAY

MODERATE

Guadalquivir – *Calle Nueva, 6 – ☎/fax 953 72 02 68 – 16 rooms – 5 700pts.* The major advantage of this small hotel is its central location. All rooms have an en-suite bathroom, telephone and TV.

Molino La Fárraga – *150m from the ruins of Santa María, at the end of calle de la Torre on camino del Ángel – Apartado de Correos (P.O. Box), 1 – ☎/fax 953 72 12 49 – 8 rooms – 7 500pts.* In the outbuildings of an 18C olive oil mill, whose machinery can still be seen under the house. Basic rooms, a garden with a small stream and a swimming pool with views of the castle and mountains.

MID-RANGE

Villa Turística de Cazorla – *Ladera de San Isicio – ☎ 953 71 01 00 – fax 953 71 01 52 – 32 apartments – 10 500pts.* This complex facing the town of Cazorla has fully equipped apartments with kitchen, bathroom, lounge and bedroom. Other features include a restaurant, swimming pool and a garden with fruit, walnut and pomegranate trees.

EATING OUT

La Sarga – *Calle del Mercado – ☎ 953 72 15 07 – closed Tues and in Sept.* Specialities in this pleasant restaurant with sweeping views of the *sierra* include orange and cod salad *(ensalada de naranja y bacalao)*, pork with honey *(cerdo a la miel)* and a flan-like dessert known as *tocinillo de San Rafael*.

TAPAS

La Montería – *Corredera, 20 – ☎ 953 72 05 42.* This popular bar is decorated with the stuffed heads of prize game. The excellent range of tapas on offer includes cured hams, cheeses and venison.

Travellers' addresses

Parque Natural de las Sierras de
CAZORLA, SEGURA Y LAS VILLAS★★★

Jaén

Michelin map 446 S 20-21-22 R 20-21-22 Q 21-22

Spain's largest nature reserve is located within the Cazorla, Segura y Las Villas *sierras*, an impressive range of mountains acting as a link between the Sierra Morena and the Cordilleras Béticas, enclosing the depression of the Guadalquivir River to the east. The 214 300ha/529 535 acres of the park are situated at an altitude of between 600m/1 968ft and 2 017m/6 616ft in a landscape characterised by steep cliffs, deep gorges and a complex network of rivers and streams. The park is also home to a number of small towns and villages which have preserved their traditional mountain culture and continue to produce the arts and crafts synonymous with this area.

The park's most impressive feature is the incredible beauty of its landscape, in which visitors have the sensation of entering a lost world where the silence is broken only by the sound of rushing water and the far-off sounds of the park's fauna. The sombre light adds to the moody atmosphere of the park, casting dark hues over the steep, heavily forested slopes and promontories.

Flora and fauna

The park's high levels of precipitation have resulted in the growth of abundant vegetation in the park. Flora found here includes the beautiful Cazorla violet, an endemic species that appears in the forests of black pine, holm and downy oak; hazel and holly. The list of native fauna is equally impressive with wild boar, stags, mountain goats and deer (all of which can be hunted during authorised periods in the Coto Nacional de Caza de Cazorla hunting reserve); predators such as the genet, stone marten, wildcat and fox; aquatic fauna such as the otter; and numerous species of fish, including trout, barbel, carp and black perch. The park is also home to a variety of birdlife (golden eagle, peregrine falcon, kite, osprey etc).

Tour – Because of its size, the park is accessible via a number of different routes. Once inside the park, however, it is advisable to head for one of the **information points**, from where attractive itineraries will enable visitors to make the most of their visit to the park's breathtaking landscapes. The largest of these information points is at the Torre del Vinagre, although others are located at **Cazorla** ⊘, Segura de la Sierra and Siles. In addition to exploring minor roads, mountain-bikers, horse-riders and hikers can also follow the extensive network of forest tracks and marked footpaths criss-crossing the park.

The two itineraries below are suggested for visitors, although many others are possible depending on which direction visitors approach the park.

SIERRAS DE CAZORLA, LAS VILLAS Y EL POZO

1 From Tíscar to the Embalse del Tranco de Beas

92km/67mi – allow one day

This route combines the artistic heritage of the towns of Cazorla and Quesada with the superb natural landscapes of the Sierra Morena.

★**Tíscar** – The **Santuario de Tíscar** ⊘ enjoys a superb site enclosed by rocks, where the sound of gushing water blends in with the birdsong emanating from distant caverns. Below this place of pilgrimage, which houses a statue of the Virgin Mary, appears the impressive **Cueva del Agua★**, a natural cave formation where a torrent of water emerges from between the rocks.

20km/12mi northwest along the C 323.

Quesada – Quesada sits on the Cerro de la Magdalena hill, its whitewashed houses adding a dash of brightness to the sombre olive groves around it. The town was the birthplace of the painter Rafael Zabaleta (1907-60); the **museum** ⊘ which bears his name displays works by this artist who was able to capture the characteristic light found here and the friendly nature of the town's inhabitants. The **Cañada de las Fuentes**, a ravine situated at an altitude of 1 400m/4 592ft on the outer limits of Quesada, is the **source of the Guadalquivir River** *(access via a track off the A 315, to the north of Quesada).*

Wall paintings from the Paleolithic era can be admired in Cerro Vitar and in the Cueva del Encajero, just a short distance from the town.

23.5km/14.5mi northeast. Take the A 315 towards Peal de Becerro, then bear right on the A 319 at a signposted junction.

★**Cazorla** – *See CAZORLA.*

After heading 1.5km/1mi northeast along the A 319, turn right at a signposted junction.

La Iruela Castle and the Sierra de Cazorla

La Iruela – Founded by the Carthaginians in the 3C BC, this small town is overlooked by the remains of a Templar castle offering superb **views**★★ of the Guadalquivir Valley. The Iglesia de Santo Domingo, a Renaissance-style church designed by Vandelvira, stands proudly at its centre.

★**The road from La Iruela to the Tranco Reservoir** – The first 17km/10.5mi stretch along the A 319 snakes its way along a corniche, providing **spectacular views**★★. The Parador de **El Adelantado** is reached via a branch road *(8km/5mi)* which winds its way uphill through forests of pine trees popular with hunters.

Continue along the A 319 running parallel to the river.

Torre del Vinagre – A number of routes head off from the **Centro de Interpretación** ⊘ inside the park. This information centre has a hunting museum displaying trophies and photographs which provide an insight into the history of hunting in the region, as well as a botanical garden where species native to the park can be seen. The horns of two stag are also exhibited, along with a photograph of how these animals were initially located.

A game reserve, the **Parque Cinegético de Collado del Almendral** ⊘, 15km/9.5mi further along the A 319, has several look-out points where the typical wildlife of the area (deer, mouflons, mountain goats etc) can be observed through binoculars early in the morning.

Embalse del Tranco de Beas – This reservoir is the first large expanse of water along the Guadalquivir River from its source. Several camping areas and hotels have been created nearby which, along with the water sports on offer, have turned the lake into one of the popular destinations within the park. Two islands stand in the middle of the reservoir: the Isla de Cabeza la Viña; and the **Isla de Bujaraiza**, with the ruins of an old Moorish castle, opposite which stands a viewpoint, the **Mirador Rodríguez de la Fuente**.

WHERE TO STAY

LA IRUELA

Sierra de Cazorla – *Carretera de la Sierra. On the outskirts of the town, heading towards the Parque de Cazorla* – ☎ *953 72 00 15* – *fax 953 72 00 17* – *57 rooms* – *8 000pts.* Although the building is of recent design, little has been done to modernise the rooms, which remain somewhat antiquated. An outdoor pool and superb views of the mountains.

SIERRA DE CAZORLA

Parador de Cazorla – *Sierra de Cazorla* – ☎ *953 72 70 75* – *fax 953 72 70 77* – *33 rooms* – *15 000pts.* In the heart of the Parque de Cazorla (the gate-keeper's lodge is 23km/14mi from the *parador*), close to an old hunting refuge. The excellent facilities and secluded location make it an ideal base for nature-lovers.

133

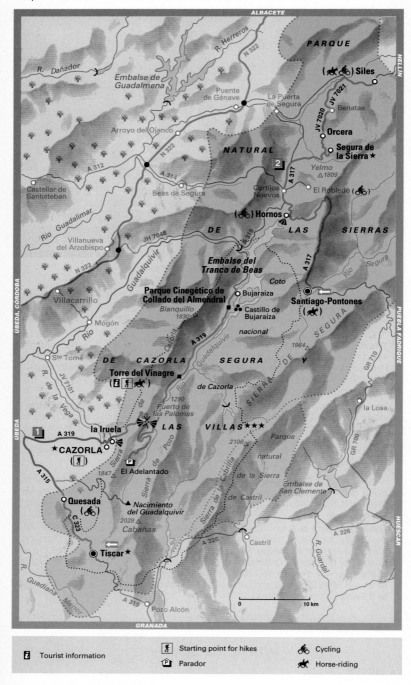

	Tourist information		Starting point for hikes		Cycling
	Parador				Horse-riding

Félix Rodríguez de la Fuente

The name of this naturalist and television presenter is indelibly linked with the Parque Natural de Cazorla. He filmed numerous wildlife programmes here, teaching viewers to love and respect this superb natural environment.

SIERRA DE SEGURA

② From Santiago-Pontones to Siles

79.5km/49.5mi – allow half a day

This itinerary passes through a series of whitewashed towns and villages dotted around the Segura de la Sierra, which has preserved vestiges of its Moorish occupation.

Santiago-Pontones – This municipality encompasses several villages scattered through the mountains. A number of archeological sites are located within its boundaries, such as the **Cueva del Nacimiento**, a cave 9 000 years old, and the **Cuevas de Engalbo**, with their impressive wall art.

From Pontones, head 27km/17mi northwest along the A 317.

Hornos – This settlement-cum-fortress consists of an attractive series of cobbled streets which are perfectly integrated inside the walls. The remains of the fortress rise above a steep cliff from where there are some spectacular **views**★ of the Tranco Reservoir and the Guadalquivir Valley. A market selling locally made artisanal products is held in Hornos on the first Saturday of every month.

24km/15mi northeast. Take the A 317, then bear right at a signposted junction.

★**Segura de la Sierra** – This picturesque village, the birthplace of the 15C poet Jorge Manrique, straddles a hill at an altitude of 1 240m/4 067ft in the shelter of its Mudéjar **castle**, whose silhouette appears to watch over the village from on high. This Moorish fortress has preserved its parade ground, a chapel (Capilla de Santa Ana) and, in particular, its keep, offering a sweeping **panorama**★★ of the Sierra de Segura.

The centre of the village is a maze of narrow alleyways lined by a mixture of low dwellings and monumental buildings, including the **town hall**, with its fine Plateresque doorway, and the **parish church**, containing a delicate, polychrome statue of the Virgin Mary carved in Gothic style from alabaster, and a recumbent Christ attributed to Gregorio Hernández. Also worthy of note are the unusual square-shaped bullring, the imperial fountain *(fuente imperial)*, emblasoned with the escutcheon of Carlos V, and, above all, the **Moorish baths** *(baños árabes)*, with three longitudinal aisles divided by horseshoe arches and topped by barrel vaults and star-shaped vault lights.

7.5km/4.5mi northwest along the JV 7020.

Orcera – The most interesting feature of this village is the pentagonal plaza del Ayuntamiento, fronted by the Iglesia de Nuestra Señora de la Asunción, with its sober Renaissance portal, and the Fuente de los Chorros, a 15C fountain. The three Santa Catalina towers, the only remaining vestiges of the former Moorish fortress, are visible on the outskirts of Orcera.

21km/13mi northeast. Follow the JV 7020 beyond Benatae, then take the JV 7021.

Siles – The village has preserved several sections of its old walls. The nearby nature reserve of Las Acebeas is an area of delightful landscapes close to the source of the Los Molinos River.

CÓRDOBA ★★★

Population 309 961
Michelin map 446 S 15

Córdoba is famous above all for its *mezquita*, an architectural masterpiece with a unique fusion of Muslim and Christian styles. Yet, the city is much more than just its mosque-cathedral; it is a symbolic city and a crossroads of cultures which is overflowing in artistic splendour and charm, as seen in its delightful Jewish quarter *(Judería)* with its narrow streets and whitewashed houses.

Córdoba stands on the banks of the Guadalquivir River, at the centre of its province, between the ranches and farmlands of the Sierra de Córdoba plateau to the north and the wheatlands and olive groves of the Campiña plains to the south. Its magnificent past has left an indelible mark on a city which has managed to preserve the beauty and sense of enchantment that has inspired numerous artists during the course of its history. The *cordobeses* are justifiably proud of their city and take great delight in sharing their treasures with visitors.

The historical centre of the city, the "quiet Córdoba" described in the poems of the 20C poet Antonio Machado, has since been joined by the wide, noisy streets of the city's modern quarters, enveloping the oldest part of the city as if to protect it from the hustle and bustle of modern life. Today, Córdoba is a prosperous city and the centre of an important agricultural and industrial region.

The month of May

In spring Córdoba becomes more beautiful than ever as it prepares itself for the numerous vibrant *fiestas* held during the course of the month.
Times are given as a guideline only and vary from year to year. For more detailed information contact the city's Tourist Office.

Cruces de Mayo – The Festival of the Crosses takes place in the first few days of the month. Large, flower-decked crosses are the centrepieces of this traditional contest involving the city's guilds and local associations. These impressive structures can be found dotted around squares and on street corners, attracting the admiring glances of locals and visitors alike.

Concurso de Patios – Córdoba's traditional *patio competition* is held during the first half of May. Dozens of patios, particularly those belonging to houses and mansions in the historical heart of the city and the San Basilio quarter, are transformed into breathtaking displays of flowers and colour for this eagerly awaited annual contest.

A Cordoban patio

136

Concurso Nacional de Arte Flamenco – The prestigious national flamenco competition is held every three years *(next contest in 2001)* and is open to singers, dancers and guitarists. If you have the opportunity, don't miss out on the chance to watch and listen to some superb flamenco performed by some of Spain's most talented artists.

The Feria – The end of the month is a time for great merriment in the city as Córdoba hosts its annual fair. The fairground's entertainment booths *(casetas)* belonging to public and private institutions, flamenco clubs and brotherhoods are the setting for the dancing of *sevillanas*, the eating of tapas and the drinking of *fino* until the early hours of the morning. The *feria* is also the occasion for Córdoba to host major bullfights attracting leading names in the bullfighting world, as advertised on the colourful posters all around the city.

HISTORICAL NOTES

Several key periods have marked Córdoba's illustrious past. Under the Romans, the city was the capital of the province of Baetica, and as such was one of the most important cities on the Iberian Peninsula. Following its conquest by the Moors, it developed into the most cosmopolitan and refined city in the Western world. The Christian Reconquest in the 13C brought with it significant changes both in terms of the city's daily life and its architecture.

Roman Córdoba

In 152 BC, Córdoba became a Roman colony and was the capital of Baetica until almost the end of the Roman Empire. Its development was further enhanced by the construction of the Via Augusta and the city's walls. Córdoba's cultural background was to spawn a number of leading intellectual figures such as **Seneca the Rhetorician** (55 BC-AD 39); his son, the stoic philosopher and preceptor to Nero, **Seneca the Philosopher** (AD 4-AD 65); and the poet **Lucan**, Seneca the Philosopher's nephew and companion to Nero in his student days, and author of *Pharsalia*, an epic poem recounting the wars between Caesar and Pompey. Christian Córdoba produced another important figure, **Bishop Ossius** (257-359), counsellor to Emperor Constantine and staunch opponent of Arianism in the Council of Nicaea, which he himself presided over.

Muslim Córdoba

Under the Moors, this melting pot of cultures was to become the most important city in the West. Following its conquest in 711, emirs from the Damascus Caliphate established themselves in Córdoba as early as 719. In 755, Abd ar-Rahman I, sole survivor of the Umayyads who had been annihilated by the Abassids, created an **independent emirate** which recognised the religious supremacy of Baghdad. The establishment of a new judicial system subsequently calmed down this volatile situation. In the 9C, during the reign of Abd ar-Rahman II, the city underwent great cultural development, led by the Iraqi poet Ziryab, a leading intellectual figure in Cordoban society.

B. Kaufmann/MICHELIN

The Caliphate – In 929, Abd ar-Rahman III proclaimed himself Caliph of Córdoba and achieved total independence, assuming full political power. Córdoba became an important administrative city, while commerce, enhanced by an extensive network of roads, resulted in the significant development of the urban economy, with strong growth in industry, agriculture and animal breeding. The 10C, a period characterised by peace and prosperity, brought with it unprecedented cultural splendour. The tolerance practised at the time allowed the three communities – Jewish, Christian and Muslim – to live peacefully and offer mutual enrichment to each other. Córdoba became the great capital of the whole of the Western world, with all political, economic, artistic and cultural power under its yoke and a population exceeding 250 000 inhabitants – some chroniclers even talk of a figure approaching one million. The city also had some 3 000 mosques, a multitude of

WHERE TO STAY

MODERATE

Séneca – *Conde y Luque, 7* – ☎ *957473234* – *12 rooms* – *5 700pts.* This quiet *hostal* with its plant-filled patio is just a stone's throw from the Mezquita. Although the decor is attractive the rooms are very basic, some with a shared bathroom.

Maestre – *Romero Barros, 4 and 6* – ☎ *957472410* – *fax 957475395* – *24 rooms* – *6 500pts.* The Maestre is one of Córdoba's better value-for-money standard hotels. Everything is new, the decor pleasant, the rooms spacious, plus it's close to the attractive plaza del Potro. The owners also run a second *hostal* with 22 rooms (4 750pts) and seven apartments (7 500pts).

MID-RANGE

Marisa – *Cardenal Herrero, 6* – ☎ *957473142* – *fax 957474144* – *28 rooms* – *9 000pts* – *Garage.* A fairly basic hotel but with an excellent location opposite the Mezquita. Ten rooms overlooking the city's major monument. Spanish-style decor. Small bathrooms.

Mezquita – *Plaza de Santa Catalina, 1* – ☎ *957475585* – *fax 957476219* – *21 rooms* – *9 850pts.* Opposite the main entrance to the Mezquita. Spacious, attractively decorated rooms with all the necessary creature comforts. Good value for money.

González – *Manríquez, 3* – ☎ *957479819* – *fax 957486187* – *16 rooms* – *9 850pts.* A small, 16C palace with comfortable, well-furnished guest rooms and a Moorish-inspired patio with restaurant. The González belongs to the same owners as the Hotel Mezquita *(see above).*

Albucasis – *Buen Pastor, 11* – ☎ *957478625* – *fax 957478625* – *15 rooms* – *9 950pts* – *Garage.* A basic hotel in a typical Cordoban house in the Judería. Access via a patio. Spacious, well-appointed rooms.

NH Amistad Córdoba – *Plaza de Maimónides, 3* – ☎ *957420356* – *fax 957420365* – *69 rooms* – *16 500pts* – *Garage.* A top-class hotel split between two 18C mansions close to the city's Moorish walls. Spacious public areas and a large Mudéjar patio. Functional yet comfortable rooms that have been tastefully decorated.

EATING OUT

El Churrasco – *Romero, 16* – ☎ *957290819.* Typical restaurant with a very pleasant patio and bar for an aperitif or a bite to eat. Grilled meats are the house speciality. The *menú del día* costs 3 500pts.

La Almudaina – *Jardines Santos Mártires, 1* – ☎ *957474342* – *closed Sun evenings.* An attractive, elegant restaurant with a delightful covered wooden patio. Andalucian specialities and international dishes.

Bodegas Campos – *Lineros, 32 (near plaza del Potro)* – ☎ *957497643* – *closed Sun evenings.* The restaurant, which occupies some old wine storehouses *(bodegas)* founded in 1908, is attractively laid out around several patios. At the entrance *(to the right)* there is a bar decorated with photos of famous visitors.

El Caballo Rojo – *Cardenal Herrera, 28* – ☎ *957475375.* One of the city's institutions situated alongside the Mezquita, with a small entrance patio. Somewhat traditional decor on the inside.

TAPAS

Judería

Casa Salinas – *Puerta de Almodóvar, 2.* A quiet tavern with a counter, two rooms and a small patio. Friendly atmosphere with *azulejo* decoration and numerous photos of the rich and famous adorning the walls.

Taberna Guzmán – *Judíos, 9 (opposite the Synagogue)* – ☎ *957290960* – *closed Thur.* A traditional bar with lots of character, *azulejo* decoration, bullfighting mementoes and posters advertising the local *feria.* Good local sausages and cheeses.

La Bacalá – *Medina y Corella (near the Mezquita).* A bar with a terrace, situated on a pleasant square. Cod tapas specialities. Flamenco background music.

Pepe "de la Judería" – *Romero, 1* – ☎ *957200744.* This bar first opened in 1928 and the counter dates from this period. Several rooms serving tapas around a patio. Restaurant on the upper floor. Tapas and Andalucian cuisine.

Plaza de la Corredera – Plaza del Potro

Salinas – *Tundidores, 3 (near plaza de la Corredera)* – *closed Sun.* Attractive bar founded in 1924 with several rooms radiating off a central covered patio. Specialities include scrambled eggs with prawns and ham *(revuelto de gambas y jamón)*, fried aubergines *(berenjenas fritas)* and braised bull's tail *(rabo de toro)*.

Sociedad de Plateros – *San Francisco, 6 (near plaza del Potro)* – ☎ *957 47 00 42* – *closed Mon.* The Sociedad de Plateros owns several bars and taverns. This one, over a century old (1872), has particular character. Very popular, particularly on Sunday lunchtimes.

Gran Capitán – Cruz Conde

San Miguel "El Pisto" – *Plaza San Miguel, 1 (next to the church of the same name).* A typical tavern dating back to 1886 with a delightful wooden bar and inner patio. A must!

Taberna San Miguel "El Pisto"

La Canoa – *Ronda de Tejares, Cajasur passageway.* A bar with large arches and wine barrels instead of tables located in a somewhat gloomy shopping arcade. *Canoa* is the name of a funnel used to refill the barrels.

Gaudí – *Av. Gran Capitán, 22* – ☎ *957 47 17 36* – *open 8-1am.* A *cervecería* with Modernist decor. A pleasant location for lunch, a snack or an aperitif. Wide selection of tapas.

CAFÉS, BARS & NIGHT-LIFE

Most of Córdoba's bars and night-clubs are found in the city centre, mainly around the avenida del Gran Capitán and in the El Brillante residential area.

Málaga Café – *Calle de Málaga, 3. Open daily, 4pm-2am (Fri and Sat, 4am; Sun 10pm).* A quiet café with classical decor and comfortable sofas and armchairs near the plaza de las Tendillas in the centre of the city. Highly recommended for evening drinks with friends.

Siena – *Plaza de las Tendillas. Open daily, 8am-midnight.* A long-established café in Córdoba's main square, with one of the city's most popular outdoor terraces. A perfect venue for a morning coffee or an evening drink.

Chato – *Calle Alhakem II, 14. Open daily, 4pm-early morning.* A bar with a modern design in the Gran Capitán area of the city with a trendy mixed-age clientele. A pleasant location for a quiet early-evening coffee or drinks in a more lively atmosphere closer to midnight.

Sojo – *Calle Benito Pérez Galdós, 3. Open daily, 8am-4am.* Popular with the over-25s, this avant-garde bar is open from breakfast time to late at night. The Sojo also organises concerts by soloists, as well as art, photography and video exhibitions. Highly recommended, whatever the hour.

El Puentecillo – *Calle Poeta Emilio Prados. In summer, open daily, 9.30pm-5am; in winter, open Thur, Fri and Sat, midnight-5am.* A small venue on the way up to the El Brillante district. Warm and inviting decor inside as well as on the small patio. Tends to be frequented by a slightly older, quieter crowd. Popular for drinks early on.

ENTERTAINMENT

Córdoba is a provincial capital with a buzzing social and cultural life. During the winter, the **Gran Teatro** *(Av. Gran Capitán, 3 –* ☎ *957 48 02 37)* hosts a regular season of concerts and theatre. In addition, the Filmoteca de Andalucía, which has its headquarters in Córdoba *(calle Medina y Corella, 5 – www.cica.es/filmo)*, organises a varied programme of cinema.

The Town Hall *(Ayuntamiento)* publishes *Qué hacer en Córdoba*, a free guide (in Spanish only) listing forthcoming cultural events in the city, which is available from Tourist Offices, hotels etc.

One of the best flamenco clubs in Córdoba is the Tablao Cardenal at calle Torrijos, 10 *(*☎ *957 48 31 12)*, opposite the Mezquita. This excellent show, featuring several award-winning dancers, is performed in a delightful outdoor patio. *Performances at 10.30pm daily, except Mon.*

SHOPPING

Córdoba's main shopping streets are concentrated around plaza de las Tendillas. These include the busy calle José Cruz Conde and Conde de Gondomar, both of which are pedestrianised. The larger department stores can be found along avenida Ronda de los Tejares, including El Corte Inglés, on the corner with avenida del Gran Capitán. The large Eroski shopping centre is located next to the municipal stadium in the Arcángel district.

The city's traditional craftwork is its gold and silver filigree, which is on sale in shops throughout the city. La Purísima, a jeweller's located in the area behind the Alcázar, has an excellent reputation for this particular work.

The municipal market or *Zoco Municipal* (www.aca-zoco.com – ☎ 957 20 40 33), laid out around a small square and along a network of narrow streets in calle Judíos, is home to a number of artisans' shops selling ceramics, leather, pottery etc (open Mon-Sat, 10am-8pm).

On almost every day of the week small markets *(mercadillos)* are held in various parts of the city. The Saturday morning market in plaza de la Corredera is popular, as is the one held on the esplanade next to the municipal stadium *(estadio municipal)* on Sunday mornings.

TRANSPORT

Airport – Avenida Aeropuerto – ☎ 957 23 23 00. Córdoba airport is only used for flights within Spain. The nearest international airport is in Sevilla (☎ 954 44 90 00) 140km/88mi to the west. The two cities are well connected by both bus and train services.

Domestic reservations: ☎ 901 333 111.

International reservations: ☎ 901 333 222.

Information: ☎ 957 47 12 27.

Trains – *Carretera Conde de Guadalhorce* – ☎ 957 49 02 02. Córdoba, along with Sevilla, has excellent connections with Madrid on the AVE *(Alta Velocidad Española)* high-speed train, with a journey time of under two hours to the Spanish capital. The city is also served by a comprehensive network of local and provincial trains, as well as regular services to other parts of the country.

RENFE (Spanish State Railways) – *Ronda de los Tejares 10* – ☎ 957 47 58 84.

City buses – AUCORSA; ☎ 957 25 57 04 or 957 25 13 93. Córdoba has an excellent local bus network covering the whole city. A single journey costs 115pts, a ten-trip ticket 810pts. Tickets entitle passengers to transfer from one bus to another. Monthly passes are also available at a cost of 4 750pts.

Inter-city buses – *Calle Federico García Lorca, 3* – ☎ 957 50 16 32. Buses depart from here to other cities in Andalucia and elsewhere in Spain.

Taxis – ☎ 957 25 19 95, 957 23 20 42, 957 47 48 71 or 957 47 51 53.

Horse-drawn carriages – An attractive way of seeing the city's main sights. Carriages can be hired from calle Torrijos (next to the Mezquita) and Campo Santo de los Mártires.

Not to be missed:

– the Mezquita illuminated at night;
– the view of the city from the top of the Torre de la Calahorra;
– the Mezquita's minaret from calleja de las Flores.

---

markets and baths and a complex sewage system. The famous university, as well as a number of libraries – the one created by Al-Hakam II was the largest of the period – and sumptuous buildings which were a source of amazement to visitors and provided inspiration for countless artists of the period, were also built under this Caliphate.

A kingdom of taifas – The first 30 years of the 11C were marked by an intense power struggle that brought about the dissolution of the Caliphate in 1031. Powerful cities declared their independence, resulting in the fragmentation of al-Andalus into small warring kingdoms, the **reinos de taifas**. However, this decline in no way diminished artistic or cultural life, which continued unabated in keeping with the Caliphal tradition. Up until its reconquest in 1236, Córdoba was itself a *taifa*. During this period, the city saw the birth of numerous personalities in the field of science (astronomy, mathematics, medicine) and philosophy, with the Cordobans Averroës (1126-98) and Maimónides (1135-1204) at the forefront of this intellectual movement. The writings of the Moor **Averroës** on the works of Aristotle had a major impact in the Western medieval world, while the Jew **Maimónides** stood out as a philosopher and physician. His *Guide of the Perplexed*, in which he establishes conciliation between faith and reason, not only found favour with Jews and Muslims, but also influenced Christian scholars, particularly St Thomas Aquinas.

Christian Córdoba

On 29 June 1236, **Fernando III the Saint** reconquered the city. The arrival of the Christians had a large impact on Córdoba's architecture with the construction of 14 parish churches under Fernando.
In the **15C**, Córdoba was the setting for Columbus' first audience with the Catholic Monarchs (1486), during which he presented plans for his expedition to the Indies. Following several years of indecision, the Crown finally gave its support to his project and in April 1492 signed the *Santa Fe Agreement* (Granada) (see p 197) which opened the way for an adventure that would change the course of history.

★★★1 THE MEZQUITA

★★★Mosque-Cathedral ⊘

Córdoba's mosque-cathedral is one of the world's most unique architectural monuments, influenced in turn by the Muslim and Christian faiths dominant in the city. The present-day Mezquita was built between the 8C and 10C above the Visigothic basilica of San Vicente. Following the Reconquest, the Christians then erected a Gothic cathedral in the very heart of this place of Muslim worship. In its capacity as mosque and cathedral, the building proudly displays the religious and architectural features of its two faiths, both of which used great sensitivity in its construction, enabling modern visitors to admire a harmonious building formed by two distinct, yet equally magnificent, parts.

Mezquita (Mosque) – The Mezquita is undoubtedly one of the world's masterpieces of Islamic art. The overall plan is that of a traditional Arab mosque, which has its origins in the house of the prophet Muhammad in Medina, with a crenellated square perimeter enclosing a patio for ritual ablution, the prayer hall and the minaret. The first Muslims to arrive in Córdoba shared the Visigothic church of St Vincent with the Christians. Soon, however, this proved insufficient and Abd ar-Rahman I (758-788) purchased the Christian part of the site. He razed the church and around the year 780 began the construction of a splendid mosque with 11 aisles each opening onto the Patio de los Naranjos. Marble pillars and stone from former Roman and Visigothic buildings were re-used in the mosque which became famous for an architectural innovation: the superimposition of two tiers of arches to give added height and space. The mosque was enlarged over the years: in 848 Abd ar-Rahman II had it extended to the present-day Capilla de Villaviciosa (Villaviciosa Chapel); in 961 Al-Hakam II built the *mihrab* (prayer-niche); and lastly, in 987, Al-Mansur gave it its present size by adding eight more aisles (recognisable by their red brick pavement).

Patio de los Naranjos – This spacious and enchanting patio, which has porticoes on three sides, takes its names from the orange trees (naranjos) planted by the Christians following the Reconquest. The attractiveness and aroma of these orange trees is one of the Mezquita's characteristic charms. Like the mosque itself, the patio was also enlarged

---

The unique structure of the Mezquita

During the Moorish period, Córdoba had around 3 000 mosques. The one admired by visitors today was the main mosque, used by Muslims for their Friday prayers. Subsequent enlargements to the building were carried out in line with the growth in the city's population.
The Mezquita has a structure which is totally different to that found in Christian churches and as such could be extended much more easily, without affecting the building's architectural style. Its simple structure, with its parallel aisles, enabled further aisles to be built, while retaining its overall unity.

CÓRDOBA

CÓRDOBA

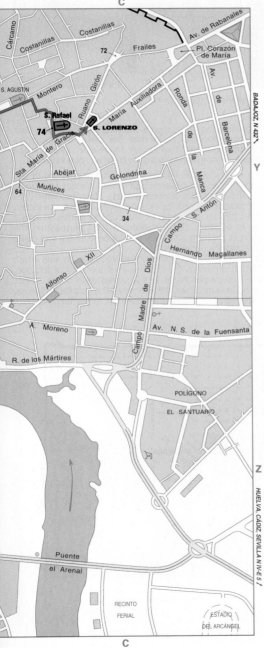

Interior of the Mezquita

according to necessity. Before commencing their prayers, Muslims would perform their ritual ablutions in the basin here to symbolically purify their five senses. The patio has managed to preserve several fountains, some of which are Mudéjar in style, and the 10C **Al-Mansur basin** (**1**). The ground is completely covered with small round pebbles.

Interior – *Entrance through the Puerta de Las Palmas*. The initial impression of the interior is truly spectacular with its forest of columns and arches. Colour and shade play a fundamental role here. The horseshoe-shaped arches – features which are Visigothic in origin – consist of alternating red (brick) and white (stone) voussoirs. This twin-coloured effect is enriched by the tones of the column shafts, in which greys and pinks predominate. In addition, the variations in light permeating the whole edifice play their own part in creating an unreal atmosphere which will make a visit to the Mezquita an unforgettable experience.

The **visit** starts in the oldest part of the building. The doorway leads into an aisle which is wider than the others and which served as the main aisle of the original mosque, leading to the *mihrab*. The aisles run perpendicular to the sacred walls of the *kiblah*, towards which Muslims would pray. In all mosques, this wall should be built facing Mecca. However, it is not known why the *kiblah* in this mosque does not follow this rule.

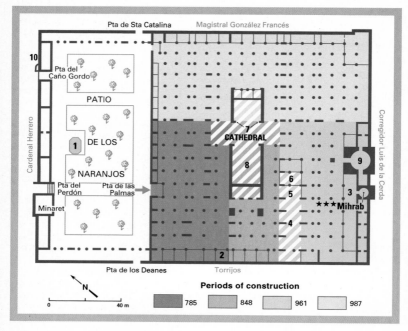

Decoration: everything except the human form

Because of their religious beliefs, Muslims could not incorporate the human body in the decorative features they used. As a result, they developed a type of decoration which maximised the use of plant and geometric motifs, with marble panels, sections of carved stucco and mosaics combining to produce unparalleled splendour. Given the sacred character of the Word, the other fundamental characteristic of Muslim art is the use of script; in the case of Islam, verses from the Koran. A superb example of this can be seen on the entrance arch to the *mihrab*, on which the rectangular surround *(alfiz)* bears inscriptions in Kufic script.

The mosque built by **Abd ar-Rahman I** extended as far as the wall of the present-day cathedral. After the Reconquest, chapels were built by the Christians in the west nave. These include the 17C **Capilla de la Purísima Concepción** (**2**), which is completely covered with marble of different colours.

In 833 **Abd ar-Rahman II** removed the wall of the *kiblah* and extended the 11 aisles to the Capilla de Villaviciosa to the south. He continued to use the same system of arcades, but what is particularly striking is the refinement in the decoration as demonstrated by the fact that in the work carried out under Al-Hakam II in and around the *mihrab*, architectural features from this period were re-used.

The expansion carried out under **Al-Hakam II** was the most sumptuous of all, involving the extension of the 11 aisles to their current dimensions. In addition, all the columns and capitals were hand carved for this particular building. The richness in ornamentation, centred around the **mihrab★★★**, is the jewel in the Mezquita's crown. In order to decorate this octagonal niche, rendered with a plaster moulding, the same Byzantine artists who created the superb mosaics decorating its entrance arch and the magnificent **cupola★★** preceding it were called upon. The three ribbed domes of the **maksourah** (**3**) – the enclosure in front of the mihrab reserved for the Caliph – rest on an unusual series of multifoil arches. However, these domes have nothing in common with Christian art, given that the ribs are interwoven, leaving a polygon in the centre – the opposite of what is seen in Romanesque or Gothic architecture. This type of dome is oriental in origin. The ceiling of the Capilla Real (Royal Chapel) followed the same design.

Al-Mansur was responsible for the last, and largest, extension of the mosque, although this did not result in the introduction of any new features. Due to the proximity of the river, this enlargement, involving the addition of a further eight aisles, was to the east and not to the south.

Christian features – The conversion of the building to Christian use brought several physical alterations, including the walling up of the aisles on the side of the Patio de los Naranjos, with the sole exception of the Puerta de las Palmas. In order to build the **first cathedral** (**4**), several columns were removed and a Gothic *artesonado* ceiling supported by pointed arches was erected in their place. Alfonso X was responsible for the chancel in the **Capilla de Villaviciosa** or **Lucernario** (**5**), and built the **Capilla Real★** (**6**), decorated in the 13C with Mudéjar stucco which nevertheless retained the harmony with the rest of the monument.

Cathedral – In the 16C, despite opposition from the cathedral chapter, Bishop Don Alonso Manrique received authorisation to build a cathedral in the middle of the mosque. However, in spite of the talent of the architects Hernán Ruiz I, Hernán Ruiz II and Juan de Ochoa, and the beauty and richness of their creation, Emperor Carlos V was far from pleased: "You have destroyed something unique", he said, "to build something commonplace".

The different styles of the 16C and 17C can be seen alongside one another with Hispano-Flemish arches and vaults, a Renaissance dome, Baroque vaulting above the choir and a Baroque high altar. Additional enrichments include the two **pulpits★★** (**7**) in mahogany, marble and jasper by Michel de Verdiguier.

The **choir** (**8**) is quite spectacular, in particular the Baroque **choir stalls★★** by Pedro Duque Cornejo (c 1750). These outstanding works of exquisitely carved mahogany offer a complete iconographic programme, depicting saints, scenes from the life of Christ and the Virgin Mary, and the Old and New Testaments, in which the Ascension of Christ, in the centre, stands out. Note also the two impressive organs from the 17C and 18C.

Treasury – *To the left of the mihrab*. The treasury *(tesoro)*, built by the Baroque architect Francisco Hurtado Izquierdo, can be found in the **Capilla del Cardenal** (Cardinal's Chapel) (**9**) and in two adjoining rooms. A monumental 16C **monstrance★** by Enrique Arfe and an exceptional Baroque figure of Christ in ivory stand out in this collection of liturgical objects.

Exterior – The **minaret** built under Abd ar-Rahman III, from the top of which the muezzin called the faithful to prayer, is enveloped in a Baroque tower dating from the late 16C and early 17C. To the side, the 14C Mudéjar **Puerta del Perdón** (Pardon Doorway), a doorway faced with bronze, opens onto the street.

Detail, cathedral vaults

B. Kaufmann/MICHELIN

A small shrine to the deeply venerated **Virgin of the Lanterns** (**10**) has been built into the north wall. This altar, surrounded by a metal grille and adorned with lanterns, is a copy of a work by Julio Romero de Torres. Its illumination at night is particularly attractive.

It is well worth walking around the exterior of the Mezquita to admire the elegant decoration on its entrance gates, most of which have now been permanently sealed. Of these, the two gates on calle Torrijos, the Puerta de San Esteban, created by Abd ar-Rahman I and one of the very first gates to the mosque subsequently modified by Abd ar-Rahman II, and the Puerta de Palacio, are particularly rich in decoration.

Callejita del Pañuelo

This attractive alleyway *(callejita)*, accessed via the plaza de la Concha *(very close to the Mezquita, along Martínez Rücker)*, is one of Córdoba's most delightful sights. Although its official name is calle Pedro Jiménez, it is known as Pañuelo (handkerchief) because at its narrowest point it has the width of a man's handkerchief placed diagonally. It comes to a dead end in a slightly wider, yet equally charming section with a small fountain, an attractive doorway and wrought-iron grilles.

Around the Mezquita

A number of attractive streets and monuments within close proximity of the Mezquita can easily be visited on foot.

Calleja de las Flores – This narrow street in the Judería is typically Cordoban in style with its arches and abundance of flowers *(flores)* and flowerpots. The street ends at a small square with a fountain, from where visitors can enjoy one of the best views of the Mezquita's tower.

Palacio de Exposiciones y Congresos – The conference and exhibition centre occupies the former Hospital de San Sebastián. It was later used as the city's orphanage and nowadays also houses the **Tourist Office**.

Its **doorway★**, with fine sculptures on the tympanum and jambs, is a work of art dating from the early 16C. The wall is adorned with an ornamental border and fretwork, thistle leaves and stringcourses. The high quality of workmanship can be seen in both the arrangement of the façade and the craftsmanship.

The sober patio is made entirely of brick and is entirely devoid of decorative features.

Museo Diocesano de Bellas Artes ⌚ – *Next to the Palacio de Exposiciones y Congresos.* The Fine Arts Museum is housed in the 18C Bishops' Palace (Palacio Episcopal) and was built on top of the former Moorish fortress. The building has an interesting patio and a double-access Baroque black marble staircase topped by a fine cupola with stucco decoration.

The rooms of the museum, on the second floor, contain a collection of sculptures, paintings, religious books and tapestries, some of which date back to the 13C. The highly restored Baroque chapel of Nuestra Señora del Pilar (Our Lady of the Pillar), can also be visited *(entrance from the patio, to the right of the staircase)*.

Triunfo de San Rafael – This, the most impressive of all the city's monuments to St Raphael, dates from the second half of the 18C. The

---

St Raphael

Devotion to the archangel Raphael has been a deep-rooted feature of the city for many centuries. It is rare to find a family without at least one family member named after him, and even the local football stadium is called El Arcángel. This devotion has its origins in the 16C, following an apparition of St Raphael *(San Rafael)*, who came forward as the protector of the city. Several original monuments, known as *triunfos* (literally "triumphs"), have been erected around the city to honour Córdoba's patron saint.

---

archangel can be seen on top of the monument, with sculptures of various allegorical figures at its base.

Puerta del Puente – This impressive monument now appears to be a triumphal arch, given that it has lost its original function as an entrance gateway on the north bank of the river. It was built in the 16C according to a classical design with its large fluted Doric columns, entablature, frieze and a curved pediment with an escutcheon supported by two warriors. The decoration can be seen on the side facing the river.

Roman bridge – The Roman bridge *(puente romano)* rises above the waters of the Guadalquivir between the Puerta del Puente and the Torre de la Calahorra. It was built under Emperor Hadrian, but has been rebuilt on several occasions, most importantly during the period of Moorish domination. The river's water mills, of Moorish origin, can be seen to the right.

A statue of **St Raphael** is visible towards the middle of the bridge, on a low, altar-like wall. It was erected here in 1651, following a serious epidemic. It is usually adorned with candles and flowers, highlighting its importance as a place of devotion.

Torre de la Calahorra: Museo Vivo de Al-Andalus ⌚ – This Moorish fortress was built at the southern end of the Puente Romano. Its early construction incorporated two towers linked by a single arch. In the 14C, Enrique II ordered their enlargement and sealed off the connecting arch. During subsequent centuries, it was to suffer further modifications.

The tower has been used for a number of purposes over the course of its history: a prison for nobles, a barracks, and even a school for children.

It now houses an **audiovisual museum** outlining the history of the Córdoba Caliphate – a period of great cultural, artistic, philosophical and scientific prosperity. Major trends in 12C and 13C thought are illustrated through information on the Christian king Alfonso X the Wise, the Jew Maimónides and the Moors Averroës and Ibn-Arabi. The museum also contains an impressive **model★** of the Mezquita as it was in the 13C. From the top of the tower, visitors can enjoy fine **views** of the city.

Cross the bridge and head along calle Amador de los Ríos to Campo Santo de los Mártires.

Excavations have also revealed some **Caliphal baths** which can be seen in the Campo Santo de los Mártires.

★Alcázar de los Reyes Cristianos ⌚ – This fortress-style residence was built by Alfonso XI in the 14C. Known as the Fortress of the Catholic Monarchs, it was the setting for an audience in 1486 between Isabel and Fernando and Columbus. The *alcázar* was also used as the headquarters of the Inquisition until 1821.

The interior contains an exceptional 3C AD **Roman sarcophagus★**, with an outstanding treatment of facial features and fabric, and an interesting collection of **mosaics★**, magnificently displayed in the Salón de los Mosaicos and Sala del Océano, highlighting the splendour of Roman Córdoba. The **baths**, Moorish in structure but built by the Christians, can also be seen *(downstairs, to the right, at the end of the corridor).*

The gardens of the Alcázar

Cross the Mudéjar patio to visit the delightful Moorish-style **gardens★** with their terraces, pools, fountains, cypress trees and flowers of every colour and scent.

The **Caballerizas Reales**, royal stables situated next to the Alcázar, were founded by Felipe II in the 16C. The present building dates from the 18C. Although it is closed to the public, it is well worth a look inside if the entrance happens to be open as you pass by.

At the end of the street, after the arch, enter the **San Basilio district**, famous for the charming patios in its typical houses. One of the most attractive patios can be found at no 50, calle San Basilio, the headquarters of the Cordoban Patio Association.

An oasis of greenery

The centre of Córdoba is not just a maze of narrow, winding streets, for one of the city's main thoroughfares has a wide stretch of greenery running through its centre. This oasis of peace and tranquillity links the avenida del Conde de Valledano, paseo de la Victoria and avenida de Cervantes.

★★Judería

The old Jewish quarter has its very own charming features and character. Time seems to have stood still in these whitewashed alleyways with their flower-filled patios, wrought-iron grilles and typical bars. It is well worth taking plenty of time to explore the district in order to fully appreciate its unique atmosphere.

City walls and Puerta de Almodóvar – The pedestrianised calle Cairuán runs parallel to the walls of the Judería, which were just a small part of the defence system protecting the city. This well-preserved section, built from ashlar stone, contrasts with the tapestry of greenery provided by the numerous cypress trees.

The Puerta de Almodóvar (Almodóvar Gate) provides access to the Jewish quarter. Its origins date back to Moorish times, although it was heavily restored in the early 19C, when an inner doorway was added. A statue of Seneca can be seen to the left of the gateway. The illumination of this area at night adds to the charms of this delightful quarter.

Walk through the Puerta de Almodóvar and follow calle Judíos.

Calle Judíos – The Street of the Jews, running parallel to the walls, is one of the Judería's most famous thoroughfares. Look out for the Bodega Guzmán, a charming bar at no 7, and the **Casa Andalusí** ⊙, a 12C Moorish house at no 12, which houses an exhibition of items used by the Moors to produce paper.

Synagogue ⊙ – Along with the two in Toledo, this synagogue *(sinagoga)* is one of the few examples of a medieval synagogue to have been preserved in Spain. Built in the early 14C, this one consists of a small square room with a balcony on one side for the women. The upper parts of the walls are covered with Mudéjar stucco and Hebrew inscriptions. The decorative motifs used are geometric and vegetal.

Zoco – *25m/80ft further along.* Access to the former Moorish market is under the brick arches of a narrow alleyway. The shops leading to its two delightful patios sell a range of typical Cordoban handicrafts.

The Jews and Córdoba

The Jews arrived in Córdoba before the Moors and took little time in transforming it into a place of influence, particularly in terms of trade and the teaching of the sciences. Following the Moorish invasion, which was generally well received by the city's Jewish population, the latter tended to concentrate in the area now referred to as the Judería (Jewish quarter), mainly consisting of the streets close to the Puerta de Almodóvar, and built a fine synagogue in calle Judíos. When Fernando III reconquered the city in 1236, the Jews maintained their influence, largely as a result of the prestige of their teaching academies. However, with rising racial hatred, their position in society gradually became more complicated. In the middle of the 13C they were forced to destroy their synagogue and soon after were compelled to pay taxes for the upkeep of the Catholic Church. They were blamed for every epidemic and disaster, until 1492, when Isabel la Católica ordered their expulsion from Spain.

A monument to **Maimónides**, the acclaimed Jewish philosopher and physician, stands in the tiny plaza Tiberiades, just a few metres further along calle Judías.

Museo Municipal Taurino ⊘ – *Plazuela de Maimónides*. The bullfighting museum is housed in the 16C Casa de las Bulas. Access is via two attractive patios: the Mudéjar-influenced entrance patio, and the finely proportioned main patio, around which the museum's rooms are arranged. The museum displays an interesting collection of items on bullfighting, including engravings, posters, photographs and mementoes of Córdoba's most famous matadors, including Lagartijo, Guerrita, Machaquito and Manolete.
The square in front of the museum is dominated by a large mansion and, to the right, the Hotel NH Amistad.
Take calle Cardenal Salazar. This typical narrow alleyway climbs slightly to the plazuela del Hospital del Cardenal.

Facultad de Filosofía y Letras – The Faculty of Philosophy and Letters occupies the former Hospital del Cardenal Salazar. Built in the early 18C, it has a Baroque stone façade bearing a cardinal's escutcheon.

From **calle Romero** *(to the rear of the square)*, the tower of the Mezquita is now visible. This street, along with **calle Deanes**, into which it runs, and the **Judería**, are part of the tourist area surrounding the Mezquita with its myriad souvenir shops.

★ ② SQUARES AND MUSEUMS: Plaza de la Corredera to Plaza de Jerónimo Paéz

Plaza de la Corredera – This large, porticoed, rectangular square, accessed via vaulted passageways, calls to mind the main squares found in Castille. For many centuries it was an important meeting place and the setting for *autos-da-fé*, fiestas, executions, markets and, well into the 19C, bullfights. The **calleja del Toril**, a narrow alleyway used as an enclosure for bulls, still exists today.
Although this sober square dates back many centuries, it has undergone significant restoration. The square visible today dates from the 17C. On Saturdays, its usual tranquillity is broken by the hustle and bustle of a busy **market**.

Plaza del Potro – The elongated plaza del Potro takes its name from the small statue of a colt *(potro)* crowning the fountain at one end of the square. This fountain dates from the 16C, although up until 1874 it was positioned on the opposite side, now occupied by a monument to San Rafael. In former times the square was a great deal livelier as the setting for the city's horse and mule fair.
The **Posada del Potro** ⊘, a charming inn described by Cervantes in *Don Quixote*, stands on the square. It is now a cultural centre dedicated to temporary exhibitions. The joint entrance to the Museo de Bellas Artes and the Museo Julio Romero de Torres, which share a landscaped patio, is located opposite the fountain.

Museo de Bellas Artes ⊘ – *To the left of the patio*. The Fine Arts Museum displays works ranging from the 14C to the 20C, predominantly by local artists. It is housed in the former Hospital de la Caridad, founded in the 15C and which, in the second half of the 19C, was already home to the early museum and the School of Fine Arts. The staircase, covered by a fine Mudéjar *artesonado* ceiling, has preserved its 16C and 17C wall paintings.
Of the works on display, the following are of particular interest: an *Immaculate Conception* by Juan Valdés Leal, which graces the former church; the collection of modern Cordoban and Spanish art dating from the second half of the 19C and first half of the 20C by the likes of Ramón Casas, José Gutiérrez Solana, Rusiñol and Zuloaga; and sculptures by the Cordoban artist Mateo Inurria.

★ **Museo Julio Romero de Torres** ⊘ – *To the right of the patio*. This mansion was the birthplace of this original painter (1880-1930). It how houses an interesting collection of his works, the main subjects of which were beautiful, dark-skinned women.

The ground floor contains a number of posters advertising *ferias* of the past, while the upper floor is devoted to his attractive female portraits such as the *La Chiquita Piconera* (The Charcoal Girl), with its magnificent psychological and intimate treatment of the feminine world, in which he pays particular attention to the gaze of his subjects. This floor also exhibits several canvases with a religious theme, such as *The Virgin of the Lanterns*, a copy of which hangs in an altar outside the Mezquita.

Follow calle San Francisco as far as calle San Fernando. To the left, after an 18C arch, the **Iglesia de San Francisco** comes into view. The church belongs to an old convent of great historical importance, although only a part of a cloister, to the left, now remains.

Return to the calle San Fernando. Pass through the Arco del Portillo into a pedestrianised area. Follow calle de Julio Romero de Torres which, after several bends, heads into plaza de los Páez.

★★**Museo Arqueológico Provincial** ⊙ – This is Andalucia's leading archeological museum. The 16C Renaissance **Palacio de los Páez**, designed by Hernán Ruiz, is an outstanding building displaying a superb collection of objects from the city and its province. It has an interesting **façade★** depicting warriors, escutcheons etc. Sadly, the limestone used in its construction has suffered significant wear and tear over the centuries.

The museum is pleasantly arranged around elegant patios. The **ground floor** is devoted to prehistoric and Iberian objects – such as zoomorphic sculptures – as well as remains from the Visigothic period. The **Roman collection★** around the patios includes toga-clad sculptures, reliefs, sarcophagi, mosaics, capitals and column tambours which bear witness to Córdoba's importance during this period in its history.

The **first floor galleries** house examples of Córdoba's Hispano-Moorish culture with interesting exhibits which include ceramics, bronzes – the 10C **stag★** (*cervatillo*) from Medina Azahara entirely decorated with plant motifs, and the small Mozarabic Abad Samson bell from the same century – and a unique collection of Moorish and Mudéjar well copings. The unusual **capital of the musicians**, decorated with human figures whose heads have been mutilated, stands out from the large collection of capitals on display.

③ PLAZA DE LAS TENDILLAS TO PLAZA DE COLÓN

Plaza de las Tendillas – This spacious square is at very heart of Cordoban life. It is dominated by the equestrian statue of Gonzalo Fernández de Córdoba, known as El Gran Capitán, and is the work of the local artist Mateo Inurria. The streaks of water gushing upwards from the pavement provide welcome cool on hot summer days and are particularly popular with young children, providing those sitting on the café terraces in the square with endless entertainment.

Iglesia de San Nicolás de la Villa ⊙ – The church was built after the Reconquest in the late 13C and early 14C. The peculiar Mudéjar-style **tower★** on the façade is of particular interest. Built in the 15C, it has a square base supporting a lofty octagonal structure with a ledge on its upper section. A modern set of bells completes the tower, but breaks its architectural harmony. A number of small reliefs depicting half-size human characters and the legend of patience and obedience can be seen on pyramidal supports at the junction of the square base and octagonal tower. The simple portal was added in the 16C.

The interior consists of three short aisles, each with two sections; the nave is topped by a wooden ceiling, while the side aisles have more modern vaulting. The apsidal end has preserved its original pointed vaulting. The church has undergone significant modification over the centuries, including the addition of the richly decorated **Capilla del Bautismo** (Baptism Chapel), with its baptism relief and oval cupola, in the middle of the 16C.

Return to plaza de las Tendillas and follow calle Ribera and calleja Barqueros.

★**Iglesia de San Miguel** ⊙ – The church, built during the reign of Fernando III in the 13C, is at the heart of the plaza de San Miguel, pleasantly laid out with café terraces in fine weather. The beauty of its Romanesque ogival façade is accentuated by the sober appearance and harmony of its architectural features. Two buttresses support the central section, which is embellished with a doorway of simple ogival archivolts and a large rose window.

The interior has three short naves, with a wooden ceiling above the central aisle, while the chancel has pointed vaults with ribs decorated with jagged indentations, and an 18C altarpiece in red marble, dominated by an Immaculate Conception. The church has preserved several Mudéjar features, particularly in the Capilla del Bautismo *(Epistle nave)*.

Behind the church, look out for one of Córdoba's oldest bars, the **Taberna San Miguel "El Pisto"**. Even if you do not plan on trying some of the tapas on offer, It is well worth having a quick look inside.

Follow calle San Zoilo, behind the church, and then head along Conde de Torres.

★ **Plaza de los Capuchinos** – The impressive calvary of **Christ of the Lanterns**, set in this whitewashed, austere square, is one of the most well-known monuments in the city. The white marble Christ was sculpted in the late 18C and was set up as part of a *vía crucis* (Stations of the Cross) created by the Capuchin monks in the square. The Iglesia de los Capuchinos and the church of the former 18C Hospital de San Jacinto, containing a venerated, and luxuriously dressed, Virgin of Pain, also front the square.

Exit the square via calle Cabrera and head to plaza de Colón.

Plaza de Colón – This pleasant square named after Columbus has an attractive fountain and gardens. An impressive Baroque building, the Palacio de la Diputación, dominates its west side.

★ **Palacio de la Diputación** – The provincial Parliament building began life as the Convento de la Merced (Convent of Mercy). Although the convent was founded in the 13C, the present Baroque building was constructed in the middle of the 18C. During the Peninsular War a century later, French troops transformed the palace into a hospital, after which it was used as a hospice for a number of years.

The surprisingly large, yet attractive, façade is composed of a large central section and two smaller wings, all of which is painted to imitate marble. The white marble doorway is enhanced by two Solomonic columns, a pediment and two belfries with bells.

Architectural features of interest inside include the patio *(entrance through the left-hand door)*, decorated in the same style as the main façade, the marble staircase, and the Baroque, stucco-adorned church *(access via the middle door)*.

Torre de la Malmuerta – This magnificent 15C octagonal tower is in fact a turret which has preserved the arch connecting it to the defensive wall. In the past it was used as a prison for the nobility as well as an astronomical observatory. Its name originates from an old legend in which a knight killed his wife for failing in her marital duties. On hearing of this act in which the knight had taken justice into his own hands, the king condemned the latter to erect this tower in memory of his wife, who had been wrongfully killed *(mal muerta)*.

★ 4 BARRIO DE SANTA MARINA

★★ **Palacio de Viana** ⊙ – This fine seigniorial palace with its adjoining outbuildings is a fine example of 14C to 19C Cordoban civil architecture. It covers an area of some 6 500m²/ 21 320sq ft, half of which is taken up by the twelve patios and the garden. A visit to the mansion, nowadays a museum, enables visitors to admire the private residence used by a noble family for several centuries. In 1980, the Caja Provincial de Ahorros savings bank purchased the palace from the Marquess and Marchioness of Viana.

Enter the palace from plaza de Don Gome, through an angled doorway consisting of two sections: a flat doorway with a broken pediment and a balcony flanked by two soldiers bearing the coats of arms of the Argote and Figueroa families. The coat of arms of the Saavedra family crowns the balcony.

The interior is enhanced by the 16C main staircase, Renaissance in style, with its magnificent Mudéjar *artesonado* ceiling from the same century, and the harmony of its furnishings. Several rooms have also preserved fine *artesonados*: the 16C Renaissance ceiling in the family's private dining room, the fine Mudéjar example in the main room, as well as that of the Marchioness' writing room.

Córdoba is famous for its **patios**, including the twelve superb examples in this palace, magnificently illustrating this deep-rooted tradition in Cordoban society. The grace, sensitivity, colour and scent of the palace's highly individual patios and garden are totally captivating.

Take calle Santa Isabel to the right, leading to plaza de Santa Marina.

Entrance to the Palacio de Viana

B. Kaufmann/MICHELIN

Palacio de Viana collections

Ground floor:
Porcelain of different provenances from the 17C to 20C.
– **Arquebuses**.

First floor:
– **Azulejos**: 236 pieces of ceramic from the 13C to 19C.
– **Cordoban leather**: the best collection of its kind, comprising articles of embossed leather and cordovans from the 15C to 19C.
– **Tapestries**: Flemish, French and Spanish – some based on cartoons by Goya.
– **Flags**.
The **library** contains over 7 000 books from the 16C to 19C.

Iglesia de Santa Marina de Aguas Santas – The 13C Church of St Marina of the Holy Waters was one of the fourteen built under Fernando III following the reconquest of the city. The austere **façade★**, divided by four heavy buttresses, shows the beauty and strength of stone in its purely architectural form, devoid of any decorative features. The trumpet-shaped portal with its smooth, slightly pointed mouldings corresponds to the early ogival style. The rose window has been restored and the tower was rebuilt in the 16C.

Opposite the church, in plaza del Conde Priego, stands a **monument to Manolete** (b Córdoba 1917 – d Linares 1947), a bullfighting legend who spent his childhood in this district. The wall to the left is part of the **Convento de Santa Isabel**.

Traditional Santa Isabel pastries

The nuns from the Convento de Santa Isabel are famous for their delicious sweets and pastries, which include almond *(almendrados)*, sultana *(sultanas)* and local Córdoba *(pasteles cordobeses)* specialities *(open 9am-12.45pm and 5-7.15pm)*.

Turn around and head along calle Rejas de Don Gome.

Note the imposing belfry on the Iglesia de San Agustín.

Continue along the same street, then along calle Pozanco, to reach plaza de San Rafael.

Plaza de San Rafael – This elongated square is home to the **Iglesia de San Rafael**, with its large neo-Classical façade.

Take the street to the right of the church as far as plaza de San Lorenzo.

★Iglesia de San Lorenzo ⊘ – This church, without doubt one of the finest in the city, appears to stand on its own, as if it is aware of its charms and wishes to highlight them to the full. Another of the Fernandine churches, its construction began in the late 13C and early 14C in early Gothic style. The original and attractive façade comprises a highly unusual portal which is rarely seen in this region, with three slightly pointed arches and a magnificent, finely worked **rose window★**. The tower forms part of the façade: the section extending to the top of the nave would have belonged to an older tower; the remainder is of later origin, and careful inspection reveals it to be slightly displaced. The colour of the stone enhances the overall charm of the church. The sober, harmonious interior consists of three aisles with pointed arches supported by cruciform pillars. The aisles are embellished with wooden ceilings and the chancel with Gothic vaulting. Illumination is provided by three high and narrow windows. The remnants of several 14C wall paintings can still be seen in the apsidal end.

5 CALLE CAPITULARES AND CALLE DE SAN PABLO

Roman temple – *Calle Capitulares, on the corner of calle Claudio Marcelo.* The imposing columns of this 1C AD Roman temple stand out impressively against the sky, providing a reminder of the splendour of Córdoba under Roman rule. All the columns are fluted and crowned with Corinthian capitals. Research has shown that the temple originally had a front portico, that it was raised on a podium and consisted of ten columns on each side, seven of which were positioned inside the inner sanctuary *(cella)*.

★Iglesia de San Pablo ⊘ – The Church of St Paul is part of the former Convento de San Pablo, founded by Fernando III to commemorate the reconquest of Córdoba on 29 June 1236, the feast day of St Paul.
The exterior doorway on calle Capitulares is Baroque in style and was built in 1706. Solomonic columns flank the entrance arch on which the image of St Paul can be seen. The doorway leads to the atrium which in turn opens onto the actual façade. The church has a carillon instead of a bell-tower.

The well-proportioned interior has three wide aisles which have retained the architectural features of the transitional Romanesque-Gothic style despite subsequent restoration. The church's Mudéjar **artesonado ceiling★** is worthy of particular note. The chapel to the left of the presbytery contains the 18C image of **Nuestra Señora de las Angustias** (Our Lady of Anguish), by the great statue sculptor Juan de Mesa, who also carved the Christ of Great Power in Sevilla. The luxuriously dressed Virgin, her face awash with tears, is holding the body of the dead Christ in her arms.
Note also, in the Epistle nave, a 15C **Mudéjar chapel** with fine *artesonado* work, the walls of which are completely covered with stucco above a frieze of *azulejos*.
Head down calle de San Pablo and turn right into calle Villalones.

Palacio de los Villalones – This impressive stone mansion has an interesting façade crowned by a gallery. The Plateresque-style decoration is concentrated around the bays. The palace is said to be the setting for a sad, and rather improbable, legend from the 17C in which the beautiful daughter of a magistrate was buried beneath the foundations of the palace. In spite of numerous excavations, her father was never able to find her. It is said that the young girl's ghost inhabits the house at night.
Exit onto plaza de San Andrés.

Plaza de San Andrés – This small square with its orange trees and simple fountain is home to the **Casa de los Luna**, also known as the Casa de Fernán Pérez de Oliva. Built in the 16C, it has two unusual corner windows. An escutcheon and a plain window can be seen above the door, which is adorned with a Plateresque-style orle. Another Fernandine church, the **Iglesia de San Andrés**, stands to the left. Although originating from the 13C, it was rebuilt in the 18C. Admire the graceful brick tower which dates from this later period.

ADDITIONAL SIGHTS

Roman mausoleum – This Roman mausoleum was discovered in 1993 during construction work in the Jardines de la Victoria. It is a robust, circular monument dating from the 1C AD, the golden age of Roman Córdoba.

Iglesia del Colegio de Santa Victoria – The monumental columns decorating the façade of this church can be seen at the end of plaza de la Compañía. The church, part of the Santa Victoria school *(colegio)*, is built in the neo-Classical style and dates from the middle of the 18C. Ventura Rodríguez was involved in the construction of the church and designed the dome.

EXCURSIONS

★★Medina Azahara (Madinat al-Zahra) ⓘ
Leave Córdoba by the A 431 (west of the map). After 8km/5mi bear right onto a signposted road.

Once on the road, the ochre-coloured mass of the **Monasterio de San Jerónimo de Valparaíso** *(private residence; not open to the public)*, founded in the 15C, can be seen. Medina Azahara was a palace-city built at the behest of Abd ar-Rahman III in 936. Chronicles written at the time contain many references to the luxury and splendour of this city, which amazed all those who visited it. However, the city had only just been completed when it was razed to the ground by the Berbers in 1013 during the war with the Caliphate of Córdoba. The city was later plundered for its materials which were then used in the construction of other buildings, until the first archeological excavations began in 1911. Although little more than 10% of the area once covered by the city remains, it is still possible to imagine what this sumptuous city must have been like.
Medina Azahara is situated in the fold of a mountain, which is why the palace-city was organised in terraces: the upper terrace contained the Alcázar, which housed the residences of the Caliph and other dignitaries, as well as administrative and military dependencies; gardens and the large reception room were situated in the middle terrace, and a mosque (excavated) and other buildings of the city were found below.

Tour – *Signposted itinerary.* The tour starts outside the north wall, marked out by square towers. Access to the interior is via an angled doorway, typical of Islamic defensive architecture.
Upper terrace – The door opens onto the **residential quarters**, to the right. The rest of the upper dwellings were built around two large square patios. To the west, at the highest point of the Alcázar, is the **Casa Real** or Royal Quarters *(Dar al-Mulk)*, currently under restoration *(not open to the public)*.
To the left of the entrance door are the **official quarters**, in which the Casa de los Visires and the Gran Pórtico stand out. The **Casa de los Visires** *(Dar al-Wuzara)* comprises a suite of rooms, including a large basilica-like hall surrounded by various dependencies and patios. The viziers held their civil audiences in the large hall. The garden in front is modern.

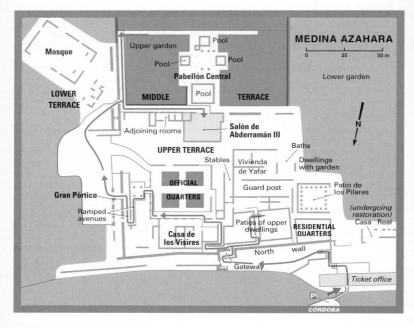

Several streets lead uphill to the impressive **portico**, the façade of a large parade ground. Only a small section of this magnificent arcade is still standing; the gateway once consisted of 15 arches and was the monumental entrance to the Alcázar, through which ambassadors would enter.

Middle terrace – The remains of the **mosque**, which stood on the lower terrace, can be seen to the left, along the path leading down from this terrace. The five aisles are at right angles to the rectangular patio, as is the base of the minaret in the northwest wall of the patio.

The middle terrace, overlooking the gardens, is dominated by the jewel of this archeological site: the **Abd ar-Rahman III Room** *(Salón de Abderramán III)*. Before entering the room, baths can be seen in the adjoining dwellings. The restoration of this richly decorated reception room gives an idea of the city's splendour in the 10C and the strong impression that it must have made on visiting dignitaries. Only the very best materials were used in the construction and embellishment of the entrance doorway and the three aisles which formed part of it. Beautiful horseshoe arches with alternating voussoirs are supported by grey and blue marble, contrasting with the large white marble flagstones used for the floor paving. The magnificent carved stone panels on the walls are also worthy of note with their geometric and plant motif decoration, including stylisations of the tree of life, a common theme in Hispano-Islamic art.

Opposite this room is the **Pabellón Central** or central pavilion, once used as a waiting room for visitors with an audience with the Caliph. The pavilion is situated in the centre of the gardens and is surrounded by four small pools.

Las Ermitas ⊘

From Córdoba, 13km/8mi on the El Brillante road.
From Medina Azahara, turn left after 10km/6mi at the first crossroads and then follow signs to Ermitas at the second.

From either direction, the **views★** of the *sierra* and the surrounding countryside are quite delightful.

This group of 13 hermitages *(ermitas)* and a single church is situated in a wild, mountainous location. It dates from the 18C, although the hermit tradition in the area goes back several centuries prior to this.

In the beautiful paseo de los Cipreses (Cypress Avenue), the skull and poetry on the **Cruz del Humilladero** serve as a reminder of the transitory nature of life and the importance of resisting sin. Once past the cross, the **Ermita de la Magdalena** can be seen to the left, along with the hermits' cemetery and the church in the distance. Entering the vestibule of the **church** *(on the right)*, note the skull once used by a hermit as a cup and plate. The rich decoration of the church – the result of donations – contrasts with the hermits' austere existence. Behind the high altar, in the room used by the hermits as a chapter-house, note also the attractive frieze of lustre *azulejos*.

The rest of the hermitage is spread over the hillside. Back at the entrance, a path leads to the **Balcón del Mundo**. From this viewpoint, dominated by an enormous Sacred Heart (1929), a magnificent **panorama★★** of Córdoba and its surrounding countryside can be enjoyed. To the right, the view extends as far as the Castillo de Almodóvar del Río, perched on a hilltop.

COSTA DE ALMERÍA★

Almería

Michelin map 446 V 20-24, U 24

This part of the Andalucian coast is characterised by extensive beaches, coves lapped by crystal-clear waters, small fishing villages that have developed into pleasant resorts, attractive tourist complexes and areas of outstanding, almost virgin, natural beauty. Along with its superb climate, little rainfall and plentiful sunshine almost all year round, the Costa de Almería is fast developing into one of the region's most popular tourist destinations.

1 From Adra to Almería

117km/73mi – allow half a day

Adra – This resort, situated at the heart of a fertile plain, was a Phoenician and Roman outpost, and has the distinction of being the last settlement on the Iberian Peninsula to be abandoned by the Moors. Adra has a fishing port, a marina, a good beach and several 17C and 18C seigniorial houses. The Iglesia de la Inmaculada Concepción contains a *Christ of the Expiration*, attributed to Alonso de Mena. The Torre de los Perdigones, a 45m/147ft-high tower which was originally part of a 19C lead foundry, now houses the town's tourist office.

20km/12mi inland along the A 347.

Berja – The Roman town of *Virgi* (which evolved into *vergel*, meaning "orchard"), nestled at the foot of the Sierra de Gádor, has a number of handsome noble Renaissance mansions and fountains. Remains of the old Roman amphitheatre are still visible.

Return to the N 340 – E 15.

The road offers attractive **views** of the Sierra de la Contraviesa to the left, with the Cerrón peak (1 238m/4 060m) in the foreground.
After a bend in the road, the "Sea of Plastic", covering almost all of the area known as the **Campo de Dalías**, comes into view. Between Adra and Almería, the N 340 – E 15 passes through swathes of plastic greenhouses, a typical feature of Almería, producing several crops a year, in addition to early grapes, vegetables and flowers.

After El Ejido, turn right.

Almerimar – This modern tourist complex of chalets, apartments and hotels also has a golf course and marina, all of which combine to create an attractive resort.

Return to the N 340 - E 15. At El Parador, bear right.

Roquetas de Mar – A fishing village which has become engulfed by tourism and been transformed into a lively resort. The remains of the old castle can be seen by the lighthouse *(faro)*. In addition to the fishing port and marina, Roquetas also has its own golf course and a water park.
The **Urbanización Roquetas de Mar** *(3.5km/2mi)* has attractive fine sandy beaches and a long palm-tree-lined promenade with views of the Gulf of Almería and Cabo de Gata. The avenida del Mediterráneo, which joins up with the paseo del Mar, is teeming with shops and restaurants.

The "Sea of Plastic"

Almerimar

EATING OUT

Náutico – *Puerto deportivo Almerimar* – ☎ *950 49 71 62*. A famous restaurant specialising in fish and seafood. Terrace with views of the marina.

Roquetas de Mar

WHERE TO STAY

Sabinal Hesperia – *Avenida Las Gaviotas* – ☎ *950 33 36 00* – fax *950 33 35 33* – *417 rooms* – *13 200pts*. In the heart of the beach area. A large hotel complex with spacious rooms overlooking the sea. A number of hotels of a similar standard are also located nearby.

EATING OUT

Al-Baida – *Avenida Las Gaviotas* – ☎ *950 33 38 21* – *closed Mon and in Jan and Feb*. A well-known local eatery serving fish and seafood. Simple decor, plus an aquarium containing live lobsters.

Aguadulce – This large resort is located in an area of abundant vegetation just 11km/7mi from Almería. It is a popular beach destination with excellent tourist facilities and a pleasant promenade. The nature reserve of Punta Entinas–Sabinar, an area of sand dunes and marshland, is to the southeast of Aguadulce. Juniper bushes, bulrushes and canes predominate in this unusual landscape.

The road from Aguadulce to Almería – The road follows the contours of the coast, hugging the cliff tops and passing through tunnels excavated in the rock. The approach towards Almería offers views of the city, the bay, the port and the fortress.

Almería – *See ALMERÍA.*

② From Almería to Mojácar
132km/82.5mi – allow one day

Níjar – *See Parque Natural de CABO DE GATA-NÍJAR.*

★★**Parque Natural de Cabo de Gata–Níjar** – *See Parque Natural de CABO DE GATA-NÍJAR.*

★**Mojácar** – *See MOJÁCAR.*

Garrucha – *See MOJÁCAR.*

The road from Mojácar Playa to Agua Amarga – *See MOJÁCAR.*

COSTA DE HUELVA★
Huelva
Michelin map 446 U 7-8-9-10, V 10

The Huelva coast is a succession of peaceful, sun-blessed beaches interrupted by the occasional delta where rivers such as the Guadiana, Guadalquivir and Tinto flow into the Atlantic. It forms part of the Costa de la Luz (Coast of Light) which extends from the Portuguese border to Tarifa, on the Straits of Gibraltar, and is the least developed stretch of southern Spain's Atlantic coastline. The coast is famous in history as the departure point for Columbus's voyage of discovery to the New World.

① From the Parque Nacional de Doñana to Palos de la Frontera
49km/30.5mi – allow half a day

★★★**Parque Nacional de Doñana** – *See Parque Nacional de DOÑANA.*
4km/2.5mi south of the El Acebuche information centre along the A 483.

Matalascañas – The road to this popular resort crosses an attractive section of the Doñana National Park. Matalascañas is one of the busiest resorts in Andalucia, with numerous apartment blocks, night-clubs, outdoor bars and a huge range of leisure facilities for summer visitors.
30km/19mi northwest along the A 494.

Mazagón – The fine-sandy **Playa de Mazagón** extends for 10km/6mi from the mouth of the Río Tinto to the Torre del Loro. This quiet beach is lined by a number of good-quality campsites and chalet complexes, but has avoided the blight of high-rise accommodation. Mazagón has its own marina offering a range of activities for visitors. The Parador de Mazagón commands delightful **views** of this Atlantic coastline.
13.5km/8.5mi northwest along the A 494.

Matalascañas

WHERE TO STAY

Hostal Victoria – *Sector 0, 18* – ☎ *959 44 09 57* – *fax 959 44 82 64* – *11 rooms – 6 000pts (8 000pts in Aug)* – *closed from mid-Sept to Mar*. Despite the building's somewhat ugly appearance, built on pillars, the rooms are pleasant and attractively decorated. Good value for money.

El Cortijo – *Sector E, Parcela 15* – ☎ *959 44 87 00* – *fax 959 44 83 75* – *53 rooms – 15 000pts*. The hotel, distinguishable by its towers, has a large swimming pool, two restaurants, an Andalucian-style bar and comfortable rooms. Organised activities in summer.

EATING OUT

The main square is lined by a number of places for lunch or dinner. Two Andalucian-style restaurants are particularly recommended: **Manolo León**, which specialises in meat dishes, and **Manolo Vázquez**, whose menu is dominated by fish and seafood.

Mazagón

WHERE TO STAY

Santa María – *Avenida de Conquistadores* – ☎ *959 53 60 18* – *fax 959 37 72 58 – 70 rooms – 12 790pts*. This hotel is immediately visible as you come into Mazagón along the Huelva road. Modern, well-appointed rooms, a bar and a restaurant.

Parador de Mazagón – *Playa de Mazagón (several kilometres from the town towards Matalascañas)* – ☎ *959 53 63 00* – *fax 959 53 62 28 – 43 rooms – 19 000pts*. This modern-style *parador* dominates Mazagón beach. Rooms with terrace and panoramic views. The restaurant serves varied cuisine, including sea bass *(lubina)*, lobster *(langosta)*, crayfish *(langostinos)*, prawns *(gambas)* and loin of pork *(solomillo de cerdo)*.

EATING OUT

El Remo – *Avenida de Conquistadores, 123 (on the outskirts of the town towards Matalascañas)* – ☎ *959 53 61 38*. One of the best restaurants in the area. A pleasant terrace with upholstered chairs and a bar overlooking the beach. The menu includes fish, seafood and grilled meats.

Palos de la Frontera

WHERE TO STAY

Santa María – *Along the Palos de la Frontera – La Rábida road* – ☎ *959 53 00 01 – 18 rooms – 6 500pts*. Just a short distance from the Monasterio de La Rábida. A small hotel with a large restaurant overlooking the Río Tinto. Unfortunately, only one double room has a view of the river.

La Pinta – *Rábida, 79* – ☎ *959 35 05 11* – *fax 959 53 01 64 – 30 rooms – 8 000pts*. A delightful small hotel with pleasant rooms in the centre of Palos.

Punta Umbría

WHERE TO STAY

Real – *Falucho, 2* – ☎ *959 31 04 58* – *fax 959 31 59 78 – 24 rooms – 6 500pts*. This small hotel is located in the pedestrianised part of town. Basic, but spotless, rooms.
The nearby **Hotel Emilio** *(calle Ancha, 21)* is of a similar standard to the Real.

Ayamontino Ría – *Avenida de La Ría, 1* – ☎ *959 31 14 58* – *fax 959 31 14 62 – 22 rooms – 7 000pts*. This hotel has several rooms overlooking the port.

Pato Amarillo – *Urbanización Everluz* – ☎ *959 31 12 50* – *fax 959 31 12 58 – 120 rooms – 12 500pts*. The Pato Amarillo has a number of rooms with views of the sea. Facilities for guests include a garden, swimming pool, bar and restaurant.

EATING OUT

Miramar – *Miramar, 1* – ☎ *959 31 12 43*. On the beach front. Although the atmosphere is somewhat noisy, smoky and lacking refinement, the Miramar serves excellent fish and seafood.

The **plaza del Mercado** is lined with numerous bars and restaurants serving fresh fish and seafood.

El Rompido

EATING OUT

Caribe II – *Calle Nao* – ☎ *959 39 90 27* – *open daily, 11am to 5pm (also open Fri and Sat evenings)*. The terrace here with views of the fishing port is an ideal place for a leisurely lunch. Fish and seafood specialities include squid *(calamares)*, red mullet *(salmonete)*, crayfish *(langostinos)* and lobster *(bogavante)*.

★**Palos de la Frontera** – This picturesque small town on the left bank of the Río Tinto was the point of departure for Columbus's voyage of discovery to the New World in 1492. It is also the birthplace of the Pinzón brothers, who sailed alongside Columbus on his epic adventure. The charm of Palos lies in its whitewashed houses, narrow alleyways and lively atmosphere which can be best enjoyed in its charming squares. It is one of the towns along the so-called "Columbus Route", as can be seen in the commemorative *azulejos* dotted around the town.

Casa-Museo de Martín Alonso Pinzón ⏱ – The former residence of this famous navigator from Palos houses some of Pinzón's personal mementoes (signed letters, navigational equipment etc), as well as a room displaying photographs, newspaper cuttings and other objects relating to the first transatlantic flight of the Plus Ultra seaplane, which flew from Palos de la Frontera to Buenos Aires in 1926.

Iglesia de San Jorge ⏱ – This fine example of 15C Gothic-Mudéjar architecture fronts an attractive small square. The church is famous as the place where Columbus prayed on the morning of his departure (3 August), and from where all his sailors exited through the Puerta de los Novios doorway before making their way to the harbour to board the ships that would take them to the New World. Behind the church stands La Fontanilla, a fountain crowned by a small Mudéjar shrine. The fountain supplied the water for the three caravels – the Niña, the Pinta and the Santa María – before they sailed from Palos under Columbus's command.

② From Huelva to Ayamonte

77km/48mi – allow one day

★**Huelva** – *See HUELVA.*

22km/14mi south along the A 497.

Punta Umbría – *Punta Umbría can be reached in summer by ferry from Huelva across the Odiel River*. This former rest centre for miners from Río Tinto is situated at the southern tip of Huelva's estuary in the middle of the salt marshes of the Paraje Natural de las Marismas del Odiel nature reserve. Nowadays it is a popular resort with a small marina and attractive beaches lapped by crystal-clear water and lined by pine groves. The early-morning fish auction held here daily is well worth attending as is the colourful fishermen's procession in honour of the Virgin Mary on 15 August every year. The **Paraje Natural de Enebrales de Punta Umbría**, an area of outstanding beauty on a sandy deposit formed by the effects of the wind off the sea, is a protected area containing several species of lizard and whitethroat in a landscape dominated by savin, juniper, mastic and hawthorn.

7km/4.5mi northwest along the A 497.

La Flecha de El Rompido

El Portil – The proximity of El Portil to Huelva and its splendid beach have resulted in the development of this section of coast into one of the province's busiest resort areas. The nearby **Reserva Natural de la Laguna de El Portil**, a lagoon nature reserve of outstanding beauty, is home to a variety of birds, including the grey heron and grebe.

9km/5.5mi northwest along the HV 4111.

El Rompido – This small fishing port has a pleasant dune-lined beach popular with summer visitors. The **Paraje Natural Marismas del Río Piedras y Flecha de El Rompido★**, a protected area of salt marsh *(marisma)* nearby, on the road towards La Antilla, has been formed from sediment carried by the river to its mouth. This reserve is home to an array of birdlife including the black-headed gull, pintail, oyster catcher and common egret.

9km/5.5mi north along the HV 4111.

Cartaya – The bright and spacious inland town of Cartaya is close to the major resorts in this part of Huelva province. The hub of the town, the **plaza Redonda**, is a tranquil square adorned with orange and lemon trees and elegant wrought-iron street lamps. All of the town's major buildings are found around the square: the 16C Iglesia de San Pedro, with its *azulejo*-decorated campanile, the town hall and the seigniorial Casa de Cultura.

7km/4.5mi southwest along the N 431.

Lepe – The town is one of the area's main agricultural centres, predominantly producing strawberries, figs and melons.

6km/4mi south along the HV 412.

La Antilla – The crowds of visitors attracted to La Antilla's delightful beaches have yet to detract from the charm of this quiet resort lined by old houses, which contrasts with the nearby Islantilla, a modern complex of apartment blocks and a luxurious golf course. The busy fishing port of **El Terrón**, just a short distance from La Antilla at the mouth of the Piedras River, is well worth visiting to watch the local fishermen tending their nets and to enjoy the excellent seafood on offer in its many restaurants.

17km/10.5mi northwest. Return to Lepe and follow the N 431.

★**Ayamonte** – *See AYAMONTE.*

COSTA DEL SOL ★★
Málaga
Michelin map 446 V 14, W 14-15-16, X 14

The Costa del Sol (Sun Coast) stretches along Andalucia's Mediterranean shore from Tarifa on the Straits of Gibraltar to the Cabo de Gata, a headland east of Almería. Every year, millions of visitors are attracted here by its wonderful climate, sandy beaches, whitewashed towns and villages and the diversity of leisure activities on offer. Sadly, the majority of the region's typical fishing communities were transformed beyond recognition in the 1970s with the massive development of the Spanish tourist industry. Yet, despite this annual influx of visitors from around the world – particularly from Northern Europe – the Costa del Sol still retains its spell-binding attraction.

Although the coast is now a year-round holiday destination popular in winter with those escaping the harsh northern winter, the Costa del Sol comes to life during the summer, when the beaches are packed, hotels are fully booked and the night-life continues until dawn. Over the past decade or so, a large number of luxurious holiday complexes have sprung up all along the coast. Many of these have been built close to the dozens of golf courses dotted along the coast, giving rise to its alternative nickname, the **Costa del Golf**, attracting famous showbiz personalities from around the world.

A delightful climate – Protected from the extremes of the inland weather systems affecting the Serranía de Ronda and the Sierra Nevada, the Costa del Sol enjoys mild winters (12°C/54°F), hot summers (26°C/79°F) and sufficient rain in winter and spring to allow subtropical crops to grow in the small alluvial plains.

From Torremolinos to Sotogrande
234km/146mi – allow two days

Torremolinos – Since the 1950s, when it started to attract numerous artists and intellectuals, Torremolinos has experienced huge growth, which reached its full potential in the 1960s with the expansion of the Spanish tourist industry. Nowadays, little remains of its traditional architecture, which has been replaced by a mass of apartment blocks, hotels and tourist complexes accommodating hundreds

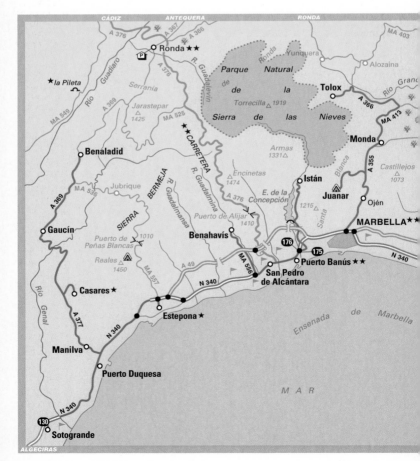

of thousands of visitors throughout the year who are attracted by the sunny climate, miles and miles of beaches, and endless choice of leisure activities in what has now developed into a lively and cosmopolitan resort. The town's commercial hub is centred around **calle de San Miguel**, with its impressive array of shops, but also the site of the **Molino de la Torre**, literally the "Mill of the Tower", the only remaining vestige of the many windmills that have lent their name to this former fishing village. The **Paseo Marítimo**, an attractive tree-lined promenade running parallel to the beach, boasts dozens of restaurants, mainly specialising in fish and seafood. Mention should also be made of the **Pueblo Andaluz**, a recently built district imitating traditional Andalucian architecture, which is fast establishing a reputation for its bars and cafés.

Benalmádena – *12km/7.5mi southwest along the N 340*. The resort of **Arroyo de la Miel**, with its succession of apartments and hotels, comes into view a mile or so before Benalmádena Costa.

Benalmádena has developed into a popular summer destination at the foot of the Sierra de Mijas. Along with its neighbouring resorts along the Costa del Sol, it now attracts the majority of its visitors from April until November, although it is still busy with expatriates and retired foreign residents over the winter months. The town has some excellent beaches, modern golf courses, a marina and myriad restaurants, night-clubs, and terraced bars and cafés.

The **old quarter** *(casco antiguo)*, a few kilometres inland, has managed to preserve the charms of a traditional Andalucian *pueblo* with its whitewashed houses, flower-decked windows and festive atmosphere. The town has an interesting **Museo Arqueológico** ⊘, displaying an interesting collection of pre-Columbian artefacts; the **Castillo de Bil-Bil**, a modern building used to host cultural events; and the 16C Torremuelle, Torrequebrada and Torrebermeja **watchtowers**.

8km/5mi west. Take the N 340 then bear onto the A 368 at exit 217.

★ **Mijas** – *See MIJAS.*

13km/8mi northwest along the A 387.

Alhaurín el Grande – This elegant town sits impressively on a hill in the Sierra de Mijas, amid a landscape of orchards, market gardens, lemon and orange trees and olive groves. The old quarter is a maze of cobbled streets lined by whitewashed houses adorned with flower-decked balconies. Alhaurín has preserved several monumental buildings from its past such as the **Arco del Cobertizo**, a Moorish gateway which was part of the town's walled defences, and the **Ermita de la Vera Cruz**, an unusual 20C chapel built in neo-Gothic style.

8km/5mi northwest along the A 366.

Coín – Coín is situated in the middle of a fertile area of citrus groves. Its main attraction is the large-proportioned 16C **Iglesia de San Juan** ⊘, containing a fine Baroque altarpiece and colourful *azulejos* on the spandrels and cornice. Other churches of interest include the 15C **Iglesia de Santa María de la Encarnación**, built above the former mosque, from which the minaret remains; the **Iglesia de San Andrés** ⊘, with its rich *artesonado* work; and the Iglesia del Santo Cristo de la Veracruz, which belonged to a former Trinitarian convent.

22km/14mi south. Return to Alhaurín el Grande and take the MA 426.

Fuengirola – Fuengirola is another of the major resorts on the Costa del Sol, with

Aerial view of the Costa del Sol

7km/4.5mi of beaches, excellent sports amenities and an impressive number of apartments, hotels, restaurants and leisure facilities attracting visitors all year round.

The **Castillo de Sohail** dominates the town from on high. The unusual name of this fortress derives from the discovery by the Moors of the star Sohail, which is known today as Canopus. The castle has preserved its 10C merloned towers and its original walls. Another of the town's noteworthy features is the **Santa Fe de los Boliches** district, with its interesting **archeological remains** – some 1C AD baths and the vestiges of a Roman villa – and the **Museo Abierto**, an outdoor art gallery formed by murals by well-known artists (Sempere, Rafael Peinado, Elena Asins etc).

28km/17.5mi southwest along the N 340.

★★ **Marbella** – *See MARBELLA.*

Excursion inland to Tolox – *See MARBELLA.*

Return to the N 340.

★★ **Puerto Banús** – *See MARBELLA.*

9km/5.5mi southwest along the N 340.

San Pedro de Alcántara – This old town, located within the municipality of Marbella, was once populated by settlers working on the cotton and sugar cane plantations owned by the Marqués del Duero. Today, it is a large resort, mainly the result of its proximity to Marbella. It has retained some impressive archeological remnants from its past, such as **Las Bóvedas** ⊘ – unusual thermal baths with an octagonal floor plan and vaulted rooms – and the **Basílica de Vega del Mar**, a 6C paleo-Christian temple with three aisles and two opposing apses containing numerous tombs with valuable funerary objects.

6km/4mi north of San Pedro de Alcántara along the MA 556, a winding **road**★★ ascends the sierra to **Ronda**★★ *(see RONDA).*

Benahavís – This inland village in the foothills of the Sierra Bermeja is on the banks of the Guadalmina River, close to the impressive Las Angosturas Canyon *(cañón).* Its name, the remains of the Castillo de Montemayor, and several old watchtowers testify to the Moorish origins of the village. Benahavís has an extraordinary number of **restaurants** for a village its size, built by British entrepreneurs in the 1980s.

Return to Pedro de Alcántara and continue southwest along the N 340 for 15km/9.5mi.

★ **Estepona** – *See ESTEPONA.*

Take the N 340 to San Luis de Sabinillas, then bear left on the A 377.

Y. Arthus-Bertrand/ALTITUDE

Manilva – Manilva extends across a gently undulating hill surrounded by vineyards just a few kilometres from the Mediterranean. Its main attraction is the **Iglesia de Santa Ana**, built in the 18C. Note the unusual mixtilinear arch over the portal.

The **coastline** to the south of Manilva has several pleasant beaches (Playa de la Paloma, Playa del Salto de la Mora, Playa Negra) between San Luis de Sabinillas and Puerto Duquesa.

15km/9.5mi northwest. Continue along the A 377, then bear right on the MA 546.

★**Casares** – The houses in this small settlement appear to be suspended above a promontory in the Sierra Crestenilla, hidden amid a fertile landscape of outstanding beauty. Casares was one of the last strongholds of the Moors in the mountains of Málaga province. Its most famous son is the father of Andalucian nationalism, **Blas Infante** (1855-1936), whose birthplace can be seen at no 51, calle Carrera *(see p 24)*.

The old **Moorish quarter**★ has preserved its labyrinthine plan, with narrow streets and typical low houses with their reddish-coloured roofs. The plaza de España is dominated by the 17C Iglesia de San Sebastián, a single-nave church with an elegant Baroque tower.

The remains of the former Moorish fortress on a rocky promontory above the old quarter stand alongside the Iglesia de la Encarnación, a 16C church badly damaged during the Spanish Civil War.

16km/10mi northwest. Return to the A 377 and continue north.

Gaucín – The village of Gaucín is impressively sited on a rocky hill in the heart of the Serranía de Ronda. With its characteristic whitewashed houses and typical narrow streets, it is a worthy member of the famed White Villages of Andalucia. The **views**★ from the remains of the old castle are particularly impressive. Gaucín is well known for its unfermented grape juice *(mosto)* and its *aguardiente*, a fiery brandy.

Benadalid – *12km/7.5mi northeast along the A 369.* This village sits in the shelter of a rocky outcrop, surrounded by extensive olive and almond groves. The strong Moorish influence is evident in the streets of Benadalid, which are decorated with *azulejos* narrating legends and anecdotes of local history. The village is crowned by the vestiges of the former Arab fortress, with its three flat cylindrical towers.

Return to San Luis de Sabinillas and rejoin the N 340.

Puerto Duquesa – *2km/1.2mi south.* This lively marina is teeming with bars, restaurants and outdoor terraces which provide a contrast to the sober appearance of the nearby Castillo de Sabinillas.

Sotogrande – *12km/7.5mi south along the N 340.* A select group of luxury housing complexes and elegant residential homes has been developed next to the famous Sotogrande golf course, which has hosted the prestigious Ryder Cup between Europe and the United States.

Casares

M. Raurich/STOCK PHOTOS

TOURIST OFFICES

Benalmádena – *Avenida Antonio Machado, 10. Benalmádena Costa.* ☎ *952 44 12 95. www.benalmadena.com*

Estepona – *Avenida de San Lorenzo, 1.* ☎ *952 80 09 13. www.pgb.es/estepona*

Fuengirola – *Avenida Jesús Santos Rein.* ☎ *952 46 74 57/46 76 25. www.pta.es/fuengirola*

Marbella – *Glorieta de la Fontanilla, Paseo Marítimo.* ☎ *952 77 14 42. www.pgb.es/marbella*
Other tourist offices are also located in the entrance arches to the town and on the motorway.

Torremolinos – *Glorieta de las Comunidades Autónomas, Playa del Bajondillo.* ☎ *952 37 19 09.*

TRANSPORT

Airport

The only airport along the Costa del Sol is in Málaga, 9.8km/6mi from the city centre.
Switchboard ☎ 952 04 84 84/04 – Arrivals ☎ 952 04 88 38/44 – Departures ☎ 952 04 88 04/42.
A bus service (operated by Portillo) runs between the airport and resorts along the coast, although a change of bus may be necessary. The local train *(tren de cercanías)* connecting Málaga with Fuengirola is another option for visitors making their own way between the two towns *(see Trains below)*. Taxis are also available twenty-four hours a day.

Although the public transport system along the coast is particularly efficient, many visitors prefer to hire a car for maximum flexibility. Two fast highways *(autovías)* run along the coast; on the most recent of these, tolls *(peaje)* are payable.

Trains

Málaga – The only railway station for long-distance services is in Málaga (avenida de Andalucía ☎ 952 87 16 73; RENFE (Spanish State Railways) Málaga ☎ 952 36 02 02).
A local service operates between Málaga and Fuengirola via La Colina, Torremolinos and Benalmádena. This service also stops at Málaga airport and a number of resorts along its route. Departures every 30min from 6.33am to 11.15pm. The journey time between Málaga and Fuengirola is 55min and tickets cost 315pts.

Benalmádena – Avenida de la Estación. ☎ 952 12 80 84

Fuengirola – Avenida Juan Gómez "Juanito". ☎ 952 12 83 15

Torremolinos – Avenida de la Estación. ☎ 952 12 80 85

Inter-city buses

One of the most popular ways of travelling to and from towns and cities along the Costa del Sol is by the efficient inter-city bus service. The **Portillo** company operates fast, comfortable transfers to every major town in the area, as well to intermediate destinations. Every town or city also has its own bus station offering departures to elsewhere in Spain and beyond.

Benalmádena – Benalmádena does not have a main bus station. **Portillo** buses connect the three parts of Benalmádena with Torremolinos from 7am to around 10.30pm, stopping at request stops en route. Tickets cost in the region of 100pts, depending on the length of journey, and can be purchased on the bus itself or at the booth in avenida Antonio Machado (near McDonald's).

Estepona – The bus station is located on avenida de España. ☎ 952 80 02 49.

Fuengirola – On the corner of avenida Matías Sáenz de Tejada and calle Alfonso XIII. ☎ 952 47 50 66.

Marbella – Buses depart from the terminal on avenida del Trapiche (☎ 952 76 44 00) to destinations around Spain and major European capitals. Marbella and Málaga bus stations are the two main terminals on the Costa del Sol.

Taxis

Benalmádena – ☎ 952 44 15 45.

Estepona – ☎ 952 80 29 00/952 80 06 39.

Fuengirola – ☎ 952 47 10 00.

Marbella – ☎ 952 77 44 88.

San Pedro de Alcántara – ☎ 952 78 38 38.

Torremolinos – ☎ 952 38 06 00.

Local buses

Benalmádena – A regular bus service operates between Benalmádena Costa, Benalmádena Pueblo and Arroyo de la Miel, stopping frequently en route. A one-way ticket costs 115pts.

Torremolinos – Two bus lines (L1 and L2) cover the whole of Torremolinos. A one-way ticket costs 110pts.

Fuengirola, Marbella and **Estepona** – There is no local bus service in these three resorts.

Marinas

Every major resort has its own marina for pleasure craft. The main ones along the Costa del Sol are as follows:

Puerto Banús – *6km/4mi from the centre of Marbella.* 915 moorings for boats ranging in length from 8m/26ft to 50m/164ft. Puerto Banús is home to some of the world's most luxurious sailing craft. The marina was opened in 1970 and is now one of the resort's most popular attractions.

Puerto Marina – This marina in Benalmádena is more recent than Puerto Banús but has developed into one of the largest moorings for pleasure craft on the Costa del Sol with a capacity for 1 000 boats. Other marinas can also be found in Estepona, Marbella and Fuengirola.

Puerto Banús

BENALMÁDENA

Where to stay

MID-RANGE

La Fonda – *Santo Domingo de Guzmán –* ☎ *952 56 86 25 – fax 952 56 86 84 – 26 rooms – 12 000pts.* An ideal location for those wishing to enjoy the pleasures of the sea in an area away from the coast's high-rise resorts. A charming hotel in the Sierra de Castillejos, overlooking the Mediterranean. Spacious rooms, indoor pool, patios and terraces with views of the hills and sea.

Cafés, bars & night-life

In Benalmádena, life is centred around the Puerto Marina and the nearby plaza Solymar. Several bars in plaza de la Mezquita de Arroyo de la Miel are also popular, although the marina and port area are the mainstays of the resort's social scene, attracting thousands of visitors twenty-four hours a day.

Benalmádena has its own casino, the **Casino Torrequebrada** *(*☎ *952 44 60 00)*, as well as a well-known funfair, **Tívoli World**, in the Arroyo de la Miel district *(open daily, Apr to Dec* ☎ *952 57 70 16)*. In summer the town organises a programme of concerts by major Spanish and international artists.

Maracas – *Puerto Marina. Open daily, 11am to 5am.* This spacious, multi-functional bar in the port area is a popular place for a coffee on the terrace, a cocktail at the bar or for dancing until dawn. A lively venue with tropical decor attracting an eclectic, mixed age group day and night.

165

Monet – *Puerto Marina. Open daily, 10am to 4am.* A café by day and pub by night. Views of the port and a large terrace full of comfortable wicker chairs. A pleasant location for an early-evening drink. At night, drinks are served at the two bars: one outside, the other indoors, where the dance floor springs into life as the night progresses.

Tabú – *Puerto Marina. Open daily, 11am to 6am.* Tabú is a café, bar and disco rolled into one, with Caribbean-inspired decoration and a huge choice of fruit juices and cocktails popular with young and old alike. Entrance to the disco costs 1 000pts (including a drink). Salsa classes for women on Thursdays and Sundays.

Disco Kiu – *Plaza Solymar, Benalmádena Costa. Open daily, midnight to 7am.* An enormous 80s-style night-club with various rooms devoted to salsa, mainstream pop and house. Popular with a young international crowd.

Shopping

Of the three parts of Benalmádena – Benalmádena Pueblo, Arroyo de la Miel and Benalmádena Costa – the latter, which includes the marina area, has the highest concentration of shops. In the late afternoon and evening, the narrow streets and small squares behind the marina are thronged with people browsing at the arts and crafts stalls selling a wide range of local handicrafts. The Avenida de Antonio Machado is also a busy shopping area. In Arroyo de la Miel, calle de las Flores and its surrounding streets contain the town's more traditional shops.

A typical **market** selling a vast array of products is held on Friday mornings in the car park of Tívoli Park, while on Sundays another market, selling mainly second-hand goods, is held at the same location.

Benalmádena Pueblo has fewer shops, although the Casa del Artesano, in plaza de España, is well worth a look, particularly on Saturdays, when local artisans can be seen making their traditional products.

ESTEPONA

Where to stay

MODERATE

La Malagueña – *Rafael, 1 –* ☎ *952 80 00 11 – 17 rooms – 6 000pts.* This family-run *hostal* on Estepona's main square has basic but adequate rooms.

MID-RANGE

Santa María – *At Km 167 on the Cádiz–Málaga road, a few kilometres from Estepona towards Málaga –* ☎ *952 88 81 77 – fax 952 88 81 80 – 37 rooms – 12 350pts – open April to Oct.* A hotel with bungalows and rooms looking out onto the garden. Swimming pool with waterfalls, a Thai restaurant and a bar overlooking the beach. Rooms are best booked ahead of time as they are often reserved in advance by travel agencies.

Eating out – tapas

La Rada – *Avenida España and calle Caridad, Edifício Neptuno –* ☎ *952 79 10 36.* A must for visitors to the town. A pleasant atmosphere and excellent fish and seafood.

Los Rosales – *Damas –* ☎ *952 79 29 45.* In an alleyway off the picturesque plaza de las Flores. This bar specialises in fish and seafood.

Cafés, bars & night-life

Calle Real, in the town centre, and the **Puerto Deportivo** (marina) are the hub of life in Estepona. In the afternoon and evening the port area is a pleasant place for a quiet drink on one of its many terraces. As night falls, the action tends to move to the quieter bars on calle Real, before heading back to the lively bars around the harbour in the early hours.

Pop and rock concerts are organised on the beach in summer.

Jazz Pub – *Puerto Deportivo, Control Tower. Open daily, 4pm to 3am.* A quiet, welcoming bar with comfortable chairs and a pleasant terrace popular with an older crowd. An excellent cocktail list and intimate music concerts on Friday and Sunday evenings.

Melodie Cool – *Calle Real, 25. Open daily, 6pm to 3am.* This small bar with its spectacular, futuristic design attracts an eclectic young crowd. An excellent bar list, including a range of beers, coffees and cocktails.

Chico Diez – *Puerto Deportivo, building 27. Open 10pm to 5am, daily in summer and weekends in winter.*

Ático – *Puerto Deportivo, upper floor. Open 10pm to 6am, daily in summer and weekends in winter.*

Sirocco – *Puerto Deportivo, upper floor. Open daily 9pm to 5am, closed Tues in winter.*

These three bars attract the 20-40 crowd, although the higher part of this age group tend to congregate at Chico Diez. Always a lively atmosphere, especially on busy summer evenings.

Shopping

The main shopping street in Estepona is the pedestrianised calle Real, in particular the section between avenida Juan Carlos I and calle Terraza. The latter, as well as several streets crossing over it (Valladolid, Granada, Córdoba, Valencia), is also home to a number of stores.

A Wednesday **market** is held on avenida Juan Carlos I from 9am to 2pm, while several arts and crafts stalls sell their wares on Sunday mornings by the marina.

FUENGIROLA

Cafés, bars & night-life

Plaza de la Constitución is at the heart of Fuengirola, and it is around this square that most of the town's bars, restaurants and night-clubs are situated. The nearby calle Miguel de Cervantes, calle Emancipación and the Paseo Marítimo Rey de España are also popular areas for night-life.

Between July and September the town hall organises a wide spectrum of cultural activities, including exhibitions, concerts and theatre performances.

Café La Plaza – *Plaza de la Constitución, 9. Open Mon to Sat, 8am to 2am.* The La Plaza café on the town's main square occupies the bottom two floors of an old house. Pleasant, traditional decor and a varied, mainly local, clientele of all ages. The café serves breakfast and a selection of tapas.

Pihama – *Calle Cervantes, 14. Open 10.30pm to 5am, daily in summer and weekends in winter.* A small but attractive venue with interesting decor and a very lively atmosphere. Popular with young twenty-somethings who tend to liven things up between midnight and 3am.

El Piso – *Avenida Condes de San Isidro, 24 (entrance on calle Estación). Open Mon to Sat, 10pm to 3am.* On the first floor of a building with good views overlooking Fuengirola's main square. A quiet, warm ambience and old-style decoration. Flamenco and Latin music concerts on Tuesdays, Wednesdays and Thursdays. A perfect bar for a relaxing evening of conversation with friends.

Mahama – *At Km 9.9 on the ring road (carretera de circunvalación), Mijas Costa. Open daily in July and Aug (Fri and Sat only in Sept), 10pm to 7am.* This huge venue is laid out around a large patio in the style of an Andalucian hacienda. Great care and attention have been given to the decor, with plentiful greenery and water, quiet areas and an enormous dance floor. Mainly frequented by locals of all ages, although the average age drops as the night progresses. If you get hungry, the grill stays open here all night.

Shopping

The commercial heart of Fuengirola is in and around plaza de la Constitución, avenida Matías Sáenz de Tejada and Ramón y Cajal, where the majority of the town's traditional shops are based. The shops in the Los Boliches district are generally more modern.

On Tuesdays, the showground *(recinto ferial)* is the setting for the largest **market** on the Costa del Sol. A small flea market selling second-hand goods is also held here on Saturday mornings.

MARBELLA

Where to stay

MODERATE

Enriqueta – *Los Caballeros, 18* – ☎ *952 82 75 52* – *15 rooms* – *6 420pts* – *closed in Jan and Feb*. A family-run *hostal* on a picturesque narrow street in Marbella's old quarter. Basic, but adequate rooms, the best and brightest of which overlook the street.

MID-RANGE

Lima – *Avenida Antonio Belón, 2* – ☎ *952 77 05 00* – *fax 952 86 30 91* – *64 rooms* – *12 000pts*. Just 60m from the beach and 100m from the old part of town.

El Fuerte – *Avenida del Fuerte* – ☎ *952 86 15 00* – *fax 952 82 44 11* – *249 rooms* – *18 800pts*. This high-standard hotel by the sea has its own tropical gardens and the remains of Marbella's 16C fortifications.

Eating out

El Balcón de la Virgen – *Remedios, 2* – ☎ *952 77 60 92*. In an attractive street lined by an endless succession of restaurant terraces. The restaurant, recognisable by the image of the Virgin Mary on the façade, is mainly popular with tourists. Andalucian cuisine.

Tapas

La Venencia – *Avenida Miguel Cano, 15* – ☎ *952 85 79 13*. A typical bar just a stone's throw from the sea with barrel tables on the pavement which always seem to be full.

Altamirano – *Plaza Altamirano, 3*. This unpretentious restaurant on a small square in the old quarter specialises in fish and seafood. *Azulejo* decoration on the façade.

Cafés, bars & night-life

The capital of the Costa del Sol offers visitors a wide range of leisure and cultural opportunities throughout the year. In the old quarter of Marbella, the picturesque, typically Andalucian narrow streets and squares are home to plenty of quiet, attractive places for a drink or bite to eat, particularly around the plaza de los Naranjos. The majority of Marbella's teenagers hang out around the town's **marina** *(puerto deportivo)*. The trendiest and most lively part of town is **Puerto Banús**, which caters to all ages and tastes. Some of the best-known night-spots, however, are out of town, along the main coast road *(autovía)*.

In summer, in particular, the town hall organises a full and varied programme of cultural events: the **Auditorio** in Parque de la Constitución is a popular venue for a range of interesting concerts and theatrical performances, while the **Galería Municipal de Arte** *(plaza José Palomo)* and the **Museo del Grabado Español Contemporáneo** *(calle Hospital Bazán)* host a number of painting and photographic exhibitions. Lastly, the **Casino de Marbella** *(in the Hotel Andalucía Plaza,* ☎ *952 81 28 44 – www.casinomarbella.com)* also stages regular shows and exhibitions, in addition to its gambling activities.

Sinatra Bar – *Puerto Banús. Open daily, 9am to 3am*. The Sinatra Bar has a pleasant terrace and tremendous views of the marina. Popular mainly with a youngish international crowd. As good a place as any to watch the luxury yachts glide past while enjoying a leisurely drink or a meal.

La Abadía – *Calle Pantaleón (close to plaza de los Naranjos). Open 9pm to 4am from 15 May to 15 Sept and during Holy Week*. Located in a small, attractive alleyway in the pedestrianised old part of town. Not that easy to find, but worth the effort. Generally frequented by the 20-35 crowd who tend to start the night here between midnight and 2am. The playlist is mainly based on the latest chart hits.

Trocadero – *Paseo Marítimo, Puerto Banús. Open 7pm to 4am daily in summer and during Holy Week*. A quiet bar by the sea with modern decor. Popular with the thirty-somethings attracted by the relaxed atmosphere and chart music.

Café del Mar/The Club – *Hotel Puente Romano. At Km 175 along the Cádiz road. Café del Mar is open 10pm to 4am and The Club midnight to 6.30am.* Both these luxurious clubs have been designed to attract a select crowd who come here for the evening, starting with a relaxed drink, followed by dinner and dancing. People generally begin the evening in the café, with its views of the Mediterranean, before making their way to dance the night away alongside the coast's rich and famous. Entry costs 3 000pts, although if you're lucky you may receive a guest invitation.

Espartaco Santoni – *Puerto Banús. Open daily, 12.30am to 5.30am.* An exotic Latin-flavoured disco always full of a varied, mainly foreign clientele in the twenty-five and upward age bracket. Mainly Latin-based sounds with the occasional live performance. Somewhat over the top, but good fun.

Olivia Valere – *At Km 0.8 on the Istán road. Open daily, 9pm to 7am.* The most exclusive and luxurious venue on the Costa del Sol. The ambience is that of a Moorish palace, with patios, terraces and gardens offering a variety of atmospheres for a quiet drink or dinner. The crowded disco often hosts live bands. *The* place for the rich and famous and Marbella's famous jet-set to be seen. Entry costs 5 000pts.

Oh! Marbella – *Beach Hotel Don Carlos. At Km 192 on the Cádiz road. Open daily, 11pm to 6am in July, Aug and during Holy Week.*
This impressively sized and glitzy night-spot – a well-known feature of Marbella night-life – has a huge dance floor and a pleasant terrace with views of the Mediterranean. Latin sounds early on followed by more commercial house tracks. A large foreign contingent in the 20-40 age range. Entry costs 3 000pts, although the club has a membership card system for frequent visitors. A great night out guaranteed.

Shopping

Marbella is also one of the best places for shopping on the Costa del Sol with all the top names in international fashion, including the most exclusive Italian, French and American names, represented here. Most of these stores are concentrated in Puerto Banús, where there is an impressive nucleus of modern, designer boutiques, and in the centre of Marbella, particularly along avenida Ricardo Soriano and Ramón y Cajal. The best indoor shopping centre on the Costa del Sol is also found in Puerto Banús.

Markets are an important feature of Marbella life, with the Monday market next to the football stadium and the large Saturday morning market next to the Nueva Andalucía bullring *(plaza de toros)* near Puerto Banús selling a whole range of goods.

SAN PEDRO DE ALCÁNTARA

Where to stay

MID-RANGE

Breakerslodge – *Avenida Mimosas, 189 – ☎/fax 452 78 47 80 – 6 rooms – 14 000pts – open June to Oct.* A pleasant, British-owned property just 300m from the sea in an area predominantly occupied by chalets. Spacious, tastefully decorated rooms.

TORREMOLINOS

Where to stay

MODERATE

Guadalupe – *Peligro, 15 – ☎ 952 38 19 37 – 10 rooms – 5 500pts (8 000pts in Aug).* A *pensión* in a narrow shopping street just 50m from the beach. Basic, but spotlessly clean rooms.

MID-RANGE

Mediterráneo Carihuela – *Carmen, 43 – ☎ 952 38 14 52 – fax 952 05 19 74 – 35 rooms – 8 000pts (12 000pts for rooms with a sea view).* Located in one of the liveliest and most attractive parts of Torremolinos. Well-appointed rooms with terraces overlooking the promenade.

Tropicana – *Trópico, 6 – ☎ 952 38 66 00 – fax 952 38 05 68 – 84 rooms – 18 000pts.* A high-quality hotel with exotic architecture. Private beach, swimming pool with garden and a restaurant (Mango).

Eating out – tapas

La Carihuela

This district extending along the beach is the most attractive – and most commercial – part of town, with dozens of bars, restaurants, hotels and shops of every description. Two restaurants worthy of mention are **Casa Juan**, which has been serving good fish and seafood for the past 30 years, and **El Roqueo**, one of the resort's most established addresses, with a terrace overlooking the *Paseo Marítimo*.

La Carihuela

Cafés, bars & night-life

By tradition, Torremolinos has always been popular with foreign tourists all year round, although visitor numbers increase significantly during the summer months. Because of this constant influx, Torremolinos hosts cultural and leisure events 12 months a year. The town hall organises a range of shows and concerts in the town's squares; a list of these, and other events, can be obtained from either the town hall itself *(ayuntamiento)* or from local tourist offices *(oficinas de turismo)*.
The majority of the resort's bars and night-clubs are found in calle San Miguel, plaza Costa del Sol and avenida Palma de Mallorca, although many locals and tourists head to the nearby marina (Puerto Marina) in Benalmádena, where the choice of night-life is far greater.

Lepanto – *Calle San Miguel, 54. Open daily, 9am to 10pm.* The Lepanto is part of a chain of cafeterias and patisseries which has outlets in both Fuengirola and Málaga. Loyal customers have been coming to this traditional tea-room for its high-quality pastries and good selection of teas for the past 35 years.

El Molino de La Torre – *Calle Cuesta del Tajo, 8. Open daily, noon to midnight.* A café-restaurant with spectacular views of the coast.

The Red Lion – *Calle Cuesta del Tajo, 30. Open daily, noon to midnight.* This typical British pub, in one of Torremolinos' busiest streets, has been popular with its compatriots since it opened in 1975. An extensive choice of imported beers, with bar food available until 10pm.

Shopping

Calle San Miguel, a busy and noisy pedestrianised street in the centre of town, is home to an impressive range of shops and boutiques. This commercial artery continues into avenida Palma de Mallorca and its adjoining streets, where an interesting cross-section of modern and traditional stores are based, such as the *pastelería* at calle Isabel Manoja, 4, founded in 1908, where visitors can purchase the typical cakes *(tortas)* made in Torremolinos. The cuesta del Tajo, a hill with impressive views down to the sea, is a popular location for stalls selling more traditional wares and souvenirs.
A Thursday morning **market** is held in El Calvario.

CUEVAS DE ALMANZORA

Almería – Population 9 114

Michelin map 446 U 23

The town of Cuevas de Almanzora is situated near the lake of the same name in an area rich in mineral deposits and archeological discoveries. The town rose to fame during the 19C following the discovery of silver in the nearby Sierra de la Almagrera. Several mansions in the old quarter, as well as the Capilla del Carmen – a chapel inside the Iglesia de Nuestra Señora de la Encarnación built by a mining company – testify to the wealth of this period in Almanzora's history. Another feature of the area are the cave dwellings close to the town.

For those interested in more active pursuits, a water park has been created on the road to Vera.

Castle – The castle was built in the 16C by the Marqués de los Vélez. It was subsequently expanded with the addition of a neo-Classical building, the Casa de la Tercia, which now houses the municipal museum. The castle's walled enclosure is still visible today.

Museo Antonio Manuel Campoy ⊙ – The museum, named after the well-known art critic for the right-wing newspaper ABC, is housed in a restored pavilion inside the castle. On Campoy's death, his private collection of contemporary Spanish art (paintings, sketches and engravings), firearms and numerous personal mementoes were bequeathed to the museum.

Museo de Arqueología ⊙ – The archeological museum, also housed within the castle, is dedicated to the El Argar culture, with a variety of finds discovered in the area (Antas, Fuente Álamo etc) on display.

Upon leaving the castle note the cave dwellings to the left.

EXCURSIONS

Vera – *6km/4mi southeast*. The Plaza Mayor is fronted by the impressive 16C **Iglesia de la Encarnación**, a church with a fortress-like appearance accentuated by the four solid cubic towers on its corners. To the left stands the **town hall**, a 19C construction with a sober stone doorway; note the standard hanging in the plenary room which was presented to the town by the Catholic Monarchs. The **Museo Histórico Municipal** ⊙ next door contains one section devoted to the archeology and history of the town, and another dedicated to its ethnography.

The naturist complex of **Vera Natura** has been developed on the nearby coast.

Huércal Overa – *25km/15mi north*. On the top of a hill on the outskirts of the town stands the square tower of the old Moorish fortress. The 18C **Iglesia de la Asunción**, housing an interesting Baroque altarpiece and the sculptures (some by Salzillo) borne aloft during the **Holy Week** processions, dominates one side of the pleasant plaza del Cura Valera. During the course of its Semana Santa celebrations, Huércal Overa's three religious brotherhoods *(cofradías)* attempt to outdo their rivals in pomp and ceremony.

Parque Natural de DESPEÑAPERROS★

Jaén

Michelin map 446 Q 19

This park, which acts as a natural boundary between Andalucia and the rest of Spain, is cut by an impressive defile *(desfiladero)* carved over the millennia by the waters of the Despeñaperros River. Its abrupt profile breaks up the uniformity of the Sierra Morena and heralds the beginning of the gentler relief of the Spanish *meseta*. According to tradition, it was into this ravine that the Christians threw the defeated Moors after the Battle of Las Navas de Tolosa, hence its unusual name *(despeñaperros* translates as "where dogs are hurled"). The entire park, which covers an area of 7 717ha/19 069 acres, rising to a maximum height of over 1 000m/3 280ft, is a superb belvedere from which to enjoy magnificent **views★★★** of its vertical walls of slate and the deep precipices dissecting it. The various **itineraries** ⊙ on offer to visitors within the park are the best way of enjoying the impressive natural beauty of Despeñaperros; some of these can only be explored on foot, others by car. The landscape here is characterised by forests of

A bird's-eye view of Despeñaperros

The Parque Natural de Despeñaperros is as fascinating for its beauty as for the ruggedness of its arid landscapes where any form of life seems impossible to sustain. This region of unusual rocky formations and outstanding panoramas is a paradise for the photographer or for those with a love of wild and natural landscapes.

oak (holm, cork and gall) and umbrella pine rising above a dense patchwork of arbutus, mastic and myrtle. This varied vegetation is an exceptional habitat for species such as the wolf, lynx, stone marten, genet, stag and wild boar, as well as the griffon vulture and the spectacular imperial eagle. The itinerary from Arroyo del Rey passes through a landscape dominated by vertical drops and fanciful formations created by the dual forces of erosion and abundant rainfall to reach the area known as "Los Órganos", where the rocks have taken on the appearance of gigantic organ pipes. Las Correderas is another interesting part of the park, and is particularly popular with hunting and fishing enthusiasts.

EXCURSIONS

Santa Elena – This small town inside the park's boundaries is, along with La Carolina, the starting point for a number of excursions.

Local sights of interest include the **Collado de los Jardines** *(5km/3mi north towards Aldeaquemada)*, an Iberian sanctuary in the heart of the mountains, and the **Cueva de los Muñecos** *(3km/2mi west towards Miranda de Rey)*, a cave in which some impressive wall paintings of animals have been discovered. The **Paraje Natural de la Cascada de Cimbarra**, an area of outstanding beauty 4km/2.5mi northwest of Santa Elena, is famous for its spectacular waterfalls *(cascadas)* and the impressive canyons *(gargantas)* through which the Guarrizas River has carved its path.

G. Torres/MARCO POLO

Cimbarra waterfalls

Parque Nacional de DOÑANA★★★

Huelva, Sevilla and Cádiz
Michelin map 446 U 9,10,11 V 10,11

With a surface area of some 50 000ha/123 550 acres, Doñana is one of Europe's largest national parks. It owes its name to Doña Ana Gómez de Mendoza y Silva, the wife of the seventh Duke of Medina Sidonia and the daughter of the famous Princess of Éboli, who first converted these lands into a private hunting ground back in the 16C and who was subsequently to retire here in her later years.

The park encompasses the salt marshes on the right bank of the Guadalquivir River, from its mouth at Sanlúcar de Barrameda to Matalascañas to the north. This large wetland, which is at its best in spring and autumn, is a paradise for over 150 African and European birds who migrate here in winter, as well as a home to several animal species including lynx, wild boar and deer.

In addition to its popularity with bird-watchers, Doñana also attracts thousands of visitors who come here to admire the contrasting landscapes within the park, where the subtle movements of the coastal dunes remove every trace of vegetation in their path, sparing perhaps a solitary tree which has been entombed by these desert-like features. However, the park is more than just an area of marshland and sand dunes, as it is also covered by impressive forests inhabited by deer, horses and wild boar.

R. Corbel/MICHELIN

Pink flamingo

Park ecosystems – Doñana has three types of ecosystem: the salt marshes, coastal dunes and the former hunting grounds *(cotos)*.

The **salt marshes**, covering an area of 27 000ha/66 717 acres, are the ideal habitat for birds which migrate to Europe over the winter. The marshland here is characterised by a high salt content and the appearance of unusual geological features such as *caños* (depressions formed by water), *lucios* (a type of lagoon that contains water all year round), *paciles* and *vetas* (small elevations of land rising out of the water and a favoured area for saltwort, one of the most typical plants found within the park).

The **sand dunes** are grouped together in formation parallel to the Atlantic. Maritime winds precipitate their advance inland at a rate of 6m/20ft per year. The land which exists between one dune and another is known as a corral *(enclosure)*, while the trees levelled by these white mountains are referred to as *cruces* (crosses).

The **cotos** are dry, undulating areas covered with various species of bush and aromatic plant such as heather, rockrose, rosemary and thyme.

Alongside these ecosystems exists another zone, known as the **vera**, an area found between the park's woodlands and marshes, made up of narrow strips of land running through its centre. The **lagoons** are another feature of the Doñana; these include the Laguna de Santa Olalla, a favourite nesting place for ducks, geese and swans, and La Dulce, a lake teeming with crustaceans – the main diet of the park's colony of pink flamingos.

Parque Natural Entorno de Doñana – This nature reserve occupies the periphery of the national park, covering 54 500ha/134 670 acres in an area that includes the saltpans of Sanlúcar and encompasses small sections of Huelva, Sevilla and Cádiz provinces. The landscape is generally flat with a predominence of eucalyptus and pine, although it does contain some marshland and several lagoons. Part of the El Rocío pilgrimage route runs through the *parque natural*; this is why it is not uncommon to see the occasional sign on tree trunks here guiding pilgrims to their destination.

VISITOR CENTRES

Because of the park's fragile ecology, entry to the park is rigorously controlled. Excursions into the park depart from four visitor centres and last approximately 3hr 30min. It is advisable to book visits in advance.

El Acebuche ⊘ – All reservations are handled by the El Acebuche information centre, which has an audiovisual presentation and an exhibition on the park's wetlands for visitors. Walks from this centre provide visitors with a closer look at the aquatic birds found in the lagoon here.

La Rocina ⊘ – La Rocina is situated just a few kilometres from the town of El Rocío, along the Almonte to Matalascañas roads. It is the departure point for the popular **Charca de la Boca walk** *(14km/9mi)*, which leads to a rest area and various hides for bird-watching, including the viewpoint known as "El Paraguas" (The Umbrella).

Parque Nacional de DOÑANA

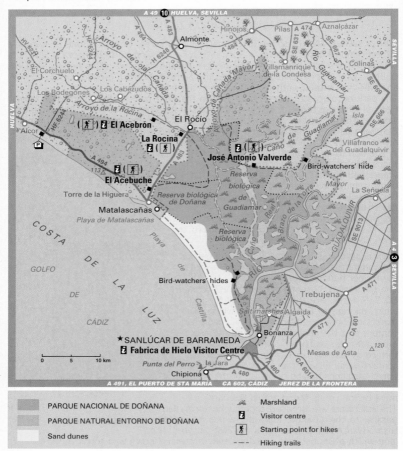

PARQUE NACIONAL DE DOÑANA

PARQUE NATURAL ENTORNO DE DOÑANA

Sand dunes

Marshland

Visitor centre

Starting point for hikes

--- Hiking trails

El Acebrón ⊙ – This centre occupies a modern building dating from 1961. It houses an exhibition entitled "Man and Doñana", an interesting presentation outlining the evolution of the park and man's presence in it. From the upper floor there are some fine views of the surrounding area. El Acebrón is the starting point for a 12km/8mi walk through attractive woodland.

José Antonio Valverde ⊙ – This centre is located within the municipality of Aznal-cázar in an area known as La Gallega. It is housed in a modern building with large windows built alongside a lagoon, enabling visitors to observe the birdlife around the centre. Audiovisual presentations provide a greater insight into the Doñana National Park, while a boutique sells mementoes of the park.

Fábrica de Hielo – *See SANLÚCAR DE BARRAMEDA.*

Excursions through the National Park

On foot – A number of different paths depart from the four information centres enabling visitors to get a closer look at the natural beauty of the park. Before choosing a particular itinerary, walkers are advised to consult with park attendants, who will be happy to provide information on the level of difficulty of the various walks and their duration. Comfortable footwear is essential.

By jeep – These visits should be booked in advance. Two visits per day are organised: one in the morning, the second halfway through the afternoon. Excursions are by four-wheel-drive vehicles and are accompanied by official park guides. Itineraries vary according to the time of year and the individual requirements of visitors.

On horseback – This interesting alternative can either be made on horseback or by horse-drawn carriage. Picnics are included for larger groups. The duration of these excursions depends on the itinerary chosen.

By boat – Excursions from Sanlúcar de Barrameda *(see p 280).*

ÉCIJA ★

Sevilla – Population 37 113
Michelin map 446 T 14

The old Roman town of Astigi is situated in the extensive Guadalquivir depression, on the left bank of the Genil River. From afar, its most striking feature is the impressive silhouette of its 11 church towers. The development of Écija's economy, which reached its peak in the 18C, resulted in the proliferation of palaces, convents and churches that line its streets today. As a result of the beauty of its towers and belfries, the influence of the Baroque style so popular here was to extend to the surrounding area.

> **"The frying-pan of Andalucia"**
> Because of its reputation as the hottest place in Andalucia during the summer, when temperatures here can easily exceed 40°C/104°F, the town has earned this less than enviable reputation.

The writer **Luis Vélez de Guevara** (1579-1644), the author of *El Diablo Cojuelo*, was born in Écija.

Fiestas – September is the month *par excellence* for fiestas in Écija. The 8th of the month sees a solemn procession in honour of the town's patron saint, the Virgen del Valle (Virgin of the Valley), while around the 21st the Feria de San Mateo is held, with its traditional fiestas, bullfights, demonstrations of horsemanship etc. The Festival de Cante Jondo, meanwhile, attracts leading performers in the world of flamenco to Écija.

Follow signs to the town centre (centro ciudad) and leave your car in the plaza de España.

Plaza de España – This pleasant and spacious landscaped square, popularly known as **El Salón** (Drawing Room) is the hub of Écija life. Three major buildings line the square: the **Iglesia de Santa Bárbara**, with its impressive choir stalls; the **Convento de San Francisco**, with houses backing onto the church; and the town hall.

Town Hall – The chapter-house contains two **Roman mosaics★**. The 16C coffered wooden ceiling was transferred here from the Convento de San Pablo y Santo Domingo.

★CHURCHES AND CONVENTS, TOWERS AND BELFRIES

★**Torre de San Juan** – The 18C tower crowning the Church of St John is, without doubt, one of the most beautiful in Écija. Note the delicacy of its Baroque decoration, due to the predominant use of *azulejos*. The result is both elegant and graceful.

★**Iglesia de Santiago** ⊘ – The Church of St James is a combination of styles: the portal leading to the atrium and the tower are both Baroque, while the remainder of the church is of Gothic-Mudéjar construction with later modifications. The interior comprises three harmoniously proportioned aisles with wooden ceilings, with the exception of the apse, which is crowned with Gothic vaulting. The Gothic **retable★** at the high altar illustrates the Passion and the Resurrection of Christ.

Iglesia de Santa María ⊘ – This church, fronting plaza de Santa María, was erected in the 18C. The handsome Baroque portal is crowned by a large arch and a **tower**, also Baroque, adorned with blue *azulejo* decoration. A series of archeological items are on display in the cloisters.

Convento de las Teresas – The convent, which occupies a 14C-15C Mudéjar palace, has a fine stone **portal** with *alfíz*, heraldic and rope decoration.

Iglesia de la Concepción ⊘ – Access to the church is through a simple, red-brick Renaissance doorway. The fine Mudéjar-style *artesonado* work on the interior is worthy of particular note.

Iglesia de los Descalzos ⊘ – The sober exterior gives no indication of the exuberant decoration which reigns in the **interior★** of this church. The building is a magnificent example of Écija Baroque, with fine **stuccowork** covering the vaults, the cupola above the transept and sections of wall.

Convento de los Marroquíes – The convent is famous for its **belfry★**, which locals consider to be the most beautiful in the town, and for the *marroquíes* biscuits still produced and sold by the nuns here.

Iglesia de Santa Cruz ⊘ – This unusual edifice stands on the plaza de la Virgen del Valle. Upon entering the church, note the series of patio-like areas formed by the walls and arches of an earlier church. The harmonious **Renaissance tower** with its attractive ceramic decoration is also impressive. The church itself is neo-Classical in style with a Greek cross

Torre de San Juan

B. Kaufmann/MICHELIN

ÉCIJA

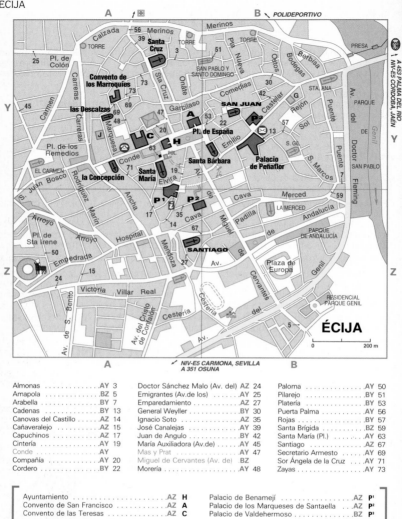

ÉCIJA

0   200 m

ground plan. The interior contains the 13C image of the **Virgin of the Valley**, the patron saint of Écija, as well as a 5C **paleo-Christian sarcophagus★**, depicting themes from the Old Testament, at one of the altars.

★PALACES

A wander through the streets of the town will reveal interesting examples of popular architecture, with inlaid columns on the corners of buildings, houses adorned with coats of arms, patios and small squares fronted by fine civil edifices.

Palacio de Peñaflor – The palace is now used as a cultural centre. It has a large, original and slightly curved **façade★** with an iron balcony and fresco decoration. The handsome pink marble doorway with its Doric and Solomonic columns and heraldic insignia is particularly impressive.

Palacio de Valdehermoso – *Calle Caballeros.* The bottom section of the fine 16C **Plateresque façade★** is noteworthy for its column shafts, which are of Roman origin. To the left of the façade, admire the delightful view of the **Torre de San Juan**.

Palacio de Benamejí ⊘ – *Calle Cánovas del Castillo.* This elegant 18C brick and marble palace is Baroque in style and comprises two storeys with towers on its corners. The marble **doorway★** consists of a delicate and continuous series of curves which are visible on the mouldings, the balcony and in the general layout of the building. A large escutcheon is the crowning feature of the palace, which now houses the **Museo Histórico Municipal**.

Palacio de los Marqueses de Santaella – *Close to the Palacio de Benamejí. Although the palace is a private club, the guard on duty may allow brief access.* It is well worth passing through the simple entrance of the palace to admire the magnificent **fresco-adorned cupola★** above the staircase.

ESTEPA ★

Sevilla – Population 11 654
Michelin map 446 U 15

This attractive small town straddling the slopes of the Cerro de San Cristóbal (St Christopher's hill) in the heart of the Sevillian countryside is crowned by the remains of its old castle, and the Iglesia de Santa María de la Asunción. This Punic, Roman and Moorish settlement, the seat of the Knights of the Order of Santiago in the Middle Ages, has numerous attractions for visitors.

★EL CERRO

Head up by car to the Cerro de San Cristóbal.

The esplanade surrounded by pine trees at the top of the hill is lined by several buildings of interest.

Walls – In former times the town walls encircled the entire Cerro de San Cristóbal. Although Moorish in origin, the line of fortifications was rebuilt in the 13C by the Order of Santiago (St James). Several towers and sections of the wall are still visible.

Torre del Homenaje – The keep was built in the 14C inside the old fortress. This massive square tower can be seen today rising amid the ruins.

Iglesia de Santa María de la Asunción – *Next to the castle ruins.* The church, which dates from the 15C and 16C, has the appearance of a church-fortress with its solid walls supported by wide buttresses and an unusual circular fortified tower. Nowadays, the building has a somewhat abandoned look to it and is no longer used as a place of worship, only opening its doors on special occasions.

Balcón de Andalucía – The esplanade in front of the church and castle is a superb balcony commanding magnificent **views**★★ of the surrounding countryside. In the foreground, dominating the rooftops of the town, which rises in staggered formation up the hill, stands the elegant Torre de la Victoria; behind the tower the view extends across a gently undulating, almost flat landscape coloured with greens and ochres to the distant horizon.

Convento de Santa Clara – This convent, standing alongside the Iglesia de Santa María, was founded at the end of the 16C and is home to an order of enclosed nuns. Its façade has a simple Baroque doorway bearing heraldic decoration. The materials used in its construction consist of a mixture of brickwork and masonry.

ADDITIONAL SIGHTS

★**Torre de la Victoria** – This handsome 18C tower stands alone following the disappearance of the church and convent of which it was part, enabling its graceful elegance to be appreciated to the full. A stone podium acts as a base for this brick construction, which comprises five sections.

Note the narrow **calle Torralba**, the entrance to which is framed by an arch, heading off to the right of the tower; this street is a perfect example of the charming cobbled alleyways rising up the hillside.

★**Iglesia del Carmen** – *Calle Mesones, next to plaza del Carmen.* This 18C church, a jewel of Andalucian Baroque, has an interesting and original stone and black ceramic **portal**★ and a fine belfry.

Portal of the Iglesia del Carmen

B. Kaufmann/MICHELIN

177

Casa-Palacio del Marqués de Cerverales – *Calle Castillejos. Private residence.* Estepa's finest example of civil architecture was built in the 18C. The decoration on the façade is concentrated around the doorway and main balcony, with Solomonic and balustered columns, escutcheons and assorted figures. The bays are framed by pilasters, while the upper storey has a truncated pediment, in the centre of which stands a decorative feature containing a human face.

The **Iglesia de la Asunción**, to the right of the palace, contains a number of interesting paintings.

ESTEPONA★

Málaga – Population 39 178
Michelin map 446 W 14

Estepona stands at the foot of the Sierra Bermeja range and is one of the Costa del Sol's major resort areas. During the summer, its population triples as a result of its numerous hotels and beaches, which stretch for 20km/12mi. The town also has a large pleasure and fishing harbour with a mooring capacity of 900 boats, a golf course, a scuba-diving centre, as well as the standard compendium of night-clubs, bars, designer boutiques and high-quality restaurants for its tens of thousands of visitors.

A series of watchtowers dating from the 15C and 16C can be seen along the coast in the immediate vicinity of the town.

★**Old quarter** – Although the *casco antiguo*, as it is known, is surrounded by an ill-assorted mix of modern buildings, it has managed to preserve the inherent charm of a small, typical Andalucian village, with its narrow streets lined by whitewashed houses adorned with wrought-iron balconies decked in flowers. The main features of interest in this part of town are the **castle ruins**, which include two towers, the Torre del Reloj and El Vigía, and the picturesque **plaza de las Flores★**, or Flower Square, one of Estepona's most characteristic sights.

Iglesia de Nuestra Señora de los Remedios ⊙ – The Church of Our Lady of the Remedies was built in the 18C in a style highlighting the influence of colonial architecture at the time. The building, part of a former Franciscan convent, has three aisles separated by

For detailed information on hotels, restaurants, bars, night-clubs and shops, consult the Travellers' addresses section under COSTA DEL SOL.

semicircular arches resting on pilasters. Its most outstanding feature is undoubtedly its Baroque **portal★★**, with unusual decoration representing the sun, the moon and the stars. An escutcheon flanked by two strange faces appears above these images. The church is crowned by a tower comprising four sections, with a pyramidal ceramic spire at its top.

Plaza de Toros – The salient feature of Estepona's bullring is its unusual asymmetrical plan.

Paraje Natural de Sierra Bermeja

The main attractions of this area of natural beauty in the hills behind Estepona are the reddish colour of its rock formations and the presence of the Spanish fir – a tree only found in Andalucia. To get to the park, follow the MA 557 towards Jubrique.

Sierra de Los FILABRES ★

Almería

Michelin map 446

The Sierra de Los Filabres mountain range is renowned for its bareness and the majestic appearance of its natural formations. The roads that wind their way through this grandiose scenery provide impressive views of the quarries that have been dug in the mountains to extract the valuable Macael marble. The stacked debris of discarded blocks of stone left by man have accumulated to form their own mountainous mounds in this desolate landscape.

TOUR THROUGH THE LAND OF MARBLE

79km/49.5mi – allow 2hr 30min

Macael – The town of Macael has lent its name to the mainly white marble proliferating in the eastern reaches of the Sierra de Los Filabres. It is the economic centre for an area comprising several small towns and villages which subsist from this valuable resource. Macael marble has been famous since time immemorial and has been used in the construction of a multitude of magnificent buildings over the centuries, including the Alhambra in Granada.

Cantoria – *14km/9mi east.* A viewpoint at the entrance to this whitewashed village provides an overview of the surrounding fertile plain of market gardens, fruit orchards and olive groves. Once inside the village, two buildings are worthy of note: the Casa del Marqués de la Romana and the Iglesia de Nuestra Señora del Carmen. On the outskirts of town stands the defunct railway station, exactly as it was when the last train pulled out of Cantoria in the 1980s.
The Palacio del Marqués de Almanzora in nearby **Almanzora** *(5.5km/3.5mi east)* is a noble residence arranged around a central patio. The village also has its own abandoned railway station, similar to the one in Cantoria.

Albánchez – *11.5km/7mi from Cantoria along the C 3325.* The whitewashed houses of this village rise up the hillside amid a landscape of thyme, broom and anthyllis.

The road to Cóbdar – *8km/5mi southwest.* The road traverses an impressive landscape dominated by mountains and open-cast marble quarries before reaching the foot of the marble rock known as Los Calares, the setting for the village of **Cóbdar**, with its attractive church. The village is popular with mountaineers who come here to scale Los Calares. For those interested in more leisurely country pursuits, a pleasant 3km/1.8mi walk takes in the remains of an old mill and fortress *(follow a path parallel to the river at the exit to Cóbdar).*

Chercos – *8km/5mi west.* This village, which is also sustained by the local quarrying activities, has preserved an old quarter, known as El Soto, at the top of the village. 3km/1.8mi to the south, perched on a mountain slope, stands the settlement of **Chercos Viejo★**.
Leave your car at the entrance to the village.
It is well worth wandering through its narrow and tranquil cobbled streets, which are overlooked by the vestiges of an old fortress *(alcazaba).* Pieces of prehistoric carved stone have been discovered on the outskirts of Chercos.

Tahal – *9.5km/6mi southwest.* The route passes through **Alcudia de Monteagud**, which has preserved its 19C threshing floors and its old public washery.
Tahal, situated at the confluence of several ravines, is a small, well-kept whitewashed village dominated by the silhouette of its sturdy 15C Moorish castle.
Return to Macael, some 19km/12mi north, along the A 349.

FUENTE OBEJUNA

Córdoba – Population 6 107

Michelin map 446 R 13

A scenic drive through the wooded landscapes adjoining the N 432 leads to the small town of Fuente Obejuna, on a hill near the source of the Guadiato River. A historical event here in the 15C was to provide the inspiration for one of the most famous plays by the Golden Age dramatist Lope de Vega.
It is well worth strolling through this historic town to admire the Renaissance mansions which bear witness to its past glories.

"Who killed the Knight Commander? Fuenteovejuna, señor"

Lope de Vega (1562-1635) immortalised the town in his play *Fuenteovejuna*, in which he relates how the town's inhabitants, pushed to breaking point by the atrocities committed by the Knight Commander Fernán Gómez de Guzmán, rebelled and subsequently murdered him. However, the judge dispatched to the town by the Catholic Monarchs to investigate the crime was only able to elicit the reply "Fuenteovejuna, señor" to his question "Who killed the Knight Commander?". Upon hearing of the outrages committed by the *comendador*, Isabel and Fernando then approved the town's conduct. This episode has remained as an example of unity and rebellion against tyranny.

Plaza Mayor – Located in the upper section of the town, the *plaza mayor* is an impressive, irregular square with a predominance of granite. Both the town hall and parish church front the square.

Iglesia de Nuestra Señora del Castillo ⊘ – This 15C church contains several interesting works of art within the frescoed walls of its three aisles. The presbytery houses a magnificent **Renaissance retable★** with high-relief sculptures representing scenes from the Life and Passion of Christ. It is dominated by the 14C statue of the Virgin of the Castle, which was discovered in a niche in the old castle walls.

The Sacrarium Chapel *(Capilla del Sagrario)* to the left of the chancel is adorned with *azulejo* panelling and houses a 16C late-Gothic **retable** with seven tablets dedicated to the life of the Virgin Mary. A second retable, Baroque in style, dominated by the Virgin of the Rosary, is situated in the chapel to the right of the chancel. The exterior has a doorway with four semicircular stilted arches resting on three columns with acanthus leaf capitals of possible Roman origin.

Casa Cardona – This unusual Modernist-style mansion house was built between 1906 and 1911.

EXCURSIONS

The road from Fuente Obejuna to Córdoba
96km/60mi along the N 432, plus a further 35km/22mi round trip to Obejo.

Bélmez – The road passes through extensive fields of sunflowers before reaching the town, nestling at the foot of a rocky outcrop crowned by a Moorish **castle** which was rebuilt after the Reconquest.

Alongside the 19C town hall stands the **Museo Histórico de Bélmez y del Territorio Minero** ⊘, occupying the site of the former public granary. The museum retraces the history of Bélmez and that of its mining activities which date back to the 18C following the discovery of a rich seam of coal in the area. Today, the town is home to a mining school.

Castle – The fortress has managed to preserve its keep and walls, the latter punctuated with cylindrical and prismatic towers. To reach the castle, follow the road leaving the square, opposite the 18C **parish church**. To the right, after 50m/55yd, note the **Ermita de la Virgen del Castillo** (Chapel of the Virgin of the Castle), from where a ramp ascends to the foot of the castle walls *(5min)*. The more daring can continue their climb along a difficult path between the rocks to the first section of wall; note the cistern *(aljibe)* on the left-hand side. Some steps lead from a patio to the terrace behind this first section. By continuing upwards *(only recommended for those with a good head for heights)*, the upper part of the castle is reached, from where magnificent **views** of Fuente Obejuna and its surroundings can be enjoyed.

The **Sierra Boyera** Reservoir *(embalse)* close to the town is a popular base for water sports enthusiasts.

View of Bélmez and its castle

Espiel – This picturesque village of cobbled streets and whitewashed houses has a town hall dating from 1792 which used to serve as a public granary. Espiel's 16C parish church, named after St Sebastian, is topped by a bell-tower which doubles as a popular nesting place for storks.

El Vacar – The ruins of an imposing rectangular fortress are visible on top of a hill to the right of the road, from where extensive views take in the Puente Nuevo Reservoir to the west. Both of the two dirt tracks heading off the main road, 100m/110yd and 200m/219yd respectively before El Vacar, lead to an esplanade providing a clearer view of the sober, bare walls of this 10C edifice.

Obejo – *Once past El Vacar, bear left towards Obejo, which is reached after 17.5km/11mi.* The **road★** to Obejo passes through some impressive mountain scenery. After a bend in the road shortly after the junction with the N 432, a delightful panorama encompassing the Guadalbarbo River comes into view. The descent into the valley is particularly tortuous, with flocks of sheep and the occasional deer visible in this landscape of oak trees, broom and rockrose. Upon reaching the river, which is traversed by a small bridge, the landscape softens, particularly when the oleander is in full bloom, adding a dash of colour to this otherwise barren mountain setting. Once over the bridge, the road climbs into mountains carpeted in olive trees. After a bend, the village of **Obejo** comes into view on high. To the left, the **Iglesia Parroquial de San Antonio Abad** ⊙, a 13C parish church, stands alongside the remains of a long-forgotten fortress. The small church is particularly charming, with three aisles separated by stilted arches resting on pillars and columns. Note the last two columns on the left-hand side, topped by **capitals★** with plant motif decoration as a reminder of their Moorish origin. Several of the bases of the columns are in fact inverted capitals. The church's most noteworthy external feature is its sober and rustic Mudéjar tower.

★★★ Córdoba – *See CÓRDOBA.*

GÉRGAL
Almería
Michelin map 446 U 22

Gérgal is situated on a fold of the Sierra de Los Filabres, some 50km/31mi to the north of Almería, and is crowned by a castle in a perfect state of repair. To reach the fortress *(a private property closed to visitors)*, follow the road bearing right to Las Aneas upon exiting the village. The fortification comprises a square crenellated tower with smaller cylindrical turrets overlooking the whitewashed village at its feet. The main feature of architectural interest is the parish church, with its Mudéjar *artesonado* ceiling in the main nave. The outlying area is particularly arid, in keeping with the rest of this part of the province.

EXCURSION

★ The road up to Calar Alto – *Allow 1hr 30min excluding a visit to the Astronomical Observatory. Follow the C 3326 for 5km/3mi, then bear right onto the AL 872 for a further 26km/16mi to Calar Alto.*
The road winds its way upwards through the Sierra de los Filabres to an altitude of 2 168m/7 111ft. Once past Aulago, to the right of the road, no further villages are encountered along the remainder of the ascent. The vegetation changes with the increase in altitude, the arid landscape gradually giving way to an extensive woodland replanted with pine trees.
The superb **views★** on both sides of the road encompass the city of Almería and Cabo de Gata to the south, the Sierra Alhamilla to the southeast, the Almanzora Valley to the north and the lofty peaks of the Sierra Nevada to the west.
On the summit of Calar Alto, the characteristic domes of an **Astronomical Observatory** ⊙ can be seen *(open to visitors one day a week)*. The centre is the ideal location from which to observe the night skies as it has the best visibility of anywhere in Europe with over 200 cloud-free nights per year.

Dome of the Astronomical Observatory

181

GRANADA★★★

Population 241 471

Michelin map 446 U 19

"Give him alms, woman, for there is no greater pain in life than being blind in Granada."

This popular saying, inscribed on a wall in the Alhambra, evokes the beauty of this city, its delightful **setting**★★★ and its monuments, the jewel of which is the Alhambra itself, one of the most magnificent artistic creations ever to have been built by man.

Granada is situated in a wide fertile plain dissected by the Genil and Darro rivers. The city spreads majestically upwards on the evocatively named hills of the Albaicín, Sacromonte and Alhambra – Granada's Moorish quarter – which overlook the modern, Christian city sitting compactly at their feet. This magnificent city, with its sumptuous monuments, is protected by the lofty, snow-capped outline of the Sierra Nevada.

Yet Granada is more than just a single monument. It is a city of history indelibly marked by its splendid Moorish and Christian past. By taking the time to wander through its old narrow streets, idle away a hot summer's afternoon in one of the city's shady squares, and explore its less-vaunted treasures, visitors will soon discover that Granada is as unforgettable as it is beautiful.

FIESTAS

Toma de Granada – The first important festival in the Andalucian calendar takes place on 2 January to commemorate a key historical event in Spanish history: Boabdil's surrender to the massed Christian armies and the subsequent capture *(toma)* of Granada by the Catholic Monarchs. The procession, headed by the standard of Fernando and Isabel, climbs up to the Torre de la Vela in the Alhambra, where the tower's bell is then rung. According to tradition, those young women who take part in the fiesta will be married by the end of the year.

San Cecilio – The saint's day of St Cecilio (1 February), the city's patron, is celebrated by a religious pilgrimage *(romería)* to the Sacromonte district, where jugs of wine and broad beans *(habas)* are distributed to the city's inhabitants next to the local abbey. This fiesta is also a time for the dancing and singing of the traditional *sevillanas*.

Semana Santa – In contrast to other Andalucian cities, Granada's Holy Week is typified by restraint and silence. From Palm Sunday to Easter Sunday, myriad processions file along the steep, cobbled Official Route *(Carrera Oficial)*, which terminates at the cathedral. Valuable Baroque statues by masters such as Diego de Siloé, Pedro de Mena, Giacomo Fiorentino and their contemporaries are carried aloft by the traditional *costaleros*, who are forced to their knees in order to squeeze their impressive floats through the cathedral's narrow ogival doorway.

Las Cruces – The Festival of the Crosses *(cruces)* on the 3 May sees the city's streets and patios adorned with flower-decked crosses.

Corpus Christi – Granada's main week of festivities, when the city hosts its annual fair *(feria)*, numerous bullfights and other events, coincides with the solemn Corpus Christi procession, when its streets are carpeted in flowers and aromatic herbs.

Festivals – The city hosts a range of important cultural events throughout the year. These include the International Theatre Festival (in May, at the Teatro Manuel de Falla), the International Music and Dance Festival (in June and July, in the Alhambra), and the International Jazz Festival (October and November).

HISTORICAL NOTES

Granada's origins are somewhat vague, although it is known that Iberian settlements existed here, and that the Romans founded a colony known as Illiberis on the Albaicín hill. Despite these periods of colonisation, the city was of little importance until the arrival of the Moors in the early 8C.

Moorish Granada – In 713 Tarik's troops conquered the city, which at the time extended across the Alhambra and Albaicín hills. During the Cordoban Caliphate, the city came under the rule of its northern neighbour, although when the latter broke up, in 1013, it became the capital of an independent kingdom *(taifa)*, governed by the **Zirite dynasty**. The Zirites strengthened the city's defences and built the El Bañuelo baths and a bridge, the Puente de Cadí.

In 1090 Granada fell into the hands of the **Almoravids**, who were subsequently overthrown by the **Almohads** in the middle of the 12C. Despite frequent internecine conflicts, the city underwent considerable development during this 150-year period, including the establishment of drainage and sewerage systems, and the further strengthening of its fortifications.

Nasrid kingdom – The rise to power of the Nasrid dynasty in 1238 heralded the beginning of the city's Golden Age. The agreement signed between Fernando III and Mohammed ibn Nasar, the dynasty's founder, through which the Moorish leader acknowledged his position as the king's vassal, resulted in a period of stability and calm.

In addition to Granada, the kingdom encompassed the provinces of Almería and Málaga, and part of the provinces of Cádiz, Sevilla, Córdoba and Jaén. During this period, its capital, Granada, prospered and entered a phase of great embellishment. The city extended its boundaries to its lower sections, and construction of the Alhambra commenced. Yusuf I (1333-53) and Mohammed V (1353-91), under whose rule the Alhambra's Nasrid palaces were built, transformed Granada into one of the leading cities of the period.

The **15C** was marked by in-fighting which facilitated the Christian's task of gradually reducing the size of the Nasrid kingdom. Following a long siege, the Catholic Monarchs took the city on 2 January 1492, closing a chapter of Moorish domination on the Iberian Peninsula lasting eight centuries.

WHERE TO STAY

MODERATE

Niza – *Navas, 16 –* ☎ *958 22 54 30 – fax 958 22 54 27 – 28 rooms – 5 500pts.* A small, fairly basic hotel, popular with backpackers. Its main attractions are its central location and price.

Los Jerónimos – *Gran Capitán, 1 –* ☎*/fax 958 29 44 61 – 30 rooms – 7 000pts.* A well-appointed hotel with modern rooms. Room 502 has a terrace with views of the Alhambra and part of the city. Good value for money.

Los Tilos – *Plaza Bib-Rambla, 4 –* ☎ *958 26 67 12 – fax 958 26 68 01 – 30 rooms – 7 500pts.* In a pleasant, pedestrianised square with a number of colourful flower stalls. Functional rooms, all with en-suite bathroom, TV and phone, and some with a view of the cathedral.

MID-RANGE

Marcia – *Plaza Nueva, 4 –* ☎ *958 22 75 36 – fax 958 22 75 33 – 44 rooms – 10 000pts.* In a centrally located square at the foot of the Alhambra. A modern hotel with carpeted rooms and wicker furniture, although the bathrooms are somewhat antiquated. A little on the expensive side for what it offers.

Carmen de Santa Inés – *Placeta de Porras, 7 –* ☎ *958 22 63 80 – fax 958 22 44 04 – 9 rooms – 12 000pts.* This former Carmelite convent in the Albaicín was extended and modified in the 17C. It has an attractive patio with an abundance of plants (lemon trees, jasmine and a grapevine). Some of the rooms have views of the Alhambra.

Palacio de Santa Inés – *Cuesta de Santa Inés, 9 –* ☎ *958 22 23 62 – fax 958 22 24 65 – 13 rooms – 12 000pts.* The architecture of this 16C building in the Albaicín district is Mudéjar inspired. Some rooms overlook the Alhambra. The delightful columned patio has preserved the remains of several Renaissance frescoes.

América – *Real de la Alhambra, 53 –* ☎ *958 22 74 71 – fax 958 22 74 71 – 12 rooms – 15 500pts.* A small hotel with a superb position in the gardens of the Alhambra. Far more modest than the nearby *parador*, but half the price. Guests are advised to book well ahead of time (at least two weeks in advance) due to the hotel's popularity and small number of rooms, most of which have views of the patio of this 19C aristocratic residence.

LUXURY

Parador de San Francisco – *Alhambra –* ☎ *958 22 14 40 – fax 958 22 22 64 – 36 rooms – 33 000pts.* A superb *parador* in the heart of the Alhambra, housed in a 15C building that was once the Convento de San Francisco, founded by the Catholic Monarchs. Even if you don't have the opportunity to stay here, it is well worth having a drink on the terrace overlooking the Generalife gardens.

EATING OUT

Mariquilla – *Lope de Vega, 2 –* ☎ *958 52 16 32 – closed Sun evenings, Mon and from 12 July to 3 Sept.* Do not be deceived by appearances: although its decor may not be anything special, the Mariquilla is one of the best restaurants in Granada and is excellent value for money.

Chikito – *Plaza del Campillo, 9 – closed Wed.* A hugely popular restaurant and bar frequented by artists and intellectuals such as García Lorca in the 1930s. The Chikito is renowned for serving local specialities and its superb cured hams.

Mirador de Morayma – *Pianista Gracia Carrillo, 2 –* ☎ *958 22 82 90 – closed Sun.* With its plant-filled terrace, dining rooms with views of the Alhambra and welcoming, rustic-style decor, this restaurant is one of the most romantic in the city…with prices to match. The menu includes local specialities such as broad beans with ham *(habas con jamón)* and lamb chops *(chuletas de cordero)*.

Ruta del Veleta – *In Cenes de la Vega, Carretera de Sierra Nevada, 50: 8km/5mi from Granada –* ☎ *958 48 61 34.* An elegant and very popular restaurant, whose decor includes dozens of ceramic jugs hanging from the ceiling. During the winter, the owners also open a restaurant they own in the Sierra Nevada.

TAPAS

Bodegas Castañeda – *Almireceros, 1-3.* At the beginning of the 20C a single family owned a huge building that took up the entire block. Sadly, the two brothers who inherited it fell out and the bar was divided up. One of them created the **Bodegas Castañeda**, a bar decorated with antique objects; the other brother opened the **Destilería Castañeda**, where customers can enjoy local tapas and one of Granada's largest selection of spirits.

Casa Enrique – *Acera del Darro, 8 – closed Sun.* The Casa Enrique is run by a friendly owner who is justifiably proud of his large wine cellar. The bar, nestled between a bank and a jewellery store in one of the city's busiest shopping streets, serves delicious cured hams and excellent wines that can be enjoyed by the glass.

Los Diamantes – *Navas, 26 – closed Sun and Mon.* This bar, in a pedestrianised street lined with bars and restaurants, specialises in excellent-quality fish and seafood.

La Trastienda – *Placeta de Cuchilleros, 11.* Founded in 1836. Once through the small entrance door, descend a couple of steps to get to a grocery store which has preserved its small counter. The excellent *chorizo* is highly recommended, either standing at the bar, or sitting down in the pleasant room to the rear.

Pilar del Toro – *Hospital de Santa Ana, 12 –* ☎ *958 22 38 47.* This old house dating from 1789 is worth a visit in its own right with its large central patio. The small counter is to the left of the entrance and the restaurant upstairs.

CAFÉS, BARS & NIGHT-LIFE

A combination of two main factors – the university and the cold temperatures here in winter – has ensured that Granada has an excellent choice of cafés and bars to idle away a quiet afternoon or evening with friends, as well as a number of lively clubs and discos which are normally busy every day of the week. The city's younger crowd tend to hang out in the bars and clubs in Pedro Antonio de Alarcón (a popular area for students) or in the area in and around carrera del Darro, near the Alhambra and Albaicín.

Bohemia Jazz Café – *Calle Santa Teresa, 17. Open daily 3pm to 2am (3am at weekends).* Popular with a cross-section of customers who come to this delightful café for a quiet drink and a chat with friends to a backdrop of jazz-inspired decoration and music. Of the four pianos here, three are true collectors' items, one of which is played several times a week by a resident pianist. Seven types of top-quality arabica coffee are available here.

El Tren – *Calle Carril del Picón, 22. Open daily 8am to 10pm.* This unusual café has a warm and friendly atmosphere and an extensive choice of teas, coffees and cakes. An electric train *(tren)* can be seen running along the tracks suspended from the ceiling, hence the café's name. A varied clientele which changes according to the time of day.

Teterías – **Calle Calderería Nueva**, between the city centre and the Albaicín, is a typical example of a street found in the Moorish quarter of any city. The small and cosy *teterías* are typical cafés which give a welcoming feel to this particular street. Two are worth mentioning: the quiet and pleasant **Pervane**, with its huge selection of teas, coffees, milk shakes and cakes; and **Kasbah**, decorated with cushions and rugs on the floor in true Moorish coffee shop style.

La Fontana – *Carrera del Darro, 19 (next to the first bridge). Open daily 4pm to 3am.* Housed in an old residence at the foot of the Alhambra and Albaicín hills, this inviting antique-adorned café is an ideal place for a quiet drink in an atmosphere dominated by lively conversation. An excellent choice of coffees, herbal teas and cocktails.

El 3er Aviso – *Plaza de Toros, 1-18. Open daily 4pm to 5am.* A surprising location inside the city's bullring, where its spacious design combines with modern, tasteful decor. The café is located on several floors, and from each floor it is possible to look down onto the floors below. Good chart music popular with the 25-45 crowd, and also quiet areas for those wanting to enjoy a chat.

El Príncipe – *Campo del Príncipe, 7. In summer open daily except Mon (Wed to Sat in winter) 11pm to 6am.* This large venue is the place to be seen for the city's in-crowd, hosting regular concerts by leading Spanish groups. Always crowded with a mix of ages. Entrance costs 2 000pts.

El Camborio – *Calle Sacromonte, 47 (on Sacromonte). Open Tues to Sat midnight to 6 or 7am.* One of Granada's oldest and most established nocturnal haunts which has been open for the past thirty years. Best approached by car or taxi as it is located in one of the city's least salubrious districts. The venue itself is quite unique with four inter-connected caves and good dance music. Popular with an eclectic crowd, though predominantly frequented by students. A good place to end the night.

ENTERTAINMENT

Granada's cultural traditions are still as strong as ever with a range of events on offer 12 months a year. The Teatro Alhambra *(calle Molinos 54,* ☎ *958 22 04 47)* hosts a varied season of theatre which is complemented by the programme of high-quality concerts at the Auditorio Manuel de Falla.

The city also organises a regular and varied range of shows and exhibitions, full details of which are listed in a monthly magazine on sale at newspaper stands around the city (100pts). The Provincial Government (Diputación de Granada) also publishes a monthly guide with details of cultural events throughout the province. This guide is readily available from tourist offices.

SHOPPING

Granada's principal shopping area is located along the main avenues in the city centre and in the adjoining pedestrianised streets. The heart of this area is centred around Gran Vía de Colón, calle Reyes Católicos and calle Recogidas, with their mix of traditional shops, modern boutiques and the occasional shopping centre, such as the Neptuno in calle Recogidas.

The former Moorish silk market, the Alcaicería, is located in the same area, next to the cathedral. Nowadays, this maze of narrow alleyways is home to souvenir and craft shops in an area that still retains its Moorish atmosphere. Another typical sight in this part of the city is the plethora of flower stalls which add a delightful splash of colour to plaza de Bib-Rambla.

The typical crafts of Granada include inlaid wood, particularly on small objects such as small boxes and jewellery cases, and pottery. Examples of these items can be found in the Alcaicería.

Shopping in the Alcaicería

This central district is also home to a number of pastry shops *(pastelerías)* selling the typical *piononos*, the traditional delicacy of Granada. Those on sale at the Pastelería Flor y Nata, in calle Reyes Católicos, are worthy of their long-established reputation.

Every Sunday a **market** selling wares of every description is held at the Campo de la Feria on the carretera de Jaén.

TRANSPORT

Airport – On the Málaga road. ☎ 958 24 52 00 and 958 44 64 11. **Information:** ☎ 958 22 75 92. The airport is on the outskirts of the city. A bus service operates between the city centre and airport, departing from plaza Isabel la Católica, next to the Banesto bank. ☎ 958 27 86 77.

Trains – The railway station is on avenida de Andalucía, ☎ 958 27 12 72. Regular services operate to most towns in Granada province and the majority of major Spanish cities. The RENFE (Spanish State Railways) booking office can be found at calle Reyes Católicos, 63. ☎ 958 22 31 19.

City buses – Buses serve all parts of the city, including the major monuments and suburbs. A one-way ticket costs 120pts; a 15-trip ticket 1 000pts; and a 30-trip coupon 2 000pts. A 30-day pass is on sale for 4 500pts.

Inter-city buses – Camino de Ronda, 47 ☎ 958 25 13 54. Buses operate to every provincial capital within Andalucia, the majority of major Spanish cities and several European capitals.

The daily 9am bus service from Granada to the Sierra Nevada leaves from the "Ventorrillo" bar on paseo de Violón, close to the Puente de la Virgen bridge. ☎ 958 81 11 06.

Taxis – ☎ 958 15 14 61 and 958 28 06 54.

Horse-drawn carriages – These can be hired near the Puerta Real for tours of Granada's main tourist sites.

INDEX OF SIGHTS AND STREETS NAMES ON PLAN OF GRANADA

The tears of Boabdil

Having handed over the keys to Granada, Boabdil, the last Nasrid king, began his journey into exile. At the place that has gone down in history with the name of The Moor's Sigh *(Suspiro del Moro)*, he stopped to cast a final glance at his beloved city, but was unable to hold back his tears. His mother is said to have rounded on him: "You weep like a woman for what you could not hold as a man". Who would not have wept in his place?

Christian Granada – Following the reconquest of Granada, the city's *morisco* population established their community on the Albaicín. However, by the end of the 15C the first in a series of conflicts had broken out following the decision to force Muslims to be baptised. As the years passed, the situation worsened, reaching a climax in 1568 when the leader of the revolt, Abén Humeya, fled to the Alpujarras mountains, where he was defeated by Don Juan of Austria, on the orders of Felipe II. Following this bloody episode, all *moriscos* were expelled from Granada.

During the **16C** and **17C**, the city experienced significant development with the razing of the maze-like network of Moorish streets to create wider streets and spacious squares, and the construction of important buildings such as the cathedral, Chapel Royal, Carlos V's palace, the Exchange, Royal Hospital, chancery and Carthusian monastery.

In the **18C**, and particularly the **19C**, Granada assumed great popularity with numerous visitors who were bewitched by its charms. Romanticism was to forge a new image for a city which was long used to having its praises sung. Its beauty, tinged with an

GRANADA

MÁLAGA, SEVILLA ✈ CÓRDOBA →

V

Ancha

de

Madrid

Av.

de

Capuchinos

Hospital Real
U

R.

Jardines del Triunfo

Av. de la Constitución

Av. Cap. Moreno

Cuesta de San Antonio

Camino de S. Antonio

Acera de S. Ildefonso

Carretera de

Veredilla de S

Larga S. Cristóbal

Cristóbal **20**

Santa Bárbara

Ventanilla

Rector López Argüeta

San Juan de Dios

SAN JUAN DE DIOS
U

San Jerónimo

Los Arandas

Santa

Capitán

SAN JERÓNIMO

Gran

Duquesa

C

U

POL

Pl. del Triunfo

76

46

Gran **G**

Elvira

Vía

44

Zenete

Convento de Sta Isabel la Real

Isabel la Real

Plaza S. Miguel Bajo

Gregorio

40

Elvira

de

San José

Cuesta de S. **B¹** S

Santos Justo y Pastor
73

78
4

Paula

Escuelas

San Jerónimo

Cárcel

Baja

Cald. Nueva

Elvira

13

Chancillería

Sta An. y S. Gil
66

Pl. de los Lobos

Málaga

36

53

CATEDRAL
12

Colón

CAPILLA REAL
1

Plaza Nueva
2

Cuesta

e

J

52

Tablas

Pl. de la Trinidad

F

K

S

Ayuntamiento Viejo

Católicos

38

Pávaneras

B²

Obispo Hurtado

Mesones

Alhóndiga

Pl.
Alcaicería

Bib. Rambla

Reyes

r

Corral del Carbón
7
77

63

de Carmen

San Matías

67

Gracia

Puentezuelas

H

16

Escudo

Navas

a

Y

Pl. de Gracia

Solarillo de Gracia

Recogidas

61

San

Puerta Real

Acera del Casino

Ángel

Ganivet

Varela

POL

68

Z

Huerta de San Vicente

MOTRIL →

Tejeiro

47

Antón

Duende

Pl. del Campillo

Pl. de Mariana Pineda

E

Carrera de la Virgen

Acera del Darro

PALACIO DE BIBATAUBÍN

3

San Jacinto

Lozano

Pedro

Antonio

Alarcón

Portón

Alhamar

Alhamar

◎ **Paseo** ◎

A **Parque de las Ciencias** ↘ B

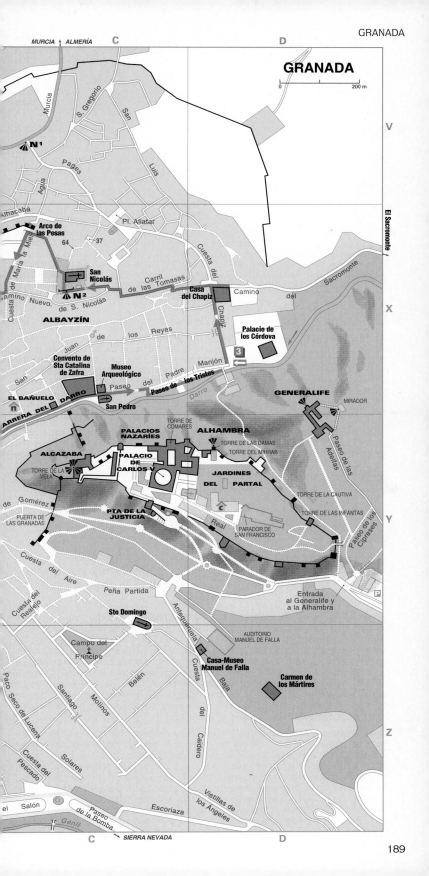

GRANADA

MURCIA / ALMERÍA

0   200 m

V

El Sacromonte

Arco de
las Pesas

64   37

San
Nicolás

N²

Casa
del Chapiz

Camino

del

Sacromonte

X

Palacio de
los Córdova

ALBAYZÍN

de   los   Reyes

3

Convento de
Sta Catalina
de Zafra

Museo
Arqueológico

Manjón

Paseo   del   Padre

Paseo de los Tristes

EL BAÑUELO

San Pedro

Darro

GENERALIFE

ARRERA   DEL   DARRO

MIRADOR

TORRE DE
COMARES

ALHAMBRA

Paseo de las Adelfas

PALACIOS
NAZARÍES

TORRE DE LAS DAMAS

TORRE DEL MIHRAB

ALCAZABA

PALACIO
DE
CARLOS

JARDINES

TORRE DE LA
VELA

DEL   PARTAL

PTA DE LA
JUSTICIA

TORRE DE LA CAUTIVA

TORRE DE LAS INFANTAS

de   Gomérez

Real

Y

PUERTA DE
LAS GRANADAS

PARADOR DE
SAN FRANCISCO

P

Cuesta   del   Aire

Paseo de los Cipreses

Peña Partida

Entrada
al Generalife y
a la Alhambra

Cuesta del
Realejo

Sto Domingo

AUDITORIO
MANUEL DE FALLA

Campo del
Príncipe

Casa-Museo
Manuel de Falla

Belén

Carmen de
los Mártires

Z

Paco Seco del Lucena

Santiago

Molinos

Solares

Cuesta del
Pescado

Vistillas de
los Angeles

Escoriaza

el   Salón

Paseo
de la Bomba

Genil

SIERRA NEVADA

C

D

aura of mysticism and exoticism, became a literary theme for renowned writers such as Victor Hugo, Alexandre Dumas and Washington Irving, who penned his famous *Tales of the Alhambra*.

However, during the 19C Granada was to receive other, less welcome visitors in the shape of French troops who destroyed parts of the city during their period of occupation. Thankfully, their attempts to destroy the Alhambra resulted in no more than the loss of some of its towers and various sections of its defensive walls.

Granada today – Nowadays, the city is the capital of a province whose main income derives from agriculture, cattle breeding and tourism. It is a lively city all year round, an atmosphere generated by the students from its respected university, and the thousands of annual visitors. The local *granadinos* believe that their city has the perfect location: on the doorstep of the Sierra Nevada with its sun-blessed ski slopes, and just an hour's drive from the Mediterranean, offering the perfect escape from the summer heat.

> **Entrance tickets**
> Visitors should ensure that they respect the **entrance time specified on their entrance ticket to the Nasrid Palaces**. Independent travellers should also be aware that due to restrictions on visitor numbers inside the Alhambra, it is advisable to book in advance or arrive at the ticket desk first thing in the morning. Tickets can also be purchased at any branch of the BBV bank in Spain, as well as their offices in London, Paris, Milan and New York. For further details, consult the Alhambra web site at www.alhambra-patronato.es

★★★ ALHAMBRA AND GENERALIFE ⏱ *half a day*

Access on foot to the Alhambra Palace and Generalife Gardens from the city centre is along Cuesta de Gomérez, from plaza Nueva. Enter the outer perimeter of the palace through the Puerta de Granadas (Pomegranate Gate), built by Machuca during the reign of Carlos V, to reach the **shrubbery★**. For visitors arriving by car or bus, the main approach up to the Alhambra branches off the road heading towards the Sierra Nevada and is clearly signposted.

★★★ Alhambra

The beautiful Calat Alhambra (Red Castle) must be one of the most remarkable fortresses ever built and the finest Moorish palace still standing anywhere in the world. It sits at the top of a wooded hill – the highest in the city – which in medieval times was known as La Sabika. "La Sabika is the crown on Granada's head... and the Alhambra (may God protect her) is the ruby on the crown" wrote the poet Ibn Zamrak (1333-93).

> **Key dates**
> The most accepted chronology for the construction of the Alhambra and Generalife is as follows:
> – late 13C: external walls;
> – early 14C: the Generalife gardens;
> – mid to late 14C: the Nasrid palaces, built during the reigns of Yusuf I (1333-54) and Mohammed V (1354-59 and 1362-91).

Visitors to the Alhambra are spellbound by its refinement and the splendour of its architecture which incorporates delightful gardens and running water into its overall plan, thus perpetuating the tradition of a Koranic Eden like no other building on Earth. However, its beauty is also full of contradictions, in that the sumptuous appearance of its individual architectural components contrasts with the poverty of the materials used to create them. It is also surprising that a political power in decline should build such a masterpiece and that the Alhambra would be so respected by those rulers who took their place in the years to come. Yet, despite its impressive dimensions, the Alhambra is a palace that has been built on a scale that can be appreciated by its modern-day visitors.

★★★ **Nasrid Palaces (Palacios Nazaríes)** – These palaces are the central nucleus of the whole fortress. Nothing on their exterior presages their internal richness or the variety and decorative originality of their *mocárabe* vaults, domes, friezes and stuccowork which, combined with the effects of water and light – both of which are used as architectural features – create a jewel of incalculable value.

The buildings are built around three courtyards: the Cuarto Dorado (Golden Room), the Patio de los Arrayanes (Myrtle Courtyard) and the Patio de los Leones (Lion Courtyard). As a result of the palace's layout, in which the individual rooms are interconnected by small passageways, the visual impact as one passes from one architectural masterpiece to the next is all the more striking.

The Mexuar – The tour begins in the rectangular **Mexuar**. The four columns at the front support a stucco-adorned entablature. An attractive frieze of *azulejos* and an epigraphic border cover the walls, which are decorated with royal coats of arms. It is thought that this room served an administrative function as a council chamber. Note the small oratory leading off the room to the rear.

Patio del Cuarto Dorado (1) – The magnificent south wall is a compendium of Nasrid art. This outstanding wall-façade comprises *azulejos* with geometric decoration, panels with vegetal features, epigraphic borders, a mocárabe frieze, a carved wood cornice and a large eave, all of which are arranged around two doors and five windows.

Opposite is the Cuarto Dorado, a wide room with tiled panelling, fine stuccowork and a beautiful wooden ceiling. The **view★** of the Albaicín from its windows is quite magnificent.

Delicate Nasrid decoration

Patio de los Arrayanes – The Myrtle Courtyard is reached via a narrow passageway, access to which is through the doorway to the left of the south wall. This delightful rectangular patio has an elongated and narrow pool bordered by myrtle bushes which reflects the massive bulk of the **Torre de Comares**; the latter offers a sharp contrast with the light, slender porticoes that give onto the **Sala de la Barca**, covered by a magnificent wooden vault with a quarter sphere at each end. The highly decorated walls are adorned with the coats of arms of the Nasrid dynasty and epigraphic inscriptions bearing the words "There is no Saviour but God". This room leads to the **Salón de Embajadores** (Hall of Ambassadors), a square-shaped room used as the audience chamber of the emirs. The richness of its decoration is quite exquisite, with its magnificent lustre *azulejo* panelling, delicate stucco with plant and geometric motifs, and numerous epigraphic strips with religious and poetic inscriptions. The remarkable **dome**, above a line of latticework windows, comprises more than 8 000 pieces of multi-coloured wood and represents the seven heavens of the Koran. Niches on three sides of the room have latticework veils allowing light to filter through.

Patio de los Leones – The justly famous Lion Courtyard dates from the reign of Mohammed V. The 11C fountain of unknown provenance at its centre is supported by 12 rough stone lions, and is surrounded by the delicate arcades of slender columns which lead to the sumptuous main state apartments. Two elegant pavilions supported by columns project over the east and west sides of the courtyard. The **Sala de los Abencerrajes** on the south side, so called after Boabdil had ordered the massacre of the rival Abencerraje family and piled their heads into the room's central basin, is adorned with a stalactite ceiling and a splendid star-shaped lantern cupola illuminated by 16 windows. The rectangular **Sala de los Reyes**, or King's Chamber, on the east side of the courtyard comprises three square sections covered with *mocárabe* cupolas, separated by richly ornamented double arches. The painted vaulting adorning the alcoves depict the pastimes of Moorish and Christian princes and probably date from the end of the 14C. The style is so atypical that it is not known whether the artist was a Christian working for the Sultan before or after the Reconquest. The **Sala de Dos Hermanas** (Hall of the Two Sisters) is a square room renowned for its honeycomb dome cupola above an octagon, and its fine *azulejos* and stuccowork. A romantic legend attributes its name to two sisters who were imprisoned within its walls. Beyond are the **Sala de los Ajimeces** and the **Mirador de Lindaraja**, both equally resplendent with their stuccowork and honeycomb decoration. Prior to the construction of Carlos V's rooms, the mirador provided views of the outskirts of Granada; nowadays, the panorama is limited to a small garden: the 16C Patio de Lindaraja.

A corridor from the Sala de Dos Hermanas passes the cupolas of the Royal Baths *(Baños Reales)* to the left, currently closed to visitors. Continue through the room used by the American writer Washington Irving during his period of residence in the Alhambra, to reach an open gallery with delightful **views★** of the Albaicín; descend the stairs to the Patio de la Reja **(2)** and the Patio de Lindaraja.

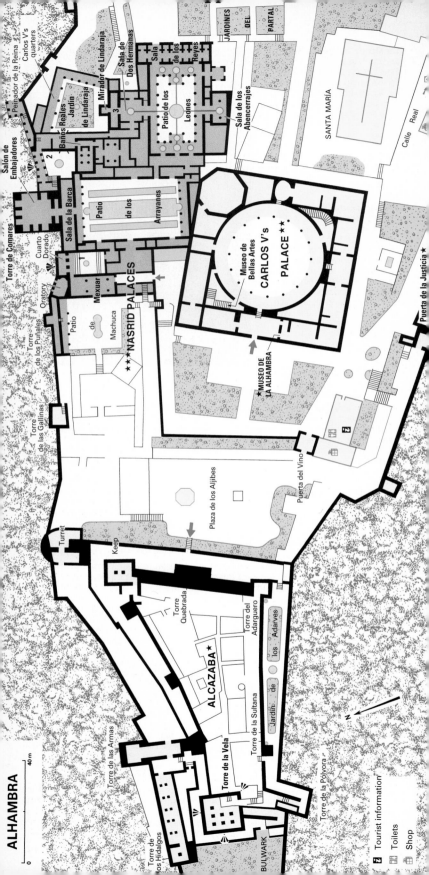

ALHAMBRA

0   40 m

Peinador de la Reina / Carlos V's quarters

Torre de Comares

Torre de los Puñales

Torre de las Gallinas

Salón de Embajadores

Baños Reales

Jardín de Lindaraja

Sala de Dos Hermanas

Mirador de Lindaraja

Sala de los Reyes

Patio de los Leones

Sala de los Abencerrajes

JARDINES DEL PARTAL

SANTA MARÍA

Calle Real

Cuarto Dorado

Sala de la Barca

Patio de los Arrayanes

Oratory

Mexuar

Patio de Machuca

★★NASRID PALACES

Museo de Bellas Artes

CARLOS V's PALACE ★★

★MUSEO DE LA ALHAMBRA

Puerta del Vino

Puerta de la Justicia ★

Plaza de los Aljibes

Turret

Keep

Torre Quebrada

Torre del Adarguero

Torre de los Adarves

ALCAZABA★

Jardín de los Adarves

Torre de la Sultana

Torre de las Armas

Torre de la Vela

Torre de los Hidalgos

BULWARK

Torre de la Pólvora

N

☐ Tourist information
☐ Toilets
☐ Shop

★★Gardens and perimeter towers – Spreading to the east of the royal palaces are the **Jardines del Partal**, terraced gardens which descend to the towers punctuating the walls. The first tower visible is the **Torre de las Damas** (Lady Tower), built by Yusuf I at the beginning of the 14C, and preceded by a graceful *artesonado* portico. The Torre del Mihrab and the former Nasrid mosque *(mezquita)* can be seen to the right. Two further towers, the Torre de la Cautiva (Captive's Tower), also dating from the reign of Yusuf I, and the later Torre de las Infantas (Infantas' Tower), have sumptuous internal decoration.

Enter the Palacio de Carlos V from the Jardines del Partal.

★★Carlos V's palace (Palacio de Carlos V) – In 1526, Emperor Carlos V ordered the construction of this palace which was financed by taxes levied on the *moriscos*. He entrusted the work to **Pedro Machuca**, who had studied in Italy under Michelangelo, and who created a design in pure Classical style. The simplicity of its plan – a circle within a square – and the harmony of its lines endow the building with an unquestionable majestic beauty. The façade comprises two storeys: a lower level of dressed stone, and an upper section adorned with Ionic pilasters.

On the main doorway of the lower level, note the medallions and superb bas-reliefs representing the triumph of peace (at the centre) and military battles (to the side). The upper storey bears the escutcheon of Spain.

The palace's outstanding feature is the large **circular patio** (31m/102ft in diameter), fronted by Doric columns on the ground floor and Ionic columns on its upper tier. The patio's charm lies in its sobriety and the beauty of its proportions, which combine to create a masterpiece of the Spanish Renaissance.

The palace contains two museums:

★Museo de la Alhambra – *Entrance to the right of the vestibule.* This pleasant museum is entirely devoted to Hispano-Moorish art and contains exhibits that demonstrate the mastery of the artists and craftsmen from the period. These include ceramics, wood carvings, panels of *azulejos* and *alicatados*, stuccowork, bronzes, fabric etc. Outstanding objects include a 10C ablutions basin, known as the Pila de Almanzor, decorated with lions and stags, the famous **blue or gazelle amphora★**, a delicate 14C masterpiece, the unusual ceramic exhibits representing animals, and replicas of household objects.

Museo de Bellas Artes – *Entrance on the upper storey of the patio.* The Fine Arts Museum contains an interesting collection of paintings and sculptures from the 15C to the 20C. Those from the 15C and 16C include works of a predominantly religious nature by renowned artists such as Sánchez Cotán, Siloé, Alonso Cano and Pedro de Mena, in addition to a magnificent still-life, *Thistle and Carrots★★*, by Sánchez Cotán, which depicts the dignity of the inanimate object with great sobriety; only Zurbarán was equal to this mastery. Both represent the culmination of the Spanish still-life tradition, so austere and so different from that of the great Dutch and Flemish masters.

The rooms devoted to the 19C and 20C contain works by Rodríguez Acosta, Muñoz Degrain, López Mezquita and Manuel Ángeles Ortiz, including a number of more avant-garde exhibits.

Puerta del Vino – The Wine Gateway, built by Mohammed V, may have been erected as a commemorative monument, given its location inside the palace walls and the fact that it did not perform any defensive function. Note the ceramic decoration on the spandrels of the horseshoe arch, and, above it, a paired window flanked by sculpted panels.

Pass through the gateway to reach the Alcazaba.

★Alcazaba – To the left of the Plaza de los Aljibes (Cistern Court), at the western-most extreme of the palace precinct, stands the Alcazaba, the oldest part of the Alhambra, with its austere, fortress-like appearance, towers and defensive walls. Three of its towers overlook the courtyard: the Torre del Adarguero, the Torre Quebrada and the Torre del Homenaje (keep). The views of the leafy Alhambra wood from the Jardín de los Adarves on the south side are particularly attractive. The parade ground inside the fortress has preserved some military remains dominated by the imposing bulk of the **Torre de la Vela** (Watchtower), the bulwark on which the Catholic Monarchs hoisted their flags upon their reconquest of Granada. The tower provides a magnificent **panorama★★** of the palace, the Generalife, Sacromonte, Granada and the Sierra Nevada. From here, the series of fortifications to the west known as the **Torres Bermejas** (Red Towers), part of the old city's defensive network, can also be seen. Although these were originally built in the late 8C and early 9C, they have been subsequently rebuilt.

★Puerta de la Justicia – Built by Yusuf I, the massive Justice Gateway is built into a tower in the outer walls. The external façade comprises a large horseshoe arch, an inner door, also with a horseshoe arch, and, above it, an inscription and a wide strip of delightful *azulejos* with an image of the Virgin and Child from the early 16C, commissioned by the Catholic Monarchs. The symbolism of the hand on the key of the outer arch and the key and rope on the internal arch remain something of a mystery.

B. Kaufmann/MICHELIN

Generalife gardens

★★Generalife

The name Generalife name derives from the Arabic *Yannat al-Arif*, for which two possible interpretations have been suggested: the "Garden of the Architect" and "the most noble of gardens". It is known that this summer residence already existed in 1319, thus predating the Alhambra Palace. The Generalife consists of a single palace surrounded by magnificent terraced **gardens** in which running water plays a predominant role once again. The avenue of cypress trees leads to the new gardens, in the centre of which stands an auditorium – the delightful setting for Granada's annual Festival of Music and Dance.

The main nucleus of the Generalife is the **Patio de la Acequia**, a long irrigation pool *(acequia)* lined with water jets and bordered by plants and flowers and with a pavilion at either end; a gallery running along its length has a mirador at its centre providing superb views of the Alhambra. The pavilion through the portico to the rear contains the Sala Regia, a room decorated with some fine stuccowork.

The Patio de la Sultana, enclosed on one side by a 16C gallery, owes its names to the so-called **"Sultana's cypress tree"**.

A meeting-place for lovers

According to legend, it was by this cypress tree that the wife of the sultan Boabdil and a leader from the rival Abencerraje family would meet. Upon hearing of these secret liaisons, the sultan ordered the well-documented massacre of the members of the Abencerraje family in the room of the palace that now bears their name.

The upper gardens above the palace contain the famous **escalera del agua**, or water staircase, part of a charming scene that highlights the refinements in taste of Moorish culture. Paseo de las Adelfas (Oleander Avenue) and paseo de los Cipreses provide an exit from this haven of tranquillity and greenery.

★★① CATHEDRAL QUARTER *allow 2hr*

★Cathedral ⊙ – *Entry from Gran Vía de Colón.* Construction of the city's cathedral began in 1518 in the middle of the old Moorish city and continued for almost two centuries. The initial project was for a Gothic cathedral similar to that in Toledo. However, the architect Diego Siloé, who replaced Enrique Egas and was entrusted with the project from 1528 until his death in 1563, made changes to the design and introduced the Renaissance style to the building.

Interior – *Entry through the ambulatory.* The interior comprises five sizeable and lofty aisles with adjoining side chapels, and an ambulatory. Enormous square pillars with engaged half columns rise up above elevated pedestals and support large sections of entablature, thereby considerably increasing the overall height. The vaulting above is Gothic in style.

The **high altar★** *(capilla mayor)* is noteworthy for its rich decoration. It is circular in plan with surprising height created by two enormous superimposed orders. In the initial design, the area above the vaulted arches, which connect the chancel with the ambulatory, contained large niches to house royal tombs; these niches were later covered by portraits of Doctors of the Church. The lower order of columns has ledges with statues of apostles and saints, while the second tier contains seven paintings by Alonso Cano representing scenes from the life of the Virgin Mary. The 16C stained glass windows above depict evangelical scenes, the majority of which are from the Passion. Note also the **silver tabernacle** in the centre of the presbytery.

A large **main arch** linking the chapel with the aisles houses the statues at prayer of the Catholic Monarchs by Pedro de Mena, and above them two medallions bearing the busts of Adam and Eve, by Alonso Cano. The impressive 18C **organs** between the first two pillars of the nave are particularly impressive.

The right transept arm opens onto the magnificent **north portal of the Chapel Royal★**, dominated by a Virgin and Child. This ornate portal by Enrique Egas is Gothic in style. Above this arch the emblems of the yoke and arrow flank the coat of arms of the Catholic Monarchs. To the left note the large altarpiece dedicated to St James, at the centre of which stands an equestrian statue of the apostle by Alonso de Mena.

Two chapels are worthy of special mention: the **Capilla de la Virgen de las Angustias** and the **Capilla de Nuestra Señora de la Antigua**. The large marble retable of the Virgin of Anguish *(angustias)* was housed in the retrochoir until 1926. At its centre the Virgin appears with the dead Christ in her arms and accompanied by several saints. The chapel of Nuestra Señora de la Antigua contains a fine 15C statue of this particular Virgin and Child at the centre of a magnificent early-18C Baroque altarpiece by Pedro Duque Cornejo. The ambulatory contains an interesting collection of choir books from the 16C to 18C.

The **Museo Catedralicio** has several notable exhibits, including a small image of the Virgin of Bethlehem, a bust of St Paul by Alonso Cano, and a bust of the Virgin and Child by Pedro de Mena.

Another delightful image of the Virgin, by Alonso Cano, can be seen at Christ's feet in the **sacristy**.

Exterior – Continue around the apse and exit the cathedral onto calle Cárcel Baja, where two doorways designed by Siloé can be seen. The lower section of the **Puerta del Perdón** (Pardon Doorway) is another example of his architectural genius, on which the figures of Faith and Justice appear against the arch, holding a tablet. Two magnificent escutcheons, one of the Catholic Monarchs *(to the left)*, the other of Emperor Carlos V *(to the right)* adorn the buttresses. The **Portada de San Jerónimo**, a portal named in honour of St Jerome, has a semicircular arch between Plateresque pilasters and medallions with cherubims in the spandrels of the arch. Above the arch, note the relief of a penitent St Jerome.

The main monumental façade overlooking the plaza de las Pasiegas was designed by Alonso Cano in 1667.

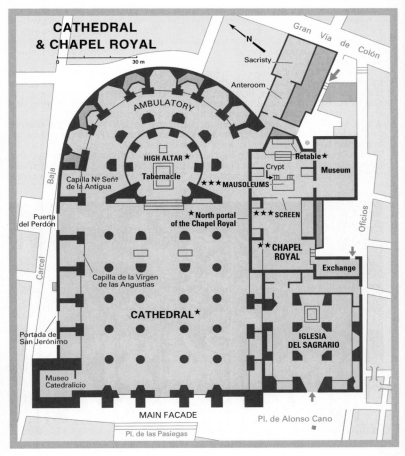

Madraza (Former University) – *In calle Oficios, opposite the Chapel Royal.* The Madraza or Muslim university was built in the 14C by Yusuf I. Following the Reconquest, the Catholic Monarchs requisitioned the building for use as Granada's city hall. The façade, late Granada Baroque in style, was created in the 18C, when the building was practically rebuilt. The decoration is mainly confined to the large balconies on the upper floor. An escutcheon between these balconies completes the decorative work.

Inside, across the inner patio, stands the former Moorish **oratory**, an attractive hall of polychrome stuccowork, *mócarabe* decoration and a delightful octagonal dome adorned with a lantern.

★★ **Chapel Royal (Capilla Real)** ⊘ – The Catholic Monarchs ordered the construction of the Chapel Royal with the express intention of being buried in the city that had bathed them in such glory. They entrusted the building work to the architect Enrique Egas, who commenced the project in 1506 and completed it 15 years later. It is a masterpiece of the Isabelline Gothic style, both in terms of its stylistic unity and the richness of its ornamentation.

> ### A historic place of rest
>
> The importance of the reign of the **Catholic Monarchs** cannot be underestimated, with their influence extending far beyond the Iberian Peninsula. This was particularly true of the discovery of America, to which they had given their financial and political support. Their marriage was also to have a determining effect on the history of Spain, by uniting the kingdoms of Castilla and Aragón into a political and geographical entity that would provide the basis for the future Spanish state and bring the country into the modern age. However, their reign is overshadowed by less glorious events, including the expulsion of Jews from the country and the establishment of the Spanish Inquisition.

The outstanding features of the **exterior** are the fine pinnacles and elegant **cresting**, the lower section of which is decorated with the letters F and Y, representing the initials of the Catholic Monarchs. The main doorway of the chapel was incorporated inside the cathedral upon the construction of the latter. Access is via the old Lonja (Exchange).

The **Lonja** is a graceful 16C Plateresque building with a rectangular ground plan and two floors. Decorative columns, adorned with spheres and spiral cord decoration, support the arches. The coat of arms of the city is emblasoned on the lower section. The upper floor gallery contains the emblems of the Catholic Monarchs and Carlos V on the carved sills.

The **interior** consists of a single nave with side chapels, with ribbed vaults supported by pillars with large bead moulding. A blue fringe with a gilded inscription adorns the upper part of the walls. However, the most characteristic decoration inside the Chapel Royal is the profusion of heraldic features with the coats of arms and emblems of the Catholic Monarchs on the walls and wrought-iron grilles.

A spectacular 16C **screen**★★★ by Master Bartolomé of Jaén encloses the chancel. In the centre, note the escutcheon and yoke and arrow of Fernando and Isabel, in addition to the scenes of the life of Christ on the upper section.

The two double **mausoleums**★★★ in the chancel, one of the Catholic Monarchs, the other of their daughter, Juana la Loca (Joan the Mad), and her husband, Felipe el Hermoso (Philip the Handsome), are quite outstanding. The first, the work of the Tuscan sculptor

Detail on the magnificent screen by Master Bartolomé of Jaén

Domenico Fancelli, was carved in Genoa in 1517 from Carrara marble, and is decorated with reliefs of apostles and medallions; those in the middle represent the baptism and resurrection of Christ. The upper part reveals the sculptures of the monarchs above angels bearing an escutcheon-adorned garland. Their epitaph is engraved on the tablet at the base of the mausoleum. The second, equally impressive mausoleum is a work carved by Bartolomé Ordóñez in 1519 on a pedestal decorated with religious scenes. The sarcophagus above it is topped by the recumbent statues of Juana and Felipe. The remains of all four figures are contained in simple coffins in the chapel's crypt.

The magnificent Plateresque **retable★** at the high altar was sculpted by Felipe Vigarny between 1520 and 1522. The artist has succeeded in endowing his figures with energetic movement and great expression. The scene is dominated by a crucified Christ accompanied by the Virgin Mary and St John. The lower register of the predella depicts the siege of Granada and the baptism of the *moriscos*. Note also the praying statues of the Catholic Monarchs attributed to Diego de Siloé.

Museum – *Access by the north arm of the transept.* Numerous objects of incalculable historical value can be seen in this museum which is housed in the sacristy. Among the exhibits on display are **Queen Isabel's sceptre and crown, King Fernando's sword**, plus an outstanding **collection of paintings★★** by Flemish (Rogier van der Weyden, Memling), Italian (Perugino, Botticelli) and Spanish (Bartolomé Bermejo, Pedro Berruguete) artists. In the rear of the museum can be found the famous **Triptych of the Passion** by the Fleming Dirk Bouts and two sculptures of the Catholic Monarchs at prayer by Felipe Vigarny.

Curia – The doorway of this 16C Plateresque-style building is adorned with an archiepiscopal escutcheon on its semicircular pediment. To the left stands the **Palacio Arzobispal**, or Archbishop's Palace, of simple design.

Iglesia del Sagrario – This 18C church was built on the site of the city's main mosque. It is known that the architect Francisco Hurtado Izquierdo was involved in its design.

Plaza Bib-Rambla – This attractive rectangular square in the centre of the city is the setting for a number of colourful flower stalls. The plaza is further embellished by attractive street-lamps and a large central fountain crowned by Neptune.

Alcaicería – In Moorish times the area was occupied by the city's silk market. It has now been rebuilt and transformed into a market for craft and souvenir shops. The Alcaicería still retains its Moorish atmosphere as a result of its narrow alleyways, horseshoe arches and Arabic-style decoration.

Corral del Carbón – This former storehouse is a Moorish construction dating from the 14C. It has a harmonious doorway with a horseshoe arch adorned with an *alfiz* surround and above it an inscription and a paired window flanked by two panels with *sebka* decoration. The doorway is crowned by a large wooden eave, while the portico is topped by *mocárabe* vaulting.

The sober internal patio is of particular interest with its three storeys of straight galleries supported by brick pillars with wooden capitals, and a simple fountain at its centre, all of which combine to create a charming scene. The building now houses the city's Tourist Office.

Casa de los Duques de Abrantes – *In placeta Tovar, to the left of the Corral del Carbón.* This 16C building has a simple Gothic-influenced doorway with heraldic decoration.

Plaza de Isabel la Católica – The square is dominated by the Monument to the Santa Fe Agreement (1892), a work by Mariano Benlliure, in which Columbus is depicted presenting his plans to Queen Isabel.

Santa Fe Agreement

On 17 April 1492, the Catholic Monarchs and Christopher Columbus signed this famous agreement in the nearby town of Santa Fe. The agreement bestowed upon Columbus the titles of admiral, viceroy and governor of all territories discovered by him.

Casa de los Tiros – Built in the mid 16C, this palace has an unusual stone façade with just five, almost round, sculptures of figures in warrior-like attire. It now houses the city's newspaper and periodicals library (Hemeroteca).

★② CARRERA DEL DARRO *allow 1hr*

This delightful street, which is bordered by the Darro River, runs from plaza de Santa Ana to paseo de los Tristes. The walk along carrera del Darro leaves the modern city behind and enters an area with a completely different appearance in which the atmosphere is more akin to a village or small town than a large city. The street skirts the right bank of the river which is spanned by several simple stone bridges providing access to Granada's mythical hills, the Alhambra and Albaicín.

Before starting the walk, several buildings in **plaza Nueva** and **plaza de Santa Ana** are worthy of special interest.

Carrera del Darro

Chancillería – The former chancery now houses Andalucia's High Court of Justice. This 16C building on plaza Nueva has a Classical façade, characterised by a combination of various architectural elements which already show Baroque undertones in their design. The marble doorway is dominated by a large Spanish coat of arms. The balustrade crowning the building was added in the 18C. The delightful and harmonious **patio★**, attributed to Siloé, is particularly attractive.

Iglesia de Santa Ana y San Gil – This small 16C church standing in plaza de Santa Ana, which is nowadays connected to plaza Nueva, was built according to plans by Diego de Siloé. The handsome bell-tower has colourful *azulejo* decoration on the arch spandrels and pinnacle section. The church portal is decorated with three niches bearing statues of St Ann and two additional female saints and a medallion of the Virgin and Child. The main features of the interior are the Mudéjar-style ceilings above the nave and chancel.

A 16C fountain, the **Pilar del Toro**, also attributed to Siloé, can be seen in the same square. It is adorned with the coat of arms of the city above a relief of a bull's head that has lent the fountain its name.

Follow carrera del Darro.

★Moorish baths (El Bañuelo) ⊘ – The baths are situated opposite the remains of the 11C bridge known as the **Puente del Cadí**, of which only a part of a fortified tower and a horseshoe arch remain.

These 11C baths have a typically Moorish structure and comprise several rooms (changing areas, a meeting and massage room, and the baths themselves). Note the star-pierced vaulting with octagonal skylights and the arcades in the last two rooms with Roman, Caliphal and Visigothic capitals. Despite their age, the baths are some of the best preserved in Spain.

The towers and walls of the Alhambra are visible from here.

Convento de Santa Catalina de Zafra – This 16C convent has a Renaissance-type doorway with a semicircular arch framed by pilasters and with medallions on the spandrels. Above it sits a niche housing a statue of the saint flanked by two coats of arms.

Museo Arqueológico ⊘ – The city's archeological museum is housed in the Casa Castril (1539), with its fine **Plateresque doorway★**, profusely decorated with heraldic motifs, scallop-shells, animals, figures etc.

Exhibits include an interesting collection of 9C BC Egyptian alabaster vases, discovered at a Punic necropolis in Almuñécar; a bull figure from Arjona, and numerous Roman artefacts and Moorish decorative objects. The museum also has a copy of the Dama de Baza, the original of which is on display in the Museo Arqueológico Nacional in Madrid.

Iglesia de San Pedro – *Opposite the museum.* The 16C Church of St Peter occupies an attractive location on the banks of the Darro, watched over by the Comares Tower *(torre)*. Two sculptures dominate its simple portal: the figure of St Peter holding the keys, and St Paul clasping a sword.

Paseo de los Tristes – Carrera del Darro runs into this avenue, which offers superb **views★★** of the Alhambra, with its towers and walls emerging from the greenery of the hill. The panorama from here is particularly impressive at night, when the palace is illuminated. Small café terraces provide the perfect setting in which to admire this memorable sight.

★★ 3 ALBAICÍN *allow 1hr 30min*

This district, which has lent its name to the hill on which it stands, is Granada's most characteristic quarter, offering magnificent views of the Alhambra at every turn. It was here that the first Moorish fortress was built in the city, although only the walls survive from this early construction. A maze of narrow alleyways wind their way up the hill between the palisades of small villas known as *cármenes*, through delightful small squares and past picturesque street corners. The Albaicín is best explored on foot in order to fully appreciate the heritage of this Moorish section of the city.

Palacio de los Córdova – *At the foot of the Cuesta del Chapiz*. An avenue of cypress trees in the garden leads to the palace, its Renaissance doorway adorned with heraldic decoration. The building is now home to the Municipal Archives.

Casa del Chapiz ⊙ – *Entrance along camino de Sacromonte*. The mansion is now the headquarters of the School of Arabic Studies. The complex is a combination of two Moorish houses from the 15C and 16C with patios and galleries. The gardens offer pleasant **views**★ of the Alhambra.

Delve deeper into the Albaicín along the Cuesta de San Agustín, which climbs between the typical *cármenes* and provides a first glimpse of the Alhambra.

> ### Cármenes
> This is the name given to the small villas found in the Albaicín. They are a more modern version of a type of Moorish residence or *carmen* which would have consisted of a house and its adjoining kitchen garden *(huerto)*.

Mirador de San Nicolás –
This terrace in front of the **Iglesia de San Nicolás** enjoys one of the best **views**★★★ of Granada's magnificent backdrop, encompassing the breathtaking beauty of the ochre-coloured Alhambra standing out against its verdant hillside, and the superb outline of the Sierra Nevada.

Pass in front of the church and follow the callejón de San Cecilio to the end, then turn right and continue through the Arco de las Pesas.

Arco de las Pesas – This simple 11C arch, standing alongside the pleasant plaza Larga, was part of the walls of the old fortress. It has a typically Moorish structure with an angled entrance.

Return through the arch. From plaza de Minas, head along Cuesta de María de la Miel, then turn right onto camino Nuevo de San Nicolás.

Convento de Santa Isabel la Real – Enter the doorway of this monastery founded by Isabel the Catholic at the beginning of the 16C to admire the church's fine, pinnacled Gothic portal bearing the coat of arms and yoke and arrow emblem of the Catholic Monarchs. The interior contains some fine Mudéjar decoration.

Plaza de San Miguel Bajo – A Christ of the Lanterns adorns this square, which is fronted by the church that has lent it its name.
Follow the street opposite the church. At the end of this street, the lower town comes into view.

Turn left and left again along calle Bocanegra, then right along calle San José.

Iglesia de San José – The church was built in the 16C above the former mosque. The 10C minaret from this earlier building still remains, although it has now been converted into a bell-tower.

Continue heading down, then look to the right immediately after some steps.

> ### Mirador de San Cristóbal
> This mirador along the Carretera de Murcia offers a superb **view**★ of the Albaicín with its typical villas or *cármenes*, the walls of the old fortress in the foreground, the Alhambra in the background and the lower town to the right.

Casa de Porras – This mansion is fronted by a simple stone doorway with heraldic decoration.
A delightful typical villa, the Carmen de los Cipreses (cypress trees), can be seen opposite. The trees that have given the house its name are visible from the street.

Head down the cuesta del Granadillo and the extremely narrow cuesta Aceituneros to emerge at the start of carrera del Darro, opposite the Iglesia de Santa Ana y San Gil.

★ 4 FROM THE UNIVERSITY TO THE ROYAL HOSPITAL
allow 2hr

University – This Baroque building, the seat of the city's university from the 18C onwards, is situated on plaza de la Universidad; the statue of its founder, Carlos V, stands proudly in the centre of the square. The building, its façade embellished by Solomonic columns, is now home to the university's Faculty of Law.

Iglesia de los Santos Justo y Pastor – The church, on the same square, belonged to the Jesuits until it was expropriated. The lower section of its 18C Baroque portal includes the reliefs of St Francis Xavier and St Francis Borgia, along with the coat of arms of the Society of Jesus above the arch; the upper tier bears a large relief depicting the conversion of St Paul.

The wall paintings on the interior are of interest, particularly those of the saints between the windows of the cupola tambour above the transept.

Colegio de San Bartolomé y Santiago – This college dates from 1621. To the left of the simple doorway, adorned with Doric columns and the sculptures of the college's patron saints, the large cupola of the Iglesia de los Santos Justo y Pastor is visible. It is well worth entering the elegant patio with its slender Doric columns and basket-handle arches.

From the corner of calle de la Duquesa and Gran Capitán the monumental **apse** of the Monasterio de San Jerónimo church comes into view.

★**Monasterio de San Jerónimo** ⊘ – *Entry along López de Argueta.* Construction of the monastery began in 1496. Two celebrated architects worked on the building: Jacopo Fiorentino, also known as Jacopo l'Indaco, until 1526, and Diego Siloé, after this date. After crossing the atrium, note the **façade** of the church before entering the monastic buildings. The upper section, bearing the coats of arms of the Catholic Monarchs, has a fine window flanked by medallions and grotesque animal figures.

Enter the monastery.

The large **cloisters**, with a garden of orange trees at its centre, was completed in

Detail on the church façade

B. Kaufmann/MICHELIN

1519 according to plans principally designed by Diego de Siloé. Robust pillars with foliated capitals support semicircular arches on the lower tier and basket-handle arches on the upper register. Another characteristic feature of the cloisters is the plethora of Plateresque and Renaissance doorways opening onto it. A stroll around the patio reveals the impressive wall of the church, with its handsome Plateresque window and the magnificent and monumental escutcheon of El Gran Capitán.

★★**Church** – The scene greeting the visitor through the fine Siloé-designed **Plateresque doorway** from the cloisters is quite a surprise, such is the rich decoration inside: vaults and domes with high-reliefs, a magnificent main retable and paintings adorning the walls, all of which combine to create a masterpiece of Spanish Renaissance architecture.

Construction of the church began during the period of Gothic influence, although the transept and apse were completed during the Renaissance, once Siloé assumed responsibility for the work. The widow of Gonzalo Fernández de Córdoba financed the building for the purpose of creating a pantheon for her husband, El Gran Capitán. Attention is first drawn to the richness of the apse, superbly illuminated by the transept windows, and the dome, with its fan vaulting and double arches with caissons decorated with busts; the squinch arches contain the statues of the four evangelists. The coffered vaulting above the transept arms is decorated with high-reliefs of biblical characters, angels, animals etc, while the vault above the high altar depicts Christ accompanied by apostles, angels and saints. The large **retable**★★, worked on by a number of artists, is a jewel of the Granadine School. It portrays saints, scenes from the life of the Virgin Mary and Christ, as well as a depiction of God the Father above some clouds on the crowning piece. The statues of El Gran Capitán and his wife at prayer are to the side, while a simple stone slab marks the burial place of Don Gonzalo. The paintings decorating the walls of the church were added in the 18C.

The **Hospital de San Juan de Dios** in calle San Juan de Dios was built between the 16C and 18C. The statue of St John of God presides over the simple portal.

★**Iglesia de San Juan de Dios** – Built in the first half of the 18C, this church is one of Granada's principal Baroque churches. The richly ornamented **façade**★ comprises a portal enclosed between bell-towers topped with spires. The niches on the lower section contain images of the archangels Gabriel and Raphael; the central part of the upper section shows the patron saint of the church accompanied by reliefs of St Ildefonsus and St Barbara.

The **interior**, access to which is via a beautiful carved mahogany doorway, has a Latin cross ground plan with side chapels, an elevated cupola above the transept and a chancel. It is magnificent in both its richness and its stylistic uniformity. The high altar is dominated by a massive Churrigueresque altarpiece of gilded wood behind which is hidden a chapel *(camarín)* whose doors are normally closed. This **camarín** is accessed via a door to the right of the altar. It consists of three lavish rooms ornamented in the most decorative of Baroque styles. The middle room houses the tabernacle with the urn containing the remains of the saint – the founder of the Order of Hospitallers, who died in 1550. The walls, awash with gilded wood, are full of reliquaries of Roman saints.

Monument to the Immaculate Conception (Inmaculada Concepción) – This monument, completed in the 17C, stands in the attractive **Jardines del Triunfo** (Triumph Gardens). The statue of a crowned Virgin Mary surrounded by beams of light on top of the column is by Alonso de Mena. The side walls of the Royal Hospital are visible behind the monument.

Hospital Real – The former Royal Hospital was founded by the Catholic Monarchs at the beginning of the 16C and is now home to the university Rectorate. The celebrated architect Enrique Egas was responsible for the first stage of its construction. In keeping with other hospitals, such as those in Toledo and Santiago de Compostela, the ground plan is of a cross within a square and four inner patios. Four Plateresque windows adorn the façade's upper storey. The entablature above the 17C marble doorway is decorated with the yoke and arrow – the emblems of the Catholic Monarchs; above it sits a Virgin and Child, flanked by the statues of Fernando and Isabel at prayer. The sculptures are the work of Alonso de Mena.

Of interest in the interior are the two patios in the left wing, decorated with heraldic motifs. From the first patio to the right, stairs lead to the university's central library *(biblioteca central)*, which occupies the large room on the first floor. The library has an open framework and a wooden coffered dome above squinch arches at its centre.

ADDITIONAL SIGHTS

★ **La Cartuja** ⊙ – Construction of the Carthusian monastery began at the beginning of the 16C. Entry is through a Plateresque portal leading into the large atrium, at the end of which is the church and other outbuildings belonging to the monastery, which can be reached through the cloisters.

The façade of the church is simple in style, with the shield of Spain visible at the top and a statue of St Bruno presiding over the portal.

Some of the outbuildings house paintings by Sánchez Cotán and Vicente Carducho, both of whom were Carthusian monks in the monastery.

Church – The church is exuberantly decorated with Baroque stucco (1662) and paintings. The nave is divided into three sections (for the monks, lay brothers and public). The areas for the monks and lay brothers are separated by a gilded screen with richly decorated doors and paintings on either side by Sánchez Cotán: *The Baptism of Christ* and *Rest after the Flight into Egypt*. The Assumption, which is visible below the baldaquin, is the work of José de Mora. Behind it is the **sacrarium**, a *camarín* decorated at the beginning of the 18C by Francisco Hurtado Izquierdo, whose style, polychrome colours and materials are all extravagantly Baroque, resulting in a decorative exuberance which is almost oppressive.

Sacristy, La Cartuja

B. Kaufmann/MICHELIN

★★Sacristy — Built between 1727 and 1764, this is one of the masterpieces of the Spanish Baroque period. The architectural elements are disguised by a rich decoration of white stucco, mixtilinear mouldings and cornices which are broken in numerous places to extraordinary effect. The strong daylight which filters through the windows emphasises the play of light and shadow created by this lavish decor. Above the apse, the dark fresco paintings of the oval cupola contrast sharply with the white stucco ornamentation elsewhere in the church. Lanjarón marble is used extensively in the room, as well as for the altarpieces of the saints in the apse. The magnificent door and the cedarwood furnishings inlaid with tortoiseshell, mother-of-pearl and silver, are by a Carthusian monk, Brother José Manuel Vázquez.

El Sacromonte — Sacromonte hill rises alongside the Albaicín quarter, opposite the Generalife. **Flamenco shows** are frequently staged in some of the cave dwellings in this gypsy troglodyte district, which is now partially abandoned.

Casa-Museo Manuel de Falla ○ — The composer Manuel de Falla (1876-1946), a passionate admirer of Granada although he only came to know the city after the age of 40, lived in this 16C house between 1919 and 1939. The house of the composer of such famous works as *Love, the Magician* and *The Three-Cornered Hat* is unchanged since the days when he lived here. The piano, guitar and furniture of this exceptional musician provide visitors with an insight into his professional and private lives.

Carmen de los Mártires ○ — The Carmelite monastery is situated on the Alhambra hill. The luxuriant terraced **gardens★** are open to the public and provide a beautiful setting for a stroll, with their Romantic 19C decor of fountains and statues and views of the city. Next to the building is a Moorish-style garden and portico.

Iglesia de Santo Domingo — This 16C church stands in the plaza de Santo Domingo. It is mainly Renaissance in style, although the building also retains some Gothic features. The façade is decorated with an elegant stone portico comprising three semicircular arches, whose spandrels are adorned with the initials of the Catholic Monarchs, their shield and that of the Emperor Carlos V. A beautiful gemelled window can be seen above the portico.

★Parque de las Ciencias ○ — The aim of this large science park is to provide visitors with a better understanding of the world in which they live. In addition to its interactive museum, the complex houses a planetarium, an astronomical observatory and a tropical butterfly collection.
Adults and children alike will enjoy learning from and interacting with the various exhibits on display. A special area, Explora, has been set aside for very young visitors (aged three to seven).

Huerta de San Vicente ○ — Fans of Federico García Lorca (1898-1936), one of the greatest of Spanish poets and writers, will enjoy this visit to his summer home. The house is situated in the Parque García Lorca, which until recently was no more than a fertile plain; it has been set out exactly as it would have been when Federico used to come here to spend the summer.

GUADIX★

Granada – Population 20 322
Michelin map 446 U 20

Guadix is a town without borders or a definite perimeter but which is nonetheless perfectly framed by the clay hills around it, and by the heights of the **Sierra Nevada** which act as a magnificent backdrop. This somewhat mysterious *pueblo* conceals many of its secrets in its troglodyte dwellings, which are only partially revealed by the white chimneys which appear everywhere at ground level, silent witnesses of a seemingly endless underground world.
As a staging post between eastern and western Andalucia, the mythical settlement of **Acci** (home to the *accitanos* tribe) saw a number of different peoples colonise the surrounding area, all of whom have left their mark on modern Guadix. The town reached its peak during the Arab period, from which its fortress *(alcazaba)* survives, although the majority of buildings visible today date from the 17C and 18C.

SIGHTS

Plaza de la Constitución — This pretty arcaded square dates from the 16C and 17C; along one of its sides stands the town hall, built at the beginning of the 17C during the reign of Felipe III.

The name Guadix

It was the Moors who gave this old Roman camp the poetic name of Guadh-Haix, which translates as "the river of life".

Cathedral ○ — Work on the cathedral started in 1597 according to designs by **Diego de Siloé**, and continued until 1715, the year in which the impressive Baroque tower was completed. This becomes obvious upon entering the church, where

WHERE TO STAY

MID-RANGE

Comercio – *Mira de Amezcua, 3* – ☏ *958 66 05 00* – *fax 958 66 50 72* – *24 rooms* – *8 000pts*. An attractive house dating from the beginning of the 20C, with large rooms and a good restaurant. Specialities here include lamb with honey *(cordero a la miel)*, Guadix soup and the delicious custard pudding known as *tocino de cielo* (literally "bacon from heaven").

Cuevas Pedro Antonio de Alarcón – *San Torcuato (on the Murcia road)* – ☏ *958 66 49 86* – *fax 958 66 17 21* – *20 caves* – *8 100pts*. Beautifully decorated caves with central heating. Although they are situated near the motorway, the natural soundproofing of these caves is excellent. Facilities include a restaurant serving typical local dishes and a swimming pool.

the Gothic architecture of the entrance aisles gives way to a Renaissance style behind the transept which reaches its highest expression in the immense dome adorned with a large lantern covering the false transept. The **Capilla de San Torcuato** *(second chapel to the left of the retrochoir)* was designed by Diego de Siloé and has an entrance arch which is referred to as a "bull's horn", because its width decreases as it curves. The **Fachada de la Encarnación★** *(facing the square)*, is a good example of the theatricality and movement of Baroque architecture. The three horizontal registers of this façade increase in complexity as they converge towards an imaginary point.

Behind the cathedral, in calle Santa María, stand the 16C **Palacio Episcopal** (Bishop's Palace), the Hospital de la Caridad and **Palacio de Villalegre** (1592), which has an attractive Renaissance doorway flanked by two solid brick towers.

★**Barrio de Santiago** – This is one of the most typical districts of the town with seigniorial mansions such as the **Palacio de Peñaflor**, built around a beautiful Renaissance patio, and in which an unusual **balcony** decorated with wood can be seen. The seminary *(seminario menor)* next door provides access to the former Arab **alcazaba** ⊙ (fortress) dating from the 11C. Although the fortress is in poor condition, a tour of it provides the best views of Guadix and the town's troglodyte district. Returning to calle Barradas, flights of steps lead to plazuela de Santiago. At the end of this small square is the **Iglesia de Santiago** ⊙, its lovely Plateresque **doorway★** crowned with the shield of Carlos V, recognisable by the two-headed eagle and the Golden Fleece. The Mudéjar ceiling inside the church is especially worthy of note. **Calle Ancha**, which leads off this square, has a number of fine 19C seigniorial mansions.

★**Barrio de las Cuevas** – The cave district is situated in the highest part of Guadix, amid a landscape of streams, gullies and small brown hills. The caves are built on different levels, so that those dwellings hollowed into the side of the hills often have their entrance on top of the roof of another cave. Solitary caves can occasionally be seen in an isolated location, occupying a single hillside.

Cueva-Museo ⊙ – *Barrio de las Cuevas (follow signs)*. This cave-museum has recreated life in a cave dwelling during the 19C. Several rooms exhibit typical farming and shepherds' tools from the region.

Barrio de las Cuevas

Museo de Alfarería ⊘ – *In the Mozarabic district of San Miguel.* This museum is housed in a cave of Moorish origin which has retained some of its historical features, including a well dating from 1650 made from Arab bricks and a large earthenware jar from 1640 buried in the floor and possibly used to store wine. The museum clearly demonstrates the rich tradition of pottery in Granada province, including the famous **accitano pitchers**.

Barrio de Santa Ana – The town's Moorish quarter is a network of narrow alleyways, lined by whitewashed houses decked in flowers and aromatic plants. The **Iglesia de Santa Ana,** built on the site of a mosque in the 15C, can be seen at the heart of the *barrio.* Next to the façade is a Renaissance fountain dating from 1567.

EXCURSIONS

Purullena – *6km/4mi on the Granada road.* The **road**★★ from Guadix crosses a beautiful landscape of tufa rock. Purullena is known for its cave dwellings and its ceramic shops which can be seen on both sides of the road running through the village. The spa of **Cortes y Graena** is reached after 6km/4mi. The road continues to **La Peza** (13km/8mi), passing through an attractive landscape of low-lying clay hills.

Cave dwellings

The special characteristics of the clay soil found in the **Guadix Basin** have made the construction of these unusual dwellings possible. Clay has the property of being easy to work and yet hardening upon contact with air. The end result is a cave which is impermeable, thermally insulated, and which maintains a constant temperature (18°C/64°F) all year round, making them cool during the hot summer months and warm during the cold winters. Guadix alone has around 2 000 inhabited caves, while one of the largest groups of cave dwellings in Europe exists in the surrounding area. The origin of these dwellings is uncertain, although it would appear that most of them were built after the Christian Reconquest and the progressive segregation imposed upon the area's *morisco* population. In Guadix, these inhabitants were gradually expelled from the Santa Ana district and subsequently occupied the cave dwellings in the troglodyte district visible today.

★**La Calahorra** – *18.5km/11.5mi southeast of Guadix on the A 92.* Hidden behind the peaks of the Sierra Nevada, like an island surrounded by a sea of almond trees, the village of La Calahorra has retained much of its historic past. One of the most spectacular approaches to the village is the route across the Sierra Nevada via the **Ragua Pass**★★ *(see p 315),* along which the contrast between the Sierra and the Altiplano can be appreciated to the full. This isolated village, crowned by an impressive fortress, stands as proudly now as it did during its time as the capital of the Marquisate of Zenete.
The desolate landscape of the Minas del Marquesado, mines which were abandoned in 1997, is visible 4km/2.5mi from the village.

★★**Castle** ⊘ – Despite the castle's robust military appearance, a feature enhanced by the castle's four cylindrical towers, one of Spain's most beautiful **Renaissance patios**★★ is hidden inside it. The patio was built at the beginning of the 15C in the artistic style of the Italian *quattrocento* and is laid out in a square plan with two sections joined by a rich **staircase**★★ comprising three flights of stairs. The decoration, particularly on the doorways and capitals, uses the full range of classical features, including mouldings, candelabra, flowers and storiated columns.

HUELVA ★

Huelva – Population 150 000
Michelin map 446 U 10

Capital of the westernmost province of Andalucia, Huelva is situated between the mouths of the Tinto and Odiel rivers, at a crossroads between routes to Portugal, Cádiz, Extremadura and Sevilla. Industry is the mainstay of the town's economy, although fishing and agriculture also play an important role. Huelva's pleasant climate and the beauty of its neighbouring beaches have transformed the town into a popular destination during the summer months. The town also has an excellent choice of shops and restaurants in the pedestrianised streets around the Iglesia de la Concepción, particularly in **calle Pablo Rada**, where locals can indulge in one of their favourite pastimes, namely enjoying the excellent local tapas.

HISTORICAL NOTES

The town has been inhabited since ancient times as a consequence of its rich mineral deposits. Towards the end of the Bronze Age, various peoples from the eastern Mediterranean settled here, including the Phoenicians and the Greeks, mixing with the indigenous population to give rise to the kingdom of Tartessus. The origins of this legendary city remain confused; however, most historians site the city close to the Tinto and Odiel rivers, around the city of Huelva, which was then known as Onuba. The city was later occupied by the Romans and in the 8C by the Muslims under the name of Guelbar. During this period Moorish settlers introduced a number of new agricultural techniques to the city, at the same time developing a range of artisanal activities, such as glazed pottery. After the reconquest led by Alfonso X the Wise in the 13C, control of Huelva exchanged hands between nobles and affluent families, creating a complex situation which lasted until the 15C; it then came under the control of the Dukes of Medina Sidonia, who initiated its final repopulation. Towards the end of the same century **Christopher Columbus** came to Huelva, an event which would later confer international fame upon the city. From this period on, the life of this tranquil town would be affected by his exploits and those under him, as Huelva became known as the cradle of

The port

the voyages of discovery. In the following centuries Huelva experienced a brief period of commercial expansion thanks to its geographical location; however, following the devastating Lisbon earthquake of 1755 and the War of Independence half a century later, the city's fortunes started to decline. The modern history of the city is marked by its proximity to the Parque Nacional de Doñana, which has had a beneficial effect on local tourism, and by the construction of a chemicals complex *(Polo Químico)*, which has provided fresh impetus to the region's industrial fabric.

WHERE TO STAY

MODERATE

Los Condes – *Alameda Sundheim, 14* – ☎ *959 28 24 00 – fax 959 28 50 41 – 54 rooms – 7 500pts*. On one of the city's main avenues. Although this building lacks any particular charm, the rooms are spacious, modern and clean. Good value for money.

MID-RANGE

Monte Conquero – *Pablo Rada, 10* – ☎ *959 28 55 00 – fax 959 28 39 12 – 166 rooms – 10 500pts*. A large hotel with all modern comforts in one of Huelva's liveliest streets. Private garage.

EATING OUT

Los Jarales – *Avenida de Huelva, 30*. This restaurant is decorated with ceramic plates and wine barrels. Specialities include paella and barbecued meats. A good local wine list. The only disadvantage is the restaurant's location on a large avenue with lots of traffic.

La Cabaña – *Pablo Rada*. La Cabaña, which specialises in barbecued meats, is situated at the heart of the city's main area for night-life. Andalucian decor.

Jeromo – *Plaza de la Merced, 6 – closed Sat in July and Aug*. Although the decor here is fairly unattractive and the square somewhat noisy due to the number of bars found here, this is one of the best fish and seafood restaurants in the city.

TAPAS

Taberna Del Condado – *Sor Ángela de la Cruz*. A typical tapas bar with barrels used as tables. A good selection of sausages, grilled fish and seafood.

Cathedral ⊙ – The main features of this building, which was constructed in 1605 and converted into a cathedral in 1953, are its Renaissance façade, the sculpture of Christ of Jerusalem and the attractive carving of the Virgen de la Cinta, the patron saint of the city, by Martínez Montañés.

Iglesia de San Pedro – This church is situated at the end of the pleasant paseo de Santa Fe on a small raised promontory. Built above the remains of an early *mudéjar* mosque, its exterior is painted in the characteristic white of Huelva's buildings. The bell-tower, which stands out against the cloudless sky, is one of the most typical sights of the city.

Iglesia de la Concepción – Badly damaged during the Lisbon earthquake of 1755, this Renaissance church is currently being rebuilt. The church contains interesting choir stalls and a number of paintings by Zurbarán.

Santuario de Nuestra Señora de la Cinta ⊙ – This quiet building, where Christopher Columbus stayed during his visit to Huelva, can be seen at the end of the elegant paseo del Conquero, on the outskirts of Huelva. The sanctuary contains some beautiful *azulejos* by Daniel Zuloaga and a fresco of the Virgin Mary, before which, according to legend, the Italian sailor prayed upon his return from America, thus fulfilling a promise made prior to his departure. The grille leading to the presbytery is also worthy of note.

Museo Provincial ⊙ – This museum presents exhibits relating to the history of Huelva from its origins to the present day. Of particular interest are the section dedicated to the Tartessian civilisation, including a number of archeological remains, and paintings by the local artist, Daniel Vázquez Díaz.

★**Barrio Reina Victoria** – The English-style houses in this district, named after Queen Victoria, were built for the families of employees of the mining company Río Tinto Company Limited. Their unusual architectural features lend an extravagant air to Huelva's otherwise uniform urban fabric.

Monumento a la Fe Descubridora – This large sculpture to the Spirit of Discovery was erected by the American artist Gertrude Vanderbilt Whitney in 1929. It is situated on the Punta del Sebo, a strip of land formed by the Tinto and Odiel rivers, directly opposite the city.

EXCURSIONS

★★**Paraje Natural de las Marismas del Odiel** – *2km/1.2mi southeast. Leave Huelva along Avenida Tomás Domínguez*. This marshland *(marisma)* of outstanding beauty, situated at the mouth of the Tinto and Odiel rivers, close to one of the city's industrial chemical facilities, has been declared a World Biosphere Reserve. It occupies a surface area of 7 150ha/17 667 acres within the municipalities of Huelva, Gibraleón, Aljaraque and Punta Umbría. In this remarkable area of tidal and continental mud flats and sandy ecosystems, the water level can rise and fall by as much as 3m/10ft, depending on the tide. The specific features of the area have resulted in a habitat that now provides a home for over 200 different species of bird despite the proximity of the nearby chemical factories, offering a spectacular sight, particularly in February and March. The area can be visited by **canoe** ⊙ and small boat which slowly cross the reserve's two main areas: El Burro and the Isla de Enmedio. Here the land appears to shift slowly and the colonies of spoonbills and herons break the silence of this exceptional natural landscape with their strident calls and sudden flight.

San Juan del Puerto – *12km/7.5mi northeast along the A 472*. The main attraction of this small town is the **Iglesia de San Juan Bautista**, a Renaissance building with three aisles, built according to a basilical plan. The church houses a Christ of Mercy, a 16C polychrome sculpture by Juan de Oviedo.

HUÉSCAR

Granada – Population 8 013

Michelin map 446 S 22

Huéscar is the geographical centre of the easternmost part of Granada province, in an area of contrasting natural landscapes ranging from the semi-desert of the region around **Orce** to the peaks of the **Sierra de la Sagra** or Sierra Seca, covered in snow in winter.
The town of Huéscar was founded in 1241 by the **Order of St James**. At the beginning of the 14C the city fell into Muslim hands until it was reconquered by **Fernando the Catholic** in 1488.

SIGHTS

Plaza Mayor – The town's main square is fronted by the town hall and a number of 19C houses. Note the unusual Art Nouveau-style house in one of the streets leading into the square.

WHERE TO STAY

GALERA

Casas–Cueva – *Avenida Nicasio Tomás, 12 (reception)* – ☎/*fax 958 73 90 68* – *22 caves* – *5 350pts*. Original and reasonably priced accommodation offering magnificent views of the grey *sierra* dotted with trees and shrubs. Pleasant caves with a living room, fireplace, bathroom and a large whitewashed bathtub.

ORCE

Laveranda – *On the Orce-Casablanca road (SE 35), 7km/4.5mi from Orce towards Vélez Blanco*– ☎/*fax 958 34 43 80* – *11 rooms* – *6 600pts*. This hotel is situated in a beautiful landscape dominated by extensive maize fields extending towards the *sierra*. The accommodation consists of an exquisitely decorated cave at an altitude of 900m/2 952ft.

Colegiata de la Encarnación – Construction of this collegiate church started in the early 16C. Although the building has some Gothic features, the dominant style is Renaissance, which reaches its purest expression in the large polygonal ceiling above the transept.

EXCURSIONS

Galera – *8km/5mi south along the A 330*. Between the 13C and 15C, Galera was a border town which changed hands regularly between the Moors and Christians; this historical fact is reflected in its layout. The lower town, built by the Christians, is ordered and built in a square pattern in contrast to the upper town, with its strong Moorish influence and maze of narrow alleyways and cave dwellings. Galera is known as the site of the 6C BC **Iberian necropolis of Tutugi**, and the **Argar settlement** ⊘ of Castellón Alto, dating from 1600 BC. The Iglesia de la Anunciación behind the town dates from the 15C.

★**Orce** – *16km/10mi southeast of Huéscar. Follow the A 330 and bear left onto the SE 34 before Galera*. Orce is situated in the eastern part of the Baza Basin, in the middle of an impressively wild and desert landscape which reveals surprising changes of light and colour. The elegant stone tower of the 16C **parish church** and the recently restored **Palacio de los Segura**, also dating from the 16C, stand out among the whitewashed houses of the town. The palace has a simple façade and an elegant patio supported by stone columns.

Museo de Prehistoria y Paleontología José Gibert ⊘ – The museum of prehistory and paleontology is housed in the **Castillo-Alcazaba de las Siete Torres**, a 16C Christian fortress with seven towers *(torres)* which has undergone much restoration. The museum exhibits numerous bones and stones from the region's archeological sites, including a piece of skull which made the town famous at the beginning of the 1980s, and an infant humerus, some 1.5 million years old, which was discovered locally. If these dates are confirmed, this find will be the oldest hominid paleontological discovery in Europe.

Fuencaliente – *2km/1.2mi from Orce, on the Galera road*. The water gushing forth from this natural spring in the middle of a desert landscape is at a constant 18°C/64°F. The spring is a pleasant spot in which to cool off in the summer.

Castril – *22km/14mi west along the A 326*. Castril is a typical mountain village at the foot of an impressive cliff and surrounded by the beautiful and largely unknown **Parque Natural de la Sierra de Castril**. The village is thought to have its origins in a small military camp founded by the Romans; its name comes from the Arabic *qastal*, or fortress. After the final reconquest in the 15C, Castril became part of the seigniory of Hernándo de Zafra, who established the town's famous glassworks, which closed in 1878. Today, these pieces of green and yellow glass are collector's items, some of which can be admired in the Museo Arqueológico de Granada. The 15C **parish church** in the centre of town is particularly worthy of note.

★**Parque Natural de la Sierra de Castril** – This natural park is the physical extension of the neighbouring Sierra de Cazorla. Its most notable characteristic is its spectacular relief, mainly the result of the deforestation caused by the glassworks. A walk of around two hours starting in the lower part of Castril skirts the river and continues around the outskirts of the village. For information on walks in the area, contact the **Visitor Centre** ⊘ *(Centro de Visitantes)*, which also houses an interesting ethnographical museum.

IZNÁJAR★

Córdoba – Population 5 200
Michelin map 446 U 17

Iznájar's magnificent **site**★, on top of a hill that juts out like a peninsula into the **Iznájar Reservoir** *(embalse)*, offers a foretaste of the charms of this small town and its superb natural surroundings.

THE TOWN

Picturesque houses line steep whitewashed streets leading to the upper part of the town which is dominated by the ochre-coloured stone of the church and the remains of the Moorish castle. The countryside surrounding Iznájar is never far from view, with several of the town's street corners providing stunning **views**.
The panorama from the castle and church quarter takes in far-distant landscapes carpeted in olive groves.

Iznájar and its reservoir

Castle – The origins of the castle date back to the 8C when the Moors built it to take advantage of this strategic site, which they named Hisn Ashar. Although it is now in ruins, the remains of sections of wall and several towers are still visible.

Biblioteca Municipal – The municipal library is housed in the former town granary, built during the reign of Carlos III.

Parroquia de Santiago – This 16C Renaissance-style parish church has been built with large pieces of ashlar stone. It is topped by a truncated tower.

Mirador de la Cruz de San Pedro – *At the end of calle Cruz de San Pedro*. This mirador offers **views**★ of the fortress and church, the lake and the town.

The lower part of the town is the setting for the **Museo Etnográfico** ⊘, an ethnographical museum displaying a collection of implements, ploughing tools and other instruments used to work the land, and the **Casa de las Columnas**, with heraldic decoration on its façade.

Embalse de Iznájar – The 30km/18mi-long Iznájar Reservoir, which is also known as the Lago de Andalucía (Lake of Andalucia), acts as a large dam for the waters of the Genil River. The eastern section of the lake is part of Granada province. The Playa de Valdearenas, on its shoreline, is a popular beach for swimmers and water sports enthusiasts.

EXCURSION

The road from Lucena to Iznájar – *See p 229.*

JAÉN

Jaén – Population 107 184
Michelin map 446 S 18

Spain's major olive-producing town sits on an undulating plain covered with olive trees at the foot of the Santa Catalina hill *(cerro)*, surrounded by the mountainous landscapes of the Sierra de Jabalcuz. The town was known to the Moors as *Geen* (on the caravan route), due to it strategic position between Castilla and Andalucia, and has had its praises sung by renowned poets such as Antonio Machado and Miguel Hernández. Jaén possesses a rich artistic and cultural heritage, as witnessed by the vestiges of its Moorish castle and its numerous Renaissance buildings, many of which were designed by the architect Andrés de Vandelvira. To soak up the atmosphere of Jaén, it is best to stroll through its varied districts such as **La Magdalena**, with its golden stone churches and Moorish atmosphere; **San Juan**, lively at night with its plentiful tapas bars; and **Santa María**, home to the town's most impressive buildings. Jaén is full of contrasts, with old monuments standing alongside elegant Renaissance palaces (Palacio de los Vilches, Palacio de los Vélez and Palacio de los Uribes), where the old town sits proudly next to the new, and where its modern shopping streets converge on an attractive park, the **Parque de la Victoria**, located next to the popular **Monumento a las Batallas** (Battles Monument).

No description of Jaén is complete without mention of its **Holy Week** celebrations, when dramatic Andalucian religious songs fill the streets. The town also has an important gastronomic tradition to uphold with local specialities such as *pestiños* (honeyed doughnuts) and *pipirrana*, a type of cold soup made with garlic, green peppers, ripe tomatoes and breadcrumbs, not forgetting the obligatory liberal measure of olive oil.

Historical notes – Jaén has been inhabited since the Paleolithic Era. Following the Roman conquest under Publius Cornelius Scipio in 207 BC it received the name of *Aurigi* until, according to legend, it was evangelised by Euphrasius, one of the 70 male apostles. In 712 the town was occupied by the Moors and then reconquered in 1246 by Fernando III the Saint who turned Jaén into a settlement of strategic importance in his struggle to liberate Andalucia from Moorish control. The seat of the bishopric was transferred here at about the same time, resulting in numerous privileges for the town which were to enhance its economic situation. From the 14C onwards, Jaén entered a period of decline which was to last until the late 19C. Nowadays, however, the town's industry, based on its olive oil production, is experiencing an upturn in fortunes.

THE TOWN *allow half a day*

★★**Cathedral** ⊙ – Built in the 16C and 17C according to plans by Andrés de Vandelvira, this building is one of the most extraordinary examples of Reniassance architecture in Andalucia. Its monumental silhouette dominates the town's old quarter, typified by its charming nooks and crannies, maze-like network of narrow streets and small squares lined by Jaén's numerous churches and convents.

★★**Main façade** – The sumptuous appearance of the ochre-coloured façade, adorned with statues of enormous proportion and delicately carved decorative detail, calls to mind the façades of some of Spain's most majestic palaces. It comprises two sections flanked by two robust square towers: the lower tier is dominated by immense engaged columns, while the upper tier is adorned with a large balustrade running

Detail, cathedral façade

WHERE TO STAY

MODERATE

Europa – *Plaza de Belén, 1* – ☎ *953 22 27 00* – *fax 953 22 26 92* – *37 rooms* – *7 500pts*. Despite its somewhat unkempt exterior, the inside of this hotel is both new and modern. Spacious rooms with all necessary creature comforts. An excellent location in the centre of Jaén.

MID-RANGE

Rey Fernando – *Plaza Coca de la Piñera, 5* – ☎ *953 25 18 40* – *fax 953 26 51 22* – *36 rooms* – *9 100pts*. Easily identifiable by its bright pink façade. Large, modern rooms and a good location next to the bus station.

Parador Castillo de Santa Catalina – *Carretera del Castillo de Santa Catalina* – ☎ *953 23 00 00* – *fax 953 23 09 30* – *45 rooms* – *17 500pts*. Jaén's impressive *parador* is housed in the 13C fortress dominating the town, with magnificent views of the mountains and extensive olive groves. Even if the hotel is full, it is well worth dining in the restaurant, adorned with ogival vaults, or spending time over a drink in its stately lounges.

EATING OUT

Casa Vicente – *Francisco Martín Mora, 8* – ☎ *953 23 22 22* – *closed Sun evening*. This picturesque 18C house has an attractive patio, a bar, and an elegant, renowned restaurant decorated with family photos and pictures of distinguished guests. Specialities include Jaén-style spinach *(espinacas)*, loin of pork *(lomo de cerdo)* and braised oxtail *(rabo de toro)*.

Mesón Nuyra – *Pasaje Nuyra* – ☎ *953 24 07 63* – *closed Sun evenings*. This typical restaurant is found inside a cave close to calle Nueva. The menu includes dishes such as suckling pig *(cochinillo)* and sirloin steak *(solomillo de vaca)*.

TAPAS

La Manchega – *Consuelo, 7* – ☎ *953 23 21 91*. This bar, founded in 1886, has remained faithful to its origins without ceding to modern tastes, and serves an excellent selection of sandwiches, sausage-based tapas and wine. Wooden stools add a rustic charm to the decor, while an old transistor radio at the back provides the music.

Río Chico – *Calle Nueva, 12* – ☎ *953 24 08 02*. This cave is in a street teeming with bars and restaurants. Excellent *raciones* including fish dishes, fried veal and ham rolls *(flamenquines)*, clams *(almejas)* and suckling calf's kidneys *(riñones de choto)*. The restaurant on the first floor has a 1 100pts fixed menu.

CAFÉS, BARS & NIGHT-LIFE

As well as the shopping area around plaza de la Constitución, the San Ildefonso area is the best place in town for a quiet drink. Jaén's young people tend to hang out in the bars and cafés along avenida de Muñoz Grandes and in the streets running off it, such as calle Santa Alicia and calle San Francisco Javier.

Café-Bar del Pósito – *Plaza del Pósito, 10. Open daily, 9am to 1.30am*. This bar is situated close to the cathedral and the town's other major monuments. It has an excellent reputation for its music, which combines jazz and flamenco, and is popular with a more affluent crowd in their twenties and thirties. Art exhibitions are occasionally held here.

Chubby-Cheek – *Calle San Francisco Javier, 7. Open daily, 4.30pm to 2am*. A café which lives and breathes jazz, both in its decor and its music. Concerts on Thursday evenings. A pleasant place for a quiet drink in the shadow of the bar's grand piano. A varied clientele, which changes as the evening progresses.

Oppidum – *Calle Los Molinos, 8. Open 5pm to 1am at weekends (11pm weekdays)*. The Oppidum has a rustic feel with the occasional touch of modern design. Popular with the 20-40 brigade who come here to enjoy the quiet, relaxed atmosphere.

Ábaco – *Avenida Muñoz Grandes, 5. Open 4pm to 7am at weekends (5am weekdays)*. This modern, meticulously decorated bar is frequented by day with those wanting a quiet drink, transforming itself at night into a popular dance venue. A wide cross-section of ages depending on the hour, ranging from those in their mid-20s to customers in their late-40s.

Trujal – *Calle Hurtado, 21. Open daily, 4pm to 3am*. This bar in the San Ildefonso district is mainly frequented by thirty-somethings. The warm, rustic decor and candlelight illumination combine to create an intimate atmosphere perfect for a quiet night out.

ENTERTAINMENT

For an up-to-date list of cultural events in Jaén and around the province, visitors are advised to consult the *Agenda Turístico-Cultural*, published monthly by the town hall and available free of charge from tourist offices. The contents of this booklet can also be found on-line at www.promojaen.es. The **Teatro Darymelia**, in calle Maestra *(☎ 953 21 91 80)*, organises an excellent programme of predominantly theatrical events.

SHOPPING

Jaén's main shopping streets are located around **plaza de la Constitución**. The trio of calle Virgen de la Capilla, calle San Clemente and paseo de la Estación are the main commercial arteries, along with other adjoining streets lined by small shops and the occasional large department store, such as **El Corte Inglés**, in calle Roldán y Marín.

Markets – An open-air market selling a wide selection of food, clothes and other goods is held on Thursday mornings at the town's showground *(recinto ferial)* near Alameda de Calvo Sotelo.

TRANSPORT

Airport – The nearest airport to Jaén is in Granada, 50min to the south along the N 323. ☎ 958 24 52 00 and 958 44 64 11.

Trains – The railway station is on paseo Virgen de Libarejos *(☎ 953 27 02 02)*. The only direct services from the town are to Madrid and Cádiz (passing through Córdoba and Sevilla).

Inter-city buses – The central bus station is on plaza de Coca de la Piñera *(☎ 953 25 01 06)*. Services operate to every provincial capital in Andalucia and to major cities around Spain.

City buses – Jaén has an extensive local bus network. A single ticket costs 90pts and a 10-trip ticket 675pts.

Taxis – ☎ 953 22 00 28, 953 26 50 17, 953 22 00 21 and 953 26 50 19.

Horse-drawn carriages – These can be hired from several locations around town for visits to Jaén's major sites of interest.

its entire width. The finely sculpted reliefs above the three doors represent the Assumption of the Virgin, the archangel St Michael and St Catherine, who is highly venerated in Jaén as it was on her saint's day that Fernando III the Saint reconquered the town from the Moors. The **balustrade**★ on the upper tier is a key element of the façade and contains a group of sculptures representing King Fernando, the four evangelists and the Doctors of the Church.

★★**Interior** – The three aisles are crowned by handsome oven vaults and separated by thick pillars with engaged Corinthian columns to create an effect of spectacular simplicity. From the transept, a magnificent work by Pedro del Portillo and Juan de Aranda covered by an impressive dome, it is possible to admire the huge size of the building in which light enhances every decorative feature, bestowing upon the cathedral an atmosphere of refined solemnity. In the centre of the main nave, cutting off the full perspective of it, stands the chancel, housing some exceptional walnut **choir stalls**★★ carved by the masterly hands of José Gallego and Oviedo del Portal, disciples of the great 16C sculptor, Alonso Berruguete. At the high altar, dominated by a noteworthy Renaissance altarpiece, the cathedral's most precious treasure can be seen: the **Veil of the Holy Face**★. According to tradition, this reliquary, which is jealously guarded inside an attractive cask, was used by Veronica to wipe the face of Christ on his way to Calvary, and upon which his features were then impressed. The veil was later brought to Spain by St Euphrasius, the bishop of Andújar.

Of the numerous side chapels – 17 in total – the most outstanding is the Capilla de San Fernando, housing a fine statue of Our Father Jesus of Nazareth. Also worthy of note are the chapter-house *(sala capitular)*, containing a fine *Sagrada Familia* by Pedro Machuca, and the **sacristy**, a work by Vandelvira, which is now home to the cathedral museum (Museo Catedralicio).

Museum ⊙ – *Access via the right arm of the transept.* The cathedral treasury has on display a number of interesting exhibits including a Flemish *Virgin and Child*, two canvases by **Ribera**, various illuminated choir books, a large collection of religious gold and silverwork, and several candelabra by Maestro Bartolomé.

Iglesia del Sagrario – This sober, neo-Classical church stands next to the cathedral. The purity of its architectural features is in contrast to the main altarpiece, a magnificent 18C Baroque work.

JAÉN

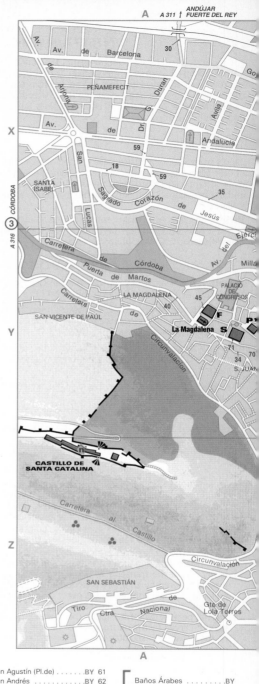

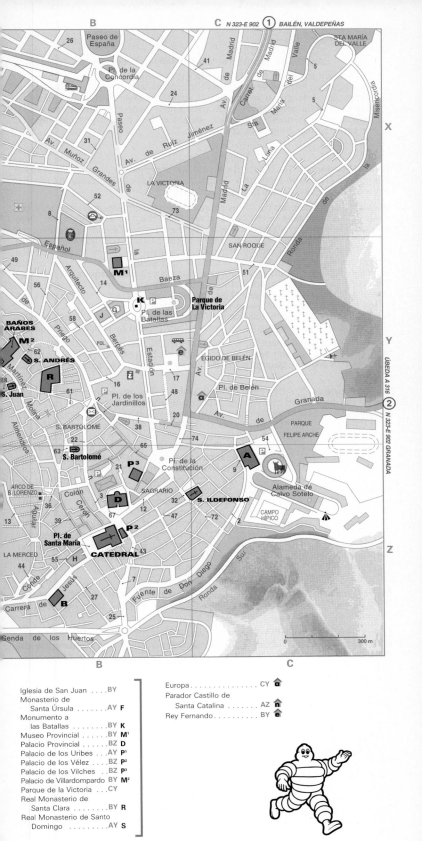

Andrés de Vandelvira, the Andalucian Brunelleschi

This brilliant architect (1509-75), a disciple of Diego de Siloé, enjoyed great prestige in his lifetime for the concept of monumentality that he brought to Andalucian Renaissance architecture. Vandelvira's style blends in perfectly with the barrenness of Jaén's landscapes, where his ornamental features are reduced to a minimum of expression, yet at the same time embracing a taste for large, bare and luminous spaces.

Palacio Provincial – The seat of the Provincial Government *(Diputación Provincial)* is a former Franciscan monastery designed by Vandelvira. The delightful internal patio is fronted by a double gallery of columns.

★**Iglesia de San Ildefonso** ⊙ – This church is the second largest in Jaén after the cathedral and was built in the Gothic style during the 14C and 15C. It has three portals: one Gothic, containing a mosaic representing the *Descent of the Virgin of the Chapel*, the patron saint of Jaén, who, according to tradition, liberated the town from a Moorish siege; a second, Renaissance in style, a work by Vandelvira; and the third neo-Classical, created by Ventura Rodríguez in the 18C. The interior has several outstanding features including a magnificent **main altarpiece**, sculpted by Pedro and Julio Roldán, in addition to a fine tabernacle by Pedro Duque Cornejo. One of its chapels, the **Capilla de la Virgen**, decorated with attractive stained glass and fresco paintings, houses an image of Jaén's patron saint.

Next to the church stands the **Casa de la Virgen** ⊙ or House of the Virgin Mary, a small museum displaying numerous works of art inspired by popular devotion.

Convento de las Bernardas ⊙ – Founded in the 17C, the convent has a Classicist-inspired portal, a pleasant inner cloisters, and a church housing the retables of the *Annunciation* and the *Assumption of the Virgin*, works by the Italian artist Angelo Nardi.

Museo Provincial ⊙ – The main building, which was constructed in 1920, incorporates the façades of the former public granary *(pósito)* – note the reliefs representing a sheaf of wheat and a bread basket – and the Iglesia de San Miguel, both dating from the 16C. Two other buildings to the side are dedicated to temporary exhibitions and to an exhibition of contemporary etchings. The museum is divided into two parts: the archeological section *(ground floor)* and the fine arts section *(first floor)*. The set of **Iberian carvings from Porcuna**★ (bulls, sphinxes, high priests and warriors) dating from the 6C BC is one of the museum's most outstanding exhibits, and represents one of the most important discoveries from the native Iberian culture. The rooms devoted to Roman art display numerous busts, amphorae, capitals and mosaics; the most impressive example of the latter is the **Bruñel** mosaic, striking in its complexity and use of colour. Also of interest are the Visigothic clasps, and the marble **sarcophagus from Martos**★, a magnificent paleo-Christian work between columned porticoes representing seven miraculous scenes from the life of Jesus – note the scenes depicting the changing of water into wine and the healing of the paralysed man. The fine arts section displays works by Pedro Berruguete, Alonso Cano, José and Federico de Madrazo, Mariano Benlliure and Antonio López *(Women in Dialogue)*.

Real Monasterio de Santa Clara – The outstanding feature of this 13C monastery is the delightful **cloisters**. The church has preserved an unusual 16C bamboo image of Christ.

Iglesia de San Bartolomé – The church was built in the 16C and 17C on the site of the former Moorish mosque. An attractive patio crowned by a **Mudéjar artesonado ceiling** of great artistic value stands behind its sober 17C façade. One of the inner chapels houses a carving of Christ of the Expiration, which is brought out in procession during Holy Week.

★**Capilla de San Andrés** ⊙ – This 16C Mudéjar chapel showing Jewish influence was built upon the orders of Gutierre González Doncel, the treasurer to Pope Leo X. Hidden behind the extraordinary whiteness of its exterior is a masterpiece of Plateresque art: the **Capilla de la Purísima Inmaculada**★★ (Chapel of the Immaculate Conception), with a minutely decorated octagonal drum supporting its star vaulting. The gilded wrought-iron **screen**★ enclosing the chapel is a work by Maestro Bartolomé (16C), a native son of Jaén.

Palacio de Villardompardo ⊙ – This elegant 16C palace was the residence of Fernando de Torres y Portugal, the Viceroy of Peru and Count of Villardompardo. The sober façade obscures an arcaded **patio**★ around which several rooms are laid out. The visit includes the **Museo de Artes y Costumbres Populares**, housed in different rooms within the palace, providing an insight into the crafts and traditional customs of the province's inhabitants (artisanal instruments, household objects, clothing etc);

the **Museo Internacional de Arte Naïf**, a museum devoted to naive art, containing an unusual collection of paintings and sculptures; a room dedicated to temporary exhibitions by local artists; and the outstanding Moorish Baths.

Interior of the Moorish Baths

★★ **Moorish Baths** – The Moorish Baths *(Baños Árabes)*, situated in the catacombs of the palace, are the best preserved of any in Spain. As a result of the excellent restoration work carried out here, it is still possible to admire the advanced level of architectural mastery achieved in this type of construction, where light pervades the semi-darkness of the individual rooms to create a pleasant sensation of calm. The complex comprises a barrel-vaulted entrance hall; a cold room adorned with a skylight which provided the room with illumination and ventilation; a warm room, crowned with a handsome hemispherical cupola with pendentives and horseshoe arches; and a hot room, which also contains various alcoves with oven vaults and star-shaped skylights.

Iglesia de San Juan – Built after the reconquest of Jaén, this church contains a noteworthy collection of Gothic carvings.

Real Monasterio de Santo Domingo ⊘ – The royal monastery was founded by Juan I above the vestiges of the former palace of the Moorish kings; the building later became the headquarters of the Inquisition. The well-proportioned Renaissance façade, another work by Vandelvira, and a 17C inner **patio★**, with its delicate gallery of arches on the ground floor and finely carved windows on the upper floor, are the building's outstanding features. Nowadays, it houses the offices of the **Archivo Histórico Provincial**, the province's historical archives.

Iglesia de la Magdalena – This Isabelline Gothic-style church dating from the 16C was built above the remains of a former Arab mosque, from which it has preserved an exquisite **patio★**, along with the pool used for ritual ablutions, and several fruit trees. In the interior, above the main altar, note the fine retable by Jacopo l'Indaco and the 18C relief of *La Magdalena*, by Mateo Medina. Opposite the church stands the **Fuente del Raudal**, a fountain that used to provide drinking water for the town's inhabitants.

Monasterio de Santa Úrsula ⊘ – The convent's church has a fine Mudéjar *artesonado* ceiling. The **candied egg yolks** *(yemas)*, produced according to traditional methods and recipes by the nuns of Santa Úrsula, are one of Jaén's main delicacies.

ADDITIONAL SIGHTS

★**Castillo de Santa Catalina** ⊘ – *5km/3mi west. Best approached by car.* This imposing Moorish fortress, which sits impressively on the top of the hill of the same name, was restored by Fernando III following the reconquest of Jaén. It was from here that the monumental walls which enclosed the whole town began. All that now remains of them are the **Puerta del Ángel**, a gateway restored in Baroque style in the 17C, and the arches of **San Lorenzo** and Consuelo. Several features have been preserved from the original edifice: the interesting **Capilla de Santa Catalina**, in one of the castle's turrets, accessed via a delicate horseshoe arch; and, in particular, the keep, a graceful structure which dominates the scene and provides stupendous **views★★** of the blue-tinged Sierra de Jabalcuz and the extensive swathes of olive groves. Today, the fortress is home to the town's *parador*.

Convento de Santa Teresa or Convento de las Descalzas – The Convent of Poor Clares or Discalced Nuns contains a handwritten copy of the *Spiritual Canticle* written by St John of the Cross. The delicious **pastries** produced by the nuns here are well worth sampling.

EXCURSIONS

La Guardia de Jaén – *10km/6mi southeast along the N 323 – E 902*. This small village of whitewashed houses sits in the shadow of its Moorish fortress. The impressive **views** from the keep take in the Cerro de San Martos, with fields of fruit, vegatables and wheat in the distance.

Parque Natural Sierra Mágina – *35km/22mi east. Exit Jaén along the avenida de Granada, follow the A 316 and A 320 towards Mancha Real, then continue along the JV 3242. Information is available at the* **Centro de interpretación de Jodar** ⊘. Known through the writer Antonio Muñoz Molina, who set several of his novels in a fictitious place he referred to as Mágina, this park forms part of the Cordillera Subbética, between the Guadalquivir Depression and the Sierra de Lucena. The 19 900ha/49 127 acres covered by the park extend across the hills and plains of Jaén in a landscape dominated by dense forests of oak, providing a natural habitat for species which include the imperial eagle, peregrine falcon and mountain goat.

JEREZ DE LA FRONTERA★★
Cádiz – Population 181 602
Michelin map 446 V 11

It may be a cliché, but it is difficult to describe Jerez without mentioning horses and sherry. Horses dominate the local festivals, while the aroma of sherry wafts through the city's streets and alleyways. Jerez is situated with its back to the sea, looking out at the fertile countryside which surrounds it, and is the earthly counterpoint to the ethereal Cádiz. The city boasts one of the finest architectural heritages of the province and a cultural life which revolves around **flamenco**; Jerez, along with Sevilla, is the birthplace of this art. The traditional Andalucian dance, the *bulería*, takes place in the town's humble gypsy quarters.

TOUR

★★Gothic Jerez

Jerez has preserved a large number of its Gothic-style buildings in its medieval quarter, including several so-called "churches of the Reconquest". *Most churches are open daily during services*.

Plaza del Mercado – The Moorish market once stood on this square, which is situated in the working-class district of San Mateo. The richly decorated **Palacio de Riquelme**, a Renaissance building from which only the façade has survived, stands out like a stage set at one end of the square. A pair of "savages" can be seen above the Corinthian columns of the lower section, accompanied by two rampant lions which have acted as symbolic protectors of these doorways since Antiquity.
The **Museo Arqueológico** and **Iglesia de San Mateo** also line this square.

Museo Arqueológico de Jerez ⊘ – The archeological museum is housed in a heavily restored 18C mansion, which has conserved an attractive façade. The rooms, arranged around a patio, present the history of the Jerez region in chronological order. The outstanding exhibit is an elegant **Greek helmet★** dating from the 7C BC which was found in the Guadalete River. The **cylindrical idols★** made from marble date from the Copper Age and were discovered in Cerro de las Vacas (Lebrija) and Torrecera; despite their simplicity they still manage to portray remarkable expression.

13C Jerez

The capture of Sevilla in 1248 by Fernando III the Saint led to the opening up of the Lower Guadalquivir Valley to Christian troops, who subsequently occupied important cities such as Arcos, Medina and Jerez de la Frontera. Jerez finally came under Castilian control on 9 October 1264, the feast day of St Dionysius, following the repression of a Mudéjar revolt. During this period, the city was surrounded by a rectangular wall, built by the Almohads, with a perimeter of more than 4km/2.5mi; remains of this defensive structure can still be seen in calle Porvera and calle Ancha. Three gates led into the city, which was divided into six parishes or *collaciones* (Cádiz only had one), named after the four Evangelists, St Dionysius (the city's patron saint) and the Saviour. The suburbs of San Miguel and Santiago, as well as the Dominican and Franciscan monasteries, stood outside the walls. From the 13C onwards, the city played a key role in the defensive border system established between the Christian and Nasrid kingdom.

JEREZ DE LA FRONTERA

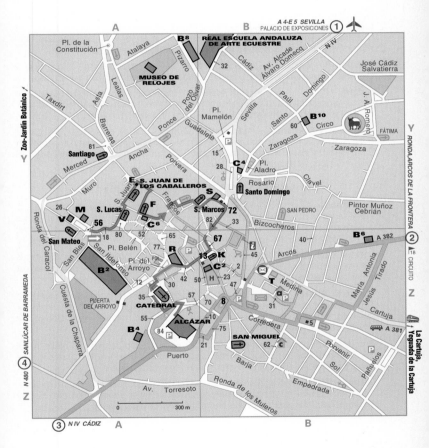

Doña Blanca .BZ 🏠   El Coloso .BZ 🏠

217

WHERE TO STAY

MODERATE

El Coloso – *Pedro Alonso, 13 – ☎/fax 956349008 – 20 rooms – 6 000pts.* Although the facilities are somewhat basic, the rooms are clean and well maintained, and the welcome extremely friendly.

MID-RANGE

Doña Blanca – *Bodegas, 11 – ☎ 956340403 – fax 956348586 – 30 rooms – 9 500pts.* A modern hotel situated in the city centre. Functional, but comfortable rooms.

Jerez – *Alcalde Álvaro Domecq, 35 – ☎ 956300600 – fax 956305001 – 116 rooms – 18 900pts.* A large hotel of a high standard with rooms overlooking the garden or the swimming pool. Its only disadvantage is its location away from the city centre.

EATING OUT

Bar Juanito – *Pescadería Vieja, 8 – ☎ 956334838.* The Bar Juanito was founded in 1943 in a pedestrianised street teeming with outdoor cafés and restaurants. The decor is typically Andalucian in style, with *azulejos* and bullfighting paintings and posters adorning the walls.

Tendido 6 – *Circo, 10 – ☎ 956344835.* Next to the bullring. This is one of the best restaurants in Jerez, serving Andalucian meat and fish specialities.

Gaitán – *Gaitán, 3–5 – ☎ 956345859.* This restaurant, decorated in a traditional, albeit kitsch and overelaborate style, is more than 30 years old. Its specialities include braised oxtail *(rabo de toro)* and veal *(ternera)*.

La Taberna Flamenca – *Angostillo de Santiago, 3 – ☎ 649383973 – closed Sun.* A large tavern located in a former wine storehouse. Dinner is served at 9pm, with the flamenco show starting at 10.30pm. Joint dinner/flamenco tickets cost 3 500pts, although tickets for the show can be bought separately.

CAFÉS, BARS & NIGHT-LIFE

La Rotonda – *Larga, 40. Open daily, 9am to 11pm.* This is a classic venue is every sense of the word, in terms of its decor, atmosphere and character. It has a pleasant outdoor terrace and excellent service. A fine selection of wines, cheeses and dried sausages, as well as a small shop selling delicious sweets.

Cafetería La Vega – *Plaza Estévez, 1. Open 9am to 11pm.* Tourists and locals mingle on the pleasant terrace of this cafeteria, situated on one of the busiest squares in central Jerez. Highly recommended at any time of day.

Cafetería Bristol – *Plaza Romero Martínez, 1. Open daily, 9am to midnight.* The presence of the **Teatro Villamarta** in the square explains the busy nature of this café, whose relaxing atmosphere is popular with theatre-goers. One of the city's favourite haunts for afternoon coffee.

Don José – *Letrados. Open daily, 4pm to midnight.* Popular with an older, more select crowd, this bar is very English in style, with a warm, classical decor. The perfect spot for a drink and a chat in a relaxed atmosphere.

Carbonería – *Letrados (behind the town hall). Open daily, 4.30pm to 3am.* A modern, avant-garde bar mainly frequented by a young clientele. Highly recommended for a drink in the late afternoon or early evening.

ENTERTAINMENT

Although Jerez's cultural and social life is mainly based around wine and flamenco, it does not neglect other cultural activities such as music and theatre. The **Teatro Villamarta** *(plaza Romero Martínez, ☎ 956329313)* offers a full programme of opera, music, dance and theatre, including flamenco.

The city's renowned flamenco clubs *(peñas flamencas)* offer residents and visitors a range of options, including shows, exhibitions, informal gatherings and recitals, such as the famous *zambombás* at Christmas. Recommended clubs in Jerez include the traditional **Peña Tío José de Paula**, at calle Merced, 11 (☎ 956303267), and the popular Peña el Garbanzo, at calle Santa Clara, 9 (☎ 956337667).

The town hall publishes a bimonthly **cultural guide** *(guía cultural)* available from newspaper kiosks and the tourist office listing detailed information on events around the city.

FIESTAS

The **Festival de Jerez**, dedicated to flamenco, is held at the end of April. The most famous fiesta in the city is the **Feria del Caballo** (horse fair) which takes place in May in the Parque González Hontória *(avenida Alcalde Álvaro Domecq)*. The **Fiesta de la Vendimia** (wine harvest festival) and the **Fiesta de la Bulería**, a festival devoted to traditional Andalucian song, are both held in September.

SHOPPING

The main shopping district in Jerez is situated around calle Larga, a pleasant pedestrianised street lined with shops. A traditional market, which has been recently restored and is well worth a visit, can be seen in plaza Estévez at one end of this street.

Jerez is an excellent place for buying equestrian equipment. Two harness shops are particularly recommended: **Arcab** *(Divina Pastora, 1 – ☎ 956 32 41 00)* and **Duarte** *(Lancería, 15 – ☎ 956 34 27 51)*.

The town is also *the* city in which to buy sherry. It is best to purchase products directly from the main wine cellars *(bodegas)* or to buy from a specialised establishment, such as La Casa del Jerez *(Divina Pastora, 1 – ☎ 956 33 51 84)*.

Markets – A large market selling a wide selection of goods is held on Monday mornings in the **Parque González Hontória**, the site of the city's annual horse fair.

TRANSPORT

Airport – La Parra airport (☎ 956 33 56 48) is located 7km/4.5mi from the city along the N-IV. The most convenient way of getting to the city from the airport is by taxi.

Trains – The railway station is at plaza de la Estación *(☎ 956 25 43 01)*. Mainline services operate to Sevilla, Madrid and Barcelona, as well as regular departures to Cádiz.

RENFE (Spanish State Railways) – The information office is located at calle Tonería, 4. ☎ 956 33 79 75.

City buses – Jerez has an extensive bus network serving all parts of the city. A single ticket costs 105pts, a 10-trip ticket 750pts, and a 20-trip ticket 1 300pts. Monthly passes are also available at a cost of 3 500pts.

Inter-city buses – The bus station is situated on calle Cartuja ☎ 956 34 52 07. Regular services operate to most towns in the province of Cádiz, as well as to Madrid, Sevilla, Málaga and Córdoba.

Taxis – ☎ 956 34 48 60.

Horse-drawn carriages – Horse-drawn carriages can be hired from several places in Jerez for visits to the main tourist sites around the city.

Iglesia de San Mateo – This is one of the first churches built by Alfonso X in the 13C, on the site of a former mosque. The present building dates from the 15C. The external walls are supported by strong buttresses.

Follow calle Cabezas to plaza de San Lucas.

Iglesia de San Lucas – The medieval origin of this church is hidden by the more recent additions to the building, particularly those added during the Baroque period. Outside the church, the tower-façade with a splayed portal is particularly striking.

Take calle Ánimas de San Lucas and turn left into calle Santa María, continuing as far as plaza Orbaneja. From here take calle Liebre to plaza Carrizosa to admire the striking façade of an 18C mansion with a curved balcony. Return to plaza Orbaneja and follow calle San Juan as far as the Iglesia de San Juan de los Caballeros.

★**Iglesia de San Juan de los Caballeros** – The present church, with its dark exterior, dates mainly from the

---

Tocino de Cielo

This delicious dessert (literally "heavenly bacon") is thought to have its origins in the Jerez wine-cellars, where local wine-producers once used beaten egg whites to clarify their wine. Not knowing what to do with the leftover egg yolks, they gave them to the neighbouring convents, where the nuns used them to make these delicious custard puddings.

15C, although features such as the façade were added in the 17C. The single-nave interior has a magnificent nine-sided 14C **polygonal apse**★, topped by a ten-rib cupola with jagged decoration, resting on a series of slender columns.

The **Centro Andaluz de Flamenco**, which is housed in Palacio Pemartín, is visible behind the church, in plaza San Juan.

Take calle Francos and turn left into calle Canto. Continue as far as plaza Ponce de León.

The old **Palacio de los Ponce de León**, with its beautiful corner **window**★★, an excellent example of the Plateresque style, stands proudly in this square.

Continue down calle Juana de Dios Lacoste and turn left into calle Almenillas. Cross calle Francos and follow calle Compañía which runs from one side of the Iglesia de la Compañía de Jesús up to the Iglesia de San Marcos.

> A selection of pastries can be bought at the **Convento de Santa María de Gracia** in plaza de Ponce de León. *Tocino de cielo* is made on request. Open 9.30am to 12.45pm and 5.30pm to 6.45pm.

Iglesia de San Marcos – Although this church was founded during the reign of Alfonso X, the present building probably dates from 1480 when the church was remodelled. The single nave visible today dates from this period and is covered by a beautiful 16C **star vault**. The apse is hidden by a 17C polygonal **retable**★ above which hangs a 19C panel representing St Mark. The other three panels date from the 16C and show strong Flemish influence. The 15C **baptismal chapel** to the left of the nave is also worthy of note.

Plaza de Rafael Rivero – This small square is bordered by the Palacio de los Pérez Luna, with its beautiful late-18C **doorway**, and next to it, the Casa de los Villavicencio, with its attractive patio.

Follow calle Tornería as far as plaza de Plateros.

Plaza del Plateros – This is one of the most atmospheric squares in old Jerez. It was an important commercial centre in the Middle Ages, as demonstrated by the names of the streets in its immediate vicinity such as *Chapinería* (clog makers), *Sedería* (silk dealers), and *Tornería* (turners). The **Atalaya tower** *(torre)* in the square was built in the first half of the 15C as a watchtower. Admire the Gothic windows with their multifoil arches on the second section of the tower facing the square.

★ **Plaza de la Asunción** – On one side of this pleasant square stands the Renaissance **Casa del Cabildo**★★, built in 1575. The façade of this former town hall consists of a main section adorned with grotesque figures and cupids, with the figures of Hercules and Julius Caesar flanked by the Cardinal Virtues. To the left is a porch or porticoed gallery, comprising three semicircular openings supported by delicate columns which contrast with the heavy Corinthian columns around the door and the windows on the opposite side. A statue dedicated to the Assumption, which dates from the middle of the 20C, has been erected in the middle of the square.

Iglesia de San Dionisio – The Church of St Dionysius, which shows strong Mudéjar influence, is dedicated to the town's patron saint. The main portal on the exterior is splayed and covered by a small roof. This rather clumsy building is adorned with unusual modillions at roof level.

Follow calle José Luis Díez down to plaza del Arroyo.

★ **Palacio del Marqués de Bertemati** – This palace has one of the most impressive façades of any building in Jerez. The **left doorway**★ comprises two sections separated by a beautiful curved wrought-iron balcony which bears the letters of the name Dávila. The first section, dedicated to the secular world, is decorated with two statues of riders on horseback. The second section is dedicated to the religious world.

★★ **Cathedral** ⊙ – The Colegial del Salvador was the first church to be consecrated after the Reconquest and in keeping with other churches in Jerez was built over a mosque. The present building is situated slightly further to the east than the original church and was the most important religious project undertaken in Jerez in the 18C;

> **Fiesta de la Vendimia**
>
> Since the 18C, the Wine Harvest Festival, one of the most important events in the Jerez calendar, has been held in the **plaza de la Asunción**, in front of the cathedral, to celebrate the pressing of the harvested grapes.

the work involved changes to the layout of neighbouring streets and the opening up of new sections of town, such as the **plaza de la Encarnación**. Its imposing silhouette, dominated by the tiled **cupola**★ above the transept, is visible from much of the city. The cathedral is eclectic in appearance, combining Baroque elements in its portals and towers with Gothic details such as vaults and flying buttresses, although the latter are purely decorative and provide no support for the building. The interior of the church is extravagantly decorated and comprises five aisles; the central nave, covered by a barrel vault, is particularly striking.

★**Alcázar** ⊘ – *In alameda Vieja*. From here there is an excellent **view**★★ of the cathedral. The old Moorish fortress was originally part of the 4km/2.5mi defensive wall built by the Almohads in the 12C; sections of this structure can still be seen around Jerez. The Alcázar is situated in the southwest corner of the walls, and is accessed via the **Puerta de la Ciudad** (City Gateway), a typical Almohad gate built at a 90° angle. The turrets are also a typical example of Almohad defensive architecture, as witnessed in the Torre Octogonal. Also visible along the fortress walls are the keep and the 15C Torre de Ponce de León. The **mosque**★★, located within the walls of the Alcázar, is a fine example of the unadorned style of the early Almohads, in which the prayer room is covered by a delightful **octagonal cupola**. The 12C baths, built in the Roman style, are visible across the garden, at the far end of the fortifications.

Main portal of the cathedral

J. Guillard/SCOPE

Camera Obscura ⊘ – This, the second camera obscura of its type built in Spain, is housed in the tower of the **Palacio de Villavicencio**. An ingenious arrangement of mirrors and lenses provides visitors with a completely different **view**★★ of Jerez. This is an ideal first stop on a tour of the city.

From Plaza del Arenal to Alameda Cristina

This walk explores the area outside the old city walls, which in the Middle Ages was occupied by the districts of San Miguel and Santiago, where a number of religious orders, including the Dominicans, founded monasteries and convents. Despite its location, this district has always played an important role in the life of the city, as demonstrated by the different styles of architecture which can be seen here. This is now one of the liveliest areas of Jerez, full of outdoor cafés and shops.

Plaza del Arenal – Once a place of leisure for the Moors, this square is still used as a meeting place and venue for public festivities. The monument in the centre of the square is in memory of **Miguel Primo de Rivera**, a native son of the city, and is a work by Mariano Benlliure.

From plaza del Arenal take calle San Miguel, which provides a good view of the Baroque tower of the Iglesia de San Miguel.

★★ **Iglesia de San Miguel** – The **San José façade**, the oldest part of the church, was built in 1480 in Hispano-Flemish style. A statue of St Joseph can be seen on the tympanum, flanked by two imposing Flamboyant pillars and crowned with an ogee arch. The main façade, dedicated to St Michael, consists of an imposing three-tiered Baroque tower, topped with an *azulejo* roof, typical of Jerez. The interior is graceful in appearance and has three aisles. The transept and main chapel are highly decorated and are covered by an elaborate star vault. The **retable**★ adorning the apse is an extraordinary late-Renaissance work by Martínez Montañés, with additional Baroque features introduced by Juan de Arce. Attached to the church is the Baroque-style **Capilla Sacramental** (Sacramental Chapel).

Return to plaza del Arenal and follow calle Lencería as far as the popular Gallo Azul building. Calle Larga leads to the Convento de Santo Domingo.

Convento de Santo Domingo – This Dominican monastery was founded during the reign of Alfonso X. Temporary exhibitions are held in its attractive Gothic cloisters.

★ **Casa Domecq** – This elegant building, built towards the end of the 18C, is a fine example of a Jerez Baroque-style palace. Its most striking feature is the highly decorative marble **doorway**★. Between the two sections of the door, note the graceful iron balustrade which rests on a curvaceous cornice and which lends dynamism to the structure as a whole.

SHERRY

The Sherry appellation – A triangular section of land between the towns of **Jerez, Sanlúcar** and **El Puerto de Santa María**. Wines produced in this area are granted **Denominación de Origen Jerez-Xerez-Sherry** appellation status and are controlled by the Consejo Regulador, a regulatory body created in 1935.

Albariza – A light-coloured soil containing loam of marine origin. Its ability to retain moisture makes it ideal for grape cultivation.

Palomino – 95% of the grapes grown in Jerez are of the Palomino variety. This particular grape was introduced to the region during the time of Alfonso X.

Pedro Ximénez – This grape variety was introduced to the area in 1680 by a soldier from the Flemish army.

Botas – Three types of barrels are used: *bocolles*, *toneles* and *botas*. The *botas* (500l) are the most commonly used and are made from American oak.

Solera and Criaderas – These are the names given to the system used to produce sherry. The *solera* is the row of large barrels *(barricas)* closest to the floor which contain the oldest wine. The rows of barrels above this bottom layer are known as *criaderas*. The wine runs from the top level (the first *criadera*) to the *solera*, in a process known as "running down the ladder".

Flor del vino – A fine layer of yeast which forms on the surface of the wine, causing fermentation and preventing oxidisation.

Sobretabla – This is the name given to the youngest wine which is placed in the first *criadera*. In essence this is the fermented must to which alcohol has been added to bring the alcohol level to 15%.

Types of sherry:

Fino – This is a dry wine which is light and straw-like in colour, with an alcohol content of 15%. An excellent accompaniment to fish and seafood.

Amontillado – An amber-coloured sherry which is both dry and aromatic. The alcohol content in amontillados is around 17%.

Oloroso – Dark in colour with a sharp aroma. Around 18% proof.

Cream – A sweet, dark sherry produced from *oloroso* sherry. A perfect dessert wine.

Pedro Ximénez – This sweet wine is ruby in colour and is made from the grape of the same name.

The main sherry bodegas ⓥ:

Pedro Domecq: Founded in 1730. The company's El Molino storehouse *(bodega)* is particularly impressive.

González Byass (Tío Pepe): Founded in 1835. Two of its *bodegas* are of particular interest: La Concha, designed by Eiffel in 1892, and La Constancia, which is full of famous signatures. Gonzalez Byass have also preserved the company's original tasting room.

William & Humbert: Storehouses and a museum. For information, ☎ 956 34 65 39.

For further information on sherry consult the **Consejo Regulador's web site** at www.sherry.org

Bodega de La Ina. Domecq

ADDITIONAL SIGHTS

★★ Museo de Relojes ⊘ – This remarkable clock museum, one of the rare examples of its type in Spain, is housed in the 19C Palacete de la Atalaya, built in Classical style. The palace is surrounded by romantic gardens in which a number of peacocks are free to wander. The museum, whose collection numbers some 300 timepieces, has its origins in the private collection of Gabia's widow, which was later acquired by José María Ruiz Mateos. The oldest clock dates from the 17C and has an **Italian casing** made from ebony and semi-precious stones. The rest of the collection comprises mainly 18C and 19C timepieces from England and France. Note the interesting and somewhat unusual 18C English sundial.

Zoo-Botanical Garden ⊘ – The zoo was founded in the 1950s in the former botanical garden *(jardín botánico)* to the north of the city. Nowadays the zoo and garden combine to create one of the most pleasant parks in Jerez. More than 400 species can be admired here, including lions, tigers and elephants. The zoo is particularly recommended for families with children.

★ Real Escuela Andaluza del Arte Ecuestre ⊘ – The **Royal Andalucian School of Equestrian Art** is located in an attractive 19C French-style palace, built by **Charles Garnier**, the architect of the Paris Opera House. The building, which is nowadays used for administrative purposes, is surrounded by magnificent, well-tended gardens. A **show★★** entitled "A Horse Symphony" takes place in the main arena, in which the impressive Cartujana horses hold centre stage. The combination of Spanish music, riders dressed in 18C costume, and magnificent horses is a spectacle not to be missed.

Iglesia de Santiago – This church, dedicated to St James, is situated in the district of the same name. The building visible today dates from the late 15C and was built above a small chapel founded by Alfonso X in the 13C. The exterior has an imposing appearance, with sturdy buttresses which end in pinnacles. The main façade is a typical example of Hispano-Flemish art which was such a feature of this period. The portal, adorned with splayed arches and completed by an ogee arch bearing the coat of arms of the Catholic Monarchs, is flanked by two Flamboyant Gothic sections. The interior consists of three aisles crowned with pointed vaults.

EXCURSIONS

★ La Cartuja ⊘ – *6km/3.5mi south along the A 381 on the Medina Sidonia road.* Started in 1478, work on this Carthusian monastery continued for most of the following century. The Renaissance doorway, completed in 1571, leads to a large paved patio to the rear of which the impressive **façade★★★** of the church stands out. This portal-retable is divided into four sections which combine to create an ensemble of great theatricality. The side intercolumniations of the two main sections are adorned with the statues of the saints of the Order, while the central axis contains a representation of the Immaculate Conception and, above the rose window, the figure of St Bruno, the founder of the Order. The single-nave interior is crowned by pointed vaulting.

★ La Cartuja Stud Farm (Yeguada de la Cartuja) ⊘ – *Leave Jerez on the Medina Sidonia road. The Finca Fuente del Suero comes into view after 6.5km/4mi.* The state-run company **EXPASA** is responsible for the breeding and training of **Cartujana horses**. On Saturdays, members of the public are able to visit the stud farm's facilities and get a closer look at these magnificent beasts. The visit also includes an exhibition of horse equipment and an opportunity to admire a team of mares.

Montecastillo Golf Club – *Next to the racetrack.* One of the best golf clubs in Spain, chosen in 1997 as the venue for the prestigious **Volvo Masters** golf tournament. For information on facilities and green fees, contact the club's web site at www.montecastillo.com

Jerez Racetrack (Circuito de Jerez) – *10km/6mi east along the A 382 towards Arcos.* Motorcycling enthusiasts come here in their thousands for the annual Grand Prix. For more information on events consult the track's web site at: www.circuitodejerez.com or ☎ 956 15 11 05.

JIMENA DE LA FRONTERA

Cádiz – Population 8 949
Michelin map 446 W 13

This attractive, yet somewhat forgotten town stands at the eastern end of the **Parque Natural de los Alcornocales**. Access from the north of the province is via a spectacular landscape of forests of cork, holm and gall oak, which only changes as you approach Jimena, giving way to pasture land set aside for the breeding of fighting bulls. The Romans founded a settlement here which they named Oba, while during the Middle Ages the fortress of Jimena developed into an important border post between Christian and Nasrid forces (hence its suffix of "de la frontera") until its final reconquest in 1454 by the Trastamara king, Enrique IV. Access to this strategic area nestled between Gibraltar to the south and the plains of Jerez to the north has always been difficult, a factor which contributed to its renown as a refuge for smugglers and highwaymen from the 19C until after the Spanish Civil War. Nowadays, Jimena is a tranquil town popular with a number of British residents who have settled here.

SIGHTS

The town straddles the slope of a hill dominated by the castle. The white-washed harmony of its houses is broken only by the red-brick neo-Classical bell-tower of the **Iglesia de Santa María La Coronada**.

Iglesia de la Misericordia – This simple, 15C Gothic church with a single nave has been sensitively restored to house the **Centro de Información del Parque Natural de los Alcornocales** ♡, providing a wealth of information on the park. It was probably the first church to have been built after the reconquest of the town.

WHERE TO STAY

MID-RANGE

El Anón – *Consuelo, 34-40* – ☎ *956 64 01 13 – fax 956 64 11 10 – 12 rooms – 7 000pts.* Small rooms, numerous steps, flower-decked patios, a typical restaurant and swimming pool with views of the mountains are the main features of this charming hotel. Highly recommended.

Castle – This castle-fortress stands on the Cerro de San Cristóbal, where it would appear that the Roman settlement of Oba once stood. The building visible today is of Moorish origin and dates from the 13C. Access to the main enclosure is through the double horseshoe arch of the imposing turret, which acted as a watchtower. The esplanade on the hill is occupied by the town cemetery, several large water tanks and the castle enclosure, dominated by its austere **keep** *(torre del homenaje)*.

Turrets

One of the new features of Almohad military architecture was the construction of turrets *(torres albarranas)*, which were often built in a forward position separate from the main body of the fortification, yet connected to it via an arch or a wall. These turrets served as watchtowers and were permanently guarded. The most famous of these is the **Torre del Oro** in Sevilla.

EXCURSIONS

★**Laja Alta wall paintings** – *In order to visit the paintings, visitors must contact a local guide.* These wall paintings are some of the most interesting to be found in Cádiz province as well as some of the best preserved, mainly due to their recent discovery and difficult access. The paintings include a series of six Phoenician sailing vessels of extraordinary beauty that have been dated to around 1000 BC.

★**Castellar de la Frontera** – The Nasrids built this village-fortress in the 13C as a defensive enclave to help protect the recently created kingdom of Granada. For two centuries, Castellar was the site of frontier battles between Moors and Christians until its final reconquest by Christian troops in 1434. However,

WHERE TO STAY

MID-RANGE

La Almoraima – *On the A 369, between the N 340 and Jimena de la Frontera* – ☎ *956 69 30 02 – fax 956 69 32 14 – 17 rooms – 10 000pts.* This magnificent country hotel is in the middle of a huge park. The residence was used as a convent in the 17C, and then as a hunting lodge for a local duke in the 19C. The rooms are soberly decorated in rustic style. Peace and quiet guaranteed.

its most difficult crisis occurred in the early 1970s when, following the construction of the **Embalse de Guadarranque**, a reservoir which flooded the local area, the majority of its inhabitants were forced to move to Nuevo Castellar, 7km/4mi to the south. The road to old Castellar winds its way up the hill on which it stands, past whitewashed houses and through a landscape of outstanding beauty to this half-abandoned village, which looks as though it has come straight out of a medieval fairy tale. Entry to the village, which is totally enclosed inside the walls of the fortress, is via the gateway to the palace of the Dukes of Arcos.

★**Parque Natural de los Alcornocales** – *Several roads criss-cross the park, offering superb views of its delightful landscapes. These include the A 375 from Alcalá de los Gazules, the CA 503 from Arcos de la Frontera, and the A 369 from San Roque (Algeciras). Others come over the Puerto Galis, which has acted as an important crossroads since early times. For information on the park,* ☎ *956 41 33 07.*

A typical street in Castellar de la Frontera

The typical vegetation of this natural park comprises holm oak, gall oak, wild olive trees and, more importantly, the cork oak, which covers almost half of the park's total area to form Europe's largest cork oak forest. The park is a paradise for nature-lovers, who can walk its numerous paths and trails, many of which are old cattle tracks. Two of the best walks here are to La Sauceda *(around 5hr)* and the somewhat more strenuous ascent of **El Picacho** *(around 3hr)*.

Cork

The extraction of cork *(corcho)* is a delicate process that calls for the experience and skill of the *corchero* or cork-stripper. The exploitation of Andalucian cork oak began in the 1830s, since when there has been little change in working methods. The instrument used to strip the cork is a special hatchet which cuts large strips of bark known as *panas*. This is the most delicate moment of the whole operation as any damage to the tree might affect the regeneration of the bark, a process which normally takes ten years. Once stripped, the cork collectors and splitters take over; it is their job to prepare the cork ready for transport for the muleteers. Cork oaks are considered ready for exploitation once they have reached 30 years and a diameter exceeding 60cm/2ft. As the average lifespan of a cork oak is 150 years, each tree normally yields around 10 harvests. Stripping normally takes place between June and September, when the cork oak is best able to regenerate itself.

LEBRIJA

Sevilla – Population 23 924

Michelin map 446 V 11

Lebrija stands on a small promontory on the banks of an area of marshland alongside the Guadalquivir Estuary. According to legend, it was founded by Bacchus, who gave it the name *Nebrissa*. Following the Roman occupation, the town was to enjoy a period of great splendour under the Moors. In 1264 Alfonso X reconquered Lebrija, heralding an era of prosperity – in the main due to its rich agricultural resources – that would last until well into the 18C. Today, the birthplace of **Elio Antonio de Nebrija** (1442-1522), the first lexicographer of the Spanish language, is a town that has embarked upon a process of industrial modernisation.

Iglesia de Santa María de la Oliva ⊙ – This former mosque, adapted for Christian worship in 1249, fronts the attractive plaza del Rector Merina. The interior is a mix of several architectural styles with its Mudéjar horseshoe arches separating the three aisles; the Gothic windows in the side chapels; the Renaissance transept and apse; and the Baroque bell-tower. It also houses a statue of the Virgin Mary, as well as a fine **main altarpiece**, a work by Alonso Cano.

> ### Júas
> These rag dolls created by the town's inhabitants are ceremoniously burned on the night of St John (23-24 June) as the centrepiece of this huge Andalucian festival in honour of John the Baptist.

Iglesia de Santa María del Castillo ⊙ – The church stands alongside the ruins of the old Moorish castle in the upper town. It is Mudéjar in style with fine original *artesonado* work and a patio that was part of the former mosque.

Capilla de la Vera Cruz ⊙ – This interesting 17C neo-Classical chapel on plaza de España, the hub of local life, houses an exquisite **crucifix** carved by Martínez Montañés.

LINARES★

Jaén – Population 58 410

Michelin map 446 R 19

The second largest town in Jaén province after Jaén itself, Linares is an old mining settlement situated in a depression at the foot of the Sierra Morena, alongside a Roman road that was part of the route between Cádiz and Rome. It extends across a landscape of extensive olive groves, the perfect lines of which have transformed the vast Jaén countryside into a precise patchwork of green, occasionally punctuated by the white outline of a distant homestead.

The town's origins date back to the Roman era, when the settlement here was known as *Linarium*. However, following the destruction of the nearby Cástulo, many mining families moved to Linares, transforming it into a prosperous town of major economic importance. Conquered by Fernando III the Saint in the mid 13C, it subsequently experienced a period of great wealth during the reign of Carlos III, a situation brought about by lead and silver mining in the local area. In recent times, the closure of several mines and the crisis in the iron and steel industry has had a detrimental effect on the local economy. Linares is the birthplace of the guitarist **Andrés Segovia**, and is also known for its bullring, in which the legendary **Manolete** was killed in 1947.

Iglesia de Santa María la Mayor – This magnificent 16C building, built above the remains of an earlier church, is a mix of Romanesque, Gothic and Renaissance styles. Of note inside are the doors of several side chapels *(the first and second on the right)*, and the fine **main altarpiece**, depicting scenes from the Old Testament.

★**Museo Arqueológico** ⊙ – The town's archeological museum is housed in the refined Palacio Dávalos, its façade crowned by a graceful watchtower. Exhibits on display include collections from the Bronze Age to the Middle Ages. Of those pieces discovered in nearby Cástulo, a 1C AD bronze **Nike**, the robes of which show delicate sculptural technique, stands out. The collection of **6C BC statuettes** from Astarté are also of particular interest.

Hospital de los Marqueses de Linares – The exuberant architecture of this building contrasts with the elegant simplicity of the square of the same name. The hospital is neo-Classical in style and dates from the early 20C. The crypt of the Marquess and Marchioness of Linares inside the building is by Coullaut Valera.

Palacio de Justicia – The façade of this imposing 18C building has profuse decoration which combines to create a superb sculptural composition. The scenes depicted are a mixture of religious themes and others showing aspects of daily life.

Manolete

On the afternoon of 29 August 1947, a bull named Islero from the Miura ranch gored to death the famous bullfighter Manuel Rodríguez Sánchez – universally known as Manolete – in the Linares bullring. This slender, elegant *torero*, who lived life to the full both in and out of the ring, has developed into one of the legendary figures of the world of bullfighting.

Iglesia de San Francisco – The austere external appearance, enhanced by the handsome façade crowned by a spire and flanked by a graceful bell-tower, contrasts with the beauty of the fine Baroque **retable** at the high altar.

Town Hall – This monumental 18C construction has an attractive porticoed atrium occupying one side of the square.

EXCURSIONS

Ruins of Cástulo – *7km/4.5mi northeast along the A 312 towards Arquillos.* Cástulo was founded by the Greeks and subsequently inhabited by the Phoenicians and Romans. It was here that Imilce, the wife of the Carthaginian, Hannibal, was born. Cástulo was one of the most prosperous settlements in this area due to the lead and silver mines in the vicinity. Today, it is an important archeological site where a number of highly prized discoveries have been unearthed.

Baños de la Encina – *11km/7mi northwest along the J 6030.* This quiet village, hidden amid olive groves and the gently undulating hills of the **Parque Natural Sierra de Andújar★** *(see p 90),* is known for its **Moorish fortress**, which overlooks the settlement from the top of its strategic rock. Vestiges of its old streets and the former mosque are still visible here. It is well worth climbing any one of the watchtowers to enjoy the superb **views** of the village and the surrounding area.

LOJA

Granada – Population 20 143
Michelin map 446 U 17

The town of Loja is situated in the fertile plain of the **Genil River**, halfway between Málaga and Granada. To the Moors, who named it Medina Lawsa, it was a place of great strategic importance for their defence of the plain extending east towards Granada. Loja was razed on several occasions during the Reconquest, although it was not until Boabdil handed over the city to the Catholic Monarchs in 1486 that Moorish domination in Loja finally came to end. The year 1800 saw the birth here of **General Narváez**, who controlled Spanish politics in an authoritative manner during the reign of Isabel II.

OLD QUARTER

Loja's historical centre stands on a small promontory, and is characterised by narrow alleyways with evocative names lined by a number of architectural treasures. Access to the old quarter is either via the Cuesta del Señor hill or by circling the impressively proportioned **Iglesia de la Encarnación**, a church built between the 16C and 18C. Above it stands the **alcazaba** ⊘, a fortress which has preserved its keep; the residence of the Christian Governors *(Caserón de los Alcaides Cristianos),* a house of simple design from the 17C; the Torre Ochavada and, on the parade ground, the remains of a cistern *(aljibe).* Calle Moraima leads to the outer limits of the medieval quarter. The view from the Mirador Arqueológico of the **Iglesia de San Gabriel**, a fine 16C Renaissance church, is particularly impressive.

Bell-tower, Iglesia de la Encarnación

B. Kaufmann/MICHELIN

> ### Annunciation façade
> The façade of the Iglesia de San Gabriel, attributed to **Diego de Siloé**, is a striking example of 16C Renaissance architecture. The lower section corresponds to the typical design of a triumphal arch, its bay flanked by paired Ionic columns, while the smaller upper tier is crowned by a pediment and flanked by Corinthian columns. In the vaulted niche, a sculptural group featuring the archangel Gabriel and the Virgin Mary represents the Annunciation – hence the name given to the portal of the church.

In plaza de Abajo, formerly known as plaza Joaquín Costa, note one of the gates, the 13C **Puerta de Jaufín**, that provided access to the fortress. To the side stands the former granary *(pósito)*, a heavily restored building that has only retained its lower section.

WHERE TO STAY

LUXURY

Finca La Bobadilla – *Along the A 328 towards Iznájar* – ☎ *958 32 18 61* – *fax 958 32 18 10* – *55 rooms* – *38 500pts.* This luxury hotel is tucked away on an estate covering some 350ha/865 acres. The suites here (costing 100 000pts/night) have hosted heads of state, including King Juan Carlos, and leading international stars such as Plácido Domingo and Tom Cruise. The estate is a village in itself and even has its own church, the bells of which ring out every morning.

EATING OUT

The nearby village of **Riofrío** has an excellent reputation for its trout which dates back to the 17C. For dessert, why not try another local speciality, the cakes known as **roscos de Loja**.
For those visitors who would like to catch their own trout, Riofrío has a fishing area, the **Coto Intensivo de Pesca**, which is open all year round. *For permits, information and reservations, contact the Albergue de Pescadores de Riofrío* ☎ *958 32 31 77.*

LUCENA
Córdoba – Population 35 564
Michelin map 446 T 16

The origins of this historic town date back to the Roman period, although it was during the 10C and 11C, under Moorish domination, that Lucena enjoyed considerable development. It became an important Jewish enclave known as "The Pearl of Sefarad" and was home to a prestigious Hebrew university. In the 18C it experienced an economic and artistic revival, developing into one of the most prosperous and active towns in the province.

SIGHTS

★Iglesia de San Mateo ⊘ – *In plaza Nueva, opposite the town hall.* It is thought that this church, built in transitional Gothic-Renaissance style, was erected over the former mosque. Hernán Ruiz I and II were both involved in its design.

Exterior – The interplay of its architectural features gives dynamism to this large church. The main façade has a fine, classically inspired Renaissance portal framed by two buttresses. A tower stands to the left, while the exterior of the Capilla del Sagrario (Sacrarium Chapel), with its characteristic cupola, is visible to the right.

WHERE TO STAY

Husa Santo Domingo – *El Agua, 12* – ☎ *957 51 11 00* – *fax 957 51 62 95* – *30 rooms* – *11 000pts.* A luxury hotel with large, comfortable rooms, housed in a former 18C convent.

EATING OUT

Araceli – *Avenida del Parque, 10* – ☎ *957 50 17 14.* Although it may not look anything out of the ordinary, this is the town's best restaurant, specialising in fish and seafood.

Interior – The interior is both spacious and harmoniously proportioned. The three aisles are topped by wooden ceilings, in contrast to the triple apse with its Gothic vaulting. A magnificent Renaissance **retable**★ presides over the presbytery. The polychrome reliefs on its five panels narrate scenes from the life of Christ and depict characters from the Old and New Testaments.

★★ **Capilla del Sagrario** – *In the Epistle nave, at the foot of the church.* This jewel of Baroque architecture dates from the first half of the 18C. The walls and cupola are covered with a variety of polychrome **stuccowork**★★ which combines to create an ensemble of unparalleled decorative exuberance. Every type of ornamental feature is represented here, including geometric and plant motifs, angels, bishops, saints etc.

Castillo del Moral – This heavily restored old fortress of medieval origin has preserved two of its towers. It is said that Boabdil was imprisoned in the octagonal Torre del Mora. The second tower, the square-shaped Torre de las Damas, was the former keep.

Iglesia de Santiago ⊙ – The Church of St James was built above the former synagogue. The brick façade, adorned with a late-Gothic portal, is supported by two buttresses. Inside, the pointed ogival arches rest upon brick pillars that appear twisted by the weight above them, creating an unusual sensation of fragility. The church also houses a sculpture of Christ tied to the column, by Pedro Roldán.

Other churches of interest in Lucena are the **Iglesia de San Juan de Dios** and the **Iglesia de San Agustín**, both fronted by handsome Baroque portals. The Iglesia de San Agustín has one of the few elliptical ground plans to be found in Andalucia.

EXCURSIONS

★ **Santuario de la Virgen de Araceli** – *6km/4mi south, on the last section of a steep road with a 20% gradient.* The road climbs up to this sanctuary at the highest point of the Sierra de Aras. From the esplanade, there is an impressive **view**★ of extensive olive groves, with the mountains acting as a backdrop.

The road from Lucena to Iznájar – *35km/22mi along the C 334.* With the exception of the first few kilometres, this road passes through a charming landscape, skirting mountains carpeted with olive trees.

After 20km/12.5mi the road passes through **Rute**, famous for its anise-flavoured liqueur, standing on a mountain fold amid delightful surroundings. A donkey sanctuary can be seen on the outskirts of the town.
The **road**★ *(15km/9.5mi)* continues through a similar landscape, with views to the right of the reservoir *(embalse)* and **Iznájar**★ *(see p 208)*, impressively positioned on top of a hill.

MÁLAGA★

Málaga – Population 528 079
Michelin map 446 V 16

The capital of the Costa del Sol enjoys a pleasant climate all year round due to the maritime influence of the Mediterranean and the protection afforded by the Montes de Málaga mountain range inland, which acts as barrier against weather systems from the north. The city sits at the mouth of the Guadalmedina River, and is dominated by the Gibralfaro, or Lighthouse Hill. The villas in the residential district of La Caleta bear witness to the city's economic power during the 19C.
Málaga is an active commercial and leisure port. In addition, its airport, one of the busiest in Spain, is the arrival point for the millions of tourists who come to the Costa del Sol every year to enjoy its beaches, glorious sunshine and dozens of golf courses dotted along the coast.

FIESTAS

Semana Santa – In keeping with Andalucia's other provincial capitals, Málaga celebrates Holy Week to the full. Its origins date back to the 16C, when local brotherhoods would take to the streets bearing aloft their religious statues.
The celebrations in Málaga take on their own particular character, with huge, colourful floats, known locally as *tronos* (thrones), which often have to be erected outside churches due to their size. Unlike Sevilla, where the bearers remain hidden beneath

WHERE TO STAY

MODERATE

Pedregalejo – *Conde de las Navas, 9 –* ☏ *952 29 32 18 – 10 rooms – 7 300pts*. A pleasant *hostal* with well-appointed rooms, albeit without air-conditioning. In May 1999 the owners opened another hotel next door in which several of the rooms have air-conditioning *(7 800pts)*.

MID-RANGE

California – *Paseo de Sancha, 17 –* ☏*/fax 952 21 51 64 – 16 rooms – 8 995pts*. Just a stone's throw from the sea but away from the city centre. A small hotel with spacious and modern rooms.

Venecia – *Alameda Principal, 9 –* ☏*/fax 952 21 36 36 – 40 rooms – 10 000pts*. Don't be deceived by appearances. Although the exterior of this hotel on one of the city's widest and noisiest thoroughfares may not look particularly inspiring, the modern interior is a welcome surprise. The quieter rooms overlooking a narrow street to the rear are particularly recommended.

Don Curro – *Sancha de Lara, 7 –* ☏ *952 22 72 00 – fax 952 21 59 46 – 120 rooms – 14 010pts*. A traditional, centrally located hotel with classically designed rooms, a restaurant and a games room.

Parador de Málaga-Gibralfaro – *Castillo de Gibralfaro –* ☏ *952 22 19 02 – fax 952 22 19 04 – 38 rooms – 19 000pts*. Málaga's *parador*, with the usual charm associated with this state-run chain, occupies a dominant position overlooking the city. If you get the chance, enjoy a drink on the bar terrace with its delightful views of Málaga and the coast.

EATING OUT

El Campanario – *Paseo de la Sierra, 36 –* ☏ *952 20 24 48 – closed Mon in winter and Sun in summer*. A restaurant serving typical fish and meat dishes with a splendid panoramic backdrop encompassing Málaga Bay.

Paseo Marítimo – El Pedregal – *Zona de Pedregalejo*. The maritime promenade, with its plentiful choice of bars and restaurants, is a pleasant area for a stroll, particularly at dusk. Two of the best are **Posada II**, which specialises in grilled meats, and **Maricuchi**, serving an excellent choice of fish and seafood.

Adolfo – *Paseo Marítimo Pablo Ruiz Picasso, 12 –* ☏ *952 60 19 14 – closed Sun*. This top-class restaurant is renowned for its high-quality local and international cuisine.

TAPAS

Orellana – *Moreno Monroy, 5 –* ☏ *952 22 30 12 – closed Sun*. Although the decor lacks imagination, the Orellana is one of the city's best-known establishments, where a lively atmosphere is always guaranteed.

La Posada – *Granada, 33*. This typical bar, at the heart of Málaga's main area for night-life, specialises in grilled meats prepared in front of customers. Under the same ownership as the **Posada II** on the Paseo Marítimo.

CAFÉS, BARS & NIGHT-LIFE

Because of its benign climate, the local *malagueños* spend much of their time outdoors and are spoilt for choice when it comes to enjoying themselves. The area around the cathedral and calle Larios in the centre has numerous old bars, lively haunts mainly frequented by Málaga's younger generations and its large contingent of foreign visitors, and quieter cafés or *teterías*, such as those found near the future Picasso Museum. In summer, locals tend to spend more of their time along the Paseo Marítimo. The city's more exclusive bars and clubs tend to be concentrated in the El Limonar district, an expensive residential area at the foot of the mountains.

Cheers – *Plaza del Obispo, 1. Open daily 10am to 2am*. This café imitates the decor of the Boston bar made famous by the television series of the same name. The wonderful terrace looks onto the majestic façade of the cathedral. Although the bar has a quiet ambience, it is mainly popular with a younger crowd.

La Tetería – *Tetería Alcazaba – Calle San Agustín, 9 and 21. Open daily, 4pm to 1am*. Two small bars, popular with a younger clientele, located in a pleasant pedestrianised street. The Moorish feel and the aroma of the many teas on offer add additional flavour to the intimate atmosphere.

Café Central – *Plaza de la Constitución, 1. Open daily, 8am to 10pm*. One of Málaga's most typical and long-standing cafeterias, frequented by a faithful batch of regulars. Although the terrace on the square is particularly pleasant, the large tea-room stands out as the café's most impressive feature.

Casa Aranda – *Calle Herrería del Rey. Open daily, 9am to 9pm.* This lively, atmospheric café has taken over every building on this narrow street. A great place for a chat with friends over *chocolate con churros.*

Siempre Así – *Calle Convaleciente 5. Open daily, 10pm to 5am.* This centrally located bar is mainly frequented by the city's jet set. From midnight onwards the dance floor fills up with people dancing to the sounds of rumbas, *sevillanas* and the latest flamenco hits.

Liceo – *Calle Beatas 26. Open daily, 10pm to 5am.* This lively bar, installed in one of Málaga's old town houses is popular with an international crowd, particularly those in their thirties. This old mansion with its 19C feel really comes to life at the weekend.

El Pimpi – *Calle Granada, 6. Open daily, 4pm to 4am.* El Pimpi, on two floors with a number of rooms, is located in a pedestrianised street in the heart of Málaga. This unmissable bar is a favourite haunt for a quiet beer, coffee or tapas in the late afternoon and early evening. Later on, the atmosphere livens up considerably with the occasional burst into song in a wine cellar-type atmosphere. The chilled sweet Málaga wine here is well worth trying.

ENTERTAINMENT

Málaga's cosmopolitan atmosphere is reflected in the choice of cultural and leisure activities on offer. The **Teatro Cervantes** *(calle Ramos María)*, which first opened its doors in 1870, offers an extensive programme of theatre and concerts (☎ 952 22 41 00), while the city's art galleries frequently host a range of exhibitions. The Palacio Episcopal *(plaza del Obispo)*, Museo Municipal *(paseo de Reding, 1)* and Centro Cultural Provincial *(calle Ollerías)* are all renowned for the quality of their exhibits.

SHOPPING

The city's main shopping streets are concentrated between calle Puerta del Mar, which runs into plaza de Félix Sáez and then becomes calle Nueva, and **Marqués de Larios**. This whole area is also home to a large number of street vendors. Look out for the many pastry shops selling the typical puff pastry cakes *(hojaldres)*, a local speciality.
A good selection of more modern stores, as well as two large department stores belonging to the El Corte Inglés chain, can be found just outside the historical centre in calle Armengual de la Mota.
Large hypermarkets such as Pryca and Continente are located on the city's outskirts.

Markets – A typical market selling everything from second-hand clothes to antiques is held on Sunday mornings in the area around the La Rosaleda football stadium.

TRANSPORT

Málaga Pablo Picasso International Airport – The city's airport is situated 9.8km/6mi southwest of the city along the coast road. ☎ 952 04 84 04 and 952 04 84 84.
The Portillo bus company operates a service between the city centre and the airport every 25min. In addition, the local train linking Málaga and Fuengirola stops at the airport, with a service every 30min. Taxis are also widely available at the airport.

Trains – The city's railway station is on avenida de Andalucía and serves all of Spain's major cities. ☎ 952 87 16 73.
The Málaga to Fuengirola train serves Torremolinos, Benalmádena, Fuengirola and other towns and resorts along its route.

RENFE (Spanish State Railways) – Calle Divina Pastora, 8. ☎ 952 84 32 26.

Inter-city buses – Paseo de Los Tilos. ☎ 952 35 00 61.
Because of the city's location at the heart of Spain's busiest tourist area, Málaga offers travellers a wide choice of departures to other parts of the country and abroad.

City buses – The local bus network (SAM) is both comprehensive and inexpensive. A single journey costs 115pts, and a 10-trip ticket 725pts.
A private network operated by **Portillo** offers periodic services to the major resorts and towns along the Costa del Sol.

Taxis – ☎ 952 32 79 50 and 952 32 80 62.

Horse-drawn carriages – These can be hired at a number of places around the city for tours of Málaga's major tourist sites.

Ferries – Málaga's port is mainly used for commercial traffic, although a passenger service does operate to Morocco. The city is also a popular port of call for many of the world's leading cruise line companies.

MÁLAGA

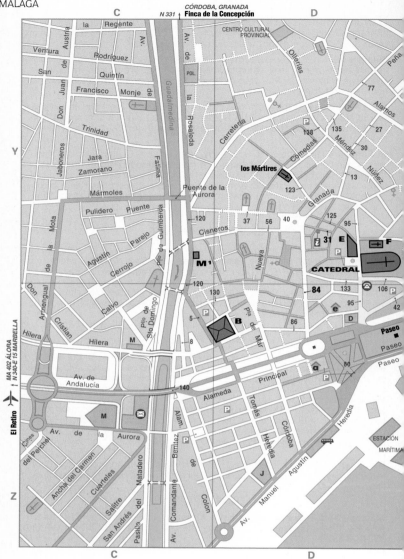

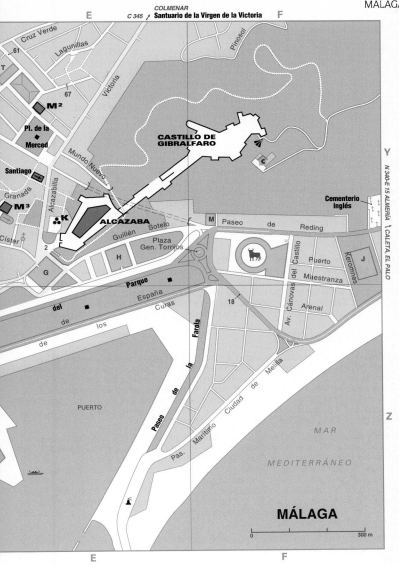

MÁLAGA

0   300 m

> ## Málaga wine
> The city's wines were highly appreciated during Antiquity. Nowadays, the best-known Málaga wines are sweet or semi-sweet with an alcohol content of between 15% and 23%. The two grape varieties used in their production are Pedro Ximénez and Moscatel. The latter, which is also highly prized as a dessert grape, is used to produce a dessert wine known as **Málaga Dulce** (Sweet Málaga). Other wines made here include the smooth **Lágrima**, and **Pedro Ximénez**, which is created exclusively from the grape of the same name.

the float, here the *costaleros* stay in full view of the spectators. The moment at which these floats are lifted aloft and subsequently "rocked" at various points along the procession is one of the most spectacular aspects of the entire week.

The most important **processions** during Holy Week are the following: Señor de los Gitanos (Easter Monday), El Cautivo (Wednesday), Cristo de la Buena Muerte and Esperanza Perchelera (Maundy Thursday). The liberation of a prisoner, a privilege granted by Carlos III to the brotherhood *(cofradía)* of Nuestro Padre Jesús el Rico, whose procession takes to the streets on the Wednesday of Holy Week, is another highlight of Málaga's devout celebrations.

The Feria – The city's annual fair, held to commemorate the capture of the city by the Catholic Monarchs, is held in the week of 15 August. It encompasses every traditional feature associated with a typical Andalucian *fiesta*: entertainment booths, copious eating and drinking, lively dancing, lots of noise and general merriment until the early hours of the morning. The fair is hugely popular, particularly with tourists enjoying a holiday on the Costa del Sol. As is customary, the city's bullfighting festival is held during the same week.

HISTORICAL NOTES

Antiquity – The Phoenicians founded a commercial colony here in the late 8C BC or early 7C BC which they named Malaca. The Greeks and Carthaginians later established trading posts on the same spot. The Romans, who conquered the city in the 3C BC, created a colony that was federated to Rome until AD 81, when it attained the status of a Roman municipality. Its port was used to export wine, oil, raisins, cereals, salted meat and fish. In the 4C, Christianity came to the city, while the 5C and 6C were marked by conflicts between rival Barbarian tribes.

Moorish domination – Following the Moorish conquest (714-16), the city came under the direct authority of Córdoba. Upon the fall of the Caliphate, control of Málaga was transferred to the kingdom of Granada. The fortress *(alcazaba)* was built in the 11C, a century in which the city enjoyed great prosperity due to the development of its textile industry. Following the periods of Almoravid and Almohad influence, Málaga saw its affairs fall under the jurisdiction of the Nasrids, in Granada, for whom the city became the main port. In the 14C, the Gibralfaro fortress was rebuilt and extended by Yusuf I. The Genoese subsequently developed the city's commercial activities, in the process opening up new trading routes.

The Christian city – The Catholic Monarchs reconquered the city in 1487 following a difficult campaign. During the 16C, under the reign of Felipe II, the new port was built which resulted in a new period of prosperity. The liberalisation of trade with the Americas in the 18C was a further boost to this coastal city.

19C – Between 1810 and 1812 the city fell into the hands of the French. The conflicts between absolutists and liberals following the return of Fernando VII were at the root of a sad event in Málaga's history: the execution of General Torrijos and his companions in 1831. However, the 19C was above all the era of the Industrial Revolution. Two wealthy bourgeois families, the Heredia (iron and steel) and the Larios (textiles), placed Málaga at the forefront of Spanish industrial development with the establishment of their factories here, resulting in the growth of a large manufacturing and working-class district to the west of the city. The recession at the end of the 19C brought about a sudden change of fortunes, sinking the city into a period of decline that was to last until the end of the 1950s, when tourism breathed new life into the local economy.

ROMAN AND MOORISH QUARTER

★**Alcazaba** ⊘ – Construction of the Moorish fortress on a hill overlooking the city was started in 1040. Today, it is one of the largest Muslim military installations to have been preserved in Spain, consisting of a double enclosure with rectangular towers. It formed part of the defensive system of the Moorish city, known as Malaka, and was connected to the surrounding walls, which have since disappeared. Access to the fortress is via a zigzag ramp which winds its way upwards from calle Alcazabilla and provides an attractive view of the whole complex with its broken sections of brick and masonry walls ascending the hill. The pleasant walkway passes through fortified gateways, some of which used Roman columns and capitals in their construction. The Arco de Cristo (Christ's Arch), where the first mass was celebrated immediately after the reconquest of the city, leads to the Moorish gardens, embellished with bougainvillaea, jasmine and honeysuckle. The **views**★ from the top of the walls take in the city and port.

★**Museo Arqueológico** ⊘ – *Under restoration*. The Archeological Museum is housed in the former palace, inside the second enclosure. The palace, Nasrid in style, is ordered around two patios and displays objects from Prehistory to the Middle Ages. Particularly outstanding are the exhibits dedicated to Roman (busts, a gigantic foot, mosaics etc) and, above all, Moorish art from the 10C to the 15C, most of which were discovered within the fortress. The museum also contains scale models of both the Alcazaba and the cathedral.

The walls and towers of the Alcazaba

Roman theatre – The remains of the Roman theatre *(teatro romano)* stand at the foot of the Alcazaba, on its west side, and bear witness to the importance of the Romans in the history of Málaga. The terraces of the cavea, which made use of the slope of the hill, are all that is left of this impressive theatre.

Close by stands the former **Aduana** (Customs House), built in neo-Classical style. The building now houses the seat of the provincial parliament.

Castillo de Gibralfaro – *Access: bus no 35. Alight at the paseo del Parque*. The remains of the 14C Gibralfaro Castle sit on a hill behind the Alcazaba, overlooking the city. The path around the broken walls provides magnificent **views**★★ of the Alcazaba, the city and the port. The walled corridor connecting the Alcazaba with the castle was built in the 14C.

View of the city and port from the Castillo de Gibralfaro

CITY CENTRE

Although the centre of Málaga has a number of interesting monuments dating from the Christian era, it has also preserved some delightful narrow streets and alley-ways – many of which are now closed to traffic – with an unmistakable Moorish air, such as the typical **pasaje Chinitas**. This lively shopping area is concentrated around **calle Marqués de Larios**, the city's main street.

★**Cathedral** ⊙ – Construction began in the 16C but was only completed in the 18C, hence the evident mix of architectural styles. Although the Renaissance influence predominates, the ground plan is Gothic and the ceilings and façade Baroque. It is thought that the design is the work of Diego de Siloé, the architect who was also responsible for Granada Cathedral.

Exterior – The main façade, fronting plaza del Obispo, is Baroque. It comprises two towers, one of which (on the right) is unfinished, hence the popular nickname of "La Manquita" (The Missing One), and three portals, created using different coloured marble with a clear decorative function in mind. On the middle portal, which is flanked by Solomonic columns, admire the relief of the Incarnation, after which the cathedral is named.

Interior – *Entry through the garden, on the left side of the cathedral.* Attention is immediately drawn to the monumental proportions of the interior, which consists of a hall-church ground plan with three aisles, side chapels and an ambulatory. In order to solve the problem of how to support the lofty naves, a novel solution was reached: namely the superimposing of supports, whereby sections of entablature supporting an upper tier of columns was placed above a lower section of pillars with engaged columns and Corinthian capitals. The naves are crowned by fine **oven vaulting**★ bearing attractive decoration. The choir contains some handsome 17C **stalls**★, partly carved by Pedro de Mena. Note also the two magnificent 18C Baroque organs and the 17C marble pulpits, decorated with ecclesiastical escutcheons. The tabernacle at the high altar dates from the 19C.

The **side chapels** also feature several works of interest: in the Epistle nave, the Capilla de los Caídos displays a fine *Dolorosa* by Pedro de Mena at the feet of a *Christ Crucified* by Alonso de Mena, both dating from the 17C; while the Capilla del Rosario is presided over by a huge canvas of the *Virgin of the Rosary* by Alonso Cano.

In the **ambulatory**, the Capilla de Nuestra Señora de los Reyes boasts a *Virgin and Child*, a gift from the Catholic Monarchs following their reconquest of the city, which is accompanied by a sculpture of its benefactors, a work by Pedro de Mena; the Capilla de Santa Bárbara houses an impressive early 15C carved and painted **Gothic retable**★; while the 18C Capilla de la Encarnación – also known as the Capilla del Sagrario (Sacrarium Chapel) – is an axial chapel created entirely from marble with four monumental agate columns.

El Sagrario ⊙ – This unusual 16C rectangular church stands in the gardens of the cathedral. Its outstanding external feature is the Isabelline Gothic **side portal**★ (giving onto calle Santa María), with its fine sculptural detail and superb technique.

The single-nave Baroque interior dates from the 18C, the century in which the church was remodelled. The superb sculpted **altarpiece**★★ in the apse is Mannerist in style and crowned by an impressive Calvary.

Ajoblanco

If you happen to be in Málaga in summer, make sure you try fried fish *(pescaíto frito)*, as well as one of the city's traditional dishes, *ajoblanco*, a local variant of *gazpacho*. The ingredients for this refreshing chilled soup include almonds, garlic, breadcrumbs, salt and olive oil. It is normally served with Moscatel grapes.

Palacio Episcopal – The city's Bishop's Palace stands on plaza del Obispo. This 18C Baroque building has a beautiful pink and grey marble doorway adorned with Corinthian columns and broken entablatures. The upper niche houses a *pietà*.

Iglesia de Santiago ⊙ – The Church of St James is situated along the narrow calle Granada, close to the plaza de la Merced. It was founded after the Reconquest and preserves from this époque a brick tower in primitive Mudéjar style with *sebka* decoration on its second section, and a portal, now sealed off, adorned with geometric *lacería* motifs. The 18C Baroque interior houses the venerated statue of **Jesus the Rich** in a chapel off the Evangelist nave; this sculpture takes its name from the wooden and silver cross supporting it. The main altarpiece is also Baroque. Pablo Picasso was baptised in this church.

Plaza de la Merced – An obelisk in memory of General Torrijos and his men, who were executed in 1831 for defending liberal ideas, stands in the centre of this square. Two identical buildings provide harmony to the northeast side of the square; one of these was the birthplace of Picasso.

Museo-Casa Natal Picasso ⊙ – The artist was born at no 15, a mid-19C building which is now a museum dedicated to this famous *malagueño*. The first floor contains a number of his drawings as well as a collection of ceramics. The remainder of the building is occupied by the offices of the Pablo Ruiz Picasso Foundation and a room dedicated to temporary exhibitions.

Palacio de los Condes de Buenavista – This sober, yet elegant 16C Renaissance palace will shortly house the new **Museo Picasso** *(opening scheduled in 2001)*.

Iglesia de los Mártires ⊙ – The church, founded in the 15C, is situated in a pedestrianised area of narrow streets lined by small shops.

The simple exterior conceals an exuberant Baroque interior created as part of restoration work carried out in the 18C. It comprises three aisles with side chapels and transept arms in the shape of an apse. An entablature with a small balcony encircles the whole church. The walls and ceilings are adorned with stuccowork, yet it is in the presbytery and transept that the most exuberant decoration is concentrated. The high altar is dominated by an altarpiece with a small chapel *(camarín)* housing the statues of St Paula and St Cyriacus, the city's patrons. An enormous coat of arms crowns the ensemble. Along calle Mártires, a small square close to the church displays a typical **Christ of the Lanterns**.

Museo de Artes y Costumbres Populares ⊙ – The city's Museum of Popular Arts and Traditions is housed in an attractive 17C inn, the Mesón de la Victoria, and provides an insight into the traditional rural and urban life of the province. The museum's rooms are arranged around a delightful patio.

The **ground floor** is devoted to exhibits of farming equipment, ironwork, bread-making, fishing and the production of oil and wine, and includes a reproduction of a typical kitchen and country dining room. On the **first floor**, the collection of clay figurines representing typical local characters is particularly fascinating. Also worthy of note are the ex-

> ### Beaches
> Málaga is blessed with a series of beaches to the east of the city from La Malagueta, at one end of the promenade, and Las Acacias, to the Playa del Palo, 5km/3mi further east. All these beaches have excellent facilities and are lined by a wide choice of bars and restaurants.

hibits of 19C bourgeois objects and furniture, traditional farming implements, local arts and crafts, household ceramic items, lace etc.

Mercado Central – Málaga's main market is an iron structure built in the 19C on the site of the former Moorish dockyards. The entrance arch from the original building is still standing today.

Paseo del Parque – This extensive stretch of greenery is a verdant botanical garden and a haven of peace and quiet amid the hustle and bustle of the surrounding streets. The plants and trees grown here, most of which are tropical or sub-tropical species, all display their name and place of origin.

In the **paseo de la Farola**, which connects with the paseo del Parque at its eastern end and skirts alongside the port, stands the **statue of the Cenachero**, a popular local figure and itinerant fish seller who is one of the symbols of Málaga. The La Malagueta quarter beyond heralds the start of the city's beach area.

ADDITIONAL SIGHTS

★**Santuario de la Virgen de la Victoria** ⊙ – *At the end of calle Compás de la Victoria*. The sanctuary was founded by the Catholic Monarchs in the 15C and rebuilt two centuries later. The church has a simple brick exterior with a portico and belfry, and an interior which is a fine example of restrained Andalucian Baroque with plant motif adornments on a number of architectural features. The single nave is flanked by side chapels, and is crowned with small galleries above the arches. Note the lamp-bearing angels which provide a complete contrast with the sobriety visible elsewhere in the church. The large 17C carved altarpiece narrates scenes from the life of St Francis of Paola, while a chapel in the Evangelist nave displays a highly expressive *Dolorosa* by Pedro de Mena. However, the two most outstanding features of the church are the small chapel *(camarín)* behind the altarpiece, and the crypt, accessed via a Baroque staircase to the right of the transept.

The **camarín**★★, at the centre of the main altarpiece, is particularly ostentatious. This masterpiece of exuberant Baroque architecture is completely covered by stuccowork decoration featuring cherubs, acanthus leaves, mirrors, coats of arms etc. It is presided over by a fine Virgin and Child – a 15C statue of German provenance – offered as a gift by the Catholic Monarchs upon their reconquest of the city.

The **crypt**★, an extraordinary pantheon created to house the tombs of the Counts of Buenavista, could not be more sombre, with its black background festooned with skeletons and skulls – the symbols of death and the fleeting nature of life.

English cemetery (Cementerio inglés) – *Avenida Pries, 1*. The cemetery has the distinction of being the first Protestant burial ground to be created in Spain. It is set in a pleasant garden occupying an area ceded by the Governor of Málaga to the British consul in 1829. The renowned poet Jorge Guillén (1893-1984) is laid to rest in the cemetery.

EXCURSIONS

★**Finca de la Concepción** ⊘ – *7km/4.5mi north*. This magnificent garden was created in the middle of the 19C by an upper-class Málaga couple, Jorge Loring and Amalia Heredia. Heredia developed a substantial collection of tropical and sub-tropical species (now numbering over 300) which she arranged to have brought to Málaga on board the boats owned by her father, and which adapted perfectly to the local climate. A visit to the estate is quite delightful, offering visitors an opportunity to wander through a forest of greenery dissected by small streams and embellished with lakes, waterfalls and Roman remains. Alongside this palatial mansion stands an impressive iron arbour covered with wisteria, ivy and bougainvillaea.

B. Kaufmann/MICHELIN

Finca de la Concepción

★**El Retiro: ornithological park and historical garden** ⊘ – *15km/9.5mi southwest. Follow signs to the airport, then bear onto the A 366 close to it. Once past Churriana, turn right along a signposted road.* Children and adults alike will enjoy a visit to this handsome estate, founded in the 17C by a local bishop. The visit consists of two parts: the ornithological park and the historical garden.

The aviaries, containing some 150 exotic and Mediterranean species, are spread over a wide area in the shade of pine trees.

The **historical garden**★ is made up of several 17C and 18C gardens, the oldest of which is the kitchen garden, now home to a number of tropical species. To its left, note the six-spouted fountain, an unusual sundial and the stream. The most spectacular section of the garden is the French-influenced garden-court. The lion fountain is the source for a impressive **water staircase**, which brings to mind the garden of a Baroque palace. The patio-garden is also well worth visiting, with its parterres and Italian statues laid out around the Genoa fountain *(fuente de Génova)*.

Parque Natural de los Montes de Málaga

This park, situated just a few kilometres to the north of the city, covers an area of 4 900ha/12 108 acres of semi-mountainous landscape dissected by streams which have carved small valleys along their path. The typical vegetation here is predominantly Mediterranean with extensive repopulated woods of Aleppo pine. These plantations were created to prevent the flooding experienced by the city of Málaga over several centuries. The road to the park is dotted with viewpoints and roadside inns where visitors can enjoy the delicious local cuisine and wine.

MARBELLA★★

Málaga – Population 98 377
Michelin map 446 W 15

Hemmed in by the Mediterranean to the south and by the backdrop of the mountains to the north, Marbella is the centre of international tourism on the Costa del Sol. Its magnificent climate, superb beaches, wealth of leisure facilities and hundreds of thousands of annual visitors have transformed this fishing port into a summer playground. The seemingly endless mass of apartment blocks line the seafront, while more luxurious holiday complexes, with their impressive chalets, mansions and even palaces, extend inland. The city has developed a reputation as the most exclusive resort along the Costa del Sol, attracting famous visitors from the world of showbusiness, adding a further glamourous dimension to this jet-setting resort.

Despite its modern opulence, Marbella has still preserved its old quarter of whitewashed houses, their façades adorned with typical wrought-iron grilles and breathtaking displays of

If you are looking for a hotel, a restaurant, the best night-spots and shopping areas, or just somewhere for a quiet drink, consult the Travellers' addresses section under COSTA DEL SOL.

addresses

flowers. The town has become a shoppers' paradise, particularly for luxury goods, and over the past few years has developed a reputation for its health clubs and farms. Mention should also be made of the superb sporting facilities on offer in and around Marbella, particularly its golf courses, for which the area is famous. To further emphasize the cosmopolitan nature of this modern resort, Marbella has two mosques, a synagogue and a number of Protestant churches.

★OLD QUARTER *allow 2hr*

Marbella's old Moorish quarter has preserved its maze-like layout of narrow, twisting alleyways, in which the whitewashed façades of old buildings are now lined by a whole host of shops, bars and restaurants.

★**Plaza de los Naranjos** – This enchanting square, the heart of the town's old quarter, is the perfect setting to unwind at an outdoor café in front of the 16C stone fountain, delightful floral displays and orange trees *(naranjos)* that adorn it. The square is fronted by several interesting buildings such as the 16C **town hall**, with its wrought-iron balconies and handsome Mudéjar doorway, the 17C **Casa del Corregidor** (Magistrate's Mansion), with its monumental stone **façade★** and elegant balcony, and the 15C **Ermita de Nuestro Señor Santiago**, the first Christian church to be erected in Marbella.

Iglesia de Santa María de la Encarnación ⊙ – The church stands in the square of the same name, at the end of the busy calle Nueva, where one of the towers from the former Moorish castle can still be seen. This Baroque-style building has a splendid stone **portal** and a large bell-tower. The interior contains a carving of St Barnabas, the patron of Marbella, and a sumptuous organ, the **Órgano del Sol Mayor**.

Aerial view of the Plaza de los Naranjos

Y. Arthus-Bertrand/ALTITUDE

239

★**Museo del Grabado Español Contemporáneo** ⊘ – The town's Contemporary Spanish Print Museum is housed in a 16C building which was formerly the Hospital de Bazán. This small museum is the only one in Spain dedicated exclusively to 20C prints. The well-presented exhibits on display include works by renowned artists such as Tàpies, Alberti, Chillida and Maruja Mallo.

Hospital de San Juan de Dios – This large hospital in calle Misericordia was founded by the Catholic Monarchs. Its oustanding features are the pleasant cloisters and the noteworthy Mudéjar *artesonado* work in the chapel.

Seigniorial mansions – The majority of these elegant and graceful residences can be seen in plaza Ancha and plaza de Altamirano. Of particular interest are the Casa de los Cano Saldaña, an imposing 16C residence, and the houses which belonged to the wealthy landowner, Enrique Grivegnée, and to Fernando Lesseps, the engineer who designed the Suez Canal.

EXCURSIONS

Villa Romana de Río Verde – *2km/1.2mi west along the N 340*. This 1C-2C Roman villa has preserved some attractive mosaic paving.

★★**Puerto Banús** – *5km/3mi west along the N 340*. This superb marina is home to some of the world's finest sailing vessels. Alongside the moorings, where an impressive collection of fast cars can normally be seen, stands a huge array of bars, restaurants, antique shops and luxury boutiques. The marina is a popular tourist attraction along this stretch of coast, attracting huge numbers of visitors, particularly on summer evenings when it is teeming with people who come here to see and be seen, enjoy a drink or meal with friends and shop in the local boutiques which stay open until the early hours of the morning. During the day, especially outside of the main holiday season, Puerto Banús is a quiet and pleasant place for a stroll, with attractive views of the coast and nearby resorts.

Istán – *15km/9.5mi northwest along the MA 409. Head west out of Marbella and follow signposts*. This former Moorish village is nestled in the gorge of the Verde River. It stands in a fertile area of terraced fields of fruits and vegetables. Its most important monument is the Iglesia de San Miguel, a 16C church with an impressive belfry.

EXCURSIONS INLAND 51km/32mi north

Ojén – *9km/5.5mi north along the A 355*. This small whitewashed town is situated in the middle of a landscape dominated by orange and pine groves. The old Moorish quarter is spread at the foot of the **Iglesia de Nuestra Señora de la Encarnación**, a 15C church with a single nave and a fine *artesonado* ceiling. Ojén is famous for its local brandy *(aguardiente)*, which has been popularised in a traditional Andalucian ballad.

Refugio de Juanar – *Continue along the A 355, then bear left*. This refuge stands in a breathtaking setting with stunning **views**★ over the forests of the Sierra Blanca.

Monda – *Return to the A 355 and continue to Monda*. The village stands on the slope of a small hill and is sheltered beneath the remains of an old Moorish fortress. The main attraction in Monda is the **Iglesia de Santiago**, a 16C church subsequently modified in the 18C. The triple-nave interior is crowned by profusely decorated vaulting.

Where to stay in Monda

Castillo de Monda – ☎ *952 45 71 42* – *fax 952 45 73 36* – *23 rooms* – *16 000pts*. If you prefer to stay away from the resorts along the Costa del Sol, this magnificent hotel, situated on the summit of the Colina de Monda hill, is a delightful hideaway. It is housed in an 8C castle with exceptional views and rooms decorated with antique furniture.

Tolox – *23km/14.5mi northwest. Follow the MA 413, bear left onto the A 366, then continue along the MA 412*. Hidden between fields of citrus fruits, the village of Tolox has an impressive position in the Sierra de Tolox, within the boundaries of the **Parque Natural de Sierra de las Nieves**. The Moorish heart of the village is dominated by the outline of the 16C **Iglesia de San Miguel** ⊘, a church with three aisles separated by semicircular arches and topped by an attractive *artesonado* ceiling. The other interesting feature of the church is the elliptical roof above the presbytery, which is decorated with paintings.

The Fuente Amargosa spa, built in 1867 in an area of exceptional beauty, stands on the outskirts of Tolox.

MARCHENA

Sevilla – Population 18 018

Michelin map 446 T-U 13

This small town in the Sevillian countryside is at the heart of an area of great archeological interest boasting a number of settlements dating back to the Bronze Age. The Moors left their imprint on the town, which enjoyed its period of greatest splendour in the 15C and 16C, under the Dukes of Arcos.

SIGHTS

Arco de la Rosa – This 15C arch was a gateway which punctuated the walls surrounding the town. It consists of a horseshoe arch framed by two rectangular bastions. Note the old section of wall still standing next to it.

★★ **Iglesia de San Juan Bautista** – The Church of John the Baptist was built in the 15C in Gothic-Mudéjar style. It fronts a pleasant square with several seigniorial doorways. The sober façade is crowned by a bell-tower topped by a spire bearing *azulejo* decoration.

The **interior** comprises five aisles: the three central ones have *artesonado* ceilings, while the two side aisles – extensions which were added during the 16C – are covered by arris vaults. The most surprising feature of the interior is the quality and quantity of **works of art** adorning the walls.

In the presbytery, an outstanding, sumptuously carved and painted **retable**★★★ narrating scenes from the life of Christ is a work created in the early 16C, with paintings by Alejo Fernández and sculptural groups by his brother, Jorge. The 16C **grille** enclosing the high altar is a work by a local workshop. The wrought-iron pulpits are 18C, as is the impressive **grille** in front of the choir. The magnificent mahogany and cedar **choir stalls**★ were carved in the 18C by Jerónimo de Balbás; male saints are represented in the upper choir, while the busts of female saints can be seen in small medallions in the upper part of the lower choir. The church's two organs, one Rococo, the other neo-Classical, stand on either side of the choir.

Iglesia de San Juan Bautista

The Capilla del Sagrario, a chapel to the left of the presbytery, is presided over by a magnificent 16C **carved retable**★★ by Roque Balduque and Jerónimo Hernández. Note the unusual arrangement of the Last Supper at its centre.

The church also contains several noteworthy statues, including an *Immaculate Conception* by Pedro de Mena *(the first chapel in the Epistle nave)* and a *St Joseph and Child (the chapel to the right of the apse)*; it is known that the figure of St Joseph at least is a work by Pedro Roldán.

★★ **Museo Zurbarán** ⊙ – *Entry through the church.* The canvases displayed were commissioned for the church sacristy and date from almost the same period as those in the Monasterio de Guadalupe, in the province of Cáceres. Nine canvases by this masterful Baroque artist (1598-1664) are exhibited in the museum: Christ, the Immaculate Conception, St Peter, St James, John the Evangelist, John the Baptist, St Paul, St Andrew and St Bartholomew. The church's monstrance and several choir books from the museum's collection are also displayed.

An interesting collection of 16C and 17C embroidery and silverware is exhibited in a separate room.

Head up to the highest part of the town.

Plaza Ducal – This square occupies the site of the former castle parade ground. It is lined by the 18C former town hall with its sober stone doorway.

Nearby, the remains of the castle can be seen, some of which are well preserved and others in ruins. Pass through the Arco de la Alcazaba, an arch dating from the 11C.

Iglesia de Santa María la Mayor or Iglesia de la Mota – The church was built within the confines of the ducal palace. It is a sombre Gothic-Mudéjar construction which was later modified, as can be seen on the tower. The façade consists of a single trumpet-shaped doorway with jagged decoration.

Other interesting buildings in the vicinity include the **Iglesia de San Agustín**, a church built during the transition from Baroque to neo-Classical, and the **Puerta de Morón**, a large fortified tower that now houses the Tourist Office and a museum dedicated to a local sculptor.

EXCURSIONS

Paradas – *8km/5mi southwest along the SE 217*. Paradas owes its name to its function as a stopping-point *(parada)* for caravans travelling to Sevilla during the Middle Ages. The main attraction of this small town is the **Iglesia de San Eutropio**, whose **museum** ○ contains an interesting collection of religious gold and silverware, illuminated books, and an outstanding *Magdalena* by El Greco.

El Arahal – *15km/9.5mi southwest along the SE 217*. This tranquil town of Moorish origin has conserved an attractive old quarter where small whitewashed houses stand alongside elegant Baroque and neo-Classical buildings. The Capilla de la Vera Cruz, an 18C chapel built in colonial style, is particularly worthy of note, as are three churches: the Mudéjar Iglesia de Nuestra Señora de la Victoria; the 17C **Iglesia de Santa María Magdalena**, with its fine set of choral books and various pieces of silverware; and the **Iglesia de San Roque**, containing several 18C altarpieces in its side chapels and at the main altar.

Morón de la Frontera – *27km/17mi south. Follow the A 364 to Montepalacio, then bear onto the A 361*. Morón de la Frontera is an agricultural town extending around the ruins of a Moorish castle, with a military base nearby. Of interest are the **Iglesia de San Miguel**, a Gothic church with a neo-Classical portal and an interior with decorative 18C Baroque features; the **Iglesia de San Ignacio**, also known as the Iglesia de la Compañía due to its construction by the Jesuit order, housing an outstanding set of Flemish canvases; and the 16C **Iglesia de San Francisco**, a Renaissance church containing several paintings by the artist **José Ribera**, "El Españoleto".

MARTOS
Jaén – Population 22 391
Michelin map 446 S 18

Martos extends across a hill amid a typical landscape of endless olive groves, upon which the local economy is entirely based. This former Iberian settlement of *Tucci* was used by their leader, Viriatus, as a winter camp in 142 BC. A little over a century later, in 27 BC, Augustus transformed it into a colony for veteran legionnaires; in the early days of Christianity, the town was the seat of a bishopric. Following five centuries of Arab domination, Martos was finally reconquered in 1225 by Fernando III the Saint, and was later ceded to the Order of Calatrava.
The town has preserved its picturesque old quarter with delightful street corners and narrow winding streets. A number of 15C and 17C ancestral homes are also dotted around Martos, giving the town an elegant and seigniorial air. The main shopping area is situated in and around plaza Fuente de la Villa.

Plaza de la Constitución – This graceful square at the heart of the old quarter is fronted by the Iglesia de Santa Marta and the town hall.

Iglesia de Santa Marta ○ – The church was built after the Christian Reconquest in Gothic-Mudéjar style, but was heavily restored in the 16C by the architect Francisco del Castillo. A handsome, Isabelline **portal** adorns the façade, while the sober interior has a hall-church ground plan with impressive monumental pillars linked by plaster-adorned arches.

Town Hall – The town's former prison is an interesting late-16C Renaissance building. Its outstanding architectural feature is the main façade, with an elegant portico of semicircular arches and a balcony adorned with reliefs.

Fortaleza de la Virgen de la Villa – This fortress rises on a steep hill on the outskirts of the town. Only two towers – the keep and the Torre de Almedina – remain from the original structure, although these imposing defensive bulwarks provide a clear idea of the size of the fortress in its prime.

★**Fuente Nueva** – This large 16C Renaissance fountain stands in a park close to the bullring *(plaza de toros)*, at the end of a wide shopping street. The work is by the sculptor Francisco del Castillo and clearly shows the influence of the Italian architect Vignola. It consists of three raised sections in the centre of which appears the town's coat of arms.

Calle Real – Modernist buildings provide a contrast to the older buildings in this street which include the large fortified tower, originally part of the defensive walls, and the Iglesia de las Madres Trinitarias, a Baroque church built in the 18C but damaged during the Spanish Civil War.

Iglesia de San Francisco – The elegant colonial-style portal is the oldest feature of the Church of St Francis.

Iglesia de Santa María de la Villa – Only the monumental four-storey tower remains from the original 13C church.

EXCURSIONS

Torredonjimeno – *7km/4.5mi north.* The centre of this agricultural town, with its well-kept whitewashed houses, is dissected by the two main roads running through it. If approaching from Martos, the modern town stands to the left, with the historical quarter to the right.
Torredonjimeno is renowned for its wrought-iron work – the town has the only bell foundry still in existence in Andalucia – and a local dish known as *encebollado*, a stew of cod, tomatoes, onions, garlic and herbs.

Old quarter – The main buildings in this part of town are the **town hall**, a 16C Renaissance edifice fronting plaza de la Constitución; the 16C **Iglesia de San Pedro**, a Renaissance church displaying the occasional Mudéjar feature; the **castle**, built in the 13C over a former Roman and Visigothic fortress; and the **Iglesia de Santa María**, a church built in the

> ### The treasure of Torredonjimeno
>
> In 1931, farmworkers discovered a chest full of valuable objects from the Visigothic period in the local area. The "Treasure of Torredonjimeno", as it has become known, is now on display in the archeological museums of Madrid and Barcelona.

16C in Gothic style, the slender silhouette of which rises above the houses in the square of the same name. An inscription at the entrance to the church confirms that it was the first place of worship to be dedicated to the Immaculate Conception.

Ermita de Nuestra Señora de la Consolación – This Renaissance-style hermitage on the outskirts of town is a popular destination for several lively pilgrimages and *romerías*.

MEDINA SIDONIA★

Cádiz – Population 10 872
Michelin map 446 W 12

Medina Sidonia stands in fertile countryside at the centre of Cádiz province, at a natural crossroads between the coast and the Andalucian hinterland, close to the **Parque Natural de los Alcornocales**. The town occupies a strategic elevated site, from where, on clear days, it is possible to make out **El Puerto de Santa María** and **Vejer de la Frontera** in the distance. Its name has evolved from two key periods in the town's history: the first under the Phoenicians; the second during the Moorish occupation of the region. The Phoenicians referred to their settlement here as Assido, while the Moors, who conquered the town in 712, named it Medina (city). Medina Sidonia was an important Roman

> ### EATING OUT
>
> **Machín** – *Plaza de la Iglesia Mayor* – ☎ *956 41 13 47 – closed Mon evenings.* Next to the **tourist office**. A terrace restaurant with views of the valley. Specialities include asparagus omelette *(tortilla de espárragos)* and braised oxtail *(rabo de toro)*.

town and the seat of one of the first Visigothic councils, the Assidonensis, in the 6C. Alfonso X the Wise reconquered it in the 13C, and in 1430 Juan II handed the town over as a dukedom to the Guzmán family. The seventh Duke of Medina Sidonia has gone down in history as the commander of the fateful Spanish Armada.

SIGHTS

★**Roman remains** ⊘ – The extraordinary system of over 30m/100ft of underground galleries formed part of the water system built by Roman engineers in the 1C AD. Although this network was discovered by chance in 1963, excavation of the site only began in 1991. It offers a glimpse of a typical Roman sewage system, with a main channel covered by a barrel-vaulted ceiling and the original tegular flooring, into which water from other, smaller galleries would be channelled. A series of cryptoporticoes (a Roman construction whose function was to raise and level out the terrain) has also been unearthed on the same site.

Medieval town

Climb calle Espíritu Santo as far as the Arco de la Pastora.

Arco de la Pastora – Along with the Arco del Sol and the **Arco de Belén**, this is one of the three gateways that have been preserved from the medieval period. Built in the 10C, it consists of a double, pointed horseshoe arch supported by two sturdy marble columns, probably Phoenician in origin.

★**Iglesia Santa María la Mayor, la Coronada** ⊘ – This fine example of so-called aristocratic Gothic architecture dates from the late 15C, although the tower was completed in 1623 in Baroque style. The present church stands above an earlier one which, in turn, was built over an Arab mosque. Access to the church is via a patio displaying strong Mudéjar influence which was part of the earlier church. The interior has a Latin cross ground plan with three aisles crowned by pointed vaults, with the exception of the transept and apse, where profusely decorated star vaulting is employed. Note the impressive **Plateresque retable**★ at the high altar by Roque Boldaque, Juan Bautista Vázquez and Melchor de Turín, depicting scenes from the life of Jesus and the Virgin Mary, with the mystery of the coronation as its central theme. To the left of the high altar stands the 17C statue of Nuestra Señora de la Paz (Our Lady of Peace), the town's patron saint. A monstrance created from Mexican silver by Martínez Montañés can be admired in the chapel to the right of the transept. Upon leaving the church, note the Plateresque doorway leading to the patio.

Alcázar and old town ⊘ – The former Moorish fortress *(alcazaba)* originally occupied the site which was transformed into a fortified Christian palace *(alcázar)* in 1264. The medieval district in which it stands was inhabited until the 16C, when it was abandoned and used as a quarry. At its zenith, it consisted of a triple walled enclosure from which several towers, an angled access gateway (a typical Almohad feature), various 16C houses and an interesting series of silos have been preserved. The entrance to this enclosure is guarded by the **Torre de Doña Blanca**, a turret which nowadays offers visitors an excellent view of the delicate cresting on the 16C church.

A tradition of pastries

Since Moorish times, Medina Sidonia has been famous for its delicious cakes, including the ever-popular **alfajor** – a type of macaroon made with almonds, eggs and honey – *tortas parda*s and *amarguillos*. Pastries can be purchased from the following convents:

Convento de Jesús, María y José – In the **medieval town**, behind Santa María (*alfajores* and *tortas pardas*). Daily from 9.30am to 12.15pm and 4.30pm to 6.15pm.

Convento de San Cristóbal – Calle Hércules, 1. This convent is situated in the **modern town**, behind the municipal market (*alfajores*, *amarguillos* and *tortas pardas*).

Modern Town

Cross the threshold of the 15C **Arco de Belén** (Bethlehem Arch) and wander through streets lined with whitewashed houses to the Medina Sidonia of the 16C to 19C.

Plaza de España – This triangular *plaza* in the centre of Medina is fronted on one side by the neo-Classical 18C **town hall**.

The nearby municipal **market**, built in 1871, is well worth visiting for its interesting architecture. To the side, the plaza de la Cruz is fronted by a late-17C Baroque church, the Iglesia de la Victoria.

Calle de Fray Félix★, or calle de la Loba as it is also known, is lined by 18C and 19C houses adorned with charming balconies and superb wrought-iron work. Outside of the walls, the 16C Iglesia de Santiago, with its fine *artesonado*, is also worthy of note.

EXCURSIONS

Ermita de los Santos Mártires Justo y Pastor ⊘ – *On the ring road on the out-skirts of Medina Sidonia.*
Founded by the bishop Pimenio in the year 630, this hermitage is one of the oldest churches in Andalucia, with a large medieval tower which is said to be Roman in origin. The interior is of singular beauty and simplicity, in which Roman features have been reused to create stelae and capitals.

Castillo de Gigonza – *4km/2.5mi north of Paterna de Rivera.* Only the keep has been preserved from this former Moorish castle.

Alcalá de los Gazules – *25km/15.5mi east along the A 381*. Alcalá appears as a splash of white on top of a hill. This small town, whose name refers to the Moorish castle *(alcalá)* that existed here until the 19C and of which only scant remains are still visible, is the gateway to the **Parque Natural de los Alcornocales**. Several buildings of note occupy the upper section of the town, including the **Iglesia de San Jorge**, with its 18C Baroque tower and Gothic façade with a representation of St George (San Jorge) on horseback above the tympanum. The 16C former **town hall** is now home to a park visitor centre, the **Centro de Interpretación del Parque Natural de los Alcornocales** ⊙, providing a wealth of information on possible excursions through this delightful protected area. The climb up to **El Picacho** and the Ruta de los Molinos (Route of the Windmills) are two of the most popular excursions from Alcalá.

Benalup – *20km/12.5mi southeast of Medina Sidonia along the A 393*. This small village has gone down in history as the site of the **Casas Viejas** incident *(see p 33)*, the name by which Benalup was previously known. In 1933, a group of anarchists disenchanted mainly with the limited success of agrarian reforms, surrounded the town. The rebellion was brutally repressed by the government under **Azaña** and was one of the catalysts behind the rise to power of the republican right in the 1934 elections.

Cueva del Tajo de las Figuras ⊙ – *8km/5mi south of Benalup along the CA 212 towards Algeciras. The caves are on the left-hand side of the road*. These caves, declared a National Monument in 1924, contain an interesting set of wall paintings which are thought to date from the post-Paleolithic period.

MIJAS★

Málaga – Population 37 490
Michelin map 446 W 16

This picturesque town, occupying an impressive position on one of the many hills of the Sierra de Mijas, stands amid a landscape of pine groves offering stunning **views**★ of the Costa del Sol. Its winding streets, charming nooks and crannies, flower-decked houses and numerous tiny squares all contribute to Mijas' popularity with thousands of annual visitors, who come here to admire its superb architecture and purchase its renowned pottery, basketwork and woven goods. A number of excellent local golf courses add to its appeal with foreign visitors.

The donkey taxi – This unusual form of transport is the most frequently used by visitors to the town. Although these colourfully decked-out animals travel at a less than breakneck pace, they are a popular aspect of local life.

Santuario de la Virgen de la Peña ⊙ – *At the entrance to the town*. This sanctuary was excavated out of the rock by an order of monks in the 16C. The hermitage, dedicated to the town's patron saint, the Virgin of the Rock, has an attractive **mirador** known as El Compás, providing visitors with delightful views of the valley and the Mediterranean.

★**Old quarter** – This district, a photographer's paradise, is made up of a small network of bright streets lined by low-roofed houses decorated with artistic wrought-iron balconies and grilles. The majority of the town's boutiques and souvenir shops can be found in calle de Charcones, calle de San Sebastián and calle de Málaga.

Walls – Sections of the old Moorish walls, part of a fortified defensive perimeter, can still be seen dotted around the town.

R. Mattès

A donkey taxi

Iglesia de la Inmaculada Concepción – The Church of the Immaculate Conception was erected in the 16C on the site of the former Arab mosque and has preserved an imposing Mudéjar tower. One of the side chapels inside the church is adorned with attractive polychrome stuccowork adorned with plant motifs.

Iglesia de San Sebastián – Built in the 18C, this single-nave church is crowned by a cupola with internal Rococo stuccowork decoration.

Museo de Miniaturas ⊘ – The town's Miniatures Museum displays a number of interesting exhibits including *The Last Supper* by Leonardo da Vinci painted on a grain of rice.

Town Hall – The town hall houses a **museum** ⊘ of agricultural tools and other items relating to life on the land.

Plaza de Toros – Despite its relatively small size, the town's bullring has an unusual rectangular design and is home to a **bullfighting museum** ⊘ *(museo taurino)*.

MINAS DE RIOTINTO★★
Huelva – Population 5 500
Michelin map 446 S 10

This small community is at the heart of an area with a mining tradition dating back to Antiquity. The landscapes here are quite magnificent, characterised by breathtakings colours, forests of holm and cork oak, and the tranquil waters of the area's numerous reservoirs and lakes, such as Cobre-Gossan, Campofrío and Agua. Added to this is the impressive sight of excavated mountain slopes, deep-red in colour, which bear witness to man's intervention. The British district of Bellavista, the town's numerous arts and crafts centres, and a fine selection of *mesones* where visitors can try local specialities such as *migas* (breadcrumbs fried in olive oil and garlic, and traditionally served with grilled sardines), *gurumelos* (a local cep mushroom), *pestiños* (honeyed doughnuts), and a whole variety of pork-based products, add to the charm of Minas de Riotinto.

★★Parque Minero de Riotinto ⊘

This mining theme park lies within the town and in the surrounding area. It displays various pieces of equipment and machinery and allows visitors to take guided tours of the mines.

★Museo Minero y Ferroviario ⊘ – This recently built mining and railway museum occupying the former British hospital provides visitors with a comprehensive history of mining and metallurgy. Exhibits include several early-20C locomotives and the popular **Maharajah's carriage★★★**, built in Birmingham, England, for a journey to India by Queen Victoria. This work of art, brought here for a visit by Alfonso XIII, is a mass of carved wood and leather, creating an overall effect of great luxury. The museum also has on display a notable collection of exhibits which enable archeologists to date the mining history of the town to the Bronze Age.

★★★Corta Atalaya ⊘ – *2km/1.2mi northwest of the town.* This huge open-cast mine measuring over 1 000m/3 280ft in length, 900m/2 950ft wide and 350m/1 150ft deep is quite a sight. From the viewpoint to one side, the **views★★★** of the striated crater are quite exceptional, with the horizontal seams visible in the side of the rock, cut in perfect straight lines by the huge mining machinery. Additional mining facilities can be visited nearby, showing visitors how gossan (mineralised iron) is extracted before being subsequently transported in enormous vehicles capable of carrying goods weighing up to 200 000kg/485 000lb.

★★Cerro Colorado – *2.5km/1.5mi northwest of the town.* This open-cast mine is the second largest in Riotinto. It is an unusual red in colour and appears to twinkle in the late evening sun, creating a picture of unexpected beauty in this imposing landscape.

The impressive Corta Atalaya mine

★★Tourist train ◷ – The train departs from an old station on the outskirts of Rio-tinto and travels to Cerro Colorado. Two trips are possible, one 10km/6mi in length, the other covering a distance of 23km/14.5mi, both running parallel to the river along a railway line built at the end of the 19C by the British Río Tinto Company Limited to transport the mineral to Huelva for export to Great Britain. This enjoy-able journey in old-fashioned carriages offers surprises at every turn, including stunning glimpses of the reddy-coloured Tinto River as it winds its way through dense woods of oak, views of the very first stations built here, and the crossing of an impressive bridge, the Puente de Salomé, from where the views of the river and the surrounding area are quite spectacular.

Bellavista district – As in Huelva, this old district of Victorian-style houses was built at the beginning of the 20C to house the huge numbers of British workers employed by the Río Tinto Company. Although it is now uninhabited, a Presbyterian church, social club and cemetery with tombstones bearing English inscriptions are still standing.

The British in Riotinto

It is a strange sensation to discover the vestiges of Anglo-Saxon culture, so out of keeping with the character of the local population and landscape, in an isolated backwater such as Riotinto. It should be remembered, however, that at the beginning of the 20C, Britain had developed into a huge economic power, partly due to its colonial possessions and to the role played in this eco-nomic development by mining operations in outposts such as Riotinto.

ADDITIONAL SIGHTS

Necrópolis de la Dehesa ◷ – *3km/2mi north along the A 461*. This large Roman cemetery dating from the 2C AD was part of the Corta de Lago settlement. A number of tombs bearing funerary inscriptions and containing an interesting array of personal effects have enabled archeologists to ascertain the social class of those buried here.

Pozo Alfredo – *1km/0.6mi northwest of the town*. This underground mine, which is connected to Corta Atalaya, will in the near future be extended to a length of 600m/1 968ft. At present, only certain parts of this sizeable project can be visited.

EXCURSIONS

Nerva – *4km/2.5mi southeast along the A 478*. Nerva owes its name to a Roman tablet dedicated to the Emperor Nerva. The village stands in an almost lunar land-scape, where the mass of mining rubble and debris infringes upon the borders of the reddy-coloured water, producing an acrid, sulphur-like odour.

Zalamea la Real – *12km/8mi southwest. Follow the A 461, then bear onto the N 435 after El Campillo.* The **road**★★ winds its way across mountain spurs, passing along its route the attractive Cobre-Gossan Reservoir *(embalse)*. Upon reaching Zalamea, a village renowned for its anise-flavoured liqueurs, it is well worth visiting the Iglesia de Nuestra Señora de la Asunción and the El Pozuelo dolmen.

Valverde del Camino – *45km/28mi southwest. Follow the A 461, then bear onto the N 435 after El Campillo.* This small community is famous for its shoe-making, which includes the manufacture of walking shoes and boots and footwear for dancers.

Shoe-making

One of the prized souvenirs to be purchased on a trip to the Sierra de Aracena, and to Valverde del Camino in particular, is a pair of leather boots or shoes. A number of local workshops still produce this high-quality footwear to exacting standards.

MOGUER ★

Huelva – Population 11 000

Michelin map 446 U 9

The beautiful town of Moguer stands on a hill on the left bank of the Tinto River, its quiet avenues lined by elegant Gothic and Baroque seigniorial houses under the clear light of the Huelva sky. Along with many places in this area, Moguer is on the so-called "Columbus Route", famous for its association with the great adventurer who set off on his voyage of discovery from the nearby port of Palos de la Frontera. Today, the town's main income is derived from fishing and agriculture; it is also famous as the birthplace of the illustrious poet and 1956 Nobel prizewinner, **Juan Ramón Jiménez** (1881-1958), whose verses adorn attractive *azulejo* panelling dotted around the town centre. Moguer was also the home town of the Niño brothers, who played an active part in Columbus's voyage of discovery. No description of Moguer is complete without mention of its gastronomic speciality, the popular *pastelillos*, a sweet made from almond paste and candied fruit.

★**Monasterio de Santa Clara** ⊙ – This 14C building, Gothic-Mudéjar in style, is one of the most important monasteries in Huelva province. It has a strong connection with the history of the Discoveries for it was here that Columbus prayed on the morning of 16 March 1493, in so doing fulfilling a promise made on the high seas when one of the three caravels accompanying him experienced difficulties during a severe storm. The interior, occupied since 1955 by an order of Conceptionist nuns, is made up of a series of monastic rooms and porticoed patios with elegant balconies, attractive orange trees and even several banana trees as a reminder of the exotic latitudes explored by Columbus. The buttressed façade of the convent fronts the **plaza de Portocarrero**, one of Moguer's most attractive squares.

Church – This simply designed church with three aisles crowned by pointed vaulting houses the **tombs of the Portocarrero family**★, the lords of Moguer. This work, one of the most outstanding examples of the Andalucian Renaissance style, was carved in Carrara marble by Giacomo, Michelangelo's master. Note also the interesting 16C main altarpiece, a fine 17C carved depiction of the Immaculate Conception, and the superb set of **tombs**★ at the high altar, including that of Beatriz de Henríquez, who partly financed the voyage of discovery.

Cloisters – This tranquil area enclosed by galleries of pointed arches is surrounded by various buildings with different functions, including the former infirmary – a large room containing priests' vestments from the 16C to 18C – and the store-room, which nowadays houses objects belonging to diocesan bishops, a 16C Gothic carving, and a skullcap worn by Pope John Paul II.

Choir and antechoir – The choir, separated from the rest of the church by a grille, has some quite exceptional 14C **Nasrid-Mudéjar choir stalls**★★. Through the use of a refined technique, the arms of these magnificently carved stalls depict the lions of the Alhambra, while the heraldic coat of arms of each nun adorns the seat backs. A small confessional box can be seen to the right. The antechoir has a fine Mudéjar-style *artesonado* ceiling and contains several 15C books of Gregorian chants in protective glass cases.

Iglesia de Nuestra Señora de la Granada – This 18C church was erected above an earlier Mudéjar temple. It stands opposite the plaza del Marqués, a pleasant square with old lamp posts and façades adorned with polychrome glazed windows. Besides the carving of Nuestra Señora de la Granada, protected by a baldaquin in the middle of the presbytery, admire also the **bell-tower**★, the only remaining vestige of the earlier church. The tower calls to mind the Giralda in Sevilla and is Moguer's principal landmark.

> ### Juan Ramón Jiménez, the 1956 Nobel prizewinner for literature
>
> It is often said that there were two sides to the character of this famous poet, who was a contemporary of Federico García Lorca: on the one hand he was a cultured poet, and on the other a straight-forward and passionate popular writer. All the bitterness and anger he used to attack his literary peers of the time evaporated when he wrote enthusiastically about the inhabitants of Moguer, its customs and its typical vocabulary.

★**Calle Andalucía** – This pedestrianised street running from plaza del Cabildo, in front of the town hall, to the **Archivo Histórico Municipal y Biblioteca Iberoamericana** ⊘ (Historical Archives and Ibero-American Library), containing a precious collection of old documents, is one of the most attractive parts of Moguer. Several buildings of note line the street: the **Teatro Felipe Godínez**, a modern theatre with a handsomely decorate façade of Sevillian *azulejos*; the chapel of the Hospital del Corpus Christi; the unusual **pasaje de Nuestra Señora de la Esperanza**, a passageway of typical houses which have retained their typical old appearance; and the Convento de San Francisco.

Convento de San Francisco ⊘ – This 15C convent, built under the initiative of Pedro Portocarrero, played an important role in the evangelisation of the New World. It has preserved a noteworthy Mannerist cloisters, a 17C belfry, as well as an interesting 18C Baroque main altarpiece inside the church.

★**Casa-Museo "Zenobia y Juan Ramón"** ⊘ – This elegant two-storey house with balconies embellished with typical Andalucian grilles was the home of the poet Juan Ramón Jiménez and his wife Zenobia. It has been transformed into a musem *(museo)* displaying photographs, furniture, books and other items relating to the life of this Nobel prizewinner.

Casa Natal de Juan Ramón Jiménez ⊘ – The birthplace *(casa natal)* of this illustrious poet can be seen in calle Ribera. Today, it is used as the setting for important literary contests.

Town Hall – This impressive construction dominates the picturesque plaza del Cabildo, with its palm trees, wrought-iron benches and old lamp posts. The building is a fine example of civil Renaissance architecture by the Italian Tommaso Bottani. The handsome two-storey porticoed **façade**★, with fine wood *artesonado* work and galleries comprising five semicircular arches, is adorned with Doric columns on its lower section and Ionic columns on its upper tier.

MOJÁCAR★

Almería – Population 4 525
Michelin map 446 U 24

This enchanting whitewashed town, inhabited since Antiquity, enjoys a superb **setting**★ on a rocky promontory offering delightful views of the Mediterranean just 2km/1.2mi to the east and the unusual rocky formations dotted around its surrounding plain.

The old quarter of Mojácar, rising up the hillside, has preserved its unmistakable Moorish character, with its narrow, cobbled streets lined by whitewashed houses adorned with colourful floral arrangements, and dotted with charming courtyards. The town was only reconquered by the Christians in 1488.

Over the past few decades, a significant foreign community, particularly from northern Europe, has settled here, giving Mojácar a cosmopolitan feel. The many small restaurants, outdoor cafés and craft shops are the other main attractions of the town, which receives tens of thousands of visitors every year, particularly during the summer months.

TOWN

Leave your car in the lower part of town and continue up on foot.

The beauty of Mojácar mainly resides in the charm of its well-maintained popular architecture and its superb vistas. It is an ideal town in which to wander aimlessly, with surprising discoveries at every turn.

The best starting point is the pleasant **plaza Nueva**, fronted by the 18C Ermita de Nuestra Señora de los Dolores, a former chapel which has now been converted into a shop. The mirador on the square is the perfect vantage point from which to admire the surrounding area. At the foot of the mirador, the remains of Mojácar la Vieja, the town's first area of settlement, can be seen on top of a hill.

The cuesta del Castillo, a street to the left of the square, heads up to the **castle mirador**; nothing is now left of the castle, although the views of the coast are well worth the climb.

The calle de la Iglesia to the right of plaza Nueva leads to the **Iglesia de Santa María**, its ochre-coloured walls standing out against the swathe of white of the houses around it. Built after the Reconquest, it has a fortress-like appearance with solid walls, a bell-tower to one side, and buttresses on the other. Several picturesque narrow streets surround the church.

WHERE TO STAY

MID-RANGE

El Puntazo – *Paseo del Mediterráneo* – ☎ *950 47 82 65* – *fax 950 47 82 85* – *59 rooms* – *8 000pts*. This white-fronted hotel by the sea offers a choice of three types of room: the smallest, without a terrace or views cost 6 880pts; medium-sized rooms with sea views are priced at 8 000pts; while the largest rooms with a terrace overlooking the Mediterranean cost 10 900pts. Rooms at the nearby **Virgen del Mar** (☎ 950 47 22 22), a hotel of equivalent standard, are priced at 10 850pts.

Mamabel's – *Embajadores, 5* – ☎ *950 47 24 48* – *9 rooms* – *8 500pts*. Mamabel's, in the centre of the town, is an interesting hotel where, according to the owner Isabel Aznar "quality comes first". When it first opened, it was just a restaurant, serving the best paella for miles around. Eight attractively decorated rooms with views of the valley and sea have since been added.

Calle de Enmedio, running parallel to calle de la Iglesia, is lined by a number of small restaurants and bars. This street passes in front of plaza del Ayuntamiento, from where it is possible to walk down to the 15C **Puerta de la Ciudad** (Town Gate), which was part of the former defensive walls. Walk through this gateway to reach the charming **plaza de las Flores** (Flowers Square).

EXCURSIONS

Garrucha – *5.5km/3.5mi north*. This former fishing village becomes very lively in summer with the influx of tourists lured here by its excellent beaches. Garrucha now has a marina and promenade, in addition to its fishing port. An 18C fortified watchtower can still be seen along the coast to the south of the resort. A golf course is currently under construction nearby.

> **Boat trips**
>
> For those wishing to take to the water, excursions to Mojácar Bay, Carboneras and the Parque Natural de Cabo de Gata are all available from Garrucha. ☎ 607 721 469 or 607 720 777.

From Mojácar Playa to Agua Amarga

Torre del Perulico

32km/20mi south. Allow 45min.

Mojácar Playa – The Mojácar municipal area covers 17km/10.5mi of beaches and coves. Mojácar Playa is a modern resort of white-washed tourist developments and complexes running alongside the coast.

Castillo de Macenas – *9km/5.5mi south, on the left-hand side of the road*. This coastal watchtower dates from the 17C. Views extend to the **Torre del Perulico** which, like many other watchtowers, was built by the Moors in the 13C and 14C to defend this stretch of coastline. From here, a dirt track running parallel to the coast to the south passes the Torre del Perulico, before reaching several nudist beaches, including the Playa de Bordonares *(3km/2mi)*.

Return to the main road.

As far as Carboneras *(13km/8mi)* the road traverses an arid mountain landscape which occasionally obscures the Mediterranean from view. Several kilometres before Carboneras, after a bend in the road, an extensive panorama of the coast can be enjoyed, extending as far as the **Torre-vigía del Rayo**, a watchtower on the horizon.

Where to stay in Agua Amarga

Family – *La Lomilla* – ☎ *950 13 80 14* – *fax 950 13 80 70* – *9 rooms* – *8 000pts.* This small hotel is always full in summer and empty in winter. The restaurant here has just one fixed menu, priced at 2 000pts, including wine and coffee.

Carboneras – This small fishing village developed around a 16C castle, the **Castillo de San Andrés**, built by the Marquess of Carpio to defend the coast. A small **market** is held in Carboneras every Thursday.

The **Casa del Laberinto** or Casa de André Block, a typical whitewashed house in front of the Playa de las Marinicas, was built in the 1960s and is frequently featured on postcards.

Upon leaving the town, note the local spa and facilities belonging to the Endesa energy company.

The boundary of the **Parque Natural de Cabo de Gata–Níjar**★★ *(see p 114)* is reached after 5km/3mi. Shortly after, a road to the left heads up to the Mesa Roldán lighthouse *(faro)* and fortified tower *(1.5km/1mi)*, very similar in design to the Castillo de Macenas in Mojácar.

Agua Amarga – Upon returning to the main road, this whitewashed seaside complex appears after a bend, its two rocky promontories framing a pretty sandy beach.

MONTEFRÍO★

Granada – Population 7 030
Michelin map 446 U 17

Montefrío is one of the prettiest towns in the western reaches of Granada province, enjoying an impressive **setting**★★ at the foot of the Sierra de la Parapanda. Its whitewashed houses with their tiled roofs sit gracefully on two hills which appear like small islands amid a sea of olive groves. Like many of its neighbouring towns and villages, it was highly coveted by both Moors and Christians during the 15C. Several Castilian kings failed in their attempts to conquer Montefrío, before the Catholic Monarchs finally succeeded in taking control of the town in 1486.

VISIT *allow 2hr*

Plaza de España – The town's main square contains three of Montefrío's most important buildings: the impressive bulk of the Iglesia de la Encarnación, the highly recommended **tourist office** and, a little further along, the **town hall**, housed in a building dating from the 18C.

Iglesia de la Encarnación – Although this surprising neo-Classical church has been attributed to Ventura Rodríguez, there is little proof to substantiate this claim. The church has a circular plan and a half-orange cupola which is visible from all over the town.

Climb up to the Villa section of town along calle del Arco Gracia.

★**Iglesia de la Villa** ◌ – This church was built on top of the hill above the remains of a **Nasrid fortress**, from which several features have been preserved, including the old cistern. The ubiquitous **Diego de Siloé** was responsible for the design of the church,

Montefrío

251

which is a combination of a Gothic structure with Renaissance ornamentation. The single nave, crowned by an elegant pointed vault, is completed by a polygonal chapel with a shell-shaped dome.

Walk down to plaza de España and follow calle Enrique Amat to placeta del Pósito.

Placeta del Pósito – The town's 18C former **granary** (*pósito*), a building of simple design, dominates this small square.

From here, head up Monte del Calvario to the Iglesia de San Antonio.

Iglesia de San Antonio – The church was originally part of the Franciscan Convento de San Antonio, which ceased its religious function and became a flour factory known as "La Máquina" following the confiscation of church property during the 19C. The **Iglesia de San Antonio de Padua** is Baroque in style with a handsome west façade in the form of a three-sectioned retable, the upper part of which contains a statue of St Anthony in a niche. From here, it is well worth walking along calle Cruz del Calvario for one of the best **views**★★ of the town.

EXCURSIONS

★**Peña de los Gitanos** – *5km/3mi from Montefrío along the Illora road. After passing the Mesón Curro to your right, continue as far as a road signposted to Peña de los Gitanos. As this is a private road and property, leave your car at the beginning of the dirt track and continue on foot (15min).*

The track climbs gently through olive groves to a fork. Take the path to the right; after passing an abandoned mine, a first area of meadow comes into view. Cross the meadow, passing a dolmen to the right, to reach a second meadow dotted with oak trees. The best-preserved megalithic tombs are located here. Several are dotted around the meadow, although the most spectacular is to the right, behind a small group of oak trees. This particular **dolmen**★ has a corridor and burial chamber with a perfectly preserved roof.

Moclín – *33.5km/21mi. Head towards Illora, then follow the NO 19 as far as the N 432. Bear left towards Alcalá la Real until you reach Puerto López.*

The road passes through the town of **Illora**, dominated by the silhouette of the enormous 16C Iglesia de la Encarnación. The road then climbs slightly, skirting narrow bends until the impressive sight of the **Castillo de la Mota**★ suddenly appears on top of a hill, dominating the small town of Moclín. This double-enclosure fortress, dating from the Nasrid period, is accessed via an angled doorway. Several buildings stand inside the fortress confines: the former 16C granary, the Iglesia de la Encarnación, from the same century, and, higher up, the remains of the keep and a cistern.

MONTILLA
Córdoba – Population 22 792
Michelin map 446 T 16

The town of Montilla, set amid a landscape of gently undulating hills, is primarily known as the centre of a large wine-producing region which is part of the Montilla-Moriles appellation.

Several historians have identified the town as the Roman settlement Munda, the site of a battle between the troops of Caesar and Pompey in AD 45. From 1375 onwards, Montilla's history is intimately linked to that of the **Fernández de Córdoba** family, who transferred the centre of their domain from Aguilar to Montilla. One of its most illustrious members was Gonzalo Fernández de Córdoba, the famous military commander known as **El Gran Capitán** (1453-1515), who took part in the capture of Granada and the campaigns to conquer the kingdom of Naples.

Montilla enjoyed its period of greatest splendour in the 16C, when influential personalities of the time such as the writer **Inca Garcilaso de la Vega** and St John of Ávila took up residence in the town. Many of Montilla's most important buildings date from this time.

The destruction of the castle – In 1508, King Fernando the Catholic ordered the razing of the seigniorial castle, which stood at the town's highest point, as a punishment for the disloyal conduct of its owner, Don Pedro Fernández de Córdoba.

The wines of Montilla-Moriles

The renown of these wines dates back to Antiquity. As a result of the region's continental climate, Montilla-Moriles wines have developed their own personality which distinguishes them from the wines produced in Jerez. The main grape variety grown in the Montilla-Moriles area is Pedro Ximénez.

Four different wines are produced here: **fino** (an extra dry, slightly bitter wine, with an attractive light gold colour); **amontillado** (an older, amber-coloured fino with a nutty aroma); **oloroso** (a fragrant, velvety-textured wine almost mahogany in colour); and **Pedro Ximénez** (a sweet ruby-coloured wine which is an ideal accompaniment for a dessert).

A visit to one of the many local **bodegas** such as **Alvear**, founded in 1729 and one of the region's oldest and best-known producers, is highly recommended.

B. Kaufmann/MICHELIN

Follow signs to the town centre (centro ciudad), then leave your car in one of the signposted car parks.

Iglesia Parroquial de Santiago – *Calle Iglesia.* This parish church dedicated to St James dates from the 16C, although it was restored during the 18C, when the façade in particular underwent significant modification. It was built using materials from the castle standing on the hill to one side which was razed by Fernando the Catholic. Note the handsome brick tower decorated with attractive blue *azulejos* around the bays, and the cupola, which is also adorned with glazed ceramics.

The area around the church, characterised by narrow, cobbled streets lined by whitewashed houses offering delightful views of the church tower, is well worth exploring. At no 2 calle Miguel Molina, stands the **Museo Histórico Local** ⊘, an interesting museum displaying historical artefacts from the local area which date from prehistory to the modern era.

Iglesia de San Francisco Solano – *Calle San Francisco Solano.* This 17C-18C church stands on the site formerly occupied by the house in which St Francis Solano was born in 1549. The peculiar **façade★**, which could easily be that of a civil building, has a porticoed atrium, with semicircular arches supported by Doric columns. A statue of the saint, the town's patron, presides over the entrance. The overall result is an elegant, symmetrical ensemble embellished by the golden hues of the stone. The tower affixed to the building was added in 1910. The bell-tower and the spire above it are totally covered by *azulejos*. The main altarpiece inside the church is worthy of note.

Town Hall – *Calle Corredera.* The town hall was built on the site of the former Convento-Hospital de San Juan de Dios, from which only the 18C church (now used as an exhibition hall), with its simple portal, remains. The interior of the town hall is embellished by a central patio with semicircular arches resting on Doric columns.

Convento de Santa Clara – Construction of the convent was ordered by Don Pedro Fernández de Córdoba, the first Marquess of Priego, who entrusted the project to the architect Hernán Ruiz the Elder. The building was completed in 1524, although the convent was subsequently extended before reaching its present size at the beginning of the 18C.

The façade of the **church** has a fine **portal★**, built in Flamboyant-Gothic style. Above the door, between two circles with crosses bearing splayed arms, the escutcheon of the Marquess and Marchioness of Priego can be seen, standing alongside the niche housing the image of St Clare. The *artesonado* ceilings above the nave and main altarpiece are the highlights inside the church.

Upon leaving the convent, pass through an arch to reach the Llano de Palacio, the setting for the **Palacio de los Duques de Medinaceli**, a contemporary of the convent, which was built by the Marquess and Marchioness of Priego as a palatial residence following the destruction of their castle.

WHERE TO STAY

MODERATE

Bellido – *Enfermería, 57* – ☎ *957 65 19 15* – *21 rooms* – *6 000pts*. A centrally located hotel with a bright-pink façade and comfortable, well-appointed rooms.

MID-RANGE

Don Gonzalo – *At Km 47 on the Córdoba–Málaga road* – ☎ *957 65 06 58* – *fax 957 65 06 66* – *29 rooms* – *8 400pts*. A modern hotel with pleasant rooms, bar, restaurant, and a garden with swimming pool to the rear.

EATING OUT

Las Camachas – *Avenida de Europa, 3* – ☎ *957 65 00 04*. One of the best-known restaurants in the area, situated in a typical Montilla house with a covered patio, an *azulejo*-adorned bar, and a *bodega* replete with barrels. The excellent menu includes specialities such as local artichokes *(alcachofas a la montillana)*, white cardoons with clams and prawns *(cardos blancos con almejas y gambas)*, partridge *(perdiz)*, the thick local gazpacho known as *salmorejo*, and braised oxtail *(rabo de toro)*.

PASTRIES

The Pastelería Manuel Aguilar *(calle Corredera, 25)* has been producing delicious pastries for over a century. Local specialities include *alfajores*, made with almonds and honey, the round, wine-based *roscos de Pedro Ximénez*, and *pastelones de cabello de ángel*, which literally translate as "angel's hair pastries".

Convento de Santa Ana – Only the 17C church with its simple doorway remains from the original convent founded in the 16C. The interior is dominated by the main altarpiece, depicting an Immaculate Conception by the renowned sculptor Pedro Roldán. The handsome belfry rising above the church is decorated with *azulejos*, although it is somewhat obscured by the new conventual buildings and houses nearby.

Casa-Museo del Inca Garcilaso ⊘ – It was in this house that the writer Inca Garcilaso de la Vega lived between 1561 and 1591 and wrote several of his important works such as *La Florida* and *Los Comentarios Reales*, as commemorated by a plaque mounted at the entrance.

The house, which has now been converted into a museum, is an interesting example of civil architecture from the period, characterised by the sober façade and golden hue of the stone used in its construction. Several pieces of furniture inside the house are original, while others are imitations.

The town centre is blessed with several fine buildings including **La Tercia**, in plaza de la Rosa, the **Teatro Garnelo** (1921), the **Colegio de las Monjas Asuncionistas** (School of Assumptionist Nuns), which was formerly the residence of the Count of La Cortina, and the **Iglesia de San Agustín**.

EXCURSIONS

Espejo – *13.5km/8.5mi northeast along the A 309*. Espejo stands on a hill beneath its imposing castle amid an undulating landscape of olive groves. It is an attractive town of whitewashed houses, cobbled streets and the occasional flight of steps.

Leave your car in paseo de Andalucía and walk up to the castle.

Castle – *Private property; closed to visitors*. The castle belongs to the ducal house of Osuna and is situated in the upper part of the town, affording magnificent **views★** of the surrounding countryside. This solid construction dates from the 15C and has a lofty keep at its centre.

The nearby **Iglesia Parroquial de San Bartolomé**, a parish church Gothic in style but modified over the centuries, contains several works by Pedro Romaña (such as the retable of St Andrés), an 18C Corpus Christi monstrance, and several pieces of gold and silverwork.

Montemayor – *14km/9mi northwest along the N 331*. The houses of Montemayor extend across a gentle hill, at the centre of which rises a well-preserved 14C Mudéjar **castle**, with its impressive keep.

Iglesia de la Asunción – The pedestrianised **plaza de la Constitución** is lined by the town hall and this impressive 16C-17C church with its Renaissance bell-tower. The remains of a Roman mill can be seen embedded in one of its walls.

Where to stay in Montemayor

Castillo de Montemayor – *At Km 35 on the Córdoba–Málaga road* – ☎ *957 38 42 53* – *fax 957 38 43 06* – *54 rooms* – *6 000pts*. The modern façade of this hotel conceals an interior designed in regional style. Swimming pool, bar, restaurant and night-club. Excellent value for money.

The outstanding features of the three-aisle interior are the richly decorated triple apse and the three Baroque cupolas. A large 17C carved Renaissance altarpiece presides over the presbytery, with Baroque chapels to the sides, each profusely decorated with stuccowork. The Capilla del Rosario (Rosary Chapel) contains some interesting gold and silverwork, including a superbly worked 18C altar frontal.

The **Museo de Ulía** *(visits are only possible when the church is open)*, a museum that has been established below the church in what were once the ossuary and the cistern, displays a variety of exhibits from the 5C BC to the 15C.

The delightful streets around the square offer an interesting insight into the popular architecture of the area, with their picturesque corners and whitewashed houses, some of which are adorned with impressive seigniorial doorways.

Fernán Núñez – *18km/11mi northwest along the N 331*. This small town is named after a local aristocratic family and was founded by its first member in the mid 13C above the former Roman settlement of Ulía. Two buildings are of interest in the town centre: the Palacio Ducal and the Iglesia de Santa Marina de Aguas Santas.

Palacio Ducal – The impressive ducal palace was built around a square in the 18C. The vermilion red of its plasterwork and the whiteness of the mouldings on the windows and cornices inject life into the building's otherwise sober decoration, which is broken only by the occasional heraldic motif.

Iglesia de Santa Marina de Aguas Santas – The interior of this 18C church has preserved its Baroque decoration of frescoes and stuccowork on the vaulting and cupolas.

La Rambla – *16km/10mi west along the N 331 and A 386*. This country town has a long-standing pottery tradition. It was here that Miguel de Cervantes worked as both a tax collector and treasurer for the royal storehouses. La Rambla has preserved monuments of interest.

Iglesia Parroquial de la Asunción – Built during the period of the Reconquest, this parish church was practically rebuilt in the 18C. The superb, finely carved **Plateresque portal**★ is the work of Hernán Ruiz I. On the interior, note the Baroque Capilla del Sagrario to the left of the chancel, with its imitation marble retable and cupola, both of which are covered with plaster. Some of the statues in the church are attributed to Martínez Montañés: St Joseph with the Infant Jesus, St Ann with the Virgin Mary, John the Baptist, and St Rose.

Nearby, also in calle Iglesia, the remains of a massive square tower which was part of the former **fortress**, can be seen.

Torre del ex-Convento de la Consolación – This fine Baroque-style brick tower bears abundant decoration, particularly on its west side, which is mainly concentrated around the windows and bays.

Colegio del Espiritú Santo – The church belonging to this school houses a sculptural jewel which is the pride and joy of La Rambla's inhabitants: the wooden carving of **Jesus of Nazareth**★ bearing a cross on his shoulders, by Juan de Mesa. This impressive sculpture shows exceptional skill in its portrayal of the subject's emotion.

Santaella – *32km/20mi west along the N 331 and A 386*. A pleasant view of this small town, which appears to be dominated by the impressive Iglesia de la Asunción, can be enjoyed from the main road.

In the main square *(plaza mayor)* to the right of the town hall, the vestiges of the former Moorish fortress are still visible.

Santaella has several seigniorial houses such as the 18C Casa de las Columnas, currently being refurbished to house the **Museo de Arqueología Local** ⊙, which at present occupies the former granary. The museum has two sections, one devoted to ethnology, the other to archeology. The latter contains the *Leona de Santaella* (The Santaella Lioness), Iberian votive offerings, an Ibero-Roman lion, Roman ceramics and a set of Visigothic monograms.

Climb the ramp in front of the castle.

The views from the top of the ramp take in the church and the surrounding countryside.

Iglesia de la Asunción – The 16C-17C Church of the Assumption is surprising in its proportions. It is well worth walking around it to fully appreciate its monumental stature. The Baroque **façade** is preceded by a wall which protects the door from the wind, preventing visitors from admiring the portal's full perspective. To the left rises a **Renaissance tower**, adorned with heraldic decoration. The wall on the northwest side has preserved its original decoration beneath a blind arch. On the interior, note the Mudéjar *artesonado* work in the Capilla de las Ánimas, several retables and the pulpit.

The 18C Baroque sanctuary of **Nuestra Señora del Valle**, housing the image of Our Lady of the Valley, the town's patron saint, can be visited on the outskirts of Santaella.

MONTORO ★

Córdoba – Population 9 489

Michelin map 446 R 16

Montoro's impressive site is best viewed from a bend on the main road, from where the full contrast between the reddish tones of its soil and the ochre and whitewash of its houses can be admired. From the undulating line of houses gently descending to the river, the Baroque tower of the Iglesia de San Bartolomé rises majestically above the rooftops. A graceful 15C bridge spans the meander in the Guadalquivir, whose course skirts the town.

Montoro on a meander of the Guadalquivir River

Visitors are advised to leave their vehicle at the entrance to the town, as driving and parking in Montoro is particularly difficult.

★**Plaza de España** – This charming square at the very heart of the old town is lined by three interesting buildings: the Iglesia de San Bartolomé, the town hall and a fine seigniorial mansion. All three are built in the characteristic stone of the area and add a sense of harmony to the square's appearance.

Iglesia de San Bartolomé ⊘ – This handsome 15C church is the dominant feature of the square with its monumental Baroque bell-tower standing proudly at its east end. Note the finely carved elegant Gothic-Mudéjar **portal**★, in the upper section of which the arch and a statue of the Virgin Child are framed by an *alfiz* surround. To the left of the doorway, embedded in the wall, a Visigothic slab can also be seen. Two coats of arms appear on the portal, while another adorns the Baroque window to the right of the façade. The triple-aisled interior contains some interesting marquetry, in addition to a delicately carved statue of the Virgin of the Rosary in a side chapel on the left-hand side. The headless statue of the archangel Raphael stands alongside the church.

Town Hall – This Renaissance building has a harmonious two-storey façade bearing the coat of arms of the ducal house of Alba-Montoro. Between the façade and the vaulted arch on its left, note the stone commemorating the order given by Felipe III to build the old prison, the edifice adjoining the town hall. The interior is crowned by some fine Mudéjar *artesonado* ceilings.

Seigniorial mansion – *To the right of the church.* It is was in this building that justice was formerly administered in Montoro. Four escutcheons can be seen on the second floor, while the heads of a man and woman above the doors denote the entrances through which the accused of each sex would have entered the building.

The area surrounding the square is a maze of narrow cobbled streets, picturesque nooks and crannies, and typical examples of popular architecture, with whitewashed houses framed by the traditional stone of the area providing a colourful contrast with the blue of the Cordoban sky. The **Casa de las Conchas** (House of the Shells) is an unusual modern building built in 1960 and, as the name would suggest, is completely covered by shells.

Handicrafts

Montoro has preserved several of its traditional handicraft workshops. Some of these can be found in calle Corredera, including those of Juan Hidalgo (no 73), dedicated to esparto grass, and the sons of Manuel Mohedo (no 39), who specialise in harness-making.

Walk along calle Bartolomé Camacho, next to the church in plaza de España, to the **Ermita de Santa María**, a 13C chapel, now home to the town's **Museo Arqueológico Local** ⊙. Upon returning to the square, there is an impressive view of the church tower.

ADDITIONAL SIGHTS

Iglesia del Carmen – *In calle El Santo*. The façade of this church, built out of local stone, is dominated by the image of St John of the Cross. Inside, the three naves are overshadowed by an 18C Baroque **retable** in the chancel, with a Virgin and Child enthroned at its centre.

Hospital de Jesús Nazareno – This hospital was built in the 17C and 18C, although it has undergone subsequent restoration on a number of occasions. It is now used as a rest home. The cupola of the church is brightly decorated in tones of blue and gold.

EXCURSIONS

Adamuz – *22km/14mi west. Take the E 5 motorway towards Córdoba. Exit at Km 367 and follow signs to Adamuz*. The road passes through an area of abundant vegetation, following the wide course of the Guadalquivir until it crosses the river at the El Salto. Continue along the opposite bank, before leaving the river behind and ascending a winding route towards Adamuz, set amid a landscape of olive groves. The town's whitewashed streets are overlooked by the Gothic **Iglesia de San Andrés**, built in red sandstone in the late 14C and early 15C. The sober appearance of the church, enhanced by the absence of decoration, is counteracted only by its impressive bulk. The main civil building is the **Torre del Reloj**, a clock tower built by the Marquess of El Carpio in 1566, but subsequently restored.

El Carpio – *16km/10mi southwest along the E 5*. The houses of El Carpio rise up a hill dominated by a 14C tower, the Mudéjar-style **Torre de Garci Méndez**. The best view of this imposing brick tower can be enjoyed from plaza de la Constitución, a pleasant square fronted by a 17C parish church and adorned with orange trees and arrangements of flowers.

Parque Natural de la Sierra de Cardeña y Montoro – *Access via the N 420*. The gentle features of this protected area to the south of the Sierra Morena give way to steeper landscapes and numerous ravines further to the west. The predominant species found here are holm oak, arbutus, the occasional downy oak, and areas replanted with pines. Local wildlife includes wolves, otters, lynx, wild boar, genet and deer. The park is also popular with hikers, due to the numerous marked paths criss-crossing the area.

NERJA★

Málaga – Population 15 326
Michelin map 446 V 18

The main tourist centre in La Axarquía *(see p 101)* is an attractive small town of Moorish origin and whitewashed alleyways perched on a promontory above the Mediterranean. This stretch of coastline at the foot of the Sierra de Almijara is characterised by steep cliffs and delightful beaches. Nerja's many bars, outdoor cafés, restaurants and night-clubs have made the town one of the most popular summer resorts along the Costa del Sol.

WHERE TO STAY

MODERATE

Cala–Bella – *Puerta del Mar, 8* – ☎ 952 52 07 00 – *fax 952 52 07 04 – several rooms – 6 500pts*. Well-appointed rooms (four of which have views of the sea) in the heart of the town. Given its price and location, advance booking is advisable.

MID-RANGE

Paraíso del Mar – *Prolongación de Carabeo, 22* – ☎ 952 52 16 21 – *fax 952 52 23 09 – 12 rooms – 12 000pts – closed mid-Nov to mid-Dec*. A small, pleasant hotel overlooking the Mediterranean. Comfortable rooms with TV, phone, air-conditioning and minibar.

EATING OUT

Pepe Rico – *Almirante Ferrándiz, 28* – ☎ 952 52 02 47 – *fax 952 52 44 98 – closed Tues, first two weeks in Dec and second week in Jan*. This Swedish-run restaurant in one of Nerja's many pedestrianised streets has a pleasant terrace for outdoor dining, as well as 10 apartments for rent *(8 300pts)*. Specialities include *solomillo de buey a la pimienta verde* (loin of ox in a green pepper sauce).

La Parrala – *Playa Burriana* – ☎ 952 52 22 89. A restaurant with a large terrace right on the beach. The house speciality is paella.

Travellers' addresses

Nerja beach

Balcón de Europa – This magnificent mirador in the historical centre of Nerja was built on the site of the old castle. It is a large landscaped square overlooking the sea with an avenue of palm trees and views of this rocky coastline. On clear days it is possible to make out the African coast in the distance.

The whitewashed 17C Iglesia del Salvador, with its impressive bell-tower, stands alongside the square.

EXCURSION

Cueva de Nerja ⊘ – *4.5km/3mi towards Motril.* Discovered in 1959, this enormous natural cave has been carved out of the marble landscape of the Sierra de Almijara. Traces of pottery, ceramics, human remains and wall paintings, some of which are exhibited in the first few rooms, indicate that the caves were inhabited during the Paleolithic era.

The cave is impressive in the scale of its chambers and the spectacular appearance of the stalactites and stalagmites formed by water infiltrating the cave over the millennia. Only a quarter of the cave's total surface area is open to the public. The **Sala de la Cascada** (Cascade Chamber), also known as the **Sala del Ballet** (Ballet Chamber), takes its name from the formations on the right-hand side. It is here that an annual **Festival of Music and Dance** is held in the second or third week of July. The chamber's main feature is its 17m/56ft central column, which appears tiny compared with its enormous 32m/105ft counterpart in the **Sala del Cataclismo** (Cataclysm Chamber), an impressively dimensioned cavern with further formations of outstanding beauty.

OSUNA★★

Sevilla – Population 17 306
Michelin map 446 U 14

This elegant town standing proudly on a hill overlooking the Sevillian countryside has an interesting history. Initially inhabited by the Iberians, who named it Urso, it was subsequently conquered by Caesar. Following the period of Moorish occupation, it was reconquered by Fernando III the Saint in 1239, and then ceded to the Order of Calatrava by Alfonso X the Wise in 1264. However, its period of greatest splendour is indelibly linked with the House of Osuna, under whose control it passed in 1562, when Felipe II granted the title of Duke of Osuna to the fifth Count of Ureña. The dukedom was to become one of the most powerful on the Iberian Peninsula, and was responsible for the embellishment of Osuna, as well as its artistic and cultural development.

★MONUMENTAL CENTRE

Follow signs to the town centre (centro ciudad) and Zona Monumental.

★**Colegiata** ⊙ – This imposing 16C Renaissance-style collegiate church stands impressively above the town. The façade is adorned with a handsome, finely sculpted Plateresque doorway.

Interior – The **church** is composed of three elegant Renaissance aisles opening out onto several chapels and a Baroque apse with an interesting retable in the same style, bearing the coat of arms of the House of Osuna. The organ dates from the 18C.
The church contains several important works of art within its walls: *Jesus of Nazareth* by the "divine" Morales, a *Christ of Misericord* by Juan de Mesa, the superb tenebrist canvas, **The Expiration of Christ**★★, by **José Ribera** "El Españoleto", and an unusually small 16C organ, which is carried during religious processions.
The **sacristy** is adorned with 16C *azulejos* and some original *artesonado* work.

Exhibits include several books of Gregorian chants dating from the 16C, and the four additional **paintings by Ribera**★★ in the possession of the collegiate church: *St Jerome*, *The Tears of St Peter*, *The Martyrdom of St Bartholomew* and *The Martyrdom of St Sebastian*, all of which were painted between 1616 and 1618. Additional works of art on view in other rooms include an *Immaculate Conception* by Alonso Cano, a silver processional cross (1534), Flemish paintings, vestments dating from the period in which the Colegiata was founded, gold and silverwork etc.

WHERE TO STAY

El Caballo Blanco – *Granada, 1* – ☎/fax 95 481 01 84 – *13 rooms* – *6 000pts.* This motel-like residence is located in the heart of Osuna. Spotlessly clean rooms, all at street level. Good value for money.

EATING OUT

La Casa Del Marqués – *San Pedro, 20* – ☎ 95 481 22 23 – *fax 95 481 24 54.* This 17C architectural jewel once belonged to the Marquess of La Gomera. The façade of the building is adorned with impressive columns, while the inner patio, opening onto a small chapel, is used as a dining area, serving typical Andalucian and Basque specialities. The bar is a delightful spot for an aperitif or after-dinner drink. The owners will shortly be opening a hotel and Andalucian restaurant, which will serve inexpensive local cuisine.

Travellers' addresses

★★**Panteón Ducal** – The ducal pantheon was built in Plateresque style in 1545 as the burial place for the Dukes of Osuna. It is approached by a delightful patio, designed in the same style. The chapel stands just below the Colegiata's main altar, and despite its tiny dimensions (8m/26ft long, 4.5m/15ft wide and 2.5m/8ft high), it comprises three aisles and a choir. It is crowned by a blue and gold polychrome coffered ceiling which has been blackened by candle smoke. The altarpiece, by Roque Balduque, represents the Burial of Christ.
The **crypt** beneath the chapel contains the tombs of the most notable Dukes of Osuna and the founders of the Colegiata (the parents of the first duke).

Former university – The old university *(antigua universidad)*, created in 1548 and in existence until 1824, was founded by Juan Téllez, the Count of Ureña and father of the first Duke of Osuna. It is a large square building made of stone; the circular towers on its corners are crowned by spires decorated with blue and white *azulejos*. Note also the attractive inner patio.

★**Monasterio de la Encarnación** ⊙ – This convent of discalced nuns was founded by the fourth Duke of Osuna in the 17C. Its outstanding feature is the magnificent **dado**★ of 17C Sevillian *azulejos* in the patio, dedicated to the five senses. This decoration continues up the stairs and on the patio's upper floor. The large collection of paintings, statuary and other objects of artistic interest includes a set of statues of the Infant Jesus, various pieces of gold and silverwork and an 18C Baroque altarpiece. The church is also Baroque in style. Like many convents in Andalucia, the nuns here produce and sell several types of delicious biscuits and pastries.

Torre del Agua – *On the way down to the Plaza Mayor*. This medieval defensive tower dates from the 12C-13C, although its origins can be traced to the Carthaginians. Nowadays, it is home to the town's **Museo Arqueológico** ⊘, displaying a range of Iberian and Roman objects discovered in Osuna, as well as reproductions of Iberian bulls and Roman bronzes (the originals can be seen in the Museo Arqueológico Nacional, Madrid).

ADDITIONAL SIGHTS

The centre of Osuna has some fine examples of civil architecture, including an impressive array of Baroque **palaces and seigniorial residences★★**.

★**Calle San Pedro** – In addition to several interesting town houses and churches, this street is lined by two magnificent palaces:

Cilla del Cabildo – This original 18C Baroque edifice was designed by Alonso Ruiz Florindo, who was also responsible for the tower *(torre)* of the Iglesia de la Merced

(see below). In both buildings he incorporated unusual pilasters with individual decoration. Above the doorway, a somewhat curious copy of the Giralda (Sevilla) dominates the façade.

Palacio de los Marqueses de la Gomera – This 18C Baroque palace has a striking cornice with a sensation of movement created by volutes and waves, in addition to a beautiful stone doorway crowned by a large escutcheon.

Antiguo Palacio de Puente Hermoso – *Calle Sevilla, 44.* The handsome 18C Baroque **portal★** adorning the façade of this former palace is embellished by the Solomonic columns on the lower tier adorned with fig leaves and bunches of grapes.
The street is also lined by several other notable civil and religious buildings.

Cilla del Cabildo

B. Kaufmann/MICHELIN

Palacio de los Cepeda – *Calle de la Huerta*. This palace is now the home of the town's law courts. It is a handsome 18C construction with an impressive main doorway and a fine cornice crowning the building. However, its most outstanding features are the *estípites* on the doorway and, in particular, the large coat of arms with the two halberdiers flanking it.

Antigua Audiencia – *Carrera Caballos, 82.* Osuna's former law courts were housed in this sober building dating from the reign of Carlos III.

★**Torre de la Iglesia de la Merced** – The church tower, designed by the same architect as the Cilla del Cabildo, is an impressive monument with a number of decorative elements.

Osuna's religious architecture is represented by numerous convents and churches (Santo Domingo, la Compañía, la Concepción etc), predominantly dating from the 17C and 18C.

PALMA DEL RÍO

Córdoba – Population 18 948

Michelin map 446 S 14

Palma del Río is situated on a plain, close to the confluence of the Guadalquivir and Genil rivers. Approaching from Córdoba along the C 431 the whitewashed **Ermita de la Virgen de Belén**, a chapel named after the town's patron saint, the Virgin of Bethlehem, can be seen on top of a small hill to the right. The views of the town from here are particularly impressive. A turning on the other side of the road leads to Palma del Río, reached after crossing a large iron and concrete bridge built in the 19C.

Follow signs to the town centre (centro ciudad), then park near plaza de Andalucía.

Plaza de Andalucía – The town's main square is lined by three major buildings: the town hall, post office *(correos)* and law courts *(juzgados)*. The most interesting constructions in the square are the **Puerta del Sol** (Sun Gateway) and the 16C **Renaissance balcony**, which was part of the Palacio de los Portacarrero, above which rises the tower of the Iglesia de la Asunción. The palace originally stood through the arch on the right-hand side.

> ### A tradition of pottery
> The town's inhabitants believe that it is the quality of the clay used in the production of the local earthenware pots that keeps the water stored in them so cool. Other typical items of pottery from Palma del Río include wine pitchers, gazpacho bowls and flowerpots.

★Town walls – These date from the 12C and formed part of an extensive walled enclosure built during the Almohad period to provide protection for the town. Substantial parts of the walls still remain intact, including several solid sections, in addition to several square towers and one octagonal one.

Museo Municipal ⊙ – The municipal museum is housed in the former royal stables. It is divided into three sections, devoted to archeology, ethnography and fine arts.

Iglesia de la Asunción ⊙ – The Church of the Assumption was built in the 18C. The exterior is dominated by an elegant **tower★**, showing clear Écijan influence in the middle of the façade, above a red-brick Baroque portal. The rich decoration on its belfry *(estípites*, frets and Solomonic columns) is enhanced by the blue-tinged tones of its *azulejos*.

The **interior★** is particularly harmonious with its wide nave and transept, above which rises a cupola, with pendentives decorated with stuccowork bearing plant motifs. The nave is supported by enormous pilasters, above which runs a cornice adorned with further stucco features. The wrought-iron balconies create a pleasant contrast, adding an element of dynamism to the overall effect. Side chapels open out from the nave, although the walls originally in place to separate them have since disappeared, leaving what now appears to be two narrow, corridor-like aisles. The church is presided over by a Baroque altarpiece.

ADDITIONAL SIGHTS

Iglesia y Convento de San Francisco – The church and convent were founded in the 16C, but underwent significant modification in the 17C and 18C. Noteworthy external features include the cupolas above the side chapels and the transept. A hospice *(hospedería)* stands alongside the church.

Other sights of interest in Palma del Río include the 18C Baroque **Capilla del Virgin del Rosario**, a chapel dedicated to the Virgin of the Rosary, in the Iglesia de Santo Domingo, and the **Hospital de San Sebastián** (now a retirement home), with its attractive patio and a church with a Mudéjar-influenced façade. On the interior, note the unusual retable of the Virgin of Sorrow (Virgen de los Dolores) and a chapel with a fine dado of old *azulejos* and a Mudéjar *artesonado* ceiling.

EXCURSIONS

Jardines de Moratalla – *11km/7mi east along the A 431*. Botanical enthusiasts will not want to miss the gardens *(jardines)* of this private estate, designed in 1918 by JN Forestier, the architect of the María Luisa Park in Sevilla.

Hornachuelos – *18km/11mi northeast. Head east along the A 431 for 10km/6mi, then bear left onto the CO 141*. This small whitewashed town in the *sierra* of the same name has preserved vestiges of the castle and walls built during the period of the Cordoban Caliphate. Several vantage points, including one in plaza de la Iglesia, offer impressive views of the mountains. Hornachuelos is renowned for its local gastronomy, which is based on venison and wild boar.
Walk along calle Palmera, so named after the palm tree *(palmera)* engraved on its pavement, to the 16C **Iglesia de Santa María de las Flores**, a church embellished with a handsome late-Gothic **portal** attributed to Hernán Ruiz I, and an 18C tower.

Las Erillas can be seen on the outskirts of Hornachuelos, heading east. This area of limestone has been eroded by water to produce some extraordinary rock formations such as the so-called *casas colgantes* or "hanging houses".

Parque Natural de la Sierra de Hornachuelos – This park covers an area of just 67ha/165 acres in the west of the province. Despite its relatively low altitude – its highest peak is the Sierra Alta (722m/2 368ft) – the rivers running through the park have sculpted a landscape of gorges and lakes, one of which (El Retortillo) is popular with swimmers. The vegetation here is mainly holm, cork and gall oak and wild olives, with poplar, alder and ash closer to water. The park is a popular area for hunting, particularly for deer and wild boar; other species found here include the black vulture and the golden eagle, as well as otters, wolves and the rare Iberian lynx.

Centro de Visitantes Huerta del Rey ⊘ – *1.5km/1mi from Hornachuelos along the CO 142*. The Huerta del Rey visitor centre has a number of rooms devoted to interactive exhibitions on the park. Information is available on the extensive network of footpaths on offer to visitors, as well as details on camping permits. The centre is also able to organise tours of the park by donkey and jeep *(advance booking required)*.

San Calixto – *16km/10mi from the visitor centre along the CO 142*. San Calixto was developed as part of Carlos III's land colonisation policy in the 18C. Its major buildings are the Palacio del Marqués de Salinas and its gardens, a 16C convent for discalced Carmelite nuns, and the Iglesia de Nuestra Señora de la Sierra, a church rebuilt in the 18C. The nuns from the convent have developed a reputation for their handicrafts, in particular embroidered table linen, trays decorated by hand and receptacles made from deerskin.

PRIEGO DE CÓRDOBA★★

Córdoba – Population 22 196
Michelin map 446 T 17

The delightful town of Priego de Córdoba is nestled at the foot of the Pico de la Tiñosa (1 570m/5 150ft) in the heart of the Subbética Cordobesa mountain range. It is considered to be the capital of Cordoban Baroque, as borne out by the numerous buildings erected during this sumptuous period in the town's history. Priego reached its economic zenith in the 18C thanks to the silk industry, which was to generate untold artistic and cultural splendour.
The town's **native sons** include the politician **Niceto Alcalá-Zamora** (1877-1949), president of the Second Republic, and the Baroque artists Juan de Dios Santaella (1718-1802) and Francisco Javier Pedrajas (1736-1817). Priego is well known for the intensity of its **fiestas**, particularly Holy Week *(Semana Santa)*, the annual International Festival of Music, Theatre and Dance (August), and the Royal Fair *(Feria Real)*, held in the first week of September.

WHERE TO STAY

MID-RANGE

Villa Turística de Priego – *In the village of Zagrilla, 7km/4.5mi from Priego* – ☎ 957 70 35 03 – *fax 957 70 35 73* – *45 rooms* – *9 350pts*. The magnificent views from this typical Andalucian village take in the surrounding mountain landscape. The villa comprises a series of apartments for between one and four guests, in a verdant setting of pomegranate trees, jasmine and a whole host of other flowers.

EATING OUT

La Fuente de Zagrilla – *In the upper part of Zagrilla, a few hundred yards from the Villa Turística* – ☎ 957 70 37 34. This restaurant serves simple, yet high-quality cuisine such as *sopa de verduras* (vegetable soup), *solomillo relleno de champiñones y jamón* (loin of pork stuffed with mushrooms and ham) and *flan con piña* (crème caramel with pineapple). The restaurant also has a small terrace overlooking a patio.

SIGHTS

Follow signs to the town centre (centro ciudad) and park near plaza de la Constitución, which is fronted by the town hall.

Hospital-Iglesia de San Juan de Dios ⊙ – *In plaza de la Constitución, to the right of the town hall.* The hospital was founded in 1637 by Juan de Herrera and completed in 1717. The first feature of interest inside the building is the attractive cloistered patio. The handsome Baroque church, with its single nave and fine echini-adorned cupola above the transept, stands to the rear, on the right-hand side. Several broken cornices run along the upper sections of the side walls, providing the church with a certain dynamism. The building is completely whitewashed, with vegetal decoration arranged in bands or garlands. The Virgin of Mercy (Virgen de las Mercedes) presides over the main altarpiece, which is also Baroque.

Castle – The significant remains of this sober and imposing fortress, of Moorish origin but modified in the 13C and 14C, can be seen from the **paseo del Abad Palomino**. The wall is punctuated with square towers, including the **keep**, with its paired windows. It is possible to walk around most of the outside of the castle, where houses can be seen built against the wall.

★**Parroquia de la Asunción** ⊙ – This 16C late-Gothic church was remodelled in the 18C in Baroque style. Note also the fine Renaissance portal on the right-hand side. The bright, spacious interior comprises three aisles crowned with arris vaults and decorated keystones, and an echini-adorned cupola above pendentives. The presbytery is dominated by an impressive carved and painted 16C Mannerist-style **retable**. Also worthy of note in the chapels are several altarpieces and a Christ attributed to Alonso de Mena.

★★**El Sagrario** – This chapel, which opens onto the Evangelist nave, is a masterpiece of Priego and Spanish Baroque. Its ground plan consists of a rectangular antechamber leading into an octagonal space surrounded by an ambulatory, in the centre of which stands the chapel. Light plays an important part in the overall scene, and is intensified by the whiteness of the walls and ceiling, inundating the central area with a dazzling brightness and creating a magical atmosphere. The interior is enhanced by the sublime **plasterwork**★★★ by the local artist Francisco Javier Pedrajas, which covers the entire chapel. Pay particular attention to the keystone of the large cupola which is adorned with numerous small heads. Lower down, a sculpture of an apostle can be seen against each pillar. The decoration combines plant motifs, rocaille work and scenes with characters illustrating themes found in both the Old and New Testaments. Despite the profuse decoration, the overall effect is one of lightness and delicacy, and is without doubt one of the highlights of a visit to Priego de Córdoba.

★★**Barrio de la Villa** – This charming quarter, dating back to medieval and Moorish times, has narrow, winding streets and flower-decked whitewashed houses. The combination of myriad colours and scents has made the Barrio de la Villa one of Andalucia's archetypal sights. A leisurely stroll along calle Jazmines, calle Bajondillo, calle Reales and through plaza de San Antonio is particularly recommended.

★**El Adarve** – This delightful balcony, which looks onto the Subbética mountain range, encircles the Barrio de la Villa to the north. The impressive **views**, attractive lamp posts, iron benches and contemplative atmosphere transport visitors back to bygone days.

Iglesia de San Pedro ⊙ – The Baroque additions to this church were completed in 1690. The interior contains some interesting statuary, including an outstanding **Immaculate Conception**★ in the *camarín* behind the main altarpiece; this statue is attributed by some to Diego de Mora, and by others to Alonso Cano. The first chapel to the side of the Evangelist nave houses an image of the **Virgin of Solitude**, while the last chapel on the Epistle nave contains a delightful wooden **recumbent Christ** (1594) attributed to Pablo de Rojas, contained inside a glass urn.

Carnicerías Reales ⊙ – The former royal abattoir and market was built in the 16C along Classical lines, and is a somewhat surprising addition to a town dominated by Baroque architecture. The simple stone doorway, presided over by the coat of arms of the Fernández de Córdoba family, is adorned with two unusual engaged columns. The square-shaped interior has a central patio and towers on its corners. To the rear, to the right of the window with views of the local countryside, a spiral staircase descends to the room where animals were slaughtered. Nowadays it is used as an exhibition hall.

Iglesia de las Angustias ⊙ – *If closed, knock on the door opposite; the nuns from the school will show visitors around.* The church was built in 1772 by Juan de Dios Santaella. Its outstanding feature is the twin-sectioned polychrome doorway with its abundant broken lines. Note also the unusual Virgin and Child in the vaulted niche and the finely worked *estípites* on the lower section. The church belfry can be seen to the left side.

The inside of the church, which is surprisingly small in size, is Rococo. The area above the altar is covered by an attractive moulded dome above pendentives. On the gilded retable, the middle sculptural group, depicting the Virgin with the dead Christ in her arms, stands out; this work is from the Granada School and dates from the late 18C. Also worthy of note are two terracotta sculptures by José Risueño beneath this work.

Follow **calle del Río**, which is lined by several seigniorial houses. The **birthplace of Niceto Alcalá-Zamora** is now home to the town's tourist office.

Fuente del Rey

B. Kaufmann/MICHELIN

Iglesia del Carmen – This church was built in the 18C in the transitional style between Baroque and neo-Classical. The façade combines elements of both styles and has a tower directly incorporated onto it. The portal, the last feature to be built, is pure neo-Classical.

★★Fuentes del Rey y de la Salud – *At the end of calle del Río*. The sight created by these two fountains, known as the Fountains of the King *(Rey)* and Health *(Salud)*, is the most well-known in Priego de Córdoba.

The older of the two, the **Fuente de la Salud★**, was sculpted in the 16C by Francisco del Castillo. It is a stone frontispiece built in Mannerist style with, at its centre, a small niche containing the Virgin of Health, hence its name. The green of the vegetation contrasts with the golden stone, helping to create a charm-

ing scene enhanced by the proximity of the lavish **Fuente del Rey★★**, which was completed at the beginning of the 19C. Both its dimensions and the richness of its design, characterised by curves and counter-curves, evoke the gardens of a Baroque palace. It is arranged on three levels with 139 jets spouting water from the mouths of the same number of masks. The sculptural groups are the work of Remigio del Mármol: the central work represents Neptune's chariot and Amphitrite. The lion fighting the snake on the top section is attributed to the neo-Classical sculptor J Alvarez Cubero.

Museo Histórico Municipal ⊘ – *Carrera de la Monjas, 6*. This local museum, housed in the birthplace of the painter and illustrator Adolfo Lozano Sidro (1872-1935), displays a number of archeological exhibits discovered in and around Priego de Córdoba.

Iglesia de la Aurora ⊘ – The former 15C church was remodelled in the 18C by Juan de Dios Santaella in Baroque style, although it has preserved its 16C tower and belfry. It has a fine polychrome marble Baroque portal on two levels, presided over by the Virgin of the Aurora between two Solomonic columns. The single-nave interior is adorned with profuse Baroque decoration.

Other Baroque churches of interest include the **Iglesia de las Mercedes** and the **Iglesia de San Francisco**, the latter fronted by a neo-Classical portal.

The Brothers of the Aurora

The brotherhood of the Iglesia de la Aurora keeps alive a time-honoured tradition every Saturday night, when it takes to the streets of Priego de Córdoba singing songs in honour of the Virgin.

EXCURSION

Carcabuey – *8km/5mi west*. Carcabuey sits at the foot of a hill crowned by the ruins of a castle and chapel amid a delightful landscape of olive groves, behind which stands the impressive backdrop of the Subbética mountain range.

Follow the street with flights of steps, which comes out opposite the town hall, then continue along a cobbled ramp.

It is well worth climbing up to the castle precinct, inside of which a chapel, the **Ermita de la Virgen del Castillo**, can be seen. The views of the town and the surrounding countryside from this elevated spot are particularly delightful. Walk around the right-hand side of the hermitage to see the remains of the castle, including its walls and turrets. The **Iglesia de la Asunción**, a solid stone construction, dominates the upper part of the town. The most impressive feature of the church, which was built in the 16C and 17C, are the two imposing buttresses connected via an arch, and its brick tower. A track leads from Carcabuey towards Luque across the **Parque Natural de las Sierras Subbéticas** (see p 117).

PUEBLOS BLANCOS DE ANDALUCÍA★★

WHITE VILLAGES OF ANDALUCIA

Cádiz – Málaga
Michelin map 446 V 12-13-14

The area occupied by the White Villages of Andalucia is one of the most beautiful, yet undiscovered parts of the Iberian Peninsula. The landscape here is predominantly mountainous, and is dotted with delightful small towns and villages of unquestionable beauty, with their narrow, maze-like streets and alleyways exuding a Moorish air, often built on steep slopes and lined by typical flower-decked houses with wrought-iron balconies. The common denominator in all these villages is their whitewashed appearance, a feature synonymous with Andalucia as a whole.

★★Arcos de la Frontera – *See p 99.*

Leave Arcos along the A 372 towards El Bosque. One of the best **views**★ of Arcos can be enjoyed from this road.

El Bosque – *30km/19mi east of Arcos.* This small town is home to the **Centro de Visitantes del Parque Natural Sierra de Grazalema** ⊙. A small botanical garden laid out in the upper part of El Bosque contains typical species of the area, such as the Spanish fir, the gall oak and the cork oak.

> **Tour**: At least three days are needed to tour the main *pueblos blancos*, including visits to Arcos and Ronda. The itinerary suggested below departs from **Arcos** and continues at a slow pace through the delightful **Sierra de Grazalema**, to **Ronda**. From here, it returns to Arcos along a road to the north, skirting mountain folds along its path.

Prado del Rey is situated 7km/4.5mi to the north from a turn-off just before El Bosque. It was founded in the 18C by **Carlos III**, hence the name "del Rey" (of the King). It has an unusual orthogonal layout – typical of the Century of Enlightenment – which is very different from that of other towns in the *sierra*.

From El Bosque, head directly to Grazalema along the A 372, passing through **Benamahoma**, a village with an old mill which now houses a small **water museum** *(museo del agua)*. The source of the Bosque River is also found in Benamahoma, with a volume of water flow exceeding 450l/99gal per second.

Ubrique – *12km/8mi along the A 373 towards El Bosque.* The **road**★ now enters the heart of the Sierra de Grazalema in what is undoubtedly the most beautiful part of the tour. The tranquil, sleepy town of Ubrique extends in a white swathe across the Cruz del Tajo Hill, in a **setting** that is one of the most attractive in the whole *sierra*. Its origins date back to the end of the 15C, when farmers from the surrounding area settled here. Today, Ubrique has developed into the main industrial and commercial centre in the area, specialising in leather goods, ranging from the more traditional leather bags and riding pouches to more modern accessories such as wallets and handbags. The upper section of the town, beyond the **plaza del Ayuntamiento**, is the more interesting, dominated by the 18C parish church of **Nuestra Señora de la O**.

Leave Ubrique on the A 374 towards Benaocaz.

The 2C AD **Roman settlement of Ocurri** ⊙ is located just 2km/1.2mi outside of Ubrique, at a spot known as the Salto de la Mora. The road then continues through a wild mountain landscape to the interesting villages of Benaocaz *(6km/4mi)* and Villaluenga del Rosario *(11km/7mi)*.

Benaocaz – Benaocaz has an attractive town hall built during the reign of Carlos III in the 18C, and a small museum, the **Museo Municipal** ⊙.

Villaluenga del Rosario – This small, tranquil village is the highest in Cádiz province. Its charm lies in its unspoilt appearance, with cobbled streets lined by whitewashed houses. The main buildings of interest in the upper part of the village are a brick tower and a neo-Classical façade giving access to the cemetery. The unusual feature of the **bullring** *(plaza de toros)* at the other end of the village is its position on the rock.

WHERE TO STAY

GRAZALEMA

Casa de las Piedras – *Las Piedras, 32 – ☎ 956 13 20 14 – 16 rooms – 4 900pts.* A small but pleasant *hostal* run by friendly owners, with excellent home cooking. Highly recommended.

Villa Turística – *El Olivar – ☎ 956 13 21 36 – fax 956 13 22 13 – 62 rooms – 7 365pts.* A rural hotel with basic but adequate rooms and apartments and magnificent views of Grazalema. Peace and quiet guaranteed.

ZAHARA DE LA SIERRA

Marqués de Zahara – *San Juan, 3 – ☎/fax 956 12 30 61 – 10 rooms – 5 650pts.* A family-run hotel in a typical town house, although the rooms have perhaps seen better days.

Grazalema: the wettest village in Spain

It is perhaps surprising to note that Spain's wettest village is not in the region of Galicia, in the northwest of the country, but here in the heart of Andalucia. This quirk of nature is due to the **föhn effect**, whereby warm clouds full of moisture from the Atlantic penetrate inland areas, only to come across the barrier of successive mountain ranges in the province of Cádiz, forcing them to rise and cool down. This then results in their condensation, giving rise to rainfall which in some places, such as **Grazalema**, can reach 45gal/sq ft.

The road continues along the La Manga defile (desfiladero), passing through delightful scenery before reaching Grazalema.

★**Grazalema** – Grazalema is without doubt one of the most beautiful and charming of all Andalucia's white villages. The approach is along a road which is surprisingly lush; once past the Los Alamillos Pass, the imposing **Peñón Grande**, a peak rising behind the village to a height of over 1 000m/3 328ft, comes into view.

The name Grazalema comes from the Arabic *Ben-Zalema*. The village has retained the layout of its streets from the Moorish period, as well as the tower of the **Iglesia de San Juan**. The tower of the 16C **Iglesia de la Encarnación** is Mudéjar in style and is the oldest in Grazalema. The pretty **plaza de España** is fronted by the **Iglesia de la Aurora**, built in the 18C during the town's period of greatest splendour; the square is also adorned with an attractive fountain. Grazalema is well-known for its tradition of basketwork and woven woollen blankets, which reached its peak in the 18C. Nowadays it is still possible to visit the **hand looms** ⊘ at the entrance to the town.

For those who do not wish to continue to Ronda, it is possible to drive directly from **Grazalema** to **Zahara de la Sierra** along the CA 531, crossing the spectacular **Las Palomas Pass**, with its dramatic **views**★.

★★**Ronda** – *See RONDA.*

Leave Ronda along the MA 428 towards Arriate.

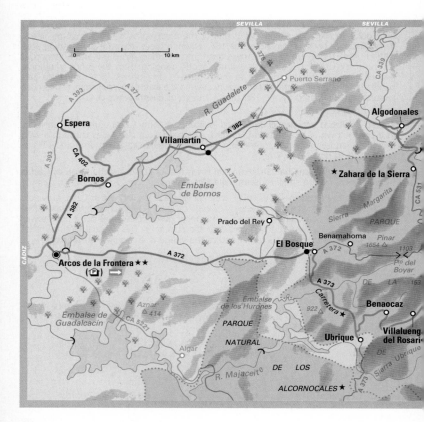

Olvera

★**Setenil** – This unique village is the only one in this part of Andalucia with troglodyte dwellings built into the rock. Unlike Guadix, no chimneys are visible here, just rows of houses which appear to support the weight of the rock from which they have been dug. Fine example of these dwellings are the **Cuevas del Sol** (Caves of the Sun) and the **Cuevas de la Sombra** (Caves of the Shade). The **tourist office** ⊘ is housed in an impressive building with a handsome 16C *artesonado* ceiling. A keep rises above the upper part of Setenil, from where the neighbouring village of Olvera is visible. The **Iglesia de la Encarnación**, higher up still, is Gothic in style and decorated with neo-Gothic frescoes.

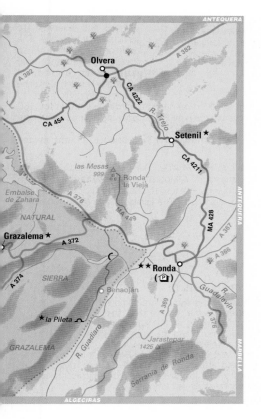

Olvera – *13km/8mi from Setenil along the CA 4222.* Olvera enjoys an impressive **site★★** on a hill, dominated by the silhouette of its imposing castle keep and the neo-Classical Iglesia de la Encarnación perched on a rocky crag. The village sits at their feet, a network of steep streets and alleyways lined by typical whitewashed houses. The triangular-shaped **castle** ⊘ was built in the late 12C and became part of the defensive network of the Nasrid kingdom. The village was conquered by Alfonso XI in 1327.

Olvera's most typical product is its superb **olive oil**, considered to be one of the finest in Spain.

Algodonales – *22km/14mi from Olvera along the CA 454.* This village is one of the best places in Spain for hanggliding.

★**Zahara de la Sierra** – Formerly known as Zahara de los Membrillos due to the importance of the local quince *(membrillo)* industry, the village enjoys an extraordinary **setting★★** on top of a hill. Zahara was an important defensive enclave for the Nasrids, and subsequently the

Christians, who conquered the village in 1483 under the command of Ponce de León. A lush landscape of vegetable gardens, as well as the recent **Zahara Dam** *(presa)*, completed in 1991, extend below the village. From the main road the outline of the 13C Nasrid castle is an impressive sight. The view from the castle encompasses stunning views of the new dam, neighbouring Algodonales and even Olvera. Once past the 16C clock tower, the village takes on the appearance of a typical Andalucian *pueblo blanco*. The Baroque **Iglesia de Santa María de Mesa** dates from the 18C.

Villamartín – Villamartín has little in common with other villages along this route with its wide, flat streets of more recent origin. The *villa* or settlement of Martín was founded in 1503 by a group of farmers who established their properties on land ceded by the city of Sevilla. The **plaza del Ayuntamiento** is the hub of the village; the **calle de El Santo** leading away from the square is fronted by several seigniorial mansions such as the **Casa-Palacio de Los Ríos**, a palatial-type residence built in the 19C, and the 16C Casa-Palacio de los Topete. The street itself is a superb example of early-20C architecture which was remodelled as part of the celebrations for the **1929 Ibero-American Exhibition** in Sevilla.

Follow calle de la Feria to the **Museo Municipal** ⊘.

The **Alberite dolmen** ⊘, dating from around 4000 BC, can be visited on the outskirts of Villamartín, 4km/2.5mi to the south. It consists of a gallery 20m/65ft long formed by large stone slabs, and a funerary chamber.

1km/0.6mi from the town, along the A 382 towards Jerez, the largest salt cedar grove in Europe can be seen.

Bornos – Bornos extends gracefully along the reservoir *(embalse)* of the same name. It is unlike many of its fellow villages along this route in that it is not surrounded by mountains, nor is it completely white. It does, however, have some of the best architecture in the whole area. The plaza del Ayuntamiento is fronted by the **Castillo-Palacio de los Ribera★** ⊘, a castle-cum-palace which is now home to the **Tourist Office** and a workshop-school. The oldest part of this castle of Moorish origin is the keep, from where the views of the rooftops and reservoir are particularly impressive. The inside of the building has an attractive Renaissance-style **patio★** with an ogival balustrade running along the upper gallery, from where there is access to one of the village's hidden treasures: a garden laid out in the 16C and one of the first of its kind designed in the pure Renaissance style. At one end, note the loggia-type gallery.

Lime

A particular feature of Andalucian architecture is the use of lime. A number of theories have been put forward to explain this practice, the origins of which can be found in the Middle Ages. When used on walls, lime acts as a consolidating agent and an insulator against fierce heat; in times past it was also used as a disinfectant against disease.

Also lining the plaza del Ayuntamiento is the **Iglesia de Santo Domingo**, a Gothic church built in the late 15C.

Espera – *10km/6mi northwest along the CA 402*. The village stands on a small outcrop in the middle of a fertile landscape. A Moorish castle, the **Castillo de Fatetar**, looks down upon the village from on high; note also the Baroque façade of a chapel, the Ermita del Cristo de la Antigua, next to it. The **Iglesia de Santa María de Gracia**, a church in the village, is also worthy of note.

Return to Arcos along the A 393.

The Spanish fir

This species, a relic of the Tertiary era, is the most common tree to be found in the local *sierra*. Known popularly as the Spanish pine, the Spanish fir *(pinsapo)* is a tree which is more commonly found in Mediterranean areas. Today, it is only found in the Sierra de Grazalema and the Serranía de Ronda in Spain, and the Rif mountains in Morocco. The Spanish fir was officially classified as an arboreal species in 1837 by the Swiss botanist Edmond Bossier. It can grow to a height of some 30m/100ft and attain a diameter of around 1m/3ft. Its branches, which grow horizontally, and its leaves, with their helicoidal shape, give the tree an unusual appearance which is quite unique in Spain.

EL PUERTO DE SANTA MARÍA★

Cádiz – Population 73 728

Michelin map 446 W 11

El Puerto de Santa María has a wealthy bourgeois appearance with its old seigniorial mansions built by the local nobility at a time when the town was an important commercial centre. It was from here that **Columbus** departed on two occasions on his journeys of discovery to the Americas; **Juan de la Cosa** also created his **Mapamundi** in the town in 1500, the first map to show the recently discovered New World. Trade with the Indies during the 16C and 17C was to make the town's fortune. During this time El Puerto de Santa María saw the constant coming and going of merchants who built small palaces and private residences here. The town has managed to preserve its ordered old quarter, predominantly built in the 18C and 19C, and best discovered on foot. In addition to its historical and artistic heritage, the modern El Puerto also has the typical *joie de vivre* of Andalucia, typified in summer when its streets are thronged with visitors from around Spain who come here to enjoy the superb local gastronomy and lively night-life.

El Vaporcito del Puerto ⊘

El Vaporcito (The Little Steamer) is the name affectionately given to the charming **Adriano III** ferry which plies the route between Puerto de Santa María and Cádiz. Its owner, Juan Fernández, came to the town from Galicia in 1927, from which time the service has operated. Prior to the construction of the Carranza Bridge, the ferry was a vital link between the two towns. The crossing takes around 40min and has the advantage of offering visitors a different perspective of Cádiz. In summer, visitors can also enjoy an evening cruise *(2hr)* in the bay of Cádiz on board El Vaporcito. The ferry departs from plaza de las Galeras Reales, with its attractive 18C **fountain**.

VISIT

Iglesia Mayor Prioral ⊘ – This priory church was founded in the 13C, during the reign of Alfonso X. The building visible today, dating from the late 15C, is a good example of the late-Gothic style employed during the reign of the Catholic Monarchs. Its outstanding feature is the **Portada del Sol★** (Sun Gateway), which opens onto plaza de España. The overall effect of this work, with its profuse Plateresque and Baroque decoration, is one of great expression. The inside of the church has suffered a number of modifications over the course of time and as such displays a mixture of styles with little coherence.

Follow calle Pagador, home to the **Museo Municipal** ⊘, *as far as calle Santo Domingo.*

Fundación Rafael Alberti ⊘ – The Rafael Alberti Foundation is devoted to the life of the late poet (1902-99), who was one of El Puerto's most famous native sons. Photographs, letters and original copies of work trace his life, and to a certain extent provide a compendium of Spanish history over the past 100 years.

Castillo de San Marcos ⊘ – Alfonso X had the first castle-church built above the main mosque of the Moorish city of *Alcanatif* in the 13C. The castle was subsequently modified and extended during the 14C and 15C, before acquiring its present form. Restoration work was carried out on the turrets and towers in the middle of the 20C. The former fish exchange *(lonja de pescado)* can be seen behind the castle.

Plaza del Polvorista – This square is fronted by the **Palácio de Imblusqueta**, a palatial 17C residence which is now home to the town hall.

Bullring ⊘ – The town's bullring, built in 1880, is one of the largest in Spain, with a diameter of 60m/197ft and seating for over 12 000 spectators. Despite its numerous external arcades, its outward appearance is one of solidity, providing a contrast with the more graceful nature of its interior.

Wine cellars

A visit to El Puerto de Santa María would not be complete without visiting one of its wine cellars:
Bodegas Osborne: For information, ☎ 956 85 52 11.
Bodegas Terry: The visit includes the **Carriage Museum** *(Museo de Carruajes)*. For information, ☎ 956 54 39 27.

Monasterio de Nuestra Señora de la Victoria – The austere external appearance of this monastery on the outskirts of the town is broken only by the exuberant decoration on the **portal★**, framed by two buttresses which develop into elaborate pinnacles. A tympanum above the door is crowned by a gable bearing the coat of arms of the Cerda family. The building has had many uses: it was a prison during part of the 19C and is now used to host official ceremonies.

WHERE TO STAY

MODERATE

Chaikana – *Javier de Burgos, 17* – ☎ *956 54 29 01* – *fax 954 54 29 22* – *25 rooms* – *6 500pts (8 500pts in Aug)*. A small, modern and spotlessly clean hotel in the centre of El Puerto de Santa María.

MID-RANGE

Los Cántaros – *Curva, 6* – ☎ *956 54 02 40* – *fax 956 54 11 21* – *39 rooms* – *12 900pts*. This well-maintained hotel, located on a small square in the town centre, owes its name to the hundred or so 17C pitchers discovered in its basement.

Dunas Puerto – *Camino de Los Enamorados* – ☎ *956 85 09 50* – *fax 956 85 02 50* – *58 rooms* – *10 000pts*. For those who prefer nature to the city, this hotel could be the answer. Bungalows with independent access in an area of greenery by the sea.

LUXURY

Monasterio de San Miguel – *Calle Larga, 27* – ☎ *956 54 04 40* – *fax 956 54 26 04* – *150 rooms* – *22 500pts*. This former Capuchin monastery dates from the 18C. The rooms are tastefully decorated and crowned by impressive vaulted ceilings. Other facilities include a swimming pool and garden.

EATING OUT

Ribera del Marisco – The attractive **plaza de la Herrería** and Ribera del Marisco are the liveliest parts of El Puerto, with numerous bars and restaurants. Popular eateries include **Casa Flores** and **Los Portales**, both of which have an excellent reputation and typical decor. Two of the town's best-known bars are **Romerijo 1** and **Romerijo 2**, where fish and seafood can be bought by weight and eaten on the terrace. Such is their popularity that it is often difficult to get a table.

El Faro del Puerto – *Carretera de Rota, 15* – ☎ *956 21 10 68* – *closed Sun evening*. This high-class restaurant located away from the noise of the town centre is one of El Puerto's most elegant establishments. International and Andalucian cuisine.

CAFÉS, BARS & NIGHT-LIFE

Most of El Puerto's bars and cafés are concentrated around Ribera del Marisco in the centre of town.

Blanco y Negro – *Ricardo Alcón, 10. Open daily from 5pm to the early hours of the morning*. This former wine storehouse, tucked away in an alleyway, is renowned for its coffee, which is roasted in El Puerto de Santa María. The café occasionally hosts art and photography exhibitions by local artists and is popular with the 25-and-over age group.

Café Central – *Luna, 41. Open 8.30am to 3pm and 5pm to midnight. Closed Sun*. The Café Central, located in the town's main pedestrianised shopping district, is frequented by a varied clientele of all ages. The outdoor terrace is a popular meeting place, while the restored 17C building which is part of the café is used as a venue for art and photography exhibitions. In winter, the café organises live performances and readings by local vocalists and storytellers.

El Convento – *Bajamar, 30. Open Mon to Sat, 11pm to 6am*. This pub-museum opposite the fish market is housed in a restored 18C convent. The smell of incense in the air and the DJ's cabin in the former pulpit are a reminder of the building's original purpose. The dance-floor is always crowded at the weekend, although during the week the atmosphere is quieter and more relaxed.

La Pescadería – *On Ribera del Marisco*. The former fish market has been transformed into a series of small bars, open until 2am, where the former fishmongers' stalls originally stood. Two of its most lively bars, particularly popular with those in their 20s and 30s, are **Barroco** and **Okendo**, at either end of the building.

SHOPPING

The main shopping district in the town centre is concentrated around three streets: **calle Luna**, **calle Palacios** and **calle Larga**. The first two head off from the **Iglesia Mayor Prioral** and are predominantly pedestrianised. This part of El Puerto is also a pleasant area in which to stroll.

Arte Sano, a boutique selling high-quality and original ceramics and basketwork, is located on calle Santo Domingo *(parallel to calle Palacios – open Mon to Fri, 10am to 2pm and on Sat mornings)*.

A small **market** selling a whole range of goods is held every Tuesday on rotonda de la Puntilla.

ENTERTAINMENT

With its excellent beaches and leisure facilities, El Puerto de Santa María has developed into a popular summer resort. The rest of the year, visitors come here to visit its wine cellars, enjoy its delicious local tapas, and perhaps play a round of golf at one of the internationally renowned courses in the area.

TRANSPORT

Airport – The nearest airport is in Jerez de la Frontera, 20km/12mi from El Puerto de Santa María along the main N IV Cádiz to Madrid road. ☎ 956 15 00 00.

Trains – The only train station is located on plaza de la Estación. The service linking Cádiz with Sevilla stops in El Puerto de Santa María every 20min. Services operate from Cádiz and Sevilla to every corner of Spain. ☎ 956 54 25 85.

Inter-city-buses – The only bus stop for long-distance services is at the bullring (plaza de toros).
The **Transportes Comes** bus company (☎ 956 21 17 63) has regular departures throughout the province and to Sevilla.

Transportes Los Amarillos (☎ 956 25 58 52) mainly operates services to destinations in the provinces of Sevilla and Málaga.

City buses – Six local bus services operate in and around El Puerto de Santa María. ☎ 956 85 75 50.

EXCURSIONS

Rota – 27km/17mi west of El Puerto de Santa María along a road skirting a large American military base. Rota is a popular resort with 16km/10mi of beaches at the northerly tip of Cádiz Bay. Its position provides protection against the strong winds which affect other towns and villages along this part of the coast.

★**Old town** – Rota's old quarter occupies a small stretch of land between two beaches, **Playa de la Costilla**★ and Playa del Rompidillo. The town, which has managed to preserve its appearance of an old fishing village, has two main monuments: the **Parroquia de Nuestra Señora de la O**, a parish church with a handsome late-Gothic **interior**★; and the **Castillo de Luna**, a castle which is now the town hall.

> ### Local specialities
>
> Rota's most typical dish is undoubtedly *urta a la roteña*, sea bream cooked with peppers, tomatoes, white wine and thyme. It is a traditional feature of one of the region's most unusual festivals, the **Fiesta de la Urta**, when locals compete to produce the best recipe for this dish. The festival has been held for the past 30 years and takes place in mid-August.

Puerto Real – 10km/6mi south of El Puerto de Santa María. This royal port (puerto real), founded by the Catholic Monarchs in 1483, enjoyed its period of greatest splendour in the 18C. Sadly, the Napoleonic invasion in 1808 was to herald the start of a century of decline for the town. The recent closure of the local shipyards has also had a serious impact on the town. Puerto Real is home to several faculties which are part of the **University of Cádiz**. Its major monument is the **Iglesia de San Sebastián**, a church built in the middle of the 16C.

La RÁBIDA★

Huelva
Michelin map 446 U 9

This small settlement of whitewashed houses built around the La Rábida monastery is located just a few kilometres from Palos de la Frontera on the left bank of the Tinto River. Like many sites in the area, La Rábida is situated along the "Columbus Route", which retraces the steps of this famous explorer.

Plans, maps and other information on La Rábida are available from the **La Casita de Zenobia** ⊙ *information and reception centre.*

MONASTERIO DE SANTA MARÍA DE LA RÁBIDA ⊙

This 14C Mudéjar-Gothic Franciscan monastery has gone down in history as the place in which Christopher Columbus stayed and, with the help of the Pinzón brothers and the monks Antonio de Marchena and Juan Pérez, planned his voyage of discovery to America, as depicted by the magnificent frescoes by **Daniel Vázquez Díaz** (1930) in various rooms on the ground floor.
Before entering the monastery, note the large white stone monument, the Columna de los Descubridores (Discoverers' Column), in a large rotunda, depicting scenes from the discoveries; this monument was erected to commemorate the 400th anniversary of this momentous event.

Monasterio de Santa María de La Rábida

*Church – Although small in dimensions, the church contains several items of great artistic value: the old frescoes which can be seen in various chapels; the polychrome wood *artesonados*, whose filigree work creates an attractive contrast with the austere appearance of the buildling as a whole; several 18C paintings by Juan de Dios, representing scenes from the life of St Francis; and, above all, the **Virgin of the Miracles***, the monastery's patron, housed in a chapel to the left of the main altar. Legend states that it was in front of this exceptional alabaster statue, a 14C figure sculpted by an Andalucian workshop, that Columbus and the crew of the three caravels prayed on the two days prior to their departure. Pope John Paul II blessed this magnificent carving as part of the celebrations commemorating the 500th anniversary of the Discoveries in 1992.

Cloisters – The Mudéjar-style cloisters comprise two galleries of columns: the lower tier was built in the 15C, while the upper crenellated section, added in the 18C, contains models of the three caravels, the Pinta, the Niña and the Santa María. Despite their fortified appearance, the cloisters retain the typical charm of Andulacian patios, with their abundant vegetation and the gentle bubbling of water from the fountain.

Dining room – A whitewashed pulpit which was formerly used for readings by lectors can be seen to the side of this austere rectangular room.

Chapter-house – This bright, spacious room crowned by an outstanding 18C Mudéjar *artesonado* ceiling has at its centre a large table which, according to tradition, was used by Columbus to discuss his plans with his advisors and assistants.

Sala de las Banderas – The Flag Room exhibits the flag of every country on the American continent as well as a recipient containing earth from each of these countries. A small room to the right exhibits a **mapamundi***, a work by Juan de la Cosa, which outlined the coast of America for the first time.

ADDITIONAL SIGHTS

*Muelle de las Carabelas ⊘ – Life-size replicas of the three caravels which transported Columbus to the New World are moored at this modern dock on the banks of the Tinto Estuary. A tour of the berths, storerooms and decks of these old vessels enables visitors to observe the detailed decoration and equipment on board, such as firearms, anchors, sails etc used by the sailors on this momentous voyage. The building at the entrance to the dock has a number of rooms with audiovisual presentations explaining different aspects of the journey, a small **museum** displaying 15C navigational tools, and a souvenir shop.

Muelle de la Reina – The small Queen's Dock is located alongside the three caravels and is dominated by the monument to Icarus of the Triumph *(Ícaro del Triunfo)*, commemorating the first transatlantic flight by the Plus Ultra seaplane from Palos de la Frontera to Buenos Aires in 1926.

Avenida de los Descubridores – This wide avenue, named in honour of the Great Discoverers, links Palos de la Frontera with La Rábida and is decorated with the coats of arms of every Ibero-American country. The Glorieta del Pueblo Argentino, a square named in honour of the Argentinian people, stands at the end of the avenue, with a glazed ceramic Aztec calendar as its centrepiece.

Parque Botánico José Celestino Mutis – The botanical garden, dedicated to this Andalucian scientist, is a maze of leafy avenues, canals and bridges displaying the most typical plant species to be found on the five continents.

Foro Iberoamericano de la Rábida – The Ibero-American forum is a building with a large open-air auditorium used as a venue for congresses, concerts and theatrical performances.

Universidad Internacional de Andalucía – This prestigious university is devoted entirely to the study of American cultures.

Plaza de Macuro – A modern sculpture in the square recalls the crossing of the Atlantic by helicopter from Macuro (Venezuela) to La Rábida.

EL ROCÍO

Huelva

Michelin map 446 U 10

This small village of whitewashed houses and sandy streets is situated within the municipal boundaries of Almonte, on the outer limits of the Parque Nacional de Doñana. For all but one weekend of the year it is a peaceful place, inhabited by a few local residents, many of whom use horses as their main mode of transport, second-homers (particularly from Almonte), members of religious brotherhoods which have their headquarters here, and a small number of shops selling religious objects and local arts and crafts. The tranquility of El Rocío is broken during Whitsun weekend, when around a million pilgrims make their way here to show their devotion to the **Virgin of the Dew** (Virgen del Rocío).

El Rocío pilgrimage

The pilgrimage to El Rocío is the largest and most famous of all religious peregrinations in Spain. For those born outside Andalucia, its profound meaning is difficult to comprehend, but for hundreds of thousands of visitors, including an increasing number of pilgrims from outside Spain attracted by its beauty and significance, the journey here is an important annual event.

According to tradition, the Church of the Virgin of the Dew was erected at the beginning of the 15C to house a statue found by a hunter in the hollow of an oak tree. In the middle of the 17C, during a large epidemic, the church developed into a place of pilgrimage which attracted the devout from far and wide, imploring the Virgin for good health.

Almonte, the nearest town to El Rocío, and Villamanrique, became the first two towns to establish brotherhoods or religious associations, which now number around 100.

"The Route" – During the course of the week preceding the feast of Pentecost, members of each brotherhood leave their headquarters and make their way towards the shrine. These pilgrims follow long-established routes on foot, in carts adorned with colourful decoration and paper flowers, on horseback and even nowadays by jeep. Women wear the traditional *rociero* skirt, decorated with one or two pleated ruffles, and hats to offer protection against the hot sun; men tend to wear a white shirt, tight-fitting trousers and a Cordoban sombrero or cap. In order to walk more easily on the sand of the Doñana, almost everyone wears leather boots. A sprig of rosemary and the medallion of the brotherhood complete the attire. Each brotherhood follows its own *simpecado*, a silver cart pulled by oxen carrying a standard bearing the image of the Virgin of the Dew. At night, when pilgrims stop along the route, the scene transforms into one of dancing and singing around open fires, with the reciting of the rosary at nightfall and celebration of mass at dawn early the next morning.

The village of El Rocío – Pilgrims arrive at El Rocío throughout the **Saturday**, where they pay homage to the White Dove (Blanca Paloma) or to Our Lady of the Marshes (La Señora de las Marismas), two of the many names given to the Virgin Mary. The **Sunday** is given over to masses, recitals of the rosary and socialising, culminating in the most eagerly awaited moment in the **early morning on the Monday of Pentecost**. Just before daybreak, youngsters from the nearby town of Almonte climb over the gate of the church and remove the statue of the Virgin, which they then process through the streets, surrounded by a security cordon to prevent pilgrims from approaching it. The night is a long one, full of emotion, fatigue and happiness, the culmination of a week of physical effort and devotion for which pilgrims have been preparing throughout the year.

A *simpecado* in front of the Ermita de la Blanca Paloma

273

WHERE TO STAY

Toruño – *Plaza del Acebuchal, 22* – ☎ *959 44 23 23* – fax *959 44 23 38* – *30 rooms* – *8 000pts.* A traditional house in the centre of the village with rooms decorated in local style. The hotel also has a typical restaurant on the ground floor.

EATING OUT

Aires de Doñana – *Avenida de la Canaliega, 1* – ☎/fax *959 44 27 19*. A rustic building with a straw roof. The restaurant enjoys views of the Ermita de la Virgen and horses grazing on the nearby marshland.

THE WINE ROUTE: from El Rocío to Niebla

36km/22.5mi – allow half a day.

The highlight of this itinerary is the tasting of excellent local white and sweet wines which fall under the Condado de Huelva appellation. It is well worth visiting the local *bodegas* to try specialities such as old *oloroso*, fruity whites, *mistela* (a flavoured brandy), *moscatel* and sweet orange wine *(vino dulce de naranja)*.

Almonte – *15km/9.5mi north of El Rocío along the A 483.* Almonte is one of the best-known towns in the province of Huelva due to the presence within its boundaries of the Parque Nacional de Doñana *(see p 173)*, the popular Matalascañas beach *(see p 156)* and, in particular, the village of El Rocío. However, much of the town's prestige stems from wine, the aroma of which is ever-present in its streets. Whitewashed houses adorned with wrought-iron grilles and resplendent doorways are a typical feature of Almonte, in front of which the carts used to transport the grapes at harvest time are a frequent sight. The **plaza Virgen del Rocío**, the hub of town life, is a delightful haven of peace and tranquillity fronted by two of Almonte's main buildings: the parish church, an attractive example of colonial-style architecture, and the town hall, with its elegant gallery of arches on the upper floor.

Bollullos del Condado – *9km/5.5mi north.* Every corner of this town appears to be devoted to wine production, with numerous old *bodegas* lining its well-maintained streets with their seigniorial air. Behind the impressive façades of these imposing buildings, visitors can learn more about ancestral wine-making techniques, and taste and purchase some of the excellent sweet and white wines produced in large vats and served in attractive earthenware cups. Bollulos is also home to several artisanal workshops producing iron utensils, carriages, gold embroidery and barrels. The town also has a number of bars and restaurants specialising in seafood. The **plaza del Sagrado Corazón de Jesús**, a picturesque square fronted by the **Iglesia de Santiago Apóstol**, with its Andalucian Baroque façade and tower, and the town hall, its attractive façade composed of two storeys of stilted arches, are worthy of note.

La Palma del Condado – *4km/2.5mi northwest.* Renowned for its excellent wines, this bright town is embellished with a number of seigniorial squares, elegant whitewashed houses and notable monumental buildings. The main event in the local calendar is the **Fiesta de la Vendimia**, the wine harvest festival held at the end of September, the origins of which date back to the 14C.

Town Hall – The former 16C Hospital of the Immaculate Conception was restored in 1929 in the Regionalist style employed for the Ibero-American Exhibition of the same year, before converting to its current use.

Plaza del Corazón de Jesús – This attractive square, dominated by the statue of the Sacred Heart of Jesus (Corazón de Jesús), a work created in 1927 by the local sculptor Antonio Pinto Soldán, is surrounded by a series of elegant, colonial-inspired buildings.

Plaza de España – This well-proportioned square is the centre of local life. One side of the plaza is bordered by the former Palacio del Señorío, the theatre and the Casa de los Arcos, while the opposite side is fronted by the Casa de Tirado, with an exquisite **grille** and *azulejos* which reproduce *Las Meninas* and *Las Hilanderas* by Velázquez. However, the most interesting construction on the square is the **Iglesia de San Juan Bautista**, a sober Baroque construction, its impressive whitewashed façade crowned by a graceful tower used as a nesting place for storks.

Iglesia del Valle – The *camarín* behind the main altar of this 15C Mudéjar-style church houses a statue of the Virgin of the Valley, the patron saint of La Palma del Condado.

★**Niebla** – *8km/5mi southwest of La Palma del Condado along the A 472. Several cultural itineraries depart from the* **Tourist Office** ⊙, *housed in the Hospital de Nuestra Señora de los Ángeles.* This old settlement, dating back to the 8C BC, is located 29km/18km from Huelva. The historical centre of Niebla is graced with several old monuments of significant interest, in particular the series of **walls★**, one of the most complete of any in Spain. Erected during the period of Almohad domination in the 12C using clay from the banks of the Tinto River – hence their reddish colour – they run for a length of 2km/1.2mi and are punctuated by a total of 50 towers and five entrance gateways. The **Iglesia de Santa María de la Granada**, built on the site of the former mosque, combines features from the earlier construction, such as the peaceful patio of orange trees which opens onto the entrance of the church, with additional Gothic elements. The **alcázar** or **Castillo de los Guzmanes**, dating from the 15C, has retained several interesting vestiges of Moorish architecture. The **Iglesia de San Martín**, divided into two by a street, is a building formerly used both as a mosque and synagogue. On the outskirts of Niebla, the Tinto River is spanned by a large Roman bridge.

RONDA★★

Málaga – Population 35 788
Michelin map 446 V 14

Ronda stands at the heart of the Serranía de Ronda in a delightful setting surrounded by lush river valleys. Its dramatic position above a deep ravine, its geographical isolation, and the legends of local highwaymen made the town a place of pilgrimage for Romantic writers during the 19C. Situated just 50km/31mi from the Costa del Sol, and with good access to other parts of Andalucia, the town has developed into a modern-day tourist destination; however, despite its huge popularity, it has retained its delightful character, typified by cobbled streets, whitewashed houses, impressive mansions and the oldest bullring in Spain.

HISTORICAL NOTES

When Moorish troops under the command of **Tarik-ibn-Zeyad** invaded the region in the early 8C, one of the first roads they followed inland was the old Roman way linking Gibraltar with the Roman settlement of **Acinipo**. Upon their arrival they founded a fortified town which they named *Izna-Rand-Onda*, nowadays known as Ronda, some 20km/12mi from this old Roman settlement. Under the Umayyads, Ronda was the capital of a Moorish region *(cora)*, and following the fall of the Caliphate, it developed

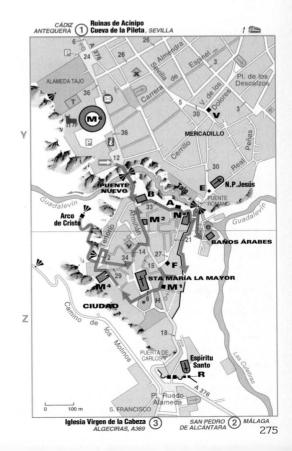

into the capital of a *taifa* kingdom. With the arrival of the Almohads, the town experienced a period of growth which continued until the Nasrid era. Christian troops finally reconquered the town in 1485.

TOUR

Getting around Ronda is quite straightforward. The **Guadalevín River**, which translates as "river of milk", cuts the town in two: on one side, stands the old Moorish quarter, nowadays referred to as **La Ciudad** (or Old Town); on the other, the more modern **Mercadillo** district. To the south, beyond the **Puerta de Almocabar**, and the Arrabal Nuevo (New District) behind it, is the San Francisco quarter, which developed in the 15C as a market area outside the walls.

★★ La Ciudad

★ Puente Nuevo – The New Bridge is perhaps the best place to start a visit of Ronda. Follow the path to the cafeteria to the rear of the *parador* for a superb view of the bridge, and of the Guadiaro river valley and the Sierra de Grazalema beyond. The bridge, built in the second half of the 18C, is a magnificent feat of engineering.

Cross the bridge and follow calle Santo Domingo.

To the left stands the Convento de Santo Domingo, the first building to be founded by the Catholic Monarchs following the reconquest of the city in 1485; the house on the right was the birthplace in 1839 of Francisco Giner de los Ríos, who founded the **Institución Libre de Enseñanza**, a liberal institution of learning.

Head down calle Santo Domingo.

Casa del Rey Moro ⊘ – According to legend, this mansion was the residence of the king of Ronda, Almonated, who it is said drank wine from the skulls of his enemies. The current building dates from the 18C. The exterior shows Mudéjar influence with its brick towers and wooden balconies. The interior contains an impressive set of Moorish steps, known as **La Mina**, which descend to the river.

WHERE TO STAY

MODERATE

Virgen de los Reyes – *Lorenzo Borrego, 13 – ☎ 952 87 11 40 – 52 rooms – 5 000pts.* An inexpensive hotel with clean, simple rooms.

Alavera – *Hoyo San Miguel – ☎/fax 952 87 91 43 – 10 rooms – 7 000pts.* In the lower part of the town next to the Moorish Baths. Although this pleasant hotel is of recent construction, all the rooms are different. Other facilities for guests include a restaurant and terrace.

MID-RANGE

San Gabriel – *José M. Hidalgo, 19 – ☎ 952 19 03 92 – fax 952 19 01 17 – 11 000pts.* A delightful, magnificently decorated mansion dating from 1736. Some of the rooms look onto a charming patio. The hotel prides itself on its friendliness and attention to detail.

La Fuente de la Higuera – *In Los Frontones: take the A 376 towards Sevilla, bear right before crossing the Guadiaro River, then follow signposts (3km/1.8mi) – ☎ 952 11 43 55 – fax 952 11 43 56 – 8 rooms – 15 000pts.* This Germanic paradise on Spanish soil was created by a German couple who decided to settle in Andalucia. Today, the ruins they purchased a number of years ago have been converted into a superb hotel with a waiting list of guests. Because of the small number of rooms, reservations are recommended well in advance.

EATING OUT

Don Miguel – *Villanueva, 4 and 8 – ☎ 952 87 10 90.* A pleasant terrace with excellent views of the Puente Nuevo, the ravine and the Guadalevín River. High-quality cuisine which includes specialities such as *rabo de toro* (braised bull's tail), *asado de ciervo* (roast venison) and *cordero a la menta* (lamb with mint sauce). A number of rooms are also available (9 500pts).

Casa Santa Pola – *Santo Domingo, 3 – ☎ 952 87 92 08.* A restaurant with several rooms overlooking the ravine. Specialities here include *carne de buey* (ox) and poultry.

Tragabuches – *José Aparicio, 1 – ☎ 952 19 02 91 – closed Mon.* This restaurant, considered by many locals to be the best in Ronda, is just a stone's throw from the *parador* and the bullring. Its kitchen, run by Sergio López, a prize-winning young chef, offers guests modern cuisine in an avant-garde setting.

★**Jardines de Forestier** – In 1912 the famous French landscapist **Forestier** who, in 1929, designed the María Luisa Park in Sevilla, was commissioned to design these attractive gardens *(jardines)*. Despite the technical difficulties he encountered due to the narrowness of the terrain, he managed to create a jewel of landscape art. The gardens are divided into three terraces which combine Moorish features, such as fountains, water and *azulejos*, with other more traditionally European elements such as pergolas and parterres.

Palacio del Marqués de Salvatierra – *The palace interior is closed to visitors.* This small mansion is a typical example of noble 18C architecture, with an exceptional **portal**★★ its most impressive feature. On the lower section, the door is flanked by two pairs of Corinthian-style columns topped by an architrave decorated with medallions. On the upper section, the

Detail on the façade of the Palacio del Marqués de Salvatierra

shafts of the columns have been replaced by attractive pairs of human figures which show strong pre-Columbian influence.

Walk down towards the old bridge. Beyond the Puerta de Felipe V, follow a stone path which heads down to the Moorish Baths.

★**Moorish Baths** ⊙ – Ronda's Moorish Baths are some of the best preserved on the Iberian Peninsula. They were built at the end of the 13C, close to the river along the Las Culebras stream *(arroyo)*, in the Arrabal Viejo, a district popular with artisans and tanners. The first part of the building, an area without a roof, leads to the baths themselves, comprising three transversal rooms topped with barrel vaults and illuminated by star-shaped lunettes. The middle room, which is divided into three naves separated by horseshoe arches and brick columns, is the most impressive in the complex. The cauldron used to heat water for the baths is still visible to the rear.

Follow a stone staircase running parallel to the walls, then pass through a 13C gateway, the Puerta de la Acijara.

★**Minarete de San Sebastián** – *In plaza del poeta Abul-Beca.* This graceful minaret is the only one which remains from the 14C Nasrid mosque which stood on this spot. Following the Christian Reconquest, this temple was subsequently dedicated to St Sebastian. Only the lower stone section dates from the Moorish period; the upper brick section is Mudéjar in style. The horseshoe arch framing the door is particularly worthy of note. The tower is the smallest minaret still standing in Andalucia.

Museo del Bandolero ⊙ – This museum is devoted to the bandits, brigands and outlaws of Andalucia, including legendary names such as Diego Corrientes and **José María el Tempranillo**, who were perceived as poor wretches, romantic travellers or bloodthirsty murderers. A video presentation *(in Spanish only)*, a series of documents and other exhibits provide visitors with an insight into these famous figures in Andalucian history.

★**Santa María la Mayor** ⊙ – The Collegiate Church of St Mary is, like many Andalucian churches from the period, dedicated to the Incarnation. It was built above the town's former main mosque following the capture of Ronda by the Catholic Monarchs in 1485. Today, only the Mihrab Arch *(in the entrance room)*, decorated with *atauriques* and calligraphic motifs, remains from the original building. The interior is divided into two sections, one Gothic, the other Renaissance.

★★**Palacio de Mondragón: Museo de la Ciudad** ⊙ – *From plaza de la Duquesa Parcent walk along calle Manuel Montero.* The palace occupies a former Moorish residence dating from the 14C, from which only the foundations have been preserved. The present building is a mixture of the Mudéjar (towers and patios) and Renaissance styles,

277

the latter best seen on the doorway of the façade. The outstanding feature on the inside is the charming **Mudéjar patio**★★ with the remains of *azulejos* and stuccowork between its arches. Nowadays, the palace also houses the town **museum**, which contains a number of interesting displays, including an exhibition on the natural habitats of the Serranía de Ronda.

Continue to plaza del Campillo. Follow the path heading down to the 18C **Arco de Cristo** (Christ's Arch), *from where there is a magnificent* **view**★★ *of the* **ravine** *(tajo) and bridge.*

Follow calle Sor Ángela to plaza del Gigante. The square is named after the barely discernible relief of Hercules adorning one of its 14C houses.

Return to calle Armiñán.

Museo Lara ◷ – Over the years, the owner of this museum, Juan Antonio Lara, has brought together an extraordinary **collection**★ of eclectic exhibits which include superb 18C enamel clocks, delightful fans, and an armoury containing an unusual seven-barrel pistol. The museum is housed in the Casa-palacio de los Condes de las Islas Batanes, fronted by an attractive façade.

Follow calle Armiñán to return to plaza de España.

El Mercadillo

This district, which developed in the 16C, is connected to **La Ciudad** via two bridges: the **Puente Nuevo** (New Bridge) and the Puente Viejo (Old Bridge). El Mercadillo is the commercial part of Ronda, with a number of pedestrianised streets such as calle Nueva, **calle Remedios**, calle Ermita and the **plaza del Socorro**, a square fronted by several attractive 19C and 20C buildings.

Bullring, Ronda

★**Bullring: Museo Taurino** ◷ – The bullring, built in 1785 by the Royal Institute of Knights (Real Maestranza de Caballería), is one of Spain's most beautiful, with a tradition to match. Its 66m/216ft diameter makes it the widest bullring anywhere in the world. Although the twin-tier interior is neo-Classical in style with Tuscan columns and a stone barrier around the ring, the overall effect is one of great simplicity. The bullring also houses an interesting **museum** devoted to bullfighting.

★**Templete de la Virgen de los Dolores** – Built in 1734, this small temple is crowned by a simple vault resting on two columns and two pilasters. Each of the columns is adorned with four half-human, half-fantastic **figures**★ with their arms interlinked and attached by the neck, all of which portray great expression.

Iglesia de Nuestro Padre Jesús – The oldest part of this heavily restored church is the tower-façade, built in the 15C in Gothic style; the roof dates from 1735. Opposite stands the **Fuente de los Ocho Caños** (Fountain of the Eight Spouts), created during the reign of Carlos III in the 18C.

ADDITIONAL SIGHTS

Iglesia del Espíritu Santo – The Church of the Holy Spirit has a sober, yet elegant façade with a fortress-like appearance which is due to its position next to the town walls. It was built upon the order of the Catholic Monarchs at the end of the 15C. The interior, which has been remodelled on a number of occasions, has a single nave crowned by a stellar vault with tiercerons.

Puerta de Almocabar – This gateway takes its name from the Arabic cemetery *(al-maqabir)* which stood in this section of the town. The gateway is flanked by two 18C towers and consists of three horseshoe arches. To one side note the **Puerta de Carlos V** (Carlos V's Gateway) and opposite, beyond the walls, the **San Francisco district**, where the outstanding monument is a 17C Franciscan convent.

EXCURSIONS

★**Iglesia Rupestre de la Virgen de la Cabeza** ☉ – *2.7km/1.7mi along the A 369 towards Algeciras. Upon leaving the town, take a signposted road to the right (after approx 700m/770yd) leading to the chapel.* This small Mozarabic monastery, probably founded by Hispano-Visigoths in the 9C, was erected on high ground on the opposite bank of the Guadalevín River, affording one of the best **views**★★ of Ronda. The monastery has been excavated out of the rock and occupies a surface area of almost 280m²/3 013sq ft. Inside the cave, the store, the monastic quarters and the church are all clearly visible. The frescoes were painted in the 18C.

In the middle of August every year the Virgen de la Cabeza (Virgin of the Head) is ceremoniously taken from the collegiate church to the chapel next to the monastery.

Ruinas de Acinipo ☉ – *19km/11.5mi along the A 376 towards Sevilla, then the MA 449 towards Ronda la Vieja.* Known popularly as **Ronda la Vieja**, the old ruined settlement of Acinipo, which was referred to by Pliny the Elder, has preserved a large 1C AD **theatre**, including part of the stage and the terraces. What appear to be the remains of a Phoenician wall and several houses with a circular floor plan dating from the 8C BC can also be seen.

★**Cueva de La Pileta** ☉ – *20km/12mi southwest. Leave Ronda on the A 376 towards Sevilla, then take the MA 555 towards Benaoján. From here, bear onto the MA 561.* The cave was discovered in 1905 by Don José Bullón Lobato when he was searching for bat droppings for use as fertiliser on his land. The importance of the discovery was such that in 1912 studies were carried out here by the eminent prehistorians **Hugo Obermaier** and **Abé Breuil**. The Pileta Cave is a limestone formation with over 2km/1.2mi of galleries, of which some 500m/550yd are open to the public. The red and black wall paintings span an extensive period of prehistory, with figurative motifs dating from the Paleolithic era (20000 BC) and symbolic art from the Neolithic period (4000 BC).

Travellers' addresses

★★**The road from Ronda to San Pedro de Alcántara** – *49km/30.5mi southeast along the A 376 – allow 1hr.* This impressive road was built in the 1970s to connect the Serranía de Ronda with the Costa del Sol. Although it does not pass through any towns or villages, it runs between two of the most spectacular mountain ranges in Málaga province: to the left the **Parque Natural de la Sierra de las Nieves**; and to the right, the **Sierra Bermeja**. The road climbs gradually though a landscape of pines and Spanish fir on its ascent to the Alijar Pass (410m/1 345ft), from where it descends steeply towards the coast.

Parque Natural de la Sierra de las Nieves – This small natural park (18 500ha/45 713 acres), which was designated a **Biosphere Reserve** in 1994, is home to the prolific **Spanish fir** *(pinsapo)*, as well as one of the largest colonies of **mountain goat** found on the Iberian Peninsula. The relief here is characterised by steep escarpments and a limestone landscape punctuated by numerous chasms. One of the world's deepest chasms, known as **GESM** (Grupo de Exploraciones Subterráneas de Málaga), is located within the confines of the park.

The cradle of bullfighting

Born in Ronda in 1695, **Francisco Romero** laid down the rules of modern bullfighting with the introduction of the cape and the **muleta**. His son Juan introduced the *cuadrillo* or supporting team and his grandson, **Pedro Romero** (1754-1839), became one of Spain's greatest bullfighters. He founded the **Ronda School**, known still for its classicism and strict observance of the rules.

SANLÚCAR DE BARRAMEDA ★

Cádiz – Population 61 382
Michelin map 446 V 10

The fishing port of Sanlúcar is a bright, tranquil town at the mouth of the Guadalquivir River. The characteristic white soil around the town produces one of Spain's best sherries, known as *manzanilla*. The two main sources of livelihood in the town are seafood and sherry, which are reflected in the layout of the town, effectively dividing it into two sections: one, the old monumental quarter, occupied by numerous sherry *bodegas*; the other, along the waterfront, where most of the town's shops and superb fish and seafood restaurants are located.

Manzanilla

This superb wine from Sanlúcar has a clear robe and a taste which is both penetrating and dry on the palate. From May onwards, the triangle of land between Sanlúcar de Barrameda, El Puerto de Santa María and Jerez is a swathe of leafy vineyards, where the main grape grown is **Palomino**. The harvest takes place in September, following which the must extracted from the grape is transferred to large metal containers, where it is transformed into the so-called *sobretabla* must, with an alcohol content of around 11%. This dry sherry is fortified up to 15% and is then transferred to American oak barrels, where the *solera* and *criadera* system *(see p 222)* begins. The difference between *manzanilla* and *fino* sherry is due to Sanlúcar's special climate, resulting in the development of a permanent layer of yeast *(flor)* which remains in place throughout the ageing process, preventing oxidation from occurring. The minimum maturing period for *manzanilla* is three years.

Bodega visits: Guided visits are offered by several companies, including **Barbadillo** *(next to the castle)*, a local institution founded in the 18C, **Pedro Romero** *(calle Trasbola, 84)* and **La Cigarrera** *(plaza Madre de Dios)*. For information on opening times, ☎ 956 38 30 32.

Historical notes – Sanlúcar's strategic position ensured its rise to fame in the 15C as a stopping point for galleys returning to Sevilla from the newly discovered Americas. It was from here, in 1519, that the expedition led by **Magellan** departed to circumnavigate the globe, to return three years later under the command of **Juan Sebastián Elcano**. This period marked the zenith in the town's history, when Sanlúcar developed into an important commercial centre. The fall from grace of the Duke of Medina Sidonia, following Portugal's independence in 1640, and the transition from the small galley to larger ships unable to negotiate Sanlúcar's sandbanks, heralded the town's decline. At the end of the 19C the sherry industry developed here, bestowing upon the town a second period of economic expansion.

WHERE TO STAY

MID-RANGE

Posada de Palacio – *Caballeros, 11 –* ☎/*fax 956 36 50 60 – 13 rooms – 9 000pts – closed in Jan and Feb.* This 17C seigniorial mansion is decorated in traditional style, with comfortable rooms complete with antique furniture. Excellent value for money.

Tartaneros – *Tartaneros, 8 –* ☎ *956 36 20 44 – fax 956 36 00 45 – 22 rooms – 10 000pts.* This attractive yellow mansion dating from the early 20C is decorated with columns and balconies.

EATING OUT

Casa Bigote – *Bajo de Guía –* ☎ *956 36 26 96.* This local institution alongside the fishing port has been run by the same family for the past 50 years and is adorned with old photos, fishing nets and other antique objects. Unsurprisingly, fish and seafood figure prominently on the menu.

PRACTICAL INFORMATION

Tourist Office – *Calzada del Ejército.* ☎ *956 36 61 10.*

Fiestas – Carnival (February), Feria de la Manzanilla (end of May), horse race (August).

Annual horse race – The horse race that has taken place on the beaches of Sanlúcar for the past 150 years is one of Spain's most exciting events, with its spectacular setting and the magical combination of water, light and superb horsemanship. Its origins date back to the 19C, a time when horse races were still something of a novelty, and as such it is considered one of the oldest races in the country. It is held every August at low tide, although the time and date vary. Further information can be obtained from the Tourist Office.

FROM PLAZA DEL CABILDO TO THE BARRIO ALTO

allow 1hr

The following itinerary includes the main sights of interest in the Barrio Alto (Upper Town).

Plaza del Cabildo – This large square with a 19C appearance is embellished with orange and palm trees. The *plaza* is the focal point of the town and is a pleasant place for a drink or leisurely meal. It is bordered on one side by the former **town hall** *(cabildo)*, an attractive 18C building.

Plaza de San Roque – This small square is one of Sanlúcar's liveliest areas and is the setting for a daily morning market.

Iglesia de la Trinidad ⊘ – The Church of the Trinity is half-hidden on the square of the same name, on the side of the plaza de San Roque. This small single-nave church contains a magnificent 15C Mudéjar **artesonado**★★ ceiling. The 17C Baroque retable includes a fine statue of Our Lady of the Sorrows.

Continue along calle Regina.

Convento de Regina Coeli – The convent was built in the early 16C by an order of Poor Clares. It has a handsome Pompeii-red façade with two elegant portals bearing the statues of St Clare and the Virgin and Child.

> ### Local pastries
> **Convento de la Madre de Dios**: The nuns from this 17C convent with its attractive Renaissance façade are famed for their **tocino de cielo** *(see JEREZ)*, which is reputed to be one of the best in the province. The entrance to the convent is on calle del Torno. Open daily except Sun from 10am-1pm and 5-7pm. The convent looks onto a pleasant colonial-style square.

Return to plaza de San Roque and follow calle Bretones. Head up cuesta de Belén, passing the municipal market along the way.

★**Covachas** – The sea air and damaged stonework have accentuated the mysterious aspect of what probably formed part of the palace of the Dukes of Medina Sidonia, built in the 15C. This recently restored complex comprises five ogee arches profusely decorated with Gothic tracery and winged dragons.

Palacio de Orleans y Borbón ⊘ – *Entrance along calle Caballeros.* This magnificent palace, which was inspired by Moorish architecture, was built in the 19C as a summer residence for the Duke of Montpensier. The overall result is a romantic building with delightful **gardens** offering attractive views of the town. The palace now houses Sanlúcar's town hall.

Parroquia de Nuestra Señora de la O ⊘ – The church was built upon the orders of Isabel de la Cerda y Guzmán, the niece of Alfonso X the Wise. Its west façade is adorned with a majestic 14C **Mudéjar portal**★★; the outstanding feature on the inside is a superb 16C **artesonado**★ ceiling, from the same century. The **Palacio de los Condes de Niebla** ⊘, the residence of the Duchess of Medina Sidonia, stands along the church.

> It is well worth strolling along callejón de las Comedias and calle Eguilaz, with their whitewashed façades and unmistakable scent of *manzanilla*.

Walk along calle Luis de Eguilaz. At no 21 note the **Casa de la Cilla**, an attractive small Baroque palace built in the 18C to collect tithes owed to the church. Since 1939 the building has been owned by the Barbadillo *manzanilla* company.

Castillo de Santiago – The oldest section of this castle is the impressive keep, built by Guzmán the Good in the 13C. The remainder of the castle, adorned with four towers, was added in the 15C. Several historical figures have stayed in the castle, including Isabel the Catholic.

THE MODERN TOWN AND BAJO DE GUÍA

The Barrio Bajo (Lower Town) was created in the 16C in response to Sanlúcar's growth following the discovery of America. The district now extends from calle Ancha down to the Guadalquivir River and is the commercial hub of the town with plenty of bars and restaurants.

Iglesia de Santo Domingo ⊘ – The church belonged to the erstwhile Convento de Santo Domingo, founded in 1548 to provide shelter for Dominicans returning from the Americas. A handsome portal, attributed to the engineer Cristóbal de Rojas, provides access to a cloistered atrium. The severity of the exterior is compensated by the Plateresque decoration on the balustrades and windows inside the church.

Continue along calle de Santo Domingo to plaza de San Francisco.

The square is fronted by the imposing 17C **Iglesia de San Francisco**.

> **Excursions by boat to the Doñana on board the Real Fernando** – The boat departs from Sanlúcar de Barrameda and docks at La Plancha, where visitors will enjoy a short walk before returning to Sanlúcar. During the course of the trip, organised by the town hall in Sanlúcar, information is provided on the national park. Tickets can be purchased at the **Centro de Visitantes Fábrica de Hielo**.

Follow calle de San Nicolás and avenida del Cabo Nobal to the avenida Bajo de Guía.

Centro de Visitantes Bajo de Guía ⊘ – This visitor centre has several rooms dedicated to the natural habitats of the Parque Nacional de Doñana on the opposite bank of the Guadalquivir, as well as a somewhat antiquated video presentation.

Centro de Visitantes Fábrica de Hielo ⊘ – The name of this visitor centre (*fábrica de hielo* translates as "ice factory") derives from its use, up to 1978, as a factory producing ice for the fresh fish arriving at the port. Inside, the two floors house attractive, modern displays on the different aspects of the **Parque Nacional de Doñana**.

EXCURSIONS

★★★**Parque Nacional de Doñana** – *See p 173.*

Bonanza – *4km/2.5mi from Sanlúcar along the CA 624.* The daily fish auction, held in Bonanza just before 5pm every afternoon, is well worth attending for a glimpse of the daily catch, the cacophony of sound and frenetic action.

Chipiona – *9km/5.5mi southwest along the A 480.* This small resort, which is relatively quiet in winter, is transformed into a popular holiday resort with the onset of summer, when its narrow streets are thronged with tourists who come here to enjoy its delightful beaches, such as **Playa de la Regla★**, and pleasant climate. The town is an ideal base from which to explore the surrounding area, although it has several sights of interest of its own, including the **Parroquia de Nuestra Señora de la O**, a church built in the 16C in Gothic style, although subsequently remodelled; only the north façade, with its interesting Isabelline Gothic portal, remains from the original building. Also well worth a

visit is the **Santuario de Nuestra Señora de la Regla** ⊘, a church rebuilt in eclectic style at the beginning of the 20C. Inside, the **cloisters** *(access via the sacristy)* have preserved their 15C structure and are decorated with interesting *azulejos* relating the history of the sanctuary. All the figures of angels are different, while the coats of arms of Spain and the Ponce de León family can be seen on the corners. Note, on one of its sides, the attractive Romanesque mullioned window from the first cloisters built during the 10C.

For the past three decades and more the lofty silhouette of this impressive metal bull has graced the tops of Spanish hillsides, establishing itself as one of the most characteristic features of the country's road network.

Originally erected in 1956 as part of an advertising campaign for the Osborne sherry and brandy company, they were on the point of disappearing from the Spanish landscape altogether in 1988, following the introduction of a law banning advertising along roads outside of urban areas. Although the company subsequently removed its name, leaving just the bulls in place, the controversy remained.

R. Mattès

Legal moves to have the bulls removed sparked a debate that received widespread media coverage, resulting in the signing of petitions and the formation of associations to preserve them. Their defenders were of the opinion that these black bulls had gone beyond their original marketing purpose and had become a decorative feature which was now an integral part of the Spanish landscape and a symbol of the country. As a result of this campaign, the regional parliament *(Junta de Andalucía)* classified the bulls as official historical monuments, thus enabling the bulls to fight another day!

SEVILLA★★★

SEVILLE – Andalucia – Population 701 927
Michelin map 446 T 11-12

The capital of Andalucia is a city of art and history which has managed to maintain its magnificent traditions without turning its back on modernity. Sevilla has been described as a feminine city which is fully aware of its charms and is happy to display them to its visitors. The *sevillanos* are passionate about where they live and take every opportunity to extol its many virtues. However, Sevilla is more than just a city: it is a way of embracing life to the full in the exuberant, festive and, above all, passionate manner for which it is famous. Sevilla is many things, perhaps too many to highlight in just a few words: it is the Guadalquivir, a river that has left its indelible mark on the city's history and acts as a mirror in which to look into its past and future; it is its impressive Holy Week and April Fair; it is Velázquez, Murillo, Don Juan Tenorio and Carmen; the scent of orange blossom; the lively gatherings of friends; and the dancing of *sevillanas* and bullfights. Sevilla is bright, it is colourful, and, in summer, it is extremely hot!

FIESTAS

During the spring, Sevilla lives for the two fiestas that have brought it international fame: Holy Week *(Semana Santa)* and the April Fair *(Feria de Abril)*. For those who have yet to experience either, it is difficult to imagine their splendour or the way in which the city's inhabitants embrace them. These two events are the two sides of the same coin: two authentic, yet totally distinct forms of expression of the Sevillian soul.

Semana Santa

Holy Week is celebrated between Palm Sunday and Easter Sunday, either in March or April, depending on the liturgical calendar. The origins of Sevilla's Semana Santa date back to the 16C, a time when the first brotherhoods or fraternities were formed to provide assistance for guild associations. Over 50 brotherhoods participate in the Holy Week processions, each carrying their own statue of Christ or the Virgin Mary.

The whole city comes out onto the street during this ceremony to relive the Passion of Christ and the pain of his mother. The spectacle is an impressive one, with the streets and street corners of the city providing a magnificent backdrop to these processions. During this extravagant religious ritual, with its breathtakingly beautiful statues atop floats exquisitely adorned with gold and silver, popular fervour comes to the fore in an atmosphere bordering on ecstasy.

The processions – These take place throughout the course of the week. Every brotherhood leaves its own church or chapel and usually carries two floats or *pasos*: one bearing Christ, the other the Virgin Mary. They make one journey *(carrera)* to the cathedral and then return to their headquarters. Each float passes along the calle Sierpes and in front of the town hall. The hundred or more floats winding their way through the city's streets, accompanied by a

Plaza de España

band of musicians, are carried by *costaleros* – young men under the tutelage of an overseer *(capataz)* – who take immense pride in transporting these holy figures and demonstrate great skill and physical prowess in this feat of endurance.

A number of these famous processions take place on the **madrugá** (the early morning of Good Friday): El Silencio, La Macarena, La Esperanza de Triana, Los Gitanos and, on the Friday afternoon, El Cachorro.

Some of the statues borne aloft in procession are priceless works of art by leading 17C sculptors, including Jesus of Great Power and Christ of Love, by Juan de Mesa; the Christ of the Passion, by Martínez Montañés; La Macarena, anonymous; the Holy Christ of the Expiration("El Cachorro"), by Francisco Antonio Gijón; and Our Father Jesus of Nazareth, by Francisco Ocampo.

Feria de Abril

Founded in the middle of the 19C as an animal fair, the April Fair soon set aside its role as a market, developing into a colourful and lively fair with its emphasis on pure enjoyment. The Feria is the major fiesta held in Sevilla, a city with a reputation for partying like nowhere else on Earth.

The April Fair takes place two or three weeks after Holy Week in the Los Remedios district, where a veritable city of light is created, illuminated by thousands of bulbs and fairy lights, with a network of streets housing the traditional *casetas*. The festivities commence late on Monday evening and in the early hours of Tuesday morning with the illumination of the fairground area, and continue until the following Sunday when a firework display draws events to a close.

During the *feria* the streets of the fairground are thronged with a high-spirited and good-humoured crowd, while inside the *casetas* the famous *fino* sherry from Jerez and *manzanilla* from Sanlúcar flow abundantly, tapas are eaten, and *sevillanas* are danced with great passion until the early hours.

During the day, the women of Sevilla do their best to upstage each other with the beauty and grace of their flamenco costumes as they dance, stroll through the

A word of advice
The Feria is created by *sevillanos* for *sevillanos*; many of the entertainment booths *(casetas)* are private and if you don't know anyone who can provide you with an introduction or ticket you may feel slightly left out of proceedings.

streets of the city with their friends and family, or wander around the *feria* area itself.

The parade is another attractive feature of this unique fiesta, with Andalucian horsemen dressed in their typical, tight-fitting costumes and wide-brimmed *sombreros cordobeses*, and carriages pulled by horses with their colourful harnesses.

The calle del Infierno in the *feria* precinct is also a popular aspect of this annual event with its range of attractions for young and old alike.

Ch. Sappa/HOA QUI

El Rocío

The list of local fiestas would not be complete without mention of **El Rocío** *(see p 273)*. This religious pilgrimage, a combination of Marian devotion and festive spirit, converges on a chapel in the village of El Rocío, to the south of Almonte in the province of Huelva. With its numerous brotherhoods, Sevilla is actively involved in this *romería*, in which pilgrims travel on foot, horseback or by cart, following the float or *simpecado*, which bears the standard of the Virgin. During the journey, these pilgrims sing and dance special pilgrimage *sevillanas* in honour of the Virgin Mary.

HISTORICAL NOTES

> "Hercules built me; Caesar surrounded me with walls and towers; and the King Saint took me."
> Inscription on the former Jerez Gate (Puerta de Jérez)

From the earliest times the history of Sevilla has been determined by its existence as a river port. Although its origins are less than clear, it is thought that the city was founded by Iberians. It later became a Greek, Phoenician and Carthaginian colony, which was subsequently overrun by the Romans in 205 BC following a long siege.

Romans and Visigoths – The first stage of Roman occupation was marked by internal disputes between various factions. However, in 42 BC, the city was conquered by Julius Caesar, who built its fortifications and presided over a period of great splendour, transforming it into one of the main cities in Baetica.

In the 5C the Vandals invaded the region; they were subsequently expelled by the Visigoths who made the city the capital of their kingdom until the court was transferred to Toledo. The 6C saw the rise of a figure of major importance, the bishop St Isidore, author of *Etymologies*, who was to have great influence on medieval European culture.

The Moors – The conquest by the Moors in 712 heralded the start of a long period of Arab domination. During the Caliphate, the city came under the control of Córdoba; upon its fall in 1031 it became a *taifa* kingdom. During the reign of Al Mutamid, Sevilla experienced a period of great cultural development. However, the difficult relations with the Christian king, Alfonso VI, resulted in him asking for help from the Almoravids who subsequently seized power of the kingdom in 1091. In the 12C, the Almohads seized control from the Almoravids and instigated a period of urban development, including the construction of both the Giralda and the *mezquita* (mosque), on the site now occupied by the cathedral.

The Reconquest – On 23 November 1248, Fernando III the Saint reconquered Sevilla and established his court in the city. Alfonso X the Wise and Pedro I did likewise, with the latter restoring and subsequently residing in the Alcázar.

No madeja do = No me ha dejado = It has not forsaken me

This emblem on the city's coat of arms was given to Sevilla by Alfonso X the Wise (1221-84) to commemorate the loyalty and support he had received from the city. The figure of eight in the emblem, representing a skein of wool *(madeja)*, creates the motto "No madeja do" or "No me ha dejado", which translates as "It has not forsaken me".

16C: The Golden Age – Following the discovery of America in 1492, Sevilla developed a monopoly on trade with the New World and became the departure and arrival point for every expedition to the newly discovered continent. Many expeditions departed from the city, including those by Amerigo Vespucci, and Magellan, who set out in 1519 and whose expedition was the first to circumnavigate the globe. 1503 saw the founding of the **Casa de Contratación**, a body established to encourage, inspect and control trade with the Americas.

Sevilla began to amass great wealth, as foreign merchants and bankers became increasingly attracted by thoughts of American gold. Palaces were built, new industries were created and the smell of money and frenetic activity attracted hustlers, villains and people from every sector of society. The population of Sevilla almost doubled during the course of the 16C, rising to a figure of some 200 000 inhabitants.

The decline – Following the plague of 1649, the city entered a period of decline which was exacerbated by the transfer of the Casa de Contratación to Cádiz in 1717.

20C – During the course of the 20C Sevilla hosted two major international exhibitions: the 1929 Ibero-American Exhibition and Expo'92, both of which were to have a significant effect on the layout of the city.

Expo'92 saw the realisation of a number of large projects, in particular the Isla de la Cartuja, the site on which the fair was held. The Isla Mágica theme park and the Centro Andaluz de Arte Contemporáneo are now housed on the site.

WHERE TO STAY

MODERATE

Sevilla – *Daoiz 5* – ☎ *954 38 41 61* – *fax 954 90 21 60* – *35 rooms* – *6 000pts.* Extremely well located on a small, pleasant square. This basic, air-conditioned hotel is a good choice for those on a budget.

Zaida – *San Roque, 26* – ☎ *954 21 11 38* – *fax 954 90 36 24* – *33 rooms* – *6 000pts.* Housed in a Mudéjar-style building. Good facilities for guests, including a lift. The quiet rooms overlooking the street have a terrace or balcony. Good value for money.

Londres – *San Pedro Mártir, 1* – ☎/*fax 954 21 28 96* – *22 rooms* – *6 500pts.* This centrally located hotel has basic but clean rooms, some with balcony. Rooms overlooking the street are generally more pleasant and, despite the hotel's central location, are relatively quiet.

MID-RANGE

La Rábida – *Castelar, 24* – ☎ *954 22 09 60* – *fax 954 22 43 75* – *87 rooms* – *9 000pts.* This hotel, with its somewhat eclectic interior decor, is hidden behind a white façade in a quiet street in the Arenal district. Dining room on the patio. Good value for money.

Corregidor – *Amor de Dios, 36* – ☎ *954 38 51 11* – *fax 954 37 61 02* – *58 rooms* – *11 000pts.* This hotel, slightly set back from other buildings in the street, has an attractive façade, large entrance hall and very comfortable rooms. Small garden.

Casas de la Judería – *Callejón Dos Hermanas, 7* – ☎ *954 41 51 50* – *fax 954 42 21 70* – *53 rooms* – *15 500pts.* A pleasant surprise in the city's old Jewish quarter. Elegant, traditional and full of colour, this charming, old hotel is housed in the former mansion of the Duke of Béjar.

Casas del Rey de Baeza – *Plaza Cristo de la Redención, 2* – ☎ *954 56 14 96* – *fax 954 56 14 45* – *44 rooms* – *17 800pts.* In a quiet part of the city. The rooms, which open onto simple patios, are perhaps a little glitzy, but are nonetheless spacious and equipped with superb bathrooms.

Doña María – *Don Remondo, 19* – ☎ *954 53 03 00* – *fax 954 21 95 46* – *59 rooms* – *19 500pts.* An old, tastefully renovated building with a view of the Giralda. Even if you're not staying here, it is well worth spending some time on its delightful terrace.

LUXURY

Los Seises – *Segovias, 6* – ☎ *954 22 94 95* – *fax 954 22 43 34* – *43 rooms* – *27 000pts.* Located on one of the patios of the Archbishop's Palace, this hotel successfully combines modern decor with the architecture of the 16C and 17C. Pool with terrace.

Casa Imperial – *Imperial, 29* – ☎ *954 50 03 00* – *fax 954 50 03 30* – *24 rooms* – *35 000pts.* The Casa Imperial is in a quiet street behind the Casa de Pilatos, occupying an interesting Baroque-style mansion. Although its original construction was started in the 16C, the current building dates from the 17C and 18C. Attractive main patio.

Alfonso XIII – *San Fernando, 2* – ☎ *954 22 28 50* – *fax 954 21 60 33* – *127 rooms* – *51 000pts.* Built in 1928 in neo-Mudéjar style. Sevilla's most luxurious and famous hotel.

EATING OUT

La Albahaca – *Plaza de Santa Cruz, 12* – ☎ *954 22 07 14* – *closed Sun.* In the city's historic centre. If you decide to eat in this former seigniorial mansion, you can select your table from a choice of three dining rooms. International cuisine. Outdoor terrace for the summer months.

Taberna del Alabardero – *Zaragoza, 20* – ☎ *954 56 06 37.* This 19C mansion houses one of the best restaurants in Sevilla, a high-class hotel with a dozen or so rooms, a very pleasant tea-room and the city's school of hotel management.

Corral del Agua – *Callejón del Agua, 6* – ☎ *954 22 48 41* – *closed Sun.* Located in a quiet street in the Santa Cruz district. This charming restaurant transports diners back in time. The plant-covered terrace is a delight in summer. Owned by the proprietor of the La Albahaca. Andalucian cuisine.

El Burladero – *Canalejas, 1* – ☎ *954 22 29 00.* A popular, top-class restaurant (and tapas bar). Sober, yet refined, decor. The house speciality here is *rabo de toro* (braised bull's tail).

TAPAS

SANTA CRUZ DISTRICT

Calle Mateos Gago – This tourist street close to the Giralda is full of bars and restaurants. One of these is the **Bodega de Santa Cruz**, popular with Sevilla's young crowd who spill out onto the street, eating and drinking. The **La Giralda** *cervecería (at no 1)* is one of this district's most traditional bars, offering a good choice of tasty *raciones*. A little further up the street is the **Bodega Belmonte** *(at no 24)*, a new bar already known for its delicious *lomo a la pimienta* (spicy loin of pork).

Las Teresas – *Ximénez del Enciso, 16*. This small, typically Sevillian tavern, whose doors open onto a picturesque narrow street, is one of the oldest in the Barrio Santa Cruz. Attractive early-19C decor and delicious tapas. The **Casa Plácido** opposite is a good place for cold tapas.

P. Wysocki/EXPLORER

Calle Mateos Gago

Puerta de la Carne – *Santa María La Blanca, 36*. A perfect location to discover one of Sevilla's most original traditions: the eating of all kinds of seafood and fried fish served, ready to eat, in paper cones.

TRIANA

Kiosco de Las Flores – *Plaza del Altozano*. A tapas bar next to the Puente de Triana, with a terrace close to the Guadalquivir. Run by the same family since 1930, it specialises in fried fish, seafood and *ortiguillas* (fried seaweed).

Sol y Sombra – *Castilla, 149-151 – closed Mon and Tues lunchtimes*. One of the most popular bars in the city. This bustling bar with its characteristic aromas of fine cheeses, cured hams and cigarette smoke, and walls covered with old and modern

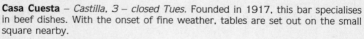

brightly coloured bullfighting posters is a must for visitors. The same owners run the restaurant next door.

Casa Cuesta – *Castilla, 3 – closed Tues*. Founded in 1917, this bar specialises in beef dishes. With the onset of fine weather, tables are set out on the small square nearby.

ARENAL and PLAZA NUEVA

Bodeguita A. Romero – *Antonio Díaz, 19 – closed Mon*. Located next to the Maestranza bullring. Famous for its exquisite *pringá* (a meat stew eaten with bread). Popular with the business community at lunchtime.

Casablanca – *Zaragoza, 50 – closed Sun*. This small bar, one of the most famous in Sevilla, is always full and is particularly popular with locals.

CENTRO

El Patio de San Eloy – *San Eloy, 9 – ☎ 954 22 11 48*. An unusual bar with several distinct sections. As you enter, there is a small wine counter on the right; the central bar offers a wide range of sandwiches *(bocadillos)* from Andalucia, Catalunya, Galicia, France, Belgium etc; while the *azulejo*-adorned benches at the back (similar to those found in an Arab bath) are the ideal place for a chat with friends. Always packed at lunchtime.

SANTA CATALINA

El Rinconcillo –

Gerona, 40. One of the oldest and most attractive bars in Sevilla. Although its origins date back to 1670, the current decor is from the 19C, including the attractive *azulejo* panelling and the wooden ceiling and counter.

ALFALFA

Bodega Extremeña –

Calle Águilas on the corner with Candilejo. An unusual showcase for products from Extremadura, in the heart of Andalucia, This small bar serves some excellent cheeses (such as the famous Torta del Casar), hams, and a whole range of sausages, chorizos and wines.

M. Raurich/STOCK PHOTOS

El Rinconcillo

CAFÉS, BARS & NIGHT-LIFE

When it comes to nightlife, the most popular areas for a drink are the city centre, particularly around the cathedral, and the attractive Santa Cruz and Arenal districts, all of which provide a magnificent historical backdrop. The working-class district of Triana, in particular the calle Betis on the opposite bank of the Guadalquivir, is also lively, with a number of bars and clubs with a local flavour. Sevilla's younger crowd tends to prefer the action in the Nervión district, with its numerous nightclubs, many of which stay open until dawn. The city's alternative crowd heads for Alameda de Hércules, where visitors will need to exercise caution at night, but which is nonetheless home to several interesting haunts, such as Fun Club, a popular concert venue, and the Habanilla café, with its large and unusual collection of old coffee pots.

In summer, the action moves down to the river, where several kilometres of bars and outdoor terraces are popular with people of all ages and tastes.

Horno San Buenaventura – *Avenida de la Constitución, 16. Open daily, 8am-10pm.* Part of a network of old furnaces over six centuries old. Particularly popular because of its proximity to the cathedral and its spacious lounge on the top floor. Its cakes are justifiably famous.

La Campana – *Plaza de la Campana, 1. Open daily, 8am-10pm.* One of Sevilla's classic cafeterias. The Rococo decor creates a pleasant atmosphere in which to enjoy La Campana's pastries, which are famous throughout the city. Varied clientele ranging from the district's senior citizens to tourists passing through the centre.

Café de la Prensa – *Calle Betis, 15. Open daily, 10-1am.* This modern café with a young and intellectual ambience is located alongside the riverbank. Its outdoor tables offer a magnificent view of both the Guadalquivir and the monumental heart of the city. Perfect for whiling away the late afternoon or for a few drinks to start the evening.

Antigüedades – *Calle Argote de Molina, 40. Open 8pm-3am.* One of Sevilla's most colourful clubs with decor which changes every month according to what's on. Another haunt popular with the young crowd, particularly thirty-somethings. Very lively around midnight.

Abades – *Calle Abades, 13. Open daily, 5pm-early hours of the morning.* This 18C palatial residence in the heart of the Barrio Santa Cruz has a number of Baroque lounges filled with antiques. A select crowd, who can enjoy a relaxing drink in elegant surroundings to the background strains of classical music.

La Carbonería – *Calle Levíes, 18. Open daily, 8pm-4am.* One of Sevilla's institutions and the key to the culture of the city's alternative crowd. Housed in a former coal warehouse in the Jewish Quarter *(Judería),* La Carbonería is split up into a number of different areas, where you can listen to a musical recital in intimate surroundings around a chimney or to authentic lively flamenco (live music every night). The venue also hosts art and photography exhibitions. A must!

El Tamboril – *Plaza Santa Cruz. Open daily, 10pm-5am.* Tucked away in a corner of the Santa Cruz district, this *taberna* is always heaving with its faithful clientele who occasionally burst into song with an impromptu *sevillana* or *rumba.* Always busy until the early hours of the morning. The Salve Rociera, a prayer to Our Lady of El Rocío, is sung at midnight every day.

Sala Mandra – *Calle Torneo, 43. Open Thur-Sat, 10pm-6am.* This modern, industrial-style venue hosts rock and pop concerts every Friday and occasionally on Thursdays, as well as some theatrical events. At the end of shows, the venue reverts to its function as a disco, with Latin sounds on Thursdays and Saturdays and more commercial music on Fridays. The most avant-garde of the city's clubs.

Voulé-Bar/Wall Street – *Calle Balbino Marrón, edificio Viapol. Open Wed-Sat, midnight-6am.* These two adjoining bars are also located in the city's favourite clubbing district for young people, Nervión. **Voulé-bar** organises regular salsa and flamenco concerts and occasionally books the odd leading band. At **Wall Street** people order drinks based on the fluctuating prices indicated on the numerous screens all along the bar. Both venues attract huge numbers of people who tend to move back and forth between both venues throughout the night. Average age between 25 and 35.

Sopa de Ganso – *Calle Pérez Galdós, 8. Open daily, 1pm-2am (6am Sat-Sun).* With its decorative emphasis on wood and its varied play list, the Sopa de Ganso is another popular night-club. A varied clientele, including a number of foreigners, come to enjoy the alternative, yet fun, atmosphere here. Always busy in the afternoon and early evening with people who come here to enjoy the great pastries.

La Sonanta – *Calle San Jacinto, 31. Open 8am-early hours of the morning.* This small bar across the river in Triana serves tapas by day and fills up with lovers of flamenco by night. Live performances on Thursdays and Fridays. Twice a year La Sonanta organises a flamenco festival. A varied public, ranging from tourists to die-hard flamenco fans.

The **paseo de las Delicias** is home to four venues (Chile, Líbano, Alfonso and Bilindo). Although not open all year round, these venues become lively in summer, when they are perfect for those who prefer to move from bar to bar. On winter afternoons they are ideal for a quiet drink in the middle of the María Luisa park, surrounded by buildings used during the 1929 Ibero-American Exhibition, while in the summer, drinking and dancing outdoors into the early hours is more the scene. The age range is between 25 and 40, but varies from one venue to the next.

ENTERTAINMENT

Sevilla is a lively and festive capital offering a whole host of varied cultural activities all year round.

Publications – Two free bilingual publications (Spanish-English) are published for tourists every month. These brochures, **Welcome Olé** and **The Tourist**, can be obtained from major hotels and tourist sites around the city. Sevilla's Town Hall also publishes a small monthly brochure listing all the city's cultural events. A monthly publication covering the whole of Andalucia, **El Giraldillo**, contains information on the region's fairs, exhibitions and theatres, as well as details on cinemas, restaurants and shops. **Web site**: www.elgiraldillo.es

The **Teatro de la Maestranza** (Paseo de Colón, 22 – ☎ 954 22 65 73 – www.maestranza.com) offers a full season of theatre and dance, including performances by leading international stars, particularly in the field of opera.

The **Teatro Lope de Vega** (Avenida María Luisa – ☎ 954 59 08 53) tends to concentrate on drama and flamenco.

The **Teatro Central** (Avenida José de Gálvez – ☎ 954 46 07 80 – www.teatrocentral.com), on the Isla de la Cartuja, is a modern building built for Expo'92. It offers a varied programme of avant-garde theatre and music including performances by some of the world's leading performers, as well as a season of flamenco. In addition to the major theatres above, Sevilla has many smaller concert halls and other venues which organise concerts and recitals.

Other cultural aspects are equally well covered in the city, which boasts a number of exhibition halls and galleries devoted to art. The exhibitions organised by the Centro Andaluz de Arte Contemporáneo in the Monasterio de la Cartuja are particularly worthy of note.

SHOPPING

Sevilla has a huge range of shops, the most traditional of which are concentrated in the historic centre, particularly along calle Tetuán, in the plaza del Duque de la Victoria, calle de San Eloy and other pedestrian areas in this district. Special mention should also be made of the historic **calle Sierpes**, with its variety of traditional and more unusual shops and boutiques, including several Foronda boutiques, selling the hand-embroidered shawls created by this famous local artisan. The Ochoa pastry shop is also located here; this local landmark is a perfect spot for breakfast or for an afternoon snack, but also has an excellent selection of take-away cakes and pastries. The streets at right angles to Sierpes and those around the nearby El Salvador church are also very popular, particular for jewellery hunters, who are spoilt for choice in the plaza del Pan and the calle Alcaicería.

In the **Los Remedios** district on the other side of the river, calle Asunción has a number of leading brand-name stores selling a whole range of goods.

The modern Nervión district is home to two large shopping centres (El Corte Inglés and Nervión Plaza), as well as several stores belonging to leading clothing chains.

Another large shopping centre has been developed in the **former Plaza de Armas railway station**, an interesting regionalist building dating from the beginning of the 20C. Here you will find the La Fábrica de Cerveza, where you can enjoy a beer while at the same time contemplating how it has been made.

Markets – Sevilla has numerous open-air markets, most of which specialise in a particular type of goods. The "jueves" (Thursday) market, in calle Feria, is a popular market for antiques and second-hand goods where you might just pick up an interesting bargain. On Sunday mornings, markets are held in several parts of the city, including plaza de la Alfalfa, a much-frequented livestock market; plaza del Cabildo, with its stalls selling stamps and old coins; and along Alameda de Hércules, where a multitude of temporary stalls selling second-hand goods are set up early in the morning to entice visitors.

Market along Alameda de Hércules

Ch. Boisvieux

TRANSPORT

Airport – The city's international airport, San Pablo, ☎ 954449000, is located 8km/5mi to the east of Sevilla along the N IV road to Madrid. Taxis and a bus service (750pts) are available for transfers between the airport and the Santa Justa railway station.

Trains – The **Santa Justa** railway station is on Avenida Kansas City. There are regular departures throughout the province, as well as to the rest of Spain, including the famous AVE high-speed train, which connects Sevilla with Madrid (via Córdoba) in just 2hr 25min. Information ☎ 954540202. Reservations ☎ 954540303.

Inter-city buses – Sevilla has two bus stations:
– Estación de Plaza de Armas (plaza de Armas): buses to the rest of the province, Huelva, elsewhere in Spain, Portugal and other European countries. ☎ 954907737.
– Estación de El Prado de San Sebastián (Prado de San Sebastián): buses to the rest of Andalucia. ☎ 954417111.

City buses – Tussam (☏ 954 22 81 77/22 53 60). This is the best way of getting around the city. A single journey costs 125pts, although it is possible to purchase a 10-trip ticket *(abono de diez viajes)*. Cost (including transfer option): 615pts, enabling passengers to transfer from one line to another within one hour; cost (excluding transfer option): 560pts.

Taxis – ☏ 954 58 00 00 and 954 57 11 11.

Horse-drawn carriages – This alternative form of transport is a pleasant way of discovering the major sites of the city. Carriages can normally be hired in plaza Virgen de los Reyes, plaza de España, avenida de la Constitución and at the Torre del Oro.

Boat trips on the Guadalquivir – Regular departures from the Torre del Oro, offering visitors to Sevilla a different view of the city. Cruises last one hour and pass the Expo'92 site.

Tourist bus – The *bus turístico* offers regular circuits of the city's main sights, stopping at each of them, enabling passengers to get on and off at leisure. Departures from the Torre del Oro.

★★★ 1 THE GIRALDA AND CATHEDRAL

★★★ Giralda ⊙

The impressive and elegant Giralda is the symbol of the city. Built at the end of the 12C this brick minaret (96m/315ft), part of the old mosque *(mezquita)*, was surmounted by three gilded spheres which sadly fell off as a result of the earthquake which struck Sevilla in the 14C. It acquired its present appearance in the 16C when the Cordoban architect Hernán Ruiz added the belfry, the three superimposed stages and the balconies. These were then crowned with an enormous weather vane, the statue of Faith, popularly known as the Giraldillo (from *girar*: to turn), from which the name of the tower has evolved.

This tower is a masterpiece of Almohad art, with the delicate yet restrained decoration so typical of this purist, austere dynasty, which shunned ostentation, yet still managed to create a harmonious style combining beauty and simplicity. The decoration on each of its four sides is organised into three vertical registers with panels of *sebka* decoration.

★★★ Cathedral ⊙

"Let us build a cathedral so immense that we will be taken for madmen", the chapter is said to have declared in 1401 when it ordered the demolition of the mosque and the construction of the new cathedral. The cathedral is impressive in its dimensions, and in terms of floor space is considered to be the third largest in the Christian world after St Peter's in the Vatican and St Paul's in London. As one of the last Gothic cathedrals to be built in Spain it shows obvious Renaissance influence.

On the massive **exterior**, it is possible to appreciate the full extent of its size. The Cristóbal (or Príncipe), Asunción and Concepción (in the Patio de los Naranjos) doorways are modern (19C and 20C), yet respect the style of the cathedral as a whole, while the Puerta del Nacimiento and Puerta del Bautismo, which open out onto the Avenida de la Constitución, include beautiful sculptures by Mercadante de Bretaña (1460). In the east end of the cathedral admire the rounded Chapel Royal (*Capilla Real* – 1575), decorated with coats of arms and, on either side, the Gothic Puerta de Palos and Puerta de las Campanillas with Renaissance-style tympana in which Miguel Perrin has made full play of perspective.

Tour of the Cathedral and the Giralda – *Entrance through the Puerta del Perdón.*

Puerta del Perdón – The Almohad arch and the door leaves are original features of this majestic entrance to the patio of the former mosque. The impressive sculptures and the relief, representing the Expulsion of the Money Changers from the Temple, were created in the 16C.

Patio de los Naranjos – This exceptional rectangular patio is planted with orange trees *(naranjos)* and was the patio used for ritual ablutions in the former mosque.

Interior – This universe of stone, stained glass and grilles is striking in its size and richness, while its extraordinary height is the result of its tall, slender pillars. The ground plan consists of five aisles – the central nave being wider and of greater height – with chapels in the side aisles. The column shafts support simple Flamboyant Gothic pointed vaults, except in the central section. The vault of the transept, also Flamboyant in style, reaches a height of 56m/184ft. A **mirror** (1) on the floor provides visitors with a striking view of these magnificent stone vaults.

Climbing the Giralda – It is possible to climb up to the tower's belfry (70m/230ft) via a ramp with 34 sections. The ascent is slow, although not particularly difficult; take your time to admire the views of the Patio de los Naranjos, the gargoyles and pinnacles of the cathedral and the Alcázar from the balconies on the way up. Your efforts will be well rewarded once you reach the outer platform at the top with a magnificent **panorama★★★** over the city.

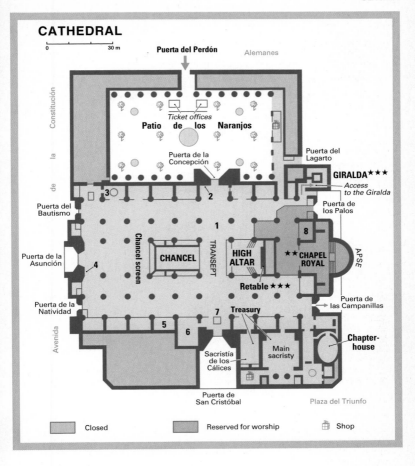

CATHEDRAL

Closed — Reserved for worship — Shop

High Altar – The high altar *(capilla mayor)*, unbelievably rich in decoration, is enclosed by a splendid 16C **Plateresque grille★★**, by Fray Francisco de Salamanca. The immense Flemish **altarpiece★★★** (1482-1525), the largest in Spain, is profusely and delicately carved with a number of colourful scenes from the life of Christ and the Virgin Mary, with the exception of the predella which is decorated with saints. The altarpiece has seven vertical panels, the widest of which is in the centre. Unfortunately, it is impossible to get close enough to admire what is one of the world's most impressive altarpieces.

Chancel – In the central nave, partly hidden by a 16C grille by Fray Francisco de Salamanca is the *coro*, with its fine 15C and 16C choir stalls. The majestic organs date from the 18C. The **trascoro**, a chancel screen of multicoloured marble, jasper and bronze, is 17C.

Treasury – The treasury is in the 16C **Sacristía de los Cálices** (Chalice Sacristy), and is surmounted by a fine vault. A number of interesting paintings are exhibited here: *Santa Justa and Santa Rufina* by Goya, a Zurbarán, a triptych by Alejo Fernández and several canvases by Valdés Leal. The anteroom of the sacristy houses the **Tenebrario**, a 7.80m/25ft, fifteen-branch Plateresque candelabrum, used during Holy Week processions.

The "Seises" – a fine tradition

The Seises are a group of 12 brightly dressed choir boys who perpetuate a tradition dating back to the 16C, in which they sing and dance in front of the cathedral's high altar during the eight days following Corpus Christi and the Feast of the Immaculate Conception. Initially the group consisted of 16 boys, hence the name. They also accompany the **Corpus Christi** procession when this stops in the plaza del Ayuntamiento and the plaza del Salvador.

SEVILLA

See overleaf for index of sights
and street names

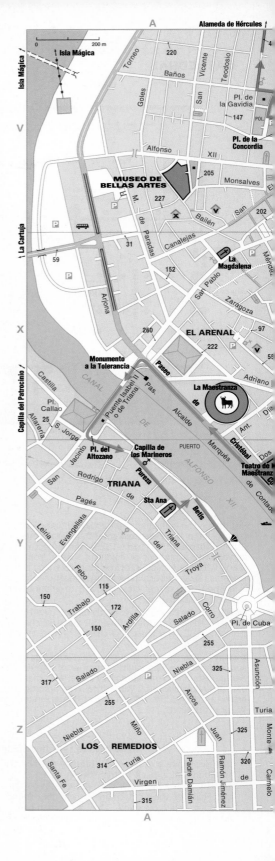

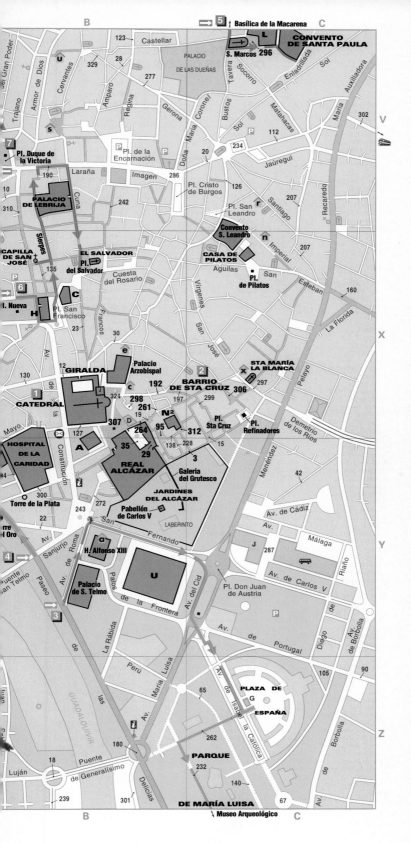

Basílica de la Macarena

CONVENTO DE SANTA PAULA
S. Marcos 296
L

Castellar
123
329
28
277
PALACIO DE LAS DUEÑAS

u
Cervantes
Armor de Dios
Gran Poder
Trajano
Amparo
Regina
Gerona
Doña María Coronel
Bustos
Socorro
Tavera
Enladrillada
Sol
María Auxiliadora

s
302
V

Pl. Duque de la Victoria
7
Pl. de la Encarnación
Laraña
Imagen
286
20
234
112
Jaúregui
Recaredo

10
190
Cuna
Pl. Cristo de Burgos
126
207
Santiago
r

PALACIO DE LEBRIJA
310
242
Pl. San Leandro
207
n

Sierpes
CAPILLA DE SAN JOSÉ
135
EL SALVADOR
Pl. del Salvador
Cuesta del Rosario
Convento S. Leandro
CASA DE PILATOS
Aguilas
Imperial

6
I. Nueva
H
C
Pl. San Francisco
23
30
Francos
Virgenes
San José
Pl. de Pilatos
San Esteban
160
La Florida

e
Palacio Arzobispal
c
GIRALDA
12
192
BARRIO DE STA CRUZ
2
STA MARÍA LA BLANCA
297
306
x
Pelayo
X

130
CATEDRAL
1
298
261
307
19
197
299
Demétrio de los Ríos

Mayo
127
324
N²
95
264
312
138 228
15
Pl. Sta Cruz
Pl. Refinadores

A
35
29
3
Menéndez
42

HOSPITAL DE LA CARIDAD
Constitución
REAL ALCÁZAR
Galería del Grutesco
JARDINES DEL ALCÁZAR

Torre de la Plata
300
272
243
Pabellón de Carlos V
LABERINTO
Av. de Cádiz
Av.
Málaga

22
Sanjurjo
San
Fernando
J
287
Av. de Carlos V
Riaño

re
l Oro
4
ente
an Telmo
Paseo
Av. de Roma
H. Alfonso XIII
a
U
Pl. Don Juan de Austria
P
de
Diego
Av. de Botbolla

3
Palacio de S. Telmo
Palos de la Frontera
Av. del Cid
Av. de Portugal

La Rábida
Perú
Maria Luisa
las
GUADALQUIVIR
65
Av. de Isabel la Católica
PLAZA DE ESPAÑA
G
105
90

18
180
Puente de Generalísimo
262
PARQUE
232
140
Borbolla
Z

239
301
Delicias
DE MARÍA LUISA
67
Av. de

Museo Arqueológico

B   C

INDEX OF SIGHTS AND STREET NAMES
ON PLANS OF SEVILLA

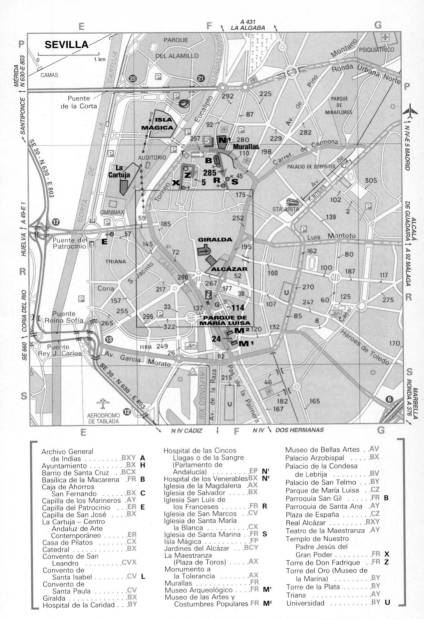

SEVILLA

1 km

Chapels and altars

Once you have seen the cathedral's major works, make sure you spend some time admiring some of its chapels, which themselves contain numerous works of art.
– **Altar de Nuestra Señora de Belén** (**2**) (Our Lady of Bethlehem): on the north side, to the left of the Puerta de la Concepción. A fine portrayal of the Virgin Mary by Alonso Cano.
– **Capilla de San Antonio** (**3**): this chapel contains several interesting canvases dominated by Murillo's *Vision of St Anthony of Padua*, on the right-hand wall. Also worthy of note are *The Baptism of Christ*, also by Murillo, and two paintings of St Peter by Valdés Leal.
– **Altar del Santo Ángel** (**4**) (at the foot of the cathedral, to the left of the Puerta Mayor): this altar is dominated by a fine *Guardian Angel* by Murillo.
– **Capilla de San Hermenegildo** (**5**) (next to the Capilla de San José): the 15C alabaster tomb of Cardinal Cervantes sculpted by Lorenzo Mercadante.
– **Capilla de la Virgen de la Antigua** (**6**) (the next chapel): larger than the others and covered with an elevated vault. A fine 14C fresco of the Virgin adorns the altar.
– **19C funerary monument to Christopher Columbus** (**7**): the explorer's coffin is borne by four pallbearers bearing the symbols of Castilla, León, Navarra and Aragón on their chest.

Aerial view of the cathedral

The **main sacristy** *(sacristía mayor)*, a fine 16C room with the floor plan of a Greek cross, contains the impressive Renaissance silver **monstrance** *(custodia)* by Juan de Arfe, measuring 3.90m/13ft and weighing 475kg/1 045lb; a *Santa Teresa* by Zurbarán and *The Martyrdom of San Lorenzo* by Lucas Jordán can be seen on the rear wall.

Chapter-house – The chapter-house *(sala capitular)*, a fine example of 16C Renaissance architecture, has an elliptical dome and a characteristic *Immaculate Conception* by Murillo.

Areas reserved for worship – *Entrance through the Puerta de Palos.* These areas include the Chapel Royal and the Capilla de San Pedro.

★★**Chapel Royal** (Capilla Real) – The Chapel Royal was built during the reign of Carlos V over an earlier chapel. The monumental stature of this Plateresque chapel is particularly impressive. It opens through an arch so high that the decoration can only be appreciated from a distance. Square in shape, it is covered by an elegant, richly ornamented coffered dome with carved busts and contains a small apse which is itself covered by a scallop shell decorated with figures. A wooden carving of the **Virgen de los Reyes**, the patron saint of Sevilla, decorates the altar, behind which, in a silver urn of great value, are the remains of Fernando III the Saint. On either side are the tombs of Alfonso X and that of his mother, Beatrice of Swabia. The Capilla Real is enclosed by a majestic grille dating from 1771.

Capilla de San Pedro (**8**) – *An incomparable series of oil paintings by* **Zurbarán** *on the life of the saint hang from the walls of this chapel, which is dedicated to St Peter.*

Palacio Arzobispal – The residence of the Archbishop of Sevilla is situated in the attractive plaza de la Virgen de los Reyes, with its monumental lantern and numerous horse-drawn carriages awaiting customers. The edifice has an elegant, late-Baroque façade built at the beginning of the 18C.

Plaza de Santa Marta – *Take the narrow callejón de Santa Marta, opposite the Palacio Arzobispal.* The alleyway offers the only access to this delightful small square, with its whitewashed façades, simple wrought-iron grilles and a small stone cross shaded by orange trees. The charming, hushed atmosphere found here is typical of that found in so many of the city's squares.

Y. Arthus-Bertrand/ALTITUDE

Archivo General de Indias ⊘ – The historical archives relating to the Spanish conquest of the Americas are housed in the former Exchange *(lonja)*, built at the end of the 16C according to plans by Juan de Herrera, the architect of El Escorial. The archives were established here by Carlos III in 1785. This sober, Renaissance-style building has two floors with architrave bays. Of particular note inside is the sumptuous 18C pink and black marble staircase. Only the upper floor, with its large rooms topped with elegant vaults, can be visited. It houses a unique collection of priceless documents on the conquest and colonisation of the Americas, as well as the signatures of Columbus, Magellan, Hernán Cortés, Juan Sebastián Elcano and others.

Plaza del Triunfo – Some of Sevilla's most impressive buildings surround this square, in the centre of which stands a "triumph" *(triunfo)* to the Immaculate Conception. One side is taken up by the Archivo General de Indias, another by the south side of the cathedral, the third by the Alcázar, with the former Hospital del Rey, now the Casa de la Provincia, on the fourth side.

★★★Real Alcázar ⊘

Entrance through the Puerta del León.

This magnificent palace is unusual for a royal residence in that it was the result of several phases of construction from the 10C onwards; as a result it has a variety of architectural styles. All that remains of the 12C Alcázar of the Almohads is the Patio del Yeso and the fortified arches separating the Patio de la Montería from the Patio del León; the rest of the building dates from the Christian period. In the 13C Alfonso X the Wise built the Gothic-style Salones de Carlos V. The main nucleus of the palace was built by Pedro I the Cruel in 1362. This masterpiece of Mudéjar art was built by masons from Granada, as can be seen in the decoration, highly influenced by the Alhambra *(see GRANADA)*, which dates from the same period. Later modifications were made by Juan II, the Catholic Monarchs, Carlos V and Felipe II.

Cuarto del Almirante – *To the right of the Patio de la Montería.* It was in the Admiral's Apartments that Isabel the Catholic founded the Casa de Contratación in 1503. The Sala de Audiencias (Audience Chamber) contains an altarpiece, the **Virgin of the Navigators★** (1531-36), painted by Alejo Fernández.

Sala de la Justicia and Patio del Yeso – *To the left of the Patio de la Montería.* The Sala de la Justicia (Justice Chamber) was built in the 14C on top of the remains of the former Almohad palace. Note the finely sculpted plasterwork *(yesería)* and the magnificent cupola. The Patio del Yeso is all that remains from the Almohad period (12C).

★★★**Palacio de Pedro el Cruel** – The narrow façade of Peter the Cruel's Palace is strongly reminiscent of the Patio del Cuarto Dorado in Granada's Alhambra, with it *sebka* decoration, fragile multifoiled arches and a large epigraphic frieze beneath its carved wood overhang.

The palace is laid out around two patios: the Patio de las Doncellas (Court of the Maidens), which was the centre of officialdom, and the smaller proportioned Patio de las Muñecas (Doll's Court), used for private life.

From here, a small hallway to the left leads to the **Patio de las Doncellas**, a rectangular, well-proportioned patio particularly noteworthy for its exquisite *yesería* decoration, which supports a gallery of foliated arches above paired columns, and its magnificent 14C *azulejo* panels. The upper storey, of Italianate design, was added under Carlos V. A number of attractive Mudéjar rooms open onto this patio: the **Salón del techo del Carlos V** (**1**) (Carlos V's Room), the palace's former chapel, with its splendid Renaissance ceiling with polygon caissons; the **Dormitorio de los Reyes Moros** (**2**) (Bedroom of the Moorish Kings), two rooms decorated with blue-toned stucco and a magnificent *artesonado* ceiling; and the **Salón de Embajadores** (**3**) (Ambassadors' Hall), the most sumptuous room in the Alcázar, with its remarkable 15C half-orange cedarwood **cupola★★★** with stucco decoration. The pendentives are adorned with

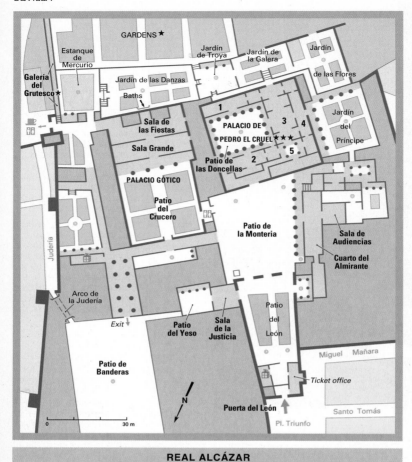

REAL ALCÁZAR

🏛 Shop   🚻 Toilets   ☕ Café

decorative Moorish motifs *(mocárabes)*. The exceptional *azulejo* panelling and the sumptuous wall decoration complete the scene. This room connects with the **Salón del techo de Felipe II** (**4**), with its magnificent Renaissance coffered cedarwood ceiling. The Salón de Embajadores leads onto the small-proportioned **Patio de las Muñecas** (**5**), whose foiled arches, with their *alfiz* surround, clearly demonstrate Granadan influence. The upper floors date from the restoration work carried out in the 19C. This patio opens into the Cuarto del Príncipe (Prince's Room).

Leave the Patio de la Montería and pass through the Corredor de Carlos V, a low-vaulted gallery.

Palacio Gótico or Salones de Carlos V – The Baroque doorway to the Gothic Palace or Carlos V's Rooms is to the rear of the **Patio del Crucero**. Built by Alfonso X in Gothic style, it underwent considerable restoration work in the 18C following the Lisbon earthquake. The **Sala Grande**, displaying part of a collection of 17C **tapestries**★★ from the Real Fábrica de Tapices in Madrid relating the Conquest of Tunis in 1535, dates from this later period. The 13C **Sala de las Fiestas**, or **Sala de las Bóvedas**, is the oldest part of the palace and retains its original structure and groin vaults *(bovédas)* from this

---

The Cuarto Real Alto

An optional 30min guided tour enables visitors to view the King and Queen of Spain's official residence in Sevilla. The various rooms, with their fine *artesonado* ceilings, contain an impressive display of 19C furniture and clocks, 18C tapestries and French lamps. Of particular note are the **Capilla de los Reyes Católicos** (Chapel of the Catholic Monarchs) – an exquisite oratory with a ceramic font, by Nicola Pisano – and the Mudéjar **Sala de Audiencias**.

era. It was here that Carlos V married Isabel of Portugal. The walls are adorned with attractive 16C *azulejo* panelling and the remainder of the tapestry collection. The large windows provide a foretaste of the palace's enchanting gardens.

★**Gardens** – The enchanting, extensive gardens are one of the best examples of this magnificent Moorish art. Like the palace's architecture, they were created over different periods; as a result, Arab, Renaissance and Baroque style are all represented here. They occupy 80% of the Alcázar's total area and are laid out in terraces with numerous ornamental basins.

Leave Carlos V's Rooms and pass by the Mercurio Pool to reach the 17C **Galería del Grutesco**★, which masks the front of an old wall. The best view of the gardens can be enjoyed from inside this gallery.

To the right, lower down, is the Jardín de las Danzas (Dancing Garden). From here, head to the baths *(baños)* of Doña María de Padilla, a large vaulted pool.

Beyond the **Pabellón de Carlos V**, a 15C pavilion, is the labyrinth, with its clipped hedges. A modern, English-style garden can be seen to the right. A quiet wander through the gardens with just the gentle bubbling of water in the background is an unforgettable experience.

The twin-columned *apeadero*, a covered room in Baroque style, leads to the Patio de Banderas.

Patio de Banderas – The Flag Court, as it is known, was formerly the parade ground *(patio de armas)* of the original Alcázar. This enclosed rectangular square, with its characteristic orange trees and a single fountain, is bordered by elegant façades, against which can be seen the silhouette of the Giralda.

★★★② BARRIO DE SANTA CRUZ

This typical quarter, with its delightful narrow, twisting streets, whitewashed houses, flower-filled patios and shady squares is the quintessential *barrio* of Sevilla. In the Middle Ages the Barrio de Santa Cruz was the city's Jewish quarter *(Judería)*. It benefited from royal protection after the Reconquest until the end of the 14C, when increasing intolerance resulted in its seizure and occupation by the Christians, who converted its former synagogues into churches.

The Barber of Seville

The city was to provide the inspiration for this comic opera, created in 1816 by the Italian composer Gioacchino Rossini (1792-1868). Written in two acts, this masterpiece tells of the attempts of Bartolo, an elderly doctor, to marry his pretty ward, Rosina. His plans are foiled by another admirer, Count Almaviva, through the help of his acquaintance, Figaro, who also happens to be Bartolo's barber.

Today, it is a haven of peace and quiet in the historical heart of Sevilla, where time seems to have stopped. Visitors will want to meander through its alleyways – resplendent in the bright sunshine, and equally delightful at night – and enjoy an unforgettable experience as they discover its many facets and the hospitality of its bars and restaurants, particularly during the *paseo*, when the quarter is imbued with its own inimitable atmosphere.

One of the best entrances to the quarter is through the **Arco de la Judería**, a covered alleyway leading to the Patio de Banderas, transporting the visitor several centuries back in time. Continue to the **callejón del Agua**, which runs alongside the district's outer wall. A less theatrical yet equally interesting route upon leaving the Patio de Banderas is through the **calle Romero Murube**, continuing along the wall of the Alcázar to the plaza de la Alianza. Having crossed the square, follow the street which becomes the twisting yet delightful **callejón de Rodrigo Caro**, ending up at the **plaza de Doña Elvira**, one of Santa Cruz's most typical squares with its *azulejo*-adorned benches shaded by orange trees and its small stone fountain at its centre. The calle Gloria leads to the lively **plaza de los Venerables**, flanked by the hospital of the same name.

★**Hospital de los Venerables** ⊘ – Founded in 1675, this hospital for priests, designed by the architect Leonardo de Figueroa, is one of the finest examples of 17C Sevillian Baroque art. It now serves as the headquarters of the FOCUS cultural foundation. Its attractive square patio is adorned with 19C *azulejos*.

The **church**★, with its single nave and barrel vault with lunettes, is covered with **frescoes**★★ painted by Valdés Leal and his son Lucas Valdés. Particularly impressive are *The Last Supper* by Valdés the Younger and, above it, *The Apotheosis of San Fernando*, by Valdés the Elder, both of which are in the apsidal end. The nave contains four Flemish works on copper and two smaller works painted on marble. Two fine statues by Pedro Roldán, *San Fernando* and *San Pedro*, are also displayed at the foot of the church. Organ concerts are frequently held in the church, hence the position of the pews.

Don Juan

This legendary character, the archetypal seducer who shows no respect for anyone or anything, appears for the first time in Tirso de Molina's *The Trickster of Seville and His Guest of Stone* (1630). It is said that he may have found his inspiration for the character in Don Miguel de Mañara, the founder of the Hospital de la Caridad *(see p 304)*.

Although the character has been re-created time and time again over the centuries by writers of the stature of Molière, Mozart, Dumas and Byron, none of whom could resist his attraction, the most well-known version in Spain is that of *Don Juan Tenorio* (1844) by Zorrilla, in whose memory the statue in the plaza de los Refinadores has been erected.

The **sacristy** contains a fresco by Valdés Leal on the theme of the triumph of the Cross. The balustrade, which appears to change position if you keep watching it as you wander around the room, is also worthy of note. Admire also the anonymous 18C Christs in ivory.

The attractive **main staircase★** is topped by an elliptical Baroque dome adorned with stuccoes bearing the papal coat of arms. Another work by Lucas Valdés, *The Presentation of the Infant Jesus in the Temple*, hangs from the walls.

Streets and squares – Many of the quarter's streets carry evocative names – such as Mesón del Moro (Moor's Inn), Gloria, Pimienta (Pepper) and Susona, from a legend describing the love affair of a disgraced Jewish woman and Christian man – or have played an important part in the city's history.

By following calle Santa Teresa – look out for no 7, the house in which Murillo lived (now an exhibition room) – or exiting plaza de Alfaro, you come to **plaza de Santa Cruz**, which has lent its name to the quarter. In the middle of the square, amid orange trees, stands an impressive iron cross, the 17C Cruz de la Cerrajería. Here, one of the city's favourite sons, Murillo, is buried. Close by are the gardens which carry his name.

The calle Mezquita leads to the majestic **plaza de los Refinadores** where, in the shade of five palm trees, a statue in honour of Don Juan Tenorio has been erected. The **plaza de las Tres Cruces**, a small, triangular square with three columns upon which stand three wrought-iron crosses, is reached via a narrow alleyway.

Calle Mateos Gago, which runs into plaza de la Virgen de los Reyes, has a number of popular bars as well as several early-20C houses. From here, you may wish to enjoy one of the most impressive views of the Giralda. It is difficult to resist the temptation of a few tapas and a beer or *fino* as you take in the delightful surroundings.

★③ PALACIO DE SAN TELMO AND PARQUE DE MARÍA LUISA

Palacio de San Telmo – This impressively wide palace, built at the end of the 17C, now serves as the headquarters of the Presidencia de la Junta de Andalucia (Regional Parliament). It was formerly a naval academy and then the residence of the Dukes of Montpensier. In the early part of the 20C it became a seminary. Its **main portal★**, one of the finest examples of Sevillian Baroque, is by the architect Leonardo de Figueroa. It is completely covered with a sumptuous decoration of reliefs and sculptures. Above, a statue of San Telmo is silhouetted against the sky.

Hotel Alfonso XIII – The most famous of all Sevilla's hotels was built for the 1929 Ibero-American Exhibition in regionalist style with neo-Mudéjar features, so in vogue at the time and visible in other buildings around the city from the same period.

University – The city's university is housed in a fine building with classical, harmonious lines and impressive dimensions, built in the 18C as Sevilla's tobacco factory. The main façade of this square, two-storey edifice fronting calle San Fernando has an attractive **portal** on two levels with paired columns, crowned by a pediment bearing a large coat of arms, on whose vertex stands an allegorical statue of an angel of the apocalypse representing Fame. The doorway arch is adorned with reliefs and medallions with the busts of Christopher Columbus and Hernán Cortés. The interior is well worth a look, with its attractive patios and monumental staircase.

The workers in the old tobacco factory are now firmly entrenched in the city's history thanks to Bizet's Carmen.

★★ Parque de María Luisa

The park, one of Sevilla's most popular outdoor areas, was a gift given to the city by the Infanta María Luisa Fernanda, the Duchess of Montpensier. It once formed part of the gardens of the Palacio de San Telmo, which at the time was the residence of the duke and duchess. The modifications resulting in its present-day appearance were carried out for the 1929 Ibero-American Exhibition by Jean Claude Nicolas Forestier. This magnificent, romantic garden with its gazebos, pools and lush and varied vegetation was further enhanced by the buildings erected for the 1929 Exhibition, which have added even more splendour to an already delightful park.

★**Plaza de España** – This magnificent creation, the work of the Sevillian architect Aníbal González, is semicircular in shape and fronted by a canal on which rowing boats can nowadays be hired. The striking features of the *plaza* are its enormous proportions and its exquisite ceramics. The brick building has two tall towers, one at each end, and a series of *azulejo* scenes, each one representing a province of Spain and illustrating an episode from its particular history.

A typical horse-drawn carriage

Plaza de América – Here we find three buildings by the same architect which were also built for the 1929 Exhibition: at one end the Pabellón Real (Royal Pavilion), in Isabelline style; and opposite, towards the centre, the Renaissance and Mudéjar pavilions.

★**Museo Arqueológico de Sevilla** ⊘ – The city's archeological museum, housed in a Renaissance pavilion, contains an interesting collection of prehistoric and Roman objects.

The prehistoric collection is displayed on the ground floor, and includes objects discovered at archeological excavations carried out around the province. The exhibits in **Room VI** are particularly impressive, comprising the 7C-6C BC **El Carambolo treasure★**, a superb collection of gold jewellery of Phoenician inspiration with a surprisingly modern design and, and the **Goddess Astarte** (8C BC), a small bronze statue bearing an inscription which is said to be the oldest script found on the Iberian peninsula.

The first floor is dedicated exclusively to the museum's **Roman collection★** (Rooms XII to XXV), the majority of which was discovered at Itálica *(see p 313)*. Exhibits include magnificent sculptures and mosaics which provide visitors with an insight into the artistic development of the Romans in the region. Other displays show a variety of objects which recreate various aspects of the Roman civilisation (domestic life, religion, commerce, coins etc).

Other items of interest in the museum include a Mercury with a large mosaic at his feet (Room XIV); an unusual collection of marble plaques with footprint markings offered at games ceremonies (Room XVI); a Venus in Room XVII; fine sculptures of Diana in Room XIX, and bronze plaques from the Roman Lex Irnitana in the annexe. The oval room (Room XX) contains an impressive statue of Trajan, while Room XXV, dedicated to funerary art, has a variety of sarcophagi, columbaria, household objects etc.

Gazebos, statues and fountains

The Parque de María Luisa is much more than just a collection of attractive buildings and long, tree-lined avenues. Its fountains, with their gentle murmuring of water, its gazebos and its statues of famous characters add an intimate, romantic air to this delightful park. The memorials to Gustavo Adolfo Bécquer and Cervantes, with its *azulejos* illustrating scenes from *Don Quixote (at one end of plaza de América)*, are just two examples of the surprises awaiting visitors as they stroll around the gardens.

Museo de las Artes y Costumbres Populares ⊘ – The Museum of Popular Art and Traditions displays a range of ethnographic exhibits such as traditional costumes worn for *romerías* and *fiestas*, a reconstruction of typical workshop scenes, musical instruments, farming tools and machinery, as well as a collection of posters for the April Fair.

★**4** THE RIVER BANK

The **paseo de Cristóbal Colón**, one of Sevilla's most pleasant avenues, runs parallel to the river between the San Telmo and Triana bridges and is lined by some of the city's most impressive sites, such as the Torre del Oro and the Real Maestranza bullring. It offers attractive views across the river to the Triana district on the opposite bank.

Torre del Oro – The Gold Tower was built by the Almohads in the 13C on the banks of the Guadalquivir. This impressive tower, along with the Torre de la Plata or Silver Tower, was originally built as part of the city's defensive system. The main part of the tower consists of a dodecagonal stone structure crowned with merlons, topped by two additional levels made from brick, the second of which was added in the 18C. The interior houses the **Museo de la Marina** ⊙, containing documents, engravings, models of boats and other items relating to maritime life.

Cruises along the Guadalquivir depart from just below the tower.

Opposite the Torre del Oro stands the **Teatro de la Maestranza**, with its unusual false façade. The Hospital de la Caridad, with its collection of important works of art, is situated just behind the theatre.

★**Hospital de la Caridad** ⊙ – The Hospital of Charity was founded in 1667 by Don Miguel de Mañara (1627-79), an extraordinary character who, having experienced a brush with death following an accident, decided to give up the licentious life he had lived until that time and devote his life to helping the poor and sick.

The whitewashed façade of the church, dazzlingly bright in the sunlight, has five murals of blue and white ceramics which, it would seem, were based on drawings by Murillo. Theological virtues predominate with Faith, Hope and Charity; the two below show St George slaying the dragon and St James (Santiago), the slayer of the Moors.

The entrance to the church is via the hospital, with its harmonious double patio adorned with panels of *azulejos* representing scenes from the Old and New Testaments.

★★**Church** – The single-nave Baroque church contains a number of artistic gems within its walls commissioned by Mañara from Sevilla's leading artists of the period. The pictorial representations of Death and Charity would have created an example of the path that the brothers of Charity would have been expected to follow.

Two **paintings**★★ by **Valdés Leal** beneath the chancel tribune are quite staggering in their severity. In *Finis Gloriae Mundi*, with its macabre realism, Valdés Leal depicts a scene in which a bishop and a knight are shown as dead and half decomposed; the scales held in the hand of Christ are a reference to the moment of judgement. *In Ictu Oculi* (In the Blink of an Eye) is an allegory of death in which the skeleton has earthly symbols at its feet (a globe, a crown, books etc). An *Exaltation of the Cross*, by the same artist, can also be seen above the choir.

In the nave, **Murillo** has illustrated the theme of Charity through several **works**★. The sense of submission to one's fellow man is exalted in the fine *St Isabel of Hungary Curing the Lepers*, and in *St John of God Carrying a Sick Man On His Shoulder*, in which the artist demonstrates his mastery of *chiaroscuro*. The two paintings of children on the side altars are also by Murillo. Also in a side altar, a 17C bleeding Christ casting a distressed glance toward the sky, by Pedro Roldán, can also be seen. The two horizontal paintings facing each other in the transept are *The Miracle of the Loaves and Fishes* (representing the giving of food to the hungry) and *Moses Smiting Water from the Rock* (representing the giving of water to the thirsty). The canvases in the dome of the transept are by Valdés Leal: in each echinus an angel bearing the symbols of passion can be seen; the Evangelists are depicted in the pendentives. Note also the fine lamp-bearing angels.

At the main altar, a splendid Baroque **altarpiece** by Pedro Roldán has at its centre a fine sculptural group representing the **Holy Burial of Christ**★★ in which the artist has interpreted with great beauty the pain in the contained emotion of the faces.

Upon leaving the hospital, note the statue of its founder opposite and, to the left, nestled between buildings, the **Torre de la Plata**, a tower which was part of the old city walls.

Return to the paseo de Cristóbal Colón and continue towards the Puente de Triana.

Carmen

This legendary character created by the French writer Prosper Merimée in 1845 was subsequently used by Bizet as the subject of his famous opera (1874), in which he narrates the story of a triangle of love and jealousy involving Carmen the cigar-maker, a brigadier and a bullfighter.

Just in front of La Maestranza, in which the tragic finale of the opera was played, a bronze statue has been erected in honour of Carmen, who has gone down in history as the personification of women's passionate love.

La Maestranza ⊙ – Sevilla's famous *plaza de toros*, with its attractive red and white façade, was built between 1758 and 1881. One interesting feature of the building is the actual bullring itself, which is not quite circular. The Puerta del Príncipe (Prince's Gate) is an important feature of La Maestranza, for it is through this gate that triumphant bullfighters are carried on the shoulders of their admiring fans. The museum displays an interesting assortment of posters, paintings, busts, bullfighters' costumes and other mementoes from the world of bullfighting.

Head down to the river.

Just before the Puente de Triana stands the **Monumento a la Tolerancia**, a large stone sculpture with the inimitable stamp of Eduardo Chillida, who spent time here in April 1992.

★**Triana**

The Triana district, one of the city's most colourful areas, is located on the other side of the Puente de Triana (or Puente de Isabel II), built in 1845. From here, there are fine **views** of the Guadalquivir and the city's major sights on the east bank.

The ceramics quarter

A number of ceramics workshops and boutiques can still be seen in the area near the plaza del Altozano occupied by the calle de Callao, calle Antillano and calle de Alfarería, perpetuating an artistic tradition which has always existed in this quarter. The façades of some of these shops and workshops are decorated with *azulejos* advertising the wares inside.

By tradition, Triana is a fishermen's and merchants' quarter, although it has also produced several famous singers and bullfighters.

To the left of the bridge, the **plaza del Altozano** has a monument to a famous *trianero* (despite the fact that he was born in calle de la Feria on the opposite bank of the river), namely Juan Belmonte (1892-1962), a key figure in the history of bullfighting. Enter the Triana district through the **calle Pureza**. At no 55, between simple yet well-maintained houses, stands the **Capilla de los Marineros**, a chapel dedicated to sailors, with a statue of the **Esperanza de Triana** (Hope of Triana), one of the most venerated statues of the Virgin Mary in the city, and whose procession rivals that of La Macarena. A Christ of the Three Falls, dating from the end of the 16C, is to the right of the high altar.

Parroquia de Santa Ana – A little further on, the Iglesia de Santa Ana in the parish *(parroquía)* of the same name is the oldest in Sevilla. The original church, founded by Alfonso X the Wise in the 13C, has undergone significant restoration and alteration work, most of which took place in the 18C.

Exterior – Because of these various modifications, it is difficult to assign a particular style to the church. The most striking feature, however, is the tower, with its multi-foiled arches in the lower sections showing clear Mudéjar influence, and its *azulejo* decoration in the upper part.

Interior – *Entrance to the side of the church, in calle Vázquez de Leca.* The interior has three elevated aisles covered with sexpartite vaults and houses a number of paintings and sculptures.

A **Renaissance altarpiece** in the chancel comprises a fine ensemble of sculptures and paintings dedicated to the Virgin Mary; several of the canvases are by Pedro de Campaña. A sculpture portraying St Anne and the Virgin and Child occupies the central vaulted niche. The Child is modern, yet the figures of St Anne and the Virgin date from the 13C, although they have undergone subsequent alteration.

The retro-choir contains the delicate **Virgin of the Rose**, created by Alejo Fernández at the beginning of the 16C. Admire also the panelling and altar, both showing attractive *azulejo* decoration, in a chapel in the Evangelist nave.

Calle Betis – This street runs alongside the river. It is well worth taking the time to stroll along it, enjoying the delightful views of the opposite bank which provide the visitor with a completely different perspective of Sevilla, with the Torre del Oro and La Maestranza in the foreground, dominated by the majestic outline of the Giralda. The street is also noteworthy for its houses, bars and open-air kiosks which combine to create a scene which has managed to retain its traditional charm. At night, with the moon reflected on the river, the street is the perfect place for a romantic stroll.

"El Cachorro"

The **Capilla del Patrocinio** ⊘ , a chapel situated at the end of the calle Castilla in the most northerly section of the Triana district, is where the **Christ of the Expiration**, commonly known as "El Cachorro", is venerated. It is said that the artist, Francisco Antonio Gijón, used a sketch of a murdered gypsy known as "El Cachorro" for the face of Christ in this late-17C masterpiece. Once he had finished carving Christ, the sculpture was so realistic that when people saw it they immediately recognised the dead gypsy, hence its name.

★5 **LA MACARENA AND CALLE SAN LUIS**

Basílica de la Macarena ⊘ – The Iglesia de Nuestra Señora de la Esperanza (Church of Our Lady of Hope), built in the middle of the 20C, contains one of Sevilla's most famous statues: **La Macarena★**. This carving of the Virgin Mary, the work of an anonymous 17C artist, looks down upon the church from the high altar. The city's inhabitants say that it was sculpted by the angels, as only they could have created a work of such magnificence. The beauty of her tearful face unleashes popular fervour during her procession, in the early morning of Good Friday. A Christ under Sentence in a chapel on the Evangelist side of the church is also venerated here and brought out in the procession alongside the Virgin.

La Macarena procession

Ch. Sappa/RAPHO

The **museum** displays a variety of cloaks and skirts, as well as the impressive floats used to carry La Macarena and Christ during the processions, providing the visitor with an idea of the splendour of these occasions.

The **Arco de la Macarena** stands opposite the church. This arch was part of the old Arab **walls** of the city. The section which has been preserved continues as far as the Puerta de Córdoba (Córdoba Gate). The walls have barbicans and are punctuated with large, square fortified towers.

Hospital de las Cinco Llagas or Hospital de la Sangre – *Opposite the Arco de la Macarena.* The former Hospital of the Five Wounds *(llagas)* or Blood *(sangre),* is now the headquarters of the Andalucian Parliament. Up until the middle of the 20C, this Renaissance-style building was Sevilla's main hospital. It is sober and harmonious in style with two floors opening out onto a square of greenery, and has towers on each corner. The building's white marble doorway is crowned by the escutcheon of the Five Wounds.

Return to La Macarena, behind which stands the 13C parish church of **San Gil**, which has undergone significant restoration over the centuries. Follow the calle de San Luis.

Iglesia de Santa Marina – This 14C brick church has a simple stone ogival portal with minor sculpted decoration and a sober Mudéjar tower with staggered merlons. A tour of the exterior reveals the church's sturdy buttresses and the large Gothic windows at the apsidal end.

★**Iglesia de San Luis de los Franceses** ⊘ – This church, the work of Leonardo de Figueroa, is one of the best examples of Sevillian Baroque architecture.
The predominant feature of the **façade** is its clear compartmentalisation: two storeys, with an octagonal tower on each side, between which stands a central cupola with ceramic decoration.
The **interior**★★ is surprising in its exuberant beauty, with murals on the magnificent cupola by Lucas Valdés and the outstanding retables by Pedro Duque Cornejo. The fine *azulejos* complete this superb ensemble, which manages to combine a richness of decoration with harmony. Note also the unusual reliquary on the frontal of the chancel.

Iglesia de San Marcos – The impressive 14C façade is a successful blend of Gothic and Mudéjar features. The attractive **Mudéjar tower**★ stands out, with its clear Giralda influence (multifoiled arches and *sebka* work on the upper frieze). The predominant building material is brick, with the exception of the stone portal which is Gothic in style and has three 18C sculptures (God the Father, the Virgin Mary and an angel), which replaced the original works, and an elegant *sebka*-style frieze lending it an unusual air.
The whitewashed interior contains a handsome 17C sculpture of **St Mark** (Evangelist nave) and an 18C **Recumbent Christ** (Epistle nave).

In the **plaza de Santa Isabel** behind the church, admire the doorway of the **convent** that has lent its name to the square, with a relief depicting the Visitation of the Virgin to her cousin Isabel. The work dates from the early 17C and is by Andrés Ocampo. The church is interesting, albeit somewhat difficult to visit as it only opens for daily mass first thing in the morning.

★**Convento de Santa Paula** ⊘ – This historic convent, home to an order of enclosed nuns, was founded at the end of the 15C and is one of the finest in Sevilla. The elegant 17C belfry, which stands proudly above the surrounding houses, acts as an invitation to discover this delightful convent which also produces its own tasty cakes and jams prepared by its Hieronymite nuns.

★ **Church** – *Entrance through the left-hand door with the azulejo depicting St Paula*. Once through the door, note the interesting atrium and the fine **portal**★ of the church, worked on by Nicola Pisano and completed in 1504. The portal is made of brick with alternating twin-coloured rows and is adorned with profuse ceramic decoration. In spite of the evident mixture of styles – Mudéjar in the use of brick, Gothic in the arches and Renaissance in the medallions and cresting – the effect is one of perfect cohesion and harmony. The escutcheon on the tympanum is of the Catholic Monarchs. The central medallion, attributed to Lucca della Robbia, represents the Birth of Jesus.

The **interior**★, with a single nave topped by a 17C *artesonado* ceiling, comprises a presbytery with Gothic vaults which are totally covered with delightful polychrome frescoes. The two niches on either side of the high altar house the tombs of the Marquess and Marchioness of Montemayor, the benefactors of this church. The brother of the Marchioness is laid to rest in a separate niche. The main altarpiece dates from the beginning of the 18C, although it has retained the image of St Paula, in the centre, from an earlier retable. Note the movement of the two lamp-bearing angels. Two altars can be seen in the nave, one opposite the other, dedicated to John the Evangelist and John the Baptist. The two finely carved sculptures are the work of Martínez Montañés. A Gothic Christ can also be seen in a large window in the Epistle nave. The enclosed choir is separated from the rest of the church by an iron grille.

★ **Museum** – *(Entrance through no 11 on the plaza)*. The museum is housed in several of the convent's high outbuildings. Two of these have fine *artesonado* ceilings. The museum contains a number of objects of great value, including canvases by **Ribera** (*St Jerome* and *The Adoration of the Shepherds*), two works by Pedro de Mena (*Our Lady of Sorrows* and *Eccehomo*), an *Immaculate Conception* by Alonso Cano, and a divine 17C crib with many figurines.

Presbytery vault, Iglesia del Convento de Santa Paula

★ 6 CENTRO

Plaza Nueva – This spacious, rectangular square is situated on the land previously occupied by the Convento de San Francisco. An equestrian statue at its centre is of Fernando III the Saint, the city's conqueror. With its tall palm trees, benches and street lamps, the square is popular with locals and tourists alike.

Town Hall (Ayuntamiento) – The west front of the town hall, which opens onto the square, is neo-Classical and dates from the 19C. The more interesting east side, which looks onto the plaza de San Francisco, has an attractive 16C **façade**★ which is pure Plateresque in style and is the work of Diego de Riaño. The delicate decoration (a mixture of classical ornamental motifs including fantastic and grotesque animals, medallions with faces, escutcheons etc) can be seen on the architraves, columns, pilasters and bay surrounds.

The attractive palace situated opposite the town hall in plaza de San Francisco is the headquarters of the Caja de Ahorros San Fernando savings bank and was formerly the seat of the Royal Court of Justice *(Audiencia)*. The classical lines of its late-16C façade are attributed to Alonso de Vandelvira.

Calle Sierpes

Calle Sierpes – This long pedestrianised street, undoubtedly the most famous in the city, is lined with a whole host of shops, both traditional and modern. Sierpes is at its most lively in the late afternoon and early evening when locals stroll along the street window-shopping or enjoy a pastry in one of its renowned *pastelerías*. When the sun is at its hottest, a protective canopy is used along the whole street to provide protection and cool for those still out and about. The famous La Campana cafeteria and pastry shop, founded in 1885, is located at the very end of calle Sierpes, at the junction with calle Martín Villa.

★**Capilla de San José** ⊙ – This exquisite chapel, built at the end of the 17C, is a masterpiece of Sevillian Baroque. Its 18C façade and belfry decorated with bright blue *azulejos* can be seen from the corner of calle Sierpes and calle Jovellanos. St Joseph with the Infant Christ in his arms can be seen on the portal. The exuberant Baroque decoration in the relatively small interior is something of a surprise, particularly that visible in the apsidal end. The large wooden **altarpiece** in the presbytery depicting angels, saints and God the Father, is a true exaltation of ornamental art. The image of St Joseph in the centre of the altarpiece is venerated here.

At the end of calle Sierpes, take calle Cuna, which runs parallel to it.

★**Palacio de la Condesa de Lebrija** ⊙ – This private residence provides visitors with an opportunity to visit a palace in a typically Sevillian layout, comprising a hallway, a central patio and an interior garden. However, once inside, a pleasant surprise awaits – a floor that appears to be completely covered with **Roman mosaics**★ from nearby Itálica *(see p 313)*. Although all the mosaics are of interest, the patio floor depicting mythological scenes is particularly impressive, as is the octagonal room with its volutes and large vases. In addition to the mosaics, the attractive patio also has elegant foiled arches, Moorish-influenced panelling and *alfiz* rectangular moulding, a colourful plinth of Sevillian *azulejos* and showcases displaying archeological remains. The **staircase**★, rich in ceramic tiles, has a mahogany banister, marble steps and an outstanding Mudéjar marquetry ceiling, which originally graced a palace in Marchena.

Continue along calle Cuna to plaza del Salvador.

Plaza del Salvador – This spacious, elongated square is dominated by the monumental parish church of El Salvador. The plaza is one of the city's most popular places for an aperitif, when it swaps its customary peace and quiet for a few hours of lively socialising, especially on Sundays.

★**Iglesia del Salvador** ⊙ – The church rises majestically on one side of the square. It was built on the site of the former main mosque, which was demolished in 1671. Construction work lasted until 1712, in accordance with plans by José Granados; the cupolas were designed by Leonardo de Figueroa. The elegant façade of the church, which combines attractive pink brick and stone, is a fine example of the ornamental Baroque style.

The sensation of vastness pervades the whole of the interior. The spacious church has a ground plan consisting of three short aisles. Note the high lanterned cupola above the transept.

Some of the city's most notable **Baroque retables**★★ (all of which date from the 18C) can be seen inside the church. The one in the chancel, dedicated to the Transfiguration of the Lord, is the work of Cayetano Acosta. This immense altarpiece covers the entire wall with unrestrained decoration that completely masks its artistic arrangement.

The frontispiece of the **Capilla del Sagrario**, the sacrarium chapel which opens onto the left transept, has been designed in the form of a gigantic retable. This is also the work of Cayetano Acosta, and is dedicated to the exaltation of the Sacred Host; it displays the same ornamental exuberance as the main altarpiece. Inside the chapel, the main object of interest is the 17C **Christ of the Passion**, by Martínez Montañés. This work, which is part of an opulent silver altarpiece, manages to create an image of serene suffering in the face of Christ.

Another fine retable, by José Maestre, with a shrine dedicated to the Virgin Mary, can be admired in the right transept.

The chapel to the right of the chancel displays the 17C **Crucificado del Amor**, by Juan de Mesa, in which the artist movingly interprets the suffering and solitude of Jesus on the Cross.

7 FROM PLAZA DEL DUQUE DE LA VICTORIA TO ALAMEDA DE HERCULES

Plaza del Duque de la Victoria is the commercial heart of this part of the city with several department stores and numerous smaller shops.

In the nearby **plaza de la Concordia**, Sevilla's town hall has created an exhibition centre in the church of the former Colegio de San Hermenegildo (1616-20), which has preserved its fine oval cupola.

Walk through plaza de Gavidia, with its statue of Daoíz, then take calle Cardenal Spínola, which leads into plaza de San Lorenzo.

Templo de Nuestro Padre Jesús del Gran Poder ⊘ – This modern church (1965), housing the magnificent statue of **Jesus of Great Power★** (1620), is situated in plaza de San Lorenzo, alongside the parish church of the same name dating from the 13C but modified four centuries later. Juan de Mesa's sculptural masterpiece is housed in a shrine surrounded by red carnations, at the feet of which the devout come to leave their offerings. The slightly inclined face of Jesus reflects with realism his great fatigue and profound sadness.

Follow calle Santa Clara, along which the convent of the same name, an enclosed order of nuns, can be seen (but not visited), and then head along calle Lumbreras. Once past the junction with calle Becas, turn around to admire the **Torre de Don Fadrique**, all that remains of the Palacio de Don Fadrique. This battlemented tower was built in the 13C in a transitional style showing both Romanesque and Gothic influence. Continue along calle Lumbreras as far as Alameda de Hércules.

Alameda de Hércules – This long boulevard was constructed in the 16C. Two statues stand at each end: those to the north were added in the 18C and show two lions bearing coats of arms; those to the south are Roman and are crowned by statues of Hercules and Julius Caesar. A **flea market** provides a lively atmosphere here on Sunday mornings.

ADDITIONAL SIGHTS

★★**Casa de Pilatos** ⊘ – The palace is one of Sevilla's most famous monuments. It is situated in the pleasant **plaza de Pilatos** to which it has lent its name. The statue in the square is of Zurbarán.

Construction of the building began at the end of the 15C. However, it was Don Fadrique, the first Marquess of Tarifa, who was responsible for most of the palace visible today. It is said that he took his inspiration from Pontius Pilate's house in Jerusalem, hence the name of the palace. It is a mixture of Mudéjar, Renaissance and Flamboyant Gothic styles, although the Mudéjar style predominates.

The delightful **patio** resembles an elegant Moorish palace with its finely moulded stuccowork and magnificent 16C lustre **azulejos★★**.

Note also that the arches are unequal and that the *azulejos* form panels that have different motifs. A fountain in the centre was carved in Genoa in the 16C. Various statues decorate the palace, including **Athena**, an original 5C BC Greek statue; the remaining statues are of Roman origin. Rounded niches in the walls contain a superb collection of busts of Roman emperors. The rooms around the patio are noteworthy for their fine *artesonado* ceilings, panels of *azulejos*, sculpted plasterwork, groined vaulting and the paleo-Christian sculpture of the Good Shepherd in the chapel, the oldest part of

Detail, Casa de Pilatos

Ch. Boisvieux

the house. The gardens can also be visited.

The sumptuous *azulejo*-adorned **staircase★★** leading up to the first floor from a corner of the patio has a remarkable half-orange **wooden dome★**.

16C frescoes representing various characters from Antiquity can be seen on the walls of the patio gallery on this upper floor. Several of the rooms have interesting ceilings, particularly the one painted by Francisco Pacheco in 1603 illustrating the Apotheosis of Hercules.

A visit to the nearby **Convento de San Leandro** is particularly recommended. Although access to the church is difficult, it is still worth a visit to buy the convent's famous **yemas**, delicious sweets made with egg yolk and sugar.

* **Iglesia de Santa María la Blanca** – This former synagogue was transformed into a church in the 14C; the simple Gothic portal remains from this period. However, the 17C saw the almost total reconstruction of the building, including the remainder of the façade and the **interior★**. The latter has three aisles separated by semicircular arches resting on pink marble columns. The barrel vaults adorned with lunettes and the dome over the transept are completely covered with delightful plasterwork decoration. The building's Baroque exuberance is balanced by the lightness of the columns, creating an effect which is both attractive and harmonious. The Evangelist nave contains a *Last Supper*, attributed to Murillo, which is surprising in its dramatic use of light, in keeping with the pure tenebrist style.

*** **Museo de Bellas Artes** ⊘ – *Entrance via the plaza del Museo.* This excellent art gallery contains one of the largest collections of Spanish paintings from the Golden Age. It is housed in the former Convento de la Merced (17C), designed by Juan de Oviedo. The Baroque doorway was added in the 18C. It is built around three delightful patios and a magnificent staircase, covered by a cupola decorated with Mannerist stucco designs.

The museum displays a number of significant works from the Middle Ages to the 20C. However, two rooms are of particular importance:

*** **Room V** – *Ground floor.* This is undoubtedly the museum's star attraction. The church, its walls decorated with paintings by the 18C artist Domingo Martínez, provides a stunning backdrop to an outstanding collection of work by Murillo and one of Zurbarán's masterpieces, *The Apotheosis of St Thomas Aquinas (in the nave).*

Murillo (1617-82), a master of both the pictorial technique and the use of light in his canvases, is the great painter of religious subjects and children. His characters, always very human, exude tenderness and gentleness in a world which avoids drama and excess. His canvases can be found in the transept and in the apse, where his

The former church, dominated by Murillo's Immaculate Conception

monumental *Immaculate Conception*, with its energetic movement, holds pride of place. It is surrounded by several notable paintings of saints: *Santa Rufina and Santa Justa*, who are clutching the Giralda, and *San Leandro and San Buenaventura*. In the right transept, a kindly *Virgin of the Cloth* is particularly interesting (admire the effect of the child moving towards you). Note also *St Francis embracing Christ on the Cross* and a further *Immaculate Conception*, also known as *La Niña (The Child)*. Among several paintings on the left-hand side, *St Anthony and Child*, *Dolorosa* and *St Felix of Cantalicio and Child* are all worth a closer look.

★★ Room X – *Upper floor*. This room is dedicated to works by **Zurbarán** (1598-1664). This artist had a particular skill for painting the shades of white of the monks' habits and the pure cloth of Christ, as admired in the fine *Christ on the Cross* (in this same room), in which the body of Christ, painted against a dark background, appears as if sculpted in relief. Zurbarán's compositions are both simple and peaceful. A certain lack of concern for perspective is apparent in some of his work, resulting in one or two inaccuracies, as can be seen in *St Hugh and Carthusian Monks at Table* which is otherwise quite outstanding. His preoccupation with the treatment of the canvas, as already seen in his depiction of the Fathers of the Church in *The Apotheosis of St Thomas Aquinas*, can equally be admired in the splendid velvet brocade in *San Ambrosio*. In addition to his paintings of saints, his *Virgin of the Caves* and *San Bruno's Visit to Urbano II* are also of interest. On display in the same room are various sculptures, including *St Dominic* by Martínez Montañés. Note also the splendid *artesonado* ceiling in the inner room.

Other rooms – **Room I** displays a number of interesting medieval works. **Room II**, once the refectory, is dedicated to Renaissance art, in particular a fine sculpture of *St Jerome* by Pietro Torrigiani, a contemporary of Michelangelo. Other works of note include Alejo Fernández's *Annunciation*, with its Flemish and Italian influence clearly evident, a painting of his son *Jorge Manuel*, by El Greco, and a diptych of *The Annunciation and Visitation* by Coffermans. Two magnificent portraits of *A Lady and a Gentleman* by Pedro Pacheco are the highlights in **Room III**.

Upper floor: Room VI (a gallery) displays a fine, richly decorated collection of female saints (anonymous, though some were painted by followers of Zurbarán), and two male saints. **Room VII** contains further works by Murillo and his disciples while **Room VIII** is entirely devoted to the other great Baroque artist **Valdés Leal**, a more expressive and dramatic painter than Murillo. European Baroque is represented in **Room IX** with, among others, Ribera's powerful *St James the Apostle*, canvases by Brueghel and the supreme *Portrait of a Lady* by Cornelis de Vos. **Room XI** (a gallery), devoted to 18C art, is enlivened by Goya's *Portrait of Canon José Duato*, and several works by Lucas Valdés. The following two rooms (**XII** and **XIII**) display 19C art, in particular some superb portraits by Esquivel, while the final room (**XIV**) shows several 20C canvases by Vázquez Díaz and Zuloaga, among others.

Iglesia de la Magdalena – The church was built in the late 17C and early 18C above an earlier building, according to designs by Leonardo de Figueroa. It is possible to see the layout of the church from the exterior, with its aisles, transept and elegant dome adorned with *azulejos*.

The **interior★**, containing a number of treasures, is particularly impressive. The paintings on the ceilings are the work of Lucas Valdés. A lanterned cupola rises majestically above the transept, while the exuberant Baroque altarpiece in the chancel dates from the early 18C; the paintings on the vaults illustrate allegories of saints. The **Capilla del Cristo del Calvario** *(to the right of the presbytery)* takes its name from the Exposed Christ, an 18C work by Francisco Ocampo. Interest in the Epistle nave is centred on the fine **high-relief of the Assumption** supported by four small angels, by Juan de Mesa (1619), and the Sacramental and Quinta Angustia chapels. The former contains canvases by **Zurbarán**: *St Dominic in Soria* and *The Miraculous Healing of the Beatified Reginald of Orleans*.

The **Capilla de la Quinta Angustia★** is situated in the vestibule of the main entrance doorway to the church. The magnificent sculpture at the altar, depicting a highly moving Descent of Christ, is attributed to the followers of Pedro Roldán. Look up to admire the three Moorish-influenced cupolas. Ten canvases of saints by Valdés Leal hang from the walls of the chapel.

In the left transept, next to the door, stands a 16C sculpture of the **Virgin of the Fever**, an elegant and maternal Virgin with the Infant Christ in her arms.

La Cartuja: Centro Andaluz de Arte Contemporáneo ⊙ – *Buses C-1 and C-2*. The Andalucian Centre for Contemporary Art is expected to open its permanent exhibition during the course of the year 2000. It is also used for temporary exhibitions.

The museum is part of an unusual complex with a complicated history. The monastery was founded at the end of the 14C in honour of an apparition of the Virgin Mary in this district. It subsequently enjoyed a period of great splendour and even visits by kings and queens and other important figures such as Columbus, who prepared his second journey of discovery to America here. During the 19C, the monastery was to undergo significant changes: the French converted it into a barracks during the Napoleonic invasion and it was later acquired by Charles Pickman, who set up a ceramics factory on the site. Although the factory closed in 1982, its chimneys and kilns are still visible today.

★ **Monastic buildings** – These mainly date from the 15C, 16C and 17C. Some have managed to preserve their original *azulejos*. The church is of particular interest with its delightful *azulejo* rosette, a sacristy with Baroque plasterwork and charming Mudéjar brick cloisters supported by slender marble columns. The monks' chapter-house, containing a number of interesting tombs, and the long refectory with an impressive 17C *artesonado* ceiling, are also well worth a visit.

★ISLA MÁGICA

The Isla Mágica theme park is spread over a 40ha/99-acre site on the Isla de la Cartuja, taking visitors on a journey back to the century of the Discoveries. The park is divided into eight areas: Sevilla, the Gateway to the Indies; Quetzal, the Fury of the Gods; The Balcony of Andalucia; The Gateway to America; Amazonia; The Pirates' Den; The Fountain of Youth; and El Dorado.

The park has a whole host of other facilities and attractions, including exciting rides, street entertainers and souvenir shops, as well as a good selection of bars and restaurants where you can catch your breath.

Isla Magica

☎ **General information 902 16 17 16** – ☎ **Reservations 902 16 00 00**
Web site: www.islamagica.es

Opening dates
Open from 19 March to 8 December. Open daily from May to mid-September; at other times open at weekends and on special occasions and holidays (contact the park for further details).

Opening times
11am- 8pm, Mon-Thur in April, May and first half of June.
11am-11pm at weekends and daily from mid-June onwards.

Admission prices
– Adults: 3 400pts
– Children between 5 and 12 and over-65s: 2 300pts
– Children under 5: free
The cost of admission includes access to all the park's attractions and shows.

The following is a list of some of the park's attractions.

Quetzal, the Fury of the Gods – An exciting journey to the Mayan world in which a plumed serpent takes you on a journey across Central America to escape the fury of the gods.

The Balcony of Andalucia – An enjoyable stroll through this miniature world highlighting the most important monuments and geographical features of the region.

Anaconda – A breathtaking water ride with spectacular descents to satisfy the most intrepid of sailors.

Iguaçu – These impressive waterfalls are bound to get your nerves tingling as you are propelled into a lagoon at speeds of over 50kph/32mph.

The Jaguar – If you still need an extra rush of adrenaline, the Jaguar is for you. This huge roller coaster with its loop-the-loops and vertigo-inducing descents reaches speed of up to 85kph/53mph.

The Fountain of Youth – A paradise for **younger visitors**. This dream-like world of lakes and streams contains most of the park's attractions for young children, including the **Tell-Tale Toad** and the **Tadpoles** with their wonderfully amusing stories.

The Rapids of the Orinoco – Why not try your hand at taming this spectacular river on board an inflatable raft.

The House of Superstition – A film created by state-of-the-art technology projected onto a gigantic spherical screen. Experience a whole new world of sensations in the House of Superstition.

EXCURSIONS

★**Itálica** ⊘ – *9km/5.5mi northwest along the E 803 – N 630. Bear left immediately after Santiponce.* The vestiges of this Roman city founded by Scipio "the African" in 206 BC stand on a hill shaded by cypress trees, dominating the Guadalquivir Plain. Itálica's golden age was in the 2C AD. Its history is indelibly linked to the Roman emperors **Trajan** (AD 53-117) and **Hadrian** (AD 76-138), both of whom were born here. Hadrian granted it the title of a colony, transforming Itálica into a monumental city. Its decline began under the Late Empire.

The archeological area corresponds to a section of the district created under Hadrian, with streets laid out according to an orthogonal plan and lined by public buildings and luxurious private houses. Several original **mosaics** have been preserved, such as those of Neptune, birds, planetary divinities etc.

Amphitheatre – This elliptical amphitheatre was one of the largest in the Roman Empire with a capacity for 25 000 spectators and is still relatively well preserved. Sections of tiered seating and the pits beneath the arena can still be seen.

The town of **Santiponce** stands on the oldest part of Itálica. The former Roman theatre can be seen at its centre.

Bollullos de la Mitación – *15km/9.5mi west along the A 49 towards Huelva, then 3km/2mi south.*

Iglesia de San Martín ⊘ – Plaza de Cuatrovitas is fronted by the town hall and the Church of St Martin, a Baroque construction dating from the 18C. The brick tower is adorned with detailed *azulejo* decoration. Inside, note the interesting **retable** with four paintings by Zurbarán.

Santuario de Cuatrovitas ⊘ – *Leave Bollullos in the direction of Aznalcázar. After 4km/2.5mi, bear left immediately after a pine grove. Continue for a further 2km/1.2mi along an unmetalled road.*

The drive to this simple sanctuary, one of few rural mosques still standing, is particularly pleasant. Built during the Almohad period in a flat landscape, its most striking features are its brick **tower** and foliated and horseshoe arch decoration. The interior contains a 16C ceramic altar frontispiece representing the Virgin and Child and the Four Evangelists.

Alcalá de Guadaira – *20km/12mi along the A 92. Drive into the town and park next to the Iglesia de Santiago.*

Iglesia de Santiago – The Church of St James was built in the 15C and 16C. Elegant ceramic decoration adorns the upper sections and the spire of the lofty bell-tower. Inside, note the presbytery, crowned with an unusual trumpet-shaped and coffered vault.

Castle – *Climb up the stepped ramps next to the church.* The remains of this important Almohad fortress stand on top of a hill, dominating the town and an extensive rolling landscape. The walls and towers of the original outer enclosure can still be seen. This pleasant site has now been transformed into a leisure area with a children's park, goalposts etc. The 14C-16C **Ermita de Nuestra Señora del Aguila**, a chapel with a solid brick tower topped by merlons, stands at its centre. Note the remains of a medieval fresco inside the chapel *(to the right of the presbytery).*

Parque Nacional de SIERRA NEVADA★★
Granada
Michelin map 446 U 19-20-21

After the Alps, the Sierra Nevada (Snowy Mountains) is the highest range in Europe, a fact that may surprise many visitors to Andalucia. Fourteen (one-fifth) of its peaks are over 3 000m/9 840ft high and it covers a total area of some 170 000ha/420 070 acres (90 000ha/222 390 acres of which are part of the national park). Snow and ice, both of which are present for much of the year, have eroded this young mountain chain during the course of time to create a sculpted, twisted profile. The highest peaks, **Mulhacén** (3 482m/11 424ft), **Veleta** (3 394m/11 132ft) and **Alcazaba** (3 371m/11 057ft) are all found in the western part of the range.

When to visit?

Any time of year is a good time to visit the Sierra Nevada. Its **ski resort** offers a range of options to visitors, including downhill skiing, various excursions, and a number of treks to some of the highest snow-capped peaks. In summer, hiking and horse riding are popular activities. Snow can start to fall in October and in some years it has even been known to snow in June; despite this, the Sierra Nevada is renowned for its glorious sunny days for two-thirds of the year, when the combination of sun, the whiteness of the snow and the blue sky create a scene of almost unparalleled beauty.

Hidalgo-Lopesino/MARCO POLO

✳✳**Sierra Nevada ski resort** – The resort was built in 1964 and held its first major sporting event, a **World Cup** downhill, in 1977. However, just two years later, the company responsible for the management of the resort was forced to consider closure due to its lack of profitability. The situation improved during the 1980s, a period which coincided with various proposals relating to the protection of the Sierra Nevada. In the 1990s the resort was chosen to host the **1995 World Skiing Championships**; however, due to a lack of snow these were postponed until the following year. The investments made for this event have transformed the resort into one of the best in Spain, with a ski area of around 60km/37.5mi, 45 runs and 20 lifts. Other options on offer here include evening skiing at weekends. The resort also has a full range of apartment and hotel accommodation in **Pradollano**.

ITINERARIES BY CAR

Construction of the first road in the Sierra Nevada began in 1914. By 1923 it had reached Pinos Genil and in 1935 the section to the Pico Veleta was officially opened. Since then, this road has been used for access to the highest peaks within the range. However, the recent designation of the Sierra Nevada as a **Natural Park** in 1989 and then a **National Park** in 1999 has resulted in severe restrictions on the use of these roads. Two control posts, one on the northern section (Borreguiles crossroads), the other to the south (Hoya del Portillo), limit access within the park for private vehicles. The two itineraries suggested below take into account these restrictions. *Visitors are, however, advised to check road conditions prior to departure.*

★★① **From Granada to El Dornajo**
Only possible in summer; allow 1hr

Leave Granada on the old mountain road *(carretera de la Sierra)*. After 8km/5mi turn off towards Pinos Genil. The road passes through an attractive landscape, skirting the Canales Reservoir *(embalse)* before reaching **Güejar-Sierra**. Head out of the village in the direction of Maitena. After crossing the Genil, the road follows the course of the river, climbing along sharp, steep bends to the Hotel del Duque, now a seminary, before arriving at the El Dornajo visitor centre.

Mulhacén

According to legend, the name of the highest peak on mainland Spain originates from a story which recounts that the king of Granada, Muley-Hacén, the father of Boabdil, is buried here. The king fell in love with a beautiful Christian maiden by the name of Zoraida, who, after the king's death in Mondújar Castle, had him buried on the highest peak of the Sierra Nevada to hide him from his enemies.

PRACTICAL INFORMATION

Before setting out...

Centro de Visitantes del Dornajo ⊘ – *At Km 23 on the Sierra Nevada road.* ☎ *958 34 06 25.* The El Dornajo visitor centre is an ideal starting point for a visit to the Sierra Nevada, with its wide range of information on the park (models, exhibitions etc), an excellent bookshop and the introduction it provides to the region's gastronomy and arts and crafts. The centre also organises a range of activities for visitors, including high-mountain hikes, excursions and bicycle hire.

Punto de información del Puerto de la Ragua – This information point is situated on the Puerto de la Ragua road – ☎ *958 76 01 06.*

Punto de Información del Parque Nacional de Sierra Nevada – **Pampaneira** – *Plaza de la Libertad* – ☎ *958 76 31 21.* The **Nevadensis** agency in Pampaneira also organises activities and tours in the Sierra Nevada and Alpujarras.

Andalucian Mountaineering Federation (Federación Andaluza de Montañismo) – ☎ *958 29 13 40.*

ACCESS

By car – The fastest and quickest route from Granada is along the A 395. In **Pradollano** visitors will have to leave their vehicles in the underground car park. A more attractive alternative is to combine the two itineraries suggested below.

By bus – The **BONAL** company operates several daily services from Granada to Pradollano, leaving from the bus stop next to the **Palacio de Congresos** – ☎ *958 27 31 00.*

WHERE TO STAY

MODERATE

Don José – *At Km 9 along the Granada road* – ☎ *958 34 04 00* – *fax 958 15 94 58 – 7 500pts.* A small and comfortable family-run hotel.

MID-RANGE

Trevenque – *Plaza de Andalucía* – ☎ *958 48 08 62* – *fax 958 48 14 03* – *10 500pts (14 200pts during the ski season).* Modern, spacious apartments with views of the mountains and an excellent location at the heart of the resort.

★★② From El Dornajo to the Borreguiles crossroads

From the **El Dornajo Visitor Centre** follow the road to the left which climbs up to the Collado de las Sabinas mountain pass, an ascent which is both steep and punctuated with sharp bends. The scenery here is one of native pines, with fine views of the Genil Valley from the road. Once past the Collado de las Sabinas pass, the road continues to Pradollano. From here it is possible to reach the Borreguiles crossroads.

ITINERARIES ON FOOT

Hiking possibilities in the Sierra Nevada are almost endless. Visitors are advised to head for the visitor centre before setting out to obtain information on the marked walks available and the length of time needed. The most popular departure points are the following: the village of Güéjar-Sierra, the El Dornajo visitor centre and the **Albergue Universitario** (University Hostal). The most interesting routes are the climb to the **Laguna de las Yeguas** lagoon and the ascents of **Pico Veleta** and **Mulhacén**.

EXCURSIONS

★**Valle del Lecrín** – *Follow the N 323 from Granada, then turn off the main road in Dúrcal.* The little-known Lecrín Valley is a delight for visitors. The road winds its way through orange groves, passing small villages nestled on the slopes of the valley along the way.

Dúrcal – This village of Moorish origin has a charming main square, the **plaza de España**.

The "ice vendors"

The name *neveros* was given to those men who supplied ice to the city of Granada in bygone days. These fearless souls would climb up to the snow-capped peaks of the Sierra Nevada in groups of around ten men and with the help of mules and donkeys would load up and transport ice to the hospitals, shops and bars in the city. They worked from dusk onwards, taking advantage of the cool of the night to return to Granada without losing any of their precious cargo due to the heat. This activity was so important that even in the 18C operating licences existed and regulations governing it were already in place. The trade in ice collapsed around 1920 with the establishment of the first ice factories.

Nigüelas – One of the prettiest settlements in the valley. The town hall is installed in the 16C Palacio de los Zayas. The town's most interesting building is the 14C **Las Laerillas oil mill** ⊘★, inside which the presses, measuring instruments, olive bins and, in particular, the large mills, can still be seen. One of these mills is known as the *molino de sangre* (blood mill), so called because it was powered by an animal; the other mill was hydraulically operated *(for entry, ask for the key at the town hall)*.

Mondújar – The Mudéjar-style church in Mondújar is crowned by an impressive tower. The neighbouring village of Lecrín, a word of Arabic origin meaning "happiness", has given its name to the valley.

The road continues along the Torrente river valley, skirting the villages of Murchas, Restábal, **Melegís** and **Saleres**. The churches in Melegís and Saleres have managed to preserve some Mudéjar *azulejos* on their towers.

Parque Natural
de la SIERRA NORTE DE SEVILLA
Sevilla
Michelin map 446 T-S-R 12-13

The park covers an area of 164 840ha/407 320 acres of outstanding natural beauty in the Sierra Morena, to the north of Sevilla, on the borders of the provinces of Huelva and Córdoba, and the region of Extremadura. It is dissected by several rivers, including the Viar, Huéznar and Retortillo, which have created a lush vegetation abounding in cork oak, horse chestnut, elm, holm oak and hazel along their path. The park's fauna is equally rich, with the presence of wild boar, harrier eagles and tawny vultures, to name but a few species.

The **Centro de Información del Parque** ⊘ in Constantina has a selection of plans, maps and other documentation on activities available within the park.

WHERE TO STAY

CAZALLA DE LA SIERRA

Las Navezuelas – *On the A 432, 3km/1.8mi from the centre of Cazalla heading towards Fábrica del Pedroso; access is via a 1km/0.6mi dirt track)* – *954 88 47 64* – *12 rooms* – *7 500pts (apartment: 11 000pts)*. A small paradise in which, according to its owner "twelve years of effort have been expended" to create the delightful residence visible today. The guest rooms have all been tastefully decorated, while the swimming pool offers a magnificent view of the Sierra Morena. A bucolic setting, where the only sound is the far-off bleating of sheep.

Posada del Moro – *Paseo del Moro* – ☏ *954 88 48 58* – *fax 954 88 43 26* – *15 rooms* – *8 000pts*. A small, pleasant family-run hotel situated opposite the Parque del Moro. The hotel also has a high-quality restaurant and a garden with swimming pool. Good value for money.

CONSTANTINA

La Casa – *José de la Bastida, 25* – ☏ *955 88 01 58* – *7 rooms* – *7 000pts*. This small, family-run *pensión* in the centre of Constantina has been charmingly maintained by its owners. Simple, but comfortable rooms at a reasonable price.

San Blas – *Miraflores, 4* – ☏ *955 88 00 77* – *fax 955 88 19 00* – *15 rooms* – *8 500pts*. A modern building, perhaps lacking in charm, but with spacious, well-appointed rooms. A small swimming pool is open to guests on the terrace

FROM LORA DEL RÍO TO GUADALCANAL
90km/56mi – allow one day

Lora del Río – *Situated outside the boundaries of the park.* This irregularly shaped town is situated on the right bank of the Guadalquivir, at the base of the foothills of the Sierra Morena. Lora is a peaceful place steeped in tradition, whose carefully maintained streets and buildings afford it a solemn air. Local delicacies include snails *(caracoles)*, *sopeaos* (a variant of the traditional *gazpacho*), and the popular *gachas con coscurros*a flour-based pureé sprinkled with breadcrumbs fried in olive oil.

Iglesia de la Asunción – This Mudéjar-Gothic church was built in the 15C above the remains of the former mosque, although it has since undergone considerable restoration. Its bell-tower, added in the 19C, is one of the tallest in Sevilla province.

Town Hall – The 18C Baroque town hall has a magnificent **façade** adorned with floral decoration.

Casa de los Leones – This fine example of Baroque civil architecture has an impressive façade and an elegant internal patio.

Casa de la Virgen – The doorway of this unusual late-18C palace is embellished with elegant marble columns.

Santuario de Nuestra Señora de Setefilla – This handsome Mudéjar sanctuary, rebuilt in the 17C, stands in an isolated mountain landscape on the outskirts of Lora del Río. It houses the statue of the highly venerated Virgin of Setefilla, in whose honour a lively pilgrimage *(romería)* is held on 8 September every year.

Constantina – *29km/18mi north along the A 455.* The town, situated in a beautiful **setting** surrounded by delightful forests and streams of crystal-clear water, owes its name to the Roman emperor Constantine. Its centre is a mix of Moorish buildings and 15C-17C noble edifices which add a touch of distinction to the town.

★**Barrio de la Morería** – The town's Moorish quarter sits at the foot of the old fortress, perched above Constantina. Its steep, narrow and winding alleyways lined by whitewashed houses and connected by numerous flights of steps have preserved all the enchantment and flavour of a typical Arab district. Amid this labyrinth, two churches are worthy of note:

> ### Cep mushrooms
> The area around Constantina is a paradise for mushroom-lovers. During the autumn, the town is inundated by visitors who come here to pick them or simply to enjoy them in one of Constantina's many bars and restaurants.

the impressive **Iglesia de la Encarnación**, an elegant Mudéjar construction with a handsome Plateresque façade on which the portal (Puerta del Pardón) is adorned with outstanding stone decorative motifs, incuding a delicate sculpture of the archangel Gabriel; and the **Iglesia de Nuestra Señora de los Dolores**, which has preserved its notable Renaissance cloisters and an interesting Baroque retable at the high altar.

Ermita de El Robledo ⊙ – *5km/3mi northeast along the SE 150.* The white Mudéjar silhouette of this chapel, set amid an isolated landscape, houses the statue of the Virgin of the Oak Wood.

El Pedroso – *18km/11mi west of Constantina along the A 452.* The town of El Pedroso, nestled in a landscape of outstanding beauty, has two impressive religious buildings: the Ermita de San Sebastián and the Iglesia de Nuestra Señora del Pino. The **views** of the surrounding mountains from the nearby hills of Monteagudo and La Lima are quite delightful.

Cazalla de la Sierra – *17km/10.5mi north along the A 432.* This delightful small town, with its charming character, is hidden away in the heart of the Sierra Morena amid a landscape of holm and cork oak forests. The centre of Cazalla is characterised by picturesque streets fronted by attractive seigniorial houses with elegant stone façades. The town is also renowned for its brandies.

Plaza Mayor – This extensive rectangular square, the hub of local life, is bordered by an impressive array of 16C popular Andalucian architecture. Also lining the square are the law courts *(Juzgado)* – note the handsome Baroque façade – and the 14C **Iglesia de Nuestra Señora de la Consolación**, crowned by a red-brick Mudéjar tower adorned with pointed and trefoil arch windows. The church interior is a mass of pillars, topped by Renaissance coffered vaults.

Convento de San Francisco – The outstanding Baroque cloisters are embellished with graceful columns supporting semicircular arches.

Ruinas de la Cartuja ⊙ – *3km/2mi north.* The monumental ruins of the former 15C Carthusian monastery are situated in an attractive setting of leafy woodland. The Mudéjar paintings in the cloisters are of particular note. The former monk-gatekeeper's lodge has been transformed into a small hotel.

Alanís – *17km/10.5mi north of Cazalla along the A 432.* Alanís stands at the heart of an impregnable mountain area, at the foot of the remains of its former medieval castle. The main buildings of interest here are the Casa de Doña Matilde Guitart, with its elegant two-storey patio, and in particular the **Iglesia de Nuestra Señora de las Nieves**, a Gothic church that has been rebuilt in neo-Classical style. The vault above the high altar is decorated with an attractive set of frescoes, while the Capilla de los Melgarejo, a chapel dating from the 16C, is adorned with some exceptional Mudéjar **azulejos**.

Guadalcanal – *11km/7mi northwest along the A 432.* This old fortified settlement has preserved interesting vestiges of its medieval walls. The Iglesia de la Asunción, a church built above the former Moorish mosque, and the Ermita de Guaditoca, a chapel which hosts an important pilgrimage, are its most outstanding architectural features.

TABERNAS

Almería – Population 3 241
Michelin map 446 U 22

Tabernas is situated in the heart of the Almerian desert, with the Sierra de los Filabres to the north and the Sierra Alhamilla to the south. The town extends across a plain at the foot of a hill crowned by the partially restored ruins of its fortress *(access via a track next to the sports centre)*. The best view of these ruins can be enjoyed from the N 340 to the east.

Like many of the religious buildings in the area, the parish church, bordering a pleasant shady square, is built of brick, and is adorned with two simple Renaissance portals.

This part of Almería is characterised by an extremely arid, rocky landscape with numerous hills; in the 1960s and 1970s this desert-like setting was popular with film-makers who came here to film a number of spaghetti westerns.

EXCURSIONS

Mini-Hollywood ⊙ – *5km/3mi southwest along the A 370; follow signposts.* This unique setting has been transformed into an American Wild West town with its wooden buildings, saloon, bank, water tank, and other typical features. Westerns such as *A Fistful of Dollars, For A Few Dollars More, A Place Called Trinity* and many others have been filmed here. A stroll along the dusty main street, with a backdrop of bare, rocky mountains behind its houses, transports visitors back to this legendary era. Nowadays, a number of shows involving staged brawls and shoot-outs in the best traditions of the Wild West are organised here.

A small zoological reserve and African museum *(Museo Africano)* can be both be visited near Mini-Hollywood.

Other film sets can also be seen along the A 370.

Spain's American West

The Tabernas desert

The town's location between two ranges of mountains produces the so-called "orographic shadow" phenomenon, which is at the origin of the sparse rainfall in the area. As a result, the vegetation and fauna found in this part of Andalucia are adapted to conditions of extreme aridity. In general, flora, such as the hardy everlasting or curry plant, is small in size, while the local fauna mainly consists of insects, toads, scorpions and hedgehogs.

From Tabernas to Los Molinos del Río Aguas

41km/25.5mi

Head east from Tabernas along the A 370 and bear right after 17km/10.5mi.

Lucairena de las Torres – This former mining town is located on the eastern edge of the Sierra de la Alhamilla. Its main attractions are its whitewashed streets, 18C parish church, a square dominated by a 100-year-old tree, and, on the outskirts of Lucainena, the smelting furnaces formerly used to extract iron. In the local museum-cum-tavern, the **Mesón Museo**, where several rooms are devoted to exhibitions by local artists, as well as a collection of traditional farming implements, visitors can sample the traditional cuisine of the area.

Return to the A 370 and continue for a further 9km/5.5mi.

Sorbas – Sorbas is an attractive town on a clay escarpment encircled by a meander in the Aguas River. The best view of its picturesque **setting**★ is from Los Molinos del Río Aguas. Because of its houses clinging to the cliff, Sorbas is known as "Little Cuenca", after the town of Cuenca in the region of Castilla-La Mancha.

Leave your car in plaza de la Constitución, in the centre of the town.

Plaza de la Constitución – This square, the hub of local life, is fronted by the 16C Iglesia de Santa María, the town hall, the house of Francisco García Roca (both dating from the 19C), and the Palace of the Duke of Alba, built in the 18C for one of the duke's administrators.

Local arts and crafts

Sorbas still maintains its tradition of pottery-making. It is particularly famous for its red ceramic earthenware, which is mainly used for cooking, due to its resistance to heat. Workshops producing this pottery can still be visited in the lower section of the town.

The town has several **miradors** overlooking the river and plain. The houses built above the ravine are particularly impressive.

Paraje Natural de Karst en Yesos ○ – *On the AL 140 towards Los Molinos del Río Aguas.* This impressive nature reserve is made up of thousands of limestone caves which have been formed by water eroding the gypsum, and is a must for all those seeking adventure. Equipment required to visit the caves, such as a torch, helmet, outer clothing and boots, are all provided on site. The tour, led by specialist guides, involves climbs, descents and a certain amount of crawling on all fours, and will enable visitors to see how gypsum is crystallised and to observe the spectacular formations created by this process.

Molinos del Río Aguas – *5km/3mi southeast of Sorbas along the AL 140.* This settlement owes its name to the numerous flour mills *(molinos)* originally found here. Once past the village, the road climbs to offer attractive views of the valley. Several foreign families settled here in the 1960s and 1970s to launch a project aimed at developing alternative techniques for use in poor, desert-like areas, such as cooking using solar power, water purification, organic farming etc.

A number of pleasant walks along marked paths *(maximum 2hr)* provide visitors with an opportunity to see irrigation ditches of Roman origin, the remains of several flour mills and the local gypsum furnaces.

TARIFA

Cádiz – Population 15 118
Michelin map 446 X 13

Tarifa is the most southerly town on the Iberian Peninsula, at a distance of just 13km/8mi from the rocky North African coast on the southern shores of the **Straits of Gibraltar**. This charming little town, popular with an alternative crowd, exudes tranquillity and a sense of well-being with its abundance of small squares and enchanting nooks and crannies. However, it is also a lively tourist centre, and because of its wild unspoilt beaches it has developed a reputation as one of the best places in the world for **windsurfing**.

A Berber name

The origins of the name Tarifa date from the time of the Moorish invasions when the Berber general **Tarif ibn Malluk** is said to have landed here in July 710 with 400 men. This incursion, the first Moorish expedition to set foot on the Iberian Peninsula, has spawned a number of legends. The reasons behind the invasion would appear to lie in a dispute between the Visigothic king, **Roderick**, and the descendants of the former king **Witiza**. Seeing the weakness of the Visigoths, the Moors, "invited" by the Witiza faction, disregarded the pacts they had made with them and embarked upon the conquest of the whole peninsula.

OLD TOWN

The entry into Tarifa's old quarter through the emblematic **Puerta de Jerez** is particularly impressive.

Castillo de Guzmán el Bueno ⊘ – Abd ar-Rahman III, the first Moorish governor, who adopted the title of Caliph, attached great importance to the control of the Straits of Gibraltar, thus enabling him to capture the strongholds of Ceuta and Melilla. Construction of Tarifa's fortress was started in the year 960. However, the castle visible today is the result of successive extensions and modifications undertaken under both Moorish and Christian rule. Access to it is via the 13C **Almohad wall** (coracha); to the right, note the **Torre de Guzmán el Bueno**, a 13C turret, from where

---

WHERE TO STAY

MID-RANGE

La Casa Amarilla – Sancho IV el Bravo, 9 – ☎ 956 68 19 93 – fax 956 68 05 90 – 8 000pts. All the apartments are different with artistic decoration provided by the owners, who have several cafés and shops in the centre of Tarifa, including the **Café Central**, La Bodega and a souvenir shop.

Hurricane – On the N 340, heading north from Tarifa towards Vejer de la Frontera – ☎ 956 68 49 19 – fax 956 68 03 29 – 34 rooms – 16 000pts. A small paradise at one of the most southerly points in Europe. The hotel is right by the sea with views of the African coast, and has a subtropical garden, swimming pool and a popular restaurant.

Dos Mares – On the N 340 – ☎ 956 68 40 35 – fax 956 68 10 78 – 17 500pts. This hotel complex near the Hurricane Hotel also enjoys views of the African coast. Accommodation is in standard rooms or bungalows, while facilities for guests include a restaurant, swimming pool, fitness room, tennis court. Bicycle hire and horse riding are also available here.

EATING OUT

Casa Juan Luis – San Francisco, 15 – closed Sun. This restaurant (and bar opposite) specialises in pork-based dishes and cured hams, with a 3 000pts menu offering an excellent choice. The **Rincón de Juan** restaurant a little further along the same street has a small terrace with several tables.

EXCURSIONS IN THE STRAITS OF GIBRALTAR

The two companies below offer whale- and dolphin-watching **excursions by boat**★ in the Straits of Gibraltar. Reservations for these trips should be made in advance.

Whale Watch – Meeting point at the Café Continental in plaza de la Alameda – ☎ 956 68 09 93.

Firmm – Pedro Cortés, 3, next to the Café Central – ☎ 956 62 70 08.

the Christian commander Don Enrique de Guzmán is said to have thrown down his dagger to besieging Moorish troops to execute his captured son rather than hand over the castle to its attackers. Access to the centre of the castle is through a 14C angled doorway. A 14C church, the **Iglesia de Santa María**, stands within the walls of the fortress.

Leave the castle and walk along calle Guzmán el Bueno to plaza de Santa María.

Plaza Santa María – This small square is bordered by the **town hall** and the **Museo Municipal**. An attractive *azulejo*-decorated fountain adorns the centre of the square.

Tarifa – a paradise for windsurfers

Follow calle de la Amargura to plaza del Viento. The **views**★★ *of Africa across the Straits from the* **Mirador del Estrecho** *are superb.*

Iglesia Mayor Parroquial de San Mateo Apóstol – The parish church of St Matthew the Apostle was built at the beginning of the 16C in Flamboyant Gothic style. The main façade, completed in the 18C, is Baroque, with a broken pediment and imposing Solomonic columns. In the surprisingly spacious interior, the central nave is crowned by a star vault, and the side aisles by groin vaulting. Note the small funerary gravestone dating from the Visigothic period at the entrance to the Capilla del Sagrario.

In plaza de Oviedo, opposite the Iglesia de San Mateo, there are numerous cafés and bars for a quiet drink.

Iglesia de San Francisco – The Church of St Francis occupies one side of the plaza del Ángel. The **tower-façade**★, Baroque in style, consists of a large Franciscan cordon resting on two columns with Corinthian capitals.

Tarifa also has a small cove next to the port known as the **Playa Chica** (small beach), and, on the other side of the Isla de las Palomas, a spectacular beach, the **Playa de los Lances**★. Opposite, on top of the Santa Catalina Hill, note the unusual building dating from the early part of the 20C.

EXCURSIONS

The road from Tarifa to Punta Paloma – *Follow the N 340 towards Cádiz.* This small stretch of road runs parallel to the sea **(Playa de los Lances)**, from which it is separated by a small copse of pine trees. Several campsites and hotels line the road, as well as a number of places where it is possible to pull over for a swim.

Garum

Since time immemorial, the Cádiz coast has been one of the main areas for tuna fishing in the whole of Spain. Phoenicians and Romans alike took advantage of the movements of shoals of tuna to the Mediterranean during the spawning months of May and June. The technique used by the Romans, and still used in Cádiz province today, is known as the **almadraba** *(see p 329)*. The salting trade was so important that many of the Roman cities along the Andalucian coast, such as Baelo, were originally outposts whose primary function was the salting of fish. Once the tunny had been cut into cubed or triangular sections, they were placed in large silos and covered with a layer of salt, where they would remain for several months before being transported throughout the Empire in a special type of amphora. The best-known and most expensive product from this industry was without doubt **garum**, a sauce produced from the head, entrails, blood and other remains of fish, and used as a condiment or even as a main dish to which oil or vinegar would then be added. For thousands of years, it has been believed that garum is endowed with special therapeutic qualities.

After 4km/2.5mi, a road to the right leads to a sanctuary, the **Santuario de Nuestra Señora de la Luz**, named in honour of Tarifa's patron saint. Two beaches, the **Playa de Valdevaqueros★** and the **Playa de Punta Paloma**, an impressive series of sand dunes, can be seen a little further along the road.

★**Ruinas Romanas de Baelo Claudia** ⊘ – *22.5km/14mi northwest. 15km/9.5mi along the N 340 and 7.5km/4.5mi along the CA 9004.*
The Roman city of Baelo Claudia was founded in the 2C BC as a salting factory. The Emperor Claudius granted it the title of a municipality in the 1C AD; the majority of the remains visible today date from this period. Baelo was a walled city, access to which was through large gateways, sections of which can still be seen. The interior of the walled area is laid out around two main streets: the *decumanus maximus* (running east to west), and the *cardo maximus* (running north to south). The public buildings were erected at the intersection of these two avenues. Of particular interest are the columns of the former basilica, the space occupied by the forum, demarcated by three temples dedicated to the Capitoline Triad (Jupiter, Juno and Minerva), a theatre of moderate dimensions and a **salting factory** alongside the beach.

ÚBEDA★★

Jaén – Population 32 524
Michelin map 446 R 19

Úbeda stands at the centre of the province of Jaén in a plain known as La Loma, between the Guadalquivir and Guadalimar Valleys. The town is one of Andalucia's architectural treasures, with numerous monuments of interest. Over the centuries, the town that has given rise to the writer Antonio Muñoz Molina and the singer Joaquín Sabina has received the highest praise from illustrious visitors and travellers such as Antonio Machado, who referred to the town as "a queen and gypsy", and Eugenio d'Ors, who compared Úbeda to the most beautiful cities in northern Italy. It is well worth spending time in Úbeda to admire the sober appearance of its palaces, its elegant squares, and the fine detail which has helped create a town where Andalucian art has attained great heights. The old Moorish quarter, the **barrio de San Millán**, provides a delightful contrast with the town's 16C masterpieces, with its maze of narrow streets where typical local products such as hand-embroidered esparto matting, rugs, pottery and lanterns made of tin and glass can still be purchased.

> **"Wandering through the hills of Úbeda"**
>
> According to legend, when Fernando III was preparing the siege of the town, one of his noblemen, who appeared not to relish the prospect of battle, appeared at his side once the fighting was over. When asked by the king the reason for his late arrival, he replied that he had got lost in the many hills around Úbeda on his approach to the town.

Historical notes – Although its origins date back to the Roman period, it was under Moorish domination that the city of Ubbadat Al Arab, which was to become one of the major cities in Al-Andalus, was founded. In 1234, Fernando III the Saint reconquered the city. In the 16C, during the reigns of Carlos I and Felipe II, Úbeda enjoyed its period of greatest splendour, a time when the town's inhabitants occupied important positions within the Empire, magnificent Renaissance buildings were erected, and many members of the nobility took up residence here, transforming Úbeda into one of the leading economic, political and cultural centres of the time.

★★OLD TOWN *allow one day*

★★**Plaza Vázquez de Molina** – This magnificent square, the monumental centre of Úbeda, is at the heart of the town's old quarter, with its sumptuous buildings and delightful streets, transporting visitors back to another era. It is lined by an impressive collection of buildings, including the Capilla del Salvador, Palacio de las Cadenas, Iglesia de Santa María de los Alcázares and the Casa del Deán Ortega, which has been converted into a *parador*. Other buildings worthy of note are the **Cárcel del Obispo** (Bishop's Prison), so called as it was here that nuns were obliged to fulfil the canonical punishments imposed by the bishop, the former granary *(pósito)*, the **Palacio del Marqués de Mancera**, the Renaissance façade of which is crowned by a quadrangular tower, and the **Casa del Regidor**.

★**Palacio de las Cadenas** ⊘ – This palace was built by Vandelvira in the middle of the 16C at the behest of Don Juan Vázquez de Molina, the nephew of Don Francisco de los Cobos, one of the leading political and cultural figures during the reigns of Carlos V and Felipe II. In 1566 it was adapted for use as a convent, work which involved changes to its original structure. It was subsequently used as a jail, before conversion to its present role as the seat of the town hall in 1868.

WHERE TO STAY

MODERATE

Victoria – *Alaminos, 5* – ☎ *953 75 29 52* – *15 rooms* – *4 800pts*. A *hostal* with plain, but clean and comfortable rooms, all of which have a private bathroom and TV, but no telephone. A friendly welcome guaranteed.

MID-RANGE

Palacio de la Rambla – *Plaza del Marqués, 1* – ☎ *953 75 01 96* – *fax 953 75 02 67* – *8 rooms* – *14 000pts*. This 16C seigniorial mansion with a magnificent Renaissance patio has been transformed into an attractive hotel with spacious rooms decorated with antique furniture. Advance booking is recommended due to the small number of rooms available.

Parador de Úbeda – *Plaza Vázquez Molina* – ☎ *953 75 03 45* – *fax 953 75 12 59* – *36 rooms* – *18 500pts*. The town's *parador* fronts one of Andalucia's finest Renaissance squares. The coat of arms of this 16C palace's first owner, Fernando Ortega Salido, is engraved on the façade.

EATING OUT

Mesón Gabino – *Fuente Seca* – ☎ *953 75 42 07*. A restaurant with a stone roof and ceiling within the walls of the fortress. Specialities here include grilled meats and pigs' ears.

TAPAS

Rincón del Jamón – *Avenida de la Constitución, 8* – ☎ *953 75 38 38*. A bar run by young people where the speciality is *tostá* (bread with olive oil) with a variety of toppings. Customers are only charged for what they eat as drinks are free.

Zoraida – *Cronista Pasquau* – ☎ *953 75 67 19*. Zoraida has a long list of regulars, and is often frequented by entire families, ranging from grandparents to young toddlers.

Josema y Anabel – *Corredera San Fernando, 46* – ☎ *953 75 16 30* – *open from 7.30am to 3pm*. Even if you're a late starter, you can always count on this bar for a restorative coffee with *churros*.

The name, meaning Palace of the Chains, derives from the iron chains between the columns around the main doorway. The building's **façade★★**, adorned with the coat of arms of the owners, has an unusual combination of decorative Andalucian features coupled with the harmony of its classical architectural orders. Note the alternating bays and pilasters which are replaced on the upper tier by caryatids and atlantes in which the influence of the French sculptor Jamete is clearly evident. The two elegant lanterns on the ends add a lighter touch to the overall effect.

The outstanding feature of the interior is the delightful Renaissance patio with its refined arcades and a central fountain. A pottery museum, the **Museo de la Alfarería** ⊙, housed in the basement, displays collections of local pottery, while the upper floor, with colourful *artesonado* work, is home to the **Archivo Histórico Municipal**, commanding pleasant views of the square and surrounding area.

★ **Iglesia de Santa María de los Alcázares** ⊙ – The church was built in the 13C above the remains of a former mosque. Its harmonious façade, crowned by two belfries, each with three large bells and an additional smaller one, adds a touch of elegance to the plaza Vázquez de Molina. Of the three doorways, the main one, the work of López de Alcaraz and Pedro del Cabo (17C), and the Puerta de la Consolada, on the left-hand side (late-16C) stand out.

The interior, which was badly damaged during the Spanish Civil War, contains several beautiful **chapels★** adorned with sculptures and profuse decoration, in particular the Capilla de La Yedra and Capilla de los Becerra, both enclosed by impressive **grilles★** designed by Master Bartolomé. Sculptures of interest in the church include a *Fallen Christ* by Mariano Benlliure and a *Christ of the Bullfighters*, from a nearby convent.

The patio of the former mosque was subsequently replaced in the 16C by handsome Renaissance **cloisters** of irregular shape with elegant pointed arches and groin vaulting.

Casa del Deán Ortega – The town's *parador* is housed in a 16C Renaissance building partly designed by Vandelvira. Hidden behind the building's sober façade is an inner patio of considerable charm.

★★ **Capilla de El Salvador** ⊙ – Designed by Diego de Siloé in 1536 and built by Andrés de Vandelvira between 1540 and 1556, this chapel is one of the finest examples of religious architecture from the Andalucian Renaissance. It was commissioned as a family pantheon by Don Francisco de los Cobos, secretary to Carlos V, who, as a result of his vast fortune and artistic leanings, became a leading figure in 16C imperial Spain.

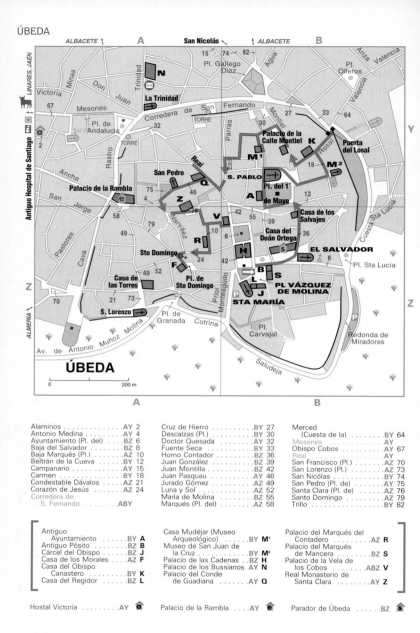

The main **façade** combines several of the principal ornamental motifs popular in Renaissance art: Christ's ascent to Mount Tabor appears above the door, while representations of St Peter and St Paul can be seen on both sides. The intrados of the inner arch is decorated with reliefs depicting mythological Greek gods. The escutcheons of the Cobos and Molina families complete the scene.

The lavish **interior**★★ comprises a single nave with vaulting outlined in blue and gold. The central part of the nave, designed as the resting place for the mausoleums of Don Francisco de los Cobos and his wife, is separated from the remainder of the chapel by a monumental grille attributed to Villalpando. The presbytery, designed by Vandelvira, is a kind of rotunda in which an immense 16C altarpiece includes a baldaquin with a sculpture of the Transfiguration by Alonso Berruguete, of which only the carving of Christ remains.

The **sacristy**★★, also by Vandelvira, is an architectural jewel, containing interesting decoration based on caissons, caryatids, atlantes and medallions, in which the stylistic influence of the Italian Renaissance is clearly visible. The harmonious south side doorway and the impressive grille enclosing the nave, a work by two local artists, are worthy of particular note.

Casa de los Salvajes – The 17C Renaissance House of the Savages, also known as Camarero Vago – Vago was the family name of the bishop's steward *(camarero)* – owes its unusual name to the two figures dressed in animal skins on the façade, supporting the coat of arms of Bishop Don Francisco de Yago, who lived in the building.

Arts and crafts

Úbeda's artisan work is one of the highlights of a visit to the town. Production is based on ceramics, earthenware and wrought-iron, as seen in the attractive lamp-posts and other decorative features adorning the town's private residences and public buildings.

Plaza del Primero de Mayo – Popularly known as the plaza del Mercado (Market Square), this plaza was the setting for the majority of public events in the town in days gone by (bullfights, *autos-da-fé*, outdoor fairs, executions, theatre performances etc). Today, the square is bordered by the former town hall and the Iglesia de San Pablo.

Antiguo Ayuntamiento – The former town hall, dating from the 17C, shows clear Palladian influence. It consists of two tiers: a lower section comprising an elegant porch with three semicircular arches and paired columns, and an upper register, in the style of a double loggia or porticoed gallery, from where the town's council presided over events in the square below.

★ **Iglesia de San Pablo** ⊘ – The harmony of the church's main portal, of Gothic design and crowned by a Plateresque bell-tower, contrasts with the **south doorway** (1511), adorned with attractive Isabelline-style reliefs. On the southwest corner, to the left of the main façade, admire the Renaissance gallery from where edicts issued by the town council were read out. Two chapels stand out inside the church: the **Capilla de las Calaveras** *(third on the right)*, with an impressive arch by Vandelvira, and the **Capilla de las Mercedes**, an Isabelline work enclosed by extraordinary **grilles**★★ created in Úbeda – note the highly imaginative scene depicting Adam and Eve.

Museo de San Juan de la Cruz ⊘ – The Museum of St John of the Cross is housed in the oratory of the same name – a Baroque room containing a sculpture of the saint. The museum is the starting-point for a guided visit through the monastery which retraces the final days of this mystical poet who died in Úbeda.

Casa del Obispo Canastero – This residence stands close to the **Puerta del Losal**, a 15C Mudéjar gateway that formed part of the town walls and provided access to the San Millán district. The mansion is Plateresque in style and is named after one of the numerous reliefs adorning the façade, representing a bishop *(obispo)* holding a basket *(canasta)*.

Palacio de la calle Montiel – The palace is one of the best examples of early Plateresque in Úbeda. The handsome façade is emblasoned with the poorly preserved coats of arms of its former owners, which indicates that those who lived in the palace supported the *comuneros* who rose against Carlos V in the early 16C.

Casa Mudéjar – This recently restored 14C Mudéjar house is home to the town's **Museo Arqueológico** ⊘, displaying archeological exhibits ranging from the Neolithic era to the period of Moorish occupation, all of which have been discovered in Úbeda and the surrounding area.

Palacio del Conde de Guadiana – Built in the early 17C, the Palace of the Count of Guadiana is crowned by a fine **tower**★ with angular balconies divided by small columns and galleries on the third floor.

Iglesia de San Pedro – The church, on the tranquil square of the same name, has preserved its original Romanesque apse. Features of interest include the harmonious Renaissance façade and several Gothic chapels.

Real Monasterio de Santa Clara – This monastery is the oldest Christian church in Úbeda (1290), although it also comprises Renaissance and Gothic-Mudéjar features.

Palacio de Vela de los Cobos – Vandelvira was commissioned by Don Francisco Vela de los Cobos, the governor of Úbeda, to build this palace in the mid-16C. Its Renaissance façade is crowned by an elegant arcaded gallery which extends to the corners of the building, where two unusual white columns have been incorporated into the construction.

Calle Real

This attractive thoroughfare, one of the most elegant in Úbeda, provides visitors with an insight into the town's architectural splendour during the 16C, when Úbeda was at its economic and artistic peak. The street is lined by monumental buildings, typical shops and refined decorative detail. Nowadays, calle Real is a favourite with residents of the city, who look upon it with great affection.

Palacio del Marqués del Contadero – Although the palace's façade dates from the late 18C, its Renaissance features bear witness to the long survival of this style in Úbeda. The upper floor is ornamented with a blunt-arched gallery.

Plaza de Santo Domingo – This pleasant square is fronted by two buildings of interest: the **Iglesia de Santo Domingo**, with its Plateresque façade, and the **Casa de los Morales**, a replica of which has been built in the Poble Espanyol (Spanish Village) in Barcelona.

ADDITIONAL SIGHTS

Casa de las Torres – The mansion formerly owned by the High Constable, Dávalos, has a Plateresque façade flanked by two monumental square towers and decorated with finely sculpted reliefs and gargoyles on the cornice.

Iglesia de San Lorenzo – The main attraction of this church is the location of its façade on the parapet of the old walls, where it is supported by the barbican of the Puerta de Granada.

Palacio de la Rambla – Situated on one side of the elegant plaza del Marqués, the façade of this palace includes the figures of two impressive life-size warriors supporting the coat of arms of the building's owners.

Iglesia de la Santísima Trinidad – The **portal**, above which a sober, three-storey bell-tower has been added, is one of the finest representations of Baroque decoration in Úbeda.

Palacio de los Bussianos – This late-16C Renaissance palace has an attractive staircase leading to a delightful gallery of pointed arches on the first floor.

Iglesia de San Nicolás – Although Gothic in style, the trumpet-shaped vault over the entrance was built by Vandelvira during the Renaissance period.

Patio, Hospital de Santiago

M. Raurich/STOCK PHOTOS

Antiguo Hospital de Santiago – *Head along calle Obispo Cobos.* Construction of the hospital was ordered by Don Diego de los Cobos, bishop of Jaén and a native of Úbeda. The façade, which is preceded by a large portico flanked by two towers, is another of Vandelvira's works, albeit more restrained in its proportions. The only decorative features are the high-relief representing St James Slayer of the Moors *(Santiago Matamoros)*, above the doorway, and the glazed ceramic medallions on the cornice. A chapel inside the building houses an impressive wooden altarpiece; the double-arcaded **patio** and the elegant staircase covered with a coffered vault, the columns of which were carved from marble brought from Italy, are also noteworthy. Nowadays, the hospital houses the **Museo de la Semana Santa** ⊙, a museum dedicated to Holy Week celebrations.

EXCURSIONS

Sabiote – *9km/5.5mi northeast along the J 6040*. This peaceful town contains a fine array of elegant houses and old, narrow alleyways. Sabiote was the place of residence of Alonso de Vandelvira, who built several mansions here for the local nobility, including the Mendoza, Melgarejo and Higuera Sabater families. However, the buildings of major interest are the 15C **Iglesia de San Pedro Apóstol**, a monumental Gothic church, and the **castle**, erected outside the walls, above the remains of the former Moorish fortress, and subsequently restored by Vandelvira.

Torreperogil – *10km/6mi east along the N 322*. Torreperogil is a charming small town with a maze of narrow, medieval streets, at the heart of which stands an attractive church, the **Iglesia de la Asunción**, with its handsome double-entrance portal and central column. A stone retable depicting the descent of Christ presides over the interior.

Villacarrillo – *32km/20mi northeast along the N 322*. This active agricultural and industrial centre is one of the oldest settlements in the province, with evidence dating its existence back to the Bronze Age.

Iglesia de la Asunción – Another 16C work by Vandelvira, erected on the base of a earlier castle, from which three monumental towers have survived. The ground plan consists of three aisles and side chapels covered with sober groined vaulting.

Casa de la Inquisición – Despite its association with the Inquisition during the Middle Ages, this monumental three-storey building has a number of redeeming features, including several attractive wrought-iron balconies on the façade, although the rooms inside the building are somewhat devoid of decoration.

UTRERA★

Sevilla – Population 45 947
Michelin map 446 U 12

Utrera is built on a small elevation at the heart of the Sevillian countryside, amid a landscape of eucalyptus groves and extensive areas of cultivated land. Although its origins date back to Roman times, its main period of development took place from the 16C onwards. A serious epidemic stunted this expansion in the middle of the 17C, heralding a decline that continued until the 19C.

Castle – This fortress of Almohad origin formed part of the walled defensive system surrounding the town. Today, only a few sections of the walls and an arch, the Arco de la Villa, to which an upper, chapel-like section was added in the 18C, remain from the original structure. An impressive keep and parade ground can also be seen within the castle's confines.

★**Iglesia de Santa María de la Asunción or Iglesia de Santa María de la Mesa** ⊘ – This Gothic church with additional Renaissance and Baroque features dominates a charming square in the centre of the town. The handsome façade is articulated around a large splayed arch, above which rises a graceful Baroque tower. The outstanding features on the interior include the **choir stalls**, a work by Duque Cornejo (1744), the main altarpiece and the noteworthy sepulchre of the Count of Arcos.

Iglesia de Santiago – This triple-nave Gothic church dates from the 15C. Its sober defensive appearance contrasts with the ostentatious decor of the **Puerta del Perdón**, an Isabelline-Gothic-style gateway with an abundance of floral ornamentation.

★**Plaza del Altozano** – This elegant square stands at the heart of Utrera. It is framed by an attractive series of three-storey 17C and 18C mansions with two-sided roofs and delicate unbroken balconies.

Town Hall – The town hall is situated on one side of the elegant plaza de Gibaxa. This old 18C palatial mansion has a magnificent Rococo façade and a number of rooms with a romantic air. Note also the collection of furniture in the Salón Azul (Blue Room).

Casa Surga – A late-18C mansion with a charming Baroque façade and rooms decorated according to the tastes of the period.

Iglesia de San Francisco ⊘ – The main feature of this 17C late-Renaissance church is the large cupola adorned with paintings.

★**Santuario de Nuestra Señora de la Consolación** ⊙ – *To reach this sanctuary on the outskirts of Utrera, exit the town along avenida de Juan XXIII.* This outstanding 17C and 18C Mudéjar-style temple occupies a former Franciscan monastery. The impressive Baroque façade and the delicate *artesonado* work inside the sanctuary are particularly worthy of note. On 8 September a popular pilgrimage *(romería)* is held here in honour of the Virgin of Solace *(Consolación)*.

EXCURSION

El Palmar de Troya – *13km/8mi southwest along the A 364.* The heretical Order of the Carmelites of the Holy Face, founded by the controversial priest Clemente Rodríguez, has its headquarters here. The centre of El Palmar is occu-

---
Suitable dress

Women who wish to attend religious ceremonies at El Palmar de Troya will need to observe a strict dress code which requires them to wear trousers and to cover their head with a veil.

---

pied by an enormous temple in which statues of various saints, presided over by a sculpture of Our Crowned Lady of El Palmar, are venerated. The best time to visit the church is in the afternoon, when mass is held in Latin in accordance with the liturgy decreed prior to that established by the Second Vatican Council.

VEJER DE LA FRONTERA★

Cádiz – Population 12 731
Michelin map 446 X 12

Vejer has a delightful position perched on a rocky crag dominating the valley of the Barbate River, just a few kilometres from the Atlantic coast. It is one of Andalucia's most picturesque *pueblos blancos*, and one with some of the strongest Moorish roots in the region. This impression is accentuated by the layout of the town, with its maze of narrow, cobbled streets, lined by whitewashed houses, enclosing verdant patios and crowned by flat terraced roofs.

VISIT ⊙

Walls – The original four gateways, built in the 15C to offer protection against Nasrid attacks and to provide access inside the town walls, have survived to this day. The **Arco de la Segur**, a basket-handle arch, marks the entrance to Vejer's old quarter.

Iglesia Parroquial del Divino Salvador ⊙ – As was the case in most Andalucian towns, Vejer's parish church was built on the site of the main mosque, from which the minaret has been preserved. The **interior★** consists of three aisles with a somewhat unusual appearance mainly due to the mixture of styles. The oldest part of the church is the apsidal end, which combines both Romanesque and Gothic features.

Convento de las Concepcionistas – This 17C convent is situated in one of Vejer's most charming corners, alongside the mysterious **Arco de las Monjas**. This 17C building, fronted by a sober, Classical façade, is now used as a cultural centre.

WHERE TO STAY

MODERATE

La Posada – *Los Remedios, 21* – ☎/fax *956 45 02 58* – *9 rooms* – *4 000pts.* A family-run hotel with pleasant rooms, three of which enjoy wonderful views of the valley. La Posada also has a number of apartments for rent *(8 000pts)*, one with a terrace.

MID-RANGE

Convento de San Francisco – *La Plazuela* – ☎ *956 45 10 01* – fax *956 45 10 04* – *25 rooms* – *9 065pts.* This 17C former convent, with its attractively decorated rooms and high ceilings, was initially occupied by an order of Poor Clares and then by Franciscan monks. Restaurant (El Refectorio).

EATING OUT

Trafalgar – *Plaza de España, 31* – ☎ *956 44 76 38.* This small restaurant with an outdoor terrace and dining-room on the first floor serves a range of tapas, as well as meat and, in particular, fish specialities. An excellent location in the centre of town.

The "Cobijado"

This name was given to the traditional garment worn by the women of Vejer up until the Spanish Civil War. Although its origins are uncertain, this simple black head-dress is also worn in a number of towns and villages in North Africa.

It is traditionally worn during the **Velada de Agosto**, a festival held in honour of the **Virgin of the Olive**, the town's patron saint, between 10 and 24 August every year.

Castle – Despite its poor state of repair, the views from the fortress are particularly impressive. Access inside the castle is via a patio.

Casa del Mayorazgo – *Private house*. This 17C Baroque residence with its simple façade has been built against the town's walls. It is possible to climb one of Vejer's defensive tower's from inside the building.

Arco de la Villa leads to plaza de España.

Plaza de España – Also known as **plaza de los Pescaítos**, due to the fish decorating the fountain at its centre, this square is one of the liveliest and most attractive in Vejer de la Frontera. It is lined by the **town hall**, surrounded by palm trees, and several whitewashed houses which give the square a colonial air.

EXCURSIONS

Although the coastline between **Chiclana** and **Zahara de los Atunes** does not include Andalucia's most attractive towns, it is nonetheless blessed with some of the area's most spectacular and under-developed beaches, popular with those seeking sun, sea and peace and quiet.

Façade of the Casa del Mayorazgo

M. Brodsky/STOCK PHOTOS

Conil de la Frontera – *15.5km/9.5mi northwest*. Like many of its neighbours along the Cádiz coast, Conil is a tranquil town where life almost comes to a standstill during the winter. In contrast, the summer sees the town transformed into a lively and popular resort, whose main attractions are its 14km/8.5mi stretch of beach and its low-key tourism. The oldest section of Conil lies between the sea and the **Puerta de Conil**. An 18C colonial-style former church, the **Iglesia de la Misericordia**, now a school, stands outside the walled section of the town.

Tuna fishing

The technique used locally to catch tuna, known as *almadraba*, derives from the Arabic word *al-madraba*. It involves a complex labyrinth of vertical nets, some of which reach lengths of several kilometres, which lead the tuna to a circular area of permanent or temporary netting. Tuna migrate through this part of the coast twice a year: on their way to the spawning grounds of the Mediterranean in spring, and upon their return to the Atlantic in the autumn.

Castillo de los Guzmanes ⊘ – Only a heavily restored tower, the Torre de los Guzmanes, remains from this fortress in plaza de Santa Catalina. Two other buildings of note border the square: a chapel, the Capilla de Jesús, and the **Museo de Raíces Conileñas** ⊘, a museum displaying exhibits relating to local life.

Beaches – Several small coves, such as the **Cala del Aceite**, are situated to the north of the town, heading towards the port, while longer, more windswept beaches, such as the **Playa de la Fontanilla** and **Playa de los Bateles**, are to the south. **El Palmar**, which is considered to be Vejer de la Frontera's beach, is a few kilometres further along the coast.

Barbate – *10km/6mi south.* Although devoid of any cultural interest, Barbate continues to be an active fishing port with a large tuna industry. The bars and restaurants in the town are renowned for their excellent fish and seafood.

★**Parque Natural La Breña and Marismas de Barbate** – *Access from Vejer along the CA 2141 or from Barbate.* The main attractions of this nature reserve and marshland are its picturesque coves, nestled between rocky cliffs, and its beaches, bordered by woods of umbrella pine. The best-known beach in the park is the **Playa de los Caños de Meca**★★.

The Battle of Trafalgar

On 21 October 1805, Admiral Villeneuve sailed out of Cádiz harbour with his Franco-Spanish fleet to confront the British, commanded by **Nelson**. After some heroic combat, in which Nelson and the Spanish **Gravina** and **Churruca** were mortally wounded, Villeneuve's fleet was destroyed, an event which sounded the death-knell for the Spanish Armada and Napoleon's hopes of defeating the British, and established Britain's supremacy at sea.

Zahara de los Atunes – *20km/12mi south.* This small fishing community (*de los Atunes* translates as "of the tunas") has some of the longest and most unspoilt beaches along the Costa de la Luz. From the 15C onwards, the town was part of the terrain controlled by the Dukes of Medina Sidonia, who exploited the tuna fishing industry which already existed here. The dukes lost control of their domain in the 19C, by which time Zahara had become no more than a small village. Only a few ruins now remain from its 15C **castle**. Today, the town lives mainly off fishing and tourism.

VÉLEZ BLANCO
Almería – Population 2 190
Michelin map 446 T 23

The area occupied by Vélez Blanco and Vélez Rubio is situated to the north of Almería province, just a few kilometres from the border with Murcia to the east. It is a region of numerous archeological remains, some of which are of great significance, such as the **Cueva de los Letreros**, a natural cave containing impressive wall paintings. The history of Vélez Blanco, and that of its neighbour Vélez Rubio, is indelibly linked with that of the Marquess of Vélez, a title bestowed upon Don Pedro Fajardo y Chacón by the Catholic Monarchs in 1506.

Vélez Blanco

WHERE TO STAY

Casa de los Arcos – *San Francisco, 2* – ☎ *950 61 48 05* – *fax 950 61 49 47* – *14 rooms* – *6 000pts*. This charming 18C seigniorial house has large bedrooms overlooking the river. A little-known address offering excellent value for money.

EATING OUT

El Molino – *Curtidores* – ☎ *950 41 50 70*. A restaurant with a good reputation specialising in grilled meats. Meals are served on the pleasant terrace during the summer months.

The town's houses extend across the slope of a hill, crowned by Vélez's majestic castle, in the foothills of the Sierra de María.

★**Castle** ⊙ – Construction of this impressive 16C fortress was ordered by the first Marquess of Vélez, who commissioned a number of Italian artists to work on the project. Sadly, one of its most impressive features, a charming Renaissance marble patio, was sold to a French antique dealer who, in turn, sold it to an American buyer. The patio was later donated to the Metropolitan Museum in New York, where it is now displayed. The castle was not designed as a traditional fortress, as demonstrated by the presence of large miradors offering superb views of the surrounding area, and the numerous openings punctuating its lofty walls. The Salón del Triunfo and the Salón de la Mitología originally contained wooden friezes depicting Caesar's triumph and the labours of Hercules. These are now on display in the Musée des Arts Décoratifs in Paris.

Centro de visitantes del Parque Natural de la Sierra de María – The visitor centre is housed in an old grain storehouse and contains a wealth of information on both the park and the nearby Cueva de los Letreros.

The Indalo

The origins of this attractive figure, the symbol of Almería, can be found in the Cueva de los Letreros, for it was here, in the 19C, that wall paintings of human figures and animals dating from around 5000 BC were discovered.

The town has two churches of interest, the 16C Iglesia de Santiago, with its fine Mudéjar *artesonado* work, and the church of the Convento de San Luis, bearing the coat of arms of the Marquisate of Vélez above the portal, as well as a large number of fountains.

EXCURSIONS

Vélez Rubio – *6km/3.5mi south*. Vélez Rubio extends across a small plain and appears dominated by the towers and dome of its parish church. Its two main streets, carrera del Carmen and carrera del Mercado, are lined by several seigniorial mansions, the Baroque church of the Convento de la Inmaculada, and the 17C Iglesia del Carmen, the oldest church in the town.

★**Parroquia de la Encarnación** ⊙ – Construction of this magnificent parish church was ordered by the 10th Marquess of Vélez in the 18C. Its monumental proportions come as something of a surprise, with two bell-towers flanking the richly decorated Baroque stone **portal**★, which is separated by pilasters and architraves. Note the coat of arms on the lower section and a fine relief of the Annunciation on the pediment. On the inside of the church, the main altarpiece and organ, both made of wood but without polychrome decoration, stand out. A St Antony of Padua, by Salzillo, is the dominant feature of the altarpiece in the Capilla de la Encarnación.

The **town hall**, an 18C seigniorial residence, lines the same square.

Museo Comarcal Velezano ⊙ – This museum devoted to local life and popular culture is housed in the former 18C Royal Hospital. It contains a large archeological collection unearthed in the surrounding area, in southeast Andalucia and even in the Sahara.

María – *9km/5.5mi northwest*. The main buildings of interest in the main square of this small whitewashed village nestled in the Sierra de María are the 16C Mudéjar-style parish church, the 18C Edificio de la Tercia and a triple-spouted basin. The village has also preserved an unusual public wash-house.

A 16C chapel, the Ermita de la Virgen de la Cabeza, is located 3km/1.8mi outside María.

Parque Natural de la Sierra de María ⊙ – The visitor centre, the **Centro de Visitantes Umbría de María**, situated 2km/1.2mi from María along the A 317, is well worth a visit. The reserve extends over an area of some 22 500ha/55 600 acres across the municipalities of Vélez Rubio, Vélez Blanco, María and Chirivel. The landscape here is steep – several sections are above 2 000m/6 560ft – and varied, with cereal crops, fields of thyme, forests of oak and pine, and even Spanish broom in the higher mountain areas. A number of recreational areas and refuges are dotted around the park.

El Rocío pilgrimage

R. Mattes

Practical Information

Planning your trip

WHEN TO GO

Spring and autumn are considered to be the best seasons for touring inland Andalucia, where temperatures can exceed 40°C/104°F between late-June and late-August. Winters inland are generally mild, although temperatures can dip dramatically at higher altitudes. The coastal resorts of the Mediterranean are popular all year round, with mild temperatures and plentiful sunshine even during the winter months.

Temperature chart – The chart below gives average daily temperatures for the main cities in Andalucia. Maximum temperatures are in blue, minimum temperatures in black.

	J	F	M	A	M	J	J	A	S	O	N	D
Almería	16	16	18	20	22	26	29	29	27	23	19	17
	8	8	10	12	15	18	21	22	20	16	12	9
Cádiz	15	16	18	21	23	27	29	30	27	23	19	16
	8	9	11	12	14	18	20	20	19	16	12	9
Córdoba	14	16	19	23	26	32	36	36	31	24	19	14
	4	5	8	10	13	17	19	20	17	13	8	5
Granada	12	14	18	20	24	30	34	34	29	22	17	12
	1	2	5	7	9	14	17	17	14	9	5	2
Huelva	16	18	20	22	25	29	32	32	29	25	21	17
	6	7	9	11	13	16	18	18	17	14	10	7
Jaén	12	14	17	20	24	30	34	34	29	22	16	12
	5	5	8	10	13	17	21	21	18	13	9	5
Málaga	16	17	19	21	24	28	30	30	28	24	20	17
	8	8	10	11	14	17	20	20	18	15	12	9
Sevilla	15	17	20	23	26	32	36	36	32	26	20	16
	6	6	9	11	13	17	20	20	18	14	10	7
Tarifa	16	17	18	20	22	24	27	27	26	23	20	17
	10	11	12	13	15	17	20	20	19	17	14	11

Formalities – Despite the law which came into force on 1 January 1993 authorising the free flow of goods and people within the EU, travellers from the UK, Ireland and countries outside the European Union require a **passport** to enter Spain. Holders of British, Irish and US passports do not need a visa for a visit to Spain of less than 90 days. Visitors from some Commonwealth countries or those planning to stay longer than 90 days should enquire about visa requirements at their local Spanish consulate. US citizens should obtain the booklet *Your Trip Abroad* (US$ 1.25) which provides useful information on visa requirements, customs regulations, medical care etc for international travellers. Apply to the Superintendent of Documents, PO Box 371954, Pittsburgh, PA 15250-7954; ☎ (202) 512-1800; fax (202) 512-2250; www.access.gpo.gov

Customs regulations – Since the birth of the single European market and the abolition of the duty-free system on certain goods, allowances for various commodities within the EU have changed. A free leaflet, **Duty Paid**, is available from HM Customs and Excise, Finchley Excise Advice Centre, Berkeley House, 304 Regents Park Road, London N3 2JY, ☎ (020) 78654400. The US Customs Service offers a free publication **Know Before You Go** for US citizens, ☎ (202) 9276724; www.customs.gov

Travel insurance – British citizens should apply for **Form E 111**, issued by the Post Office, which entitles the holder to urgent treatment for accident or unexpected illness in EU countries. This form should be presented to the relevant medical services prior to receiving treatment. For further information in the UK, contact the Department of Health and Social Security ☎ (0191) 2187777. Visitors are strongly advised to take out additional travel insurance to cover against any expenses not covered by form E 111, as well as lost luggage, theft, cancellation, delayed departure etc.
Non-EU travellers are advised to check with their insurance companies about taking out supplementary medical insurance with specific overseas coverage.

Pets (cats and dogs) – A general health certificate and proof of rabies vaccination should be obtained from your local vet before departure.

By air – A number of Spanish and international airlines operate direct scheduled services to airports in Andalucia. These include:
Iberia Airlines: 27-29 Glass House St., London, W1R 6JU ☎ (020) 78300011; fax (020) 74131262; www.iberia.com; direct flights from London Heathrow to Málaga and Sevilla. Reservations within the US and Canada: ☎ 800-772-4642 (calls to this toll-free number are charged at the usual international rate for callers outside the US).
British Airways: Waterside, PO Box 365, Harmondsworth, UB7 0GB, England; ☎ 08457733377; www.britishairways.com; flights to Málaga, Sevilla and Gibraltar, some of which are operated by their franchise holder GB Airways.
Reservations within the US and Canada: ☎ 1-800-AIRWAYS.

A number of low-cost airlines also offer inexpensive flights to several Andalucian cities from the UK. Some airlines only allow bookings to be made via the Internet, while others offer small discounts for Internet bookings:

Go: ☎ 0845 60 54321; www.go-fly.com; flights from London Stansted to Málaga.
Buzz: www.buzzaway.com; flights from London Stansted to Jerez de la Frontera.
EasyJet: ☎ 0870 6000 000; www.easyJet.com; flights from London Luton to Málaga.
Hundreds of weekly charter flights also operate to Andalucian cities, particularly Málaga and Almeria, from all over the UK.

By sea – Brittany Ferries and P&O Ferries both operate services to northern Spain.
Brittany Ferries run a ferry service between Plymouth and Santander (leaving Plymouth on Mondays and Wednesdays, returning from Santander on Tuesdays and Thursdays; journey time: 24hr). Motorists need to allow a further two days to reach Andalucia from northern Spain. For reservations, contact:
Brittany Ferries: Millbay Docks, Plymouth PL1 3EW, Devon, England ☎ (08705) 360 360; www.brittany-ferries.com
Estación Marítima, 39002 Santander, Spain ☎ 942 36 06 11.
P&O Portsmouth offers a twice-weekly crossing from Portsmouth to Bilbao (leaving Portsmouth on Tuesdays and Saturdays, returning from Bilbao on Mondays and Thursdays; journey time: 30hr). For reservations contact:
P&O Portsmouth: Peninsular House, Wharf Road, Portsmouth PO2 8TA, England ☎ (08702) 424 999; www.poportsmouth.com
Santurtzi, Cosme Echevarrieta, 48009 Bilbao, Spain ☎ 944 23 44 77.

Under the Channel then on through France – An alternative to the cross-Channel ferry services is the **Channel Tunnel.**
The high-speed undersea rail link carries passengers without cars from London to Paris (**Eurostar** – 3hr), from where it is possible to travel on by train *(see below)*.
It also ferries motorists and their cars through the tunnel (**Eurotunnel** – 35min) on specially designed double-decker wagons. The Calais terminal is linked by slip-roads to the French motorway network (the distance to Madrid by road is about 1 600km/just under 1 000mi, from where it is a further 550km/344mi to both Sevilla and Málaga.
For information, contact Eurostar, ☎ 0990 186 186; www.eurostar.com or Eurotunnel, ☎ 08705 353 535; www.eurotunnel.com

By rail – British Rail offers a wide range of services to the Channel ports and French Railways (SNCF) operates an extensive network of lines including many high-speed passenger trains to the Spanish border, from where connections are possible to Madrid and southern Spain. A direct Paris-Madrid Talgo service departs the French capital daily for Madrid, leaving at about 9pm (journey time: 12-13hr). Regular AVE high-speed and Talgo services operate between Madrid and major Andalucian cities.
For information, contact: Rail Europe, The French Rail House, 10 Leake St., London SE1 7NN ☎ (08705) 848 848; fax (0990) 717 273; www.sncf.co.uk

By bus – Regular long-distance bus services operate from London to all major towns and cities in Andalucia.
For information, contact: Eurolines UK, 4 Cardiff Road, Luton, Bedfordshire, England, LU1 1PP; ☎ (01582) 404 511; fax: (01582) 400 694; www.eurolines.co.uk

Travelling in Andalucia

BY CAR

The Andalucian road network has improved considerably in recent years. Today, the region has over 24 000km/15 000mi of motorways *(autopistas)*, dual carriageways *(autovías)* and other roads of varying categories. The most important road in Andalucia is the A 92 dual carriageway, which crosses southern Spain from east to west, connecting, either directly or via other *autovías*, every provincial capital in the region. Due to the excellent condition of roads in the region and, with the exception of some of the roads along the Mediterranean during the summer months, the relatively low volume of traffic on them, private car is the best means of transport for getting around the region for those with time to spare.
The maximum speed limits in Spain are as follows:
120kph/75mph on motorways and dual carriageways;
100kph/62mph on the open road (with a hard shoulder of at least 1.5m/5ft);
90kph/56mph on the open road (without a hard shoulder);
50kph/31mph in built-up areas.

Road information – The **National Traffic Agency** (Dirección General de Tráfico) is able to provide information in English on road conditions, driving itineraries, regulations etc. For further information ☎ 900 12 35 05 (toll-free) or consult the agency's web site at www.dgt.es
Tele-Ruta: ☎ 91 535 22 22. **Roadside assistance** – **RACE** (Spanish Royal Automobile Club) ☎ 900 11 22 22 and 91 593 33 33.

Car hire – Vehicles in Spain can be hired through the offices of all major international car hire companies around the world. Alternatively, cars can be hired at major airports, train stations, large hotels and in all major towns and cities around Andalucia:

Avis ☎ 901 13 57 90; www.avis.com

Europcar ☎ 901 10 20 20; www.europcar.com

Hertz ☎ 901 10 10 01; www.hertz.com

Most companies will only rent out vehicles to drivers over the age of 21. A valid driving licence is required.

Documents – On the whole, motorists need only have a current driving licence from their country of origin and valid papers (vehicle documentation and valid insurance) to drive in Spain, although in certain situations an International Driving Permit may be required. If in doubt, visitors should check with the AA or RAC in the United Kingdom or with the American Automobile Association in the US.

Insurance – Those motorists entering Spain in their own vehicles should ensure that their insurance policy includes overseas cover. Visitors are advised to check with their respective insurance companies prior to travel. Motorists are also advised to take out adequate accident and **breakdown** cover for their period of travel overseas. Various motoring organisations (AA, RAC etc) will be able to provide further details on options available. Bail bonds are no longer necessary, although travellers may wish to take this precaution (consult your insurance company). Members of the American Automobile Association should obtain the free brochure, *Offices to Serve You Abroad*, which gives details of affiliated organisations in Spain.

If the driver of the vehicle is not accompanied by the owner, he or she must have written permission from the owner to drive in Spain.

Driving regulations and general information – The minimum driving age is 18. Traffic drives on the right. It is compulsory for passengers in both front and rear seats to wear **seat belts**. Motorcyclists (on all sizes of machine) must wear safety helmets. It is now a legal requirement for motorists to carry two red warning triangles, in addition to a spare tyre and a set of replacement bulbs.

Motorists should note that it is illegal to use a **mobile phone** when driving, unless the vehicle is fitted with a hands-free unit. Heavy on-the-spot fines are frequent for those caught using hand-held phones.

Road maps – Michelin map 990 at a scale of 1:1 000 000 covers the whole of Spain, while map 446 at 1:400 000 covers Andalucia.

Route planning – Michelin has created a web site to help motorists prepare their journey. The service enables browsers to select their preferred route (fastest, shortest etc) and to calculate distances between towns and cities: **www.michelin–travel.com**

BY BUS

A large number of bus companies operate services within Andalucia and to other parts of Spain and Europe. The address and telephone numbers of bus stations and major bus companies are listed in the **Travellers' addresses** section found under the major towns and cities in this guide.

BY TRAIN

Since 1992, communications to and from Andalucia have been revolutionised by the construction of the AVE *(Alta Velocidad Española)*, a 250kph/156mph high-speed train linking Madrid with Córdoba (1hr 45min) and Sevilla (2hr 15min).

The AVE's infrastructure has also had a beneficial effect on the region's high-tech Talgo, a train with a top speed of 200kph/125mph which connects several Andalucian cities (Málaga, Algeciras, Cádiz and Huelva) with the Spanish capital in just a few hours.

RENFE (Spanish State Railways): ☎ 902 24 02 02 (information available 24hr a day; reservations from 5.30am to 11.55pm); www.renfe.es

---

Al-Andalus Express

This magnificent train, consisting of carriages from the 1920s and 1930s which have been refurbished to a luxurious standard, has every comfort the traveller could possibly imagine for this unforgettable journey through Andalucia. Facilities on board the train include two dining cars, a lounge and recreation car, a bar, five sleeping cars, two shower cars and one car for staff.

During the course of the one-week journey (departures from either Sevilla or Madrid), passengers visit Jerez de la Frontera, Carmona, Ronda, Antequera, Granada and Córdoba. Meals not eaten on board the train are taken in the region's very best hotels and restaurants.

The train operates from April to June and from September to November. Prices vary according to the date of travel, category of accommodation and the itinerary chosen, ranging from around 240 000 to 390 000pts per person.

Further information can be obtained from Iberraíl ☎ 91 571 96 66 or at www.alandalusexpreso.com

AVE: information and reservations:
Madrid ☎ 91 328 90 20.
Córdoba ☎ 957 40 02 02.
Sevilla ☎ 954 54 02 02.

Local trains – RENFE's regional train network includes a number of routes of particular interest to visitors.

"Green" railway stations *(Estaciones verdes)* – Several stations have been designated as "green stations" due to their proximity to the region's nature reserves, or because of their relevance for hikers, mountain-bikers or for nature-lovers wishing to discover the beauty of rural Andalucia. Information regarding timetables is available from railway stations in the region's provincial capitals. Additional tourist information can be obtained on-line at www.renfe.es/medio-ambiente

Province	Green station	Line
Almería	Gádor	Linares-Almería
Cádiz	Jimena de la Frontera	Bobadilla-Algeciras
Córdoba	Aguilar de la Frontera	Córdoba-Málaga
Granada	Guadix	Linares-Almería
Huelva	San Juan del Puerto-Moguer	Sevilla-Huelva
Jaén	Andújar	Alcázar-Sevilla-Huelva
Málaga	Ronda	Bobadilla-Algeciras
Málaga	Fuente de Piedra	Córdoba-Málaga; Sevilla-Málaga
Sevilla	Cazalla-Constantina	Mérida-Sevilla
Sevilla	Lebrija	Sevilla-Cádiz

Train & visit to Isla Mágica – This package includes a return train ticket from various stations around Andalucia to Santa Justa station in Sevilla, plus entry to the Isla Mágica theme park. Discounts are available for children and the over-65s. Information can be obtained from any RENFE station in Andalucia.

Tren de la Naturaleza – The "Nature Train" two-day package is available for group visits to the **Parque Natural de la Sierra de Cazorla-Úbeda** from Madrid. The package includes return travel by regional express train, local transfers by bus, food and accommodation. For further information and prices, contact Viajes Mundo Libero ☎ 91 473 34 29.

BY AIR

Andalucia has several excellent airports. The largest is in Málaga, with an annual capacity of some 12 million passengers. Sevilla airport, which was extended and refurbished for Expo'92, is able to handle 4 million passengers every year.
Almería ☎ 950 21 37 15/950 23 86 84.
Córdoba ☎ 947 21 41 00.
Granada ☎ 958 22 52 00/958 44 64 11.
Jerez de la Frontera ☎ 956 15 00 00/956 15 00 83.
Málaga ☎ 952 04 84 84.
Sevilla ☎ 954 44 90 00.

These airports handle thousands of foreign scheduled and charter flights, alongside services operated by the following Spanish airlines:
Iberia ☎ 902 400 500 (information and reservations); www.iberia.com
Air Europa ☎ 902 401 501 (information and reservations); www.air-europa.com
Spanair: ☎ 902 13 14 15; www.spanair.com

BY FERRY

Andalucia's main ports for commercial traffic are found in Algeciras, Cádiz, Málaga and Almería, from where several ferry companies operate services to other parts of Spain.

Trasmediterránea – The largest ferry company in the country, with a weekly service from Cádiz to the Canary Islands and daily crossings to Ceuta and Melilla from Almería, Málaga and Algeciras.
Information and reservations: ☎ 902 45 46 45; www.trasmediterranea.es
Port authorities:
Recinto del Puerto – 11201 Algeciras.
Parque Nicolás Salmerón, 19 – 04002 Almería.
Avenida Ramón Carranza, 26 – 11006 Cádiz.
Estación Marítima Recinto del Puerto. Local E1 – 29016 Málaga.

General information

Currency – The unit of currency in Spain is the peseta. In September 2000, the **exchange rate** was 262pts to the pound (178 to the US dollar). Coins come in the following denominations: 5, 10, 25, 50, 100, 200 and 500pts, with notes in 1 000, 2 000, 5 000 and 10 000 values. Visitors should be aware of the variety of Spanish coins, with a number of denominations (particularly 5, 25, 100 and 200pts) represented by several different designs. There are no restrictions on the amount of currency (Spanish or other) that foreigners may bring with them into Spain. They may leave Spain with the currency equivalent of up to 500 000pts.

Following the launch of the Euro at the beginning of 1999 and in preparation for its full introduction in Spain in 2002, many prices now appear in both pesetas and Euros. In September 2000, 1 Euro was valued at 166.39pts.

Changing money, credit cards – Travellers' cheques and foreign cash can be exchanged at banks and exchange offices *(cambios)*. International credit cards are accepted in most shops, hotels and restaurants. Visitors can also obtain cash from bank machines using credit and debit cards. A pin number will be required to use this service. Visitors should note that Eurocheques are sometimes difficult to change and are becoming somewhat obsolete.

Banks – Banks are generally open Mondays to Fridays, 9am to 2pm and on Saturdays from 9am to 12.30pm. These times are subject to change, especially in summer.

Time differences – Spain is one hour ahead of GMT.

The Spanish keep very different hours from either the British or North Americans. As a general rule, restaurants serve lunch from 1.30pm to 3.30pm and dinner from 9pm to 11pm.

Post Offices – Post Offices *(correos)* are open weekdays from 9am to 2pm. The main post offices in large cities and those in international airports have a 24-hour service. Stamps *(sellos)* are sold in post offices and tobacconists *(estancos)*. **THE RED GUIDE ESPAÑA PORTUGAL** gives the post code for every town covered.

Telephones – Public telephones accept 5, 25, 50, 100, 200 and 500pts coins as well as phonecards *(tarjetas telefónicas)*, available in 1 000 and 2 000pts denominations from tobacconists. For **international calls**, dial 00, then the country code (44 for the United Kingdom, 353 for Ireland, 1 for the United States), followed by the area code (minus the first 0 of the STD code when dialling the UK), and the number.

For calls within Spain, dial the full 9-digit number of the person you are calling.

When calling Spain from abroad, dial the international access code, followed by 34 for Spain, then the full 9-digit number.

Shops – These are generally open weekdays 10am to 1.30pm and 5pm to 8pm (some department stores stay open during the lunch hour). Some shops are closed on Saturday afternoons and most all day Sunday.

Monuments, museums and churches – Monuments and museums are generally open 10am to 1.30pm and 4pm to 7pm. Some churches are only open during services early in the morning or in the evening. For specific opening times of monuments and museums in Andalucia, consult the Admission Times and Charges section of this guide.

Entertainment – When two performances of a show are scheduled, the afternoon performance generally starts at 7pm or 7.30pm (4.30pm on Sundays and holidays) and the evening show at 10pm or 10.30pm.

Tipping – Bar, restaurant and café bills always include service in the total charge. Nevertheless, it is customary to leave an extra 10%. It is also usual to tip taxi drivers and porters.

Public holidays – As in other autonomous communities around Spain, Andalucia has its own local and regional public holidays in addition to those celebrated across the whole country. Local festivals vary from one municipality to the next, although the entire region commemorates Andalucia Day *(Día de Andalucía)* on **28 February**. National holidays are celebrated on the following dates:

1 January: New Year's Day
6 January: Epiphany
19 March: St Joseph
Maundy Thursday
Good Friday
1 May: Labour Day
15 August: Assumption of the Virgin
12 October: Spanish National Holiday
1 November: All Saints
6 December: Spanish Constitution Day
8 December: Immaculate Conception
25 December: Christmas Day

Electrical current – 220 volts AC (some of the older establishments may still have 110 V). Plugs are two-pin.

Water – Water is generally safe to drink although many people prefer mineral water *(agua mineral)*.

Accommodation

Travellers' addresses – This section, which has been added to a number of towns and cities in this guide, offers a choice of hotels in three categories to suit all budgets. Prices are based on a double/twin room:
– The **Moderate** category includes rooms at less than 8 000pts. These are usually small, simple hotels with a basic level of comfort.
– The **Mid-range** covers hotels with rooms at between 8 000 and 20 000pts with a certain amount of character.
– In the **Luxury** category we have included hotels with particular charm, offering a high degree of comfort and ensuring a memorable stay. Naturally, the cost of these hotels is in keeping with the high level of facilities provided (over 20 000pts).

Hotels – **THE RED GUIDE ESPAÑA PORTUGAL** is revised annually and is an indispensable complement to THE GREEN GUIDE ANDALUCIA, with additional information on hotels and restaurants including category, price, degree of comfort and setting. Towns underlined in red on Michelin map 446 are listed in the current edition of THE RED GUIDE ESPAÑA PORTUGAL with a choice of hotels and restaurants. The Spanish Tourist Board also publishes an annual hotel guide. Further details are also listed in the Useful Addresses section in this guide *(see p 340)*. Bear in mind that hotel prices do not include 7% VAT and that they may vary according to the season.

Discounted rates – Many chains and hotels catering to business travellers often offer reduced rates at weekends. It is also possible to purchase vouchers for one or several nights at advantageous prices. For further information on these special offers, contact the following:

NH Hoteles ☎ 902 115 116 (24hr); www.nh-hoteles.es. Special weekend rates from 5 000pts per person per night in over 75 participating hotels in 36 towns and cities.
Halcón Viajes ☎ 902 300 600 (information and reservations); www.halconviajes.com. Individual vouchers (for a one-night stay for one or two people) with a discount on the official rate.
Hoteles Meliá ☎ 971 224 500; www.solmeliá.com. Discounts via the MAS loyalty card and special weekend offers.

Paradors – Almost all of the state-run network of luxury hotels are in restored historic monuments (castles, palaces, monasteries etc) in magnificent locations. Out of season the network introduces special offers for guests, although this varies according to the location. In addition, with the "Tarjeta Amigos de Paradores" loyalty card (☎ 91 374 26 00) guests are able to accumulate points which can be exchanged for free stays. For more information, contact Paradores de Turismo, calle Requena, 3, 28013 Madrid ☎ 91 561 66 66; www.parador.es. The official UK representative is Keytel International, 402 Edgware Road, London W2 1ED ☎ (020) 76160300; fax (020) 76160317; paradors@keytel.co.uk. *Paradors* are indicated on Michelin maps 990 and 446 by the symbol 🅿.

Parador, Úbeda

R. López-Alonso/STOCK PHOTOS

Rural accommodation – The Andalucian Network of Rural Accommodation **(Red Andaluza de Alojamientos Rurales)**, or RAAR, is a private owners' association offering a choice of over 300 addresses for those interested in a holiday in the heart of the Andalucian countryside. The RAAR publishes a practical guide listing details of every type of accommodation available, including rooms in private houses, hostels for groups, entire houses for rent and farm campsites. Reservations can be made directly with the individual owners, through travel agents or via the RAAR reservations centre ☎ 902 44 22 33; fax 950 27 16 78; www.raar.es.
The Association of Rural Hotels in Andalucia **(Asociación de Hoteles Rurales de Andalucía)**, or AHRA, is a group of some 50 small **rural hotels** dotted around the region. The association operates a system of rural vouchers *(bonos rurales)* that can be bought for 5 000pts each. To contact the AHRA reservations centre ☎ 953 75 58 67; fax 953 75 60 99.

Youth tourism – The **Inturjoven** organisation, set up by the regional parliament (Junta de Andalucía), manages a large network of youth hostels and organises a wide range of sporting, cultural and tourist activities. The network of 20 youth hostels belonging to this association is located at strategic centres in cities, along the coast and in the mountains across Andalucia.

An individual or group hostelling card obtainable from any hostel or from the Inturjoven reservations centre is required to stay in any of the hostels within the network. Cards issued to members of the IYHF (International Youth Hostel Federation) are also accepted. Reservations can be made via phone, fax, e-mail or post.

Andalucia Youth Hostel Network (Red de Albergues Juveniles de Andalucía): Central de Reservas: Miño, 24. 41011 Sevilla ☎ 954 27 70 87; fax 954 27 74 67. For further information, consult the Inturjoven web site at www.inturjoven.com.

Camping and caravanning – The Junta de Andalucía *(see Further reading – Tourism)* publishes a comprehensive camping and caravanning guide listing the facilities available at every accredited site in the region. Camping outside of authorised sites is permitted in some areas. Contact individual town halls for further information.

Eating out

Andalucian gastronomy is recognised throughout Spain for its quality and diversity. The information provided in the Food and Wine section of this guide *(see p 61)* will enable visitors to discover the traditional dishes and wines of each part of the region.

Travellers' addresses – The restaurants listed in the Travellers' addresses section of several towns and cities have been chosen for their surroundings, ambience, typical dishes or unusual character. Given the region's reputation for tapas, we have also included a list of tapas bars where visitors can enjoy an aperitif or meal throughout the day and late into the evening. For a wider selection of restaurants and more detailed gastronomic information, consult **THE RED GUIDE ESPAÑA PORTUGAL.**

Useful addresses

Spanish Embassies and Consulates

Spanish Embassy, 39 Chesham Place, London SW1X 8SB ☎ (020) 7235 5555; fax (020) 7259 5392.
Spanish Consulate, 20 Draycott Place, London SW3 2RZ ☎ (020) 7589 8989; fax (020) 7581 7888; consulates also in Manchester and Edinburgh.
Embassy of Spain, 2375 Pennsylvania Avenue NW, Washington DC 20037 ☎ (202) 452 0100; fax (202) 833 5670; consulates in Boston, Chicago, Houston, Los Angeles, Miami, New Orleans, New York and San Francisco.

Foreign Embassies and Consulates in Spain

American Embassy: Serrano 75, 28006 Madrid ☎ 91 587 2200.

American Consulates: Málaga (Avenida Juan Gómez 8, Ed Lucía 1°C, 29640 Fuengirola ☎ 952 47 48 91); Sevilla (Paseo de las Delicias 7, 41012 Sevilla ☎ 954 23 18 85).

Australian Embassy: Plaza Descubridor Diego de Ordas 3, 28003 Madrid ☎ 91 441 9300.

Australian Consulate: Sevilla (Federico Rubio 14, 41004 Sevilla ☎ 954 22 09 71).

British Embassy: Calle Fernando el Santo 16, 28010 Madrid ☎ 91 700 82 00.

British Consulate-General: Centro Colón, Marqués de la Ensenada 16, 2a, 28004 Madrid ☎ 91 308 52 01.

British Consular offices: Málaga (Calle Duquesa de Parcent 8, Málaga) ☎ 952 35 23 00); **Sevilla** (Plaza Nueva 8B, 41001 ☎ 954 22 88 75); **Granada** (Carmen de San Cristóbal, Carretera de Murcia, 18010 Granada ☎ 958 27 47 24).

Canadian Embassy: Calle Núñez de Balboa 35, 28001 Madrid ☎ 91 423 32 50.

Canadian Consulate: Málaga (Plaza de la Malagueta 3-1, 29016 Málaga ☎ 95 221 33 46).

Embassy of Ireland: Ireland House, Paseo de la Castellana 46, 4a, 28046 Madrid ☎ 91 576 3500.

Honorary Irish Consulates: Málaga (Galerias Santa Monica, Avenida Los Boliches 15, 29640 Fuengirola ☎ 952 47 51 08); **Sevilla** (Plaza de Santa Cruz 6, 41004 Sevilla ☎ 954 21 63 61).

Spanish National Tourist Offices

London: 22-23 Manchester Square, London W1M 5AP, ☎ (020) 7486 8077; fax (020) 7486 8034; 24-hour brochure line: 09001 669920 (60p per minute); londres@tourspain.es; www.tourspain.co.uk; www.uk.tourspain.es.

New York: 666 Fifth Avenue, New York, NY 10103, ☎ (212) 265 8822; fax (212) 265 8864.

Chicago: Water Tower Place, Suite 915 East, 845 North Michigan Avenue, Chicago, IL 60611, ☎ (312) 642 1992; fax (312) 642 9817.

Los Angeles: 8383 Wilshire Blvd, Suite 960, Beverly Hills, CA 90211, ☏ (213) 658 7188/7192; fax (213) 658 1061.

Miami: 1221 Brickell Avenue, Miami, FL 33131, ☏ (305) 358 1992; fax (305) 358 8223.

Toronto: 2 Bloor St West, 34th Floor, Toronto, Ontario M4W 3E2, ☏ (416) 961 3131; fax (416) 961 1992.

Madrid: Secretaría General de Turismo, calle José Lázaro Galdeano 6, 28036 Madrid, ☏ 91 343 35 00.

Andalucian Regional Tourist Offices

Centro Internacional de Turismo de Andalucía – Carretera Nacional 340, Km 189.6; 29600 Marbella (Málaga), ☏ 952 83 87 85; fax 952 83 63 69; www.andalucia.org

Dirección General de Turismo de Andalucía (Andalucia Tourist Board) – Avenida República Argentina, 25, 41011 Sevilla, ☏ 954 55 84 11; info@andalucia.org; www.andalucia.org

Tourist Information Centres – All Andalucian towns and cities have a Tourist Information Centre, known as the "Oficina de Turismo" or simply "Turismo", marked on Michelin town plans with an 🛈. The addresses and telephone numbers of these centres can be found in the Admission Times and Charges section in this guide, as well as in the **THE RED GUIDE ESPAÑA PORTUGAL.**

Sur in English

This free weekly newspaper is available across Southern Spain. It includes a whole host of useful information for English-speaking residents and visitors alike, including news, classified ads, TV listings etc. For further information, contact **Sur in English**, Avenida Dr. Marañón, 48, 29009 Málaga, ☏ 952 64 96 00; fax: 952 61 12 56; sureng@surenglish.com; www.surenglish.com

---

Séneca Reservations Service – The **Séneca** booking system operates exclusively in Andalucia, enabling visitors to book a range of services including hotels, restaurants, bicycle rental, horse-riding, entrances to various sites and even boat berths at the region's marinas.

Séneca: Carretera Nacional 340, Km 189.6, 29600 Marbella (Málaga), ☏ 952 83 66 25; fax 952 83 39 86; seneca@seneca-web.com

---

The Moorish Legacy

The Moorish Legacy (*El Legado andalusí*) initiative has been developed to provide information for visitors on the Moorish occupation of the Iberian Peninsula and their major achievements. This includes a series of exhibitions, the creation of 11 official tourist routes through al-Andalus (Andalucia, Murcia, Portugal and North Africa), the publication of works relating to this period and the detailed cataloguing of all aspects of Moorish architecture.

El Legado andalusí: Molinos, 65, 18009 Granada, ☏ 958 22 59 95; fax 958 22 86 44; www.legadoandalusi.es

---

Disabled visitors – The **Confederación Coordinadora Estatal de Minusválidos Físicos de España (Servi-Cocemfe)**, a state-run association for the disabled, provides information on facilities at tourist sites around Andalucia and elsewhere in Spain. The body also has a leisure department which organises activities for the disabled. Eugenio Salazar 2, Madrid, ☏ 91 413 70 10. For information specific to Andalucia, contact the **Confederación Andaluza de Minusválidos Físicos**, Alfarería, 126 A, 41010 Sevilla, ☏ 954 33 03 11. **Rompe Barreras Travel**, a travel agent based in Madrid, is able to organise travel arrangements and a range of holidays adapted to disabled visitors, ☏ 91 551 36 22; fax 91 552 62 07.

Useful numbers

Tourist Information (in English) – ☏ 901 300 600; available daily 10am to 8pm. This service is only available within Spain.

Spanish Directory Enquiries – ☏ 1003.

International Directory Enquiries – ☏ 1025.

Junta de Andalucía (Regional Government) information – ☏ 900 50 92 92.

Weather information – ☏ 906 36 53 65.

Speaking clock – ☏ 093.

Emergency Services – ☏ 061.

Lost credit cards:
Visa and Mastercard – ☏ 902 11 44 00.
American Express – ☏ 91 572 03 03.

Leisure activities

Water parks, fun-fairs and zoos

A wide range of leisure facilities are available to visitors close to major towns and cities, along the Costa del Sol and even in Andalucia's national parks and nature reserves. Families in particular will enjoy spending a few hours at the many water parks, zoos, fun-fairs and botanical gardens scattered across the region. Further information can be obtained from Tourist Offices and in publications such as the free weekly English newspaper, **Sur in English**, available across Southern Spain *(see p 341)*.

Hiking and mountain-biking

It is often said that if there's an abundance of anything in Andalucia, it is nature and sunshine. What is certain is that walkers and cyclists are spoilt for choice in one of

Hiking in the Alpujarras

Spain's best regions for these two pursuits. Details of over 200 walking itineraries and 120 cycling routes are listed in the following guides published by the Andalucia Tourist Board: *Bicycle* (600pts); *Rural Andalucía* (1 200pts) and *Hiking* (600pts) *(see Further reading – Tourism)*. Information can also be obtained on-line at www. andalucía.org

Additional details on hiking in the Alpujarras can be obtained on-line at:
www.walking.co.uk/alpujarr.htm

Andalucian Cycling Federation (Federación Andaluza de Ciclismo): Edificio La Compañía 4, 11403 Jerez de la Frontera (Cádiz) ☎ 956 34 88 12.

Beaches

Andalucia has the geographical advantage of bordering both the Atlantic and the Mediterranean. This fact, coupled with the 25 protected areas situated along its two coasts, ensures that the region is able to offer visitors a diversity of landscape and beaches which is unique in Spain.

Atlantic coast – This coastline, which is also known as the **Costa de la Luz** (Coast of Light), extends from the Portuguese border to the Straits of Gibraltar. It covers a total length of 330km/206mi, split between the provinces of Huelva and Cádiz. In general, its beaches are popular mainly with Spanish visitors, particularly families. Days are hot, the evenings cooled by ocean breezes, and the sea temperature cooler than that of the Mediterranean. The 15 beaches in **Huelva** province are characterised by their golden sand, clear water, surf, sand dunes and pine forests. A number of resorts, such as **Isla Canela**, have excellent sporting and sailing facilities, while other wild and isolated stretches of coast are only accessible on foot from the larger resorts. Some of the Atlantic coast's best-known beaches include **Isla Cristina**, with its long-standing fishing tradition; **La Antilla**, a 22km/14mi stretch close to Lepe; **El Rompido**, with its enormous dunes and pine forests offering superb views; **Punta Umbría**, famous for its marina; **Mazagón**, with its steep cliffs; and the renowned **Matalascañas**, the beach bordering El Rocío and the Parque Nacional de Doñana.

The **Cádiz coast**, the most southerly in Spain, stretches for a total of 200km/125mi. Its beaches of fine, golden sand are lined by some of Spain's most historic towns and cities such as Sanlúcar de Barrameda, Rota, El Puerto de Santa María and Cádiz, enabling visitors to combine time on the beach with cultural visits to these fascinating places. To the south of the beach at **Bajo de Guía**, on which horse races are held in summer, the resort of **Chipiona** has four beaches which have been popular for many years. El Puerto de Santa María, within the boundaries of which the glitzy **Puerto Sherry** marina has been built, has some excellent beaches of its own, such as **La Puntilla** and **Valdelagrana**, while those close to Cádiz itself, (**La Victoria**, **La Caleta** and **Cortadura**) are heaving during the summer months with inhabitants of the city. Also worthy of mention are the recently created tourist complex of **Sancti Petri**, and the series of delightful beaches near Conil (**Caños de Meca**, **Zahara de los Atunes** and **Bolonia**) which have thus far escaped the blight of mass tourism. The only drawback for sun-worshippers on this coast is the strong wind, a feature of the local climate that attracts thousands of windsurfers here every year.

Mediterranean coast – This coastline includes several areas with differing geographical characteristics, all of which have a similar climate which is both hot and dry. The waters of the Mediterranean are generally calm, warm and crystal clear.

Costa del Sol – The section of the Sun Coast in the province of Málaga is the leading tourist destination in Andalucia *(see p 160)*. The western section, which runs from Gibraltar to the city of Málaga itself, contains over 50% of all hotel accommodation along the Andalucian coast, as well as 13 marinas, a huge range of leisure and sporting facilities, and countless tourism-related services. Paradoxically, the majority of the beaches here are pebbly. There is less pronounced tourist development along the eastern stretch of the province, in an area also known as La Axarquía *(see p 101)*, where accommodation tends to be more apartment-based. The major resorts along this coastline, with its small beaches and numerous cliffs, are **El Rincón de la Victoria, Nerja** and **Torre del Mar**.

Costa Tropical – The coastline of Granada province is known as the Tropical Coast due to its sub-tropical climate, resulting from the protection afforded it by the high peaks of the Sierra Nevada. The beaches along this stretch are particularly varied, ranging from small coves protected by high cliffs to enormous beaches such as those found in Almuñécar. Tourism here is concentrated in **Almuñécar**; Salobreña, with its two large beaches, the more developed **Playa del Peñón** and the wilder **Playa de La Guardia**; in Motril (**Playa de Poniente** and **Playa de Granada**); in Castell de Ferro and La Rábita.

Costa de Almería – The Almerian Coast represents a quarter of the entire Andalucian coastline. Most of the tourist development here is between Adra – including the immense sandy beaches of **Balanegra** and **Balerma** and the resort of **Almerimar** – and Aguadulce. The onward stretch from Aguadulce to Almería comprises an impressive series of steep cliffs. To the east of the provincial capital, the Mediterranean is bordered by the Parque Natural de Cabo de Gata, with its superb beaches, such as **Morrón de los Genoveses**, and the attractive small resort of **San José**.

Sport

With its myriad sporting possibilities and benign climate Andalucia is a year-round paradise for all outdoor pursuit enthusiasts.

WATER SPORTS

From sailing to scuba-diving and water-skiing to windsurfing, Andalucia is able to offer a whole range of sporting options for beginners and more experienced water sports enthusiasts alike.

Andalucian Sailing Federation (Federación Andaluza de Vela), Avenida de la Libertad, Puerto Sherry, 11500 El Puerto de Santa María (Cádiz), ☎ 956 87 48 05.

Andalucian Water-Skiing Federation (Federación Andaluza de Esquí Náutico), Plaza de San Miguel, 13, 29620 Torremolinos (Málaga), ☎ 952 44 42 34.

Marinas

Andalucia's seafaring tradition, which has been admirably demonstrated over the centuries, has seen the development of over 30 superb marinas along the region's 836km/522mi of Atlantic and Mediterranean coastline, in addition to the two river ports in Sevilla.

Many of these ports also have sailing, scuba-diving and windsurfing schools; some even have rowing and canoeing facilities.

Two guides published by the Junta de Andalucía – *Nautical Guide* (600pts) and the *Pleasure Craft Harbours brochure* (100pts) – list information on every port and marina in Andalucia, as well as the facilities available *(see Further reading – Tourism)*. Further information can be obtained on-line at www.puertosdeandalucia.com

B. Kaufmann/MICHELIN

La Duquesa (Costa del Sol)

Scuba-diving

In addition to the schools located at various marinas along the Andalucian coast, the region also has six scuba-diving clubs for more experienced divers.

It should be noted that the areas renowned for diving in the Atlantic and Mediterranean are very different. The waters of the Atlantic are relatively cold, visibility varies between 15m/50ft-20m/65ft and almost nothing, with dangerous currents making it advisable to dive with a local instructor. By contrast, the Mediterranean is characterised by warmer temperatures, good visibility and more tranquil sea conditions.

Further information can be obtained on-line at www.andalucia.org or by contacting the **Andalucian Scuba-Diving Federation** (Federación Andaluza de Actividades Subacuáticas), Playa de las Almadrabillas, 10, 04007 Almería, ☎ 950 27 06 12; fax 950 27 62 99.

RIVER FISHING

Jaén and Granada are the two most popular provinces for fishing in Andalucia, with rivers and lakes teeming with trout and, in some areas, carp and crayfish. In general, the season starts on 15 March and ends on 15 August, although some areas are open all year round. Fishing enthusiasts must be in possession of a relevant fishing licence.

Andalucian Fishing Federation (Federación Andaluza de Pesca), Apartado de Correos 71, 14080 Córdoba, ☎ 95 725 30 59; fax 95 726 16 54.

Andalucian Institute for Agrarian Reform (Instituto Andaluz de Reforma Agraria), Avenida República Argentina, 25, 41011 Sevilla, ☎ 954 27 00 73/01 85.

Andalucian Environmental Agency (Agencia de Medio Ambiente de la Junta de Andalucía), Avenida de Eritaña, 2, 41013 Sevilla, ☎ 954 62 86 11/72 02.

SKIING

The Sierra Nevada ski resort, one of the most popular in Spain, is easily accessible by car (just 30min from Granada along Europe's highest road), bus (local services and a daily Madrid-Sierra Nevada service), train (the nearest railway station is just 33km/21mi away) and plane (Granada, Málaga and Sevilla airports). The resort has 61km/38mi of marked runs and all the facilities expected of a major ski resort. Further information on skiing in the Sierra Nevada is available from the following:

Cetursa Central Office (Oficina Central de Cetursa), Plaza de Andalucía, 18196 Sierra Nevada, Monachil Granada ☎ 958 24 91 11; fax 958 24 91 46; agencia@cetursa.es.

Cetursa – Madrid (Delegación de Cetursa), Paseo Pintor Rosales, 32, 28008 Madrid, 91 548 44 00; fax 91 547 77 98; www.cetursa.com.

Andalucian Winter Sports Federation (Federación Andaluza de Deportes de Invierno), Avenida de la Constitución, 27, 18014 Granada, ☎ 958 13 57 48; fax 958 13 57 49.

HORSE-RIDING

The horse has long been a part of Andalucian culture. This tradition continues today throughout the region, perhaps most visibly during the pilgrimage to El Rocío, at the "mares' auction" (saca de las yeguas) held on 26 June every year in the Parque Natural de Doñana, the rounding-up of the bulls contests in Villamanrique and Sevilla (April), and the horse-races on the sands of Sanlúcar de Barrameda. Mention should also be made of the mule- and horse-drawn carriage exhibitions held in Andalucia's main bullrings as part of the region's annual fair celebrations.

Major international competitions in Andalucia include the Trofeo del Sol show-jumping competition, organised over the winter in a number of locations along the Costa del Sol, and the polo tournaments in Sotogrande (Cádiz), played during July and August.

The annual Jerez Horse Fair *(Feria del Caballo de Jerez)*, held in May, and the SICAB, an international show in Sevilla every November, are the two most important events in the Andalucian equine calendar. The Royal Andalucian School of Equestrian Art, also in Jerez, has weekly shows featuring its magnificent Cartujana horses.

For those who prefer participating to spectating, Andalucia offers equestrian-lovers an excellent choice of options, including cross-country treks lasting several days, stays on horse farms, in country houses and rural hotels, as well as courses in breaking in horses and equestrian techniques.

The Horse brochure (see Further reading – Tourism), available from Tourist Offices and the organisations below, provides further information on horse-riding in the region.

Andalucian Equestrian Federation (Federación Hípica Andaluza), Adriano, 25, 41001 Sevilla, ☎ 954 56 16 33; fax 954 56 16 33.

Association of Andalucian Equestrian and Rural Tourism Companies (Asociación de Empresas de Turismo Ecuestre y Rural de Andalucía), Isla de la Cartuja, 41092 Sevilla, ☎ 954 48 89 00; fax 954 48 89 11.

HUNTING

The hills and mountains of Andalucia offer rich pickings for hunters. Very few parts of Europe offer such a variety of large game, including wild boar (Doñana), mountain goat (Cazorla, Sierra Nevada, Ronda), deer (Serranía de Cádiz) and mouflon, the latter raised in enclosures. Smaller game is also hunted, such as hare (traditionally on horseback accompanied by hunting dogs), quail and partridge. Further information is contained in the *Hunting* brochure *(see Further reading – Tourism)*, available from regional offices *(Delegaciones Provinciales)* of the Ministry of Agriculture and Fisheries *(Consejería de Agricultura y Pesca)* and from provincial hunting federations *(Federaciones Provinciales de Caza)*.

Andalucian Hunting Federation (Federación Andaluza de Caza), Los Morenos, 29300 Archidona (Málaga), ☎ 952 71 48 71/65; www.fac.es.

GOLF

Golfers are attracted to Andalucia in their tens of thousands by the superb golfing conditions and the high quality of the 60 courses scattered around the region. The majority of these are located along the Costa de la Sol – one of which, Valderrama, hosted the 1997 Ryder Cup 1997 – although excellent courses can also be found close to the cities of Sevilla, Huelva, Cádiz, Granada and Almería.

Details on the specific aspects of each course are listed in the *Golf* brochure *(see Further reading – Tourism)* published by the Andalucian Tourist Board.

Andalucian Golf Federation (Federación Andaluza de Golf), Sierra de Grazalema, 33 – 5 – 1ºB, 29016 Málaga, ☎ 952 22 55 99; fax 952 22 03 87; www.golf-andalucia.net.

Golf on the Costa del Sol

SPA RESORTS

The region's 11 spa resorts offer a range of facilities for visitors which combine rest and relaxation, cultural activities and health treatments in beautiful natural surroundings. Four of these are located in the province of Granada, two in Málaga, Almería and Jaén, and one in Cádiz. In addition, five "Curhoteles" (four in Málaga province and one in Almería) offering a high level of comfort provide guests with the very latest techniques in health treatment.

Andalucian Spa Association (Asociación de Balnearios de Andalucía), ☎ 950 31 74 13. Additional information can be found in the *Spas and Cure Hotels* guide *(see Further reading – Tourism)* or on-line at www.andalucia.org

National and Natural Parks

The considerable efforts made by the regional government *(Junta de Andalucía)* to protect the region's natural environment over the past few years has been rewarded recently with the awarding of national park status to the Sierra Nevada. This increases to two the number of national parks (along with the Parque Nacional de Doñana) in Andalucia.

National Parks	Provinces	Ha/acres	☏ Information	Page no
Doñana	Huelva-Sevilla-Cádiz	54 250/ 134 051	955 29 95 20	*173*
Sierra Nevada	Granada-Almería	171 646/ 424 137	955 00 34 00	*313*

Natural parks				
Cabo de Gata-Níjar	Almería	29 000/ 71 659	950 25 12 52	*114*
Sierra María-Los Vélez	Almería	22 500/ 55 597	950 25 12 52	*331*
La Breña y Marismas de Barbate	Cádiz	2 957/ 7 306	956 27 48 42	*330*
Bahía de Cádiz	Cádiz	10 000/ 24 710	956 27 48 42	*not in guide*
Los Alcornocales	Cádiz-Málaga	170 025/ 420 131	956 27 48 42	*225*
Sierra de Grazalema	Cádiz-Málaga	51 695/ 127 738	956 27 48 42	*266*
Sierra de Cardeña y Montoro	Córdoba	41 245/ 101 916	957 23 25 04	*257*
Sierra de Hornachuelos	Córdoba	67 202/ 166 056	957 23 25 04	*262*
Sierras Subbéticas	Córdoba	31 568/ 78 004	957 23 25 04	*117*
Sierra de Baza	Granada	52 337/ 129 324	958 24 83 02	*111*
Sierra de Castril	Granada	12 265/ 30 306	958 24 83 02	*207*
Sierra de Huétor	Granada	12 428/ 30 709	958 24 83 02	*not in guide*
Sierra de Aracena y Picos de Aroche	Huelva	184 000/ 454 664	955 11 04 75	*97*
Despeñaperros	Jaén	7 717/ 19 068	953 22 31 54	*171*
Sierras de Andújar	Jaén	60 800/ 150 236	953 22 31 54	*90*
Sierras de Cazorla, Segura y Las Villas	Jaén	214 336/ 529 624	953 72 01 25	*132*
Sierra Mágina	Jaén	199 000/ 491 729	953 22 31 54	*216*
Montes de Málaga	Málaga	4 900/ 12 107	952 04 11 48	*238*
Sierra de las Nieves	Málaga	18 592/ 45 940	952 04 11 48	*279*
Sierra Norte de Sevilla	Sevilla	164 840/ 407 319	954 25 50 96	*316*

For further information contact the following bodies:

Andalucian Department for the Environment (Consejería de Medio Ambiente – Junta de Andalucía), Avenida Manuel Siurot, 50, 41013 Sevilla, ☏ 955 00 34 00/35 00; fax 955 00 37 77; www. cma.junta-andalucia.es

Those interested in environmental issues may wish to contact the following library:

Department for the Environment library (Biblioteca de la Consejería de Medio Ambiente), Avenida de Eritaña, 1, 41013 Sevilla, ☏ 954 55 05 50; fax 954 62 38 00; biblioteca@cma.junta-andalucia.es

Calendar of events

Practically every day something is celebrated or commemorated somewhere in Andalucia.
The list below includes some of the more well-known events in the region, although exact dates should be checked with the appropriate Tourist Office.

Granada ....Commemoration of the capture of Granada

Cádiz and elsewhere in Cádiz province; Isla Cristina and Ayamonte (Huelva) ....Carnival

In many towns and cities ..Candlemass processions

Throughout Andalucia, particularly in Sevilla, Málaga, Córdoba and Granada ....Processions

Sevilla...............................April Fair

Andújar (Jaén) ....Virgen de la Cabeza pilgrimage

Granada ....International Theatre Festival

El Puerto de Santa María ..Spring and Fino Wine Fair

Jerez .... Horse Fair

Sanlúcar de Barrameda (Cádiz) ....Manzanilla Fair

Córdoba ....May Crosses, Patio Competition, Annual Fair. National Flamenco Contest (held every three years)

Almonte (Huelva) ....El Rocío pilgrimage

Granada ....Processions
Flamenco Festival (the oldest in Spain)

Granada ....International Music and Dance Festival

Several towns and villages along the Mediterranean, particularly Almería...........Seafaring processions

Nerja (Málaga)..................Nerja Caves Festival

Sevilla's April Fair

Y. Travert/DIAF

Further reading

History

A Concise History of the Spanish Civil War – Paul Preston (Fontana 1996)
Admiral of the Ocean Sea: A Life of Christopher Columbus – Samuel Eliot Morison (Little Brown & Co 1991)
A Traveller's History of Spain – Juan Lalaguna (The Windrush Press 1999)
Franco: a Biography – Paul Preston (Fontana 1995)
Imperial Spain 1469-1716 – JH Elliott (Penguin Books 1990)
Modern Spain, 1875-1980 – Raymond Carr (Oxford Paperbacks 1981)
Moorish Spain – Richard Fletcher (Phoenix Press 1994)
Spain 1516-1598 – John Lynch (Blackwell Publishers 1994)
Spain 1808-1975 – Raymond Carr (Oxford University Press 1982)
The Arab Conquest of Spain 710-797 – Roger Collins (Blackwell Publishers 1994)
The Inquisition – Michael Baigent & Richard Leigh (Viking 1999)
The Hispanic World in Crisis and Change, 1598-1700 (A History of Spain) – John Lynch (Blackwell Publishers 1994)
The New Spaniards – John Hooper (Penguin Books 1995)
The Sephardim – Lucien Gubbay and Abraham Levy (Carnell Ltd 1992)
The Spanish Civil War – Alun Kenwood (Ed) (Berg Publishers 1993)
The Spanish Inquisition – Cecil Roth (WW Norton 1964)
The Spanish Labyrinth – Gerald Brenan (Cambridge University Press 1990)
The Spanish Seaborne Empire – JH Parry (University of California Press 1990)

Travel

Alhambra – Michael Jacobs, Francisco Fernandez (Frances Lincoln 2000)
Andalucia – Michael Jacobs (Pallas Athene 1999)
A Selection of Wild Flowers of Southern Spain – Betty Molesworth Allen (Mirador 1993)
A Visit To Spain And North Africa – Hans Christian Andersen (Peter Owen 1975)
Birds of Iberia – Clive Finlayson, David Tomlinson (Santana Books 1993)
Driving Over Lemons: an Optimist in Andalucia – Chris Stewart (Penguin Books 1999)
Wines of Spain – Jan Read (Mitchell Beazley 1997)
Iberia – James A Michener (Fawcett Books 1983)
In The Glow of the Phantom Palace – Michael Jacobs (Pallas Athene 1999)
On the Shores of the Mediterranean – Eric Newby (Picador 1985)
South from Granada – Gerald Brenan (Penguin Books 1992)
Spain – Jan Morris (Penguin Books 1986)
Spanish Journeys: A Portrait of Spain – Adam Hopkins (Viking 1993)
Tapas & More Great Dishes from Spain – Janet Mendel (Santana Books 1997)
The Face of Spain – Gerald Brenan (Penguin Books 1987)
The Pillars of Hercules – Paul Theroux (Penguin Books 1996)
Wild Olives – William Graves (Pimlico 1996)

Tourism

The Andalucian Tourist Board publishes a wide range of tourist brochures and pamphlets in English on various aspects of tourism in Andalucia. Further details on these can be obtained from tourist offices or online at www.andalucia.org

Art & Literature

A Rose for Winter – Laurie Lee (Penguin Books 1971)
The Barber of Seville & The Marriage of Figaro – Beaumarchais, John Wood (Trans) (Penguin Books 1972)
Blood Wedding – Federico García Lorca, David Johnston (Trans) (Hodder & Stoughton Educational 1989)
"Carmen" and Other Stories – Prosper Merimée, Nicholas Jotcham (Trans) (Oxford Paperbacks 1998)
Flamenco: Gypsy Dance and Music from Andalusia – Claus Schreiner (Ed), Mollie Comerford Peters (Trans) (Amadeus Press 1990)
Gypsy Ballads – Federico García Lorca, RG Havard (Ed) (Aris & Phillips 1990)
Lorca: a Dream of Life – Leslie Stainton (Bloomsbury 1999)
Oh, Andalucia – R Vernon (Minerva Press 1997)
Picasso – Timothy Hilton (Thames & Hudson 1975)
Selected Poems as Trueblood – Antonio Machado (Harvard University Press 1988)
Sunny Morning – Serafín Álvarez Quintero, Joaquin Álvarez Quintero, William-Alan Landes (Ed), Lucretia Xavier Floyd (Trans) (Players Publishers 1996)
Tales of the Alhambra – Washington Irving (This book is currently out of print in the UK, but is generally available from local lending libraries and in bookshops in Granada)
The House of Bernarda Alba – Federico García Lorca, Rona Munro (Ed) (Nick Hern Books 1999)
The Houses and Palaces of Andalusia – Monteros, Venturi (Cartago 1998)
The Three-cornered Hat – Pedro Antonio de Alarcon, Alexander Tulloch (Ed) (Everyman Paperbacks 1995)
Selected Poems of Luis Cernuda – Luis Cernuda, Reginald Gibbons (Ed) (Sheep Meadow Press 2000)
Velázquez in Seville – David Davies (Ed), Enriqueta Harris (Ed) (Yale University Press 1996)

Admission times and charges

As admission times and charges are liable to alteration, the information below is given only as a general guideline.

The following list details the opening times and charges (if any) and other relevant information concerning all sights in the descriptive part of this guide accompanied by the symbol ◷. The entries below are given in the same order as in the alphabetical section of the guide.

The prices quoted apply to individual adults with no reduction. Special conditions for both times and charges are generally granted to groups if arranged beforehand.

Charges for admission are given in pesetas: pts.

Given the great wealth of Spanish painting and sculpture, museums are often re-arranging their exhibitions or undergoing restoration so it is always worthwhile to telephone ahead of time to confirm admission times.

Opening times for churches are only given if the interior is of special interest. As a general rule, avoid visiting a church during a service; however, some are only open at these times in which case you are expected to be as discreet as possible.

For information on public holidays see the Calendar of events. Details on local feast days and festivals may be obtained from Tourist Information Centres.

Although admission prices are given in pesetas (pts), visitors should be aware that in January 2002 the peseta will be replaced by the Euro, with 1€ equal to approximately 167pts. See conversion table below.

€	Pts	Pts	€
1	166.39	200	1.20
3	499.17	300	1.80
5	831.95	500	3.01
7	1 164.73	1 000	6.01
10	1 663.90	1 300	7.81
11	1 830.29	1 500	9.02
15	2 495.85	2 000	12.02
20	3 327.80	2 500	15.03

A

AGUILAR DE LA FRONTERA 🗓 Cuesta de Jesús, 2 – 14920 – ☏ 957 66 00 00

Parroquia de Nuestra Señora del Soterraño – Visits by prior appointment. ☏ 957 66 00 14.

Excursions

Laguna de Zoñar: Centro de Visitantes Zoñar – For visits, ☏ 957 33 52 52.

Puente Genil: Museo Arqueológico y Etnográfico – Open 10.30am-1.30pm. No charge. Closed Mon. ☏ 957 60 69 05.

ALCALÁ LA REAL 🗓 Paseo de los Álamos – Fortaleza de la Mota – 23680 – ☏ 953 58 22 17

Fortaleza de la Mota: Museo Arqueológico – Open in winter 10am-1.30pm and 3.30-6.30pm; in summer 10am-1.30pm and 5-7.30pm. Closed 1 Jan and 25 Dec. ☏ 953 58 22 17.

ALGECIRAS 🗓 Calle Juan de la Cierva – 11207 – ☏ 956 57 26 36

Museo Municipal – Open 10am-2pm and 5-8pm. ☏ 956 63 00 36.

Excursions

Gibraltar:

Gibraltar Museum – Open Mon-Fri 10am-6pm; Sat 10am-2pm. Closed Sun and public holidays. £2. ☏ 956 77 42 89.

Upper Rock – Open 9.30am-7pm. Entrance includes Moorish castle, Upper Rock Nature Reserve, Great Siege Tunnel, Apes' Den and St. Michael's Cave. £5 (£2.50 for children; 50 pence for vehicles. ☏ 956 77 49 50 or 956 74 50 00.

Cable-car – Open 9.30am-5.15pm (last descent at 4.15pm). £5.

ALHAMA DE GRANADA

Iglesia de la Encarnación – Open for worship in the afternoon. ☏ 958 35 00 60.

ALMERÍA
🅱 Parque de Nicolás Salmerón – 04002 – ☏ 950 27 43 55

Alcazaba – Open 9.30am-6.30pm; 16 June to 30 Sept 10am-2pm and 3-8pm. Closed 1 Jan and 25 Dec. 250pts. No charge for citizens of the European Union. ☏ 950 27 16 17.

Cathedral – Open 10am-5.30pm. Closed to tourists on Sun and public holidays. 300pts. ☏ 689 67 90 03.

Museo de Almería: Biblioteca Villaespesa – Open 9am-2pm. Closed Sat-Sun and public holidays. ☏ 950 23 50 10.

Museo de Almería: Archivo Histórico – Open 9am-2pm. Closed Sat-Sun and public holidays.

Excursion

Los Millares: Archeological site – Open 9am-2pm and 6-9pm; Fri and Sat 9am-2pm. Closed Sun and Mon. ☏ 608 95 70 65.

Castillo de ALMODÓVAR DEL RIO

Ring the bell; the guard will show you around the castle. For information, ☏ 957 71 36 02 (town hall).

ALMUÑÉCAR
🅱 Avenida Europa – Palacete La Najarra – 18690 – ☏ 956 63 11 25

Palacete de la Najarra: Tourist Office – Open 10am-2pm and 4-7pm in winter; 10am-2pm and 6-9pm in summer. ☏ 958 63 11 25.

Castillo de San Miguel – Open 10am-2pm and 4-7pm in winter; 10am-2pm and 6-9pm in summer. ☏ 607 86 54 66.

Cueva de los Siete Palacios: Museo Arqueológico – Open 10.30am-1.30pm and 4-6pm; Sun and public holidays 10.30am-2pm. 300pts. ☏ 958 83 86 05.

Excursions

Salobreña: Castle – Open 10.30am-1.45pm and 4-7pm; in summer 10am-noon and 3.30-10pm. ☏ 958 61 27 33 or 958 61 03 14.

Las ALPUJARRAS

Pampaneira: Centro de Visitantes – Open 10.30am-2pm and 4-7pm. ☏ 958 76 31 27.

Capileira: Museo Alpujarreño de Artes y Costumbres Populares – Open 11.30am-2.30pm; Sat 4-7pm (8pm in summer). Closed Mon. ☏ 958 76 30 51.

ANDÚJAR

Town Hall – Open 8am-3pm. Closed Sat-Sun and public holidays.

Palacio de los Niños de Don Gome – Open 7-9pm (mornings by prior appointment); Sat-Sun 11am-1pm. ☏ 953 50 05 30.

Excursions

Centro de Visitantes del Parque Natural Sierra de Andújar – Open Tues to Sun 10am -1pm and 6.30-9pm. Closed Mon. ☏ 953 50 02 79.

Santuario de la Virgen de la Cabeza – Museo – Sat 11am-1pm and 4-8pm; Sun 9am-2pm and 4-6pm; Mon to Sat visits by prior appointment only. ☏ 953 54 90 15.

ANTEQUERA
🅱 Plaza de San Sebastián, 7 – 29200 – ☏ 952 70 25 05

Alcazaba – Open 10am-2pm. Closed Mon.

Colegiata de Santa María – Open 10am-2pm. Closed Mon.

Iglesia del Carmen – Open 10am-2pm (from 11.30am Mon); Sat 10am-2pm and 4-7pm. 200pts. ☏ 952 70 25 05 or 609 53 97 10.

Museo Municipal – Guided tours (40min) 10am-1.30pm and 4-6pm; Sat-Sun 11am-1.30pm. Closed Mon and public holidays. 200pts. ☏ 952 70 40 21.

Convento de San José – Open Tues to Fri 10am-12.30pm and 4.30-6.30pm; Sat 10am-12.30pm; Sun 11am-12.30pm. Closed Mon. 300pts (museum). ☏ 952 84 19 77.

Iglesia de San Sebastián – Open for services at 9.30am and 7.30pm; Sun and public holidays 9.30am, 11am and 7pm.

Iglesia de San Agustín – Open 11am-1pm. Closed Mon.

Convento de Nuestra Señora de los Remedios – Closed for restoration.

Menga and Viera dolmens – Open 10am-2pm and 3-5.30pm; Tues 3-5.30pm; Sun and public holidays 10am-2pm. Closed Mon (the Dolmen de Viera is temporarily closed for restoration). ☏ 952 70 25 05.

Excursions

El Romeral dolmen – Open 9am-3.30pm; Sat 9am-3pm; Sun 9.30am-2pm. Closed Mon and Tues. ☎ 952 70 25 05.

Centro de Recepción "El Torcal" – Open 10am-2pm and 4-6pm. ☎ 952 03 13 89.

Archidona:

Ermita de la Virgen de Gracia – Open 10am-2pm and 4-8pm in winter; 10am-2pm and 5-10pm in summer.

Iberian pigs

Iglesia de Santa Ana – Visits by prior arrangement. ☎ 952 71 40 82.

Iglesia de las Escuelas Pías – Visits by prior arrangement. ☎ 952 71 40 82.

Punto de información del Parque de Ardales – Open 9am-10pm. ☎ 952 11 24 01.

Cueva de Doña Trinidad Grund – Visits by prior arrangement. ☎ 952 45 80 87.

ARACENA ⓘ Plaza de San Pedro – 21200 – ☎ 959 11 03 55

Gruta de las Maravillas – Guided tours (60min) 10.30am-1.30pm and 2.30pm-6pm. 875pts. ☎ 959 12 83 55.

Museo Geológico Minero – Open 10.30am-6pm. No charge. ☎ 959 12 83 55.

Castle – Open 9am-7pm.

Cabildo Viejo: Centro de Información – Open 10am-2pm and 4-6pm in winter; 10am-2pm and 6pm-7pm in summer. Closed Mon and Tues. ☎ 959 12 88 25.

Sierra de ARACENA AND PICOS DE AROCHE

Information Centres:

Castillo de Aroche – Visits by prior arrangement with the town hall. ☎ 959 14 02 01.

Castillo de Cortegana – Open 10am-2pm and 4.30-6.30pm. Closed Mon. 200pts. ☎ 959 13 16 56.

Town Hall (Almonaster) – Open 9.30am-6.30pm. ☎ 959 14 30 03.

Cabildo Viejo (Aracena) – *See ARACENA.*

Almonaster La Real: Mosque – Open 11am-7pm. No charge.

ARCOS DE LA FRONTERA ⓘ Cuesta de Belén – 11630 – ☎ 956 70 22 64
ⓘ Plaza de San Sebastián, 7 – 11630 – ☎ 952 70 25 05

Iglesia de Santa María de la Asunción – Open 10am-1pm and 3.30-6.30pm in winter; 10am-1pm and 4-5pm in summer; Sat all year around 10am-2pm. Closed Sun and public holidays in Jan, Feb and Dec. 150pts. ☎ 956 70 00 06.

Iglesia de San Pedro – Open 10am-1pm and 4-7pm.

La AXARQUÍA

Cueva del Tesoro or Cueva del Higuerón – Open 10am-2pm and 3-6pm in winter; 10am-2pm and 5-9pm in summer. 500pts. ☎ 952 40 77 50.

B

BAENA ⓘ Plaza de España, 9 – 14850 – ☎ 957 66 50 10

Iglesia del Convento Madre de Dios – Open for services at 1pm (7pm on Thur). ☎ 957 67 09 10.

Iglesia de Guadalupe – Open 8-10.15am, 11.30am-2pm and 5.30-8pm. Entrance via the sacristy. ☎ 957 67 09 44.

Antiguo Convento de San Francisco: Church – Open Mon, Tues and Thur 10am-1pm and 5-7.30pm. ☎ 957 67 01 42.

Excursions

Zuheros: **Museo Arqueológico and castle** – Visits Sat-Sun and public holidays from 16 Apr to 14 Sept at 12.30pm, 1.30pm, 2.30pm, 6.30pm, 7.30pm and 8.30pm; visits at 12.30pm, 1.30pm, 2.30pm, 4.30pm, 5.30pm and 6.30pm in winter. ☎ 957 69 45 14/ 45 (town hall).

Cueva de los Murciélagos – Visits from 16 Apr to 14 Sept at 11am, noon, 1pm, 6pm and 7pm; visits at 11am, noon, 1pm, 4pm, 5pm and 6pm in winter. ☎ 957 69 45 45 – 639 15 78 86.

BAEZA ⊞ Plaza del Pópulo – 23440 – ☎ 953 74 04 44

Cathedral – Open 10am-1pm and 4.15-6pm; 1 June to 30 Sept 10.30am-1pm and 5.15-7pm. No charge. ☎ 953 74 04 44.

Palacio de Jabalquinto – Open 10am-1pm and 4-6pm. Closed Mon.

Iglesia de Santa Cruz – Open 11am-1pm and 4-6pm; Sun and public holidays noon-2pm.

Former University – Open 10am-1pm and 4-6pm. Closed Mon.

Iglesia de San Andrés: Sacristy – Open for services at 7.30pm; Sun and public holidays at 11.30am. ☎ 953 74 04 44.

BAZA ⊞ Plaza Mayor – 18800 – ☎ 958 70 05 63

Museo Municipal – Open 9am-2pm and 5-8pm. No charge. ☎ 958 70 20 10 (Dept of Culture).

Moorish baths – Open daily. If closed, go to calle Caniles, 19 (Señor Mateo or Señora Manuela).

Excursion

Parque Natural de Sierra de Baza: Centro de Visitantes – Open 10am-2pm and 4-6pm. Closed Mon and Tues. ☎ 958 86 10 13.

BELALCÁZAR ⊞ Plaza de la Constitución, 11 (town hall) – 14280 – ☎ 957 14 60 04

Iglesia Parroquial de Santiago – Open at 6.30pm (7.30pm in summer); Eucharist at 7.30pm (9pm in summer); Sunday Eucharist at 11am.

Convento de Santa Clara – Visits by prior arrangement. ☎ 957 14 61 24.

Excursion

Hinojosa del Duque: Parroquia de San Juan Bautista – Closed for restoration. ☎ 957 14 05 74.

C

Parque Natural de CABO DE GATA-NÍJAR

Níjar: Iglesia Parroquial – Open 10am-8pm. ☎ 950 36 01 34.

Centro de Visitantes Amoladeras – Open 10am-2pm and 5-9pm in summer; 9.30am-3.30pm the rest of the year; Sat-Sun and some public holidays 10am-6pm. ☎ 950 16 04 35 or 950 38 02 99.

CABRA ⊞ Calle Santa Rosalía, 2 – 14940 – ☎ 957 52 01 10

Museo Arqueológico – Open 10.30am-1pm and 6.30-8pm; Sat-Sun and public holidays visits by prior arrangement. ☎ 957 52 01 10.

Excursions

Ermita de la Virgen de la Sierra – Open daily. ☎ 957 52 01 10 (Dept of Culture).

CÁDIZ ⊞ Calle Calderón de la Barca, 1 – 11003 – ☎ 956 21 13 13
⊞ Plaza de San Juan de Dios, 11 – 11005 – ☎ 956 24 10 01

Iglesia de Santa Cruz – Open for services at noon and 7pm (the church is normally open before Mass). ☎ 956 28 77 04.

Casa de la Contaduría: Museo Catedralicio – Closed for restoration. Reopening scheduled during 2000. ☎ 956 21 13 13 (Tourist Office).

Teatro Romano – Open 11am-1.30pm. Closed Mon and public holidays. ☎ 956 21 22 81.

Cathedral – Open 10am-1pm; closed Sun and public holidays. 100pts. Museum open 10am-12.30pm (until it is transferred to the Casa de la Contaduría); closed Sun and Mon. 500pts. ☎ 956 28 61 54.

Oratorio de la Santa Cueva – Closed for restoration. Reopening scheduled during 2000. ☎ 956 22 22 62.

Iglesia de San Francisco – Open for services at 11.30am and 7.30pm. ☎ 956 21 37 10.

CÁDIZ

Museo de Cádiz – Open 9am-8pm; Sun and public holidays 9.30am-2.30pm. Closed Mon, Tues 9am-2pm (except visits booked by prior arrangement) and public holidays. 250pts. No charge for citizens of the European Union. ☎ 956 21 22 81.

Oratorio de San Felipe Neri – Guided tours 10am-1.30pm. Closed Sun and public holidays. 150pts. ☎ 956 21 16 12.

Museo Iconográfico e Histórico – Open 9am-1pm and 4-7pm; 15 June to 15 Sept 9am-1pm and 5-8pm; Sat-Sun 9am-1pm. Closed Mon and public holidays. No charge. ☎ 956 22 17 88.

Hospital de Mujeres – Open 10am-1pm. Closed Sat-Sun and public holidays. 100pts. ☎ 956 22 36 47.

Torre Tavira – Open 10am-8pm (6pm 15 June to 15 Sept); last guided visit at 5.30pm. 500pts. ☎ 956 21 29 10.

Castillo de Santa Catalina – Open 10am-7pm; Sat 10am-2pm. Closed Sun and public holidays. No charge.

Excursions

San Fernando: Museo Histórico Municipal – Open 10am-2pm and 6-9pm. Closed Sat-Sun and public holidays. No charge. ☎ 956 89 37 02.

CARMONA

🛈 Plaza de las Descalzas – 41410 – ☎ 954 14 22 00 – 954 19 09 55
🛈 Arco de la Puerta de Sevilla – 41410 – ☎ 954 19 09 55

Iglesia de San Pedro – Open 7.30am-9pm; Sat-Sun and public holidays noon-2pm and 5-7pm (tower open on Sat-Sun and public holidays).

Convento de la Concepción – Open 10am-1pm and 6-7pm. Closed on Mon, Tues and Wed morning.

Town Hall – Open 8am-3pm. ☎ 954 19 09 55.

Iglesia del Salvador – Open 10am-2pm and 4.30-6.30pm. Closed Wed, Thur, 1 Jan and 25 Dec. 200pts.

Iglesia de Santa María la Mayor – Open 10am-2pm. Closed Sun and Mon. ☎ 954 14 08 11.

Convento de Santa Clara – Open Sat-Sun 10am-1pm.

Roman necropolis – Open 9am-5pm; 16 June to 16 Sept 8.30am-2pm; Sat-Sun 10am-2pm. Closed Mon and public holidays. 250pts. No charge for citizens of the European Union. ☎ 954 14 08 11.

La CAROLINA

Iglesia de la Inmaculada Concepción – Only open during services; if closed, contact the priest who lives next to the church.

CAZORLA

🛈 Calle Juan Domingo, 2 – 23470 – ☎ 953 72 05 15

Castillo de la Yedra – Open 9am-8pm (3-8pm Tues); Sun and public holidays 9am-3pm. Closed Mon. No charge.

Sierra de CAZORLA

🛈 Calle Juan Domingo, 2 – 23470 – ☎ 953 72 01 15

Cazorla: Information Point – Open 8am-2.30pm. Closed Sat-Sun and public holidays. ☎ 953 72 01 25.

Tíscar: Santuario de Tíscar – Open for services 11.30am-12.30pm. ☎ 953 71 36 06.

Quesada: Museum – Open 11am-2pm and 5-7pm. ☎ 953 73 38 24.

Torre del Vinagre: Centro de Interpretación – Open 11am-2pm and 5-8pm in winter; 11am-2pm and 4-6pm in summer. Closed Sat-Sun and Mon. No charge. ☎ 953 71 30 40 or 953 72 01 15.

Parque Cinegético de Collado del Almendral – For information, ☎ 953 71 01 20.

Mezquita, Córdoba

R. Mattès

CÓRDOBA ⓘ Calle Torrijos, 10 -
14003 – ☎ 957 47 12 35
ⓘ Plaza Judá Levi – 14003 –
☎ 957 20 05 22

Mosque-Cathedral – Open Jan
and Dec 10am-5pm; Feb and
Nov 10am-5.30pm; Mar and
July to Oct 10am-6.30pm; Apr
to June 10am-7pm; Sun and
public holidays 10am-2pm.
800pts (includes entrance to
the cathedral, mosque and
treasury). ☎ 957 47 05 12 or
957 47 56 13.

**Museo Diocesano de Bellas
Artes** – Open 9.30am-1.30pm
and 3.30-5.30pm (9.30am-
3pm June and July); Sat
9.30am-1.30pm. Closed Sun
and public holidays. 150pts (no
charge for those with tickets to
the mosque). ☎ 957 47 93 75.

**Torre de la Calahorra: Museo Vivo
de Al-Andalus** – Open 10am-6pm;
1 May to 30 Sept 10am-7.30pm.
500pts. ☎ 957 29 39 29.

**Alcázar de los Reyes Cris-
tianos** – Open 10am-2pm and
5.30-7.30pm; 1 May to 30
Sept 10am-2pm and 6-8pm;
Sun and public holidays all year

May Cross

B. Kaufmann/MICHELIN

round 9.30am-2.30pm. Closed Mon. 425pts. No charge Fri. ☎ 957 48 50 01.

Casa Andalusí – Same opening times as Torre de la Calahorra.

Synagogue – Open 10am-2pm and 3.30-5.30pm; Sun and public holidays 10am-
1.30pm. No charge. ☎ 957 20 29 28.

Museo Municipal Taurino – Open 15 Oct to 1 May 10am-2pm and 4.30-6.30pm;
2 May to 1 July 10am-2pm and 5.30-7.30pm; 2 July to 14 Oct 10am-2pm and 5.30-
7.30pm; Sun and public holidays all year round 9.30am-3pm. Closed Mon, 1 Jan, Good
Fri and 25 Dec. 450pts. No charge Fri. ☎ 957 20 10 56.

Posada del Potro – Open 9am-2pm and 5-8pm. Closed Sat-Sun and public holidays.
No charge. ☎ 957 48 50 01 (Dept of Culture).

Museo de Bellas Artes – Open 9am-8pm (Tues 3-8pm); Sun and public holidays 9am-
3pm. Closed Mon. 250pts. No charge for citizens of the European Union. ☎ 957 47 33 45.

Museo Julio Romero de Torres – Open 10am-2pm and 5.30-7.30pm; July and Aug
8.30am-3pm; Sun and public holidays 9.30am-2.30pm. Closed Mon. 450pts.
☎ 957 49 19 09.

Museo Arqueológico Provincial – Open 9am-8pm (Tues 3-8pm); Sun 9am-1pm.
250pts. No charge for citizens of the European Union. ☎ 957 47 40 11/ 76.

Iglesia de San Nicolás de la Villa – Open 10.30-11.30am, at 6.30pm, 7.30pm and
8.30pm; no visits during religious services. ☎ 957 47 68 32.

Iglesia de San Miguel – Open for services at 7am, noon and 7pm.

Palacio de Viana – Open 10am-1pm and 4-6pm; 16 June to 30 Sept 9am-noon. Closed
Sat afternoons, Sun, public holidays and 1 to 15 June. 500pts. ☎ 957 48 01 34.

Iglesia de San Lorenzo – Open 10am-1pm and 5.30-8.30pm. ☎ 957 48 34 79.

Iglesia de San Pablo – Open 9-9.30am, 10.30am-1pm, 5.30-6.30pm and 8.30-9pm;
no visits during religious services. ☎ 957 47 12 00.

Excursions

Medina Azahara – Open 1 May to 30 Sept 10am-2pm and 6-8.30pm; 1 Oct to 30
Apr 10am-2pm and 4-6.30pm; Sun and public holidays 10am-2pm. Closed Mon.
☎ 957 32 91 30.

Las Ermitas – Open 10am-1.30pm and 3-6pm; Apr to Sept 10am-1pm and 4.30-
5.45pm; Sun 9am-1.30pm and 4.30-7.45pm. Closed Mon. 320pts. ☎ 957 33 03 10.

COSTA DE HUELVA

Palos de la Frontera:

Casa-Museo de Martín Alonso Pinzón – Open 10am-1.30pm and 5-8pm. Closed Sat-Sun and public holidays. No charge. ☎ 959 35 01 99.

Iglesia de San Jorge – Visits by prior arrangement. ☎ 959 35 01 99 (Casa-museo).

COSTA DEL SOL

Benalmádena: Museo Arqueológico – Open 10am-2pm and 4-7pm in winter; 10am-2pm and 5-8pm in summer. Closed Sat-Sun and public holidays. No charge. ☎ 952 44 85 93.

Coín:

Iglesia de San Juan – Open 10am-1.30pm and 5-7pm. ☎ 952 45 32 11 (Tourist Office).

Iglesia de San Andrés – Open 7-8pm for services.

San Pedro de Alcántara: Las Bóvedas – Guided tours (1hr 30min) Thur and Sat at noon; visit also includes the Basílica de Vega del Mar. ☎ 952 78 13 60.

CUEVAS DE ALMANZORA

Museo Antonio Manuel Campoy – Open 10am-1.30pm and 5-8pm; Sun 10am-1.30pm; July to Sept 10am-1.30pm and 6-9pm. Closed Sun (July to Sept), Mon and public holidays. No charge. ☎ 950 45 80 63.

Museo de Arqueología – Same opening times as Museo Antonio Manuel Campoy. ☎ 950 45 80 63.

Excursions

Vera: Museo Histórico Municipal – Open 10am-2pm and 5-8pm. Closed Sat afternoons, Sun and public holidays. No charge. ☎ 950 39 31 42.

D

Parque Natural de DESPEÑAPERROS

For information on tours and itineraries, ☎ 953 12 50 18.

Parque Nacional de DOÑANA

Visitor Centres:
El Acebuche – Open 8am-7pm (9pm June to Sept). ☎ 959 44 87 11.
La Rocina – Open 9am-1pm and 4-7pm (9pm June to Sept). ☎ 959 44 23 40.
El Acebrón – Closed for restoration. ☎ 959 44 23 40.
José Antonio Valverde – Open 10am-6.30pm (8.30pm June to Sept). ☎ 959 44 87 39.

E

ÉCIJA
🛈 Avenida Andalucía – 41400 – ☎ 955 83 30 62
🛈 Calle Cánovas del Castillo (Palacio de Benamejí), 4 – 41400 – ☎ 955 90 29 33

Iglesia de Santiago – Open 11am-1pm and 6-7pm. ☎ 955 90 29 33.

Iglesia de Santa María – Open 9.30am-12.30pm and 5.30-8pm. ☎ 955 83 04 30.

Iglesia de la Concepción – Open 10am-1pm.

Iglesia de los Descalzos – Currently closed for restoration.

Iglesia de Santa Cruz – Open 10am-1pm and 5-7pm.

Palacio de Benamejí – Open 9.30am-1pm and 4.30-6.30pm; June to Sept 9am-2pm; Sat-Sun and public holidays 9am-2pm. Closed Mon.

ESTEPONA
🛈 Paseo Marítimo P. Domínguez – 29680 – ☎ 952 80 09 13

Iglesia de Nuestra Señora de los Remedios – Open for services at 8pm (8.30pm in summer); Sun and public holidays at 11am, noon and 8pm.

F

FUENTE OBEJUNA
🄸 Calle Luís Rodríguez, 27 – 14290 – ☎ 957 58 49 00

Iglesia de Nuestra Señora del Castillo – Open 10am-1pm; if closed, ☎ 957 58 41 63.

Excursions

Bélmez: Museo Histórico de Bélmez y Territorio Minero – Open 10am-2pm. Closed Sat-Sun and public holidays. ☎ 957 36 90 42.

Obejo: Iglesia Parroquial de San Antonio Abad – If closed, the person living opposite the church will show you around. ☎ 957 36 71 76.

G

GÉRGAL

Excursion

Astronomical Observatory – Visits on Wed by prior arrangement. ☎ 950 23 09 88 – 950 22 55 66.

GRANADA
🄸 Calle Mariana Pineda – 18009 – ☎ 958 22 59 90 – 958 22 66 88

Alhambra and Generalife – Open 1 Mar to 31 Oct 8.30am-8pm (and 10-11.30pm Tues to Sat); 1 Nov to 28 Feb 8.30am-6pm; ticket office closes 1hr 15min before last visit. 1 000pts (1 125pts if tickets bought in advance from branches of the BBV bank anywhere in Spain). The same ticket covers all parts of the Alhambra and Generalife gardens. ☎ 958 22 75 25. Theme visits on Fri for small groups if booked by the preceding Mon. For information and bookings, ☎ 958 22 09 12.

Cathedral – Open 10.30am-1.30pm and 3.30-6.30pm; Sun 3.30-6.30pm; 1 Apr to 30 Sept 10.30am-1.30pm and 4-7pm; Sun 4-7pm. 300pts. ☎ 958 22 29 59.

Chapel Royal – Open 10.30am-1pm and 3.30-6.30pm; Sun and public holidays 11am-1pm and 3.30-6.30pm; 1 May to 30 Sept 10.30am-1pm and 4-7pm. Closed 2 Jan (morning), Good Fri and 12 Oct (morning). 250pts. No charge on Sun morning. ☎ 958 22 78 48.

Iglesia del Sagrario – Open for services at 9am and 9.30am; Sun and public holidays at 10am, noon and 1pm.

Moorish baths – Open 9am-2pm and 5-7pm; Sat 9am-2pm. Closed Sun, Mon and public holidays. ☎ 958 22 23 39.

Museo Arqueológico – Open 9am-8pm (Tues 3-8pm); Sun 9am-2.30pm. Closed Mon and public holidays. 250pts. No charge for citizens of the European Union. ☎ 958 22 56 40.

Casa del Chapiz – Open 8am-8pm. Closed Sat-Sun and public holidays. ☎ 958 22 22 90 or 958 22 47 54 (Dept of Culture).

Monasterio de San Jerónimo – Open 10am-1.30pm and 3-4.30pm; 1 Apr to 30 Sept 10am-1.30pm and 4-7.30pm. 250pts. ☎ 958 27 93 37.

La Cartuja – Open 10am-1pm and 3.30-6pm (4-8pm in summer); Sun and public holidays 10am-noon and 3.30-6pm (4-8pm in summer). 250pts. No charge Sun. ☎ 958 16 19 32 (10am-noon).

La Cartuja: Sacrarium

B. Kaufmann/MICHELIN

GRANADA

Casa-Museo Manuel de Falla – Open 10.15am-2.45pm. Closed Mon and public holidays.

Carmen de los Mártires – Open Mon to Fri 10am-2pm and 4-6pm in winter; 11am-2pm and 5-7pm in summer. Sat-Sun 10am-6pm. Closed on public holidays. No charge. ☎ 958 22 79 53.

Parque de las Ciencias – Open 10am-7pm; Sun and public holidays 10am-3pm. Closed Mon, 1 Jan, 1 May and 24 and 25 Dec. 400pts (250pts for the planetarium). ☎ 958 13 19 00.

Huerta de San Vicente – Open 10am-1pm and 4-7pm. Closed Mon.

GUADIX
🚩 Avenida Mariana Pineda – 18500 – ☎ 958 66 26 65

Cathedral – Open 9am-1pm and 4-6pm; 1 June to 30 Sept 11am-1pm and 5-7pm. Closed to visitors on Sun and public holidays. ☎ 958 66 08 00.

Alcazaba – Open 9am-2pm and 4-7pm; Sat 9am-2pm. Closed Sun and public holidays. 100pts. ☎ 958 66 01 60.

Iglesia de Santiago – Open for services at noon and 7pm. ☎ 958 66 08 00.

Cueva-Museo – Open 9am-2pm and 4-7pm; Sat-Sun 10am-2pm. Closed Sun and public holidays.

Museo de Alfarería – Open 10am-2pm and 5-8.30pm; Sun 11am-2pm. ☎ 958 66 47 67.

Excursions

La Calahorra: Castle – Open Wed 10am-1pm and 4-6pm. ☎ 958 67 70 98.

H

HUELVA
🚩 Avenida de Alemania, 12 – 21001 – ☎ 959 25 74 03
🚩 Avenida de Italia – 21001 – ☎ 959 24 56 16

Cathedral – Open for services at 7pm; Sun at 11am and 7pm. ☎ 959 24 30 36.

Santuario de Nuestra Señora de la Cinta – Open 9am-7.30pm (8.30pm in summer). ☎ 959 25 11 22.

Museo Provincial – Open 9am-8pm; Sun 9am-3pm. Closed Mon. No charge. ☎ 959 25 93 00.

Excursions

Paraje Natural de las Marismas del Odiel: Canoe excursions – Open 10am-2pm and 6-8pm (reception office). Closed Sat-Sun and public holidays. Advanced booking necessary. ☎ 959 28 06 36.

HUÉSCAR
🚩 Calle Mayor – 18830 – ☎ 958 74 00 11/ 73

Excursions

Galera: Argar settlement – Open Sat-Sun and public holidays 10.30am-1pm and 4-6pm; at other times by prior arrangement. ☎ 958 73 92 73.

Orce: Museo de Prehistoria y Paleontología José Gibert – Open 11am-2pm and 4-6pm; 1 June to 30 Sept 11am-1pm and 6-8pm. Closed Mon. 200pts. ☎ 958 74 61 71 (Tourist Office).

Castril: Visitor Centre (Parque Natural de la Sierra de Castril) – Open in winter Thur, Fri, Sat-Sun and public holidays 9am-2pm and 4-6pm; in summer 9am-2pm and 6-8pm; at other times by prior arrangement. ☎ 958 34 44 51 – 607 39 19 23.

I – J

IZNÁJAR
🚩 Calle Julio Burell – 14970 – ☎ 957 53 40 33

Museo Etnográfico – Visits by prior arrangement. ☎ 957 53 40 02 – 957 53 40 33.

JAÉN
🚩 Calle Arquitecto Bergés, 1 – 23007 – ☎ 953 22 27 37

Cathedral – Open 8.30am-1pm and 4.30-7pm in winter; 8.30am-1pm and 5-8pm in summer. Closed Sun afternoons in summer. ☎ 953 23 42 33.

Museum – Same opening times as the Cathedral. 200pts. ☎ 953 23 42 33.

Iglesia de San Ildelfonso – Open 8.30am-noon and 6-8.30pm. ☎ 953 19 03 46.

Casa de la Virgen – Closed for restoration.

Convento de las Bernardas – Open 8.30am-1pm and 4.30-8.30pm. ☎ 953 24 38 54.

Museo Provincial – Open 10am-2pm and 4-7.30pm; Sat-Sun 10am-2pm; 1 June to 15 Sept 9am-2pm; Sun 10am-2pm. Closed Mon and public holidays. 250pts. No charge for citizens of the European Union. ☎ 953 25 06 00.

Capilla de San Andrés – Open for services on Sun mornings; on other days by prior arrangement. ☎ 953 23 74 22.

Palacio de Villardompardo – Open 9am-8pm; Sat-Sun 9.30am-2.30pm; last visit 30min before closing time. Closed Mon and public holidays. No charge. ☎ 953 23 62 92.

Olive groves

B. Kaufmann/MICHELIN

Real Monasterio de Santo Domingo – Open 8.30am-2.30pm (1.30pm in summer). ☎ 953 23 85 00.

Monasterio de Santa Úrsula – Open 8-9am. ☎ 953 19 01 15.

Castillo de Santa Catalina – Open 10am-2pm in winter; 10.30am-1.30pm in winter. Closed Wed and Fri. No charge.

Excursions

Parque Natural Sierra Mágina: **Centro de Interpretación de Jodar** – For information, ☎ 953 78 76 56

JEREZ DE LA FRONTERA   🛈 Calle Larga, 39 – 11403 – ☎ 956 33 11 50

Museo Arqueológico de Jerez – Open 10am-2pm and 4-7pm; 10am-2.30pm 15 June to 30 Sept; Sat-Sun and public holidays all year round 10am-2.30pm. Closed Mon, 1 and 6 Jan, Good Fri and 25 Dec. 250pts (no charge on first Sun of the month and on 9 Nov. ☎ 956 34 13 50.

Cathedral – Open 6-8pm; Sat-Sun and public holidays 11am-2pm. ☎ 956 34 84 82.

Alcázar – Open 16 Sept to 30 Apr 10am-6pm; 1 May to 15 Sept 10am-8pm; last visit 30min before closing time. Closed 1 Jan and 25 Dec. 200pts. ☎ 956 33 73 06.

Camera Obscura – Same opening times as the Alcázar. 500pts.

Sherry bodegas:

Pedro Domecq – Visits by prior arrangement. 500pts on weekday mornings; 750pts on weekday afternoons, Sat-Sun and public holidays. ☎ 956 15 15 00.

González Byass – Visits at 10am, 11am, noon, 1pm, 5pm, 6pm and 7pm; Sat-Sun and public holidays at 10am, 11am, noon and 1pm. 900pts (1 000pts on Sat-Sun and public holidays). ☎ 956 35 70 16/35 70 00.

Williams & Humbert – Visits from 10am-2pm; Sat-Sun and public holidays by prior arrangement. 375pts. ☎ 956 34 65 39.

Sandeman *(bodega indicated on plan, p 217)* – Visits by prior arrangement 10am-4pm (5pm May to Nov); Sat 10am-2pm. ☎ 956 30 11 00 or 956 31 29 95.

Museo de Relojes – Open 10am-2pm. Closed Sat (in Aug) and Sun. 400pts. ☎ 956 18 21 00.

Zoo-Botanical Garden – Open 10am-6pm. Closed Mon. 200pts. ☎ 956 18 23 97 or 956 18 42 07.

Real Escuela Andaluza del Arte Ecuestre – Guided tours including visit of facilities and training sessions 11am-1pm. Horse show on Thur at noon (additional show on Tues in winter). Closed Sat-Sun and public holidays. 600pts; horse show: 1 500pts or 2 500pts. ☎ 956 31 95 35 or 956 31 11 11.

JEREZ DE LA FRONTERA

Excursions

La Cartuja – Temporarily closed for restoration. ☎ 956 15 64 65.

La Cartuja Stud Farm – Visits (1hr 30min–2hr) Sat at 11am. 1 500pts (800pts for children). ☎ 956 16 28 09.

JIMENA DE LA FRONTERA

Centro de Información del Parque Natural de los Alcornocales – Open 10am-5pm; Sat-Sun and public holidays 11am-3pm and 4-6pm. ☎ 956 64 05 69.

L

LEBRIJA
🛈 Calle Tetuán, 15 – 41740 – ☎ 955 97 40 68

Iglesia de Santa María de la Oliva – Open 10am-2pm and 6-9pm. ☎ 955 97 23 35.

Iglesia de Santa María del Castillo – Closed for restoration.

Capilla de la Vera Cruz – Visits by prior arrangement. ☎ 955 97 40 68 (Tourist Office).

LINARES

Museo Arqueológico – Open noon-1.30pm (2pm Sun). ☎ 953 54 40 04.

LOJA
🛈 Calle Duque de Valencia, 1 – 18300 – ☎ 958 32 39 49

Alcazaba – Closed for restoration. ☎ 958 32 39 49 (Tourist Office).

LUCENA
🛈 Calle Castillo del Moral – 14900 – ☎ 957 51 32 82

Iglesia de San Mateo – Open 9am-1pm and 7-8.30pm. ☎ 957 51 32 82 (Tourist Office).

Iglesia de Santiago – Open 7-8.30pm. ☎ 957 51 32 82.

M

MÁLAGA
🛈 Pasaje de Chinitas, 4 – 29015 – ☎ 952 21 34 45
🛈 Avenida Cervantes, 1 – 29015 – ☎ 952 60 44 10

Alcazaba – Open 8.30am-7pm. Closed Tues. ☎ 952 221 60 05.

Museo Arqueológico – Closed for restoration. ☎ 952 21 60 05 or 952 22 04 43.

Cathedral – Open 10am-12.45pm and 4-6.45pm. Closed Sun, 1 Jan and 25 Dec. ☎ 952 21 59 17.

El Sagrario – Open 9.30am-12.30pm and 6-7.30pm. ☎ 952 21 34 45 (Tourist Office).

B. Kaufmann/MICHELIN

Iglesia de Santiago – Open 9am-1.30pm and 6-8pm.

Museo-Casa Natal Picasso – Open 11am-2pm and 5-8pm in winter; 11am-2pm in summer. Closed Sat-Sun and public holidays. No charge. ☎ 952 21 50 05.

Iglesia de los Mártires – Open 8am-1.15pm and 7-8pm (for services); on public holidays, services at 9am, 1pm and 8pm.

Museo de Artes y Costumbres Populares – Open 15 June to 30 Sept 10am-1.30pm and 5-8pm; rest of the year 10am-1.30pm and 4-7pm; Sat all year round 10am-1.30pm. Closed Sun. ☎ 952 21 71 37.

Santuario de la Virgen de la Victoria – Open 8am-1pm and 4-8pm. Closed Mon.
☎ 952 25 26 47.

Excursions

Finca de la Concepción – Open 1 Apr to 20 June 10am-6.30pm; 21 June to 10 Sept 10am-7.30pm; 11 Sept to 20 Oct 10am-5.30pm; 21 Oct to 10 Dec 10am-4.30m; 11 Dec to 31 Mar 10am-4pm. Closed Mon. 435pts. ☎ 952 25 21 48/07 45.

El Retiro – Open Nov to Mar 9am-6pm (7pm in Apr, May, Sept and Oct; 8pm in June, July and Aug). 1 250pts. ☎ 952 62 16 00.

MARBELLA
🔖 Glorieta de la Fontanilla – 29600 – ☎ 952 77 14 42
🔖 Plaza de los Naranjos – 29600 – ☎ 952 82 35 50

Iglesia de Santa María de la Encarnación – Open 8.30am-2.30pm and 7-9pm.
☎ 952 77 31 36.

Museo del Grabado Español Contemporáneo – In winter open 11am-2pm and 5.30-8.30pm; Sun and Mon 11am-2pm; in summer 11am-2pm and 6-9pm; closed Sat-Sun and public holidays. 300pts. ☎ 952 82 50 35.

Excursions inland

Tolox: Iglesia de San Miguel – Open 11am-8pm.

MARCHENA
🔖 Calle San Francisco, 43 – 41620 – ☎ 955 84 61 67

Iglesia de San Juan Bautista: Museo de Zurbarán – Open 3-9pm. 200pts (museum).
☎ 954 84 32 57.

Excursions

Paradas: Museum (Iglesia de San Eutropio) – Visits by prior arrangement. ☎ 954 84 90 39.

MARTOS

Iglesia de Santa Marta – Open 10am-12.30pm and 6-7.30pm.

MEDINA SIDONIA
🔖 Plazuela de la Iglesia Mayor – 11170 – ☎ 956 41 00 05

Roman remains – Open Oct to May 10am-1.30pm and 4.30-7pm; June to Sept 10am-1.30pm and 5.30-8pm. Closed Mon.

Iglesia Santa María Mayor, la Coronada – Guided tours (30min) 10.30am-2.30pm and 3.30-8pm (9pm June to Sept). 250pts. ☎ 956 41 03 29.

Alcázar – Open Oct to May 11.30am-1.30pm and 4.30-6.30pm; June to Sept 11.30am-1.30pm and 5.30-7.30pm.

Excursions

Ermita de los Santos Mártires Justo y Pastor – Visits by prior arrangement.
☎ 956 41 24 04.

Alcalá de los Gazules: Centro de Interpretación del Parque Natural de los Alcornocales – Open 8am-3pm. ☎ 956 42 02 77.

Benalup: Cueva del Tajo de las Figuras – Open 10.30am-2pm and 3-6.30pm; Tues 3-5.30pm; Sun 10.30am-1pm. Closed Mon and public holidays. ☎ 956 42 41 29 (town hall).

MIJAS

Santuario de la Virgen de la Peña – Open 9am-6pm. ☎ 952 48 50 22.

Museo de Miniaturas – Open 10am-7pm (10pm in summer). 400pts. ☎ 952 48 95 00.

Town Hall: Museum – Open 9am-3pm. ☎ 952 48 59 00.

Bullfighting Museum – Open 10am-5.30pm (10pm in summer). 500pts (museum and bullring); 250pts (museum). ☎ 952 48 55 48.

MINAS DE RIOTINTO

Parque Minero de Riotinto – Open 10am-3pm; Sat-Sun and public holidays 10am-6pm. 1 300pts (includes visit to museum, Corta Atalaya and railway). ☎ 959 59 00 25.

Museo Minero y Ferroviario – *See Parque Minero de Riotinto.*

Corta Atalaya – *See Parque Minero de Riotinto.*

Tourist train – *See Parque Minero de Riotinto.*

Necrópolis de la Dehesa – Visits by prior arrangement. ☎ 959 59 00 25.

Riotinto

MOGUER

Monasterio de Santa Clara – Open 10am-1pm and 4-7pm. Closed Sun, Mon and public holidays. 250pts. ☏ 959 37 01 07.

Archivo Histórico Municipal y Biblioteca Iberoamericana – Open 9am-3pm. ☏ 959 37 21 93/ 4.

Convento de San Francisco – Visit to the cloisters only by prior arrangement. ☏ 959 37 27 13.

Casa-Museo "Zenobia y Juan Ramón" – Open 10.15am-1.15pm and 5.15-7.15pm; Sun and public holidays 10.15am-1.15pm. 250pts. ☏ 959 37 21 48.

Casa Natal de Juan Ramón Jiménez – Visits by prior arrangement. ☏ 959 37 24 77 (Tourist Office).

MONTEFRÍO

Iglesia de la Villa – Open 10am-2pm and 4-6pm. ☏ 958 33 60 04 (Tourist Office).

MONTILLA

Museo Histórico Local – Open Sat-Sun and public holidays 10.30am-1.30pm; at other times by prior arrangement. ☏ 957 65 24 62 or 957 65 59 81.

Casa-Museo del Inca Garcilaso – Open 10am-2pm. Closed Sat-Sun and public holidays (except by prior arrangement with the Tourist Office). ☏ 957 62 23 54.

Excursions

Santaella: Museo de Arqueología Local – Open Sat 5-7.30pm; Sun and public holidays 11am-1pm.

MONTORO

Iglesia de San Bartolomé – Open 11am-2pm and 5-8pm.

Museo Arqueológico Local – Open Sat-Sun and public holidays 11am-1pm; at other times by prior arrangement. ☏ 957 16 00 89.

N

NERJA

🚩 Calle Carmen, 1 – 29780 – ☏ 952 52 00 90

Excursion

Cueva de Nerja – Open 10.30am-2pm and 4-6.30pm (8pm July and Aug). 650pts. ☏ 952 52 95 20.

OSUNA

🛈 Calle Sevilla, 22 – 41013 – ☎ 954 81 22 11

Colegiata – Guided tours (45min) 1 Oct to 30 Apr 10am-1.30pm and 3.30-6.30pm; 1 May to 30 Sept 10am-1.30pm and 4-7pm. Closed Mon, 1 and 6 (afternoon) Jan, Maundy Thur, Good Fri and 24 (afternoon), 25 and 31 (afternoon) Dec. 300pts. ☎ 954 81 04 44.

Monasterio de la Encarnación – Open 10am-1.30pm and 3.30-6.30pm in winter; 9am-1.30pm and 4.30-7.30pm in summer. Closed Mon. ☎ 954 81 11 21.

Torre del Agua: Museo Arqueológico – Open 10am-1.30pm and 3.30-6.30pm in winter; 10am-1.30pm and 4.30-7.30pm in summer. ☎ 954 81 04 44/81 12 07.

P

PALMA DEL RÍO

🛈 Plaza de Judá Levi – 14700 – ☎ 957 20 05 22
🛈 Calle Cardenal Portocarrero – 14700 – ☎ 957 54 43 70

Museo Municipal – Open 4-7pm; Sun 10am-2pm. No charge.

Iglesia de la Asunción – Open 5-8pm in winter; 10am-2pm in summer; Sun and public holidays 11am-2pm (all year). ☎ 957 64 43 70.

Excursion

Centro de Visitantes Huerta del Rey – Open 10am-2pm and 4-7pm. Closed Mon. ☎ 957 33 82 33.

PRIEGO DE CÓRDOBA

🛈 Calle Real, 46 – 14800 – ☎ 957 59 44 27
🛈 Calle Río, 3 – 14800 – ☎ 957 70 06 25

Hospital-Iglesia de San Juan de Dios – Open 9am-9pm.

Parroquia de la Asunción – Visits by prior arrangement 11am-1.30pm and 7.30-9.30pm. ☎ 957 54 07 13 (Señor José Mateo Aguilera).

Iglesia de San Pedro – Open 10am-1pm.

Carnicerías Reales – Open 1-2pm and 7-10pm.

Iglesia de las Angustias – Open 10am-1pm.

Museo Histórico Municipal – Open 10am-2pm and 6-8pm; Sat-Sun 11am-2pm. ☎ 957 54 09 47.

Iglesia de la Aurora – Open 10am-1pm.

PUEBLOS BLANCOS DE ANDALUCIA

El Bosque: Centro de Visitantes del Parque Natural Sierra de Grazalema – Open 9am-2pm; Fri, Sat-Sun and public holidays 9am-2pm and 4-6pm. ☎ 956 71 60 63.

Ubrique: Roman settlement of Ocurri – Temporarily closed for restoration. ☎ 956 73 11 85.

Benaocaz: Museo Municipal – Open Sat-Sun and public holidays 11am-1.30pm and 6-8.30pm. No charge. ☎ 956 12 55 00.

Grazalema: Hand looms – Open 8am-2pm and 3-6.30pm; Fri 8am-2pm (shop also open in the afternoon). Closed Sat-Sun and public holidays. ☎ 956 13 20 08.

Setenil: Tourist Office – Open 10.30am-2pm and 4-7pm; Sun and public holidays 10.30am-7pm. Closed Mon. ☎ 956 13 42 61.

Olvera: Castle – Open 10am-2pm and 4-7pm (9pm in summer); Sat-Sun and public holidays 10am-5pm. 100pts. ☎ 956 12 08 16 (Tourist Office).

Villamartín:

Museo Municipal – Open 10am-2pm and 4-6pm in winter; 10am-2pm and 6-9pm in summer. Closed Mon and Tues. 120pts.

Alberite dolmen – For information, ☎ 956 36 61 10.

Bornos: Castillo-Palacio de los Ribera – Open in winter 10am-2pm and 4-7pm; Sat 10am-1pm; in summer 10am-2pm and 3-8pm; Sat-Sun and public holidays 10am-1pm. ☎ 956 72 82 74.

EL PUERTO DE SANTA MARÍA

B Calle Guadalete, 1 – 11500 –
☎ 956 54 24 75/ 13

El Vaporcito del Puerto – Departures from 15 Sept to 30 Nov and 1 Feb to 31 May at 9am, 11am, 1pm and 3.30pm; 1 June to 14 Sept at 9am, 11am, 1pm, 3.30pm and 7.30pm (evening departure at 9.45pm); additional service at 5.30pm on Sun and public holidays. Services depart from Plaza de las Galeras Reales. ☎ 956 54 24 13.

Iglesia Mayor Prioral – Open 10am-noon and 7-8.30pm.

Museo Municipal – Open 10am-2pm. Closed Sun and public holidays. ☎ 956 54 27 05/54 27 75.

Fundación Rafael Alberti – Open 10.30am-2.30pm. Closed Sat-Sun and public holidays. 300pts. ☎ 956 85 07 11.

Castillo de San Marcos – Open Sat 11am-1.30pm; visits on other days by prior arrangement. ☎ 956 85 17 51 (Bodegas Caballero).

Bullring – Open 11am-1.30pm and 6-7.30pm. Closed Mon, public holidays and day after bullfights. No charge.

R

La RÁBIDA

Centro de Información y Recepción "La Casita de Zenobia" – Open 10am-2pm and 5-9pm; Sat-Sun and public holidays 10am-8pm; Sept to Apr 10am-7pm. Closed Mon. ☎ 959 53 11 37.

Monasterio de Santa María de la Rábida – Open 10am-1pm and 4-6.15pm in winter; 10am-1pm and 4.45-8pm in summer. ☎ 959 35 04 11.

Muelle de las Carabelas – Open 10am-2pm and 5-9pm (Sept to Apr 10am-7pm); Sat-Sun and public holidays 10am-8pm. Closed Mon. ☎ 959 53 05 97/53 03 12.

El ROCÍO

Niebla: Tourist Office – Visits from 9.30am-2pm and 4-6pm. ☎ 959 36 22 70.

RONDA

B Plaza de España, 1 – 29400 – ☎ 952 87 12 72
B Palacio de Mondragón – Plaza de Mondragón – 29400 – ☎ 952 87 08 18

Casa del Rey Moro: Jardines de Forestier – Open 10am-6pm. 500pts.

Moorish Baths – Open 9am-2pm and 4-6pm; Apr to Sept 8.30am-1.30pm and 4-7pm); Sun 10.30am-1pm. Closed Mon. ☎ 952 87 38 89.

Museo del Bandolero – Open 10am-8pm (9pm in summer). 300pts. ☎ 952 87 77 85.

Santa María la Mayor – Open 10am-7pm (8pm in summer; 9pm in Aug and during local festival in Sept). 200pts. ☎ 952 87 22 46.

Palacio de Mondragón: Museo de la Ciudad – Open 10am-7pm (6pm Nov to Mar); Sat-Sun and public holidays 10am-3pm. 250pts. ☎ 952 87 84 50.

Museo Lara – Open 10am-8pm. 500pts. ☎ 952 87 12 63.

Bullring: Museo Taurino – Open 10am-6pm in winter (7pm in spring and autumn; 8pm in summer). 400pts. ☎ 952 87 41 32.

Excursions

Iglesia Rupestre de la Virgen de la Cabeza – Open 10am-6pm (7pm in spring and summer); Sat-Sun and public holidays 10am-3pm. 200pts. ☎ 649 36 57 72.

Ruinas de Acinipo – Open 10am-6pm (Apr to Sept 11am-7pm); Fri, Sat-Sun 9am-7pm; public holidays 10am-2.30pm. No charge.

Cueva de la Pileta – Guided tours (1hr) 10am-1pm and 4-6pm. 800pts. Reduced entrance for groups booked by prior arrangement. ☎ 952 16 73 43.

S

SANLÚCAR DE BARRAMEDA **B** Calzada del Ejército – 11540 – ☎ 956 36 61 10

Iglesia de la Trinidad – Open 10am-1.30pm. Closed to visitors on Sun.

Palacio de Orleans y Borbón – Open 10am-2pm; Sat-Sun and public holidays by prior arrangement. ☎ 956 38 80 00.

Parroquia de Nuestra Señora de la O – Open at 7.30pm for mass; Sun at 9am, noon and 7.30pm.

Palacio de los Condes de Niebla – Visits Sun and Mon by prior arrangement. ☎ 956 36 01 61.

Iglesia de Santo Domingo – Open 10am-noon and 3.30-8pm. Closed to visitors during services. ☎ 956 36 04 91.

Centro de Visitantes Bajo de Guía – Open 9am-3pm. ☎ 956 36 07 15.

Centro de Visitantes Fábrica de Hielo – Open 9am-8pm. ☎ 956 38 16 35.

Excursions

Chipiona: Santuario de Nuestra Señora de la Regla – Open 8am-noon and 5-6.30pm. Closed to visitors Sat-Sun.

SEVILLA

🛈 Avenida Constitución, 21 – 41004 – ☎ 954 22 14 04
🛈 Paseo de las Delicias, 9 – 41012 – ☎ 954 23 44 65

Giralda and Cathedral – Open Wed-Sat 11am-5pm; Sun 2-6pm. Closed 1 and 6 Jan, 30 May, Corpus Christi, 15 Aug, 8 and 25 Dec. Restricted opening times on Tues, Maundy Thur and Good Fri. 700pts; no charge on Sun. ☎ 954 56 33 21.

Archivo General de Indias – Open 10am-1pm (8am-3pm for research purposes). Closed Sat-Sun and public holidays. No charge. ☎ 954 21 12 34.

Real Alcázar – Open 1 Oct to 31 Mar 9.30am-6pm; Sun and public holidays 9.30am-2.30pm; 1 Apr to 30 Sept 9.30am-8pm; last entrance 1hr before closing time. Closed Mon, 1 and 6 Jan, Good Fri, 25 Dec and for official ceremonies. 600pts (Cuarto Real Alto: 400pts). ☎ 954 22 71 63.

Hospital de los Venerables – Guided tours (20min) 10am-2pm and 4-8pm. Closed 1 Jan, Good Fri and 25 Dec. 600pts. ☎ 954 56 26 96.

Museo Arqueológico de Sevilla – Open Tues 2.30-8pm; Wed to Sat 9am-8pm; Sun 9am-2.30pm. Closed Mon and public holidays. 250pts. No charge for citizens of the European Union. ☎ 954 23 24 01.

Museo de las Artes y Costumbres Populares – Open 9am-8pm; Sun and public holidays 9am-2.30pm; Tues 3-8pm. Closed Mon. 250pts. No charge for citizens of the European Union. ☎ 954 23 25 76/55 40.

Museo de la Marina – Open 10am-2pm; Sat-Sun and public holidays 11am-2pm. Closed in Aug and 1 and 6 Jan. 100pts. No charge on Tues for citizens of the European Union. ☎ 954 22 24 19.

Hospital de la Caridad – Open 9am-1.30pm and 3.30-6.30pm; Sun and public holidays 9am-1pm. 400pts. ☎ 954 22 32 32.

La Maestranza – Open 9.30am-2pm and 3-6pm. 400pts. ☎ 954 22 45 77.

Barrio de Santa Cruz

Capilla del Patrocinio – Open 10.30am-1.30pm and 6-9pm; Sun 10.30am-1.30pm. ☎ 954 33 33 41.

Basílica de la Macarena – Open 9.30am-1pm and 5-8pm (basilica closes at 9pm). Closed during and for two weeks prior to Holy Week in preparation for processions. 300pts (museum). ☎ 954 37 01 95.

SEVILLA

Iglesia de San Luis de los Franceses – Open 9am-2pm; Fri and Sat 9am-2pm and 5-8pm. ☎ 954 55 02 07.

Convento de Santa Paula – Open 10.30am-12.30pm and 3.30-6.30pm. Closed Mon and public holidays for certain religious ceremonies. ☎ 954 53 63 30.

Capilla de San José – Open 7-9pm; Sun 11am-noon. ☎ 954 22 31 42/ 32 42.

Palacio de la Condesa de Lebrija – Open 11am-1pm and 5-8pm; Sat 10am-1pm. 500pts. ☎ 954 21 81 83.

Iglesia del Salvador – Open 9-10am and 6.30-9pm. ☎ 954 21 16 79.

Templo de Nuestro Padre Jesús del Gran Poder – Open 8am-1.30pm and 6-9pm. ☎ 954 38 45 58.

Casa de Pilatos – Open 9am-6pm (7pm in summer). 500pts each floor. ☎ 954 22 52 98/ 50 55.

Museo de Bellas Artes – Open 9am-3pm (Tues 3-8pm); Sun 9am-3pm. Closed Mon and public holidays. 250pts. No charge for citizens of the European Union. ☎ 954 22 18 29/22 07 90.

La Cartuja: Centro Andaluz de Arte Contemporáneo – Open 10am-8pm; Sun 10am-3pm; guided tours at 11am, noon, 5pm and 6pm. Closed Mon and some public holidays. 300pts. No charge on Tues for citizens of the European Union. ☎ 955 03 70 70.

Excursions

Itálica – Open 9am-5.30pm; Sun 10am-4pm; 1 Apr to 30 Sept 9am-8pm; Sun 9am-3pm. Closed Mon. 250pts. No charge for citizens of the European Union. ☎ 955 99 73 76/99 65 83.

Bollullos de la Mitación: Iglesia de San Martín – Open 7-9pm; Sun and public holidays 11am-noon and 5-7pm (for services).

Santuario de Cuatrovitas – Open Sat-Sun and public holidays 10am-1pm and 5-7pm; at other times contact the lady in charge of the sanctuary in the house opposite.

SIERRA NEVADA

Centro de Visitantes del Dornajo – Open 9.30am-2.30pm and 4.30-8pm. ☎ 958 34 06 25.

Excursion

Nigüelas: Las Laerillas oil mill – Visits by prior arrangement. ☎ 958 77 76 07 (town hall).

Parque Natural de la SIERRA NORTE DE SEVILLA

Constantina: Centro de Información del Parque – Open 10am-2pm and 4-6pm; Fri 4-6pm. Closed Mon, Tues and Wed. ☎ 955 88 12 26.

Ermita de El Robledo – Visits by prior arrangement. ☎ 955 88 12 97.

Cazalla de la Sierra: Ruinas de la Cartuja – Open 9.30am-3pm and 4-6pm (8pm in summer). Closed 24 Dec. 500pts. ☎ 954 88 45 16.

T

TABERNAS   🄸 Plaza del Pueblo, 1 (Town Hall) – 04200 – ☎ 950 36 50 02

Excursions

Mini Hollywood – Open 10am-9pm. ☎ 950 36 52 36.

Paraje Natural de Karst en Yesos – For information. ☎ 950 36 44 81.

TARIFA   🄸 Paseo de la Alameda – 11380 – ☎ 956 68 09 93

Castillo de Guzmán el Bueno – Open 10am-5pm (6pm in summer). ☎ 956 68 46 89.

Excursions

Ruinas Romanas de Baelo Claudia – Visits from 16 Sept to 30 June at 10am, 11am, noon, 1pm, 4pm and 5pm; 1 July to 15 Sept at 10am, 11am, noon, 1pm, 5pm and 6pm; Sun at 10am, 11am, noon and 1pm. Closed Mon, 1 and 6 Jan, 24, 25 and 31 Dec. ☎ 956 68 85 30.

U

ÚBEDA

🄸 Avenida Cristo Rey, 2 – 23400 – ☎ 953 75 08 97

Palacio de las Cadenas – Open 9am-2pm and 5-9pm. ☎ 953 75 04 40.

Museo de la Alfarería – Open 10.30am-2pm and 4.30-7pm; Sun and public holidays 10.30am-2pm. Closed Mon. 50pts. ☎ 953 79 12 97.

Iglesia de Santa María de los Alcázares – Closed for restoration.

Capilla de El Salvador – Open 10am-2pm and 4-6.30pm. Closed Mon. 350pts. ☎ 953 75 08 97.

Iglesia de San Pablo – Open for services 7-9pm.

Museo de San Juan de la Cruz – Open 11am-12.45pm and 5-6.30pm. Closed Mon. No charge. ☎ 953 75 06 15.

Casa Mudéjar: Museo Arqueológico – Open 10am-2pm and 3-7pm; Sun 10am-2pm. Closed Mon. ☎ 953 75 37 02.

Roman ruins, Baelo Claudia

Museo de la Semana Santa – Open 9am-3pm and 3.30-10pm. Closed Mon. ☎ 953 75 08 42.

UTRERA

Iglesia de Santa María de la Mesa – Open for services at 6.30pm. Sat-Sun at noon. ☎ 954 86 03 30.

Iglesia de San Francisco – Open 6-9pm. Sun 4-9pm. ☎ 955 86 09 31.

Santuario de Nuestra Señora de la Consolación – Open 9am-2pm and 4-6.30pm. ☎ 954 86 03 30.

V

VEJER DE LA FRONTERA

🄸 Calle San Filmo, 6 – 11150 – ☎ 956 45 01 91

Visit – Guided tours (2hr) covering all the town's main monuments. 500pts. ☎ 956 45 01 91.

Iglesia Parroquial del Divino Salvador – Open 10.30am-1.30pm and 7.30-10pm.

Excursions

Conil de la Frontera:

Castillo de los Guzmanes – Visits by prior arrangement. ☎ 956 44 09 11 (Señor Fermín Muñoz).

Museo de Raíces Conileñas – Open 1 July to 15 Sept 10pm-midnight. No charge. ☎ 956 44 05 01.

VÉLEZ BLANCO

Castle – Open 11am-1.30pm and 4-6pm. ☎ 950 41 50 01 (town hall).

Excursions

Vélez Rubio:

Parroquia de la Encarnación – Open 5-8pm. Closed Mon.

Museo Comarcal Velezano – Open 9am-2pm and 4-8pm. ☎ 950 41 25 60.

Parque Natural de la Sierra de María: Centro de Visitantes Umbría de María – Open 9am-1pm and 3-5pm. Closed Sat-Sun. ☎ 950 52 70 05.

Glossary

Castilian Spanish is spoken throughout Andalucia. Visitors to the region will also find that a number of words and names, such as those bearing the prefixes *al* (the), *cala* (castle or fort) and *gaudal* (river), have evolved from Arabic.

GENERAL WORDS

Terms of address

yes, no	sí, no
good morning	buenos días
good afternoon	buenas tardes
goodbye	hasta luego, adiós
please	por favor
How are you?	¿qué tal?
thank you (very much)	(muchas) gracias
excuse me	perdone
I don't understand	no entiendo
Sir/Mr., you	señor, Usted
Madam/Mrs.	señora
Miss	señorita

Time

when?	¿cuándo?
what time?	¿a qué hora?
today	hoy
yesterday	ayer
tomorrow morning	mañana por la mañana
tomorrow afternoon	mañana por la tarde

Shopping

how much?	¿cuánto (vale)?
(too) expensive	(demasiado) caro
a lot, little	mucho, poco
more, less	más, menos
big, small	grande, pequeño
credit card	tarjeta de crédito

Correspondence

post box	buzón
post office	Correos
telephone	teléfono
letter	carta
post card	(tarjeta) postal
poste restante	lista (de Correos)
stamp	sello
telephone call	conferencia
tobacco shop	estanco, tabacos

On the road, in town

coche	car
gasolina	petrol
a la derecha	on the right
a la izquierda	on the left
obras	road works
peligro, peligroso	danger, dangerous
cuidado	beware, take care
dar la vuelta a	to go round, tour
después de	after, beyond
girar	to go round, to circle

FOOD AND WINE

For further useful hotel and restaurant vocabulary, consult the current edition of THE RED GUIDE ESPAÑA PORTUGAL.

aceite, aceitunas	oil, olives
agua con gas/sin gas	sparkling/still water
ajo	garlic
alcachofa	artichoke
alergia: tengo alergia a	allergy: I'm allergic to...
alubias	beans
anchoas	anchovies
arroz	rice
atún	tuna
ave	poultry
azúcar	sugar
bacalao	cod
berenjena	aubergine/eggplant
café con leche	coffee with hot milk
café solo	black coffee
calamares	squid
cangrejo	crab
carne	meat
cebolla	onion
cerdo	pork
cerveza	beer
chorizo	spicy sausages
cordero (lechal)	mutton (lamb)
crema (de leche)	cream
ensalada	green salad
entremeses	hors-d'oeuvre
fiambres	cold cooked meats
gambas	prawns
garbanzos	chick peas

guisantes	garden peas
helado	ice cream
hígado	liver
huevo: huevos al plato	egg: fried eggs
jamón	ham
judías verdes	French beans
langostino	(king) prawns
leche	milk
legumbres	vegetables
limón	lemon
mantequilla	butter
manzana	apple
mariscos	seafood
naranja	orange
nuez (nueces)	nut(s)
pan	bread
patatas	potatoes
pescado	fish
pimienta (negra)	(black) pepper
pimiento (rojo/verde)	(red/green) pepper
plátano	banana
pollo	chicken
postre	dessert
potaje	soup
queso	cheese
sal	salt
salchichas	sausages
sandía	water-melon
setas/hongos	mushrooms
ternera	veal

tortilla	omelette	vino blanco/rosado/tinto	white/rosé/red wine
trucha	trout	zanahoria	carrot
vaca/buey	beef	zumo de frutas	fruit juice
vegetariano/a	vegetarian		

SITES AND SIGHTS

See also architectural terms in the Introduction, p 44.

where is?	¿donde está?
may one visit?	¿se puede visitar?
key	llave
light	luz
sacristan	sacristán
guide	guía
porter, caretaker	guarda, conserje
open, closed	abierto, cerrado
alcazaba	Muslim fortress
alcázar	Muslim palace
aljibe	cistern
alrededores	environs, outskirts
alto	pass, high pass
ayuntamiento	town hall
audiencia	audience, court
balneario	spa
barranco	gully, ravine
barrio	quarter
bodega	wine cellar/store
cabo	cape, headland
calle	street
calle mayor	main street
camino	road, track
campanario	belfry
capilla	chapel
capitel	capital
carretera	main road
cartuja	Carthusian monastery
casa	house
casa consistorial	town hall
castillo	castle
castro	Celtic village
ciudad	town, city
claustro	cloister
colegio, colegiata	college, collegiate church
collado	pass, high pass
convento	monastery, convent
cruz	cross, Calvary
cuadro	picture
cueva, gruta, cava	cave, grotto
desfiladero	defile, cleft
embalse	reservoir, dam
ermita	hermitage, chapel
estación	station
excavaciones	excavations
finca	property, domain
fuente	fountain
gargantas	gorges
gruta	cavern, grotto
hoz	defile, narrow pass, gorge
huerto, huerta	vegetable/market garden
iglesia (parroquial)	(parish) church
no entry, not allowed	prohibido
entrance, exit	entrada, salida
apply to	dirigirse a
wait	esperar
beautiful	bello, bonito, hermoso
storey, stairs, steps	piso, escalera

imagen	religious statue/sculpture
isla	island, isle
lago	lake
mezquita	mosque
monasterio	monastery
monte	mount, mountain
mirador	belvedere, viewpoint, lookout point
museo	museum
nacimiento	source, birthplace
palacio (real)	(royal) palace
pantano	artificial lake
parroquia	parish, parish church
paseo	avenue, esplanade, promenade
paso	sculptured figures: the Passion
plaza	square
plaza mayor	main square
plaza de toros	bullring
portada	portal, west door
pórtico	portal, porch
pósito	granary
presa	dam
presbiterio	chancel, presbytery
pueblo	village, market town
puente	bridge
puerta	door, gate, entrance
puerto	pass, harbour, port
ría	estuary
río	river, stream
romano; románico	Roman: Romanesque
romería	religious pilgrimage
santuario	church
siglo	century
talla	carved wood
tapices	tapestries
techo	ceiling
tesoro	treasury, treasure
torre	tower, belfry
torre del homenaje	keep
torrente	mountain stream, torrent
valle	valley
vega	fertile plain
vidriera	window: plain or stained glass
vista	view, panorama

Index

U – V

W – Y – Z